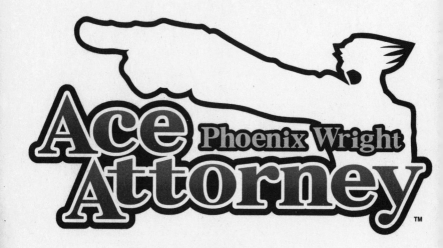

Ace Phoenix Wright Attorney ™

VOLUME TWO

Story by Kenji Kuroda
Art by Kazuo Maekawa
Supervised by CAPCOM

Translated and adapted by Alethea Nibley and Athena Nibley

Lettered by North Market Street Graphics

KC
KODANSHA COMICS

This book is a faithful translation of the book
released in Japan on June 6, 2007.

Phoenix Wright: Ace Attorney Volume 2 is a work of fiction. Names, characters, places, and incidents are the products of the author's imagination or are used fictitiously. Any resemblance to actual events, locales, or persons, living or dead, is entirely coincidental.

A Kodansha Comics Trade Paperback Original.

Published in the United States by Kodansha Comics, an imprint of Kodansha USA Publishing, LLC., New York.

Publication rights for this English edition arranged through Kodansha Ltd., Tokyo.

First published in Japan in 2007 by Kodansha Ltd., Tokyo.

ISBN 978-1-935-42970-8

Printed in the United States of America.

www.kodanshacomics.com

2 3 4 5 6 7 8 9

Translators: Alethea Nibley and Athena Nibley
Lettering: North Market Street Graphics

CONTENTS

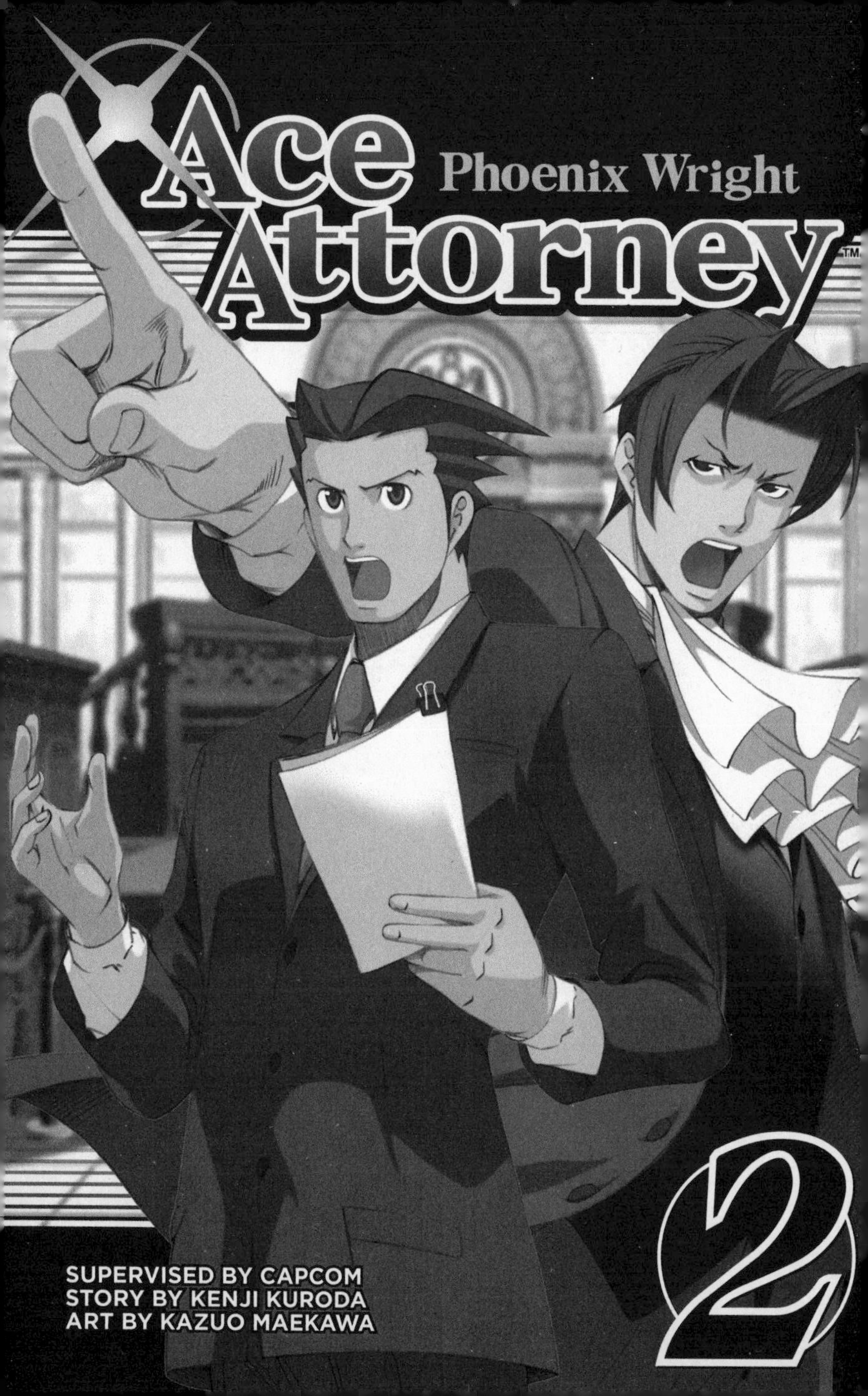
Phoenix Wright
Ace Attorney™
2
SUPERVISED BY CAPCOM
STORY BY KENJI KURODA
ART BY KAZUO MAEKAWA

CHARACTER INTRODUCTIONS

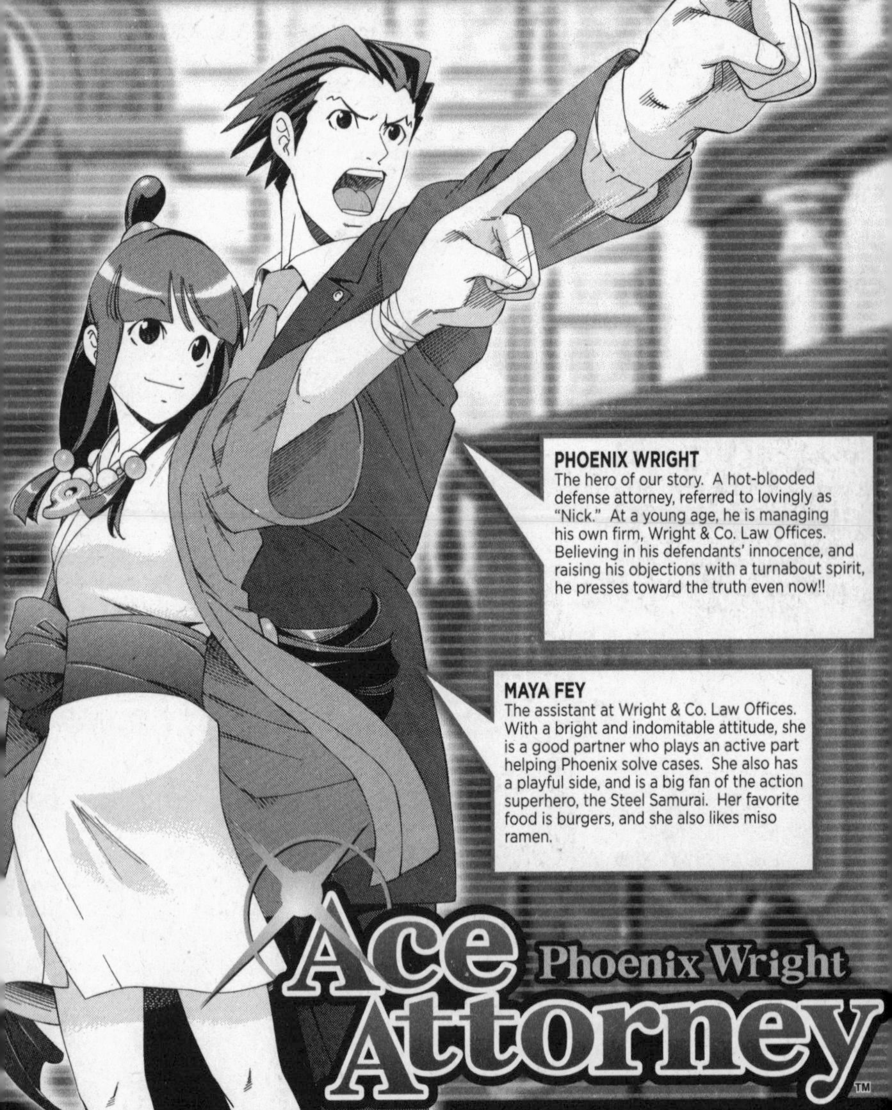
Phoenix Wright Ace Attorney™

PHOENIX WRIGHT
The hero of our story. A hot-blooded defense attorney, referred to lovingly as "Nick." At a young age, he is managing his own firm, Wright & Co. Law Offices. Believing in his defendants' innocence, and raising his objections with a turnabout spirit, he presses toward the truth even now!!

MAYA FEY
The assistant at Wright & Co. Law Offices. With a bright and indomitable attitude, she is a good partner who plays an active part helping Phoenix solve cases. She also has a playful side, and is a big fan of the action superhero, the Steel Samurai. Her favorite food is burgers, and she also likes miso ramen.

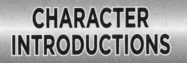

The characters, laws, and court procedures in this work are all fiction. Accordingly, the court system of this story is set in the near future, where the demand for expedited trials creates a different system than that of present-day.

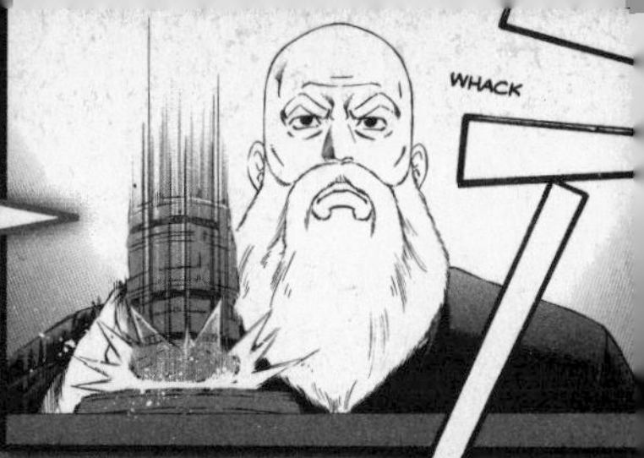
WHACK

THE JUDGE
The court judge, who looks dignified but actually is not. He has a habit of gullibly swallowing every scenario fed to him by Phoenix or Edgeworth. His name is unknown.

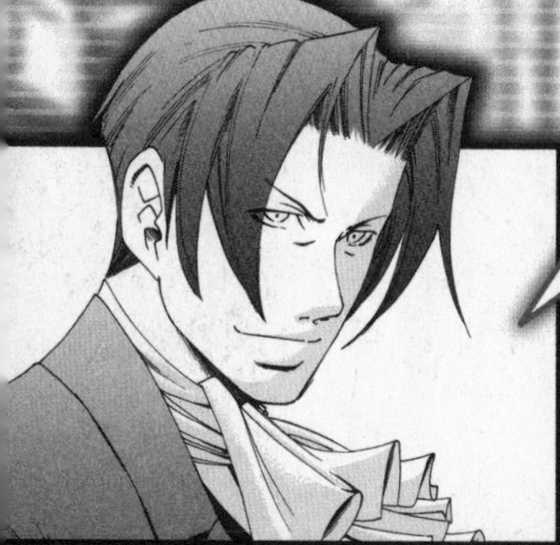

MILES EDGEWORTH
Phoenix's greatest rival. He has been known as a genius prosecutor ever since he started out in the profession. In fact, he and Phoenix knew each other as children, and were the best of friends, bound together by trust.

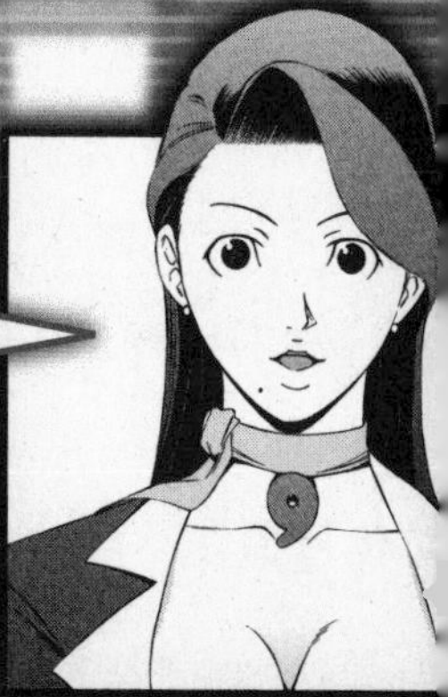

MIA FEY
Maya's older sister. Phoenix's boss and mentor, who gave him helpful advice. She was a very accomplished defense attorney, but she lost her life investigating a case.

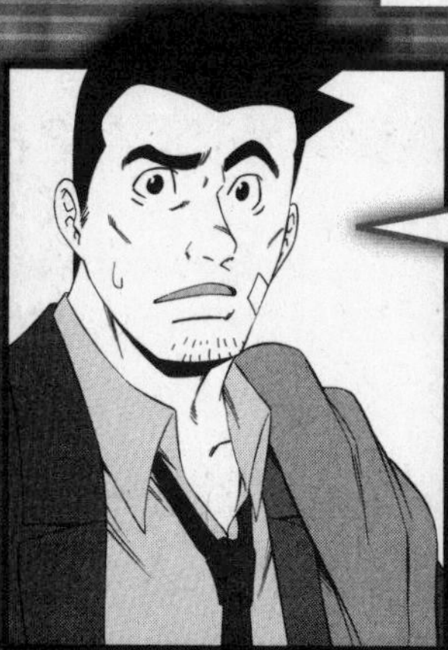

DICK GUMSHOE
A detective in charge of murder investigations. He's a few cards shy of a deck, and sometimes misses important clues. Every time he does, he gets a paycut, so his salary is very low.

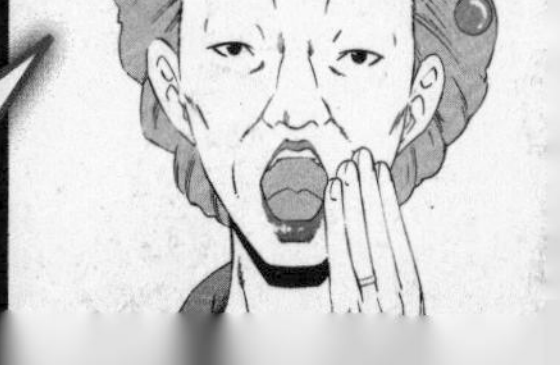

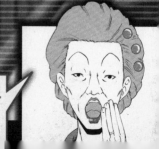

WENDY OLDBAG
A security guard who shoos away onlookers, lecturing with the stern tone of an old neighborhood gossip. Very submissive to good-looking men.

TURNABOUT GALLOWS CASE FILE

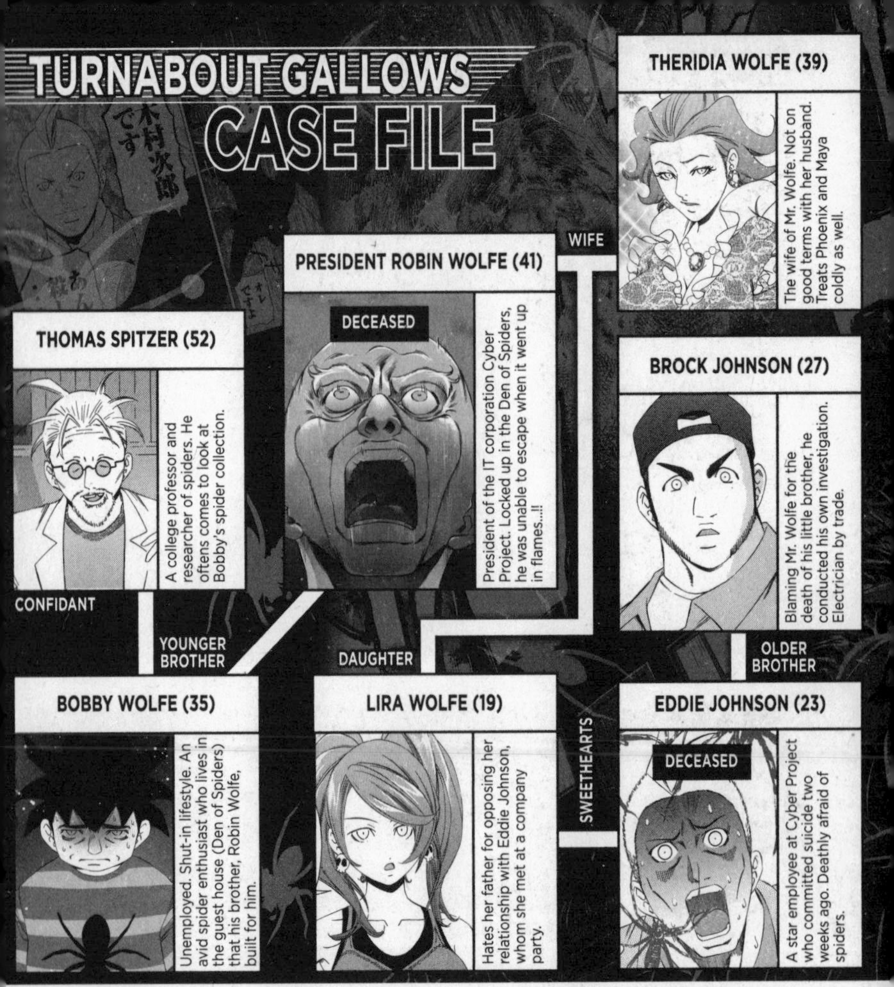

THERIDIA WOLFE (39)
The wife of Mr. Wolfe. Not on good terms with her husband. Treats Phoenix and Maya coldly as well.
WIFE
PRESIDENT ROBIN WOLFE (41)
DECEASED
President of the IT corporation Cyber Project. Locked up in the Den of Spiders, he was unable to escape when it went up in flames...!!
THOMAS SPITZER (52)
A college professor and researcher of spiders. He oftens comes to look at Bobby's spider collection.
CONFIDANT
BROCK JOHNSON (27)
Blaming Mr. Wolfe for the death of his little brother, he conducted his own investigation. Electrician by trade.
YOUNGER BROTHER
DAUGHTER
OLDER BROTHER
BOBBY WOLFE (35)
Unemployed. Shut-in lifestyle. An avid spider enthusiast who lives in the guest house (Den of Spiders) that his brother, Robin Wolfe, built for him.
LIRA WOLFE (19)
Hates her father for opposing her relationship with Eddie Johnson, whom she met at a company party.
SWEETHEARTS
EDDIE JOHNSON (23)
DECEASED
A star employee at Cyber Project who committed suicide two weeks ago. Deathly afraid of spiders.

SUMMARY Phoenix and Maya were invited to the home of Robin Wolfe, president of the IT corporation Cyber Project. However, the Wolfe family is giving Mr. Wolfe the cold shoulder. They strongly suspect that President Wolfe is the very man who drove Eddie Johnson to suicide two weeks ago.

Two weeks ago, Mr. Wolfe took Eddie to his guest house to lecture him. The guest house was the home of his spider-loving younger brother. But Eddie was deathly afraid of spiders, and when he is forced into an arachnid breeding ground, then...!? Before going home that night, Eddie killed himself.

President Wolfe dismisses all accusations, but Brock, brother of the late Eddie, visits the Wolfe home. Brock joined Phoenix and Maya in their investigation of the Den of Spiders, and found unusual restraining devices!! Suspicion builds toward Mr. Wolfe, but the man himself is shut up in his study and refuses to answer questions.

But somehow the president finds himself restrained and alone in the Den of Spiders! What's more, when he regains consciousness, he looks up and sees a spider man skittering across the ceiling...!?

Mr. Wolfe manages to contact his family through an intercom and get them to turn off the breaker, thus releasing the restraints. But at the moment they do, the Den of Spiders goes up in flames!! Mr. Wolfe is found dead, but not from smoke inhalation--he was hit on the back of the head...!!

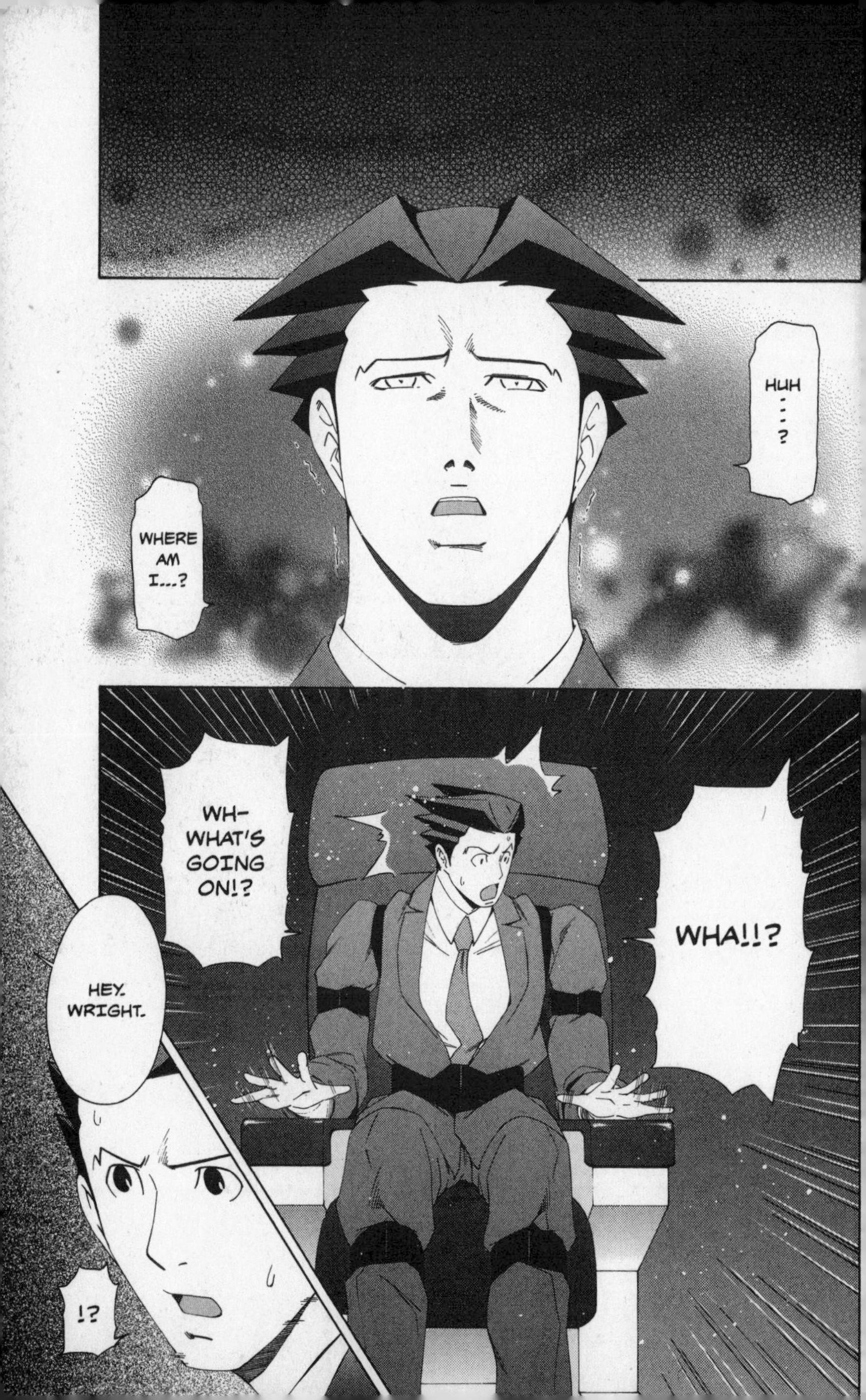
HUH...?
WHERE AM I...?
WHA!!?
WH- WHAT'S GOING ON!?
HEY. WRIGHT.
!?

Chapter 4
TURNABOUT GALLOWS 3

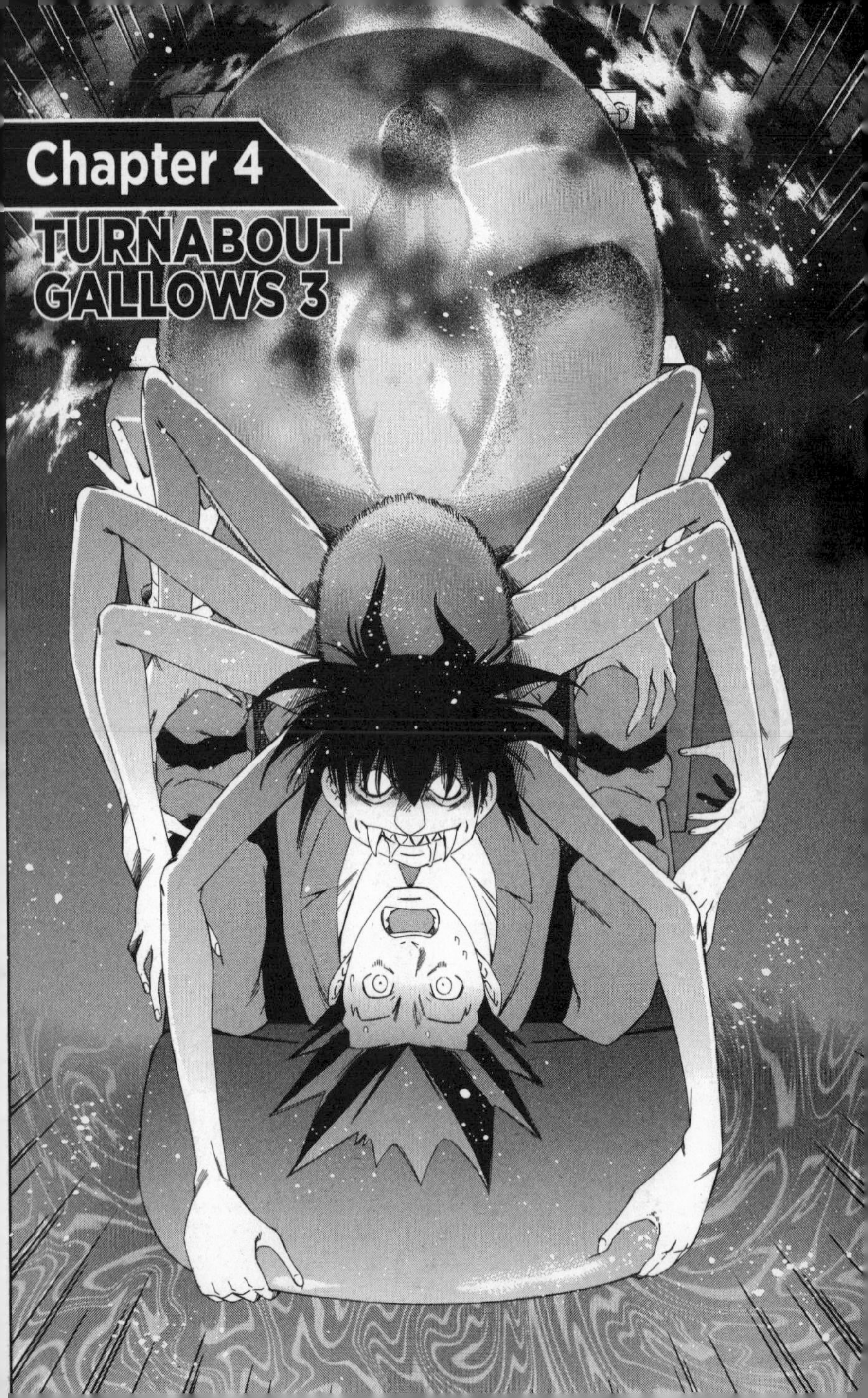

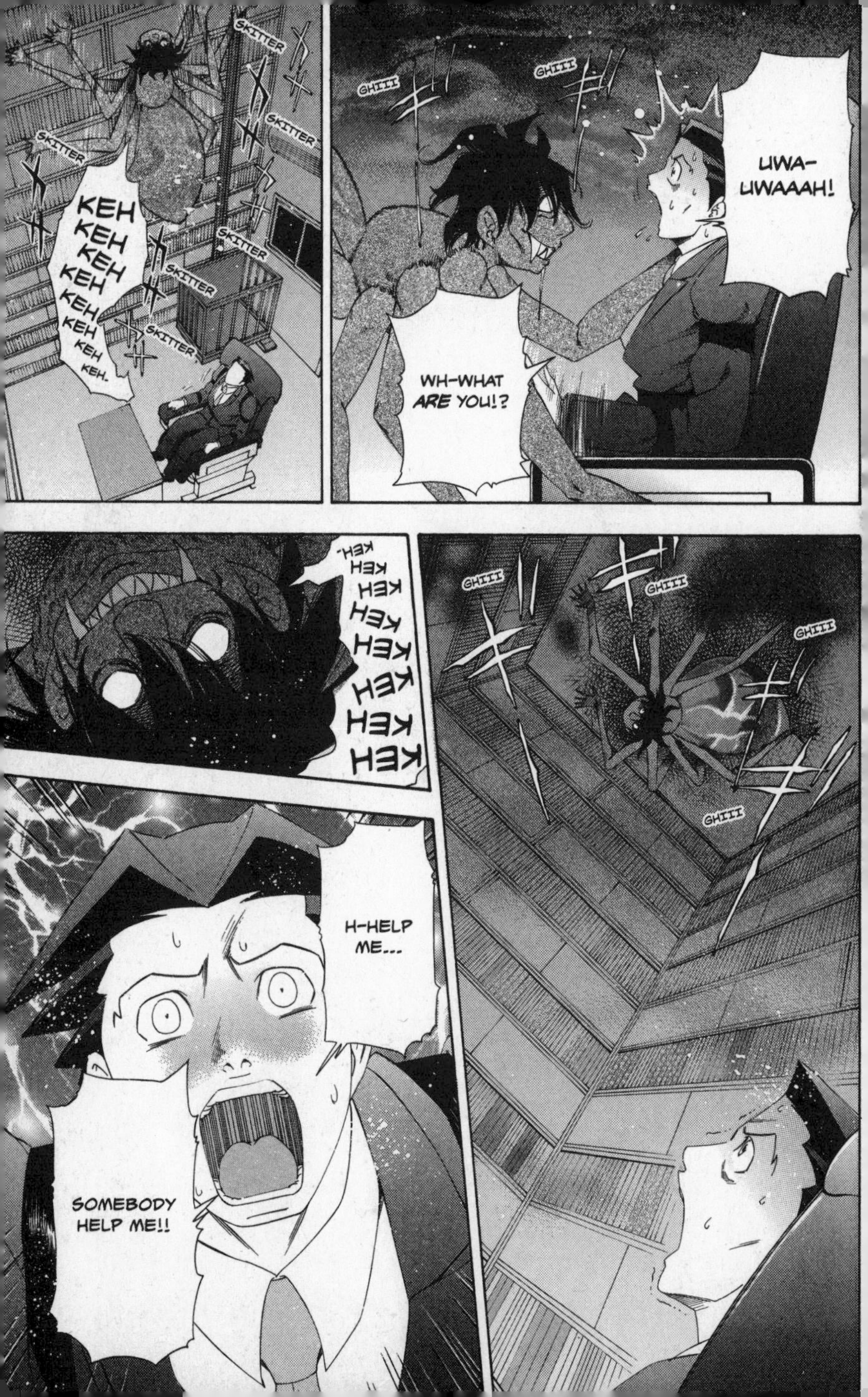
GHIII
GHIII
UWA-UWAAAH!
WH-WHAT ARE YOU!?
SKITTER
SKITTER
SKITTER
SKITTER
SKITTER
SKITTER
KEH KEH KEH KEH KEH KEH KEH KEH.
GHIII
GHIII
GHIII
GHIII
KEH KEH KEH KEH KEH KEH KEH KEH.
H-HELP ME...
SOMEBODY HELP ME!!

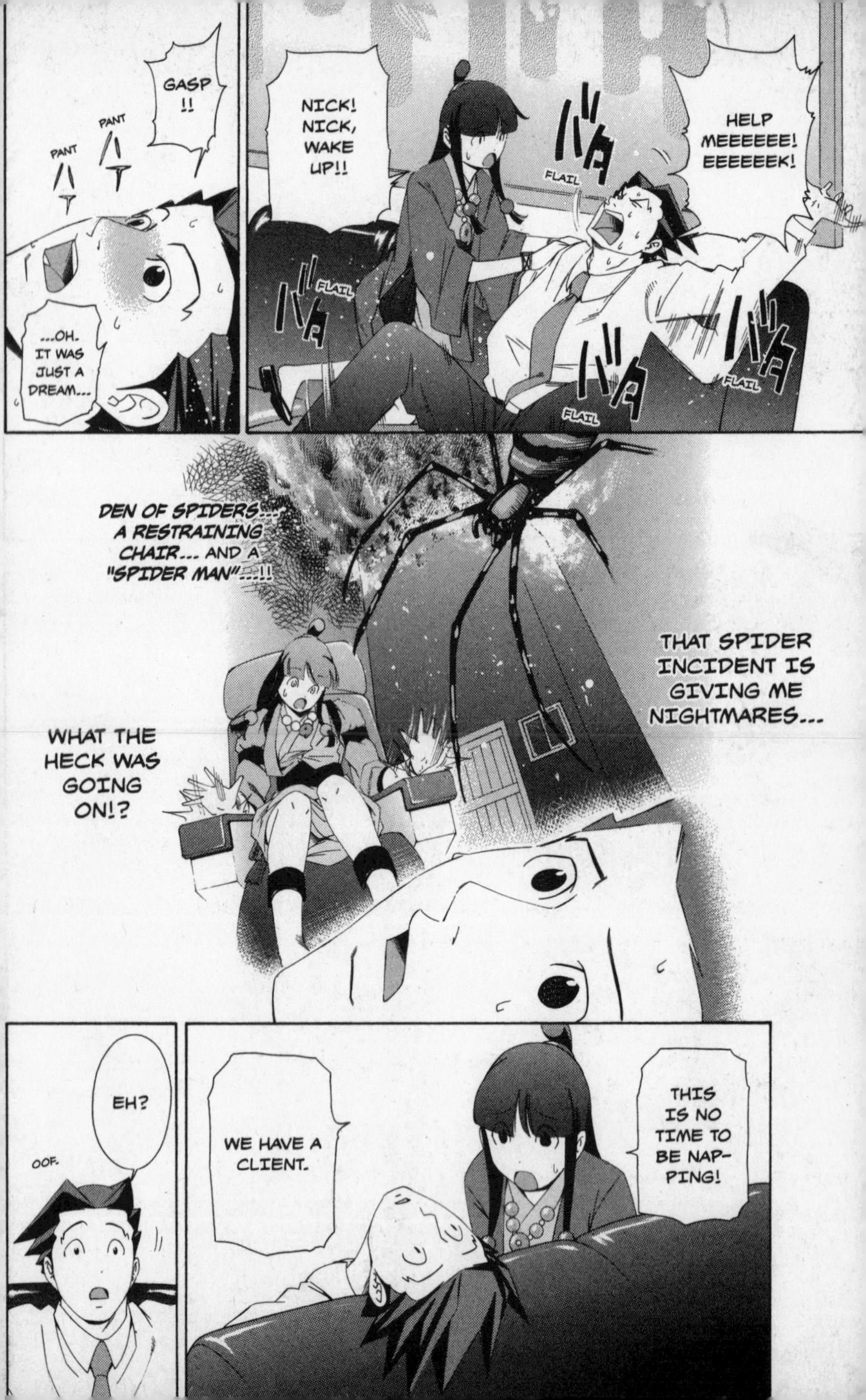
HELP MEEEEEEE! EEEEEEK!
バタ FLAIL
NICK! NICK, WAKE UP!!
バタ FLAIL
バタ FLAIL
バタ FLAIL
GASP!!
ハァ PANT
ハァ PANT
...OH. IT WAS JUST A DREAM...
THAT SPIDER INCIDENT IS GIVING ME NIGHTMARES...
DEN OF SPIDERS... A RESTRAINING CHAIR... AND A "SPIDER MAN"...!!
WHAT THE HECK WAS GOING ON!?
THIS IS NO TIME TO BE NAP-PING!
WE HAVE A CLIENT.
EH?
OOF.

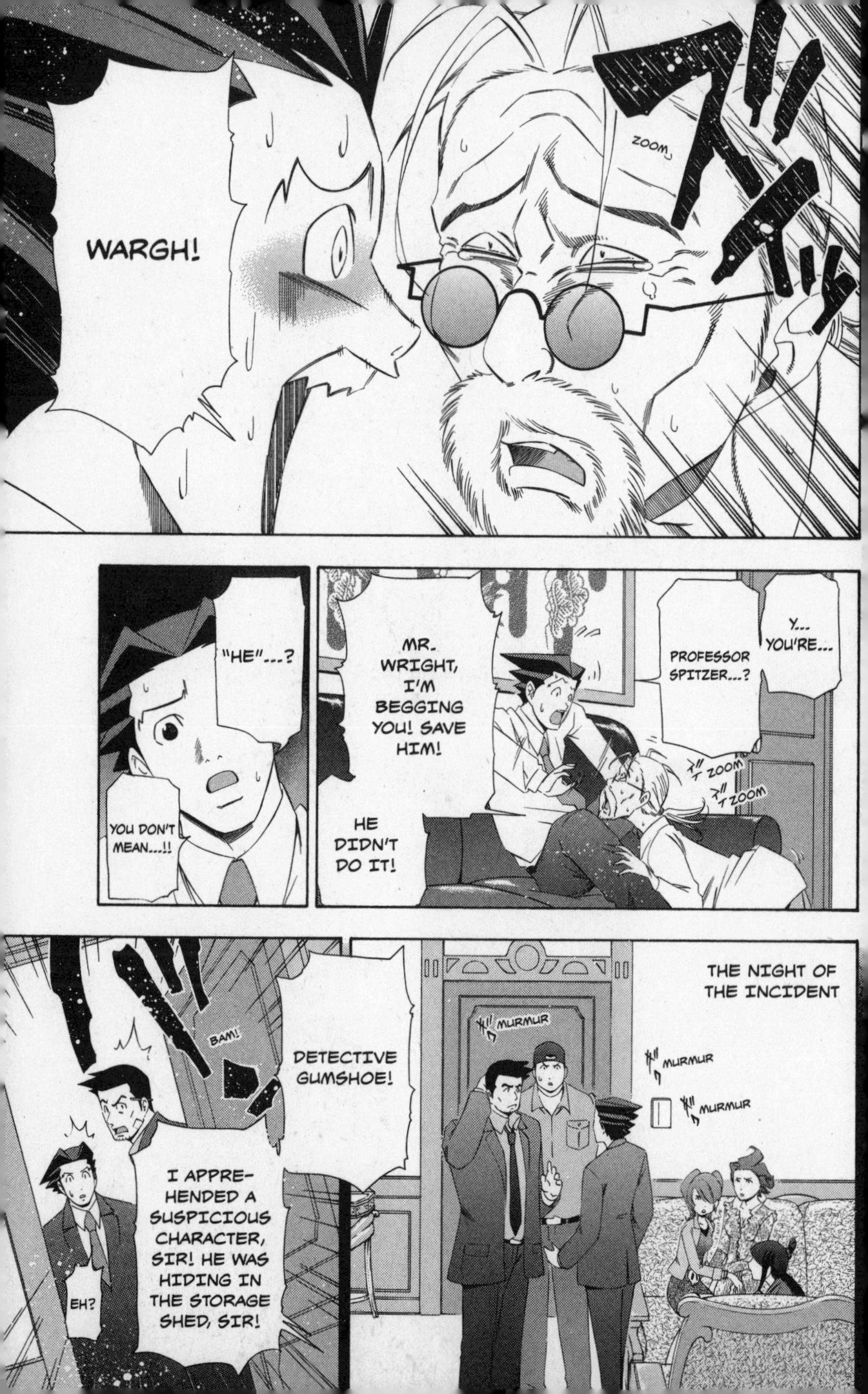
ZOOM
WARGH!
Y... YOU'RE...
PROFESSOR SPITZER...?
MR. WRIGHT, I'M BEGGING YOU! SAVE HIM!
ZOOM
ZOOM
HE DIDN'T DO IT!
"HE"...?
YOU DON'T MEAN...!!
THE NIGHT OF THE INCIDENT
MURMUR
MURMUR
MURMUR
BAM!
DETECTIVE GUMSHOE!
I APPREHENDED A SUSPICIOUS CHARACTER, SIR! HE WAS HIDING IN THE STORAGE SHED, SIR!
EH?

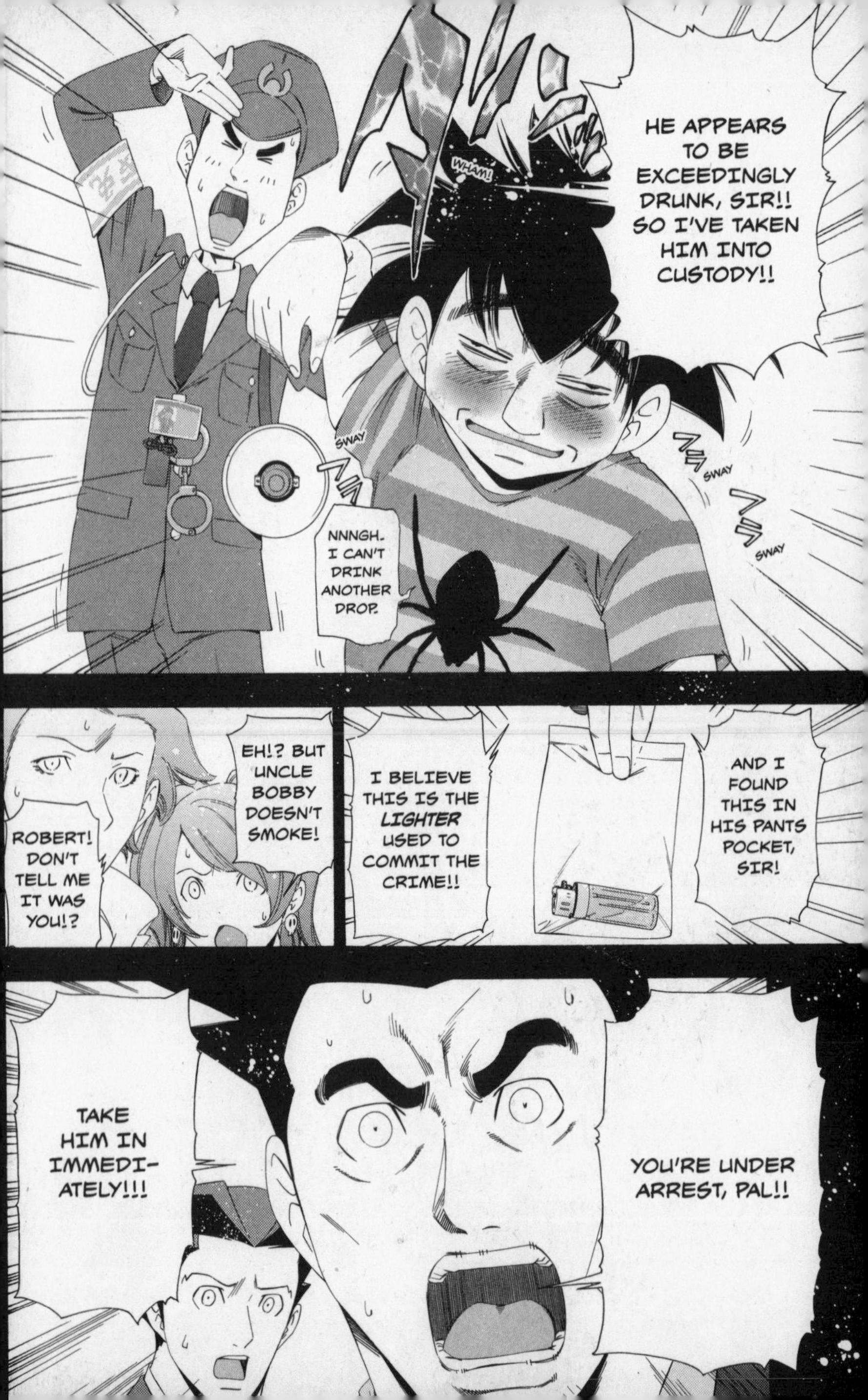
HE APPEARS TO BE EXCEEDINGLY DRUNK, SIR!! SO I'VE TAKEN HIM INTO CUSTODY!!
WHAM!
SWAY
SWAY
SWAY
NNNGH. I CAN'T DRINK ANOTHER DROP.
AND I FOUND THIS IN HIS PANTS POCKET, SIR!
I BELIEVE THIS IS THE *LIGHTER* USED TO COMMIT THE CRIME!!
EH!? BUT UNCLE BOBBY DOESN'T SMOKE!
ROBERT! DON'T TELL ME IT WAS YOU!?
YOU'RE UNDER ARREST, PAL!!
TAKE HIM IN IMMEDIATELY!!!

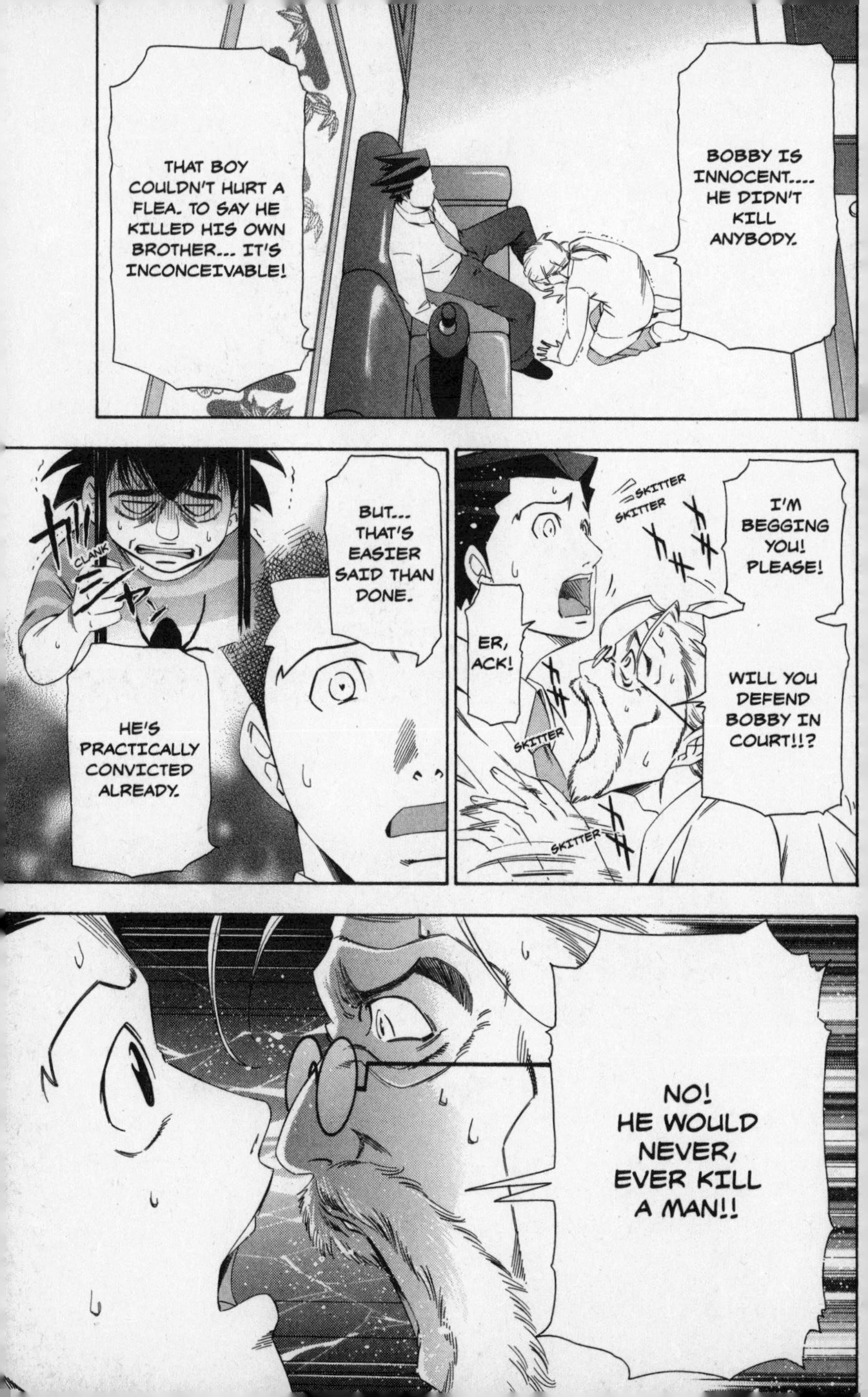
BOBBY IS INNOCENT.... HE DIDN'T KILL ANYBODY.
THAT BOY COULDN'T HURT A FLEA. TO SAY HE KILLED HIS OWN BROTHER... IT'S INCONCEIVABLE!
SKITTER
SKITTER
I'M BEGGING YOU! PLEASE!
ER, ACK!
WILL YOU DEFEND BOBBY IN COURT!!?
SKITTER
SKITTER
BUT... THAT'S EASIER SAID THAN DONE.
CLANK
HE'S PRACTICALLY CONVICTED ALREADY.
NO! HE WOULD NEVER, EVER KILL A MAN!!

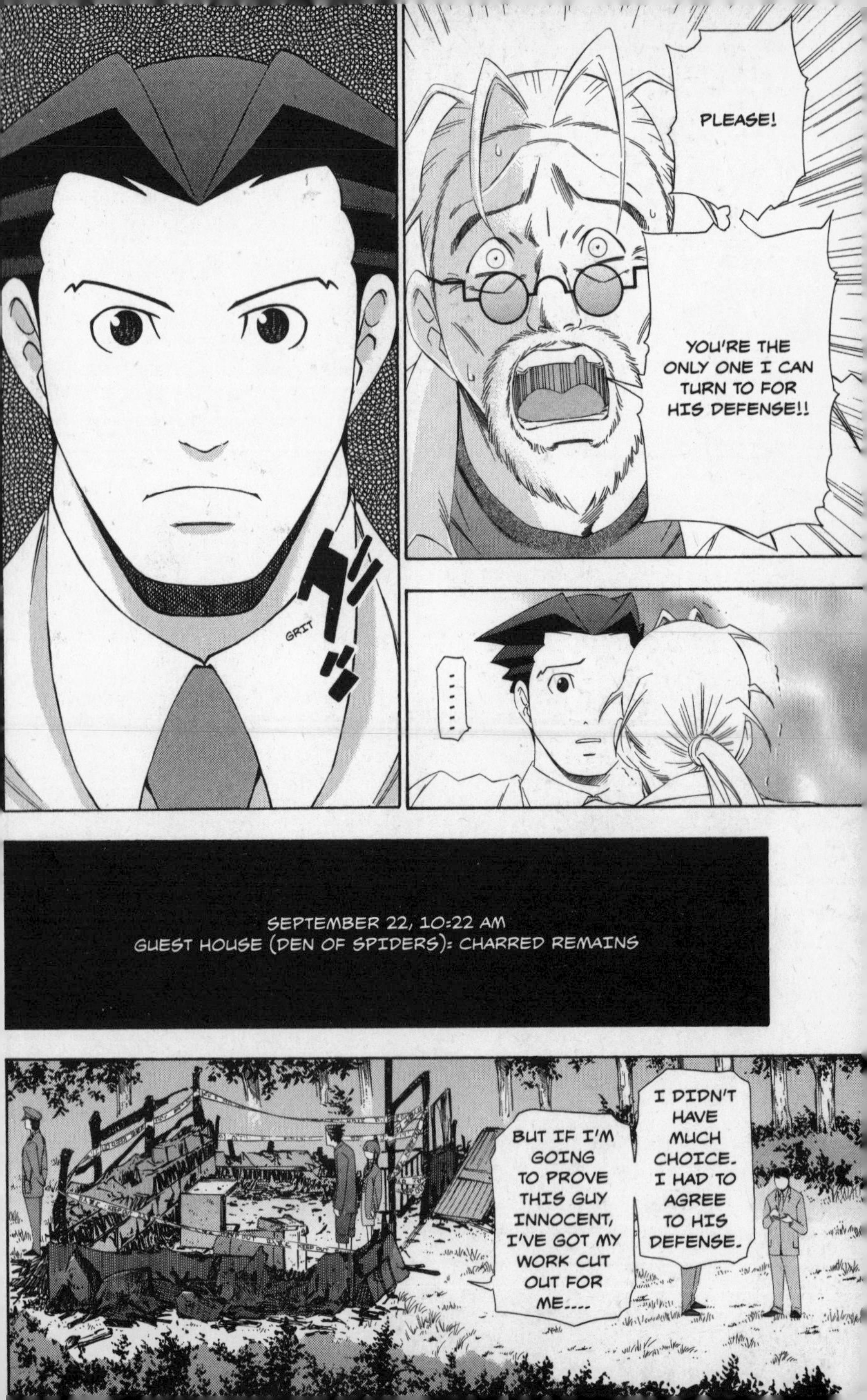
PLEASE!
YOU'RE THE ONLY ONE I CAN TURN TO FOR HIS DEFENSE!!
......
GRIT
SEPTEMBER 22, 10:22 AM
GUEST HOUSE (DEN OF SPIDERS): CHARRED REMAINS
I DIDN'T HAVE MUCH CHOICE. I HAD TO AGREE TO HIS DEFENSE.
BUT IF I'M GOING TO PROVE THIS GUY INNOCENT, I'VE GOT MY WORK CUT OUT FOR ME....

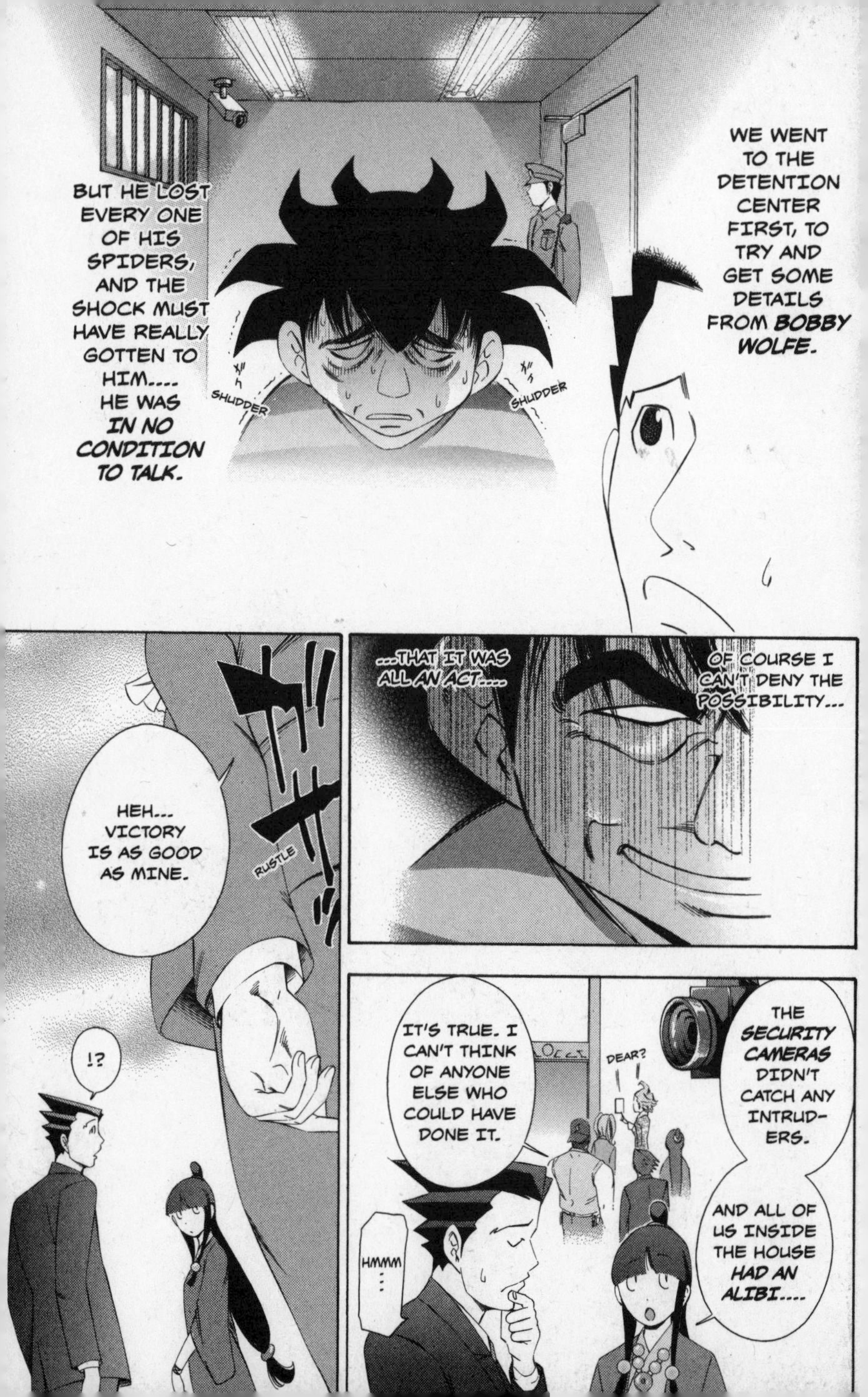
WE WENT TO THE DETENTION CENTER FIRST, TO TRY AND GET SOME DETAILS FROM BOBBY WOLFE.
BUT HE LOST EVERY ONE OF HIS SPIDERS, AND THE SHOCK MUST HAVE REALLY GOTTEN TO HIM.... HE WAS IN NO CONDITION TO TALK.
SHUDDER
SHUDDER
OF COURSE I CAN'T DENY THE POSSIBILITY...
...THAT IT WAS ALL AN ACT....
THE SECURITY CAMERAS DIDN'T CATCH ANY INTRUDERS.
AND ALL OF US INSIDE THE HOUSE HAD AN ALIBI....
DEAR?
IT'S TRUE. I CAN'T THINK OF ANYONE ELSE WHO COULD HAVE DONE IT.
HMMM...
HEH... VICTORY IS AS GOOD AS MINE.
RUSTLE
!?

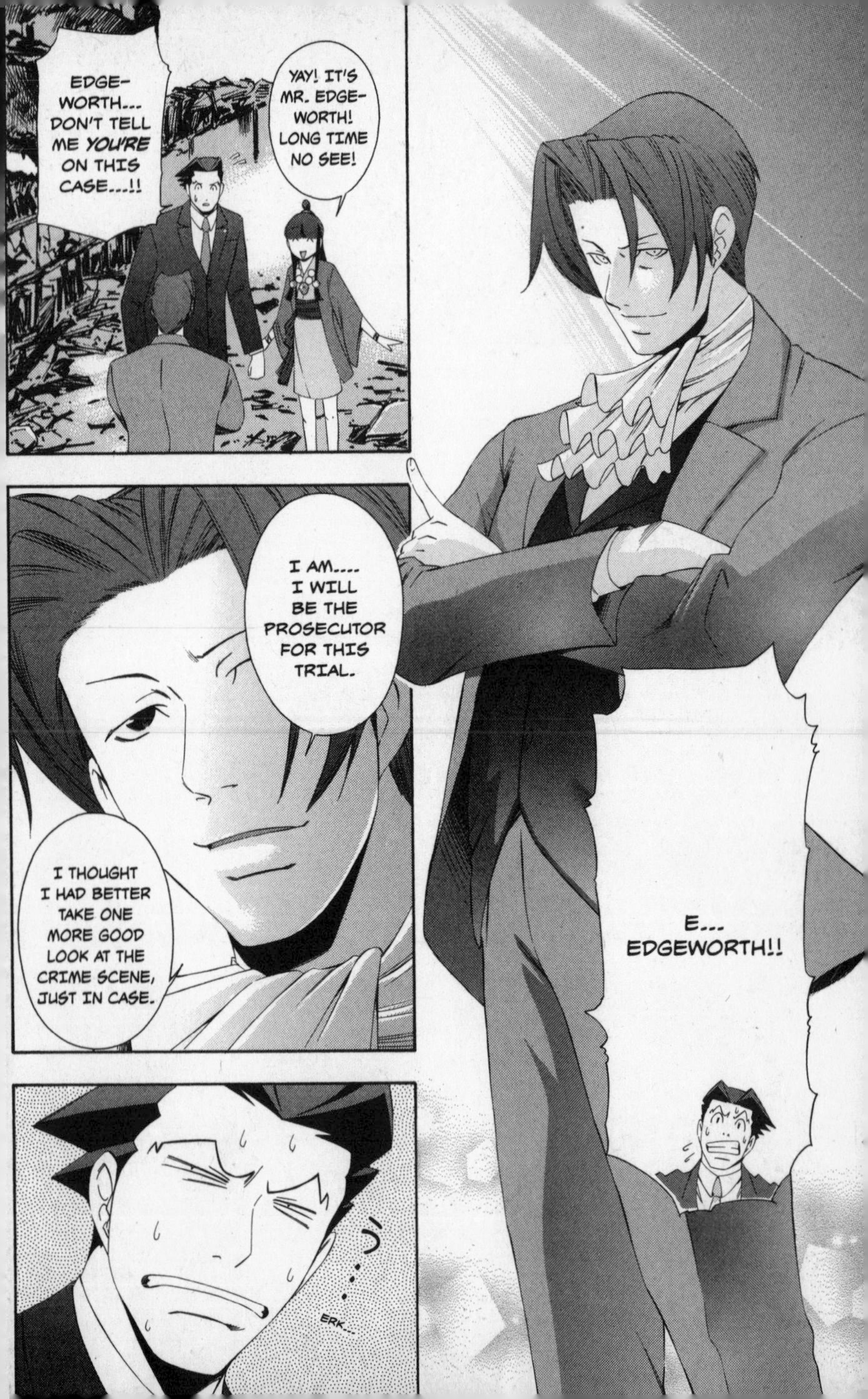
E... EDGEWORTH!!
YAY! IT'S MR. EDGEWORTH! LONG TIME NO SEE!
EDGEWORTH... DON'T TELL ME *YOU'RE* ON THIS CASE...!!
I AM.... I WILL BE THE PROSECUTOR FOR THIS TRIAL.
I THOUGHT I HAD BETTER TAKE ONE MORE GOOD LOOK AT THE CRIME SCENE, JUST IN CASE.
ERK...

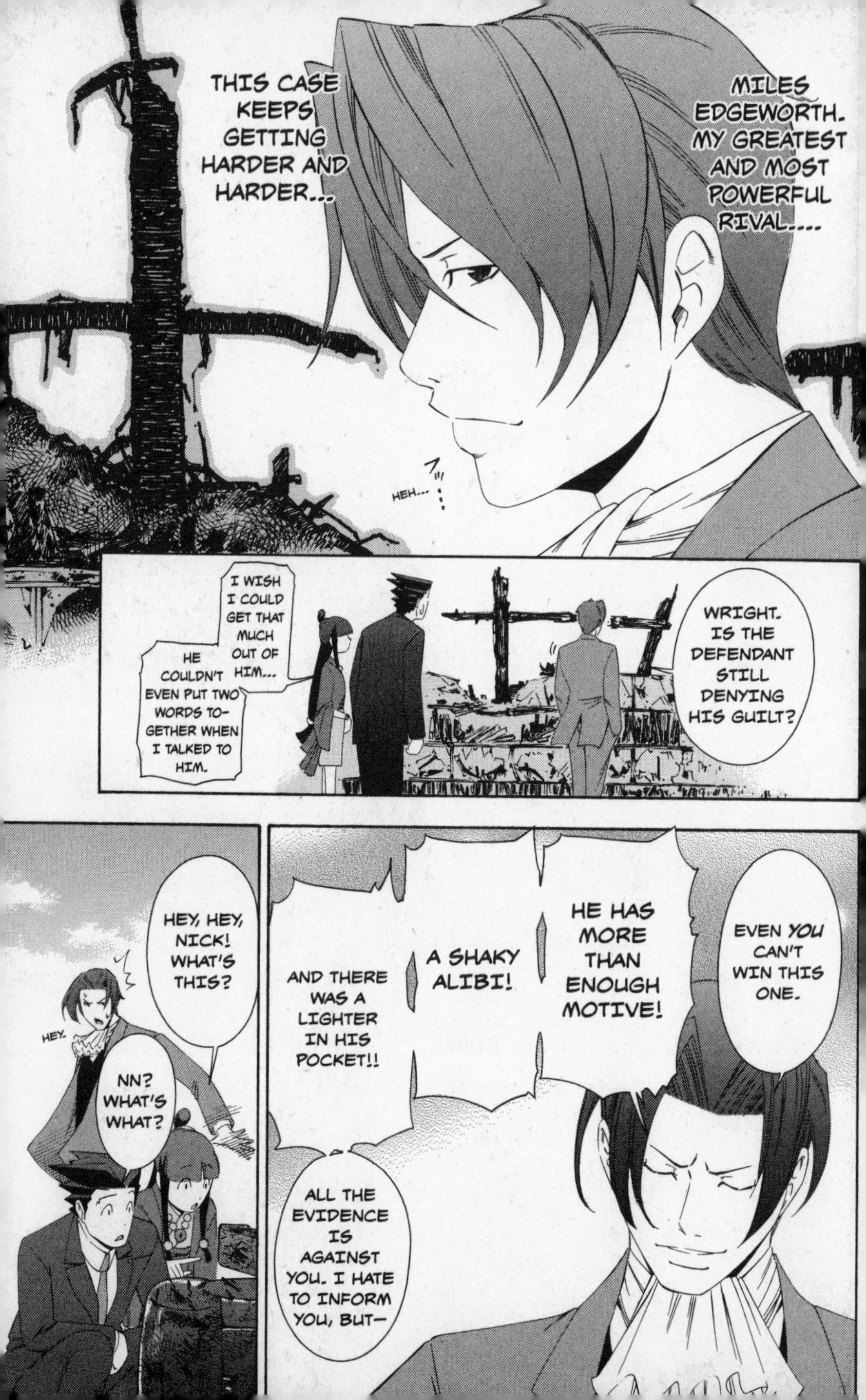
MILES EDGEWORTH. MY GREATEST AND MOST POWERFUL RIVAL....
THIS CASE KEEPS GETTING HARDER AND HARDER...
HEH...
WRIGHT. IS THE DEFENDANT STILL DENYING HIS GUILT?
I WISH I COULD GET THAT MUCH OUT OF HIM...
HE COULDN'T EVEN PUT TWO WORDS TO-GETHER WHEN I TALKED TO HIM.
EVEN YOU CAN'T WIN THIS ONE.
HE HAS MORE THAN ENOUGH MOTIVE!
A SHAKY ALIBI!
AND THERE WAS A LIGHTER IN HIS POCKET!!
ALL THE EVIDENCE IS AGAINST YOU. I HATE TO INFORM YOU, BUT—
HEY, HEY, NICK! WHAT'S THIS?
HEY.
NN? WHAT'S WHAT?

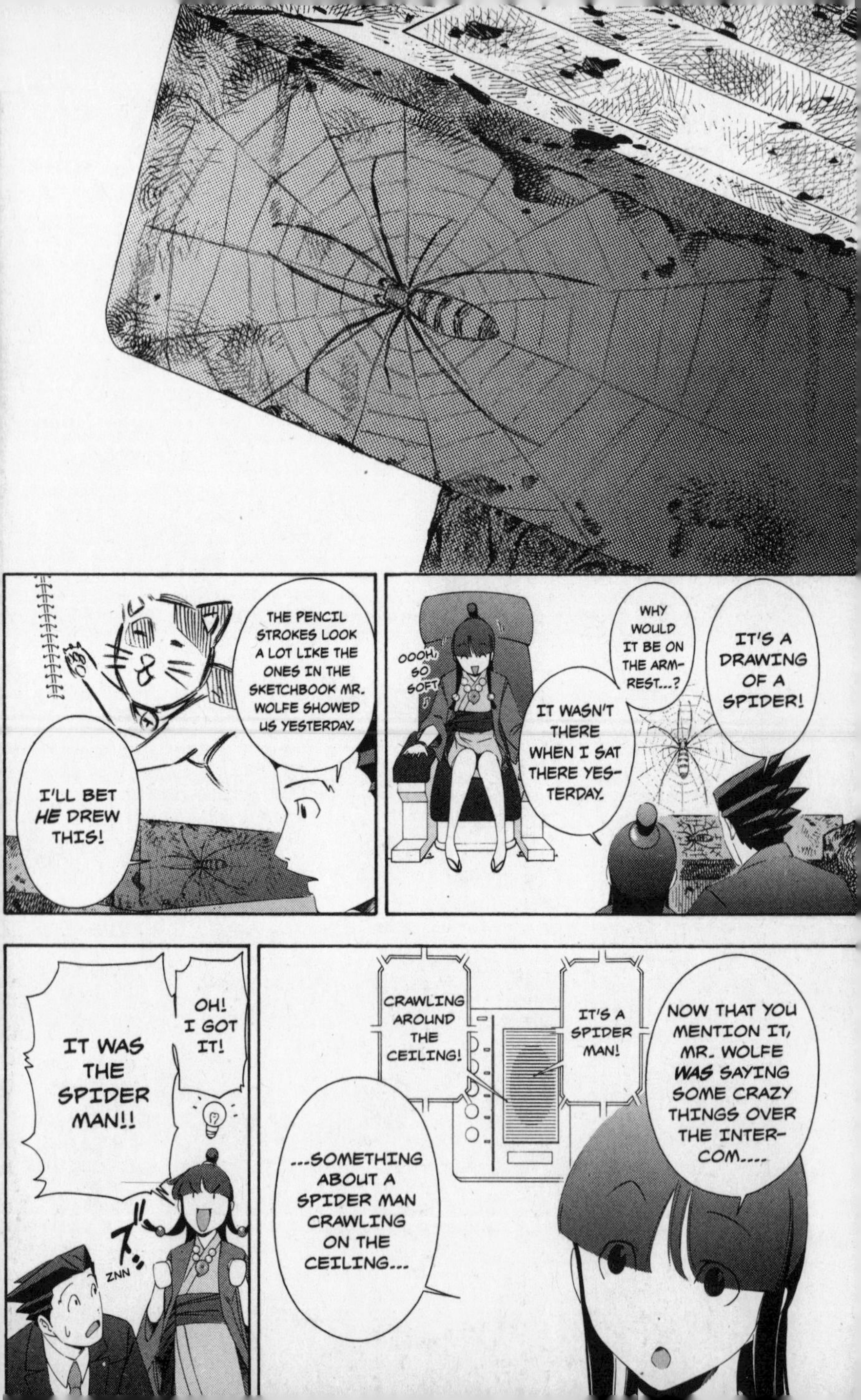
IT'S A DRAWING OF A SPIDER!
WHY WOULD IT BE ON THE ARM-REST...?
IT WASN'T THERE WHEN I SAT THERE YES-TERDAY.
OOOH, SO SOFT
THE PENCIL STROKES LOOK A LOT LIKE THE ONES IN THE SKETCHBOOK MR. WOLFE SHOWED US YESTERDAY.
I'LL BET *HE* DREW THIS!
NOW THAT YOU MENTION IT, MR. WOLFE **WAS** SAYING SOME CRAZY THINGS OVER THE INTER-COM....
IT'S A SPIDER MAN!
CRAWLING AROUND THE CEILING!
...SOMETHING ABOUT A SPIDER MAN CRAWLING ON THE CEILING...
OH! I GOT IT!
IT WAS THE SPIDER MAN!!
ZNN

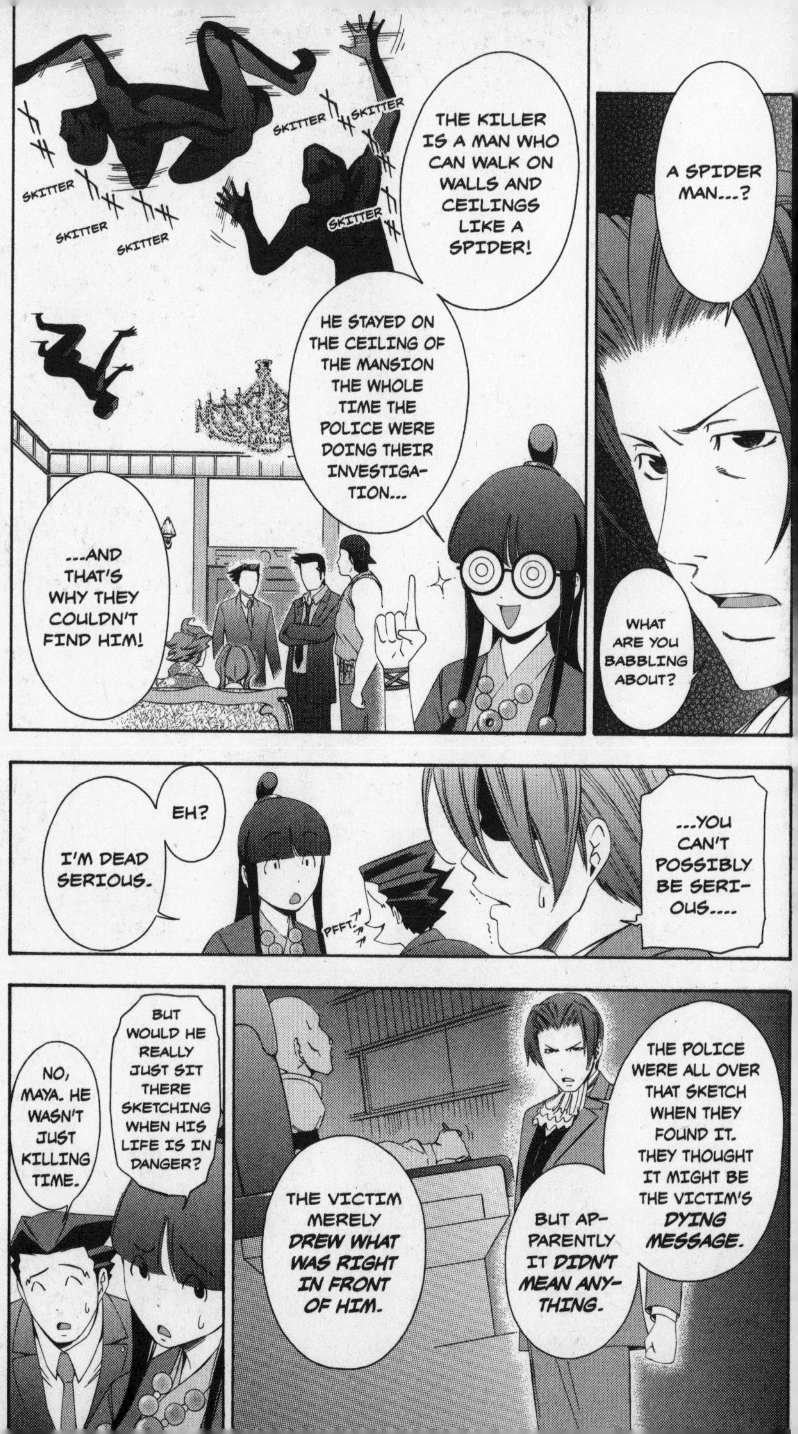
A SPIDER MAN...?
WHAT ARE YOU BABBLING ABOUT?
THE KILLER IS A MAN WHO CAN WALK ON WALLS AND CEILINGS LIKE A SPIDER!
SKITTER
SKITTER
SKITTER
SKITTER
SKITTER
SKITTER
HE STAYED ON THE CEILING OF THE MANSION THE WHOLE TIME THE POLICE WERE DOING THEIR INVESTIGA-TION...
...AND THAT'S WHY THEY COULDN'T FIND HIM!
...YOU CAN'T POSSIBLY BE SERI-OUS....
PFFT
EH?
I'M DEAD SERIOUS.
THE POLICE WERE ALL OVER THAT SKETCH WHEN THEY FOUND IT. THEY THOUGHT IT MIGHT BE THE VICTIM'S *DYING MESSAGE*.
BUT AP-PARENTLY IT *DIDN'T MEAN ANY-THING*.
THE VICTIM MERELY *DREW WHAT WAS RIGHT IN FRONT OF HIM*.
BUT WOULD HE REALLY JUST SIT THERE SKETCHING WHEN HIS LIFE IS IN DANGER?
NO, MAYA. HE WASN'T JUST KILLING TIME.

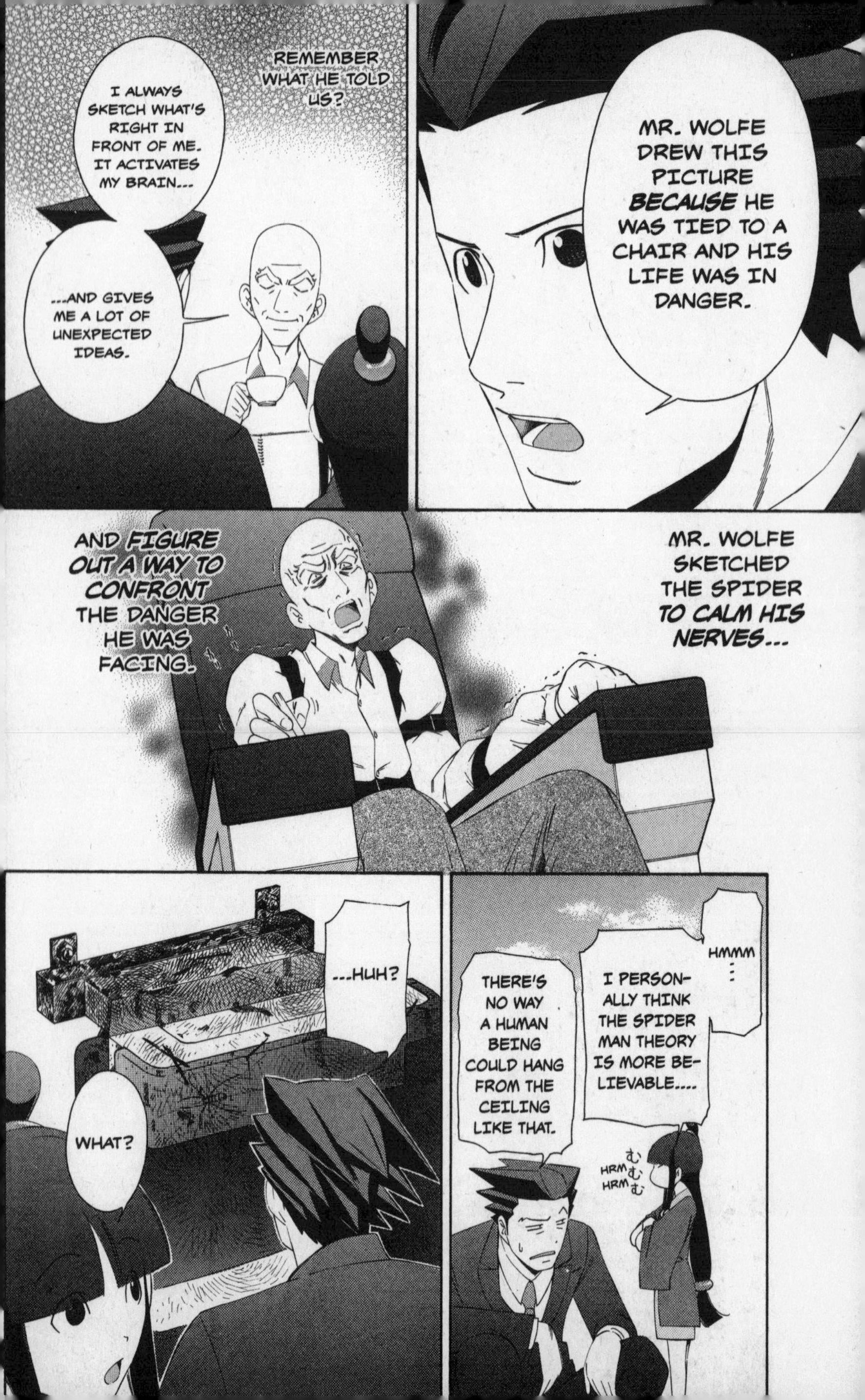
MR. WOLFE DREW THIS PICTURE BECAUSE HE WAS TIED TO A CHAIR AND HIS LIFE WAS IN DANGER.
REMEMBER WHAT HE TOLD US?
I ALWAYS SKETCH WHAT'S RIGHT IN FRONT OF ME. IT ACTIVATES MY BRAIN...
...AND GIVES ME A LOT OF UNEXPECTED IDEAS.
MR. WOLFE SKETCHED THE SPIDER TO CALM HIS NERVES...
AND FIGURE OUT A WAY TO CONFRONT THE DANGER HE WAS FACING.
HMMM
I PERSON-ALLY THINK THE SPIDER MAN THEORY IS MORE BE-LIEVABLE....
THERE'S NO WAY A HUMAN BEING COULD HANG FROM THE CEILING LIKE THAT.
HRM HRM
むむむ
...HUH?
WHAT?

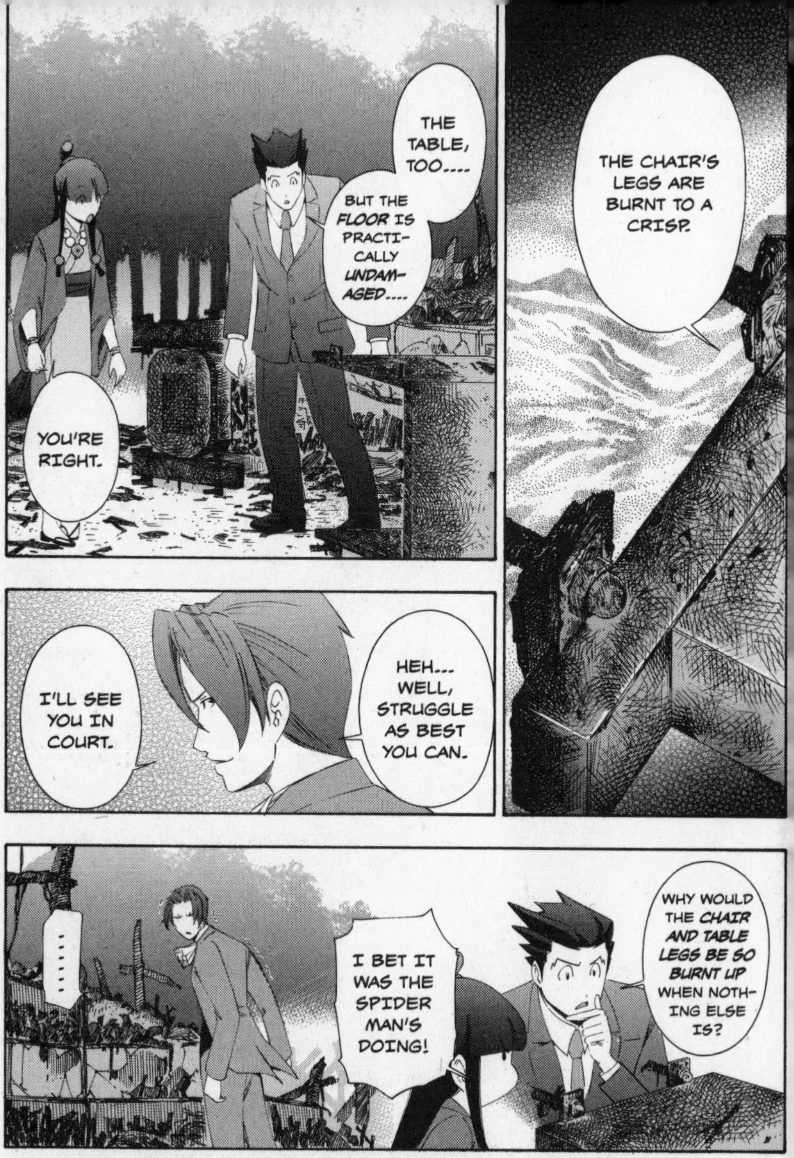
THE CHAIR'S LEGS ARE BURNT TO A CRISP.
THE TABLE, TOO....
BUT THE *FLOOR* IS PRACTICALLY *UNDAMAGED*....
YOU'RE RIGHT.
HEH... WELL, STRUGGLE AS BEST YOU CAN.
I'LL SEE YOU IN COURT.
WHY WOULD THE *CHAIR AND TABLE LEGS BE SO BURNT UP* WHEN NOTHING ELSE IS?
I BET IT WAS THE SPIDER MAN'S DOING!
......

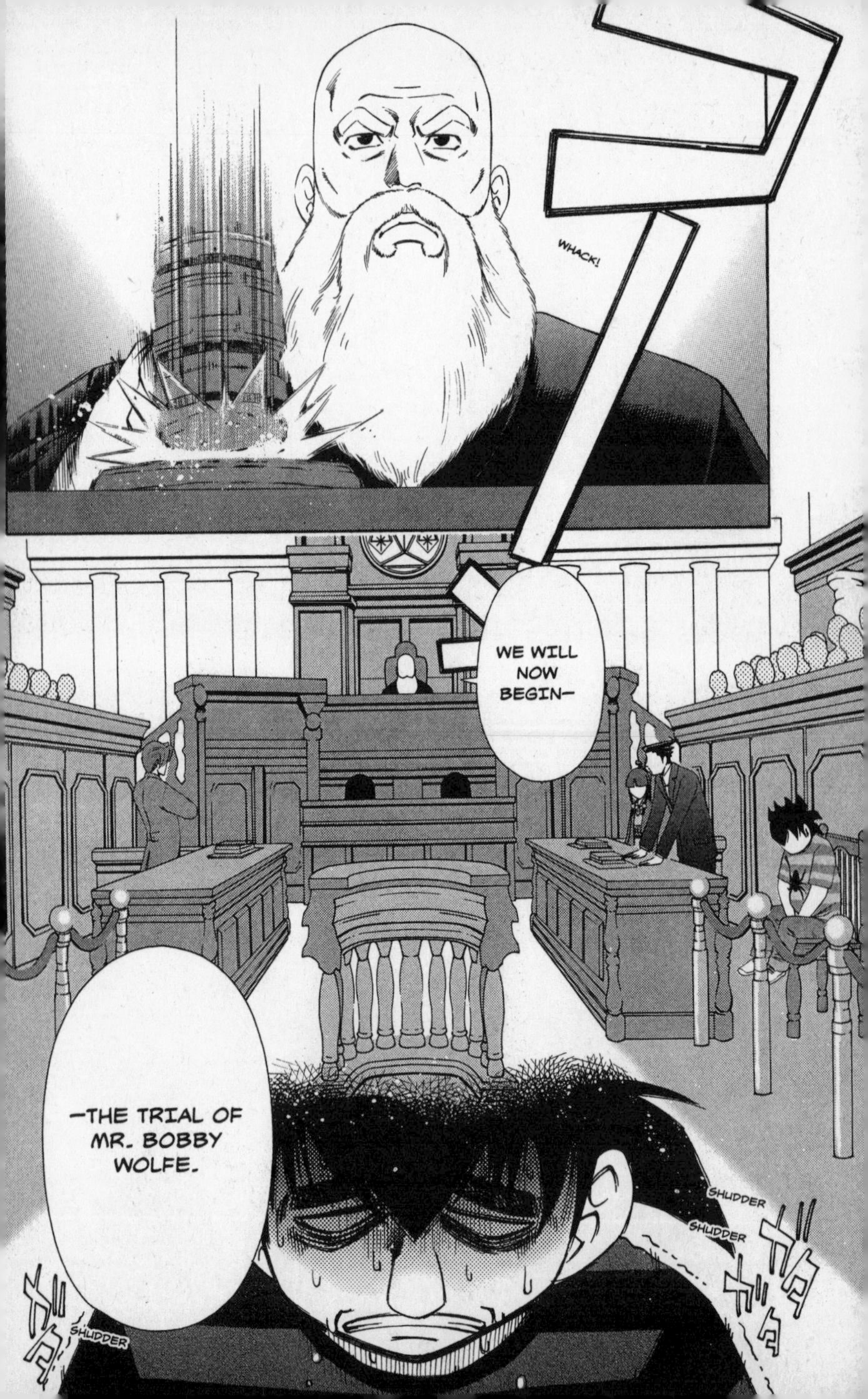
WHACK!
WE WILL NOW BEGIN—
—THE TRIAL OF MR. BOBBY WOLFE.
SHUDDER
SHUDDER
SHUDDER

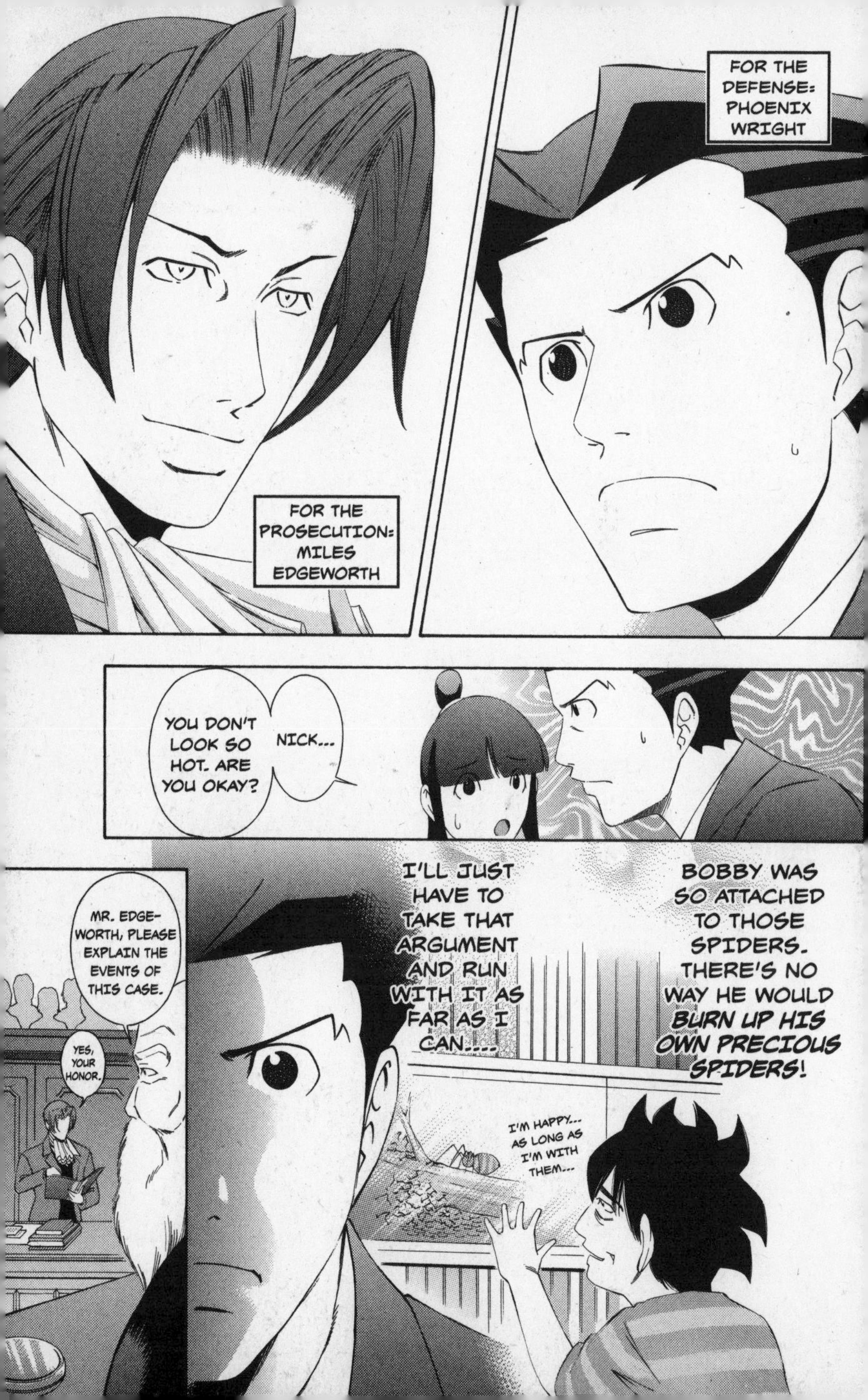
FOR THE DEFENSE: PHOENIX WRIGHT
FOR THE PROSECUTION: MILES EDGEWORTH
NICK...
YOU DON'T LOOK SO HOT. ARE YOU OKAY?
BOBBY WAS SO ATTACHED TO THOSE SPIDERS. THERE'S NO WAY HE WOULD *BURN UP HIS OWN PRECIOUS SPIDERS!*
I'LL JUST HAVE TO TAKE THAT ARGUMENT AND RUN WITH IT AS FAR AS I CAN....
I'M HAPPY... AS LONG AS I'M WITH THEM...
MR. EDGEWORTH, PLEASE EXPLAIN THE EVENTS OF THIS CASE.
YES, YOUR HONOR.

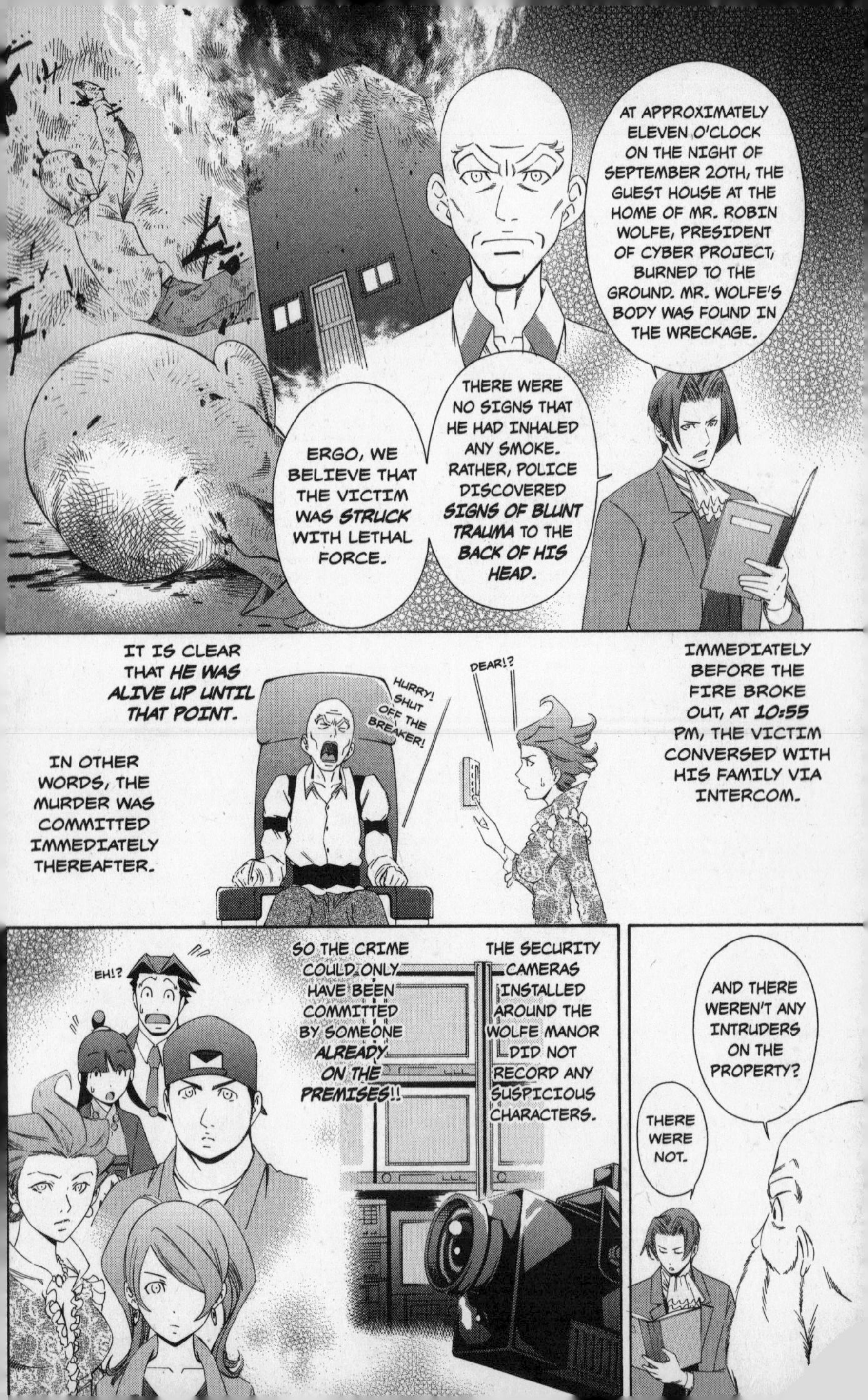
AT APPROXIMATELY ELEVEN O'CLOCK ON THE NIGHT OF SEPTEMBER 20TH, THE GUEST HOUSE AT THE HOME OF MR. ROBIN WOLFE, PRESIDENT OF CYBER PROJECT, BURNED TO THE GROUND. MR. WOLFE'S BODY WAS FOUND IN THE WRECKAGE.
THERE WERE NO SIGNS THAT HE HAD INHALED ANY SMOKE. RATHER, POLICE DISCOVERED SIGNS OF BLUNT TRAUMA TO THE BACK OF HIS HEAD.
ERGO, WE BELIEVE THAT THE VICTIM WAS STRUCK WITH LETHAL FORCE.
IMMEDIATELY BEFORE THE FIRE BROKE OUT, AT 10:55 PM, THE VICTIM CONVERSED WITH HIS FAMILY VIA INTERCOM.
DEAR!?
HURRY! SHUT OFF THE BREAKER!
IT IS CLEAR THAT HE WAS ALIVE UP UNTIL THAT POINT.
IN OTHER WORDS, THE MURDER WAS COMMITTED IMMEDIATELY THEREAFTER.
AND THERE WEREN'T ANY INTRUDERS ON THE PROPERTY?
THERE WERE NOT.
THE SECURITY CAMERAS INSTALLED AROUND THE WOLFE MANOR DID NOT RECORD ANY SUSPICIOUS CHARACTERS.
SO THE CRIME COULD ONLY HAVE BEEN COMMITTED BY SOMEONE ALREADY ON THE PREMISES!!
EH!?

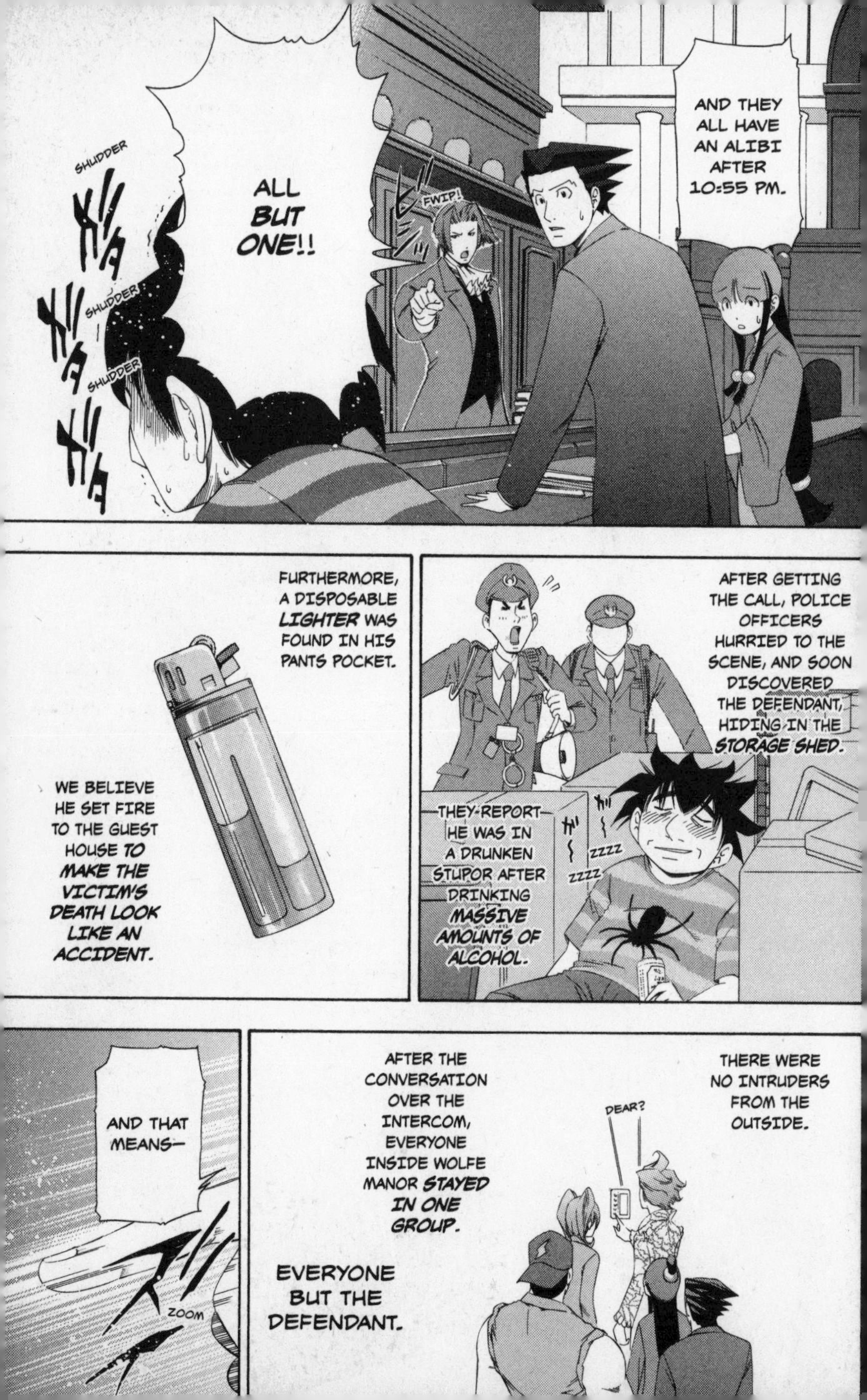
AND THEY ALL HAVE AN ALIBI AFTER 10:55 PM.
FWIP!
ALL BUT ONE!!
SHUDDER
SHUDDER
SHUDDER
AFTER GETTING THE CALL, POLICE OFFICERS HURRIED TO THE SCENE, AND SOON DISCOVERED THE DEFENDANT, HIDING IN THE STORAGE SHED.
THEY REPORT HE WAS IN A DRUNKEN STUPOR AFTER DRINKING MASSIVE AMOUNTS OF ALCOHOL.
ZZZZ
ZZZZ
FURTHERMORE, A DISPOSABLE LIGHTER WAS FOUND IN HIS PANTS POCKET.
WE BELIEVE HE SET FIRE TO THE GUEST HOUSE TO MAKE THE VICTIM'S DEATH LOOK LIKE AN ACCIDENT.
THERE WERE NO INTRUDERS FROM THE OUTSIDE.
AFTER THE CONVERSATION OVER THE INTERCOM, EVERYONE INSIDE WOLFE MANOR STAYED IN ONE GROUP.
DEAR?
EVERYONE BUT THE DEFENDANT.
AND THAT MEANS—
ZOOM

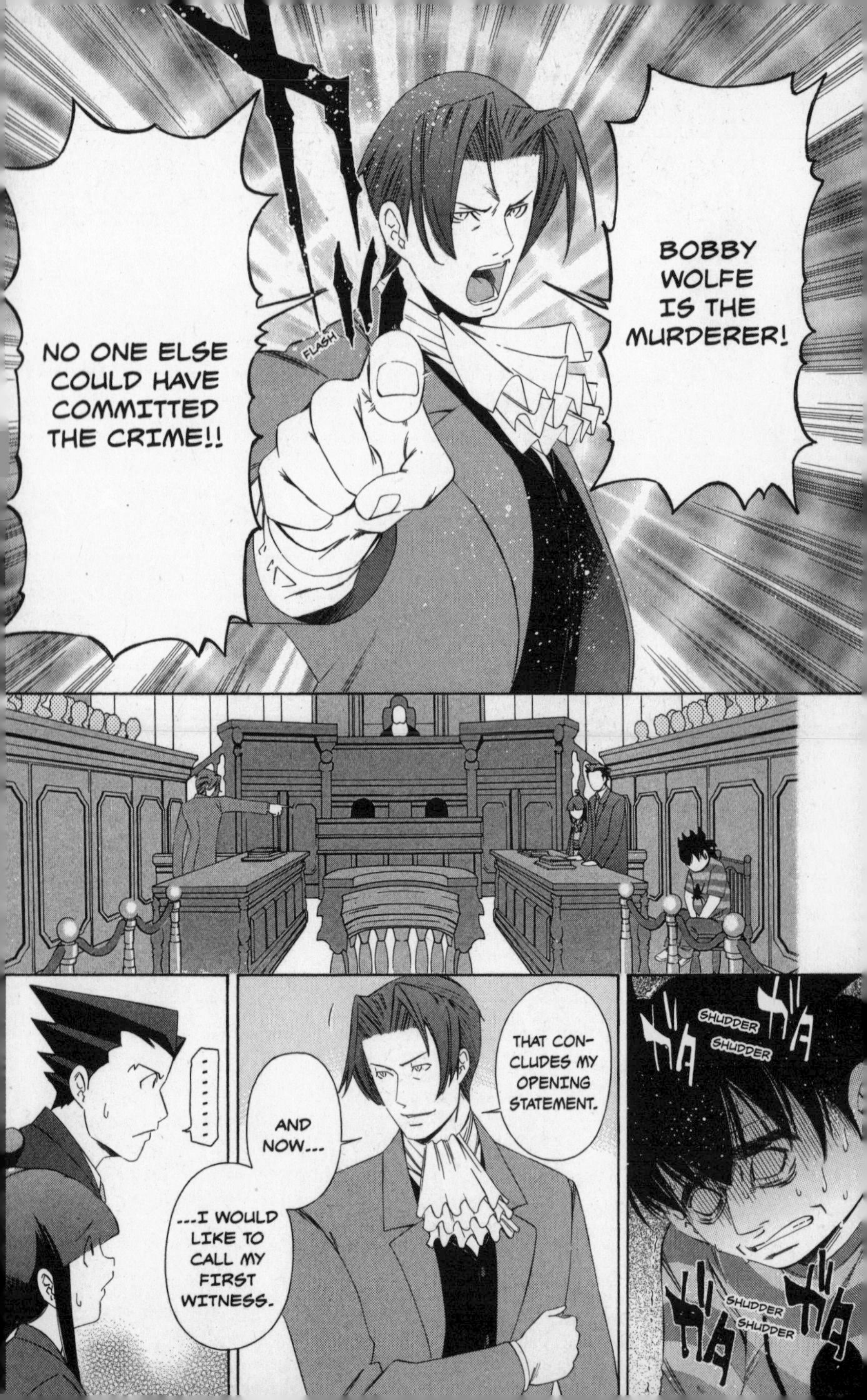
BOBBY WOLFE IS THE MURDERER!
FLASH
NO ONE ELSE COULD HAVE COMMITTED THE CRIME!!
SHUDDER SHUDDER
SHUDDER SHUDDER
THAT CON-CLUDES MY OPENING STATEMENT.
AND NOW...
...I WOULD LIKE TO CALL MY FIRST WITNESS.
......

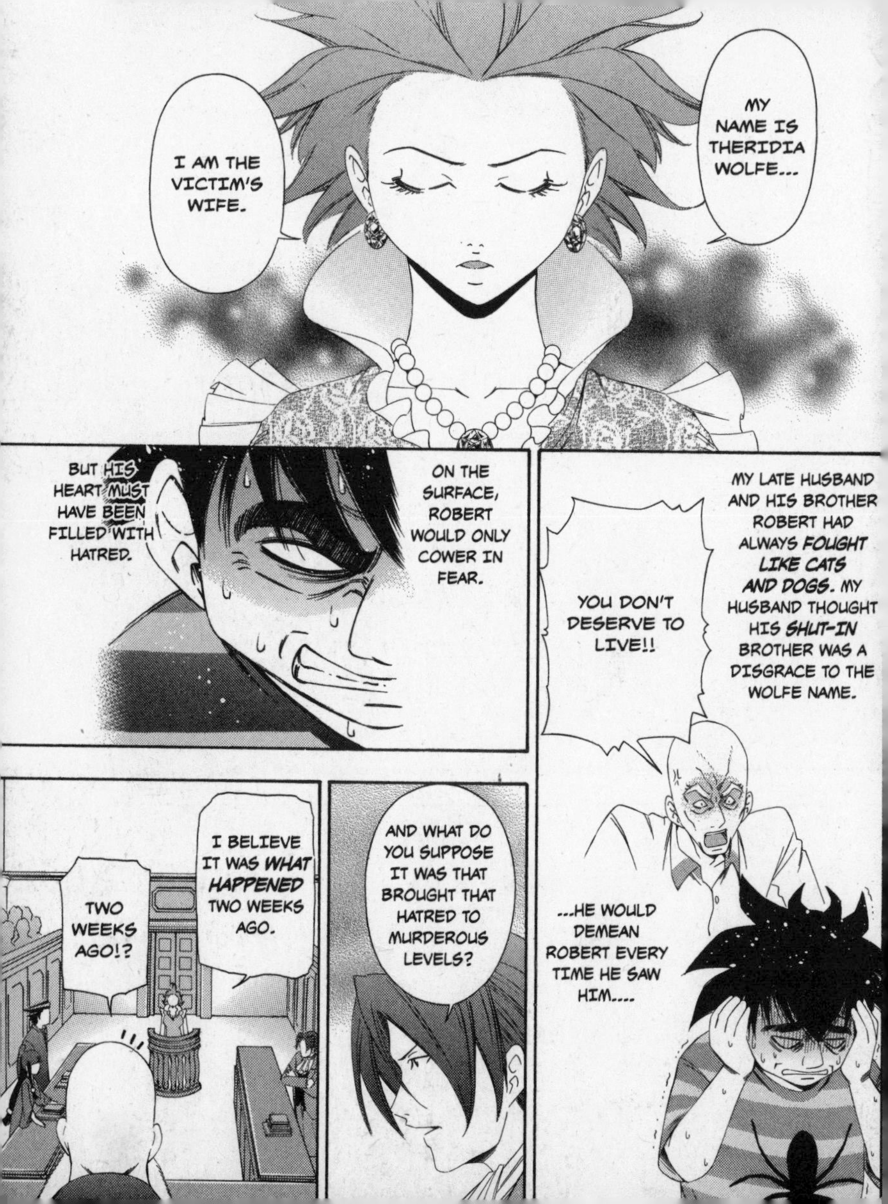
MY NAME IS THERIDIA WOLFE...
I AM THE VICTIM'S WIFE.
MY LATE HUSBAND AND HIS BROTHER ROBERT HAD ALWAYS *FOUGHT LIKE CATS AND DOGS*. MY HUSBAND THOUGHT HIS *SHUT-IN* BROTHER WAS A DISGRACE TO THE WOLFE NAME.
YOU DON'T DESERVE TO LIVE!!
...HE WOULD DEMEAN ROBERT EVERY TIME HE SAW HIM....
ON THE SURFACE, ROBERT WOULD ONLY COWER IN FEAR.
BUT HIS HEART MUST HAVE BEEN FILLED WITH HATRED.
AND WHAT DO YOU SUPPOSE IT WAS THAT BROUGHT THAT HATRED TO MURDEROUS LEVELS?
I BELIEVE IT WAS *WHAT HAPPENED* TWO WEEKS AGO.
TWO WEEKS AGO!?

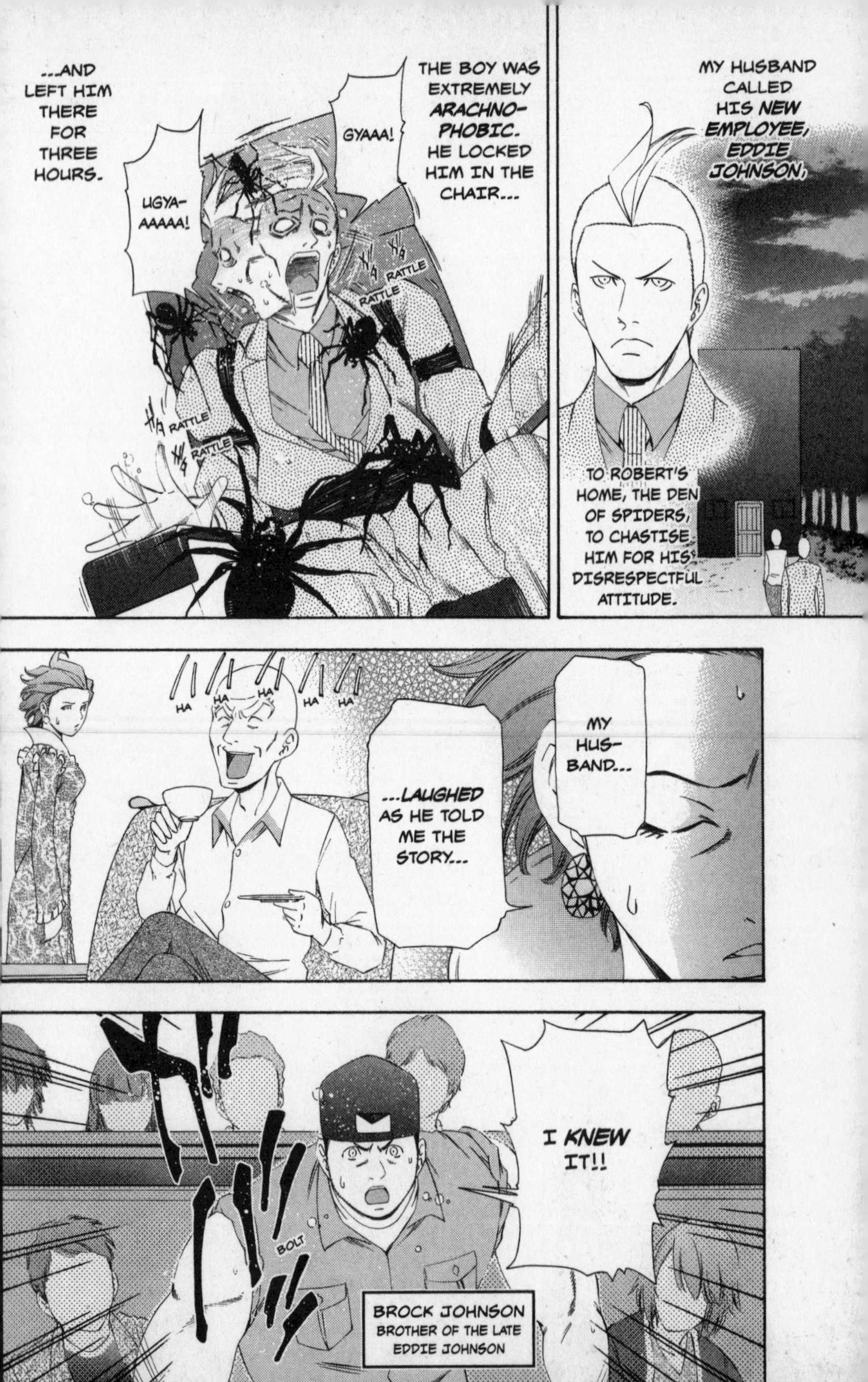
MY HUSBAND CALLED HIS NEW EMPLOYEE, EDDIE JOHNSON,
TO ROBERT'S HOME, THE DEN OF SPIDERS, TO CHASTISE HIM FOR HIS DISRESPECTFUL ATTITUDE.
THE BOY WAS EXTREMELY ARACHNOPHOBIC. HE LOCKED HIM IN THE CHAIR...
GYAAA!
RATTLE RATTLE
...AND LEFT HIM THERE FOR THREE HOURS.
UGYA-AAAAA!
RATTLE RATTLE
MY HUSBAND...
...LAUGHED AS HE TOLD ME THE STORY...
HA HA HA HA HA HA
I KNEW IT!!
BOLT
BROCK JOHNSON
BROTHER OF THE LATE EDDIE JOHNSON

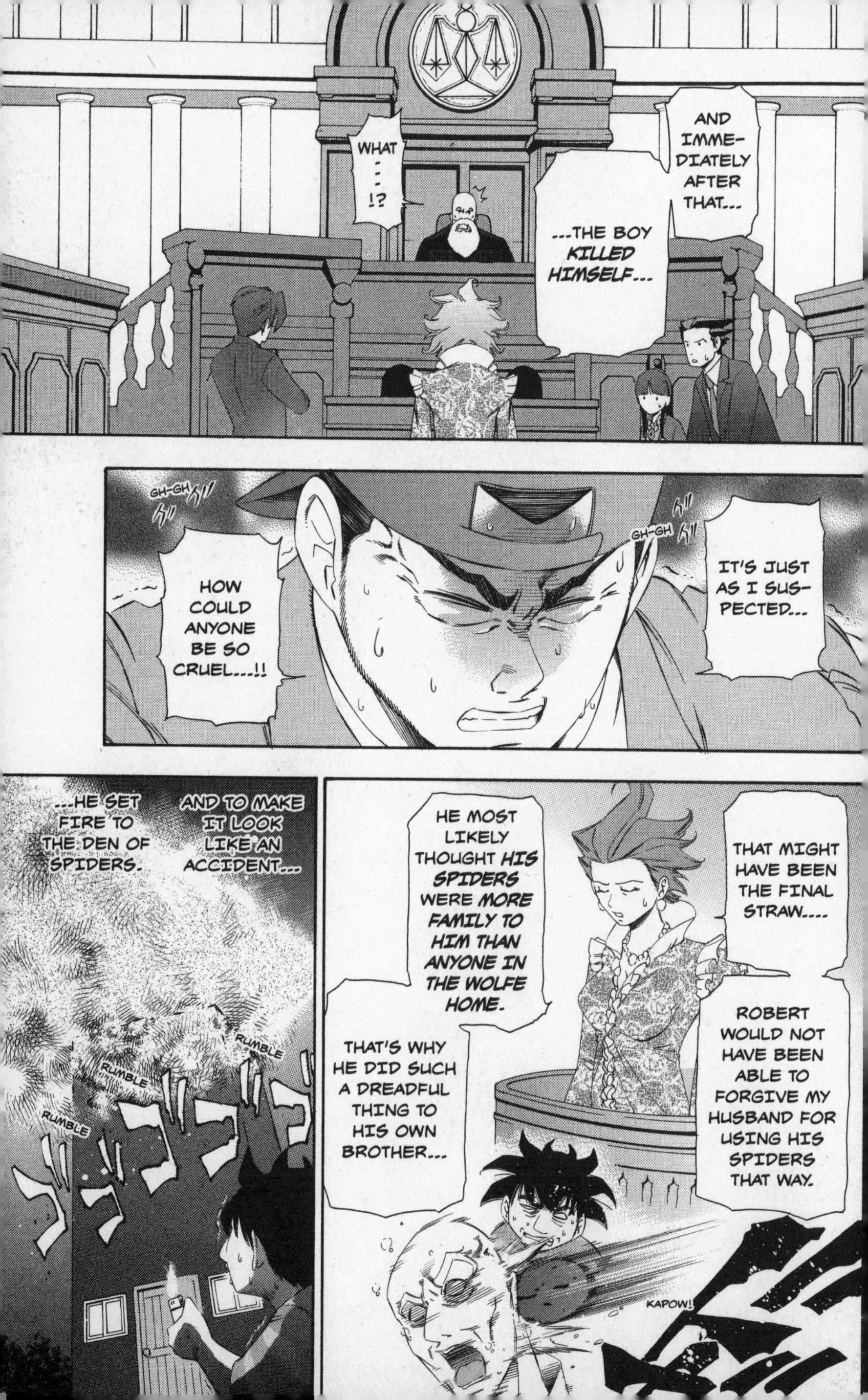
AND IMMEDIATELY AFTER THAT...
...THE BOY KILLED HIMSELF...
WHAT...!?
GH-GH
IT'S JUST AS I SUSPECTED...
HOW COULD ANYONE BE SO CRUEL...!!
GH-GH
THAT MIGHT HAVE BEEN THE FINAL STRAW....
HE MOST LIKELY THOUGHT HIS SPIDERS WERE MORE FAMILY TO HIM THAN ANYONE IN THE WOLFE HOME.
ROBERT WOULD NOT HAVE BEEN ABLE TO FORGIVE MY HUSBAND FOR USING HIS SPIDERS THAT WAY.
THAT'S WHY HE DID SUCH A DREADFUL THING TO HIS OWN BROTHER...
KAPOW!
AND TO MAKE IT LOOK LIKE AN ACCIDENT...
...HE SET FIRE TO THE DEN OF SPIDERS.
RUMBLE
RUMBLE
RUMBLE

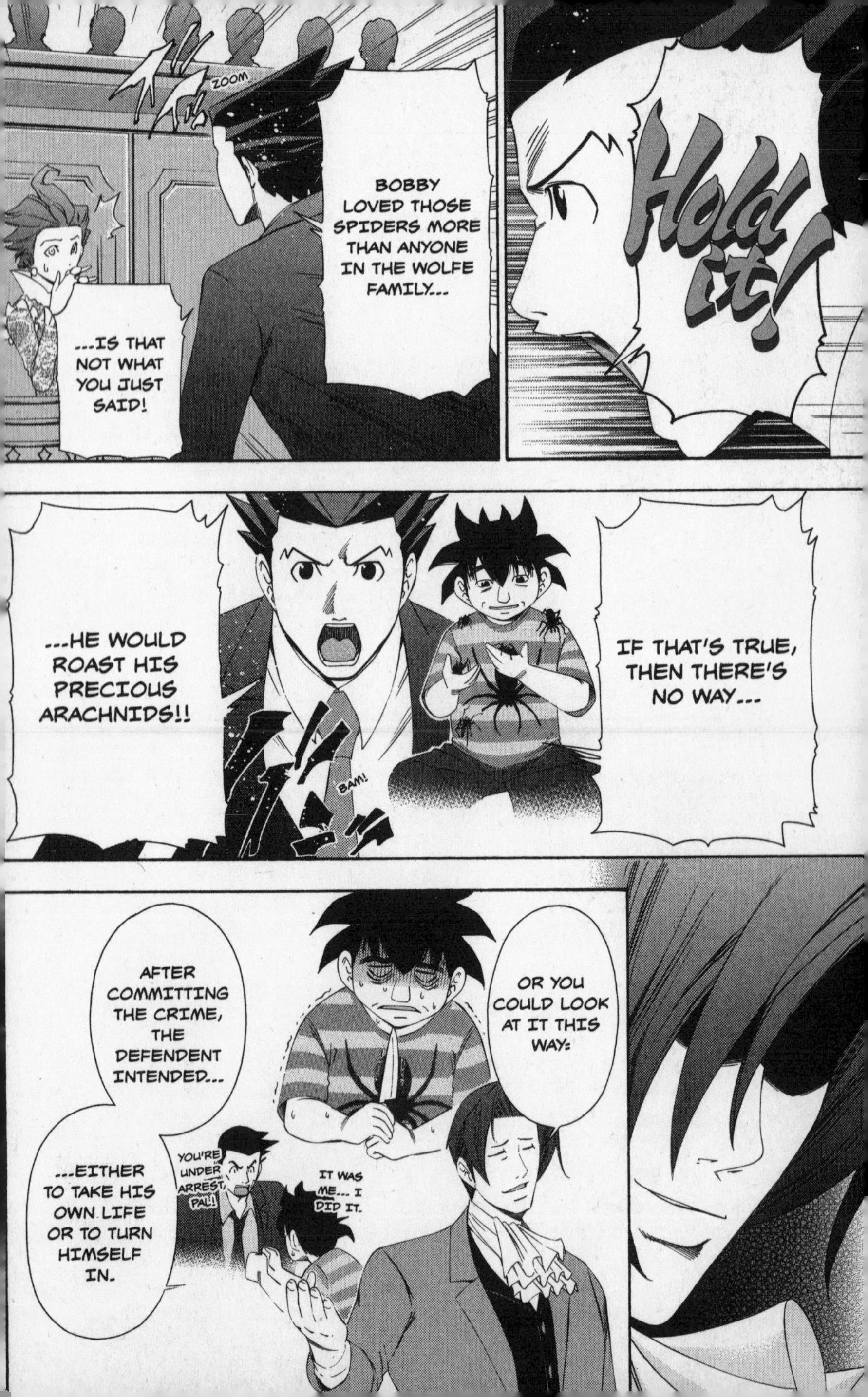
Hold it!
ZOOM
BOBBY LOVED THOSE SPIDERS MORE THAN ANYONE IN THE WOLFE FAMILY...
...IS THAT NOT WHAT YOU JUST SAID!
IF THAT'S TRUE, THEN THERE'S NO WAY...
...HE WOULD ROAST HIS PRECIOUS ARACHNIDS!!
BAM!
OR YOU COULD LOOK AT IT THIS WAY:
AFTER COMMITTING THE CRIME, THE DEFENDENT INTENDED...
IT WAS ME... I DID IT.
YOU'RE UNDER ARREST, PAL!
...EITHER TO TAKE HIS OWN LIFE OR TO TURN HIMSELF IN.

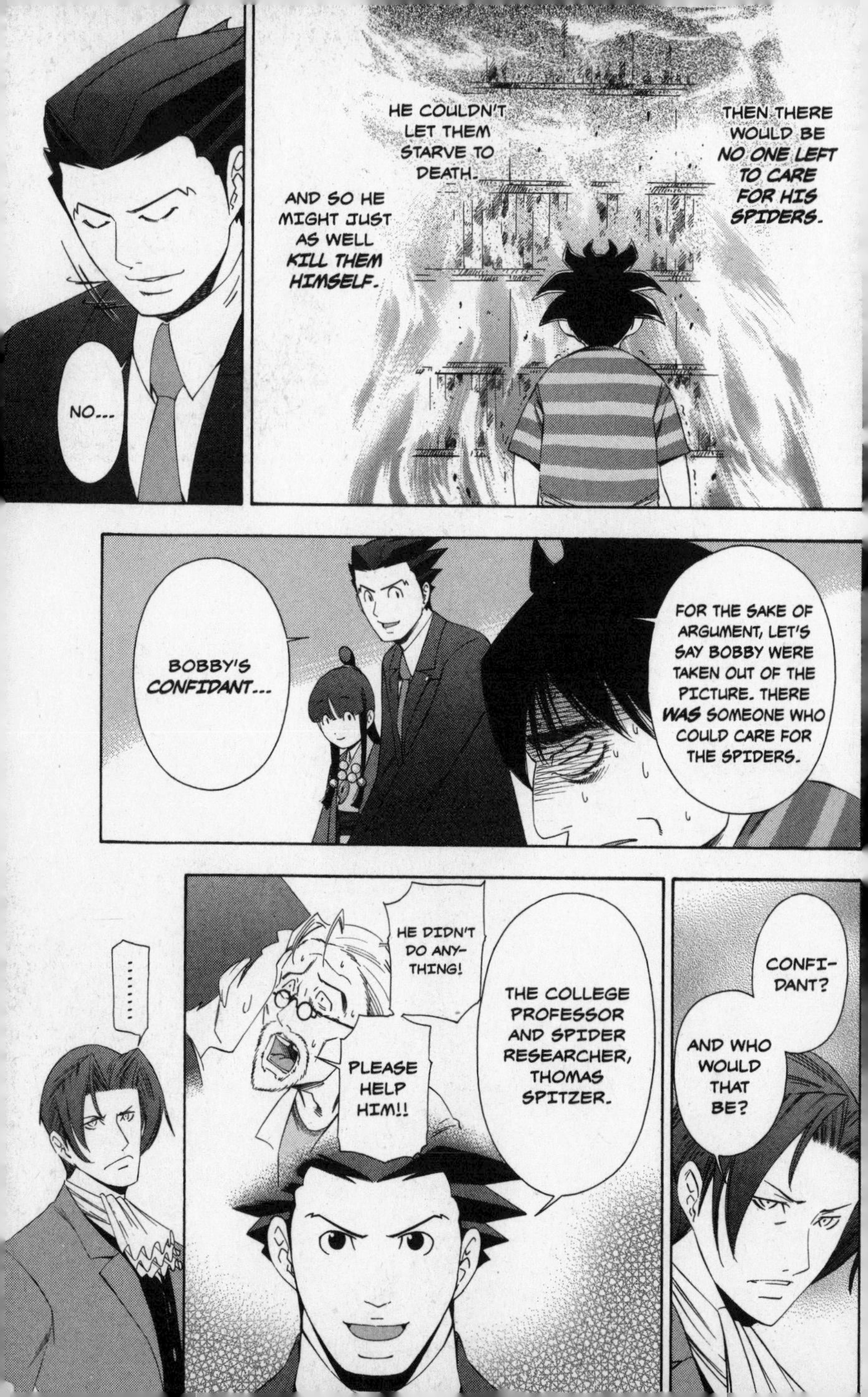
THEN THERE WOULD BE NO ONE LEFT TO CARE FOR HIS SPIDERS.
HE COULDN'T LET THEM STARVE TO DEATH.
AND SO HE MIGHT JUST AS WELL KILL THEM HIMSELF.
NO...
FOR THE SAKE OF ARGUMENT, LET'S SAY BOBBY WERE TAKEN OUT OF THE PICTURE. THERE WAS SOMEONE WHO COULD CARE FOR THE SPIDERS.
BOBBY'S CONFIDANT...
CONFI-DANT?
AND WHO WOULD THAT BE?
THE COLLEGE PROFESSOR AND SPIDER RESEARCHER, THOMAS SPITZER.
HE DIDN'T DO ANY-THING!
PLEASE HELP HIM!!
....

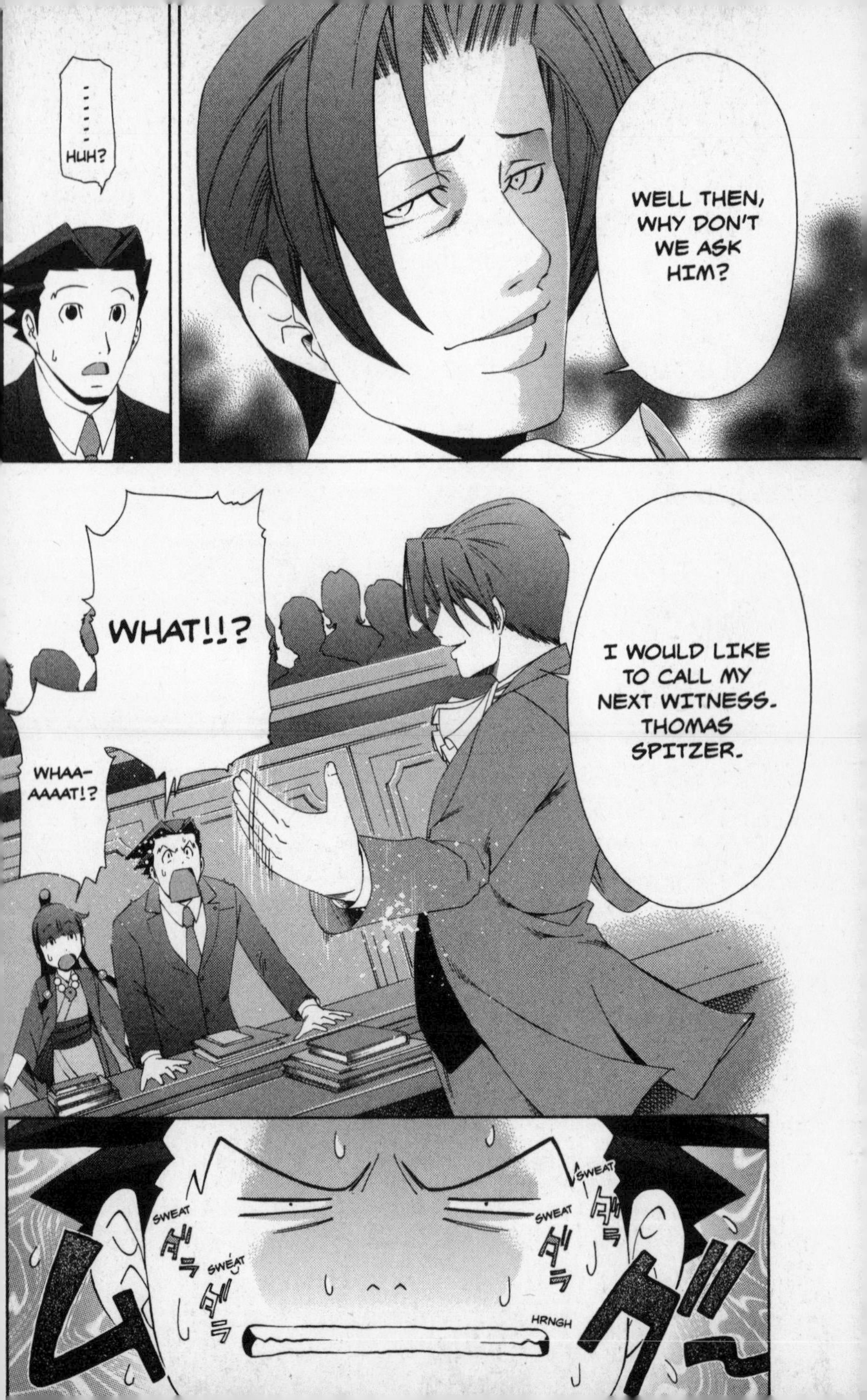
WELL THEN, WHY DON'T WE ASK HIM?
......
HUH?
I WOULD LIKE TO CALL MY NEXT WITNESS. THOMAS SPITZER.
WHAT!!?
WHAA-AAAAT!?
SWEAT
SWEAT
SWEAT
SWEAT
HRNGH

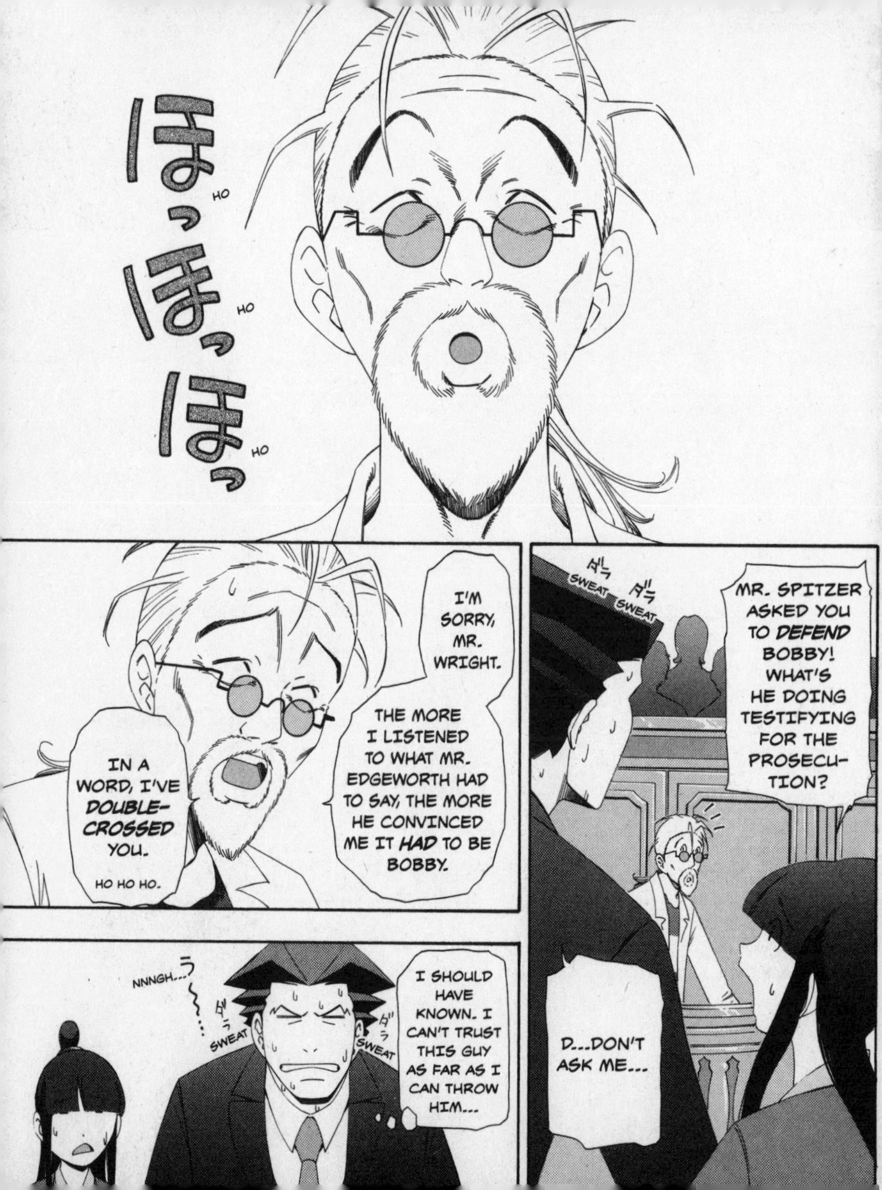
ほっ HO
ほっ HO
ほっ HO
ダラ SWEAT
ダラ SWEAT
MR. SPITZER ASKED YOU TO *DEFEND* BOBBY! WHAT'S HE DOING TESTIFYING FOR THE PROSECUTION?
D...DON'T ASK ME...
I'M SORRY, MR. WRIGHT.
THE MORE I LISTENED TO WHAT MR. EDGEWORTH HAD TO SAY, THE MORE HE CONVINCED ME IT *HAD* TO BE BOBBY.
IN A WORD, I'VE *DOUBLE-CROSSED* YOU.
HO HO HO.
ダラ SWEAT
I SHOULD HAVE KNOWN. I CAN'T TRUST THIS GUY AS FAR AS I CAN THROW HIM...
ダラ SWEAT
う NNNGH...

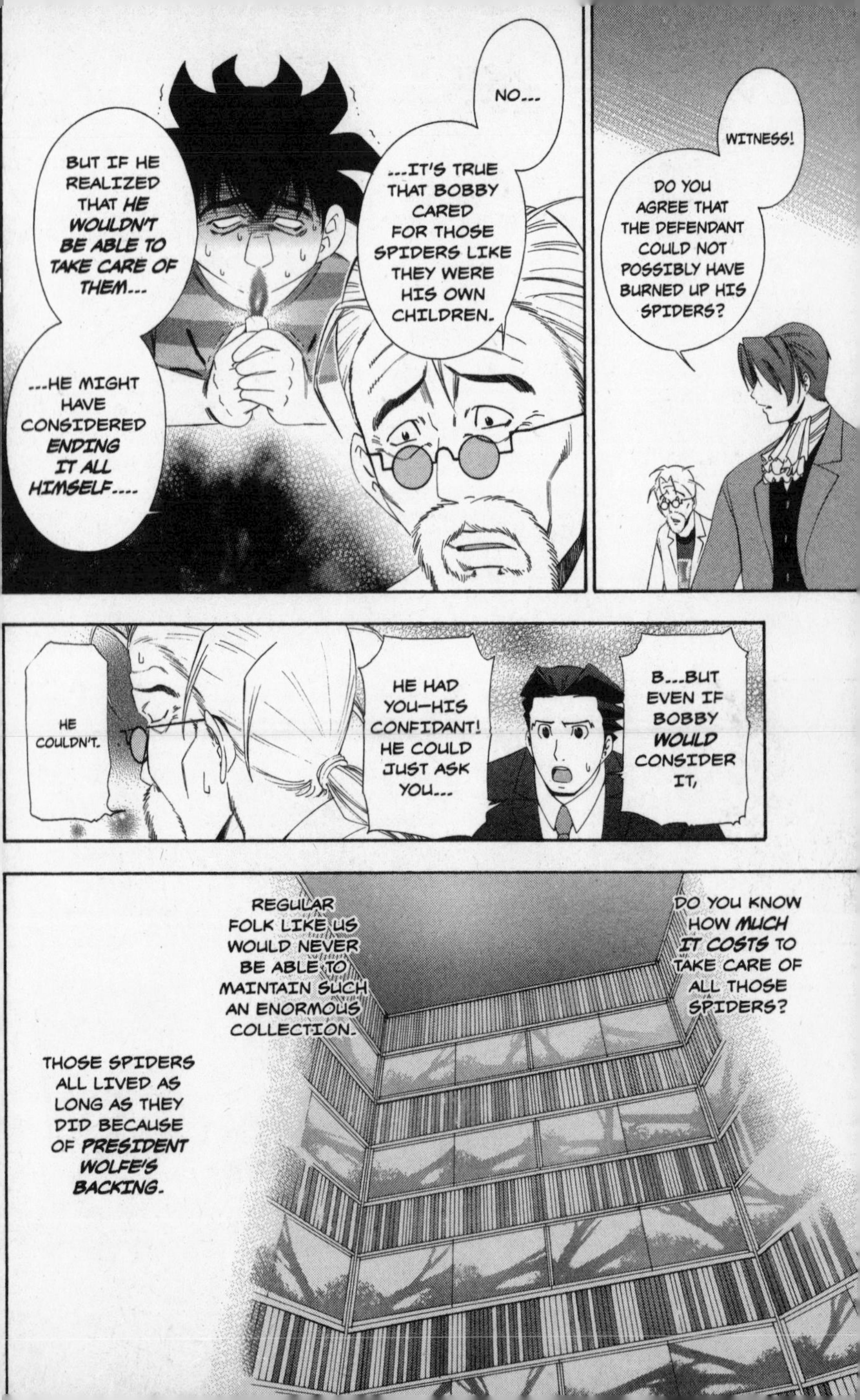
WITNESS!
DO YOU AGREE THAT THE DEFENDANT COULD NOT POSSIBLY HAVE BURNED UP HIS SPIDERS?
NO...
...IT'S TRUE THAT BOBBY CARED FOR THOSE SPIDERS LIKE THEY WERE HIS OWN CHILDREN.
BUT IF HE REALIZED THAT HE WOULDN'T BE ABLE TO TAKE CARE OF THEM...
...HE MIGHT HAVE CONSIDERED ENDING IT ALL HIMSELF....
B...BUT EVEN IF BOBBY WOULD CONSIDER IT,
HE HAD YOU—HIS CONFIDANT! HE COULD JUST ASK YOU...
HE COULDN'T.
DO YOU KNOW HOW MUCH IT COSTS TO TAKE CARE OF ALL THOSE SPIDERS?
REGULAR FOLK LIKE US WOULD NEVER BE ABLE TO MAINTAIN SUCH AN ENORMOUS COLLECTION.
THOSE SPIDERS ALL LIVED AS LONG AS THEY DID BECAUSE OF PRESIDENT WOLFE'S BACKING.

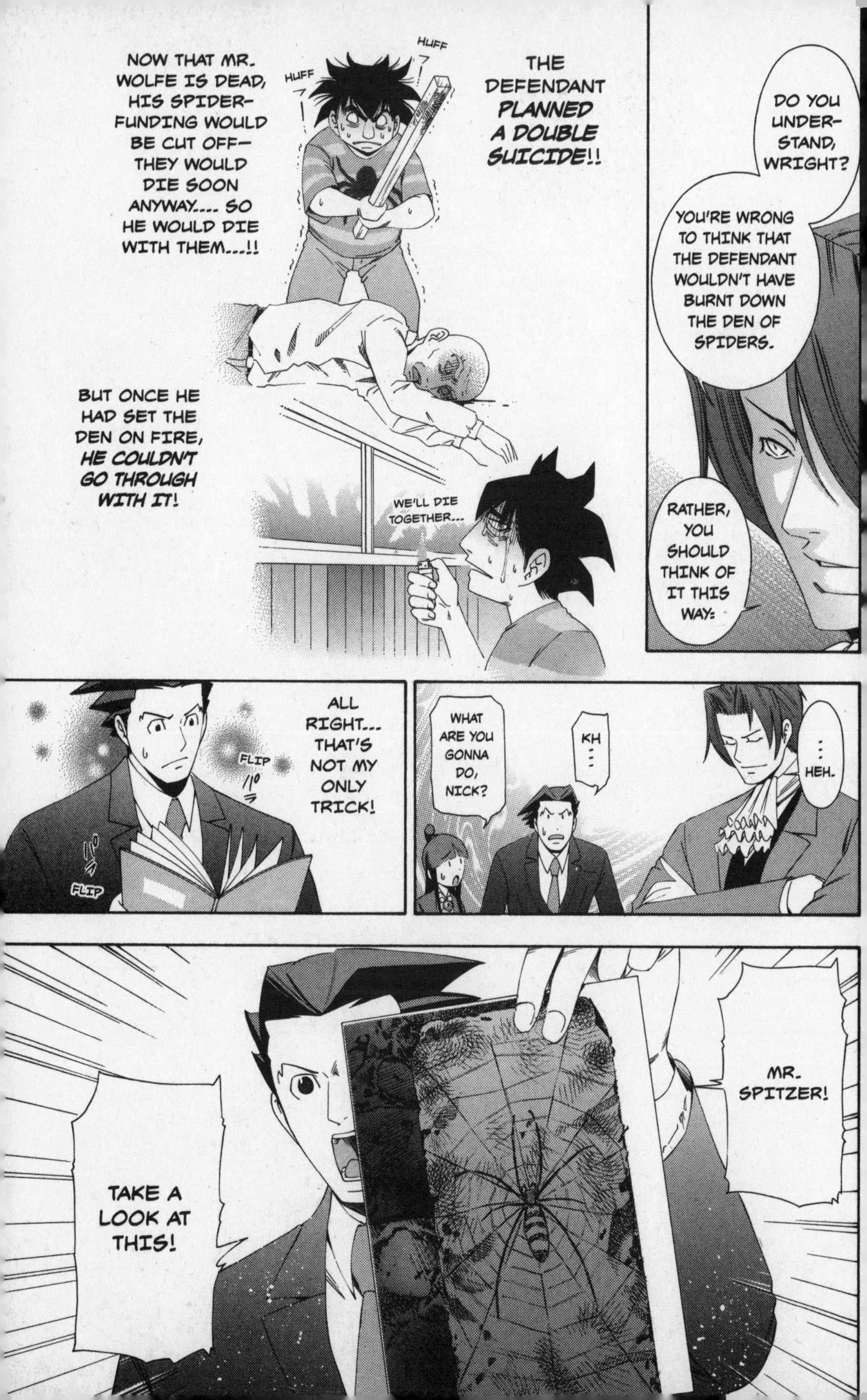
DO YOU UNDERSTAND, WRIGHT?
YOU'RE WRONG TO THINK THAT THE DEFENDANT WOULDN'T HAVE BURNT DOWN THE DEN OF SPIDERS.
RATHER, YOU SHOULD THINK OF IT THIS WAY:
THE DEFENDANT PLANNED A DOUBLE SUICIDE!!
HUFF
HUFF
NOW THAT MR. WOLFE IS DEAD, HIS SPIDER-FUNDING WOULD BE CUT OFF—THEY WOULD DIE SOON ANYWAY.... SO HE WOULD DIE WITH THEM...!!
BUT ONCE HE HAD SET THE DEN ON FIRE, HE COULDN'T GO THROUGH WITH IT!
WE'LL DIE TOGETHER...
...HEH.
KH...
WHAT ARE YOU GONNA DO, NICK?
ALL RIGHT... THAT'S NOT MY ONLY TRICK!
FLIP
FLIP
MR. SPITZER!
TAKE A LOOK AT THIS!

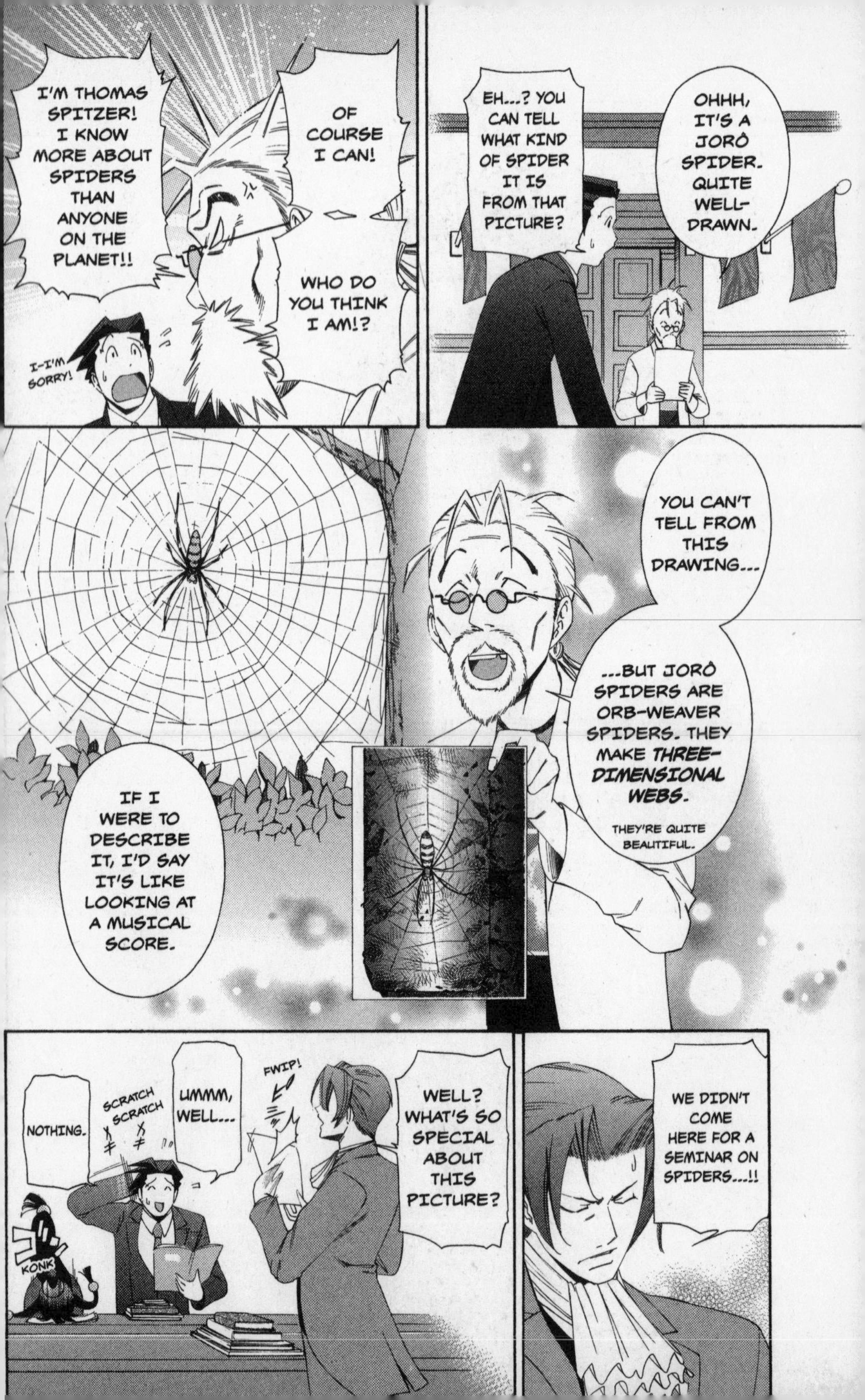

OHHH, IT'S A JORÔ SPIDER. QUITE WELL-DRAWN.
EH...? YOU CAN TELL WHAT KIND OF SPIDER IT IS FROM THAT PICTURE?
OF COURSE I CAN!
WHO DO YOU THINK I AM!?
I'M THOMAS SPITZER! I KNOW MORE ABOUT SPIDERS THAN ANYONE ON THE PLANET!!
I-I'M SORRY!
YOU CAN'T TELL FROM THIS DRAWING...
...BUT JORÔ SPIDERS ARE ORB-WEAVER SPIDERS. THEY MAKE THREE-DIMENSIONAL WEBS.
THEY'RE QUITE BEAUTIFUL.
IF I WERE TO DESCRIBE IT, I'D SAY IT'S LIKE LOOKING AT A MUSICAL SCORE.
WE DIDN'T COME HERE FOR A SEMINAR ON SPIDERS...!!
WELL? WHAT'S SO SPECIAL ABOUT THIS PICTURE?
FWIP!
UMMM, WELL...
SCRATCH SCRATCH
NOTHING.
KONK

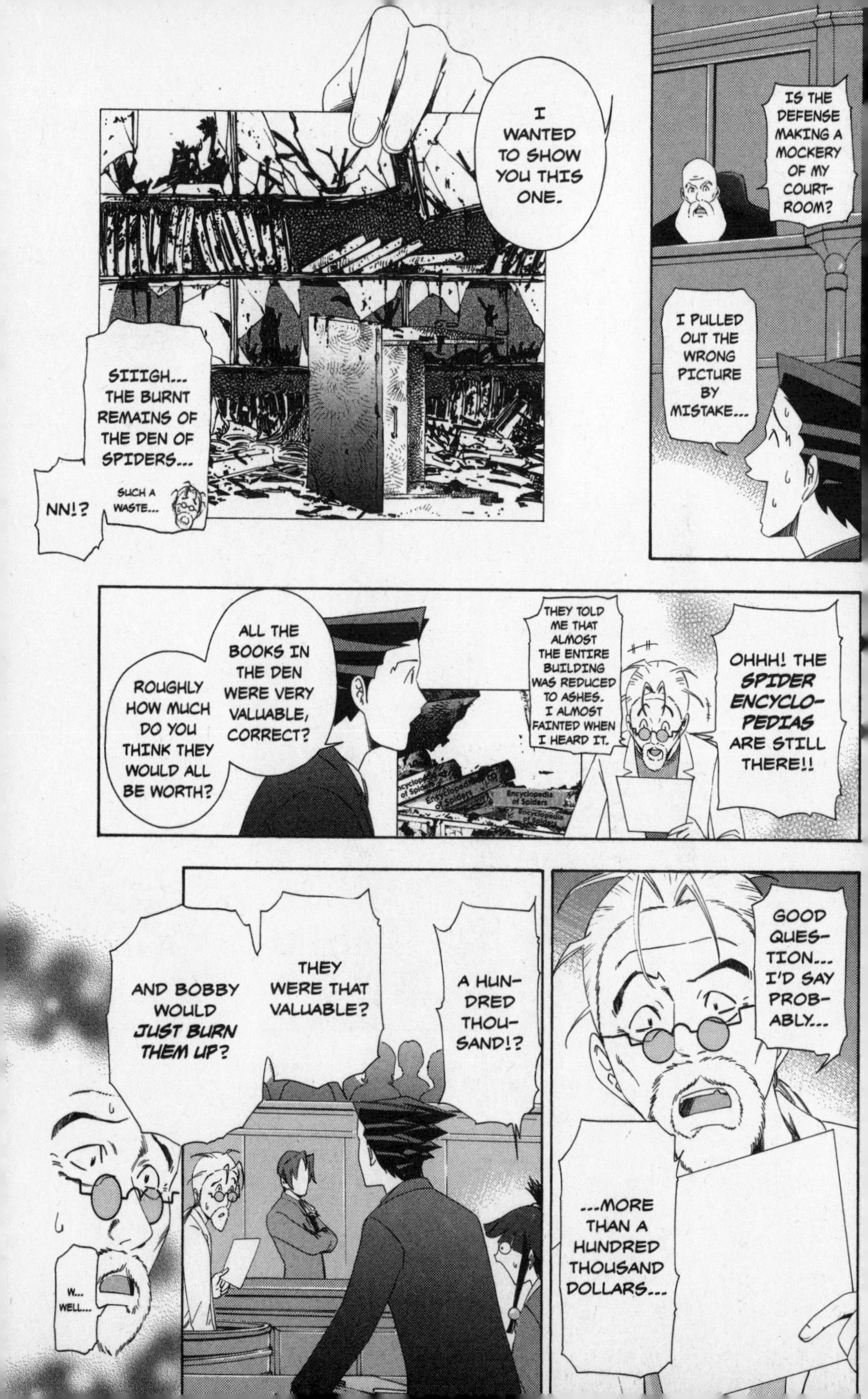
IS THE DEFENSE MAKING A MOCKERY OF MY COURTROOM?
I PULLED OUT THE WRONG PICTURE BY MISTAKE...
I WANTED TO SHOW YOU THIS ONE.
SIIIGH... THE BURNT REMAINS OF THE DEN OF SPIDERS...
SUCH A WASTE...
NN!?
OHHH! THE *SPIDER ENCYCLOPEDIAS* ARE STILL THERE!!
THEY TOLD ME THAT ALMOST THE ENTIRE BUILDING WAS REDUCED TO ASHES. I ALMOST FAINTED WHEN I HEARD IT.
ALL THE BOOKS IN THE DEN WERE VERY VALUABLE, CORRECT?
ROUGHLY HOW MUCH DO YOU THINK THEY WOULD ALL BE WORTH?
GOOD QUESTION... I'D SAY PROBABLY...
...MORE THAN A HUNDRED THOUSAND DOLLARS...
A HUNDRED THOUSAND!?
THEY WERE THAT VALUABLE?
AND BOBBY WOULD *JUST BURN THEM UP*?
W... WELL...

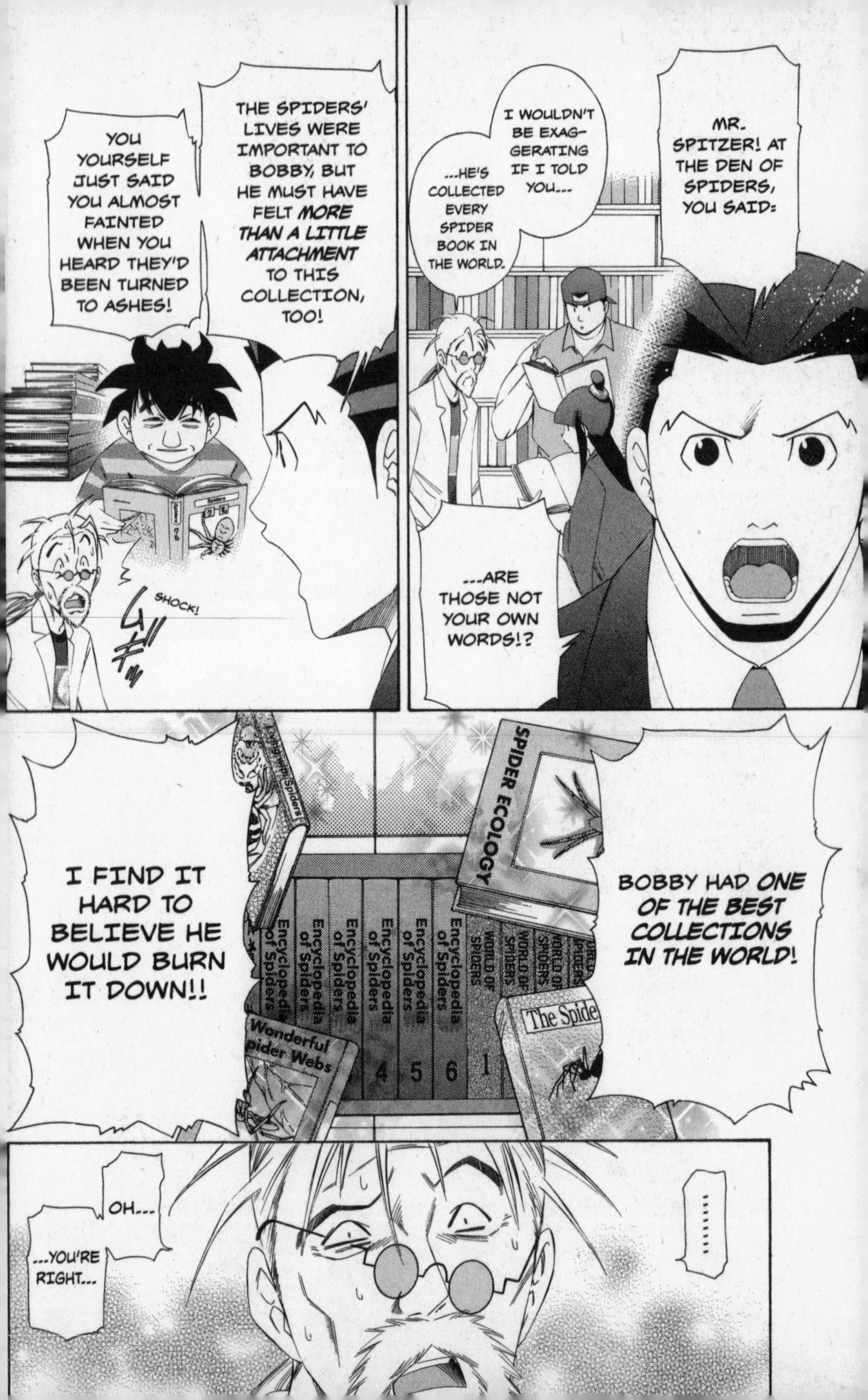
MR. SPITZER! AT THE DEN OF SPIDERS, YOU SAID:
I WOULDN'T BE EXAG-GERATING IF I TOLD YOU...
...HE'S COLLECTED EVERY SPIDER BOOK IN THE WORLD.
...ARE THOSE NOT YOUR OWN WORDS!?
THE SPIDERS' LIVES WERE IMPORTANT TO BOBBY, BUT HE MUST HAVE FELT MORE THAN A LITTLE ATTACHMENT TO THIS COLLECTION, TOO!
YOU YOURSELF JUST SAID YOU ALMOST FAINTED WHEN YOU HEARD THEY'D BEEN TURNED TO ASHES!
SHOCK!
BOBBY HAD ONE OF THE BEST COLLECTIONS IN THE WORLD!
SPIDER ECOLOGY
Living with Spiders
Encyclopedia of Spiders
WORLD OF SPIDERS
The Spide
Wonderful Spider Webs
I FIND IT HARD TO BELIEVE HE WOULD BURN IT DOWN!!
......
OH...
...YOU'RE RIGHT...

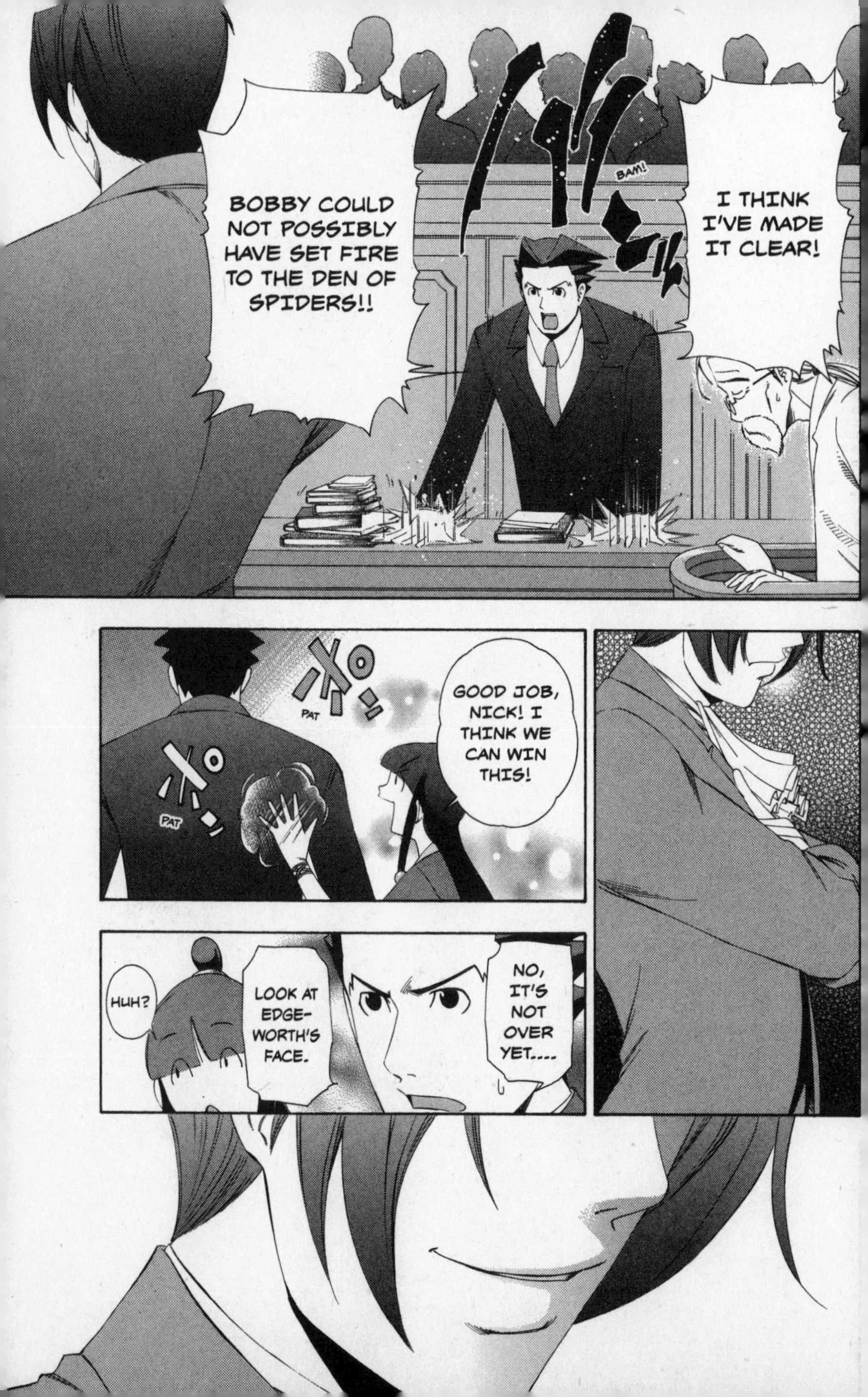
I THINK I'VE MADE IT CLEAR!
BAM!
BOBBY COULD NOT POSSIBLY HAVE SET FIRE TO THE DEN OF SPIDERS!!
GOOD JOB, NICK! I THINK WE CAN WIN THIS!
PAT
PAT
NO, IT'S NOT OVER YET....
LOOK AT EDGE-WORTH'S FACE.
HUH?

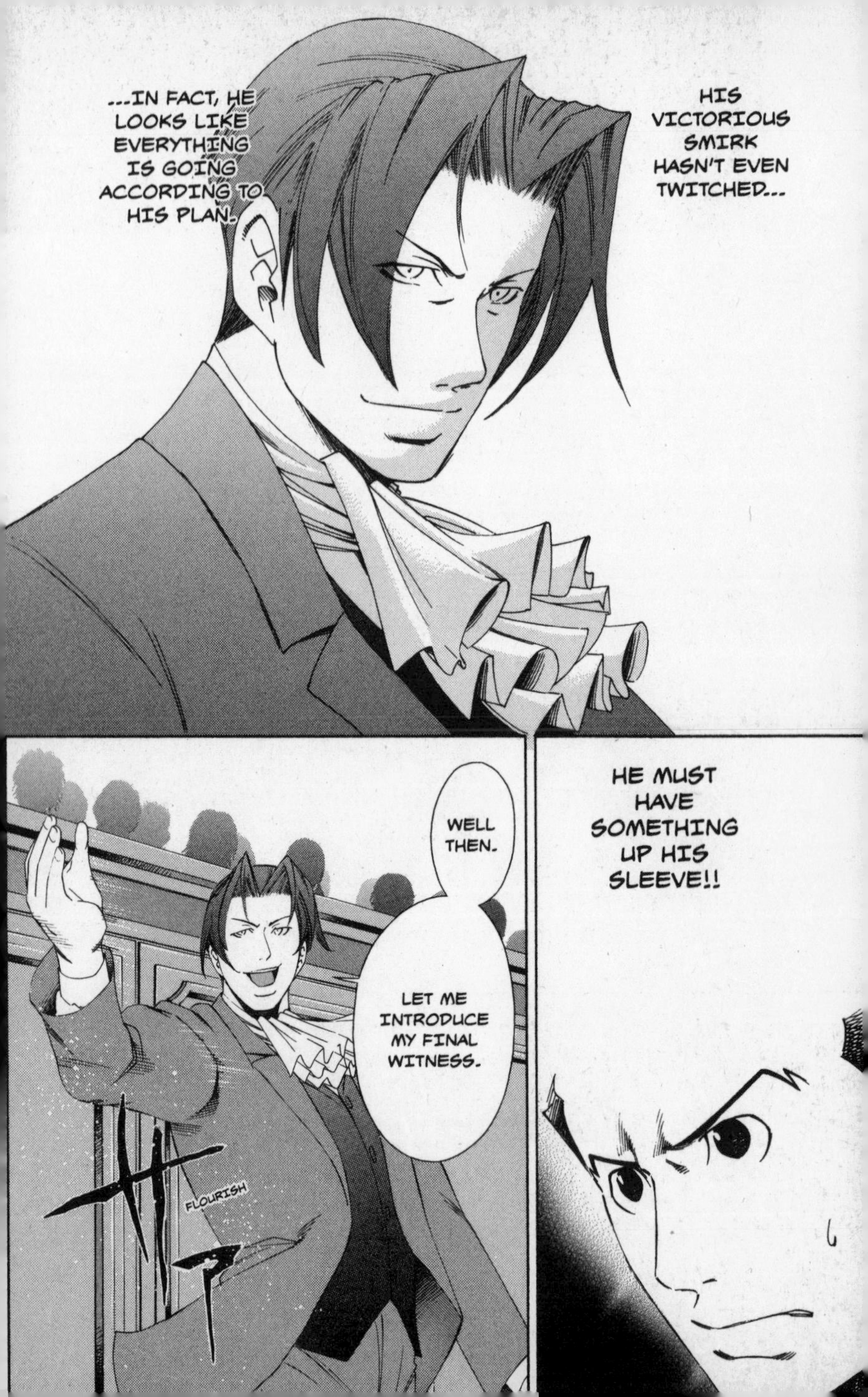
HIS VICTORIOUS SMIRK HASN'T EVEN TWITCHED...
...IN FACT, HE LOOKS LIKE EVERYTHING IS GOING ACCORDING TO HIS PLAN.
HE MUST HAVE SOMETHING UP HIS SLEEVE!!
WELL THEN.
LET ME INTRODUCE MY FINAL WITNESS.
FLOURISH

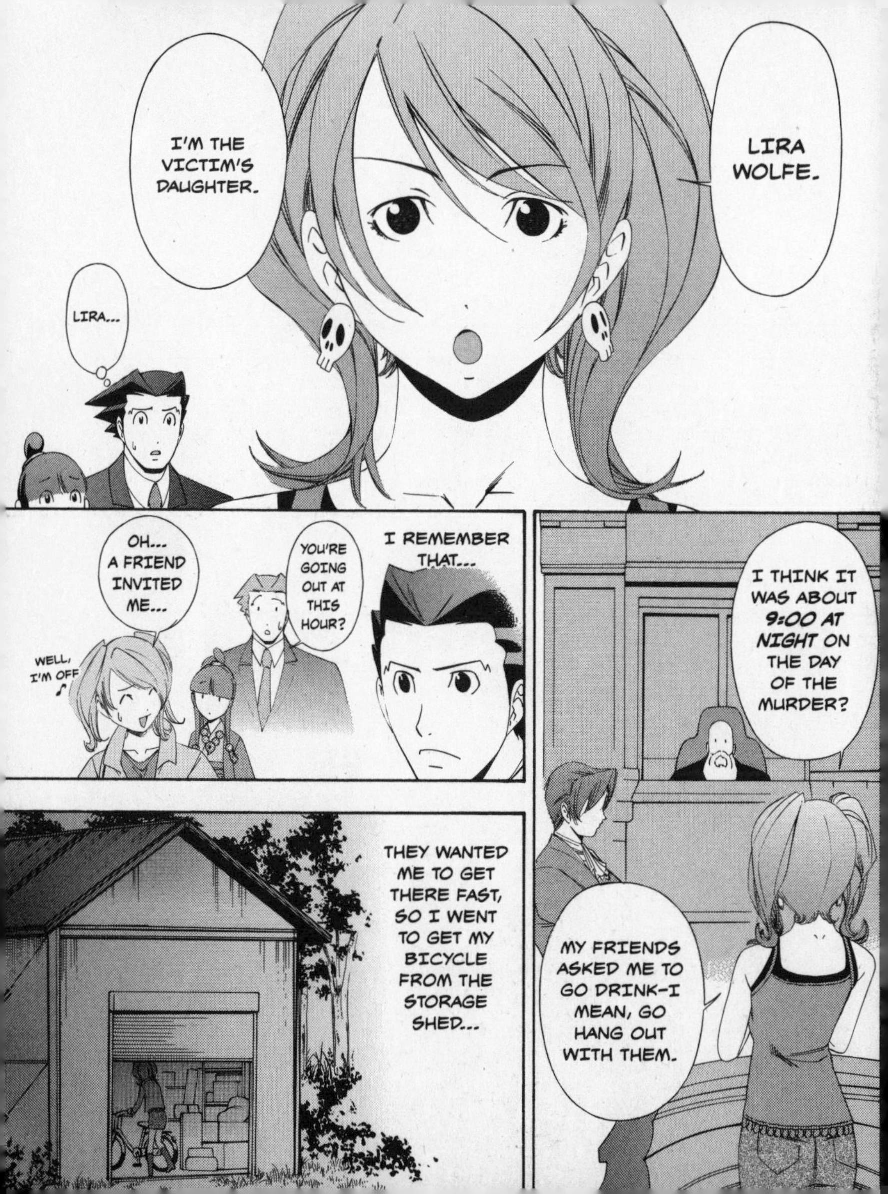
LIRA WOLFE.
I'M THE VICTIM'S DAUGHTER.
LIRA...
I THINK IT WAS ABOUT 9:00 AT NIGHT ON THE DAY OF THE MURDER?
MY FRIENDS ASKED ME TO GO DRINK—I MEAN, GO HANG OUT WITH THEM.
I REMEMBER THAT...
YOU'RE GOING OUT AT THIS HOUR?
OH... A FRIEND INVITED ME...
WELL, I'M OFF ♪
THEY WANTED ME TO GET THERE FAST, SO I WENT TO GET MY BICYCLE FROM THE STORAGE SHED...

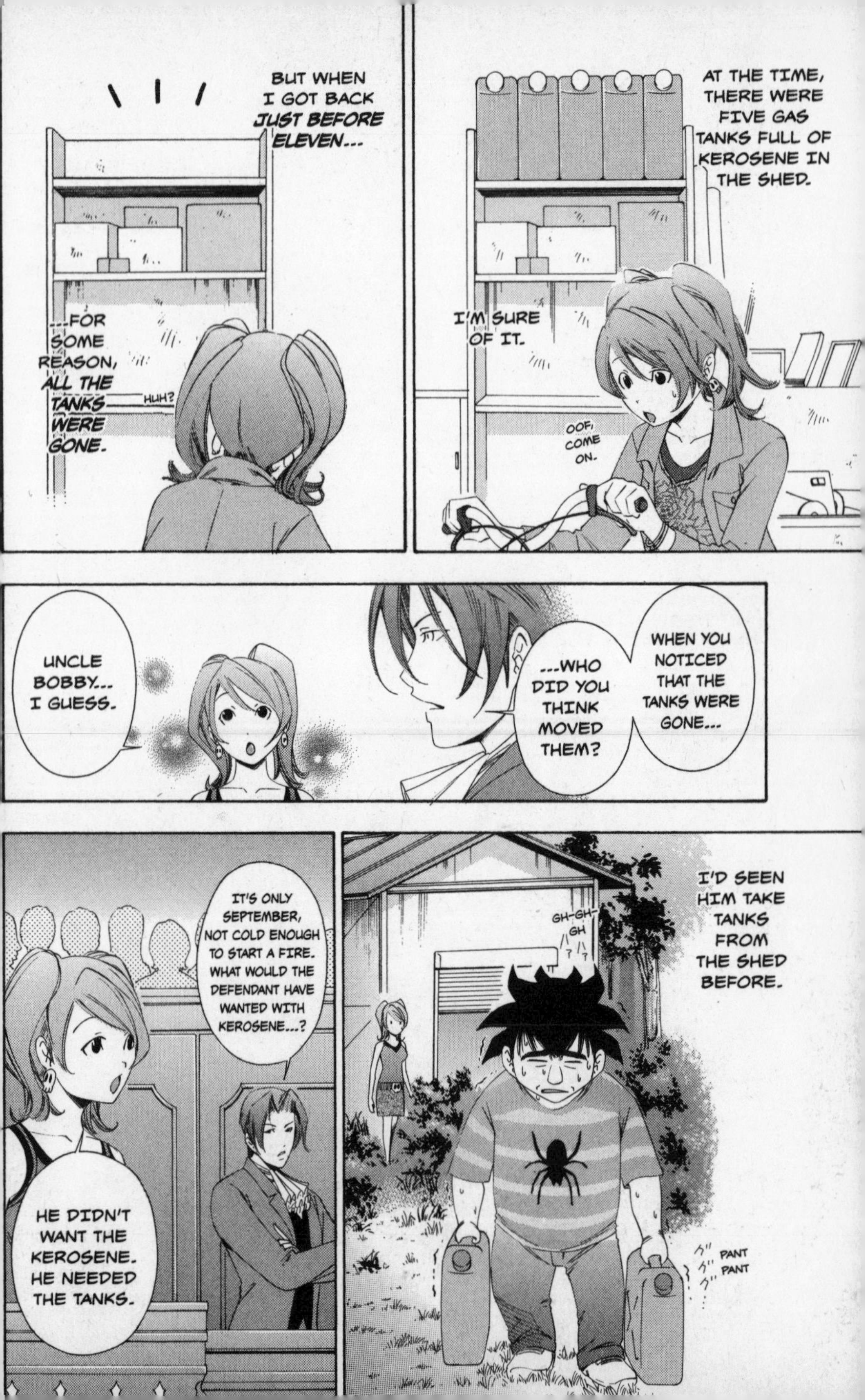
AT THE TIME, THERE WERE FIVE GAS TANKS FULL OF KEROSENE IN THE SHED.
I'M SURE OF IT.
OOF, COME ON.
BUT WHEN I GOT BACK JUST BEFORE ELEVEN...
...FOR SOME REASON, ALL THE TANKS WERE GONE.
HUH?
WHEN YOU NOTICED THAT THE TANKS WERE GONE...
...WHO DID YOU THINK MOVED THEM?
UNCLE BOBBY... I GUESS.
I'D SEEN HIM TAKE TANKS FROM THE SHED BEFORE.
GH-GH-GH
PANT PANT
IT'S ONLY SEPTEMBER, NOT COLD ENOUGH TO START A FIRE. WHAT WOULD THE DEFENDANT HAVE WANTED WITH KEROSENE...?
HE DIDN'T WANT THE KEROSENE. HE NEEDED THE TANKS.

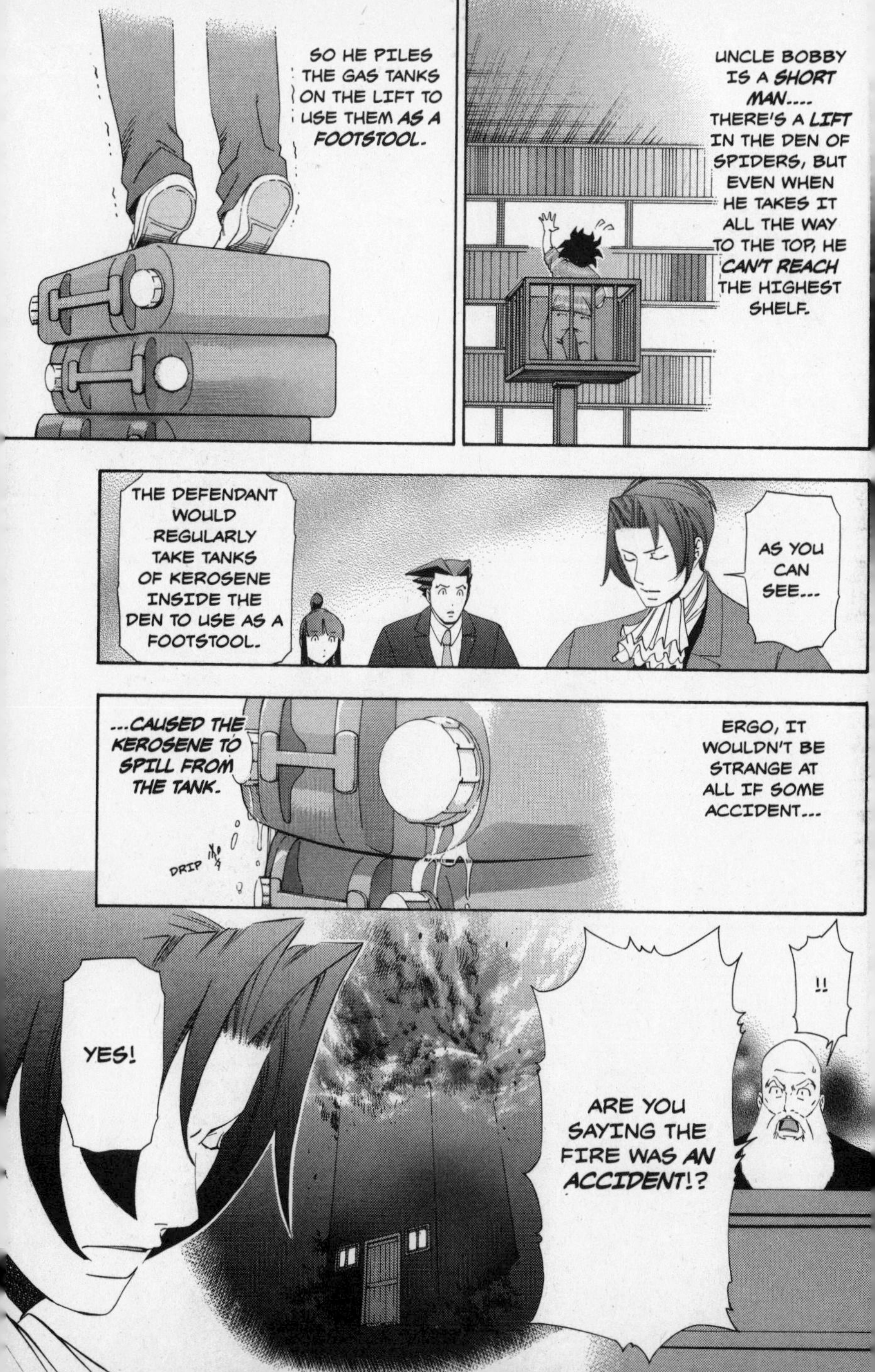
UNCLE BOBBY IS A SHORT MAN.... THERE'S A LIFT IN THE DEN OF SPIDERS, BUT EVEN WHEN HE TAKES IT ALL THE WAY TO THE TOP, HE CAN'T REACH THE HIGHEST SHELF.
SO HE PILES THE GAS TANKS ON THE LIFT TO USE THEM AS A FOOTSTOOL.
AS YOU CAN SEE...
THE DEFENDANT WOULD REGULARLY TAKE TANKS OF KEROSENE INSIDE THE DEN TO USE AS A FOOTSTOOL.
ERGO, IT WOULDN'T BE STRANGE AT ALL IF SOME ACCIDENT...
...CAUSED THE KEROSENE TO SPILL FROM THE TANK.
DRIP
!!
ARE YOU SAYING THE FIRE WAS AN ACCIDENT!?
YES!

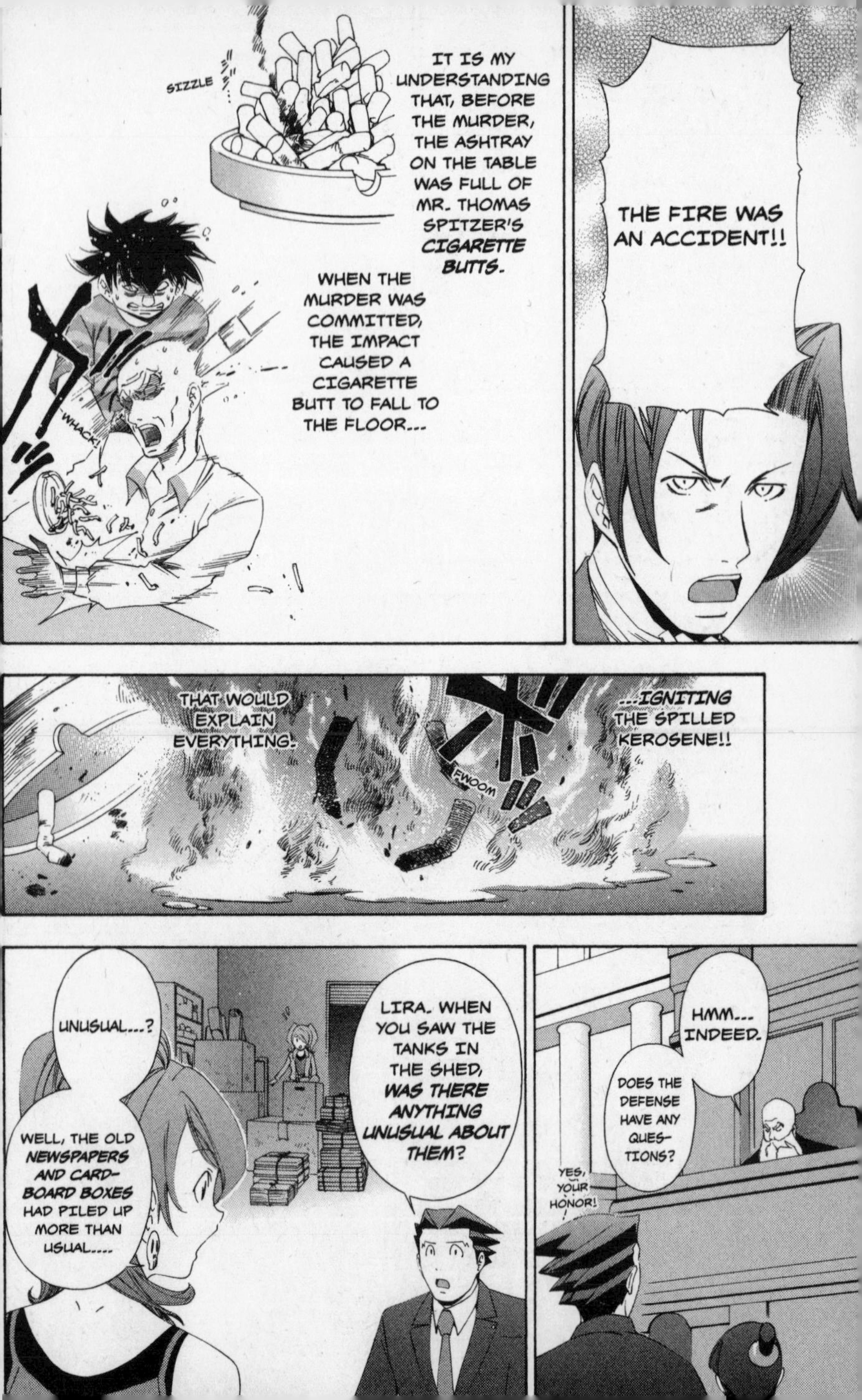

THE FIRE WAS AN ACCIDENT!!
IT IS MY UNDERSTANDING THAT, BEFORE THE MURDER, THE ASHTRAY ON THE TABLE WAS FULL OF MR. THOMAS SPITZER'S CIGARETTE BUTTS.
SIZZLE
WHEN THE MURDER WAS COMMITTED, THE IMPACT CAUSED A CIGARETTE BUTT TO FALL TO THE FLOOR...
WHACK!
...IGNITING THE SPILLED KEROSENE!!
FWOOM
THAT WOULD EXPLAIN EVERYTHING.
HMM... INDEED.
DOES THE DEFENSE HAVE ANY QUES-TIONS?
YES, YOUR HONOR!
LIRA. WHEN YOU SAW THE TANKS IN THE SHED, WAS THERE ANYTHING UNUSUAL ABOUT THEM?
UNUSUAL...?
WELL, THE OLD NEWSPAPERS AND CARD-BOARD BOXES HAD PILED UP MORE THAN USUAL....

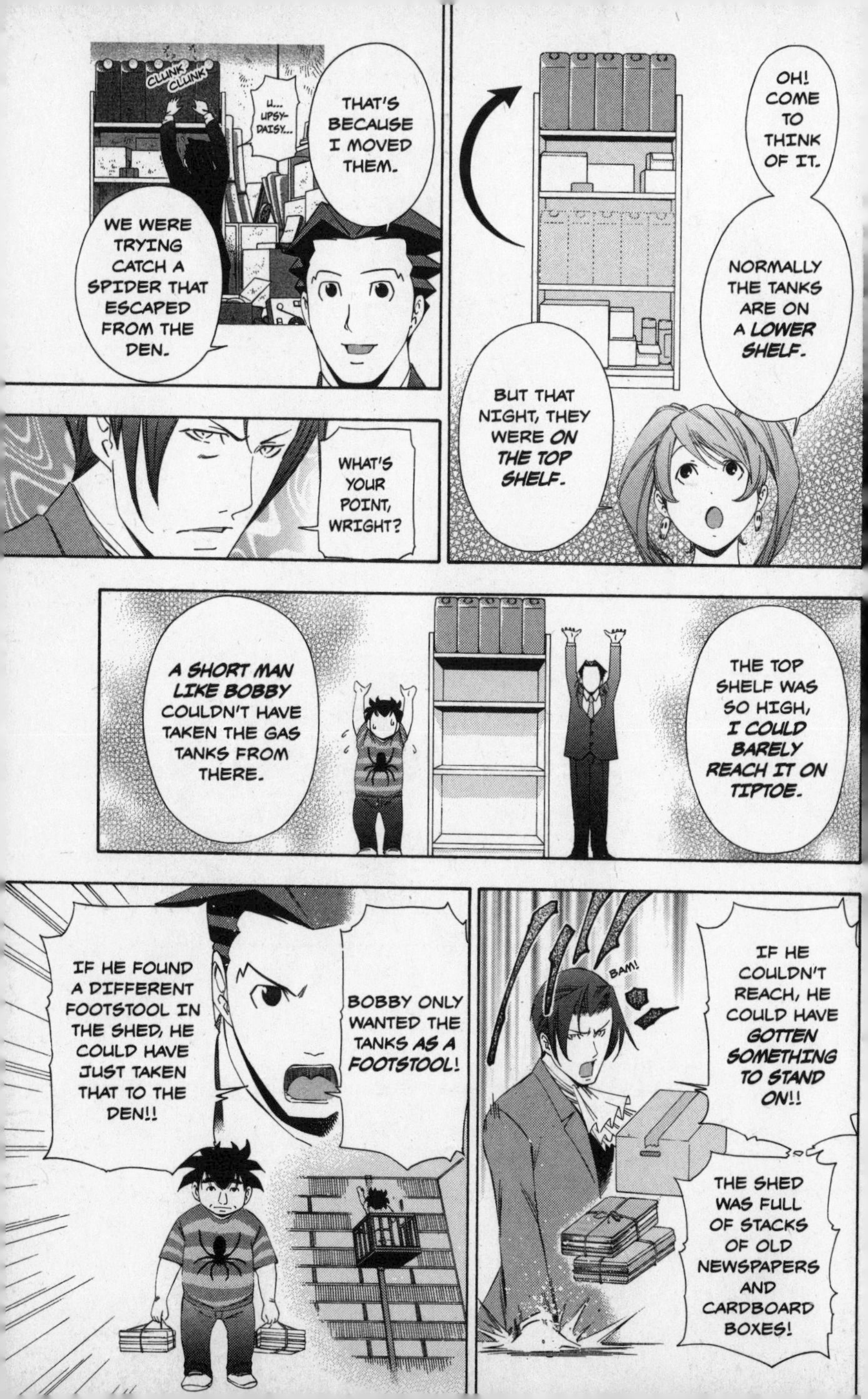
OH! COME TO THINK OF IT.
NORMALLY THE TANKS ARE ON A LOWER SHELF.
BUT THAT NIGHT, THEY WERE ON THE TOP SHELF.
THAT'S BECAUSE I MOVED THEM.
U... UPSY-DAISY...
CLUNK CLUNK
WE WERE TRYING CATCH A SPIDER THAT ESCAPED FROM THE DEN.
WHAT'S YOUR POINT, WRIGHT?
THE TOP SHELF WAS SO HIGH, I COULD BARELY REACH IT ON TIPTOE.
A SHORT MAN LIKE BOBBY COULDN'T HAVE TAKEN THE GAS TANKS FROM THERE.
BAM!
IF HE COULDN'T REACH, HE COULD HAVE GOTTEN SOMETHING TO STAND ON!!
THE SHED WAS FULL OF STACKS OF OLD NEWSPAPERS AND CARDBOARD BOXES!
BOBBY ONLY WANTED THE TANKS AS A FOOTSTOOL!
IF HE FOUND A DIFFERENT FOOTSTOOL IN THE SHED, HE COULD HAVE JUST TAKEN THAT TO THE DEN!!

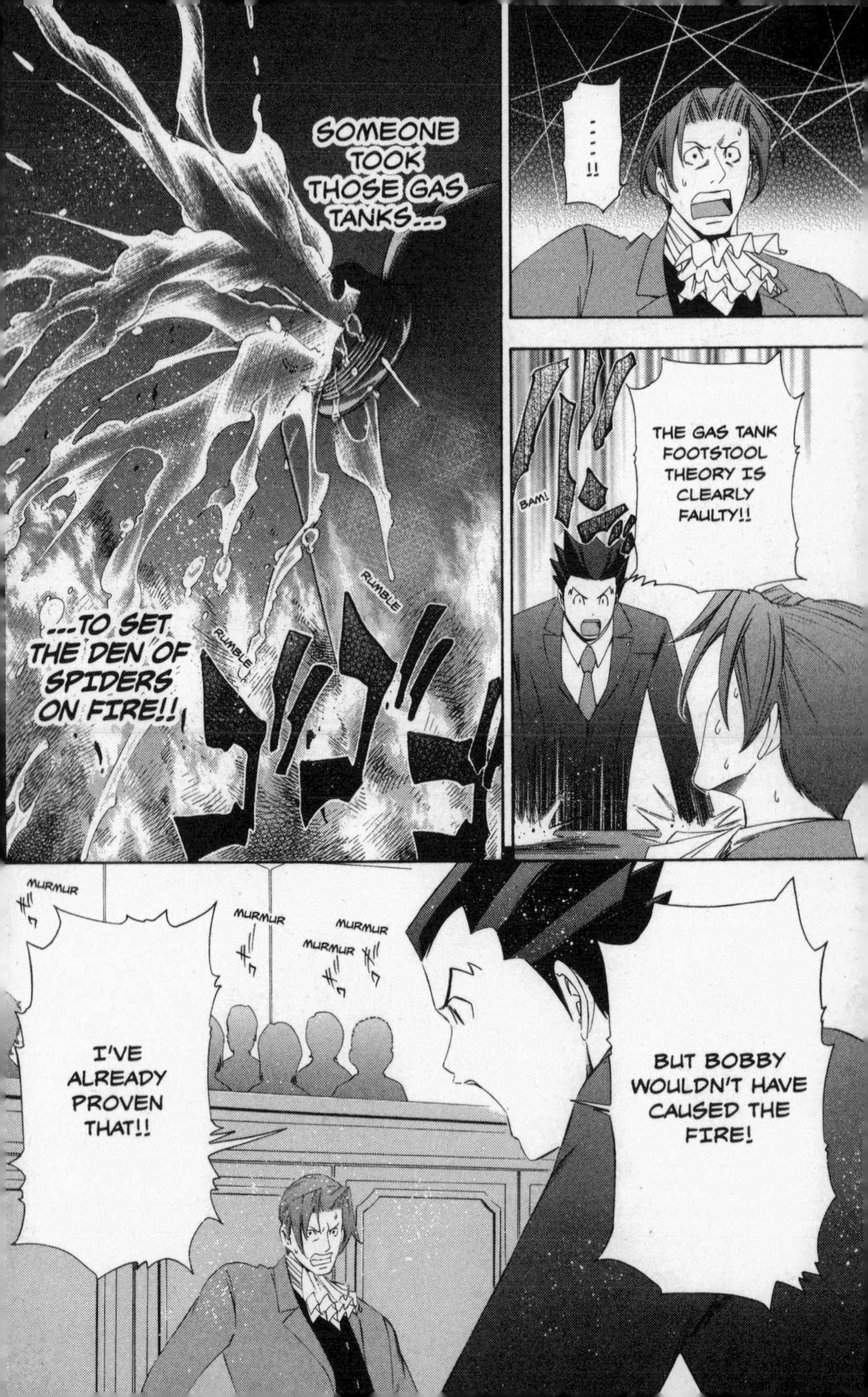
......!!
BAM!
THE GAS TANK FOOTSTOOL THEORY IS CLEARLY FAULTY!!
SOMEONE TOOK THOSE GAS TANKS...
RUMBLE
RUMBLE
...TO SET THE DEN OF SPIDERS ON FIRE!!
MURMUR
MURMUR
MURMUR
MURMUR
BUT BOBBY WOULDN'T HAVE CAUSED THE FIRE!
I'VE ALREADY PROVEN THAT!!

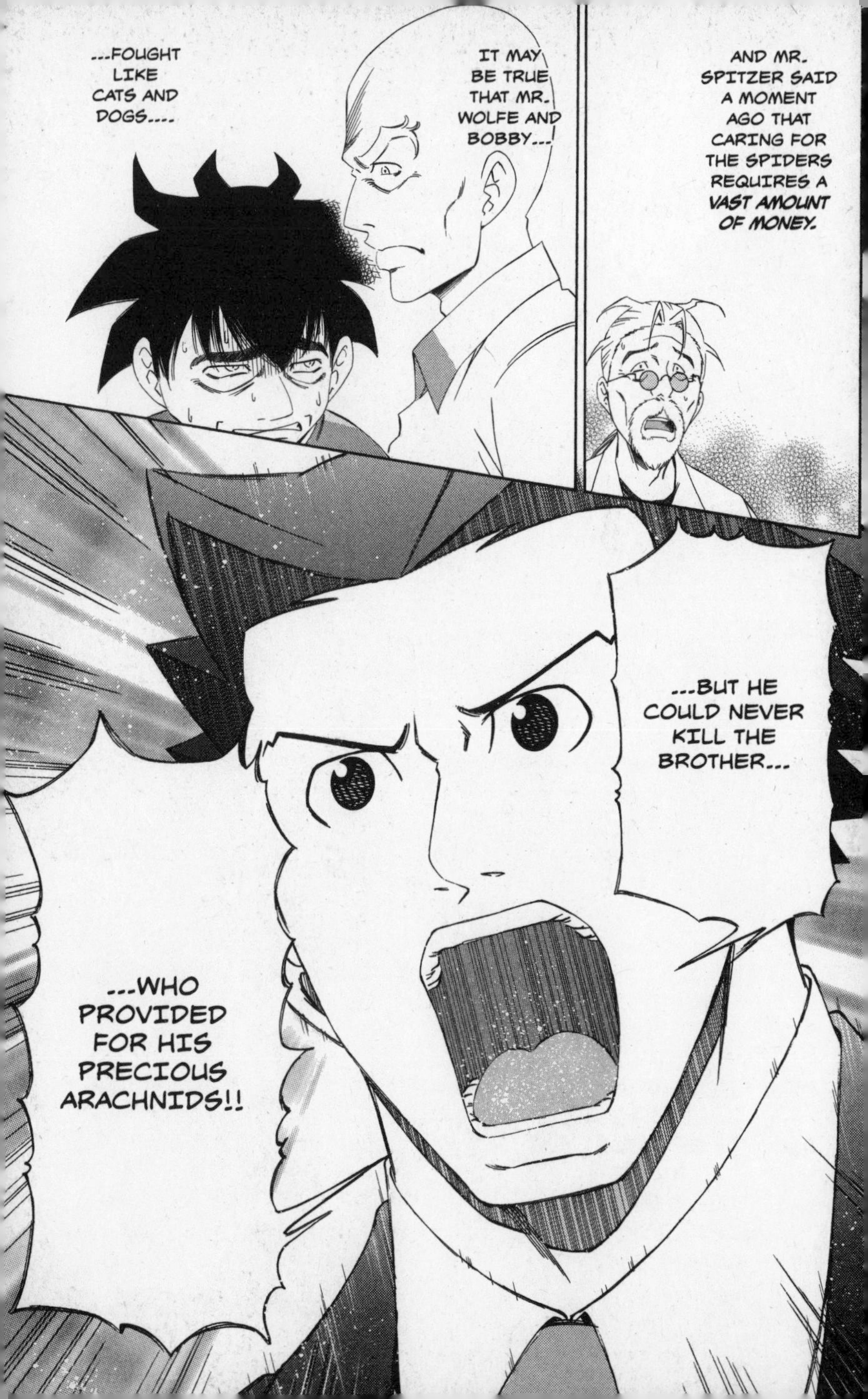
AND MR. SPITZER SAID A MOMENT AGO THAT CARING FOR THE SPIDERS REQUIRES A *VAST AMOUNT OF MONEY.*
IT MAY BE TRUE THAT MR. WOLFE AND BOBBY...
...FOUGHT LIKE CATS AND DOGS....
...BUT HE COULD NEVER KILL THE BROTHER...
...WHO PROVIDED FOR HIS PRECIOUS ARACHNIDS!!

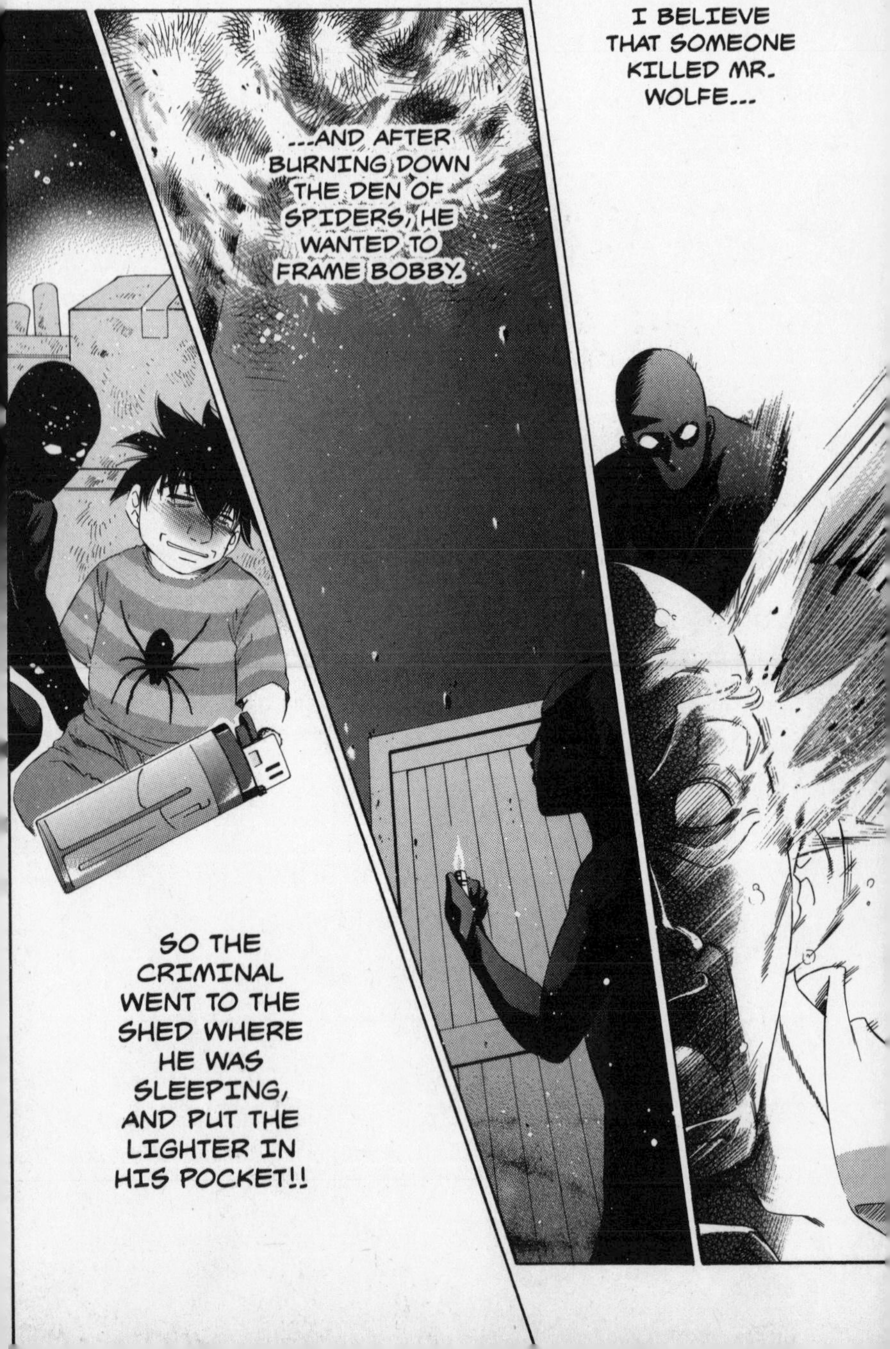
I BELIEVE THAT SOMEONE KILLED MR. WOLFE...
...AND AFTER BURNING DOWN THE DEN OF SPIDERS, HE WANTED TO FRAME BOBBY.
SO THE CRIMINAL WENT TO THE SHED WHERE HE WAS SLEEPING, AND PUT THE LIGHTER IN HIS POCKET!!

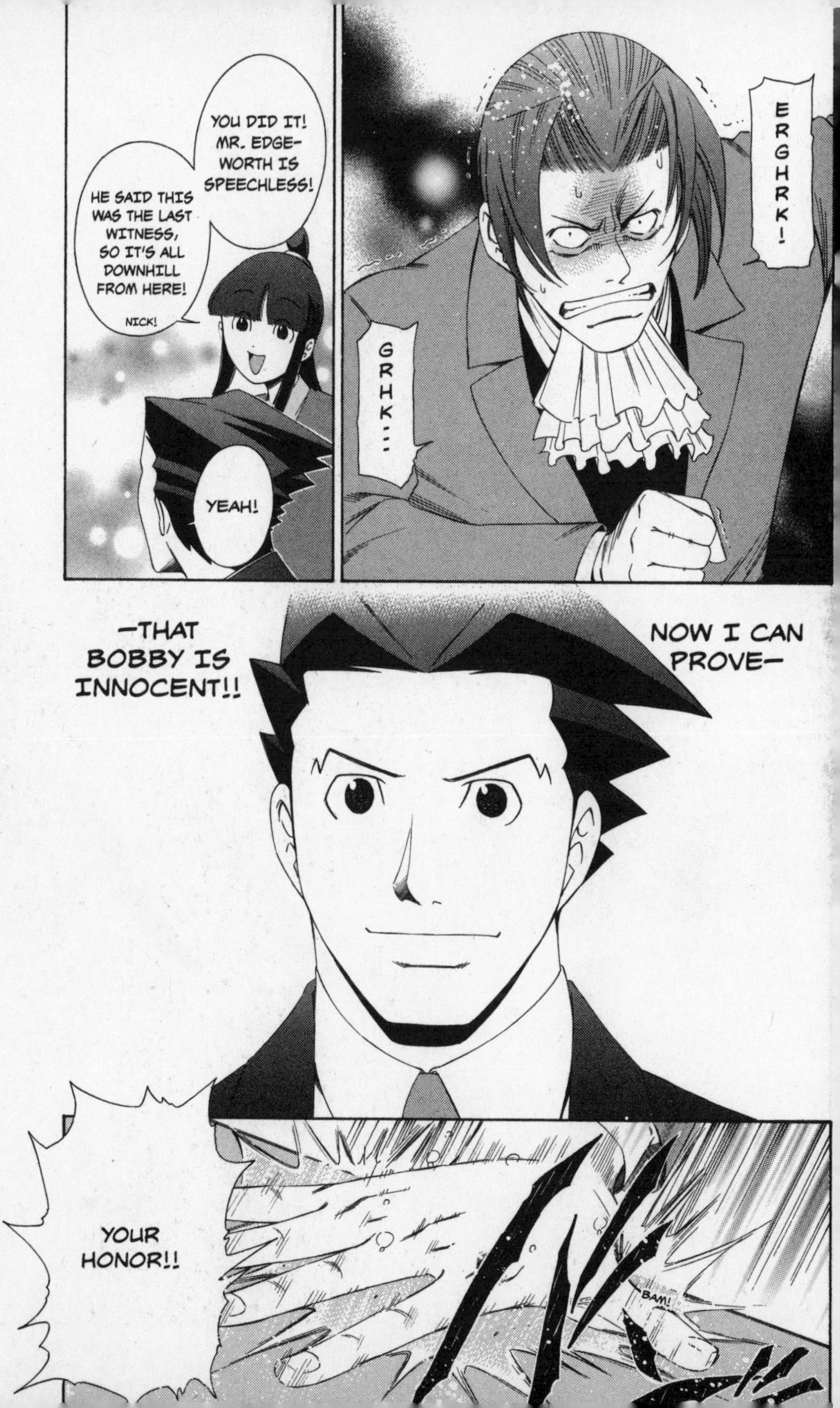
ERGHRK!
GRHK...
YOU DID IT! MR. EDGE-WORTH IS SPEECHLESS!
HE SAID THIS WAS THE LAST WITNESS, SO IT'S ALL DOWNHILL FROM HERE!
NICK!
YEAH!
NOW I CAN PROVE—
—THAT BOBBY IS INNOCENT!!
YOUR HONOR!!
BAM!

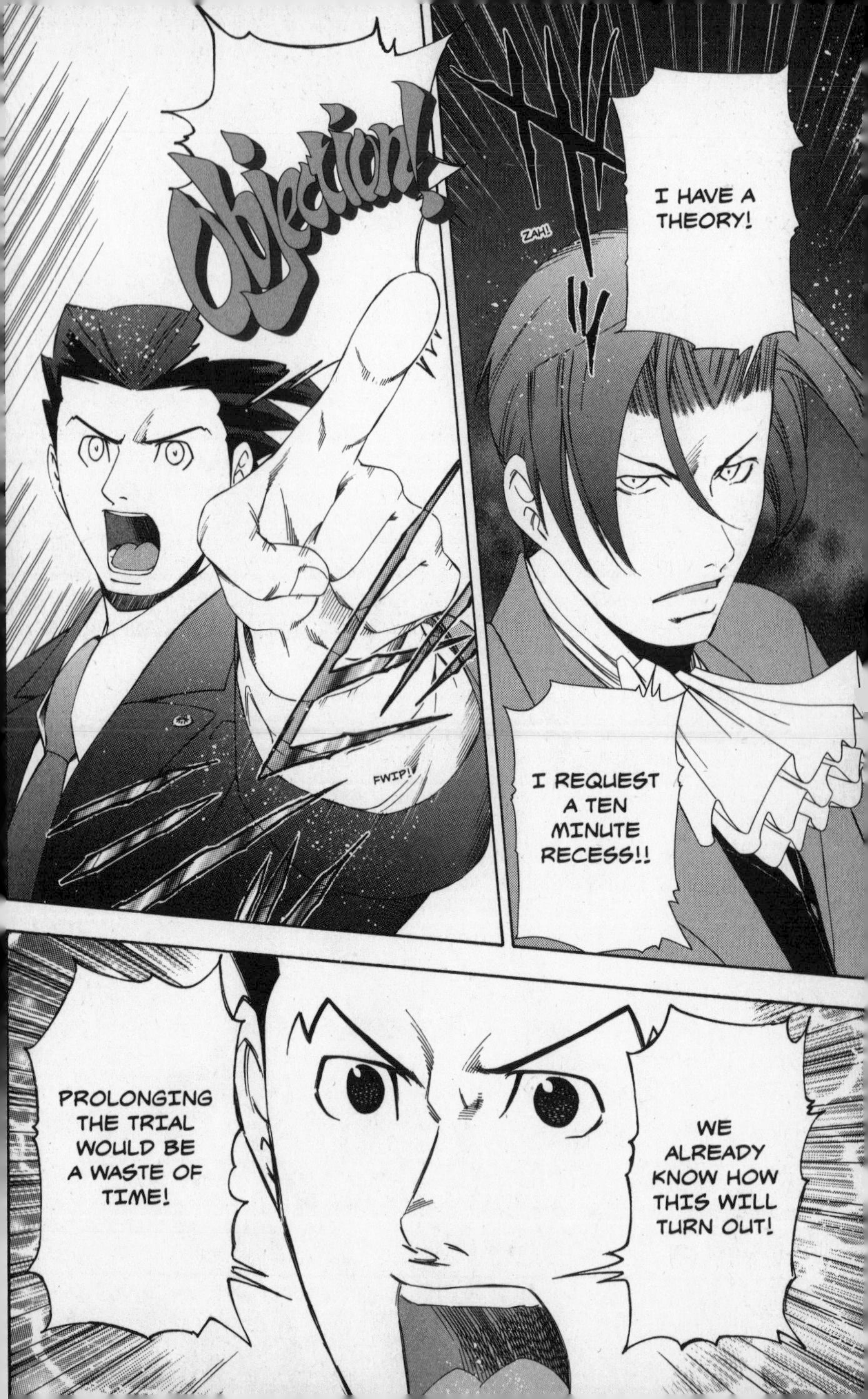
I HAVE A THEORY!
ZAH!
I REQUEST A TEN MINUTE RECESS!!
Objection!
FWIP!
WE ALREADY KNOW HOW THIS WILL TURN OUT!
PROLONGING THE TRIAL WOULD BE A WASTE OF TIME!

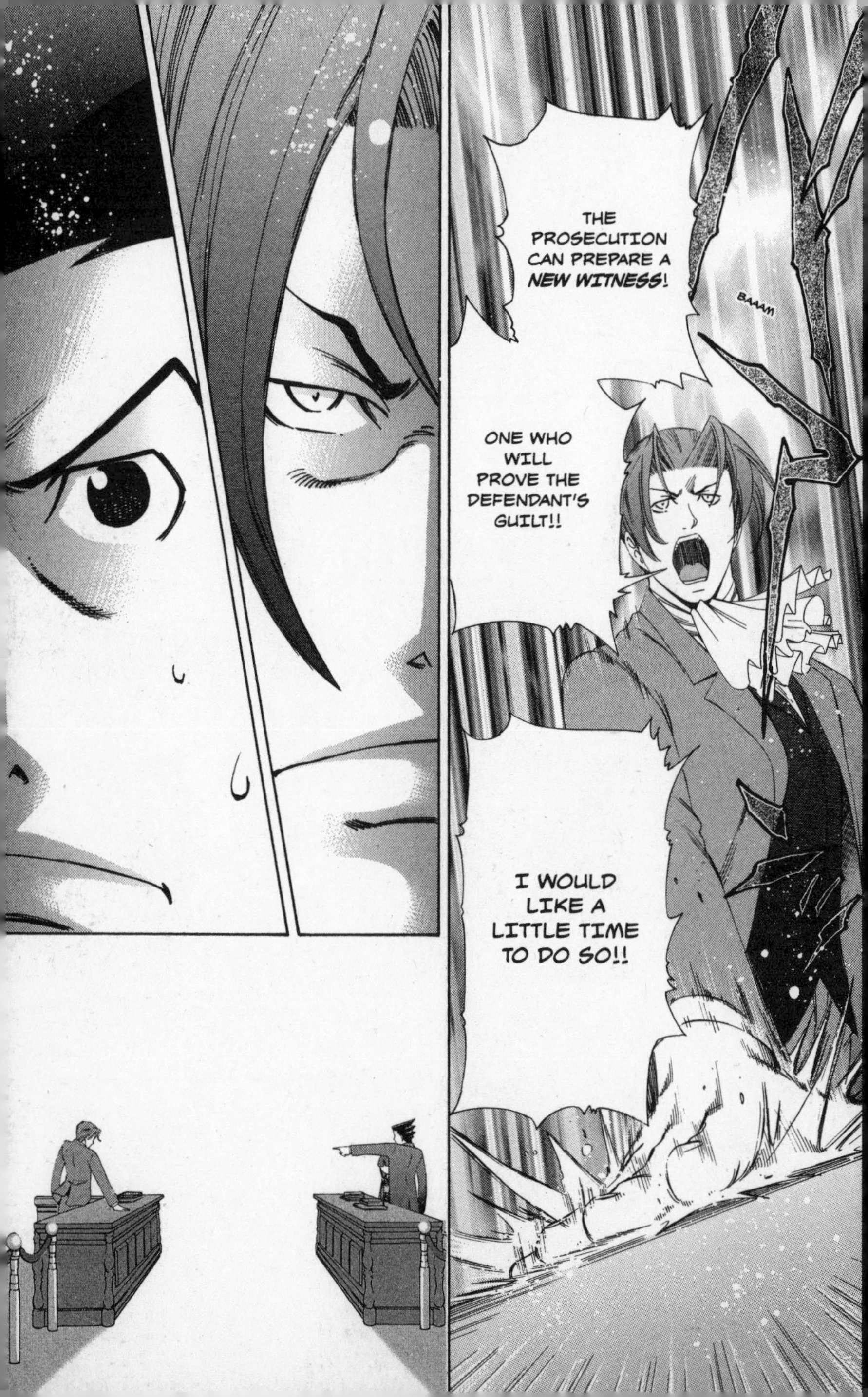
THE PROSECUTION CAN PREPARE A NEW WITNESS!
BAAAM
ONE WHO WILL PROVE THE DEFENDANT'S GUILT!!
I WOULD LIKE A LITTLE TIME TO DO SO!!

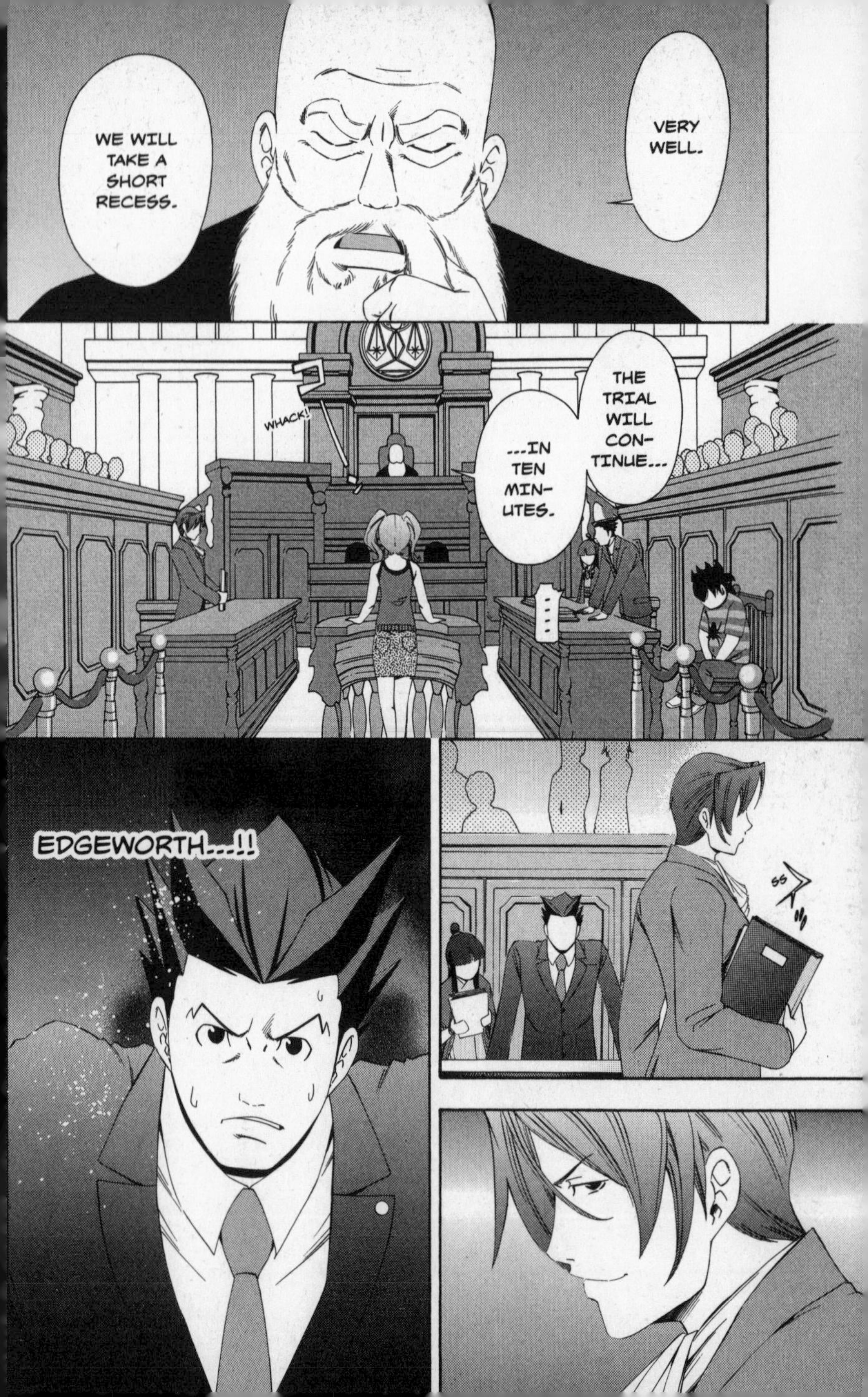
VERY WELL.
WE WILL TAKE A SHORT RECESS.
THE TRIAL WILL CONTINUE...
...IN TEN MINUTES.
WHACK!
SS
EDGEWORTH...!!

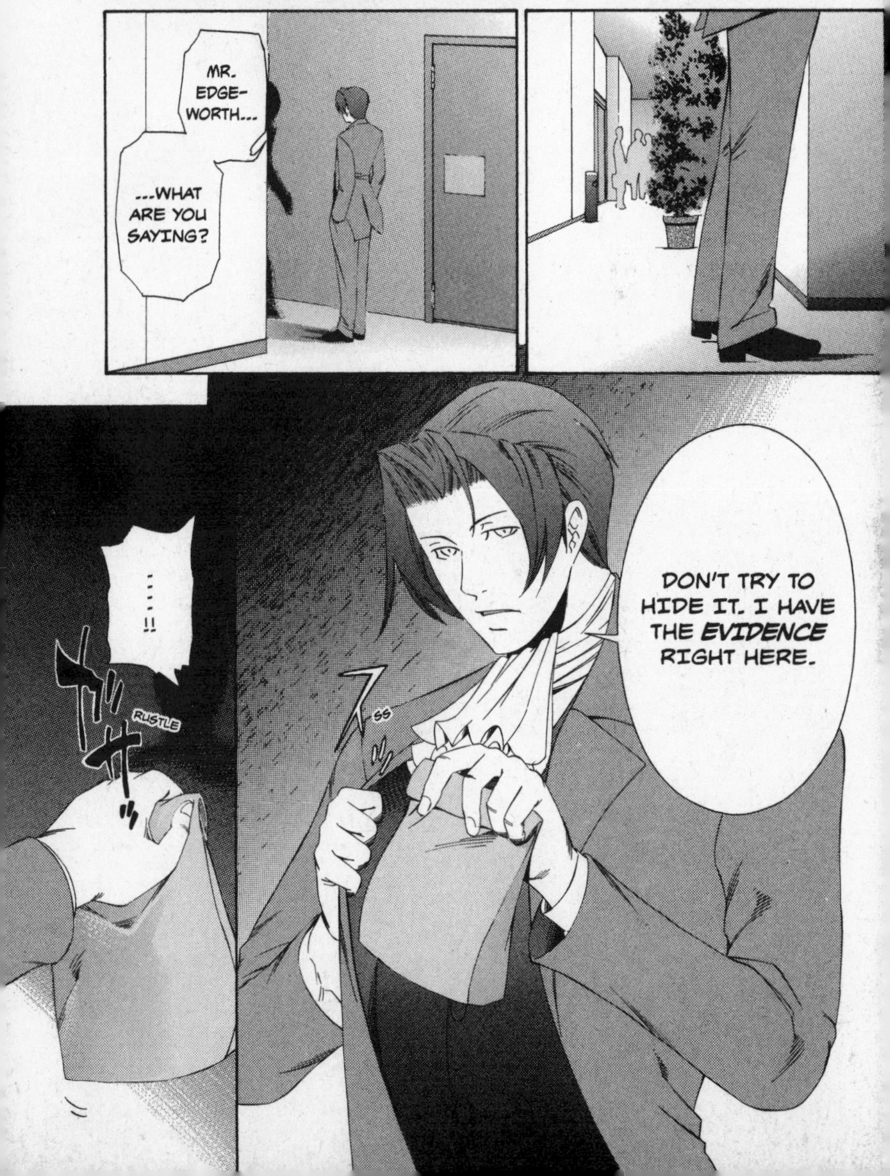

MR. EDGE-WORTH...
...WHAT ARE YOU SAYING?
DON'T TRY TO HIDE IT. I HAVE THE *EVIDENCE* RIGHT HERE.
SS
.....!!
RUSTLE

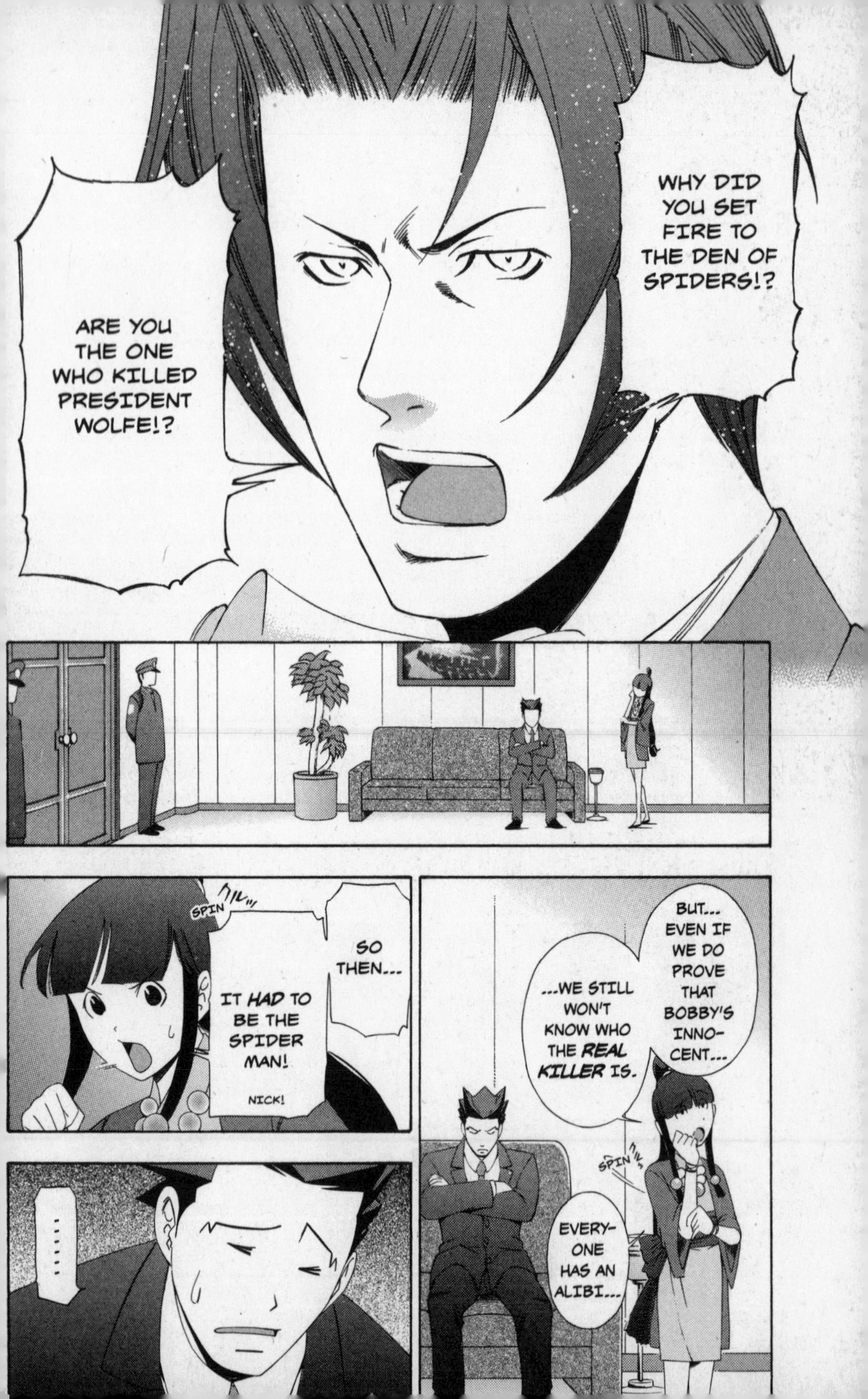
WHY DID YOU SET FIRE TO THE DEN OF SPIDERS!?
ARE YOU THE ONE WHO KILLED PRESIDENT WOLFE!?
BUT... EVEN IF WE DO PROVE THAT BOBBY'S INNO-CENT...
...WE STILL WON'T KNOW WHO THE *REAL KILLER* IS.
SPIN
EVERY-ONE HAS AN ALIBI...
SPIN
SO THEN...
IT *HAD* TO BE THE SPIDER MAN!
NICK!
......

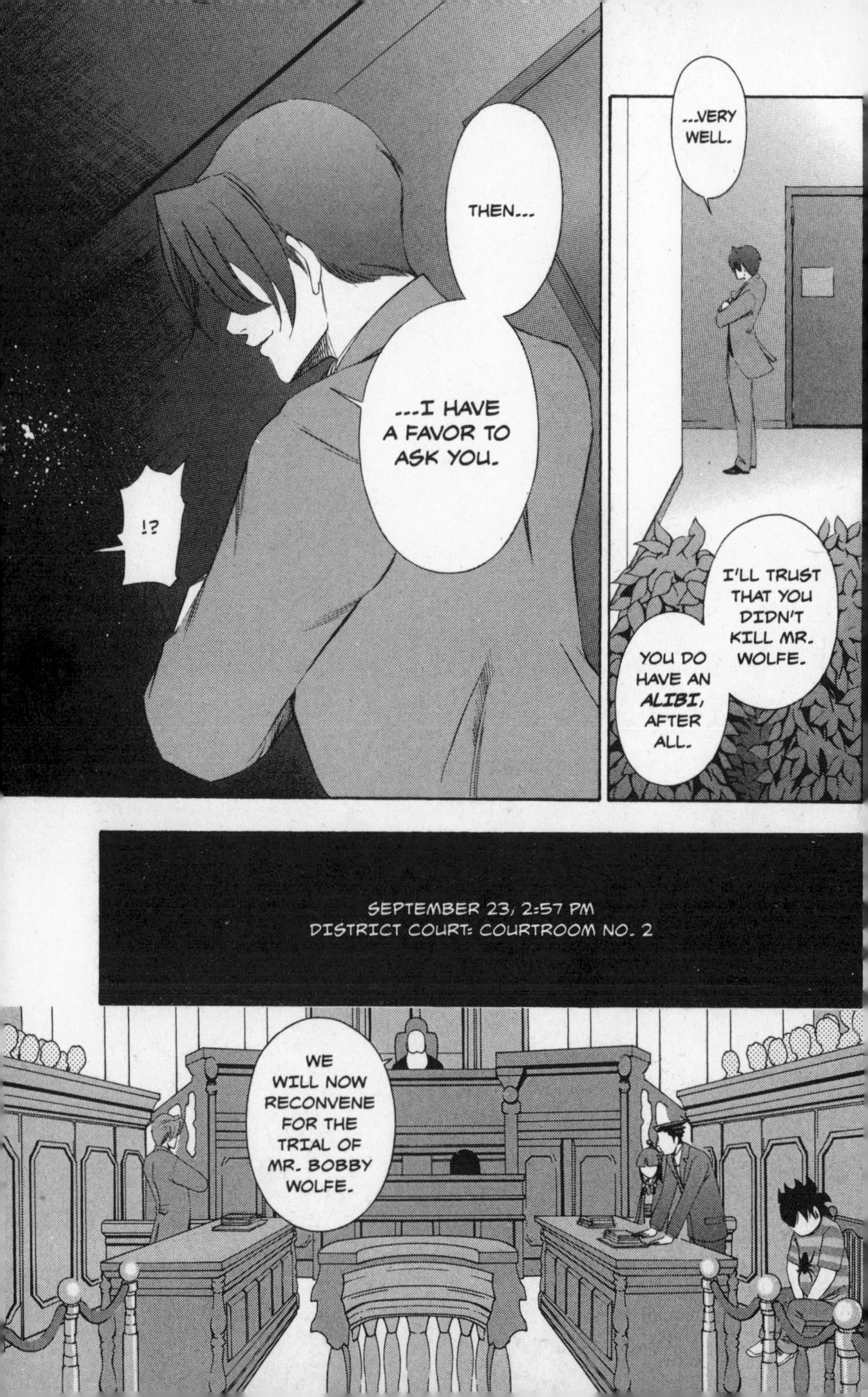
...VERY WELL.
I'LL TRUST THAT YOU DIDN'T KILL MR. WOLFE.
YOU DO HAVE AN ALIBI, AFTER ALL.
THEN...
...I HAVE A FAVOR TO ASK YOU.
!?
SEPTEMBER 23, 2:57 PM
DISTRICT COURT: COURTROOM NO. 2
WE WILL NOW RECONVENE FOR THE TRIAL OF MR. BOBBY WOLFE.

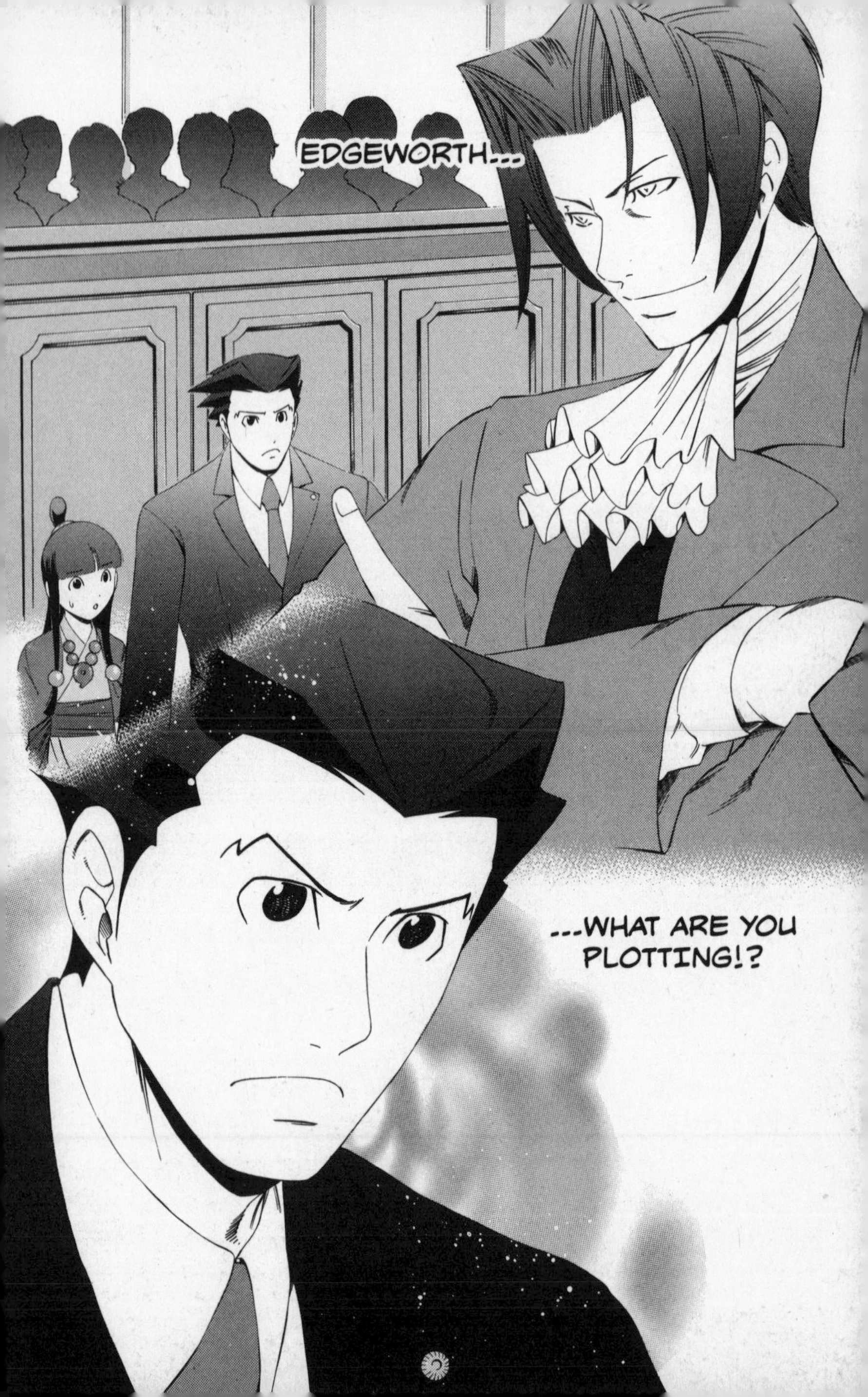
EDGEWORTH...
...WHAT ARE YOU PLOTTING!?

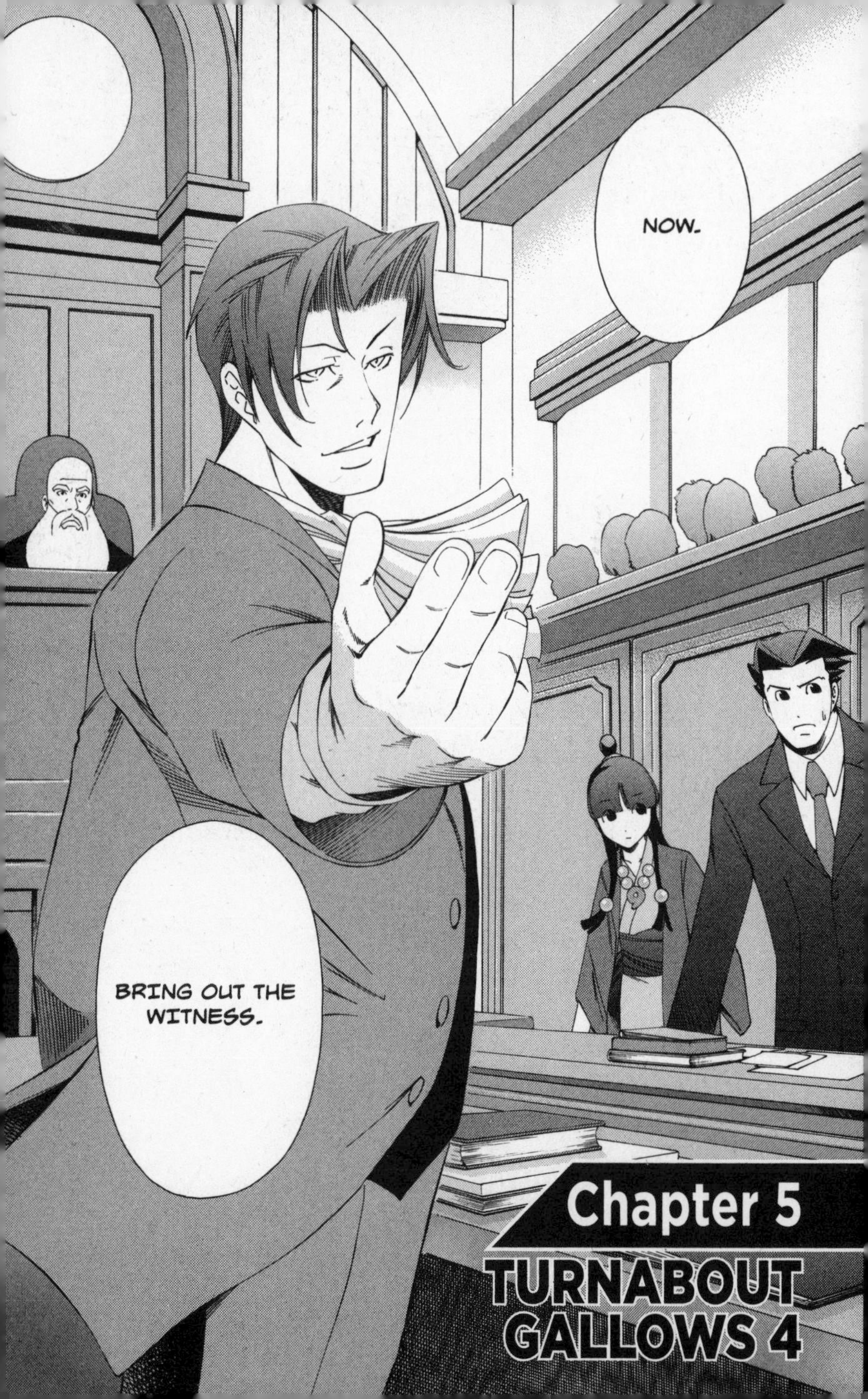
NOW.
BRING OUT THE WITNESS.

Chapter 5
TURNABOUT GALLOWS 4

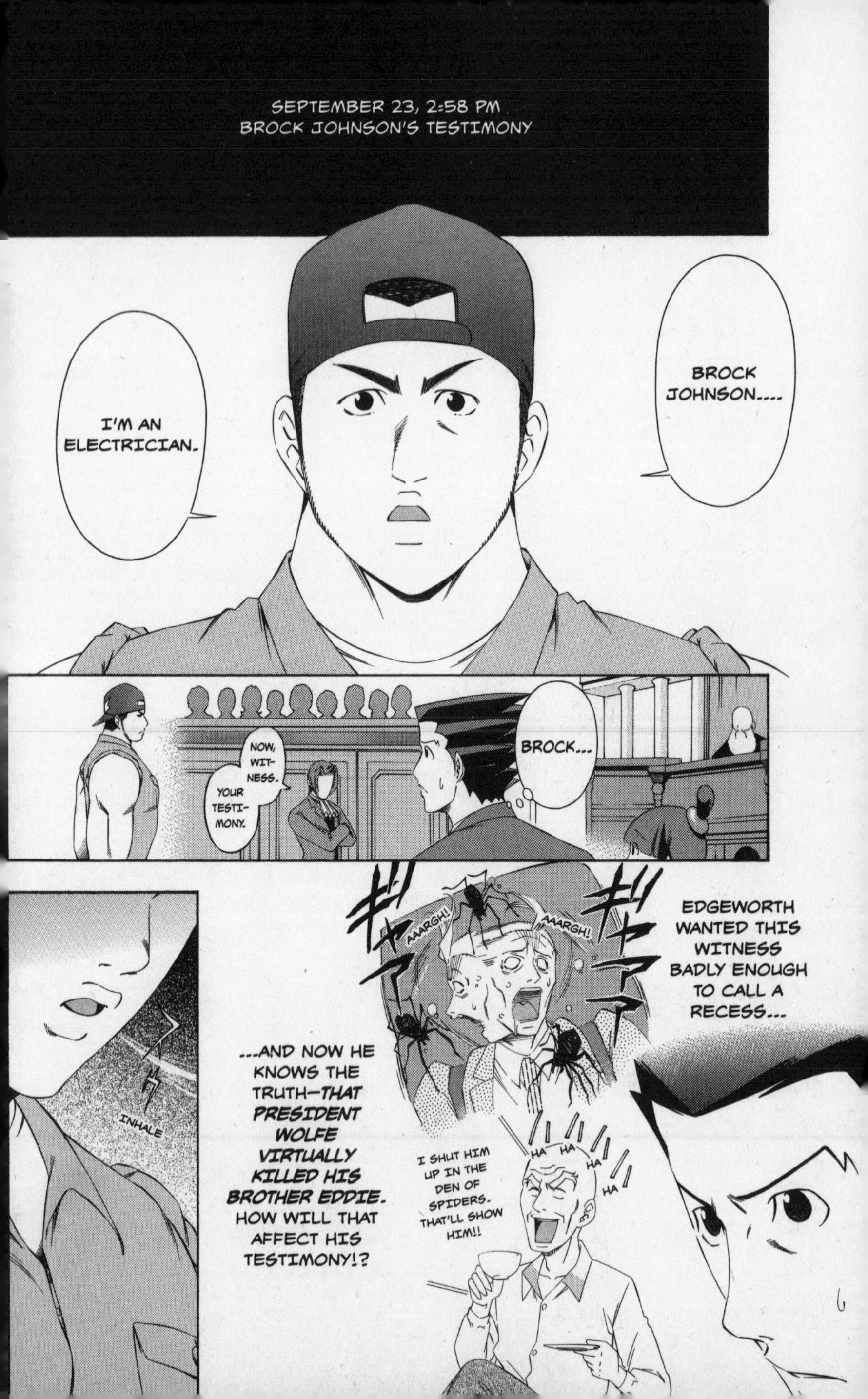
SEPTEMBER 23, 2:58 PM
BROCK JOHNSON'S TESTIMONY
BROCK JOHNSON....
I'M AN ELECTRICIAN.
BROCK...
NOW, WITNESS. YOUR TESTIMONY.
EDGEWORTH WANTED THIS WITNESS BADLY ENOUGH TO CALL A RECESS...
AAARGH!
AAARGH!
...AND NOW HE KNOWS THE TRUTH—THAT PRESIDENT WOLFE VIRTUALLY KILLED HIS BROTHER EDDIE. HOW WILL THAT AFFECT HIS TESTIMONY!?
HA HA HA HA
I SHUT HIM UP IN THE DEN OF SPIDERS. THAT'LL SHOW HIM!!
INHALE

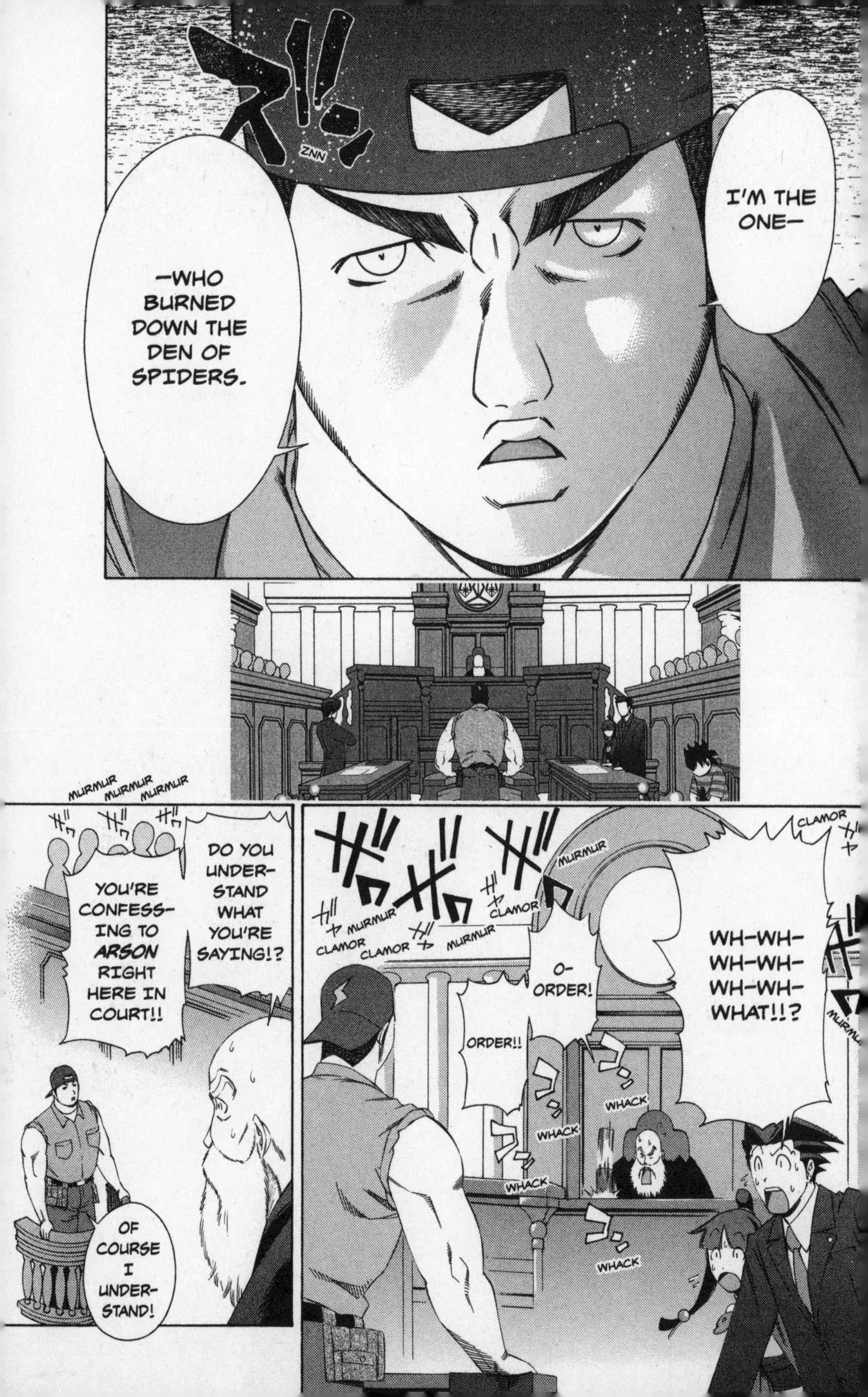
ZNN
I'M THE ONE—
—WHO BURNED DOWN THE DEN OF SPIDERS.
MURMUR MURMUR MURMUR
CLAMOR
WH-WH-WH-WH-WH-WH-WHAT!!?
MURMUR
O- ORDER!
ORDER!!
CLAMOR
MURMUR
CLAMOR CLAMOR MURMUR
WHACK
WHACK
WHACK
WHACK
DO YOU UNDERSTAND WHAT YOU'RE SAYING!?
YOU'RE CONFESSING TO *ARSON* RIGHT HERE IN COURT!!
OF COURSE I UNDERSTAND!

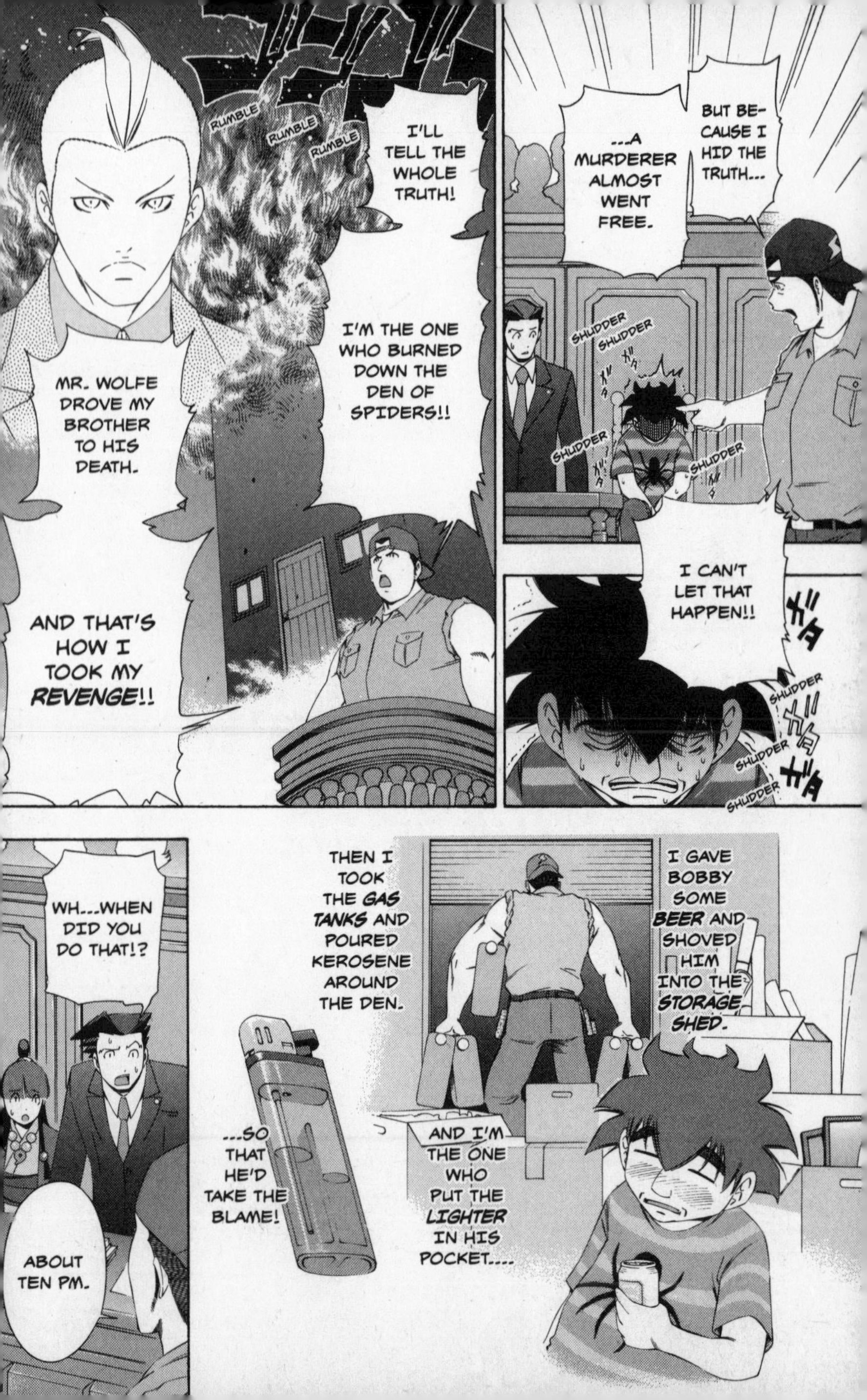
BUT BE-CAUSE I HID THE TRUTH...
...A MURDERER ALMOST WENT FREE.
SHUDDER SHUDDER
SHUDDER
SHUDDER
I CAN'T LET THAT HAPPEN!!
SHUDDER
SHUDDER
SHUDDER
RUMBLE RUMBLE RUMBLE
I'LL TELL THE WHOLE TRUTH!
I'M THE ONE WHO BURNED DOWN THE DEN OF SPIDERS!!
MR. WOLFE DROVE MY BROTHER TO HIS DEATH.
AND THAT'S HOW I TOOK MY *REVENGE*!!
I GAVE BOBBY SOME *BEER* AND SHOVED HIM INTO THE *STORAGE SHED*.
THEN I TOOK THE *GAS TANKS* AND POURED KEROSENE AROUND THE DEN.
AND I'M THE ONE WHO PUT THE *LIGHTER* IN HIS POCKET...
...SO THAT HE'D TAKE THE BLAME!
WH...WHEN DID YOU DO THAT!?
ABOUT TEN PM.

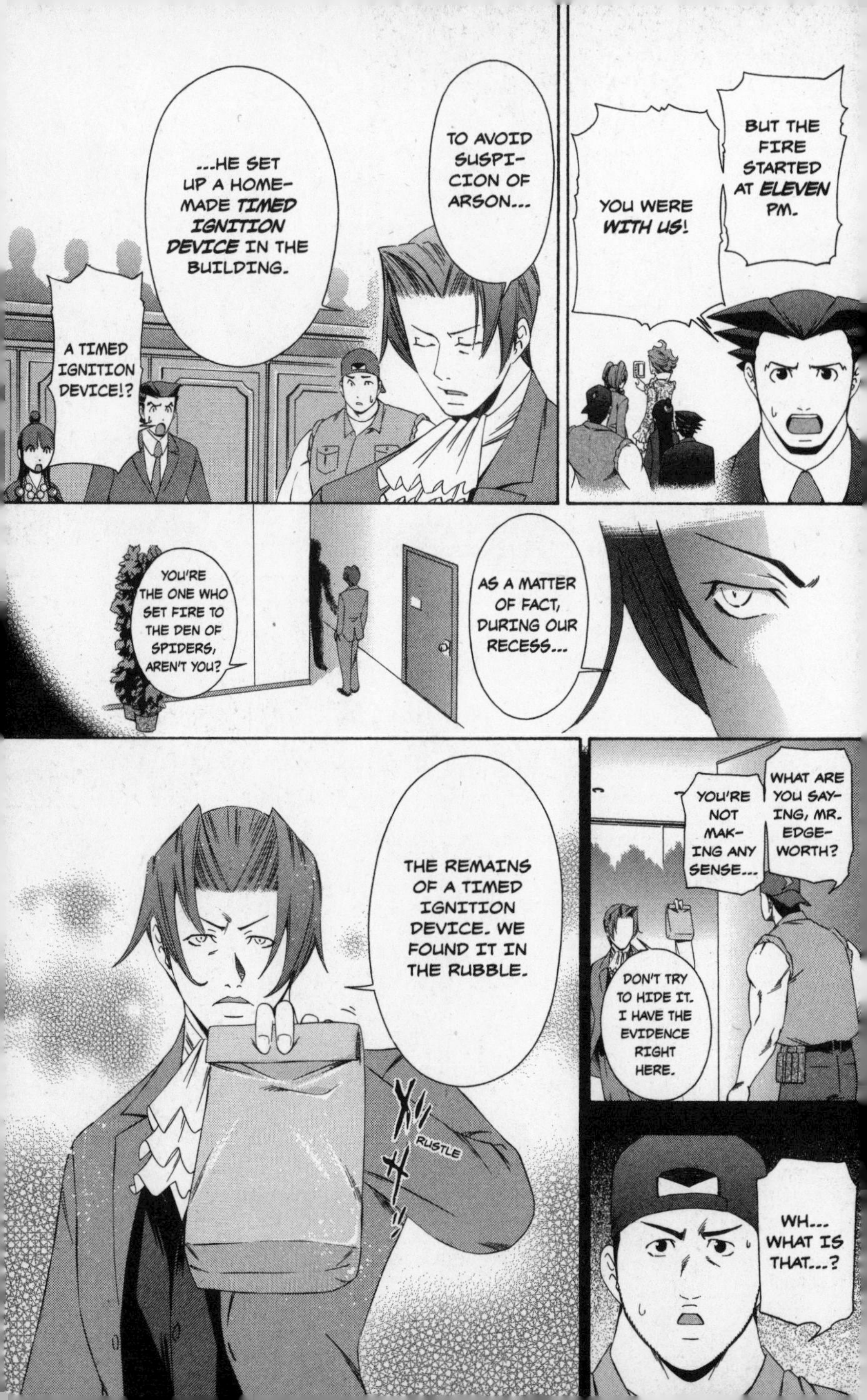
BUT THE FIRE STARTED AT ELEVEN PM.
YOU WERE WITH US!
TO AVOID SUSPICION OF ARSON...
...HE SET UP A HOMEMADE TIMED IGNITION DEVICE IN THE BUILDING.
A TIMED IGNITION DEVICE!?
AS A MATTER OF FACT, DURING OUR RECESS...
YOU'RE THE ONE WHO SET FIRE TO THE DEN OF SPIDERS, AREN'T YOU?
WHAT ARE YOU SAYING, MR. EDGEWORTH?
YOU'RE NOT MAKING ANY SENSE...
DON'T TRY TO HIDE IT. I HAVE THE EVIDENCE RIGHT HERE.
WH... WHAT IS THAT...?
THE REMAINS OF A TIMED IGNITION DEVICE. WE FOUND IT IN THE RUBBLE.
RUSTLE

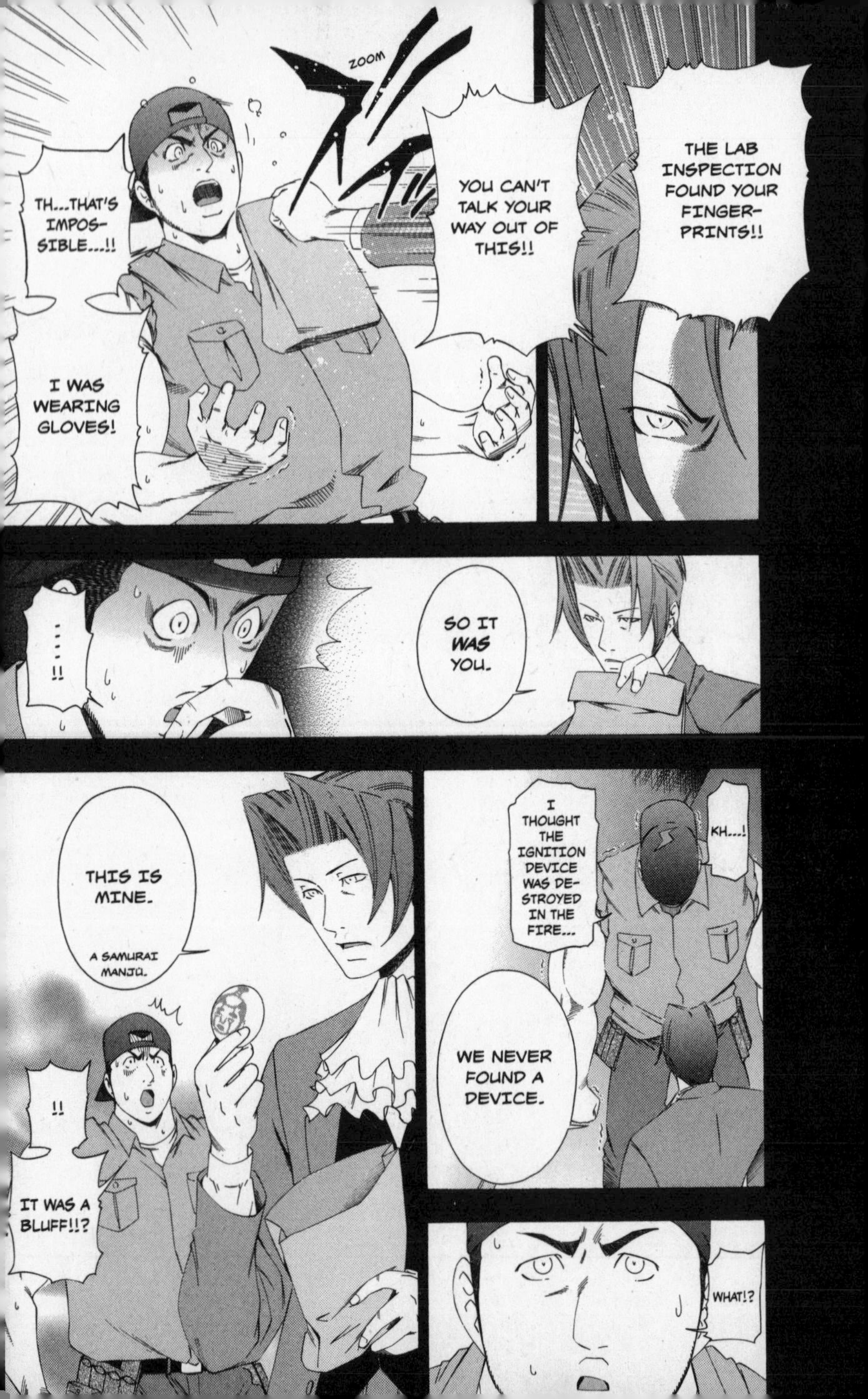
THE LAB INSPECTION FOUND YOUR FINGERPRINTS!!
ZOOM
YOU CAN'T TALK YOUR WAY OUT OF THIS!!
TH...THAT'S IMPOSSIBLE...!!
I WAS WEARING GLOVES!
SO IT WAS YOU.
......!!
KH...!
I THOUGHT THE IGNITION DEVICE WAS DESTROYED IN THE FIRE...
WE NEVER FOUND A DEVICE.
WHAT!?
THIS IS MINE.
A SAMURAI MANJŪ.
!!
IT WAS A BLUFF!!?

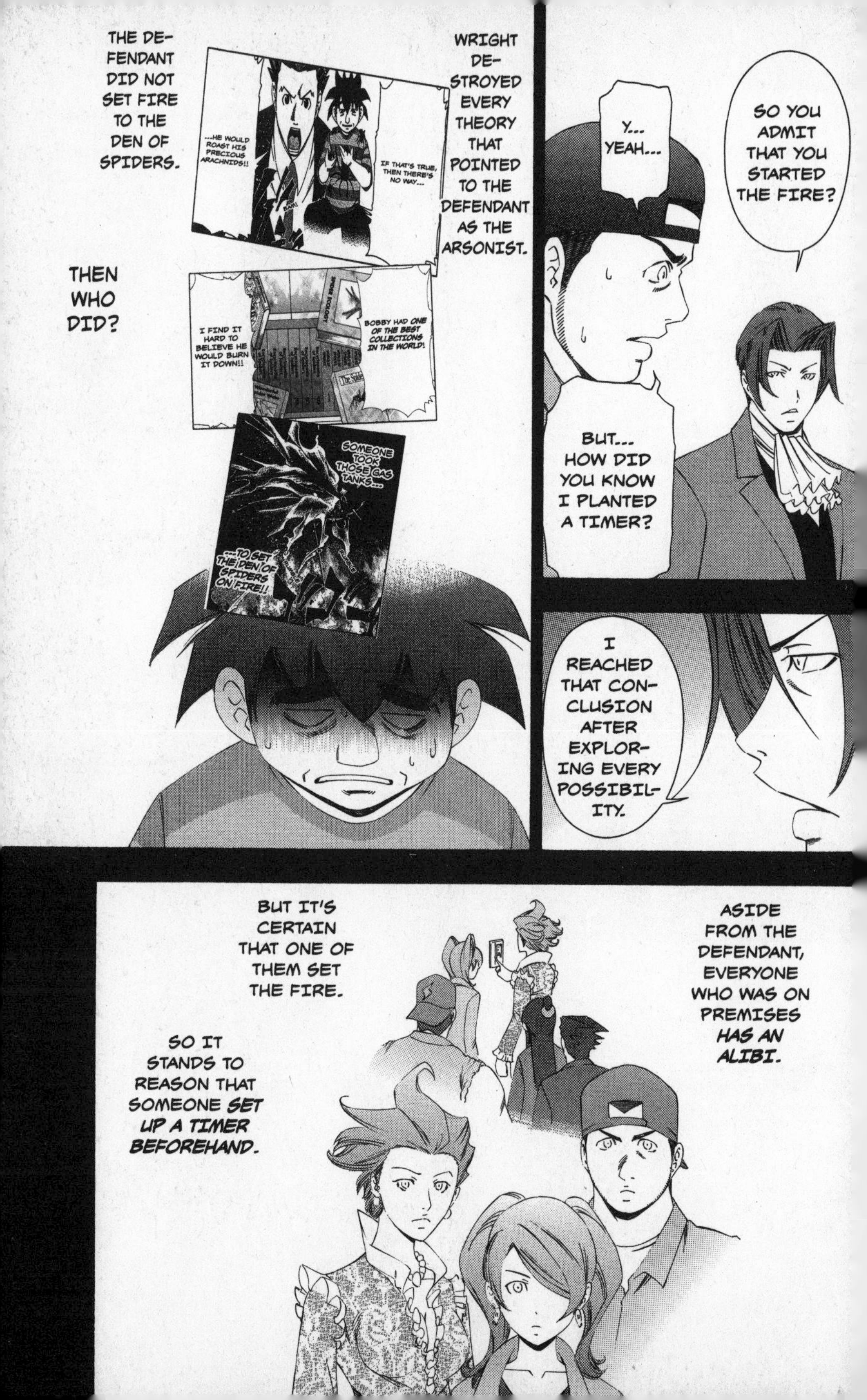
SO YOU ADMIT THAT YOU STARTED THE FIRE?
Y... YEAH...
BUT... HOW DID YOU KNOW I PLANTED A TIMER?
I REACHED THAT CONCLUSION AFTER EXPLORING EVERY POSSIBILITY.
WRIGHT DESTROYED EVERY THEORY THAT POINTED TO THE DEFENDANT AS THE ARSONIST.
THE DEFENDANT DID NOT SET FIRE TO THE DEN OF SPIDERS.
IF THAT'S TRUE, THEN THERE'S NO WAY...
...HE WOULD ROAST HIS PRECIOUS ARACHNIDS!!
BOBBY HAD ONE OF THE BEST COLLECTIONS IN THE WORLD!
I FIND IT HARD TO BELIEVE HE WOULD BURN IT DOWN!!
SOMEONE TOOK THOSE GAS TANKS...
...TO SET THE DEN OF SPIDERS ON FIRE!!
THEN WHO DID?
ASIDE FROM THE DEFENDANT, EVERYONE WHO WAS ON PREMISES HAS AN ALIBI.
BUT IT'S CERTAIN THAT ONE OF THEM SET THE FIRE.
SO IT STANDS TO REASON THAT SOMEONE SET UP A TIMER BEFOREHAND.

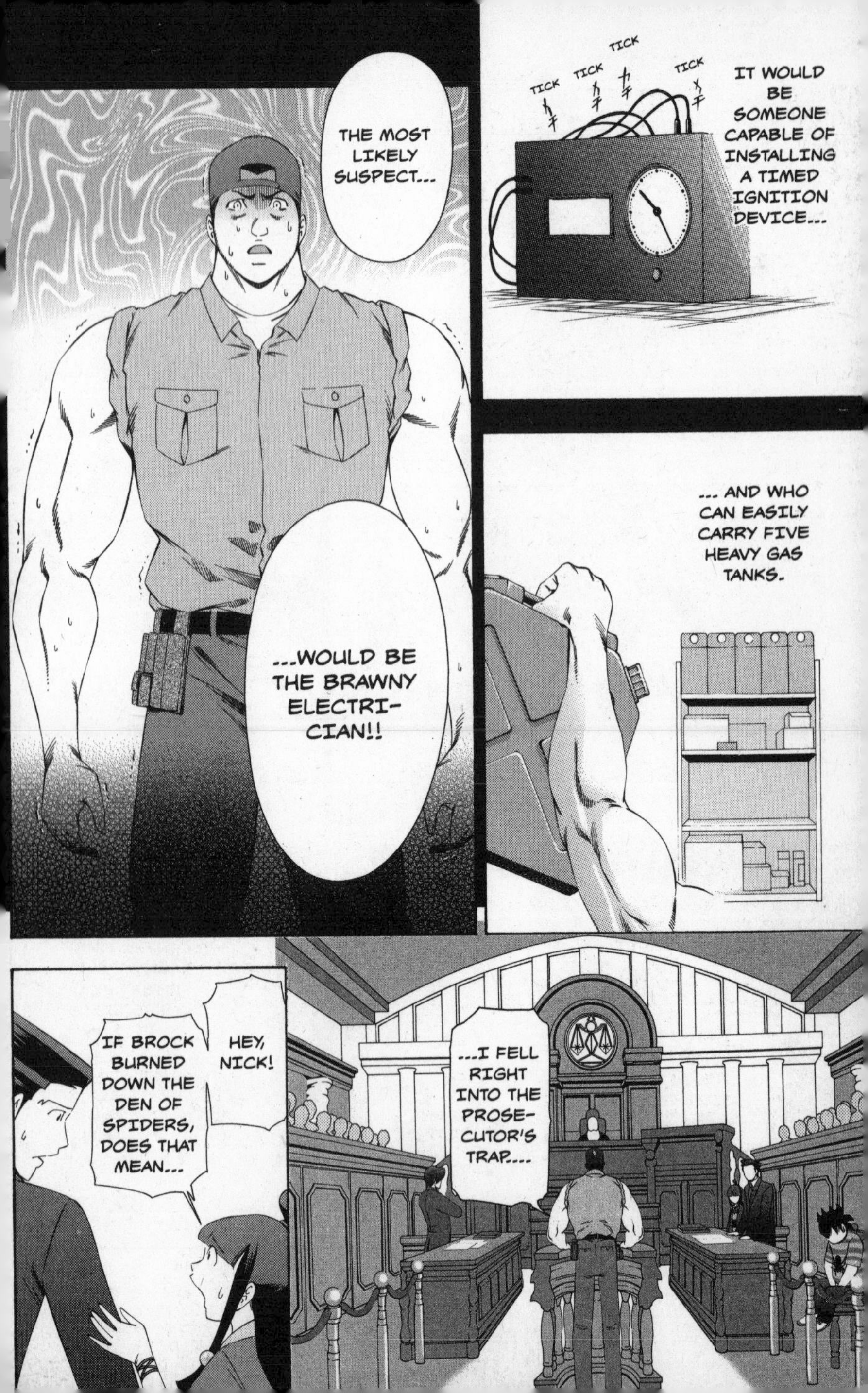
TICK
TICK
TICK
TICK
IT WOULD BE SOMEONE CAPABLE OF INSTALLING A TIMED IGNITION DEVICE...
... AND WHO CAN EASILY CARRY FIVE HEAVY GAS TANKS.
THE MOST LIKELY SUSPECT...
...WOULD BE THE BRAWNY ELECTRICIAN!!
...I FELL RIGHT INTO THE PROSECUTOR'S TRAP...
HEY, NICK!
IF BROCK BURNED DOWN THE DEN OF SPIDERS, DOES THAT MEAN...

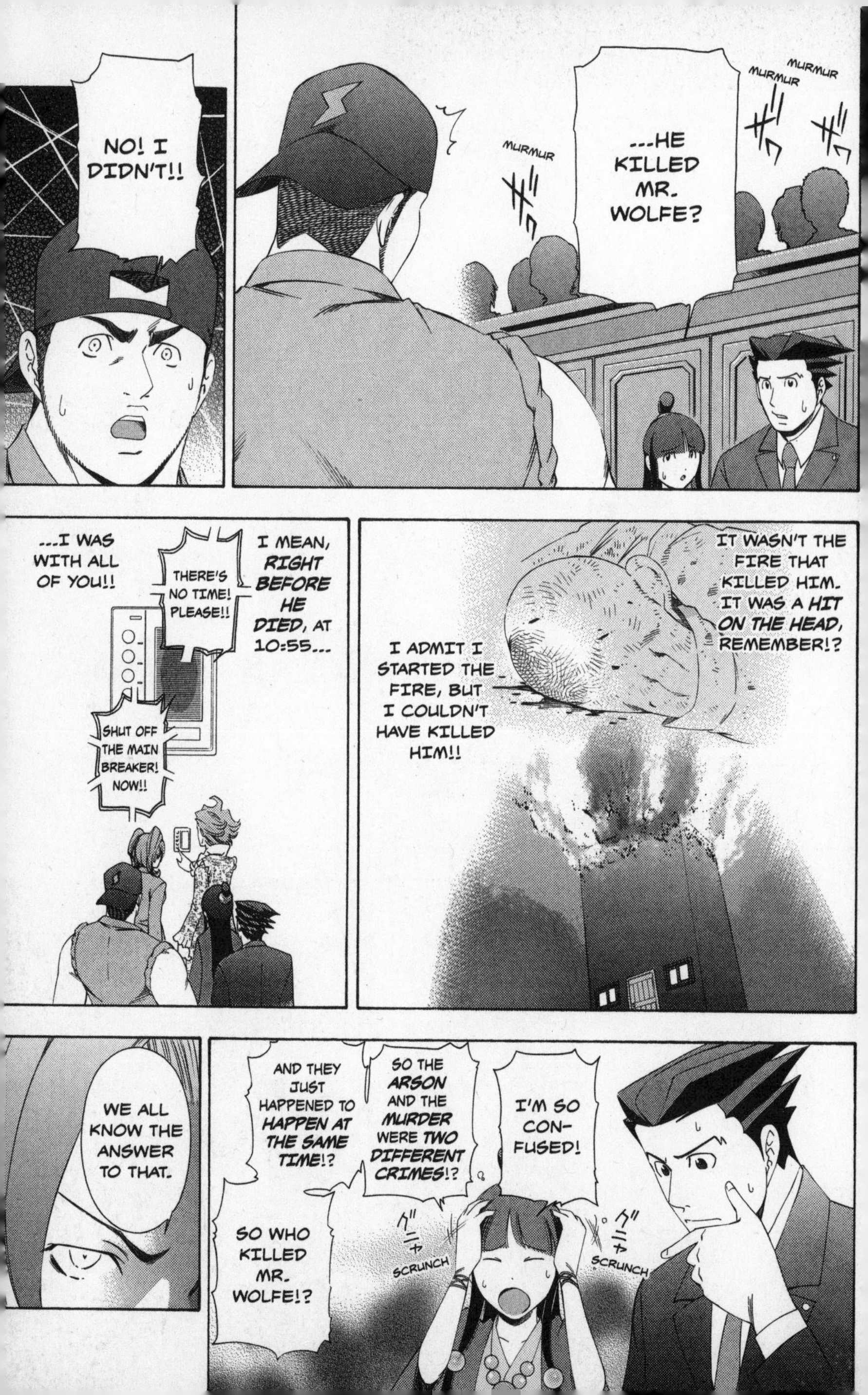
MURMUR
MURMUR
---HE KILLED MR. WOLFE?
MURMUR
NO! I DIDN'T!!
IT WASN'T THE FIRE THAT KILLED HIM. IT WAS A *HIT ON THE HEAD*, REMEMBER!?
I ADMIT I STARTED THE FIRE, BUT I COULDN'T HAVE KILLED HIM!!
I MEAN, *RIGHT BEFORE HE DIED*, AT 10:55...
THERE'S NO TIME! PLEASE!!
...I WAS WITH ALL OF YOU!!
SHUT OFF THE MAIN BREAKER! NOW!!
I'M SO CON-FUSED!
SO THE *ARSON* AND THE *MURDER* WERE *TWO DIFFERENT CRIMES*!?
AND THEY JUST HAPPENED TO *HAPPEN AT THE SAME TIME*!?
SO WHO KILLED MR. WOLFE!?
SCRUNCH
SCRUNCH
WE ALL KNOW THE ANSWER TO THAT.

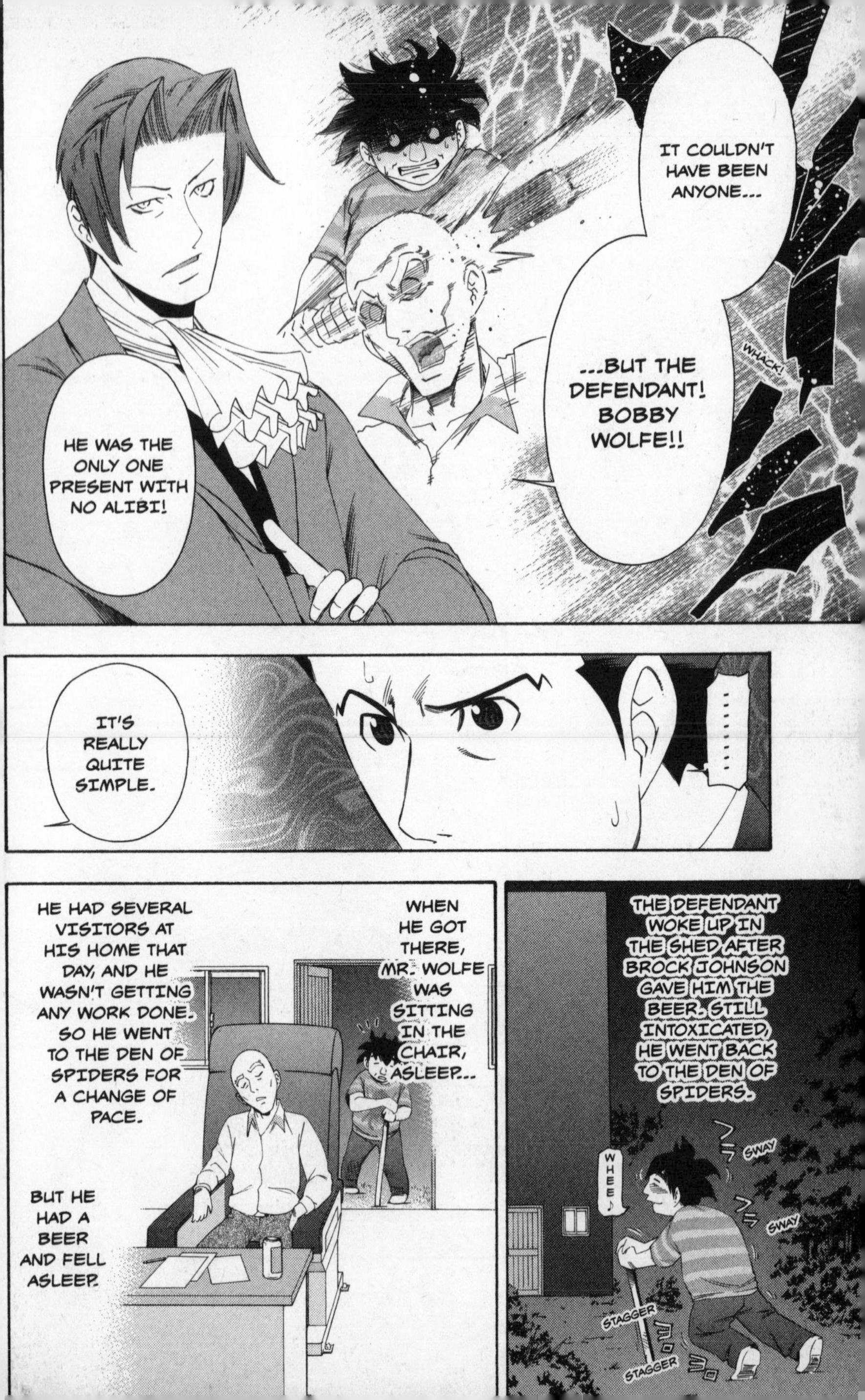
IT COULDN'T HAVE BEEN ANYONE...
...BUT THE DEFENDANT! BOBBY WOLFE!!
WHACK!
HE WAS THE ONLY ONE PRESENT WITH NO ALIBI!
IT'S REALLY QUITE SIMPLE.
THE DEFENDANT WOKE UP IN THE SHED AFTER BROCK JOHNSON GAVE HIM THE BEER. STILL INTOXICATED, HE WENT BACK TO THE DEN OF SPIDERS.
SWAY
WHEE♪
SWAY
STAGGER
STAGGER
WHEN HE GOT THERE, MR. WOLFE WAS SITTING IN THE CHAIR, ASLEEP...
HE HAD SEVERAL VISITORS AT HIS HOME THAT DAY, AND HE WASN'T GETTING ANY WORK DONE. SO HE WENT TO THE DEN OF SPIDERS FOR A CHANGE OF PACE.
BUT HE HAD A BEER AND FELL ASLEEP.

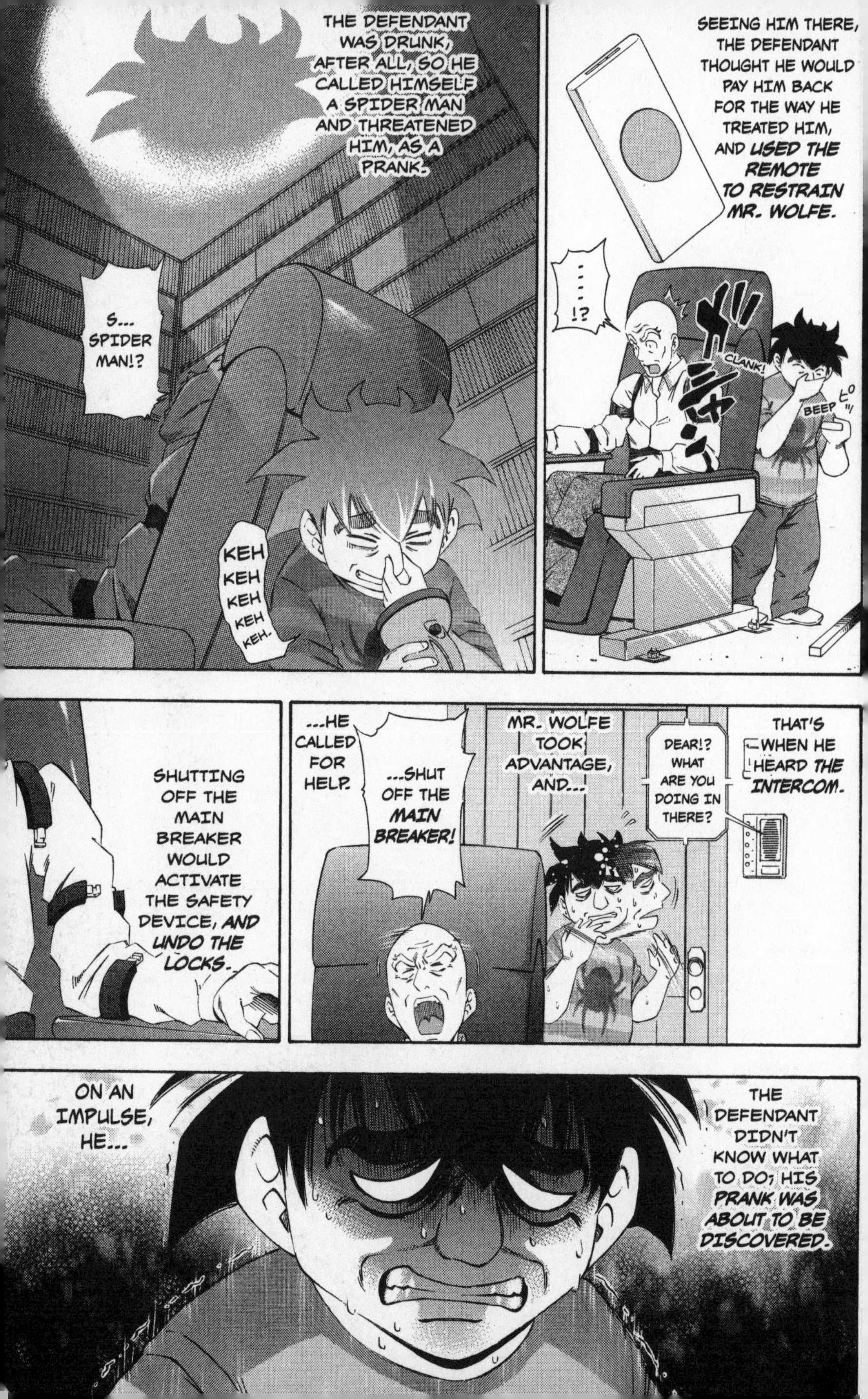
SEEING HIM THERE, THE DEFENDANT THOUGHT HE WOULD PAY HIM BACK FOR THE WAY HE TREATED HIM, AND USED THE REMOTE TO RESTRAIN MR. WOLFE.
......!?
CLANK!
BEEP
THE DEFENDANT WAS DRUNK, AFTER ALL, SO HE CALLED HIMSELF A SPIDER MAN AND THREATENED HIM, AS A PRANK.
S... SPIDER MAN!?
KEH KEH KEH KEH KEH.
THAT'S WHEN HE HEARD THE INTERCOM.
DEAR!? WHAT ARE YOU DOING IN THERE?
MR. WOLFE TOOK ADVANTAGE, AND...
...HE CALLED FOR HELP.
...SHUT OFF THE MAIN BREAKER!
SHUTTING OFF THE MAIN BREAKER WOULD ACTIVATE THE SAFETY DEVICE, AND UNDO THE LOCKS.
THE DEFENDANT DIDN'T KNOW WHAT TO DO; HIS PRANK WAS ABOUT TO BE DISCOVERED.
ON AN IMPULSE, HE...

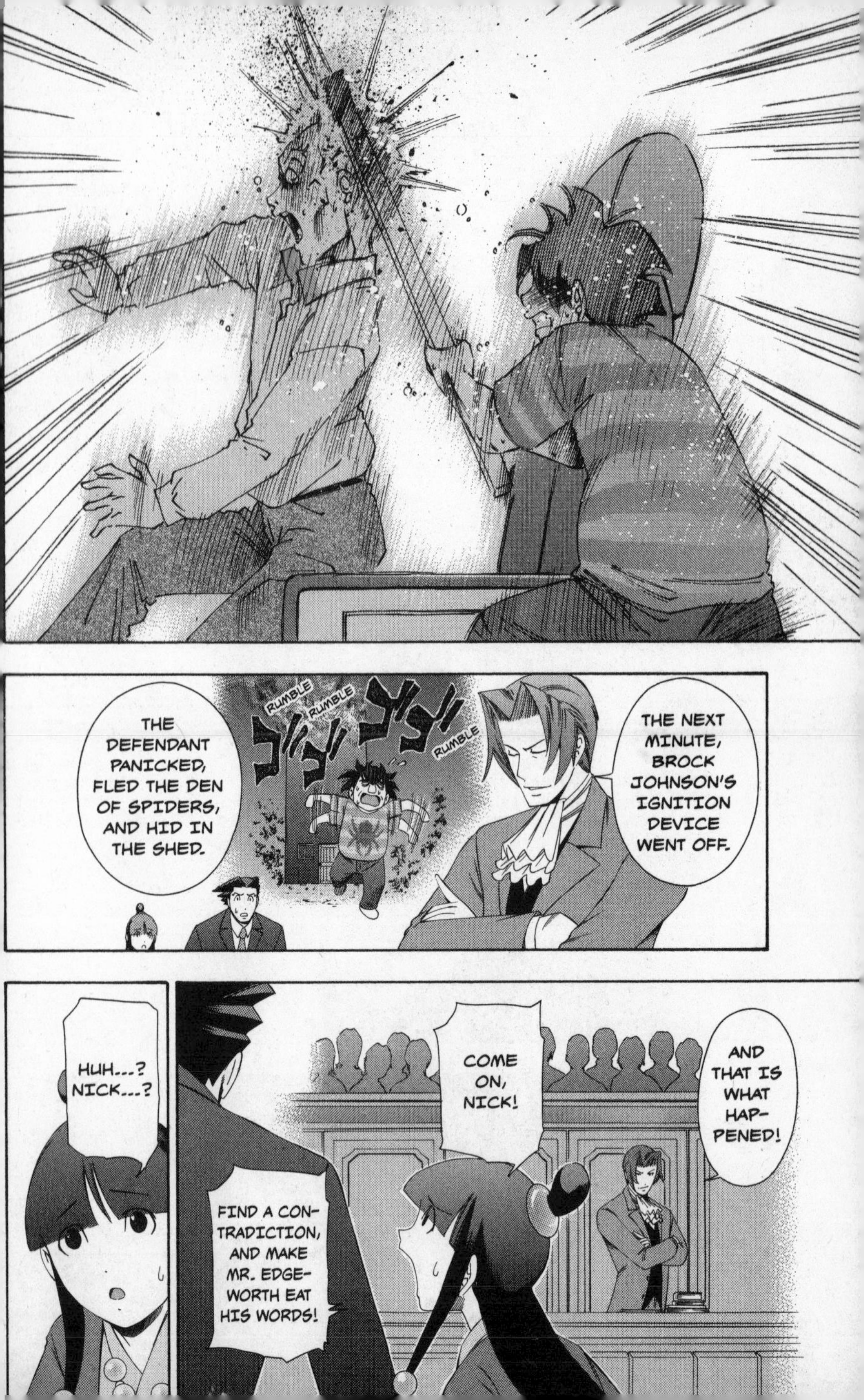
THE NEXT MINUTE, BROCK JOHNSON'S IGNITION DEVICE WENT OFF.
RUMBLE
RUMBLE
RUMBLE
THE DEFENDANT PANICKED, FLED THE DEN OF SPIDERS, AND HID IN THE SHED.
AND THAT IS WHAT HAP-PENED!
COME ON, NICK!
FIND A CON-TRADICTION, AND MAKE MR. EDGE-WORTH EAT HIS WORDS!
HUH...? NICK...?

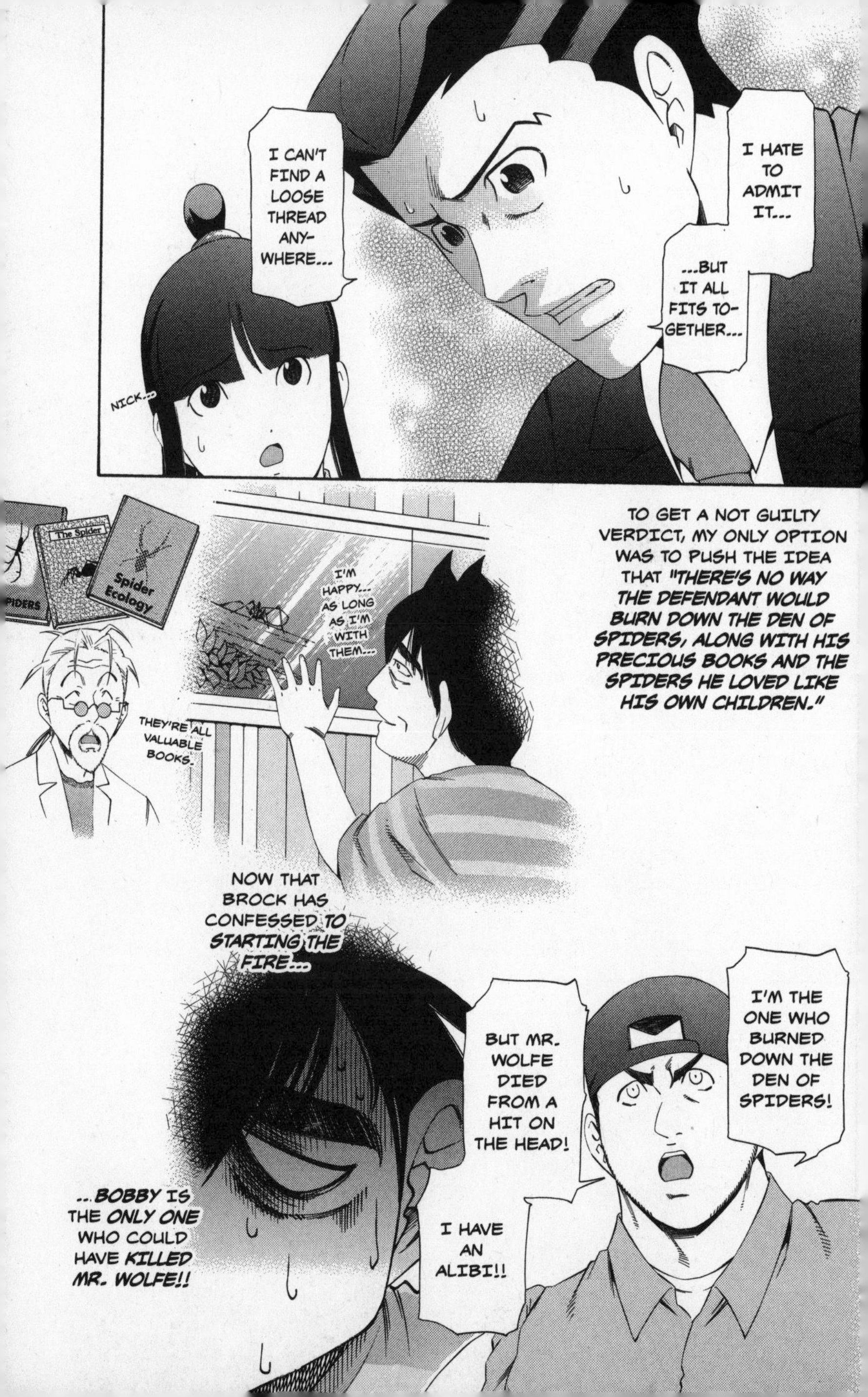
I HATE TO ADMIT IT...
...BUT IT ALL FITS TOGETHER...
I CAN'T FIND A LOOSE THREAD ANYWHERE...
NICK...
TO GET A NOT GUILTY VERDICT, MY ONLY OPTION WAS TO PUSH THE IDEA THAT "THERE'S NO WAY THE DEFENDANT WOULD BURN DOWN THE DEN OF SPIDERS, ALONG WITH HIS PRECIOUS BOOKS AND THE SPIDERS HE LOVED LIKE HIS OWN CHILDREN."
I'M HAPPY... AS LONG AS I'M WITH THEM...
Spider Ecology
The Spider
SPIDERS
THEY'RE ALL VALUABLE BOOKS.
NOW THAT BROCK HAS CONFESSED TO STARTING THE FIRE...
I'M THE ONE WHO BURNED DOWN THE DEN OF SPIDERS!
BUT MR. WOLFE DIED FROM A HIT ON THE HEAD!
I HAVE AN ALIBI!!
...BOBBY IS THE ONLY ONE WHO COULD HAVE KILLED MR. WOLFE!!

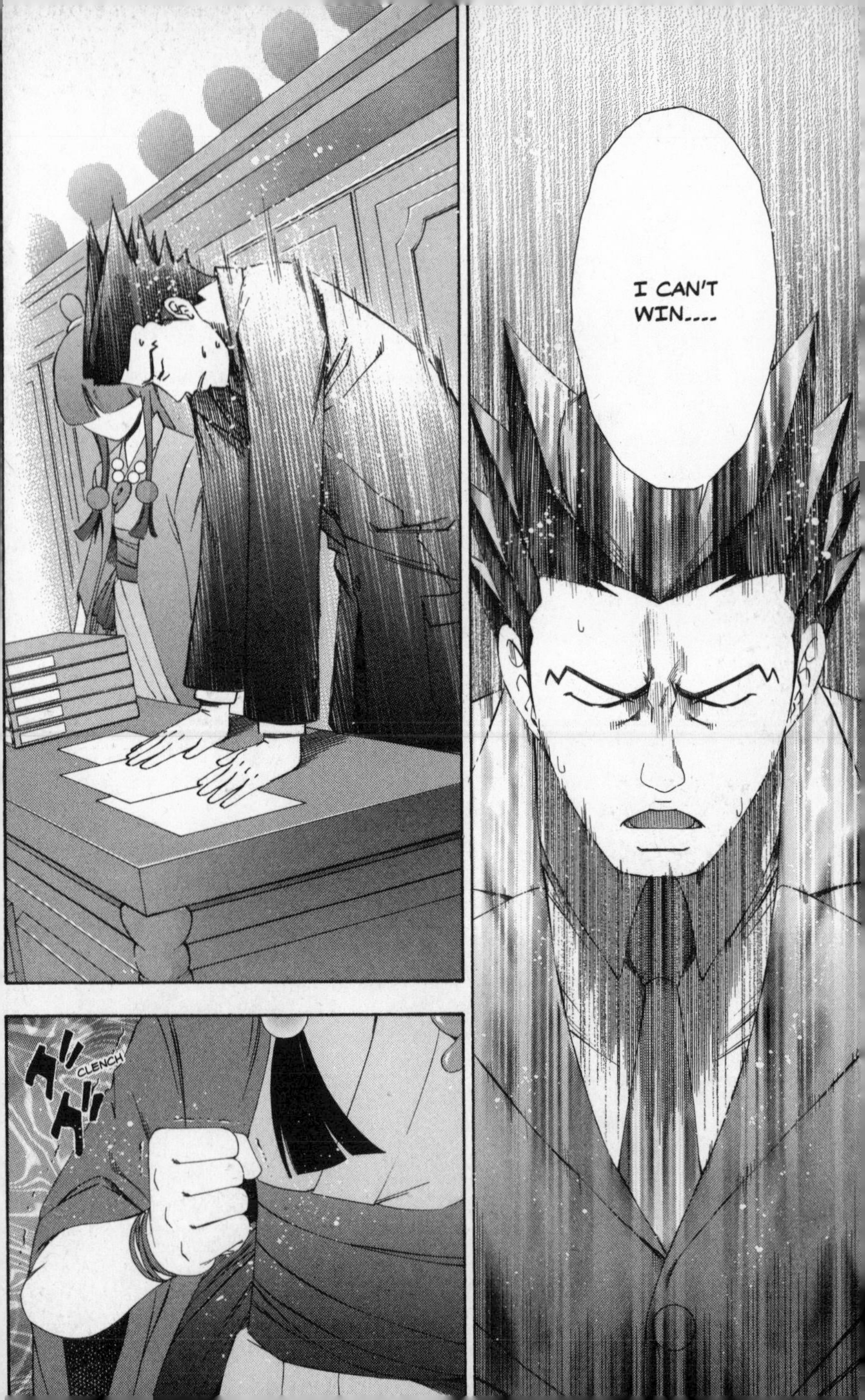
I CAN'T WIN....
CLENCH

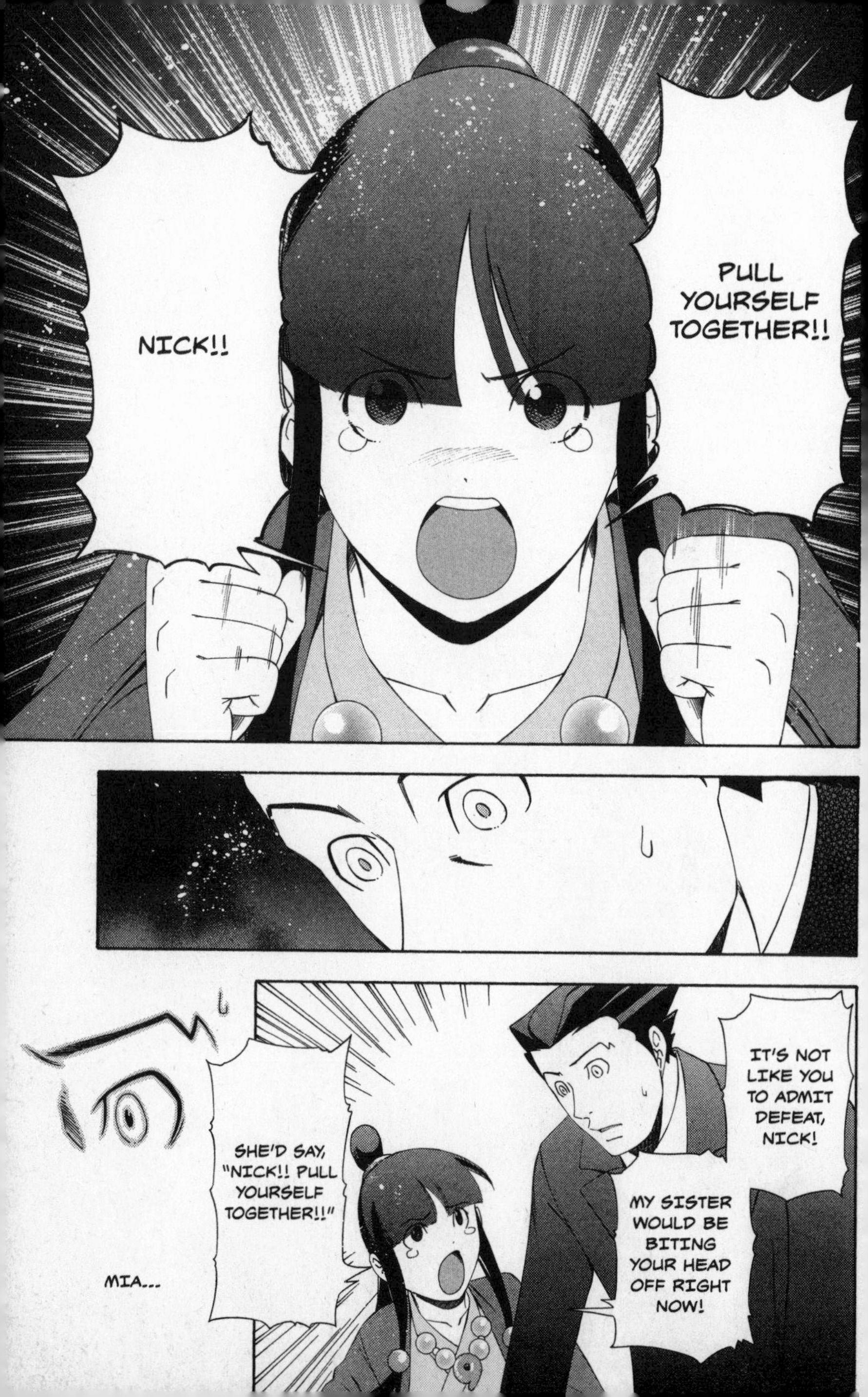
PULL YOURSELF TOGETHER!!
NICK!!
IT'S NOT LIKE YOU TO ADMIT DEFEAT, NICK!
MY SISTER WOULD BE BITING YOUR HEAD OFF RIGHT NOW!
SHE'D SAY, "NICK!! PULL YOURSELF TOGETHER!!"
MIA...

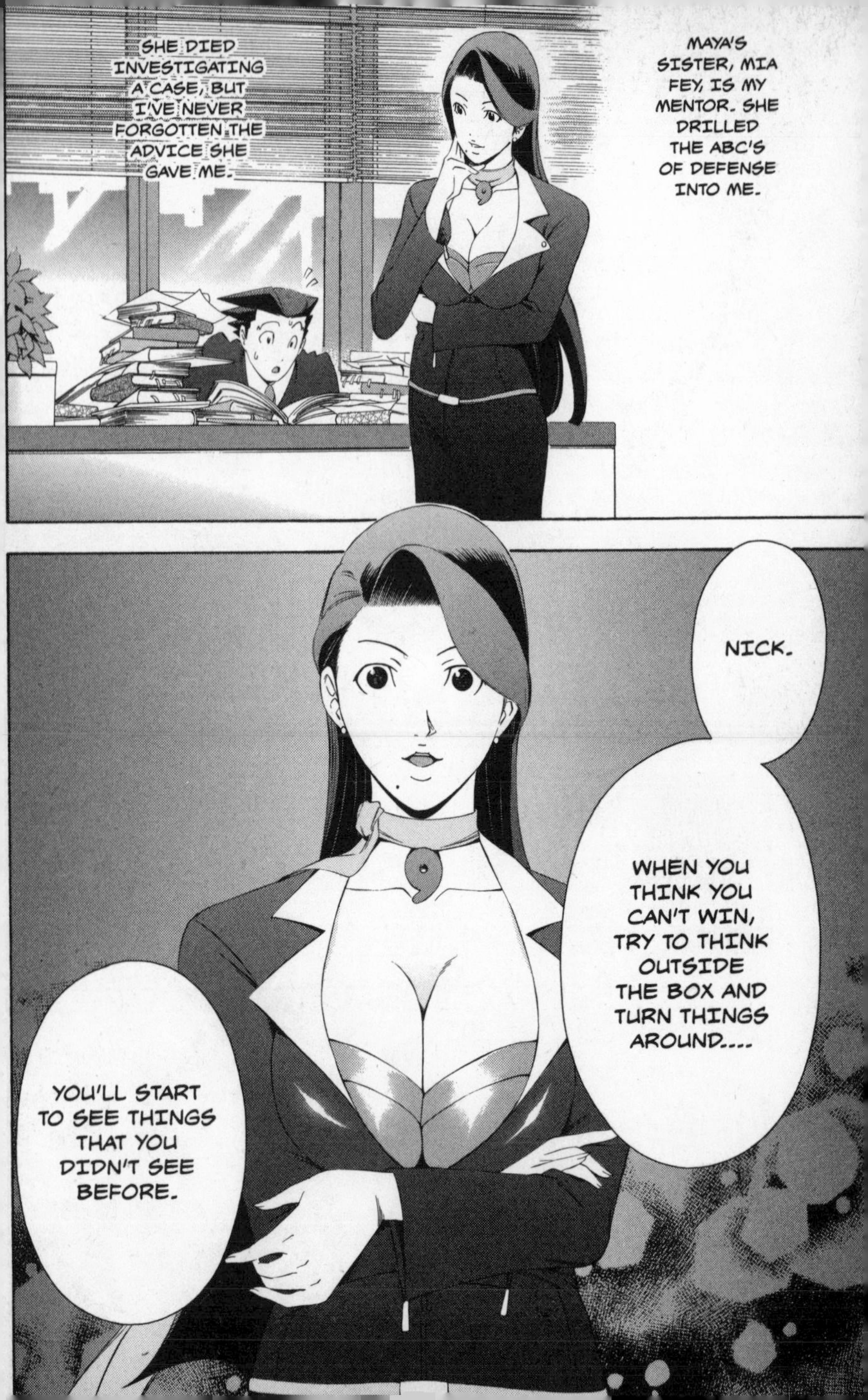
MAYA'S SISTER, MIA FEY, IS MY MENTOR. SHE DRILLED THE ABC'S OF DEFENSE INTO ME.
SHE DIED INVESTIGATING A CASE, BUT I'VE NEVER FORGOTTEN THE ADVICE SHE GAVE ME.
NICK.
WHEN YOU THINK YOU CAN'T WIN, TRY TO THINK OUTSIDE THE BOX AND TURN THINGS AROUND....
YOU'LL START TO SEE THINGS THAT YOU DIDN'T SEE BEFORE.

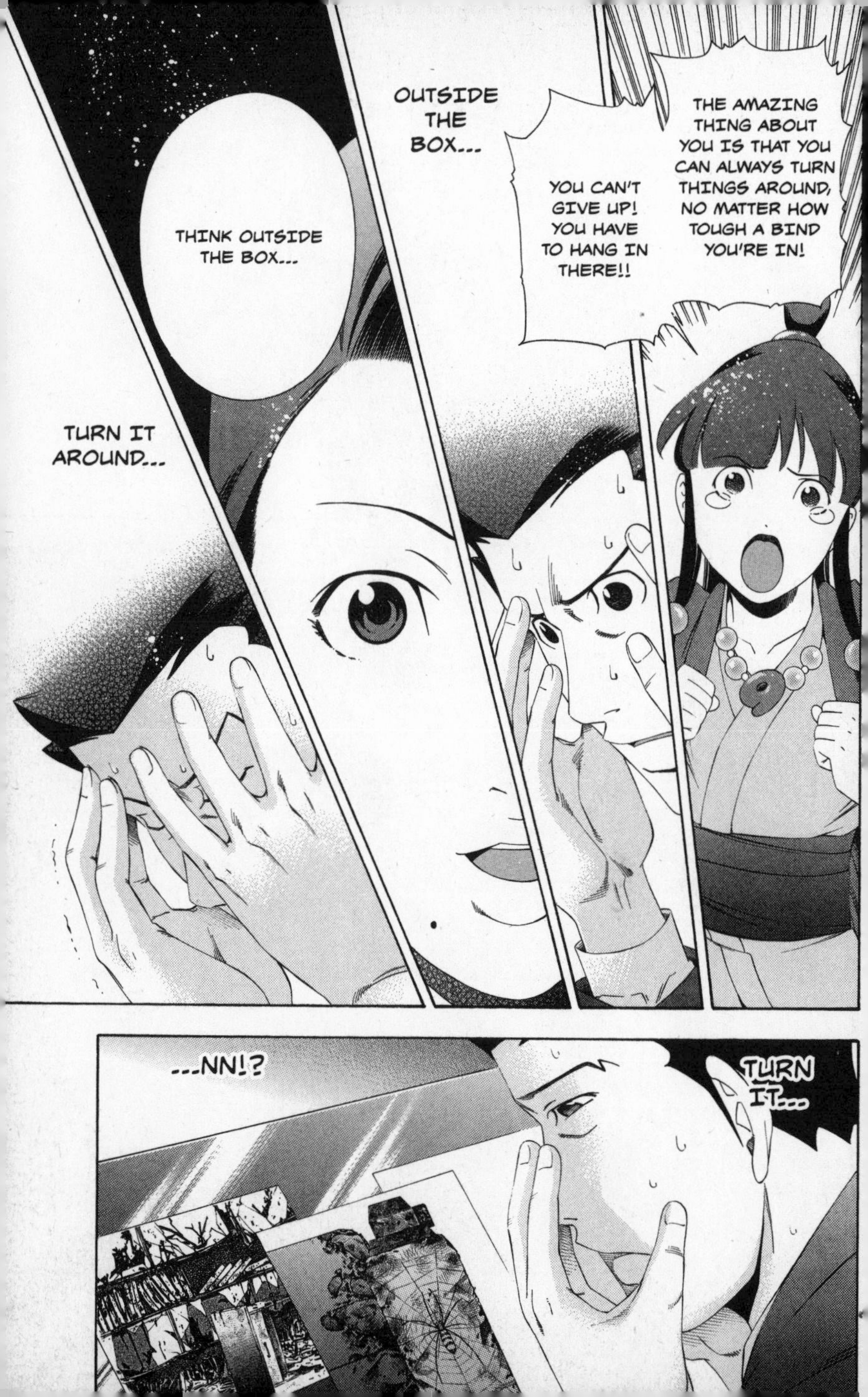
THE AMAZING THING ABOUT YOU IS THAT YOU CAN ALWAYS TURN THINGS AROUND, NO MATTER HOW TOUGH A BIND YOU'RE IN!
YOU CAN'T GIVE UP! YOU HAVE TO HANG IN THERE!!
OUTSIDE THE BOX...
THINK OUTSIDE THE BOX...
TURN IT AROUND...
TURN IT...
...NN!?

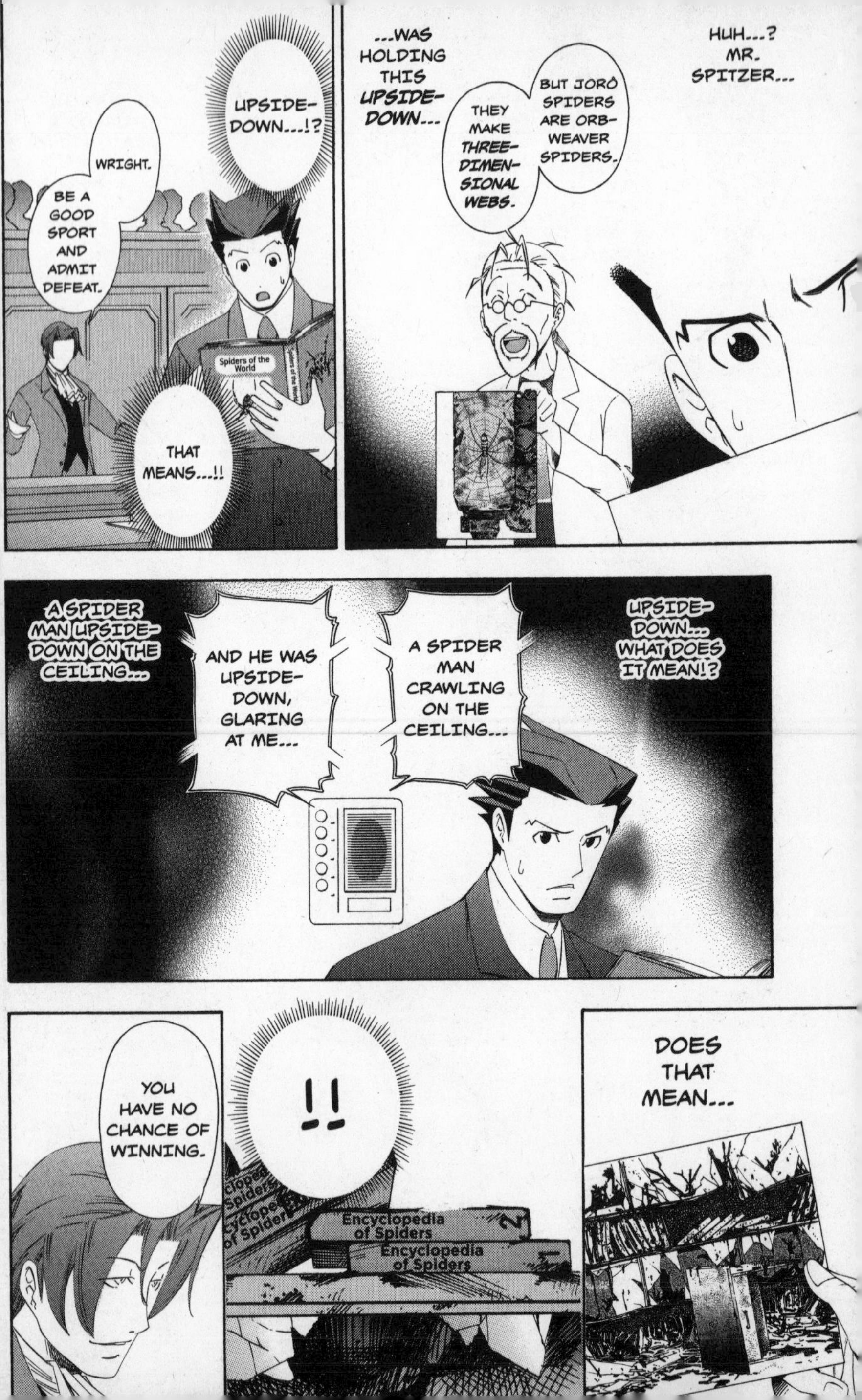
HUH...? MR. SPITZER...
BUT JORÔ SPIDERS ARE ORB-WEAVER SPIDERS.
THEY MAKE THREE-DIMENSIONAL WEBS.
...WAS HOLDING THIS UPSIDE-DOWN...
UPSIDE-DOWN...!?
WRIGHT.
BE A GOOD SPORT AND ADMIT DEFEAT.
Spiders of the World
THAT MEANS...!!
UPSIDE-DOWN... WHAT DOES IT MEAN!?
A SPIDER MAN CRAWLING ON THE CEILING...
AND HE WAS UPSIDE-DOWN, GLARING AT ME...
A SPIDER MAN UPSIDE-DOWN ON THE CEILING...
DOES THAT MEAN...
!!
Encyclopedia of Spiders
Encyclopedia of Spiders
YOU HAVE NO CHANCE OF WINNING.

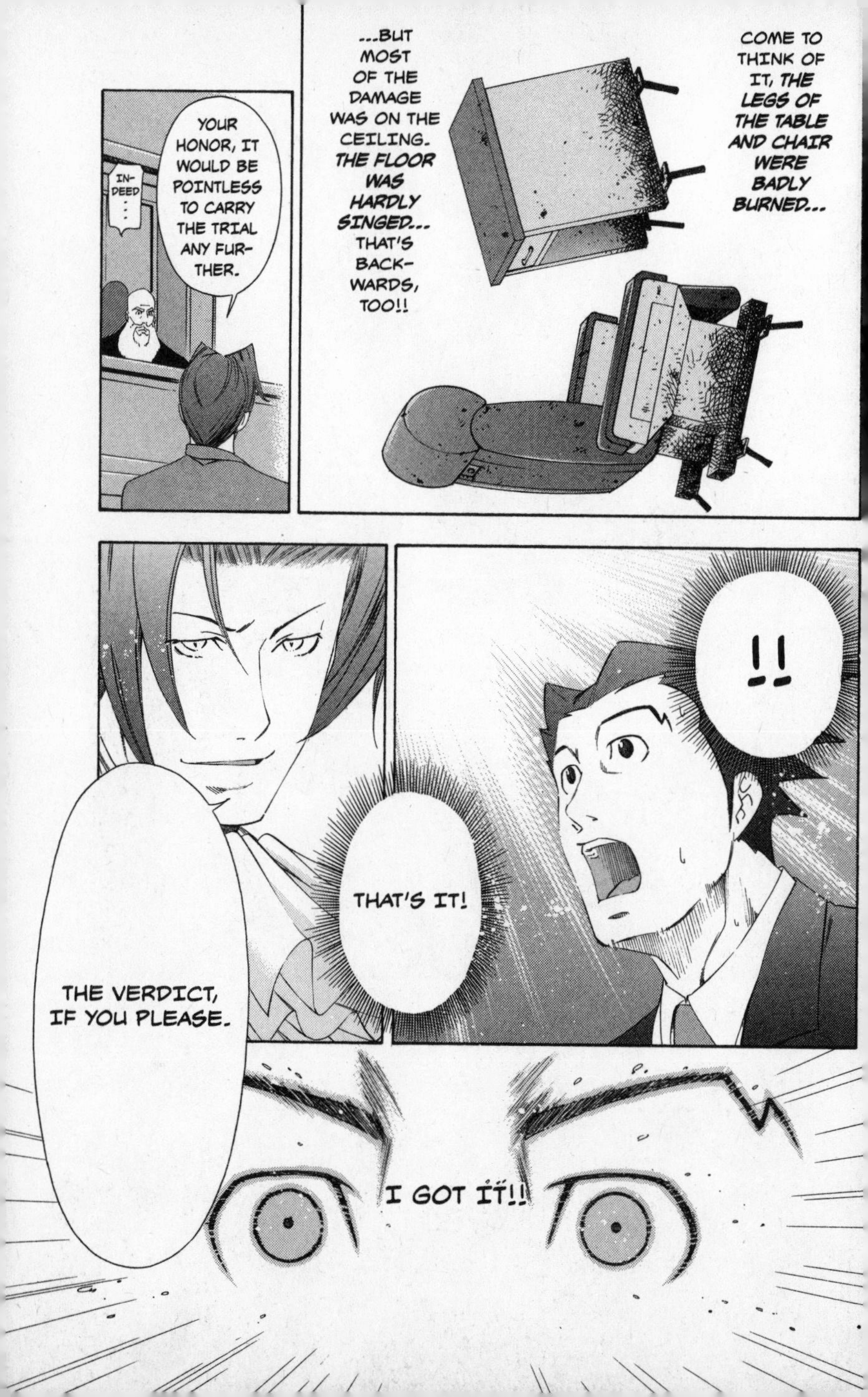
COME TO THINK OF IT, THE LEGS OF THE TABLE AND CHAIR WERE BADLY BURNED...
...BUT MOST OF THE DAMAGE WAS ON THE CEILING. THE FLOOR WAS HARDLY SINGED... THAT'S BACKWARDS, TOO!!
YOUR HONOR, IT WOULD BE POINTLESS TO CARRY THE TRIAL ANY FURTHER.
INDEED...
!!
THAT'S IT!
THE VERDICT, IF YOU PLEASE.
I GOT IT!!

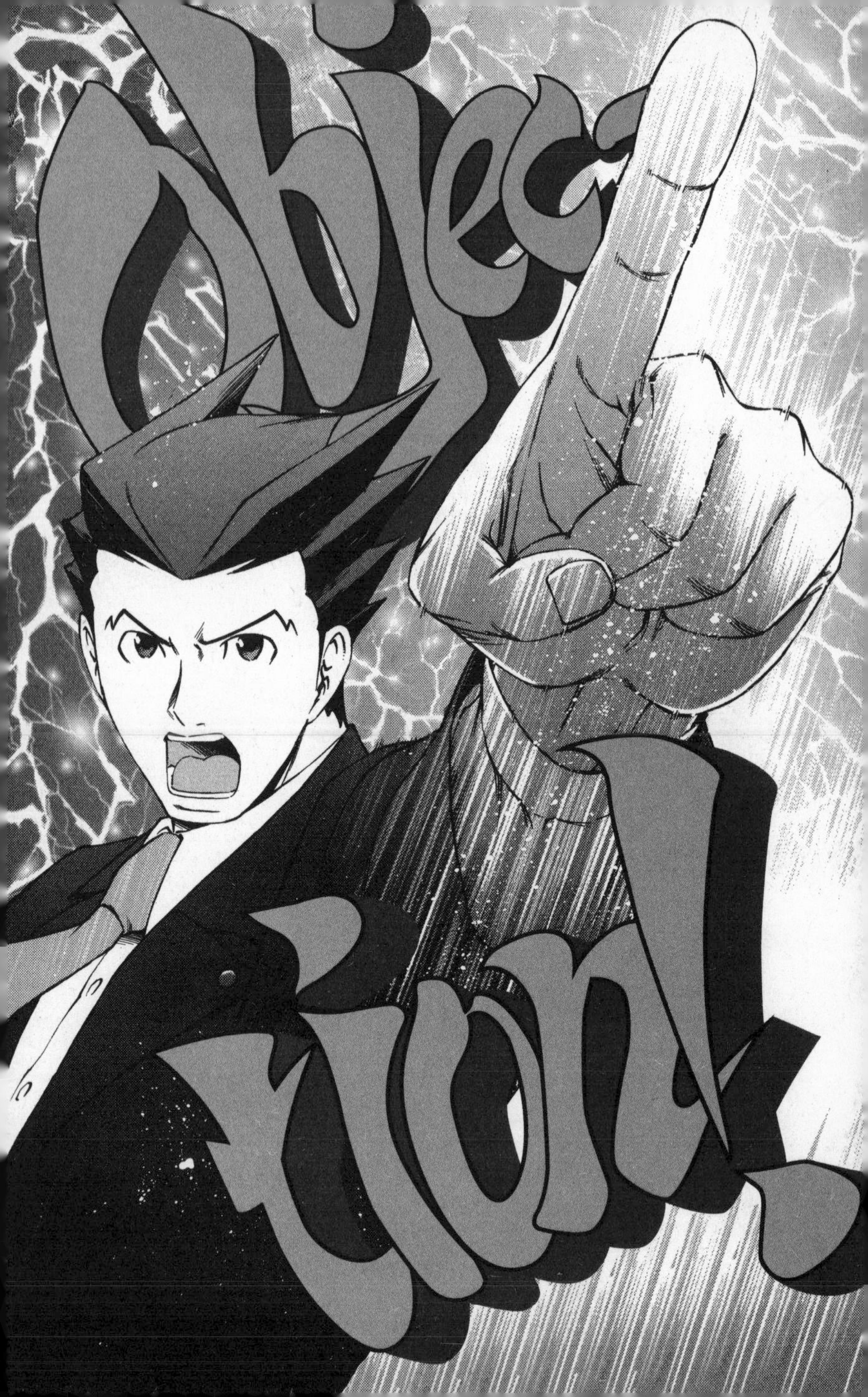
Objection!

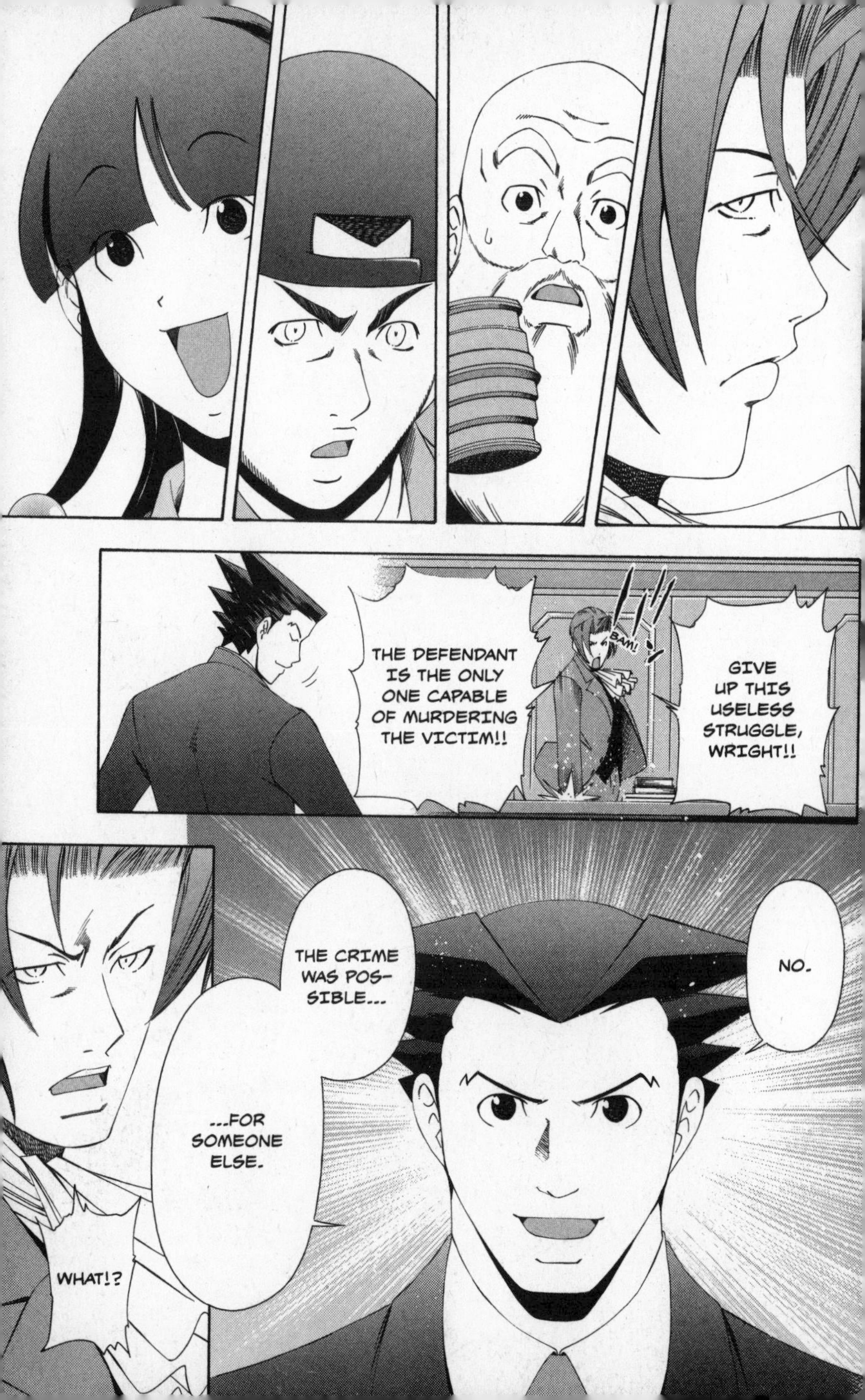
BAM!
GIVE UP THIS USELESS STRUGGLE, WRIGHT!!
THE DEFENDANT IS THE ONLY ONE CAPABLE OF MURDERING THE VICTIM!!
NO.
THE CRIME WAS POS-SIBLE...
...FOR SOMEONE ELSE.
WHAT!?

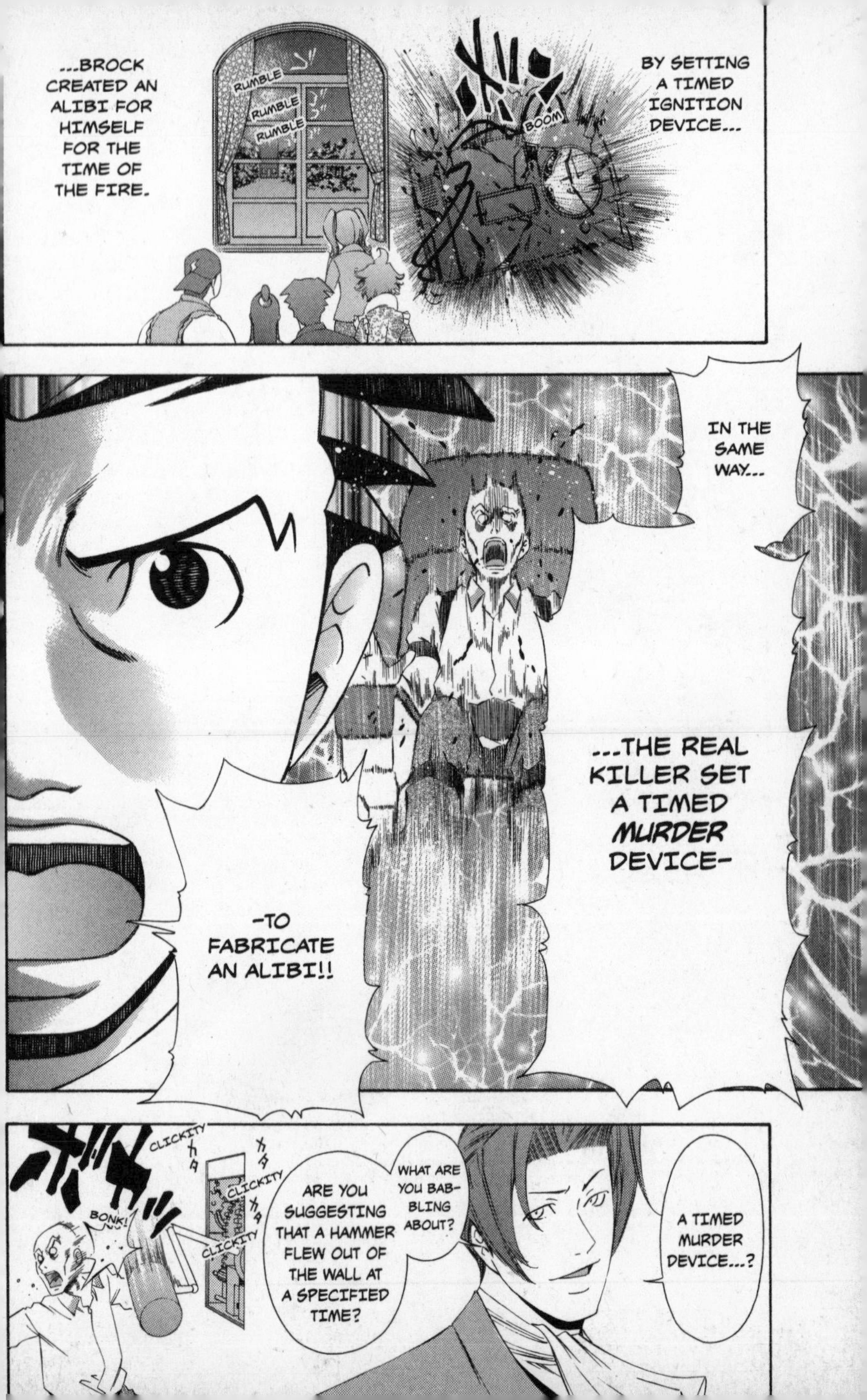
BY SETTING A TIMED IGNITION DEVICE...
BOOM
RUMBLE
RUMBLE
RUMBLE
...BROCK CREATED AN ALIBI FOR HIMSELF FOR THE TIME OF THE FIRE.
IN THE SAME WAY...
...THE REAL KILLER SET A TIMED *MURDER* DEVICE-
-TO FABRICATE AN ALIBI!!
A TIMED MURDER DEVICE...?
WHAT ARE YOU BABBLING ABOUT?
ARE YOU SUGGESTING THAT A HAMMER FLEW OUT OF THE WALL AT A SPECIFIED TIME?
CLICKITY
CLICKITY
CLICKITY
BONK!

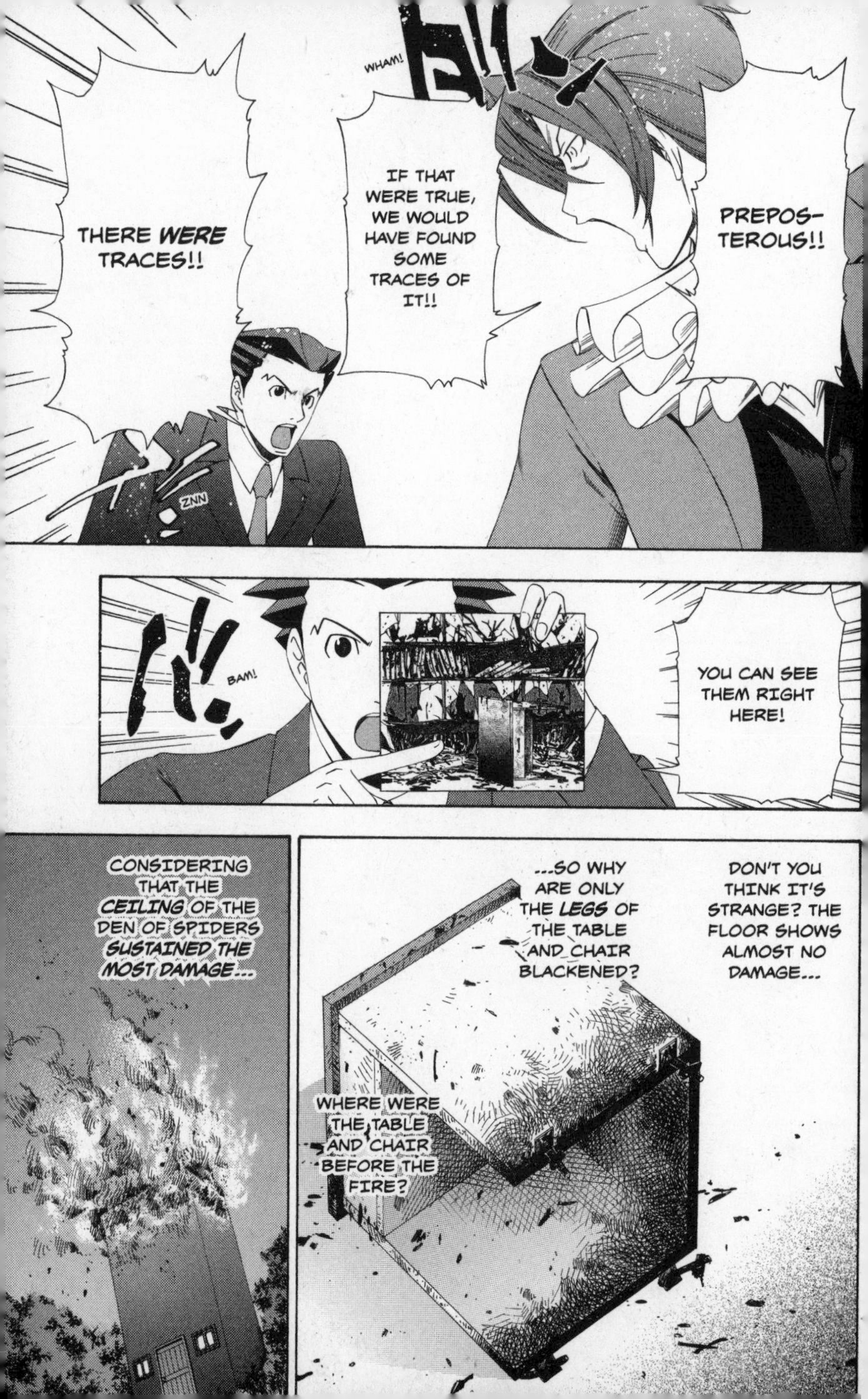
WHAM!
PREPOS-TEROUS!!
IF THAT WERE TRUE, WE WOULD HAVE FOUND SOME TRACES OF IT!!
THERE *WERE* TRACES!!
ZNN
YOU CAN SEE THEM RIGHT HERE!
BAM!
DON'T YOU THINK IT'S STRANGE? THE FLOOR SHOWS ALMOST NO DAMAGE...
...SO WHY ARE ONLY THE *LEGS* OF THE TABLE AND CHAIR BLACKENED?
WHERE WERE THE TABLE AND CHAIR BEFORE THE FIRE?
CONSIDERING THAT THE *CEILING* OF THE DEN OF SPIDERS *SUSTAINED THE MOST DAMAGE*...

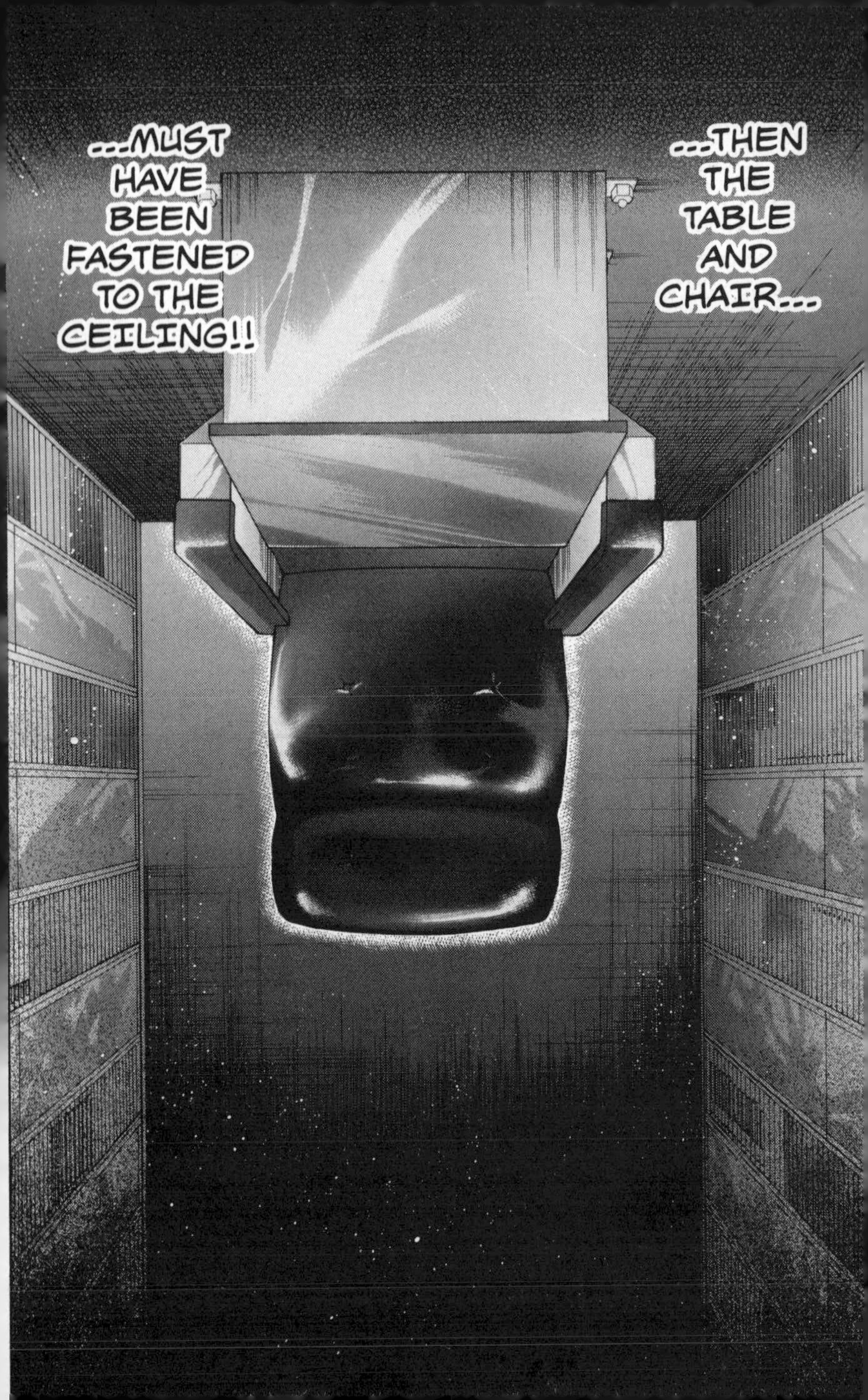
...THEN THE TABLE AND CHAIR...
...MUST HAVE BEEN FASTENED TO THE CEILING!!

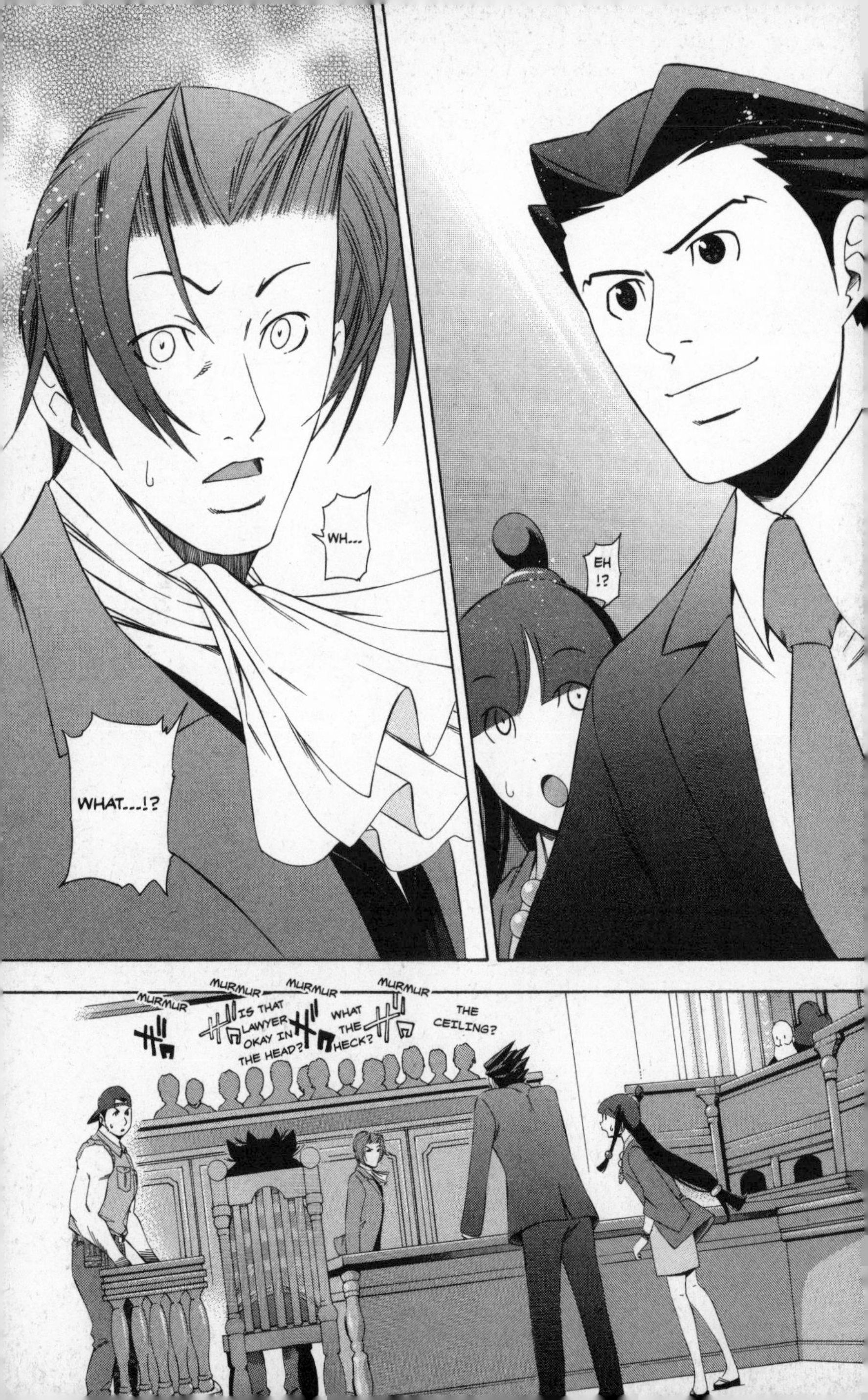
EH
!?
WH...
WHAT...!?
THE CEILING?
MURMUR
WHAT THE HECK?
MURMUR
IS THAT LAWYER OKAY IN THE HEAD?
MURMUR
MURMUR

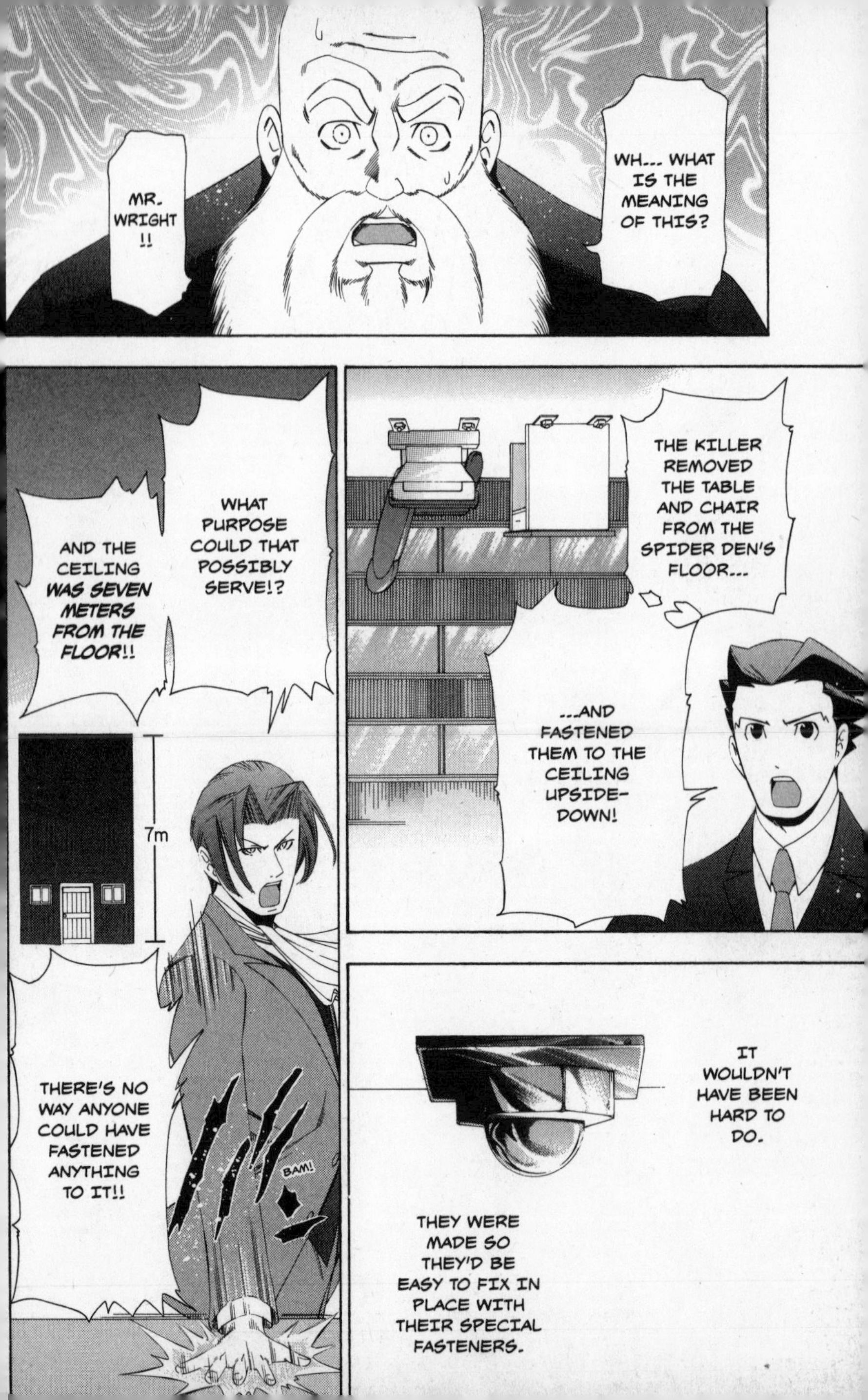
WH... WHAT IS THE MEANING OF THIS?
MR. WRIGHT !!
THE KILLER REMOVED THE TABLE AND CHAIR FROM THE SPIDER DEN'S FLOOR...
...AND FASTENED THEM TO THE CEILING UPSIDE-DOWN!
WHAT PURPOSE COULD THAT POSSIBLY SERVE!?
AND THE CEILING *WAS SEVEN METERS FROM THE FLOOR*!!
7m
THERE'S NO WAY ANYONE COULD HAVE FASTENED ANYTHING TO IT!!
BAM!
IT WOULDN'T HAVE BEEN HARD TO DO.
THEY WERE MADE SO THEY'D BE EASY TO FIX IN PLACE WITH THEIR SPECIAL FASTENERS.

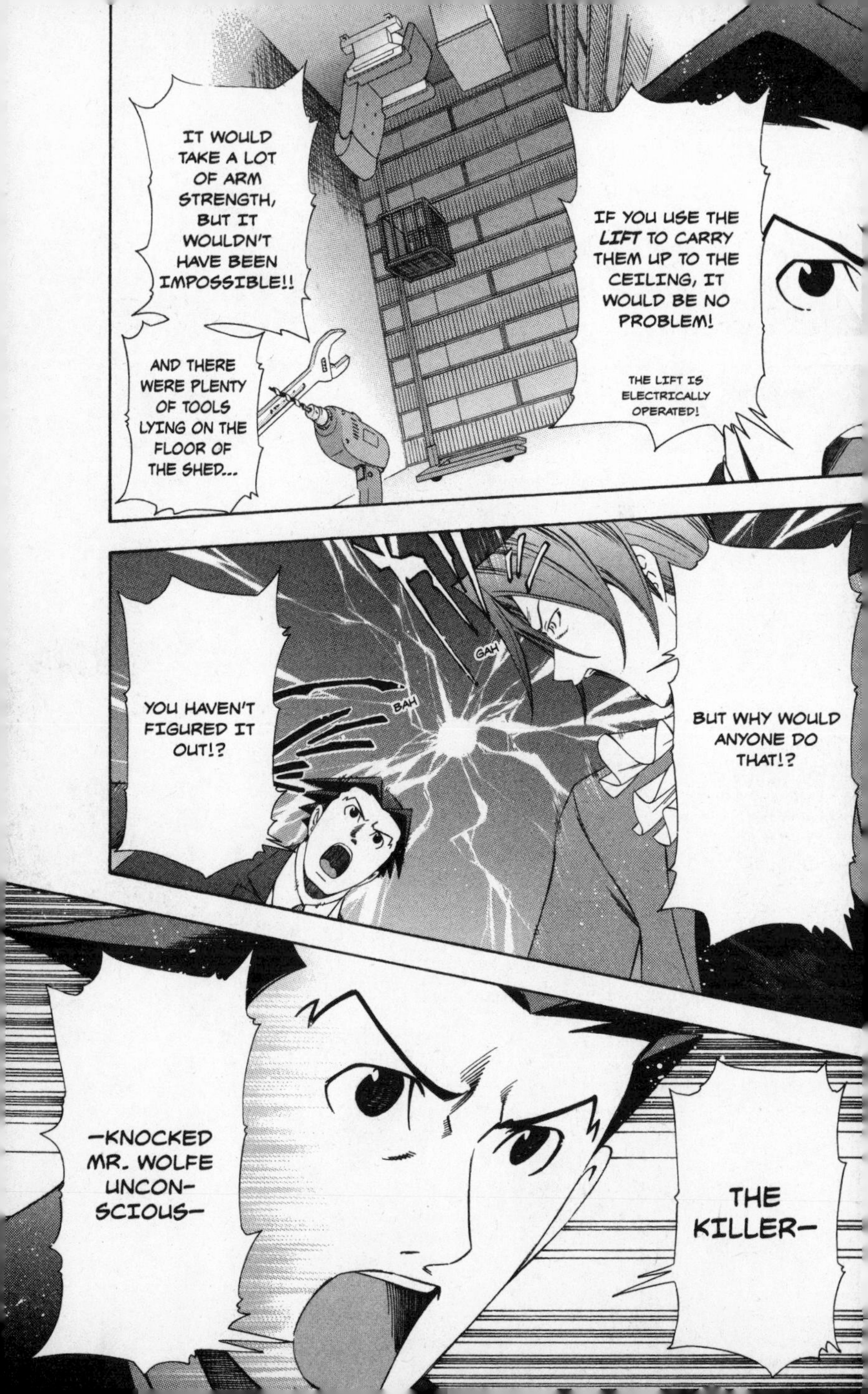
IF YOU USE THE *LIFT* TO CARRY THEM UP TO THE CEILING, IT WOULD BE NO PROBLEM!
THE LIFT IS ELECTRICALLY OPERATED!
IT WOULD TAKE A LOT OF ARM STRENGTH, BUT IT WOULDN'T HAVE BEEN IMPOSSIBLE!!
AND THERE WERE PLENTY OF TOOLS LYING ON THE FLOOR OF THE SHED...
BUT WHY WOULD ANYONE DO THAT!?
GAH
BAH
YOU HAVEN'T FIGURED IT OUT!?
THE KILLER—
—KNOCKED MR. WOLFE UNCON-SCIOUS—

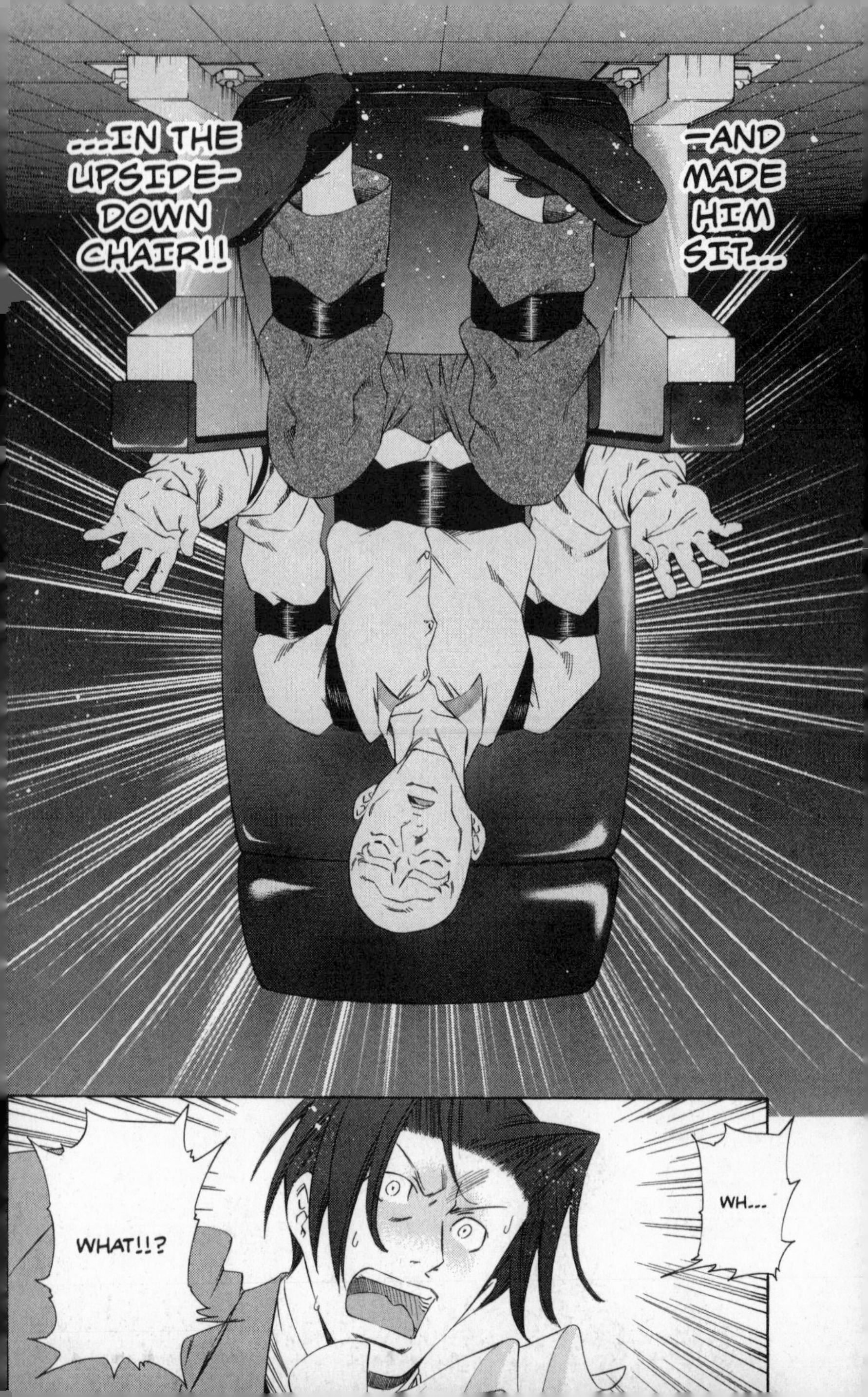
—AND MADE HIM SIT...
...IN THE UPSIDE-DOWN CHAIR!!
WH...
WHAT!!?

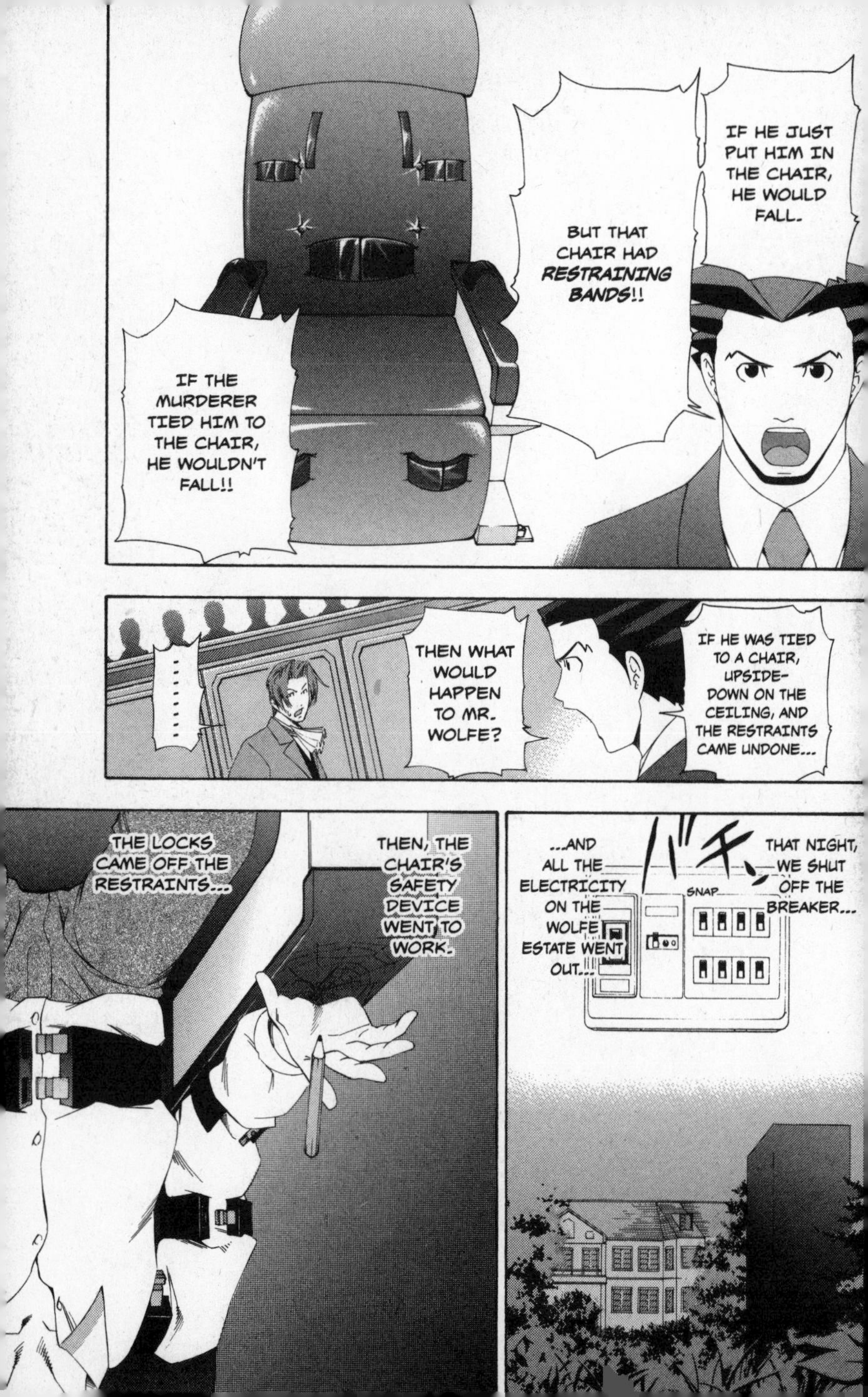
IF HE JUST PUT HIM IN THE CHAIR, HE WOULD FALL.
BUT THAT CHAIR HAD RESTRAINING BANDS!!
IF THE MURDERER TIED HIM TO THE CHAIR, HE WOULDN'T FALL!!
IF HE WAS TIED TO A CHAIR, UPSIDE-DOWN ON THE CEILING, AND THE RESTRAINTS CAME UNDONE...
THEN WHAT WOULD HAPPEN TO MR. WOLFE?
....
THAT NIGHT, WE SHUT OFF THE BREAKER...
バチ
SNAP
...AND ALL THE ELECTRICITY ON THE WOLFE ESTATE WENT OUT...
THEN, THE CHAIR'S SAFETY DEVICE WENT TO WORK.
THE LOCKS CAME OFF THE RESTRAINTS...

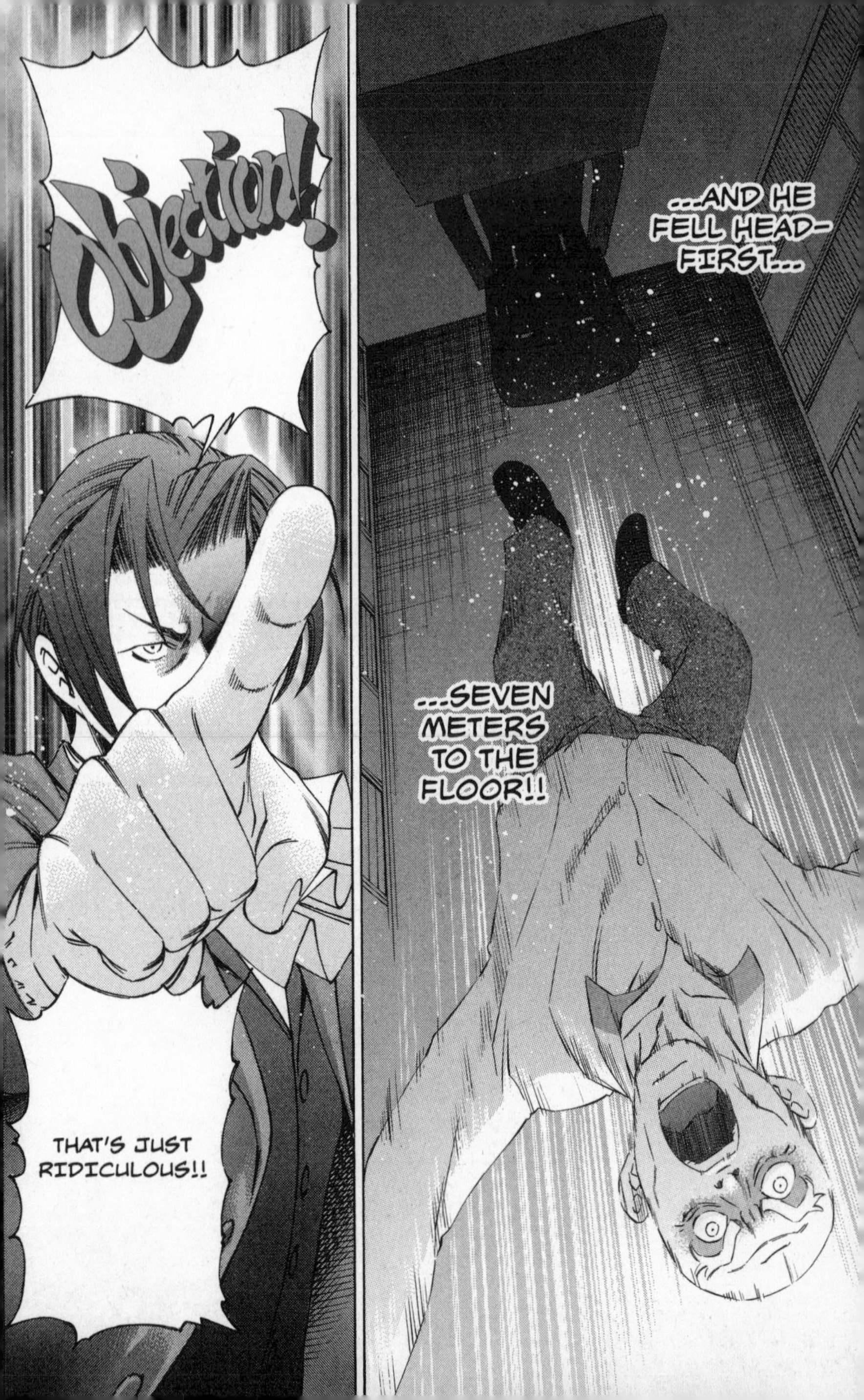
...AND HE FELL HEAD-FIRST...
...SEVEN METERS TO THE FLOOR!!
Objection!
THAT'S JUST RIDICULOUS!!

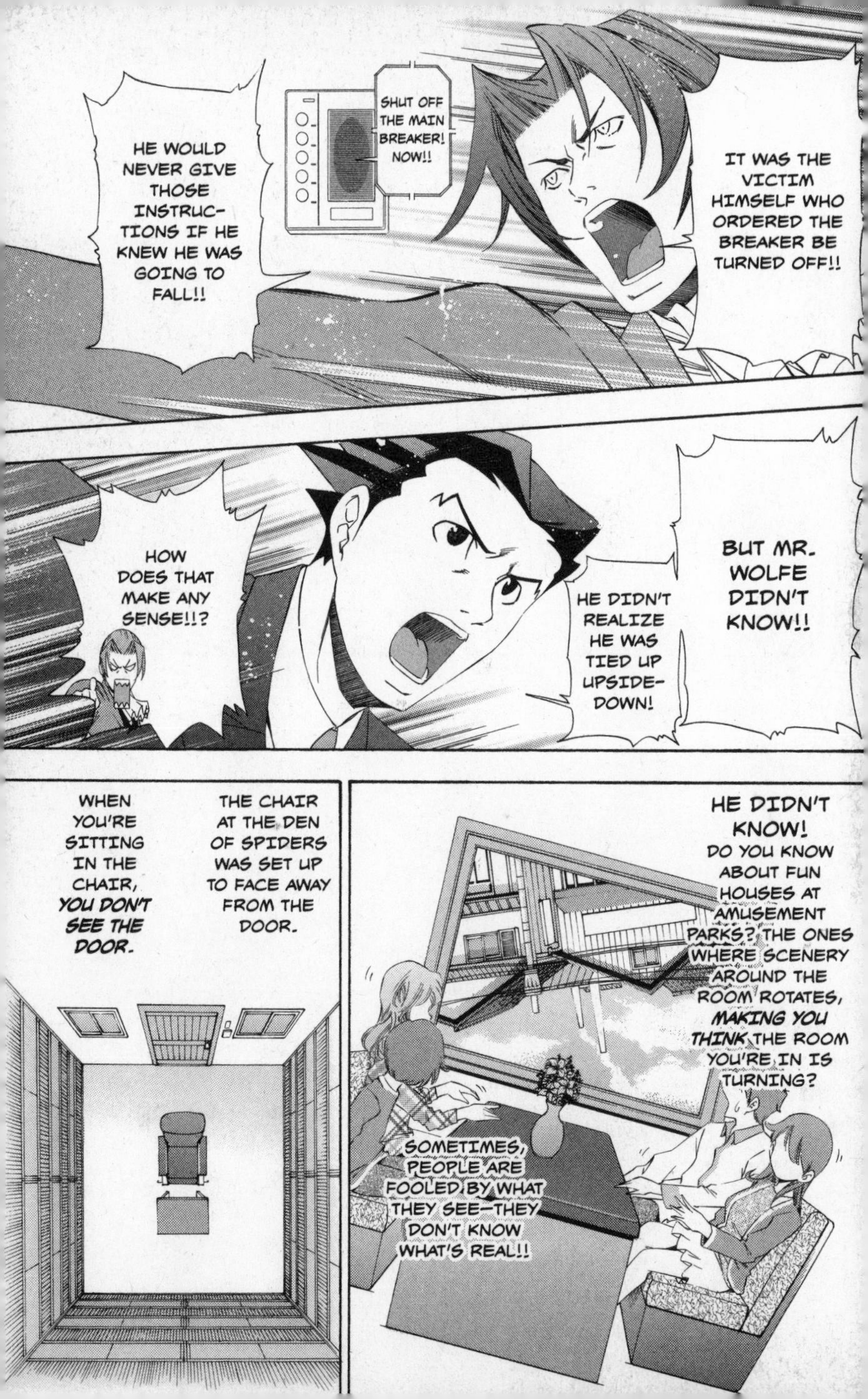
IT WAS THE VICTIM HIMSELF WHO ORDERED THE BREAKER BE TURNED OFF!!
SHUT OFF THE MAIN BREAKER! NOW!!
HE WOULD NEVER GIVE THOSE INSTRUC-TIONS IF HE KNEW HE WAS GOING TO FALL!!
BUT MR. WOLFE DIDN'T KNOW!!
HE DIDN'T REALIZE HE WAS TIED UP UPSIDE-DOWN!
HOW DOES THAT MAKE ANY SENSE!!?
HE DIDN'T KNOW! DO YOU KNOW ABOUT FUN HOUSES AT AMUSEMENT PARKS? THE ONES WHERE SCENERY AROUND THE ROOM ROTATES, *MAKING YOU THINK* THE ROOM YOU'RE IN IS TURNING?
SOMETIMES, PEOPLE ARE FOOLED BY WHAT THEY SEE—THEY DON'T KNOW WHAT'S REAL!!
THE CHAIR AT THE DEN OF SPIDERS WAS SET UP TO FACE AWAY FROM THE DOOR.
WHEN YOU'RE SITTING IN THE CHAIR, *YOU DON'T SEE THE DOOR*.

EVEN IF THE WHOLE DEN OF SPIDERS WAS ACTUALLY UPSIDE-DOWN...
...IF ALL YOU SAW WERE THE TABLE AND SHELVES THAT WERE ALWAYS THERE...
...WOULD YOU REALIZE RIGHT AWAY THAT YOU WERE UPSIDE-DOWN...!?
MR. WOLFE WAS TIED TO THE CHAIR. HE COULDN'T MOVE HIS HANDS, FEET, SHOULDERS OR WAIST.
IN THAT CONDITION, IT'S UNLIKELY THAT HE WOULD HAVE NOTICED THAT THE DEN OF SPIDERS WAS UPSIDE-DOWN.
OF COURSE, GRAVITY WOULD STILL BE IN EFFECT, SO ALL THE BLOOD WOULD HAVE RUSHED TO HIS HEAD, MAKING HIM DIZZY...
HUFF
MY... MY HEAD...
HUFF
HUFF
...SO HEAVY... NNGH...
...MR. WOLFE WOULD HAVE BEEN DAZED, AND EASILY TRICKED BY HIS SENSE OF SIGHT!!

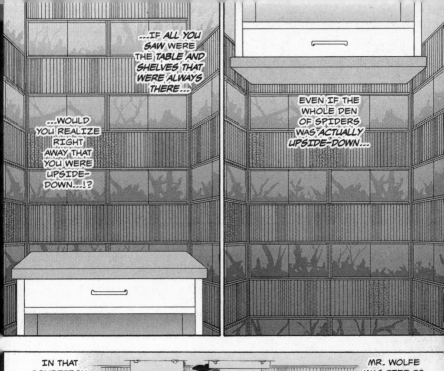

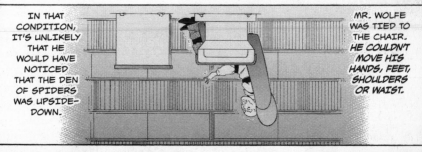

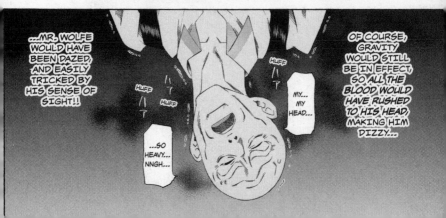

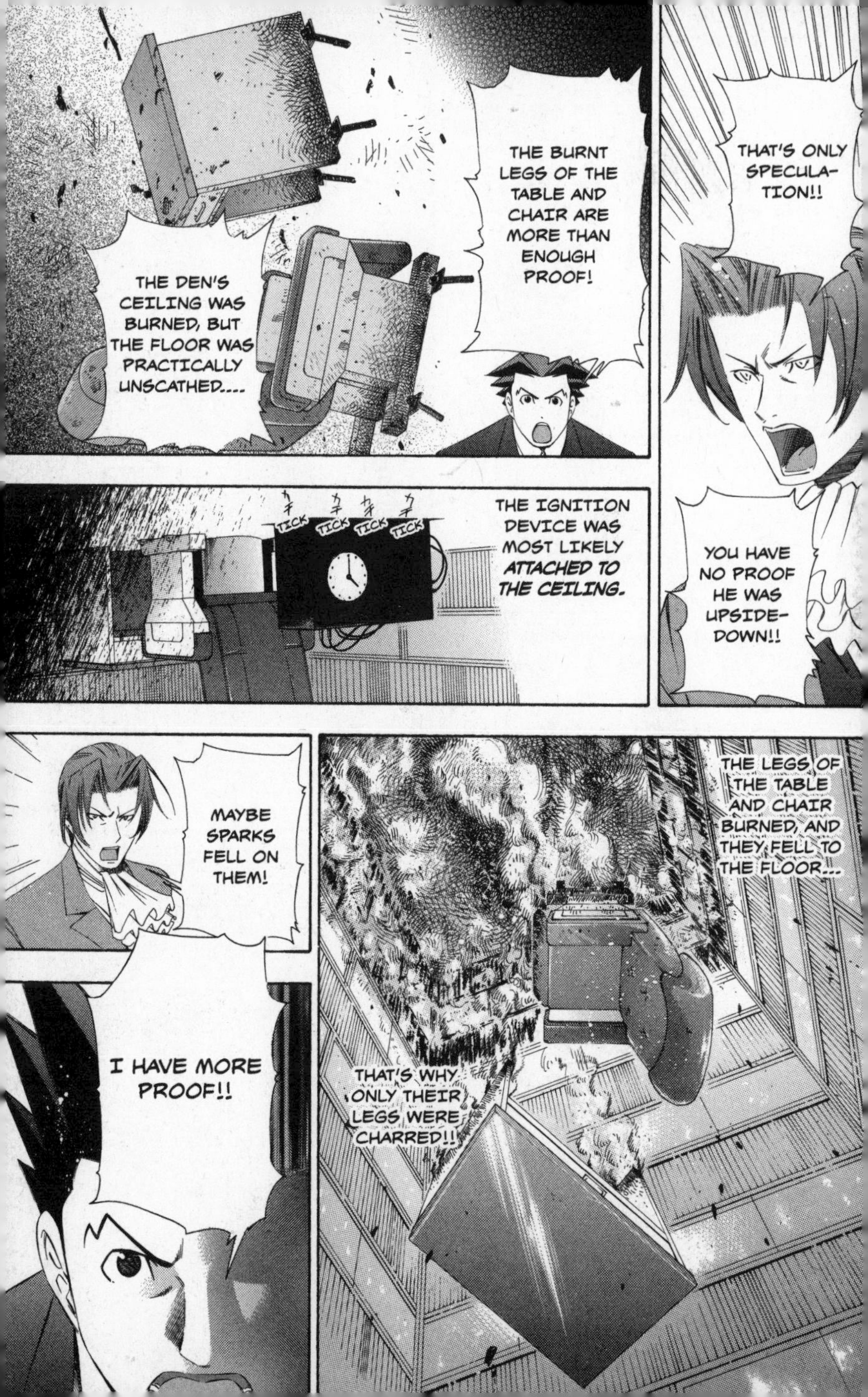
THE DEN'S CEILING WAS BURNED, BUT THE FLOOR WAS PRACTICALLY UNSCATHED....
THE BURNT LEGS OF THE TABLE AND CHAIR ARE MORE THAN ENOUGH PROOF!
THAT'S ONLY SPECULA-TION!!
YOU HAVE NO PROOF HE WAS UPSIDE-DOWN!!
TICK TICK TICK TICK
THE IGNITION DEVICE WAS MOST LIKELY *ATTACHED TO THE CEILING.*
THE LEGS OF THE TABLE AND CHAIR BURNED, AND THEY FELL TO THE FLOOR...
THAT'S WHY ONLY THEIR LEGS WERE CHARRED!!
MAYBE SPARKS FELL ON THEM!
I HAVE MORE PROOF!!

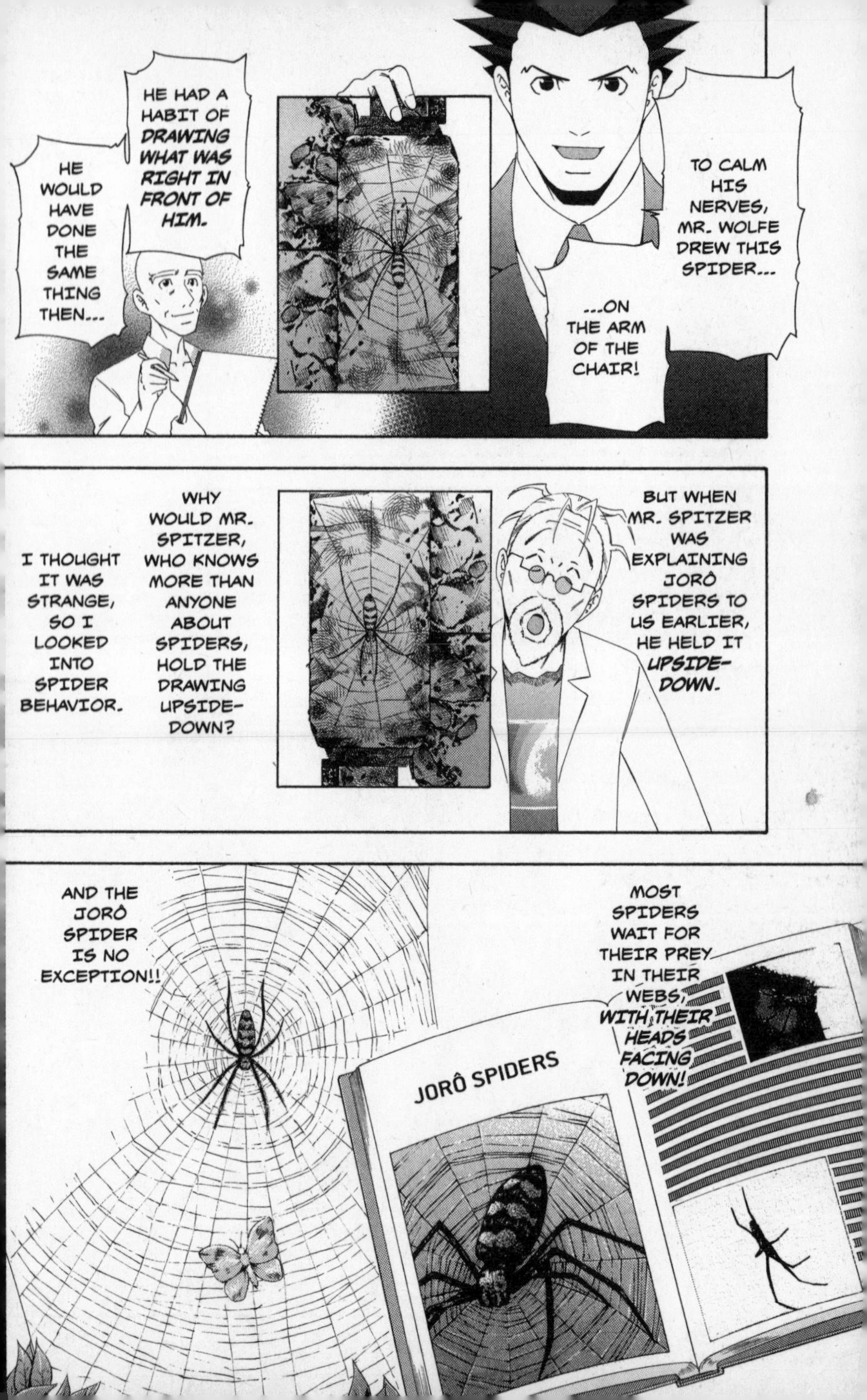
TO CALM HIS NERVES, MR. WOLFE DREW THIS SPIDER...
...ON THE ARM OF THE CHAIR!
HE HAD A HABIT OF DRAWING WHAT WAS RIGHT IN FRONT OF HIM.
HE WOULD HAVE DONE THE SAME THING THEN...
BUT WHEN MR. SPITZER WAS EXPLAINING JORÔ SPIDERS TO US EARLIER, HE HELD IT UPSIDE-DOWN.
WHY WOULD MR. SPITZER, WHO KNOWS MORE THAN ANYONE ABOUT SPIDERS, HOLD THE DRAWING UPSIDE-DOWN?
I THOUGHT IT WAS STRANGE, SO I LOOKED INTO SPIDER BEHAVIOR.
MOST SPIDERS WAIT FOR THEIR PREY IN THEIR WEBS, WITH THEIR HEADS FACING DOWN!
JORÔ SPIDERS
AND THE JORÔ SPIDER IS NO EXCEPTION!!

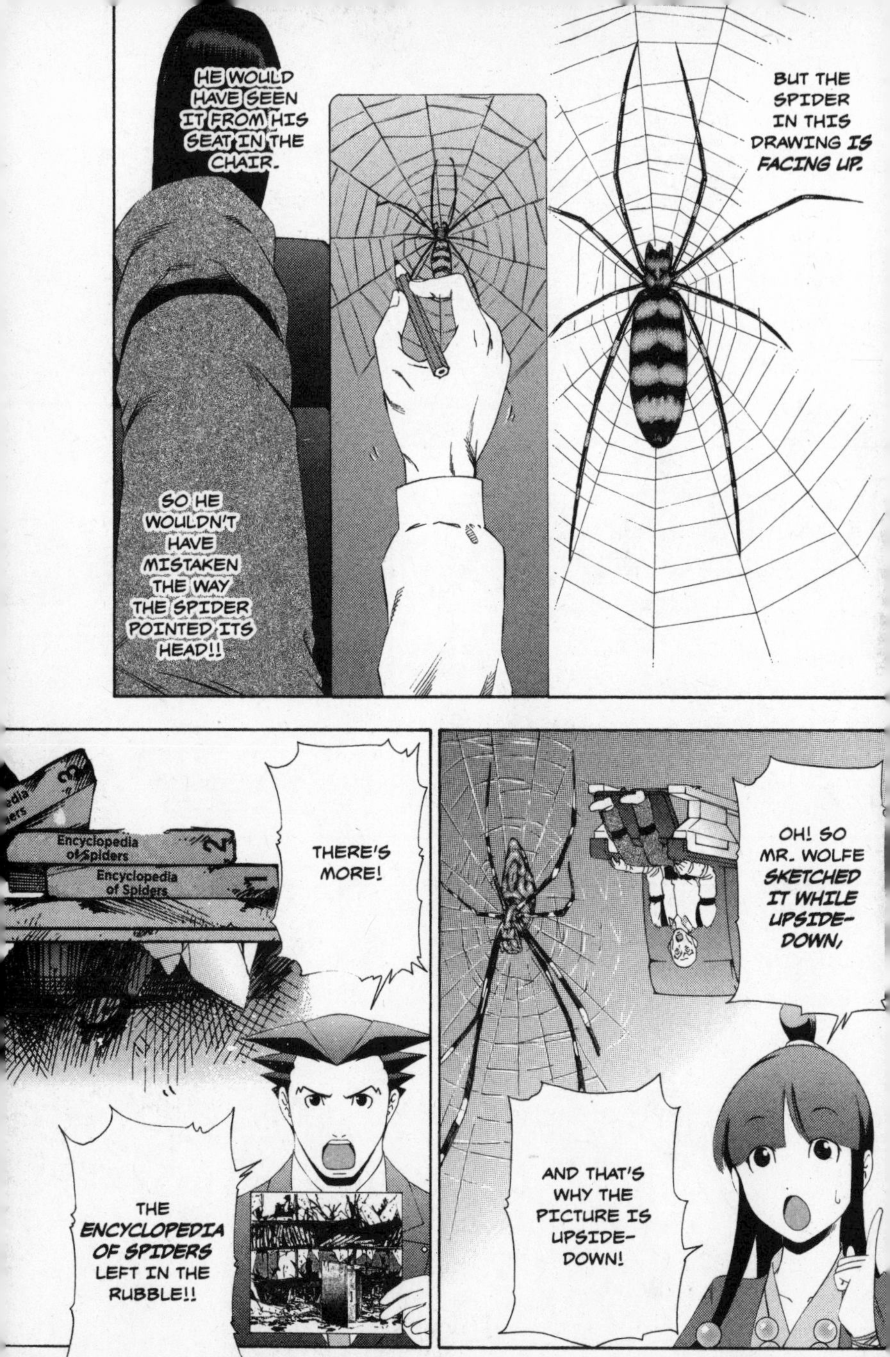
BUT THE SPIDER IN THIS DRAWING *IS FACING UP.*
HE WOULD HAVE SEEN IT FROM HIS SEAT IN THE CHAIR.
SO HE WOULDN'T HAVE MISTAKEN THE WAY THE SPIDER POINTED ITS HEAD!!
OH! SO MR. WOLFE *SKETCHED IT WHILE UPSIDE-DOWN,*
AND THAT'S WHY THE PICTURE IS UPSIDE-DOWN!
THERE'S MORE!
Encyclopedia of Spiders 2
Encyclopedia of Spiders 1
THE *ENCYCLOPEDIA OF SPIDERS* LEFT IN THE RUBBLE!!

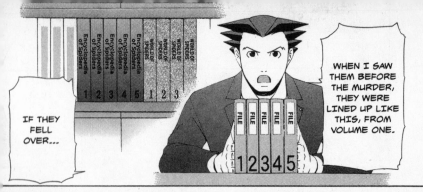

WHEN I SAW THEM BEFORE THE MURDER, THEY WERE LINED UP LIKE THIS, FROM VOLUME ONE.
IF THEY FELL OVER...
...THEY'D END UP LIKE THIS.
OR LIKE THIS.
BUT IF YOU LINE THE BOOKS UP THE WAY THEY ARE IN THE PICTURE...
...AND STAND THEM BACK UP...
...THE BOOKS...
...ARE UPSIDE-DOWN!!
GASP!!

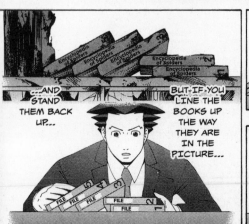

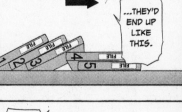

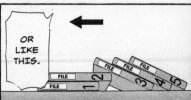

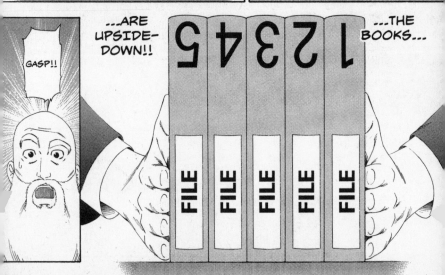

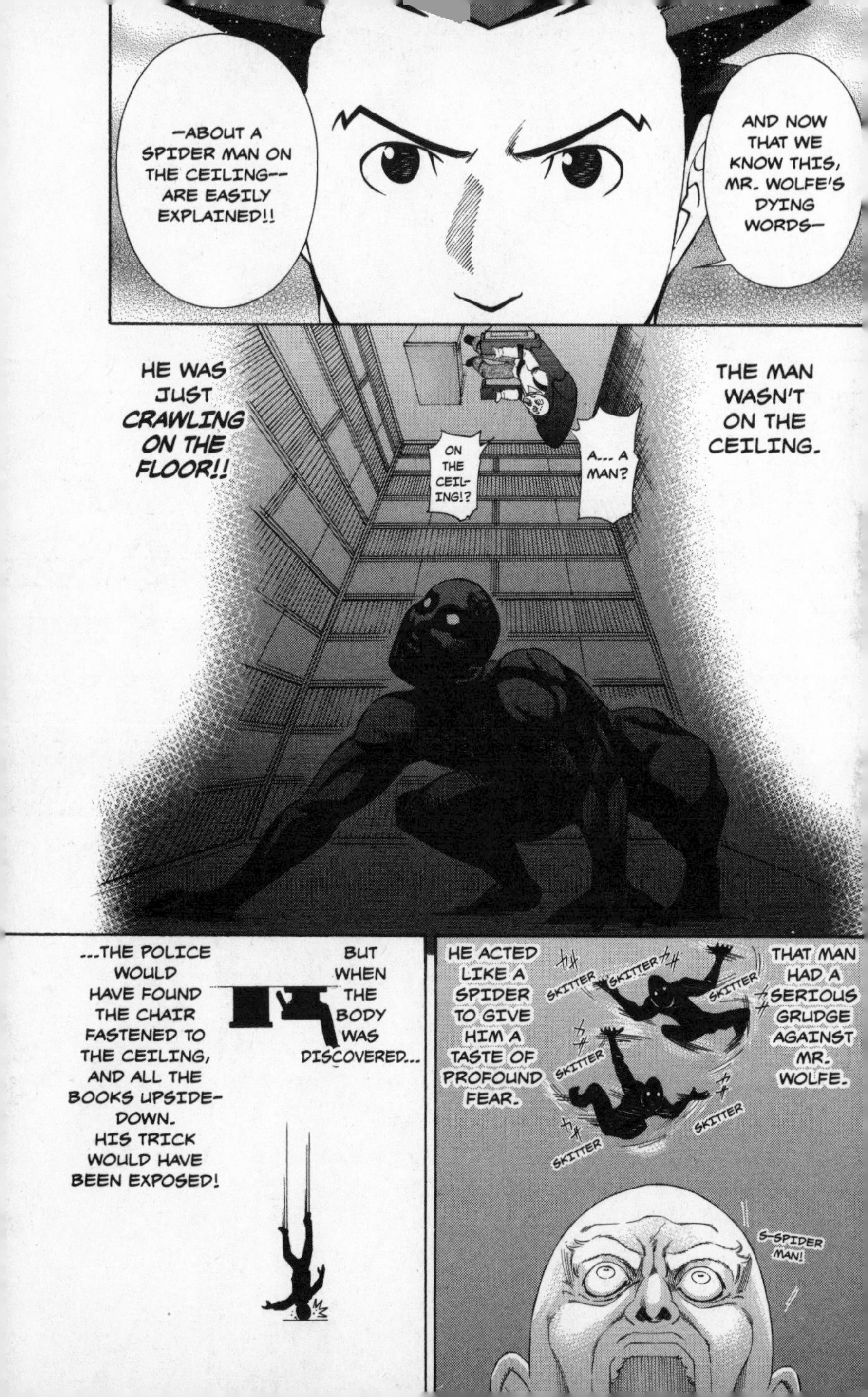
AND NOW THAT WE KNOW THIS, MR. WOLFE'S DYING WORDS—
—ABOUT A SPIDER MAN ON THE CEILING-- ARE EASILY EXPLAINED!!
THE MAN WASN'T ON THE CEILING.
A... A MAN?
ON THE CEIL-ING!?
HE WAS JUST *CRAWLING ON THE FLOOR!!*
THAT MAN HAD A SERIOUS GRUDGE AGAINST MR. WOLFE.
SKITTER
SKITTER
SKITTER
SKITTER
SKITTER
SKITTER
HE ACTED LIKE A SPIDER TO GIVE HIM A TASTE OF PROFOUND FEAR.
S-SPIDER MAN!
BUT WHEN THE BODY WAS DISCOVERED...
...THE POLICE WOULD HAVE FOUND THE CHAIR FASTENED TO THE CEILING, AND ALL THE BOOKS UPSIDE-DOWN. HIS TRICK WOULD HAVE BEEN EXPOSED!

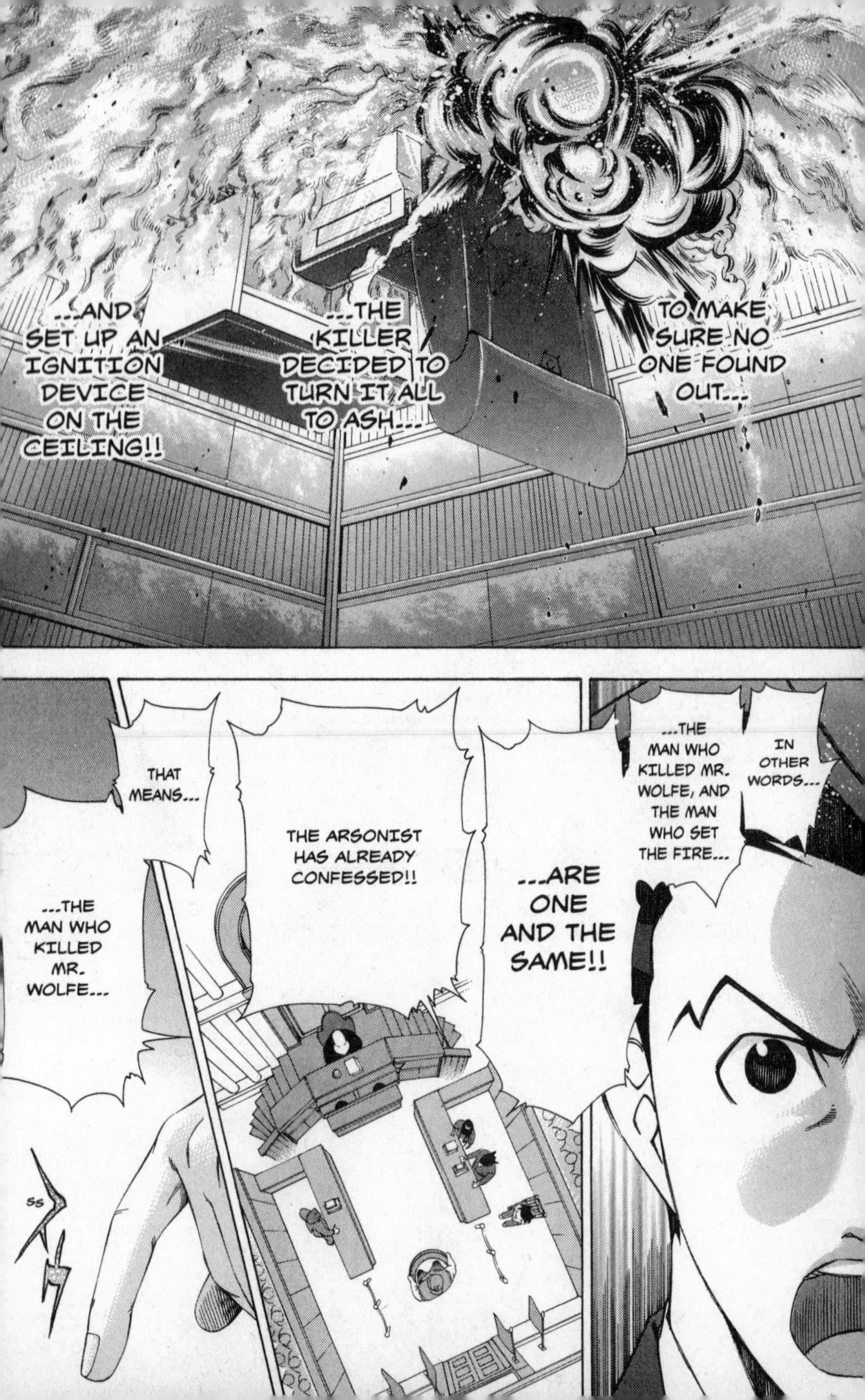
TO MAKE SURE NO ONE FOUND OUT...
...THE KILLER DECIDED TO TURN IT ALL TO ASH...
...AND SET UP AN IGNITION DEVICE ON THE CEILING!!
IN OTHER WORDS...
...THE MAN WHO KILLED MR. WOLFE, AND THE MAN WHO SET THE FIRE...
...ARE ONE AND THE SAME!!
THE ARSONIST HAS ALREADY CONFESSED!!
THAT MEANS...
...THE MAN WHO KILLED MR. WOLFE...
SS

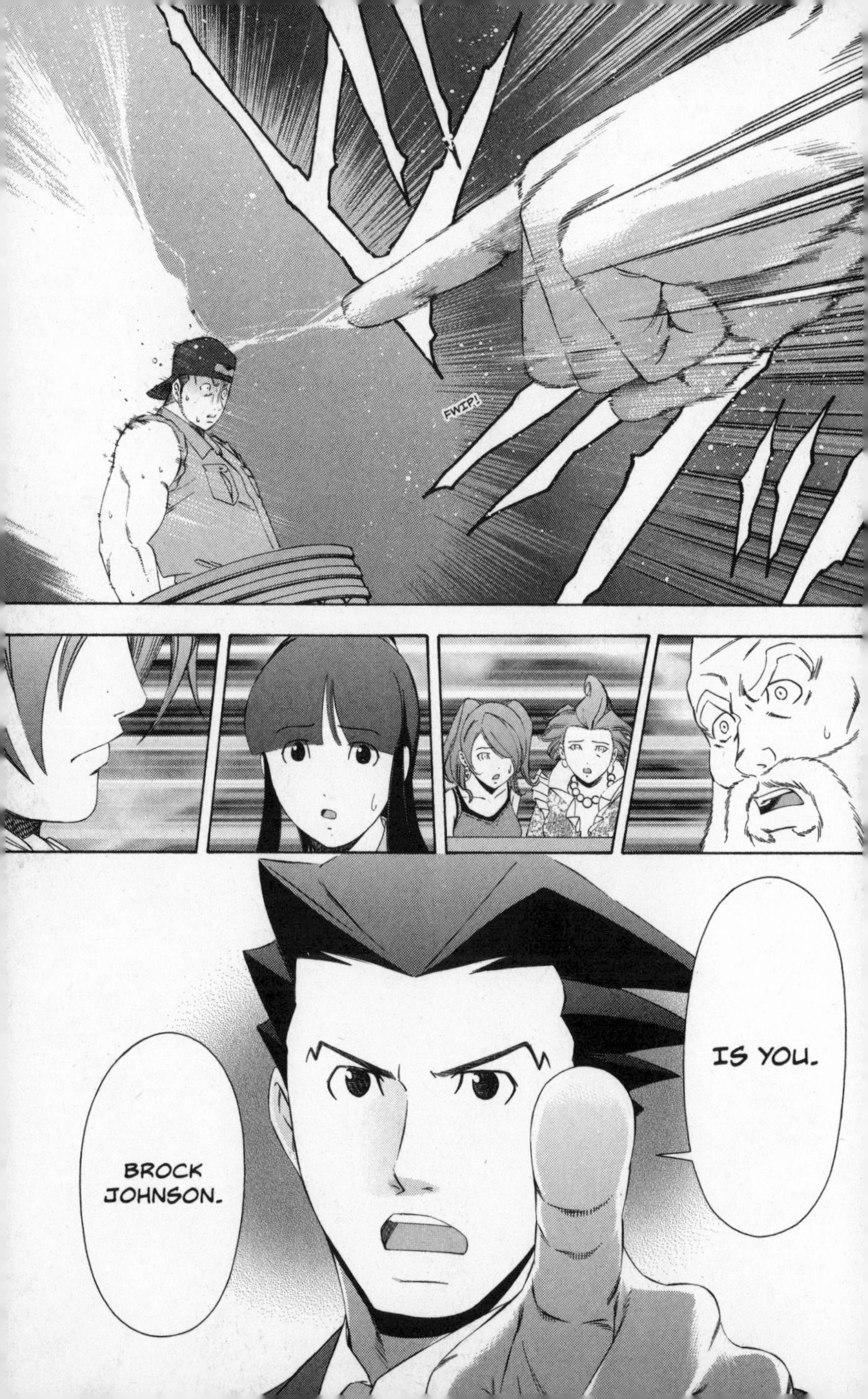
FWIP!
IS YOU.
BROCK JOHNSON.

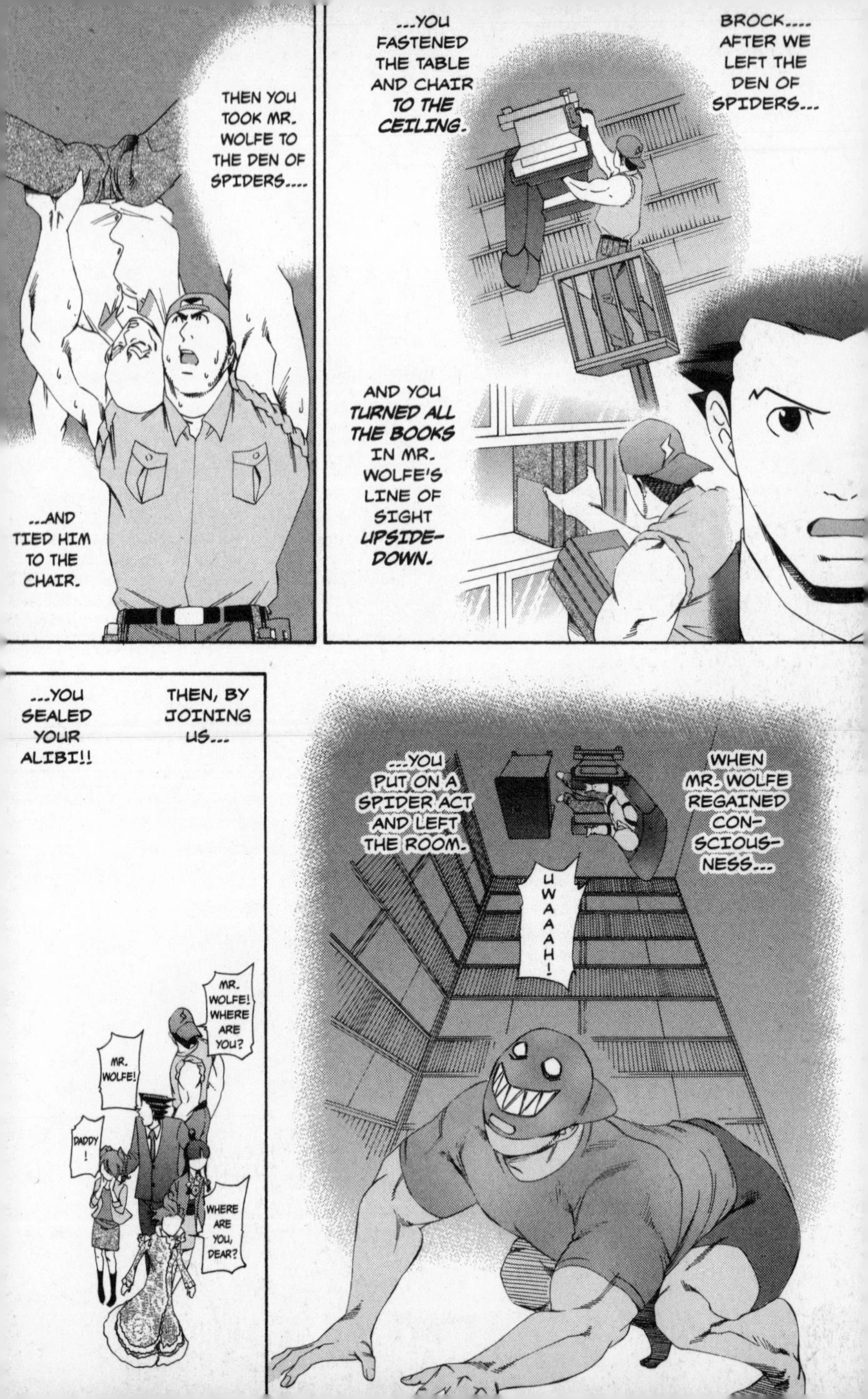
BROCK.... AFTER WE LEFT THE DEN OF SPIDERS...
...YOU FASTENED THE TABLE AND CHAIR TO THE CEILING.
AND YOU TURNED ALL THE BOOKS IN MR. WOLFE'S LINE OF SIGHT UPSIDE-DOWN.
THEN YOU TOOK MR. WOLFE TO THE DEN OF SPIDERS....
...AND TIED HIM TO THE CHAIR.
WHEN MR. WOLFE REGAINED CON-SCIOUS-NESS...
...YOU PUT ON A SPIDER ACT AND LEFT THE ROOM.
UWAAAAH!
THEN, BY JOINING US...
...YOU SEALED YOUR ALIBI!!
MR. WOLFE! WHERE ARE YOU?
MR. WOLFE!
DADDY!
WHERE ARE YOU, DEAR?

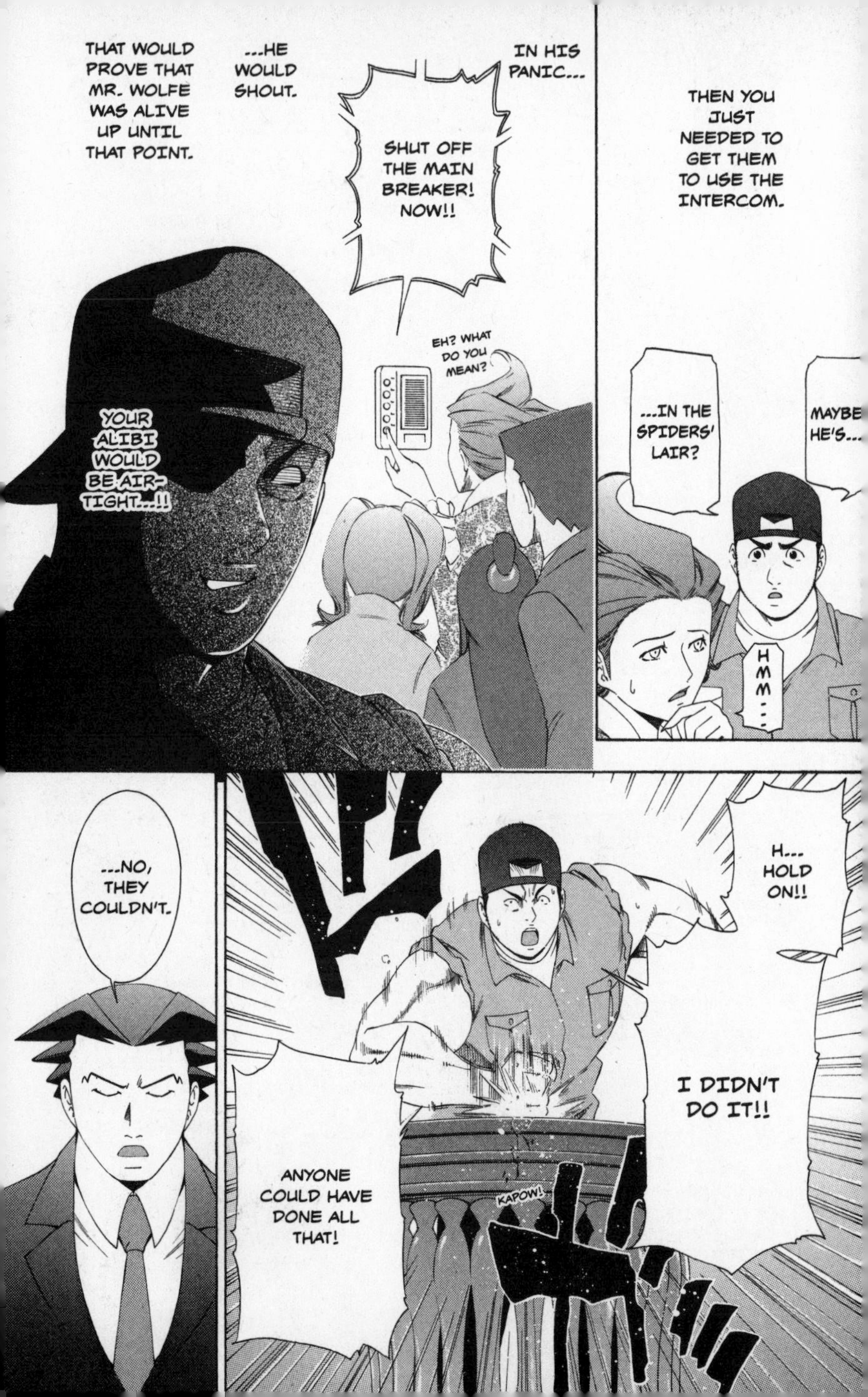
THEN YOU JUST NEEDED TO GET THEM TO USE THE INTERCOM.
MAYBE HE'S...
...IN THE SPIDERS' LAIR?
HMM...
IN HIS PANIC...
...HE WOULD SHOUT.
SHUT OFF THE MAIN BREAKER! NOW!!
THAT WOULD PROVE THAT MR. WOLFE WAS ALIVE UP UNTIL THAT POINT.
EH? WHAT DO YOU MEAN?
YOUR ALIBI WOULD BE AIR-TIGHT...!!
H... HOLD ON!!
I DIDN'T DO IT!!
KAPOW!
ANYONE COULD HAVE DONE ALL THAT!
...NO, THEY COULDN'T.

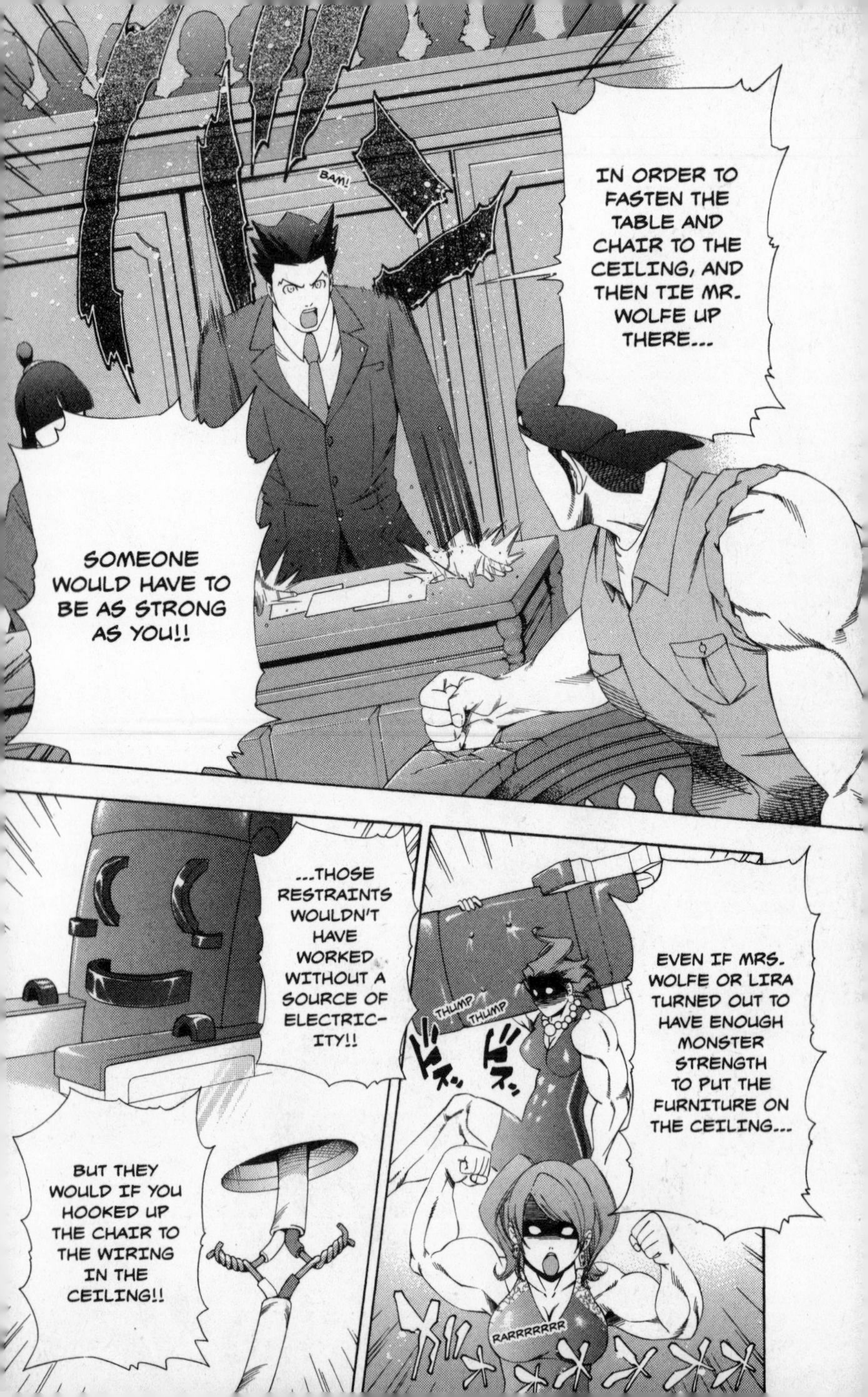
BAM!
IN ORDER TO FASTEN THE TABLE AND CHAIR TO THE CEILING, AND THEN TIE MR. WOLFE UP THERE...
SOMEONE WOULD HAVE TO BE AS STRONG AS YOU!!
EVEN IF MRS. WOLFE OR LIRA TURNED OUT TO HAVE ENOUGH MONSTER STRENGTH TO PUT THE FURNITURE ON THE CEILING...
THUMP THUMP
ドスッ ドスッ
RARRRRRRR
...THOSE RESTRAINTS WOULDN'T HAVE WORKED WITHOUT A SOURCE OF ELECTRIC-ITY!!
BUT THEY WOULD IF YOU HOOKED UP THE CHAIR TO THE WIRING IN THE CEILING!!

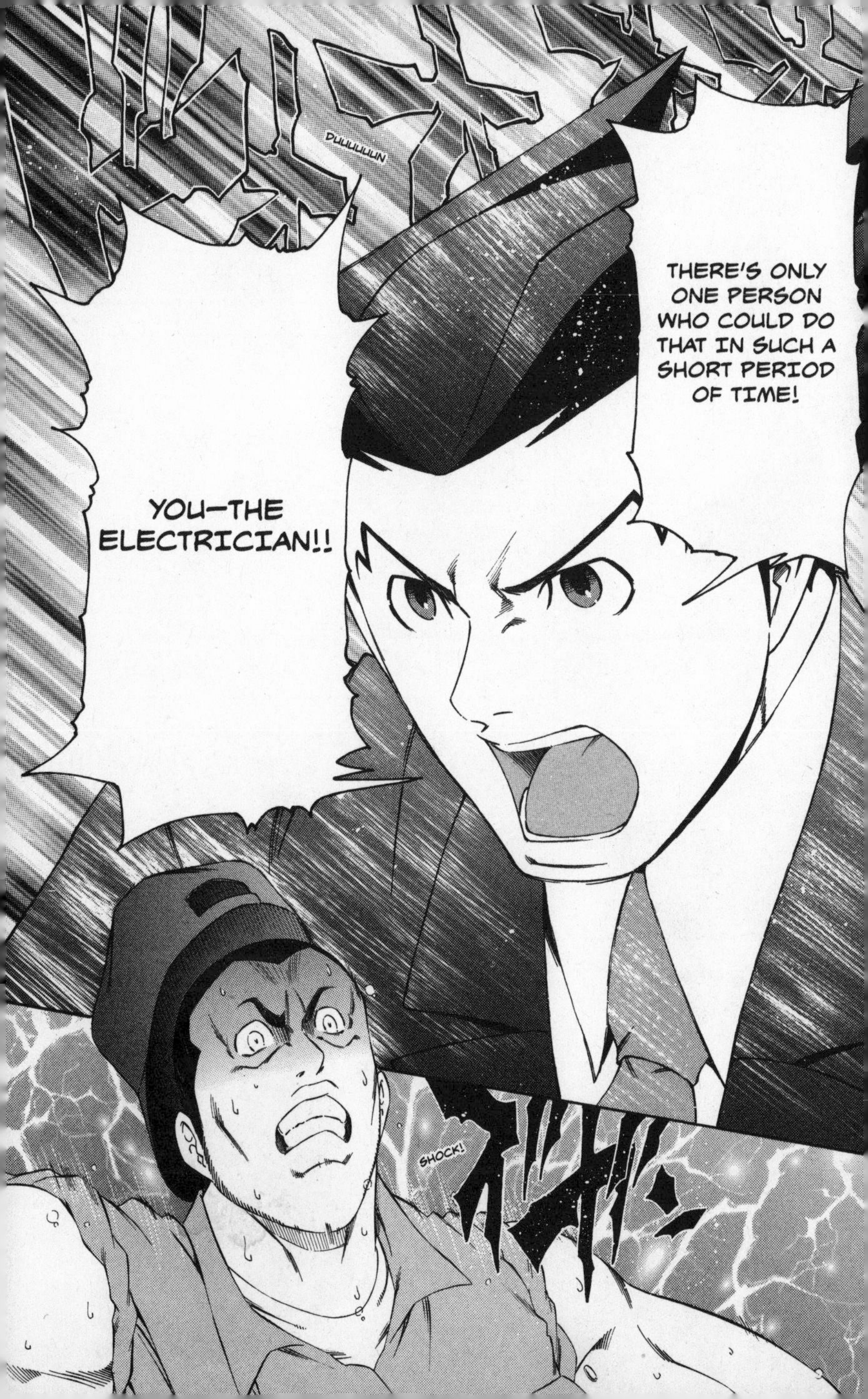
DUUUUUUUN
THERE'S ONLY ONE PERSON WHO COULD DO THAT IN SUCH A SHORT PERIOD OF TIME!
YOU—THE ELECTRICIAN!!
SHOCK!

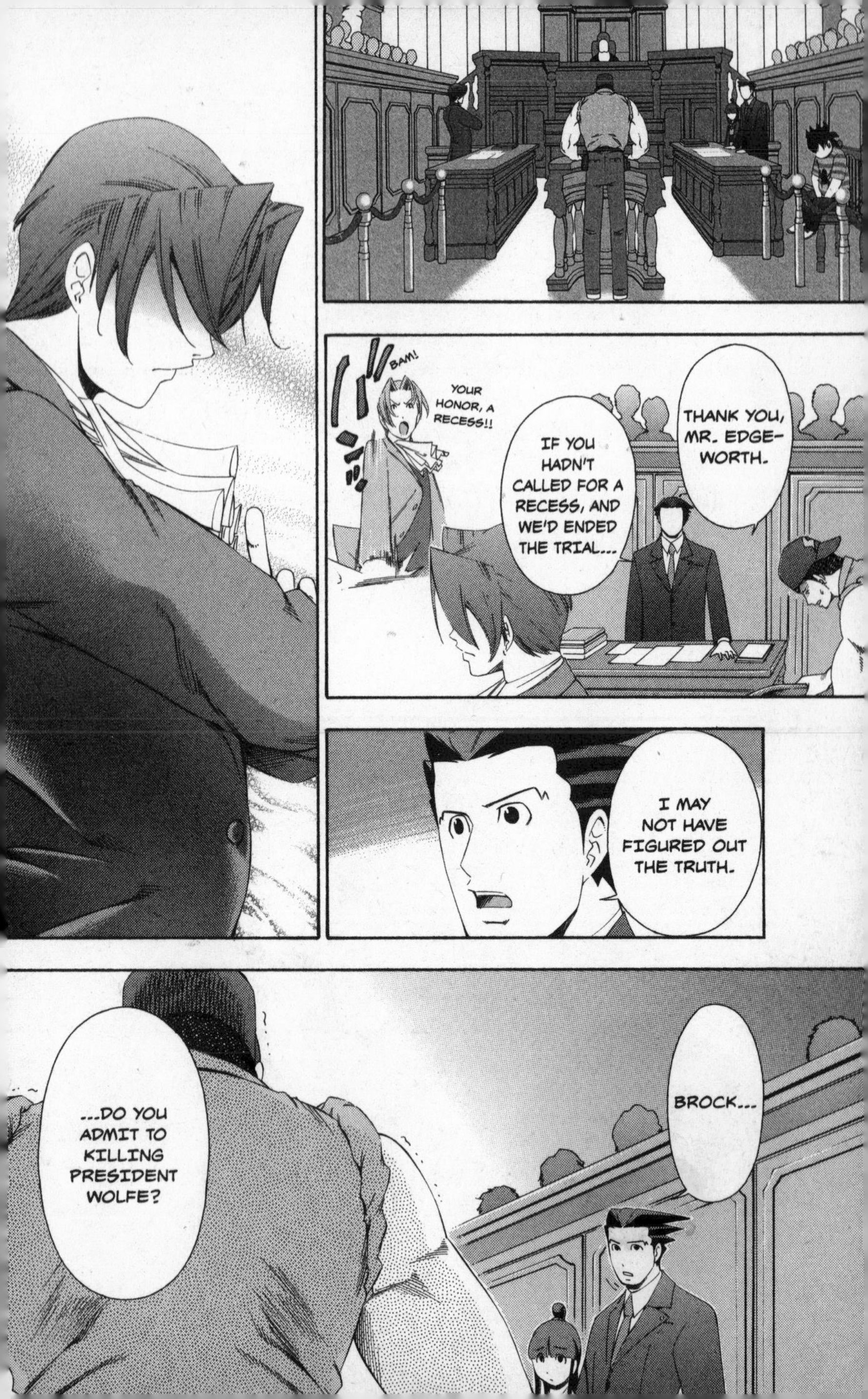
THANK YOU, MR. EDGE-WORTH.
BAM!
YOUR HONOR, A RECESS!!
IF YOU HADN'T CALLED FOR A RECESS, AND WE'D ENDED THE TRIAL...
I MAY NOT HAVE FIGURED OUT THE TRUTH.
BROCK...
...DO YOU ADMIT TO KILLING PRESIDENT WOLFE?

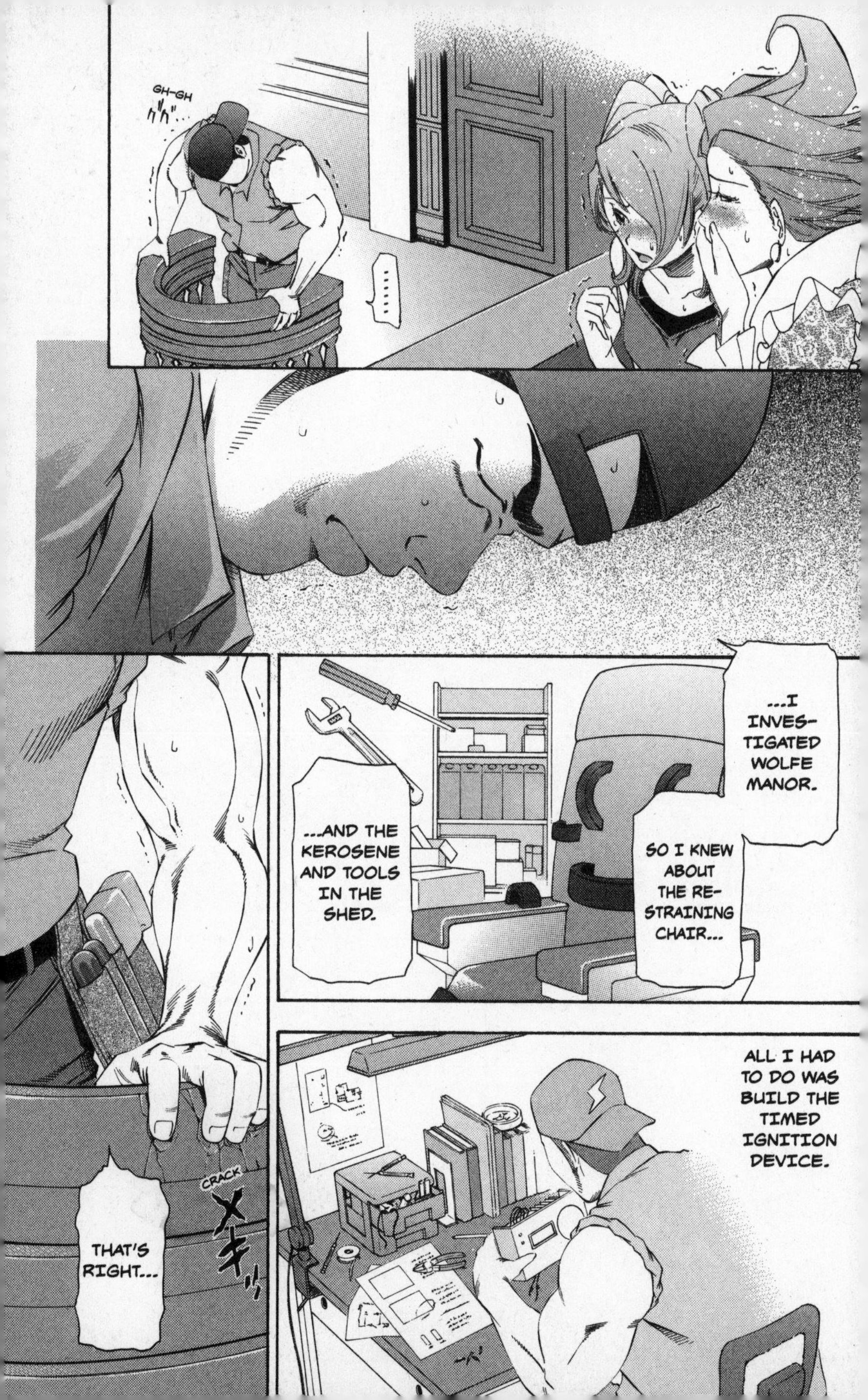
GH-GH
......
...I INVESTIGATED WOLFE MANOR.
SO I KNEW ABOUT THE RESTRAINING CHAIR...
...AND THE KEROSENE AND TOOLS IN THE SHED.
ALL I HAD TO DO WAS BUILD THE TIMED IGNITION DEVICE.
CRACK
THAT'S RIGHT...

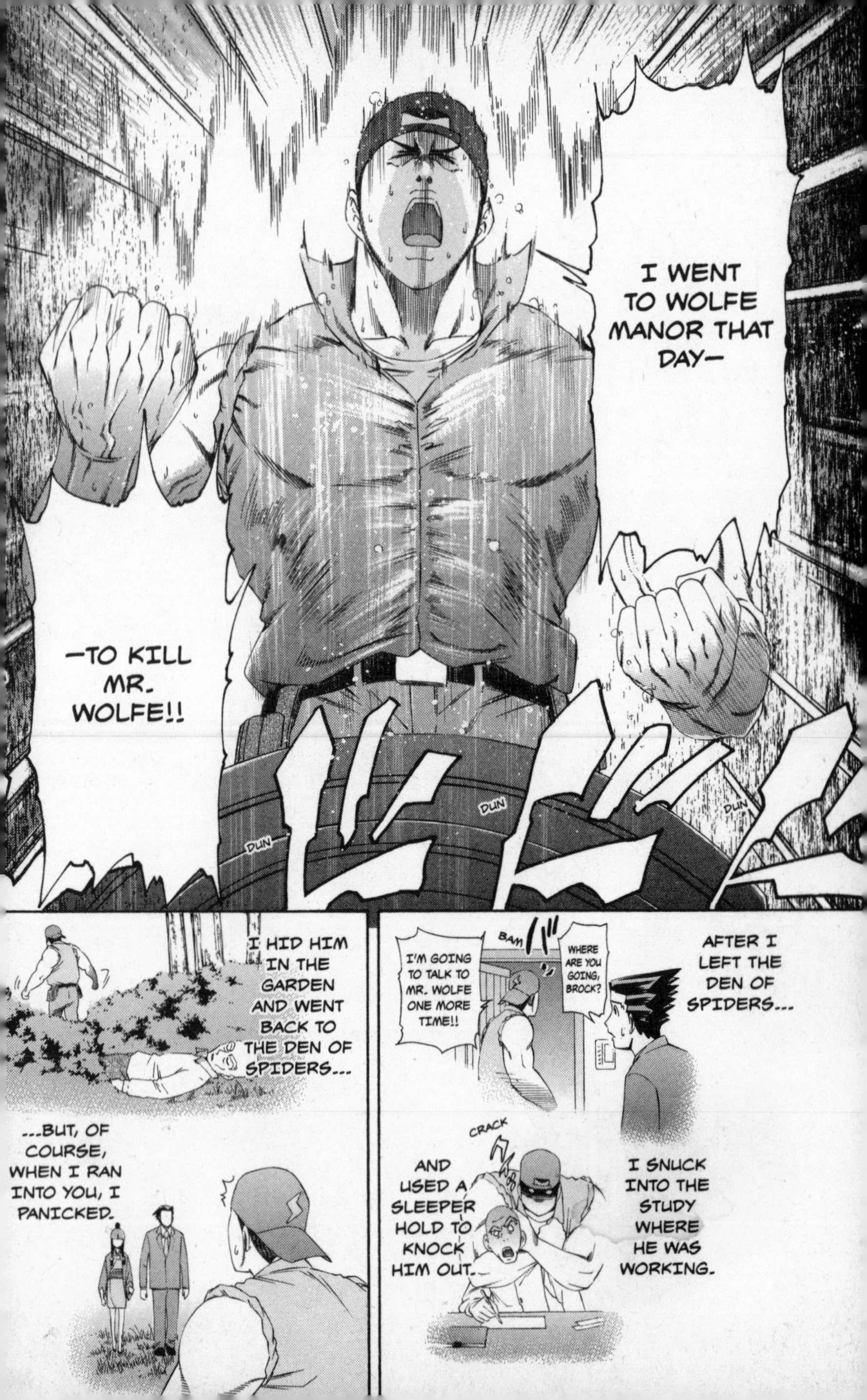
I WENT TO WOLFE MANOR THAT DAY—
—TO KILL MR. WOLFE!!
DUN
DUN
DUN
AFTER I LEFT THE DEN OF SPIDERS...
WHERE ARE YOU GOING, BROCK?
BAM
I'M GOING TO TALK TO MR. WOLFE ONE MORE TIME!!
I SNUCK INTO THE STUDY WHERE HE WAS WORKING.
CRACK
AND USED A SLEEPER HOLD TO KNOCK HIM OUT.
I HID HIM IN THE GARDEN AND WENT BACK TO THE DEN OF SPIDERS...
...BUT, OF COURSE, WHEN I RAN INTO YOU, I PANICKED.

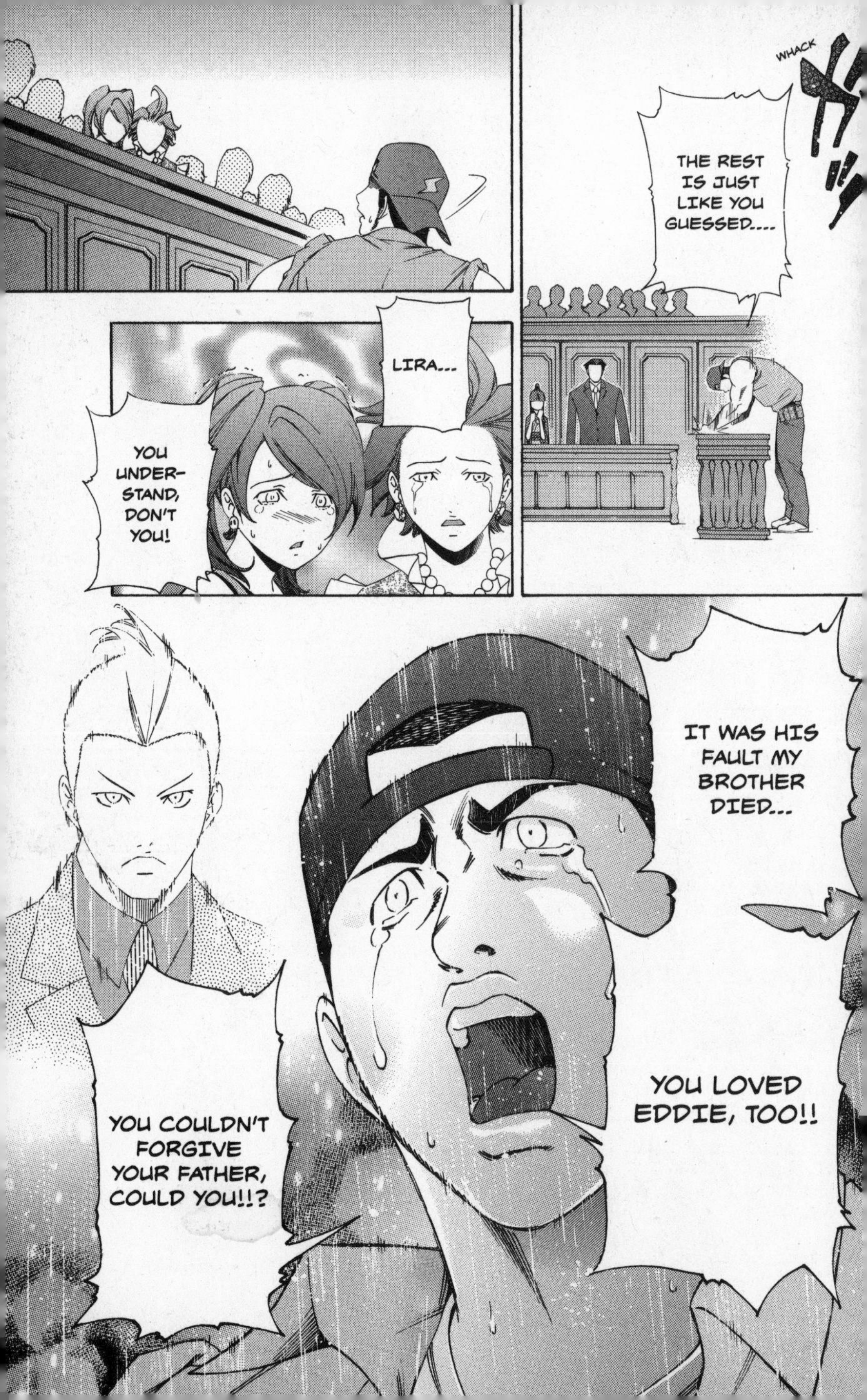
WHACK
THE REST IS JUST LIKE YOU GUESSED....
LIRA...
YOU UNDER-STAND, DON'T YOU!
IT WAS HIS FAULT MY BROTHER DIED...
YOU LOVED EDDIE, TOO!!
YOU COULDN'T FORGIVE YOUR FATHER, COULD YOU!!?

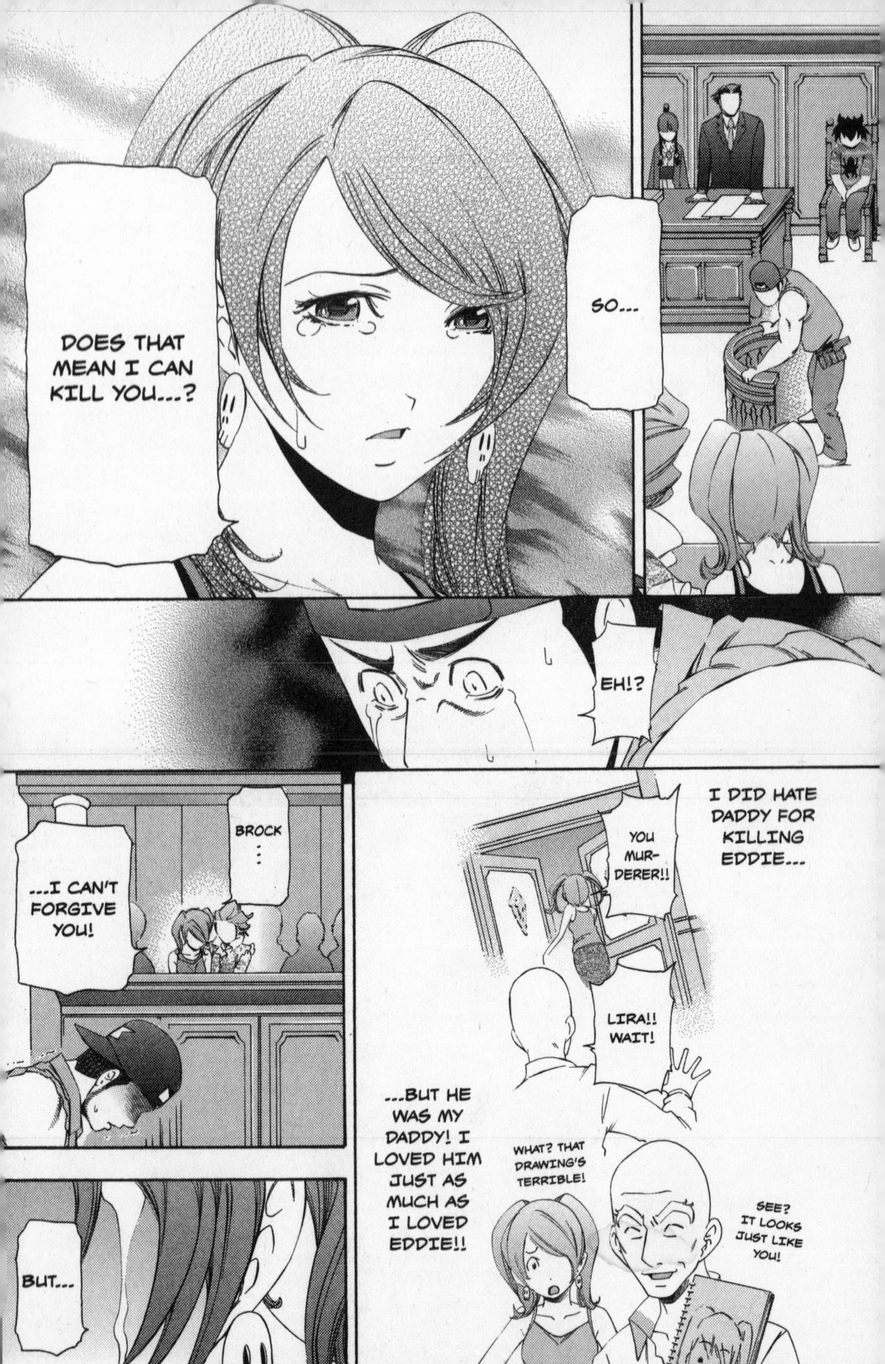
SO...
DOES THAT MEAN I CAN KILL YOU...?
EH!?
I DID HATE DADDY FOR KILLING EDDIE...
YOU MUR-DERER!!
LIRA!! WAIT!
SEE? IT LOOKS JUST LIKE YOU!
WHAT? THAT DRAWING'S TERRIBLE!
...BUT HE WAS MY DADDY! I LOVED HIM JUST AS MUCH AS I LOVED EDDIE!!
BROCK...
...I CAN'T FORGIVE YOU!
BUT...

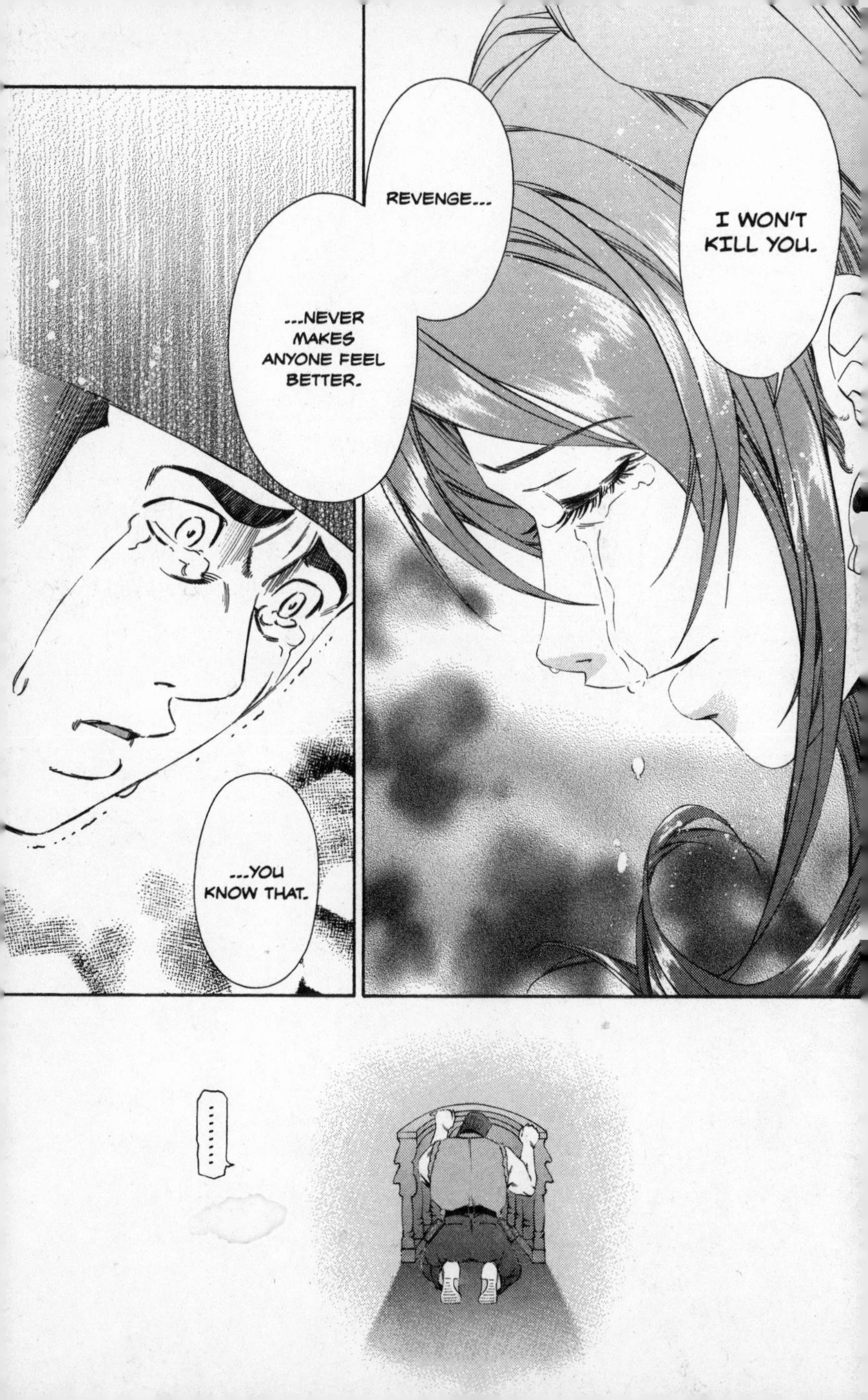
I WON'T KILL YOU.
REVENGE...
...NEVER MAKES ANYONE FEEL BETTER.
...YOU KNOW THAT.
....

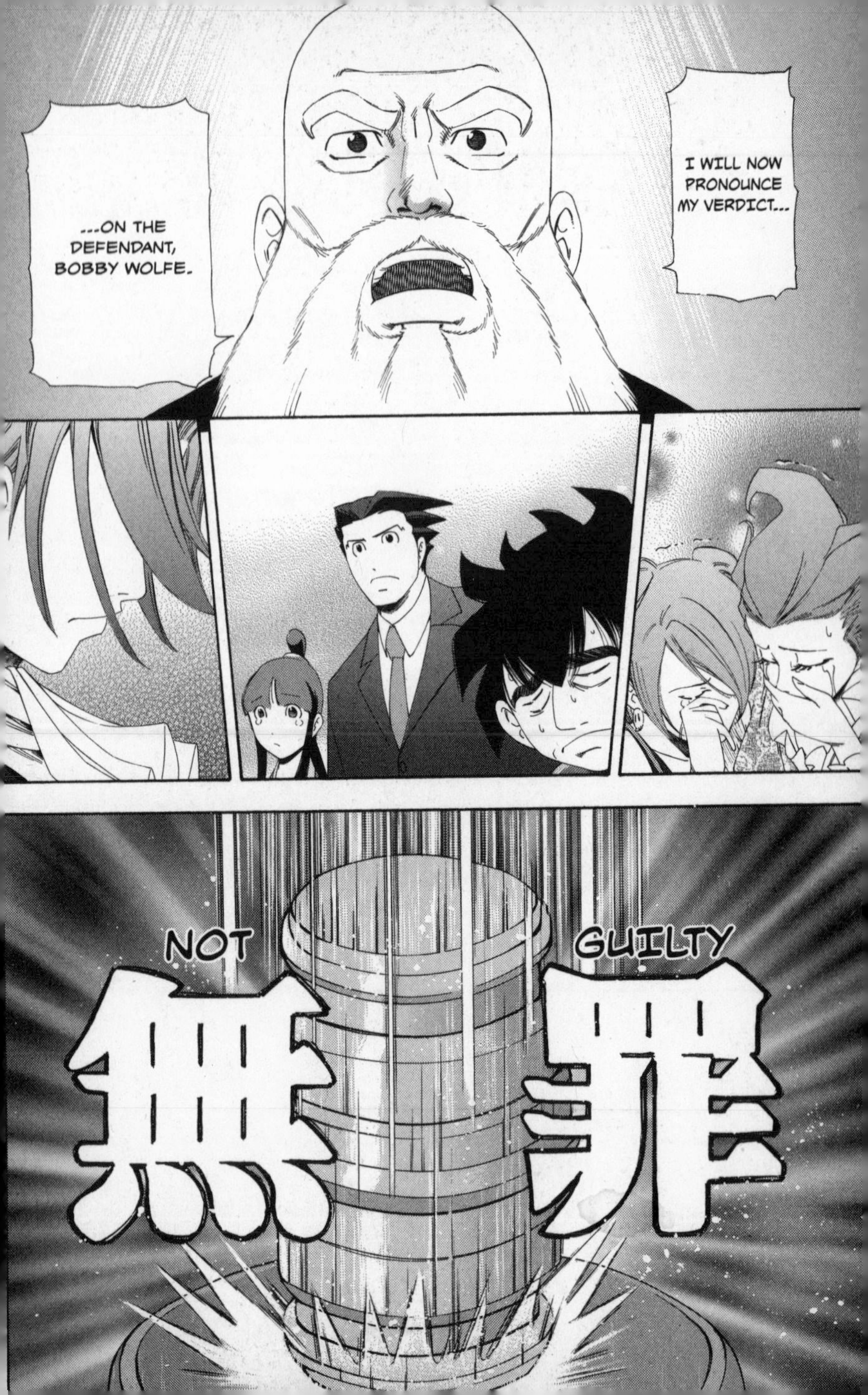
I WILL NOW PRONOUNCE MY VERDICT...
...ON THE DEFENDANT, BOBBY WOLFE.
NOT
GUILTY
無罪

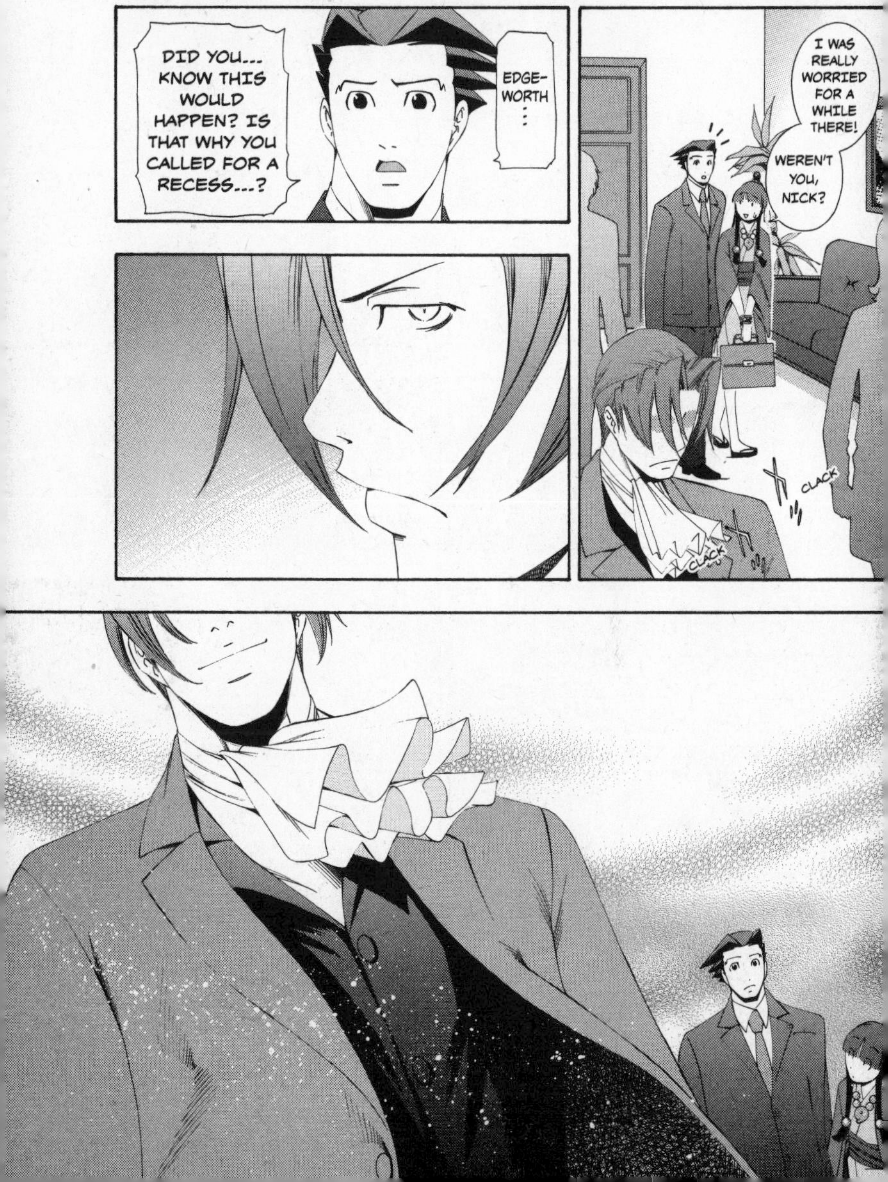
I WAS REALLY WORRIED FOR A WHILE THERE!
WEREN'T YOU, NICK?
CLACK
CLACK
EDGE-WORTH...
DID YOU... KNOW THIS WOULD HAPPEN? IS THAT WHY YOU CALLED FOR A RECESS...?

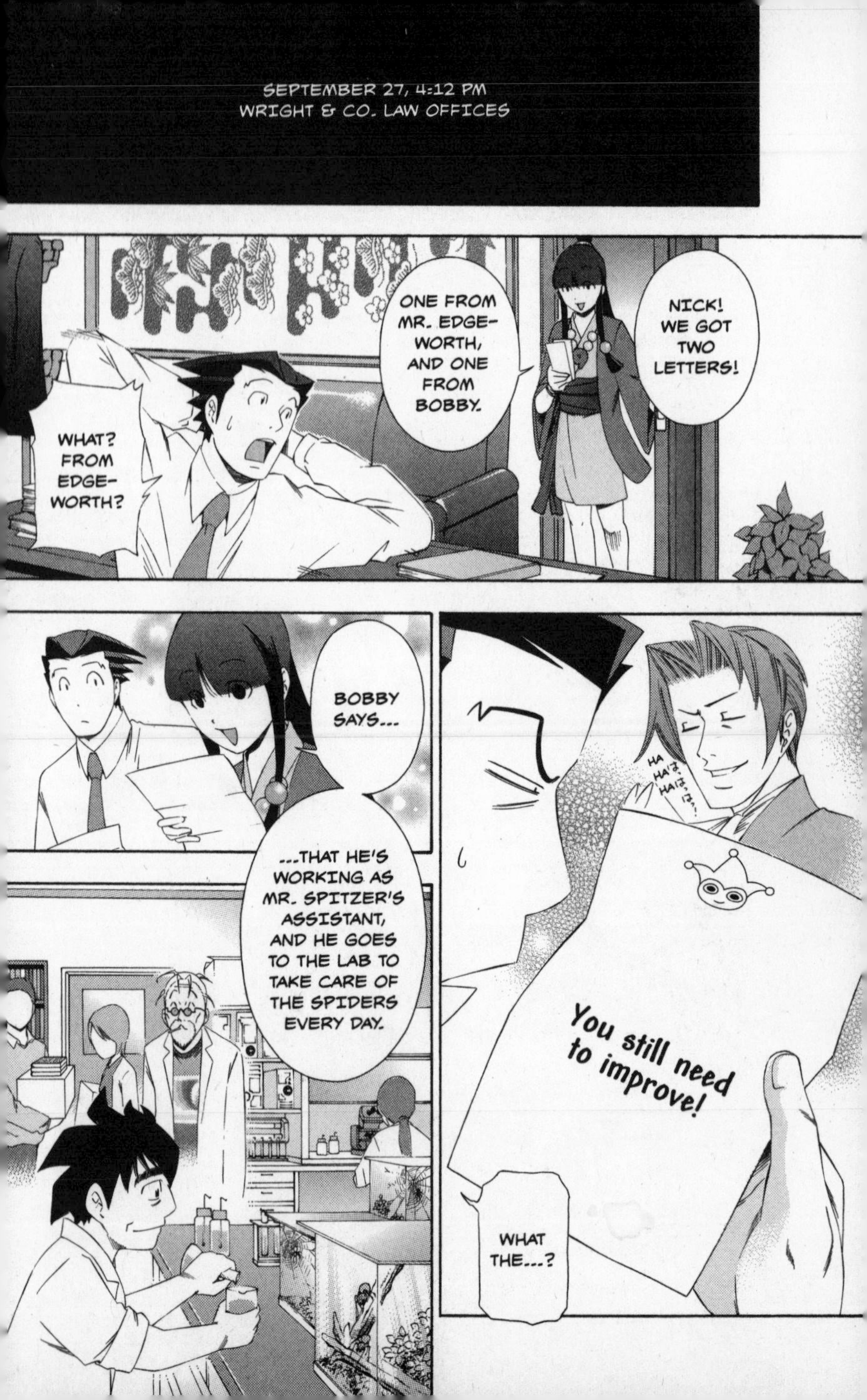
SEPTEMBER 27, 4:12 PM
WRIGHT & CO. LAW OFFICES
NICK! WE GOT TWO LETTERS!
ONE FROM MR. EDGEWORTH, AND ONE FROM BOBBY.
WHAT? FROM EDGEWORTH?
HA HA HA
You still need to improve!
WHAT THE...?
BOBBY SAYS...
...THAT HE'S WORKING AS MR. SPITZER'S ASSISTANT, AND HE GOES TO THE LAB TO TAKE CARE OF THE SPIDERS EVERY DAY.

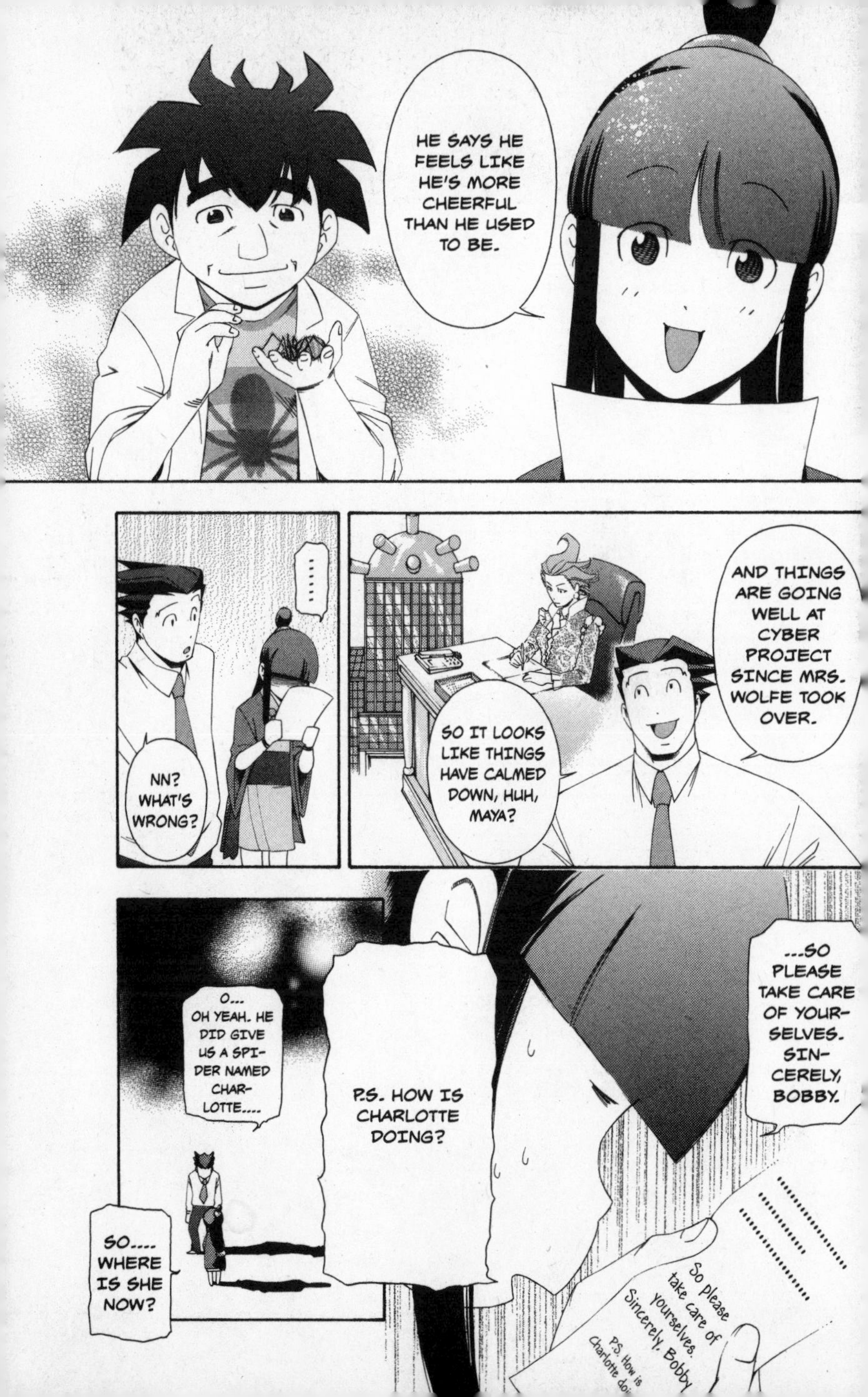

HE SAYS HE FEELS LIKE HE'S MORE CHEERFUL THAN HE USED TO BE.
AND THINGS ARE GOING WELL AT CYBER PROJECT SINCE MRS. WOLFE TOOK OVER.
SO IT LOOKS LIKE THINGS HAVE CALMED DOWN, HUH, MAYA?
......
NN? WHAT'S WRONG?
...SO PLEASE TAKE CARE OF YOURSELVES. SINCERELY, BOBBY.
So please take care of yourselves. Sincerely, Bobby
P.S. How is Charlotte doi
P.S. HOW IS CHARLOTTE DOING?
O... OH YEAH. HE DID GIVE US A SPIDER NAMED CHARLOTTE....
SO.... WHERE IS SHE NOW?

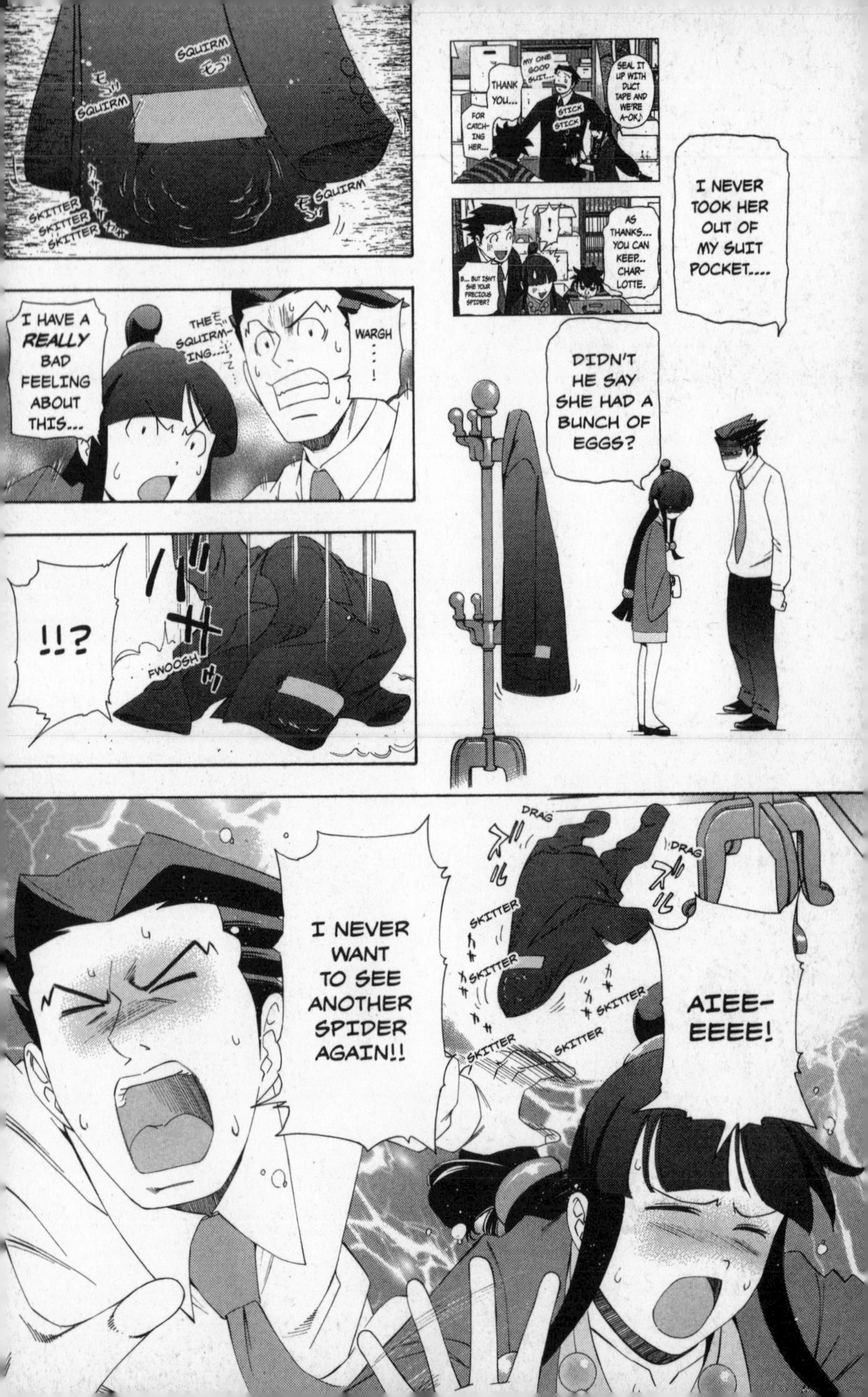
SEAL IT UP WITH DUCT TAPE AND WE'RE A-OK♪
MY ONE GOOD SUIT...
THANK YOU...
FOR CATCHING HER...
STICK
STICK
AS THANKS... YOU CAN KEEP... CHAR-LOTTE.
B... BUT ISN'T SHE YOUR PRECIOUS SPIDER?
I NEVER TOOK HER OUT OF MY SUIT POCKET....
DIDN'T HE SAY SHE HAD A BUNCH OF EGGS?
SQUIRM
SQUIRM
SQUIRM
SKITTER
SKITTER
SKITTER
WARGH...!
THE SQUIRM-ING...!
I HAVE A REALLY BAD FEELING ABOUT THIS...
FWOOSH
!!?
DRAG
DRAG
AIEE-EEEE!
SKITTER
SKITTER
SKITTER
SKITTER
SKITTER
I NEVER WANT TO SEE ANOTHER SPIDER AGAIN!!

Ace Phoenix Wright
Attorney

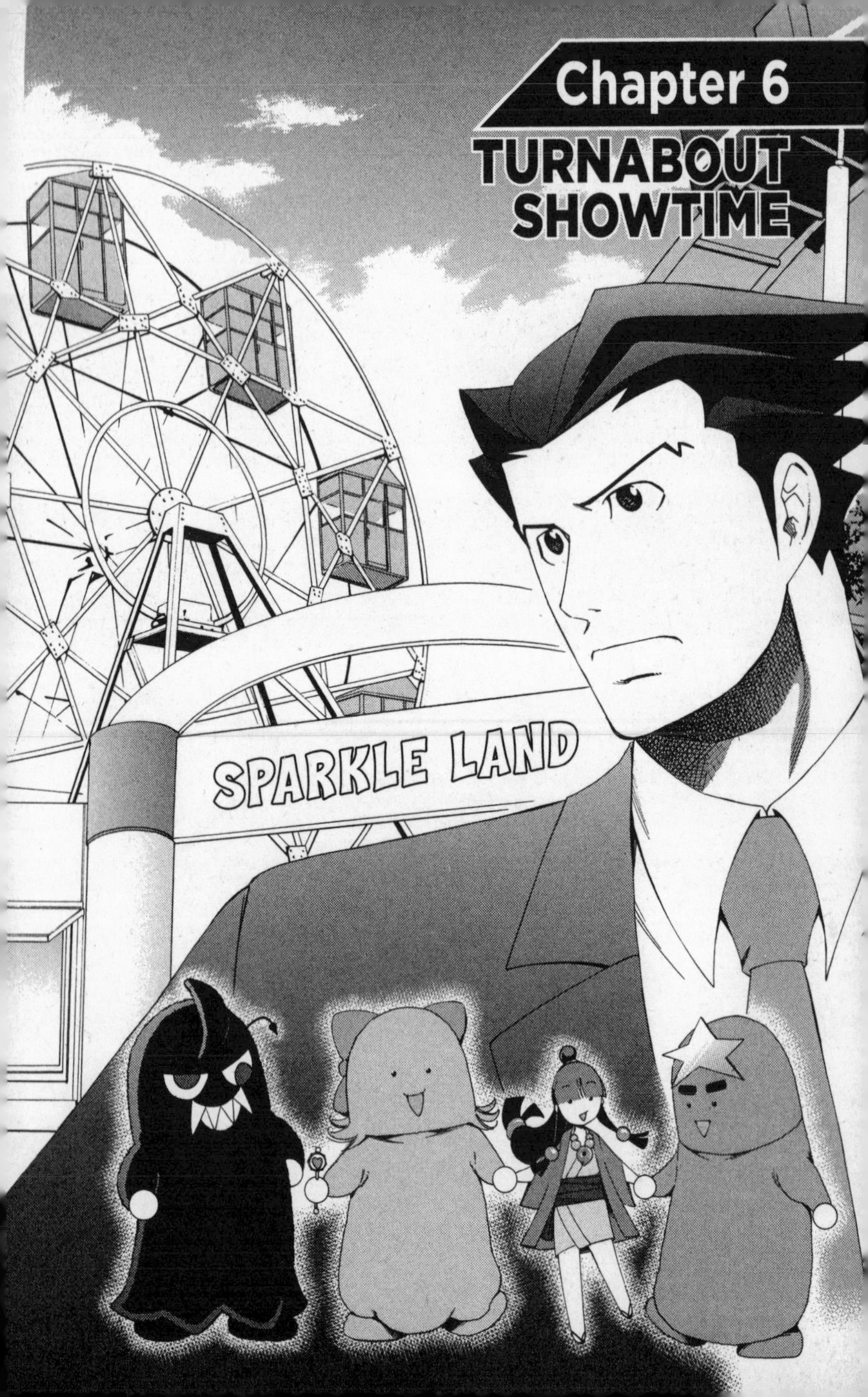
Chapter 6
TURNABOUT SHOWTIME
SPARKLE LAND

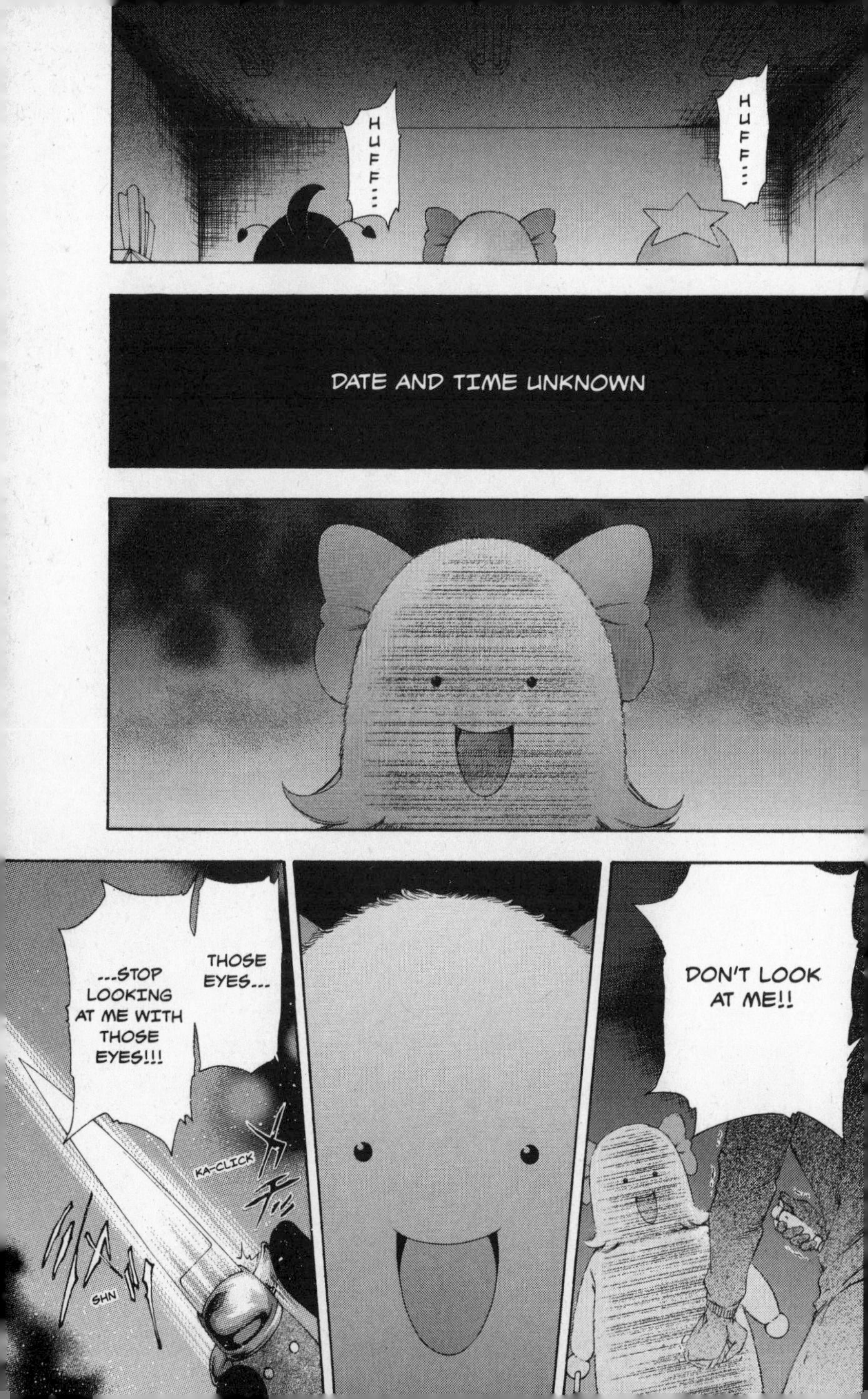
HUFF...
HUFF...
DATE AND TIME UNKNOWN
DON'T LOOK AT ME!!
THOSE EYES...
...STOP LOOKING AT ME WITH THOSE EYES!!!
KA-CLICK
SHN

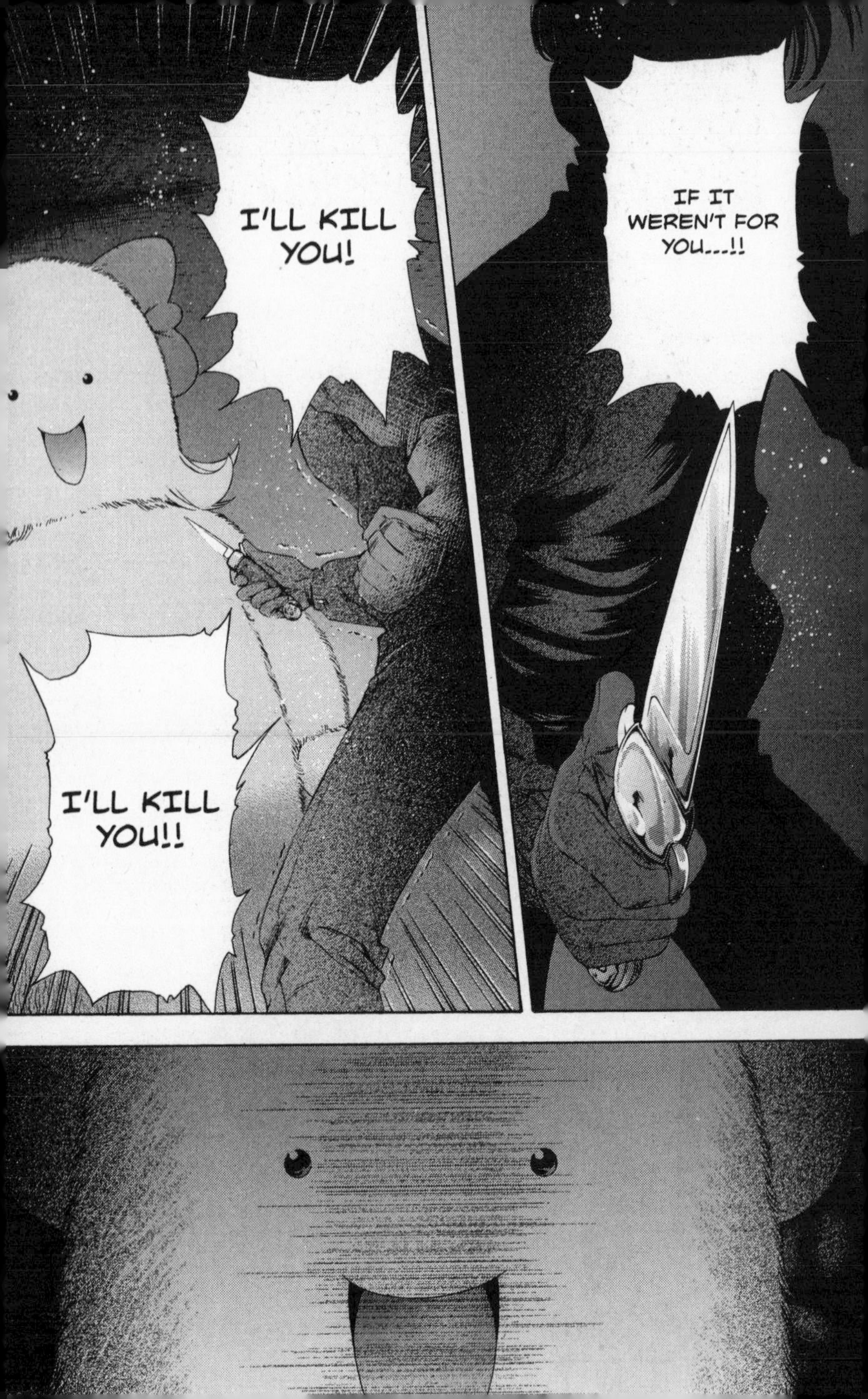
IF IT WEREN'T FOR YOU...!!
I'LL KILL YOU!
I'LL KILL YOU!!

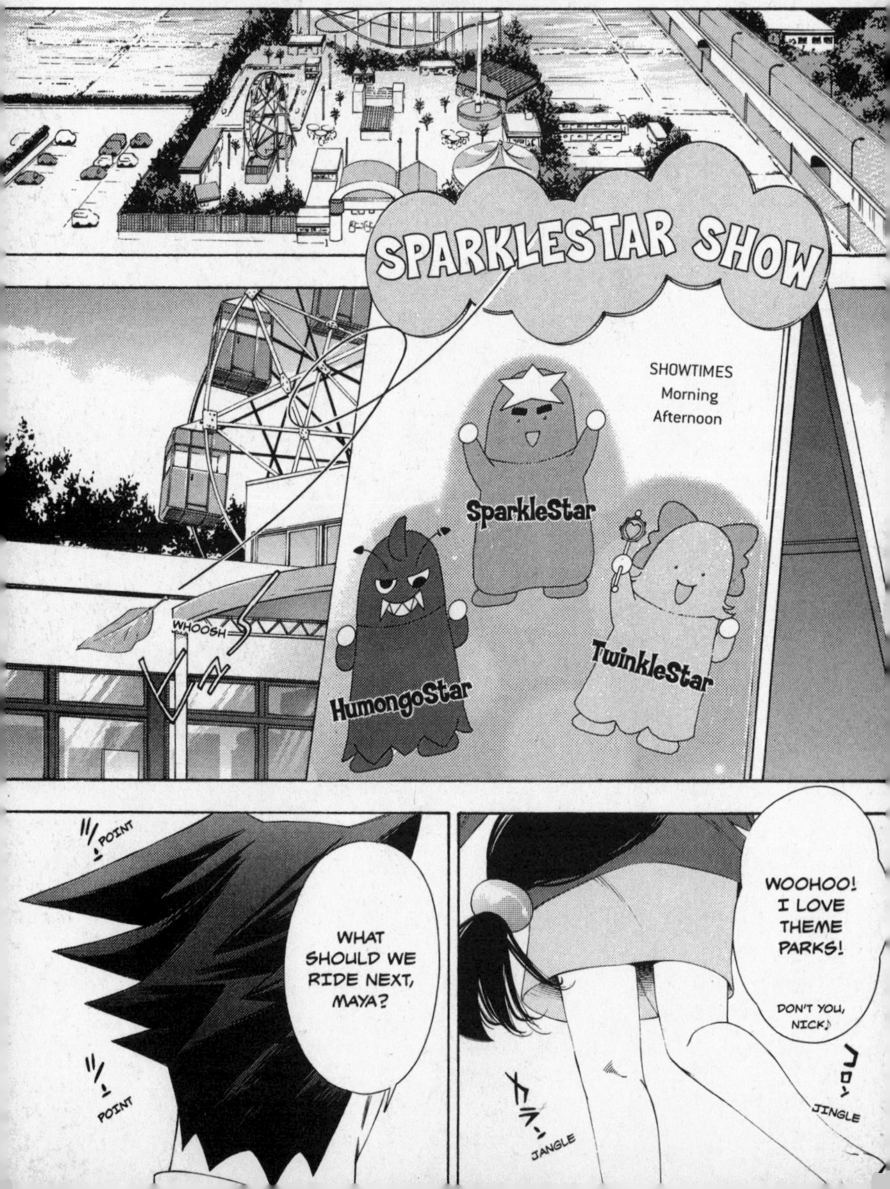
SPARKLESTAR SHOW
SHOWTIMES
Morning
Afternoon
SparkleStar
TwinkleStar
HumongoStar
WHOOSH
WOOHOO! I LOVE THEME PARKS!
DON'T YOU, NICK♪
JINGLE
JANGLE
POINT
WHAT SHOULD WE RIDE NEXT, MAYA?
POINT

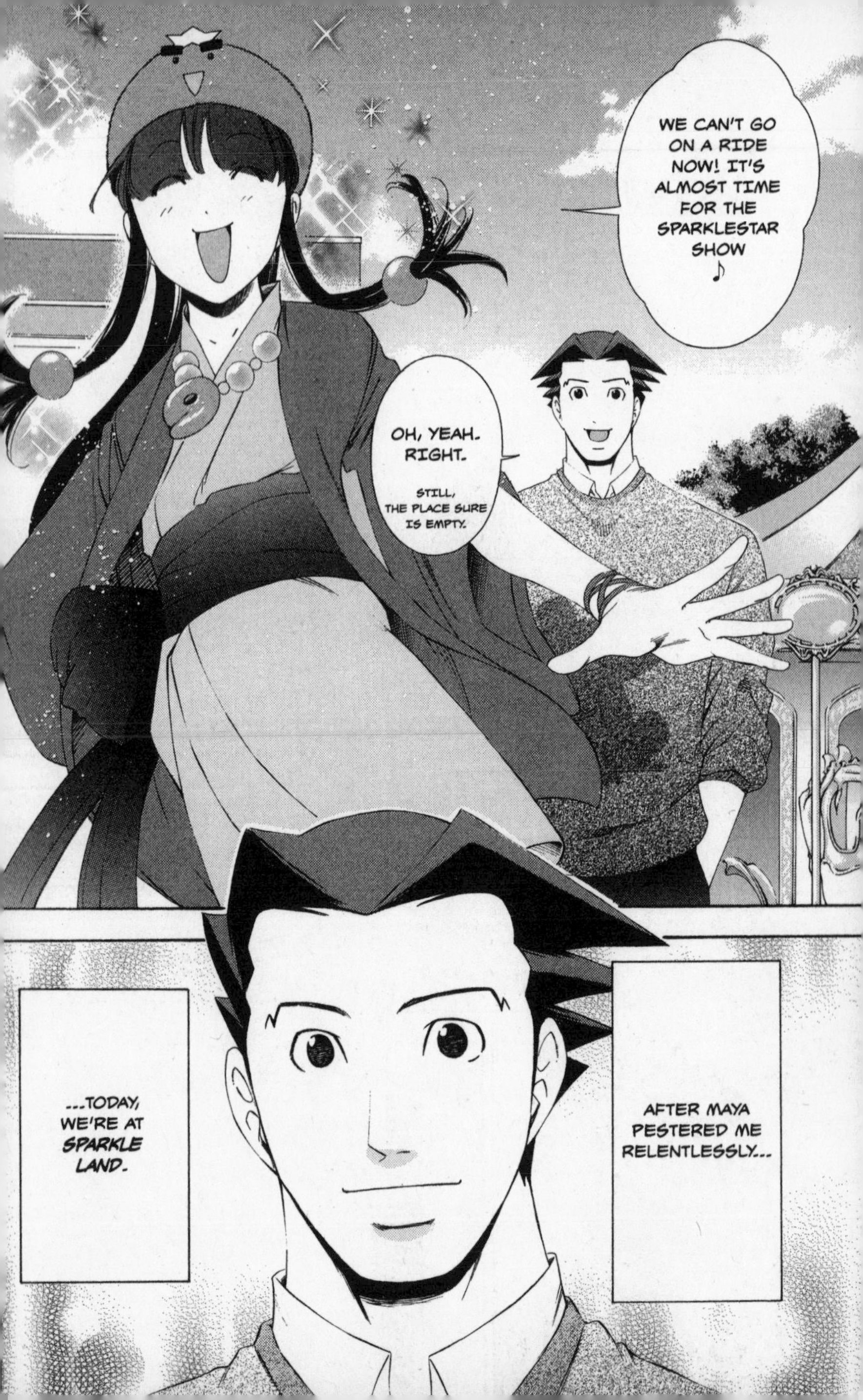
WE CAN'T GO ON A RIDE NOW! IT'S ALMOST TIME FOR THE SPARKLESTAR SHOW ♪
OH, YEAH. RIGHT.
STILL, THE PLACE SURE IS EMPTY.
AFTER MAYA PESTERED ME RELENTLESSLY...
...TODAY, WE'RE AT *SPARKLE LAND*.

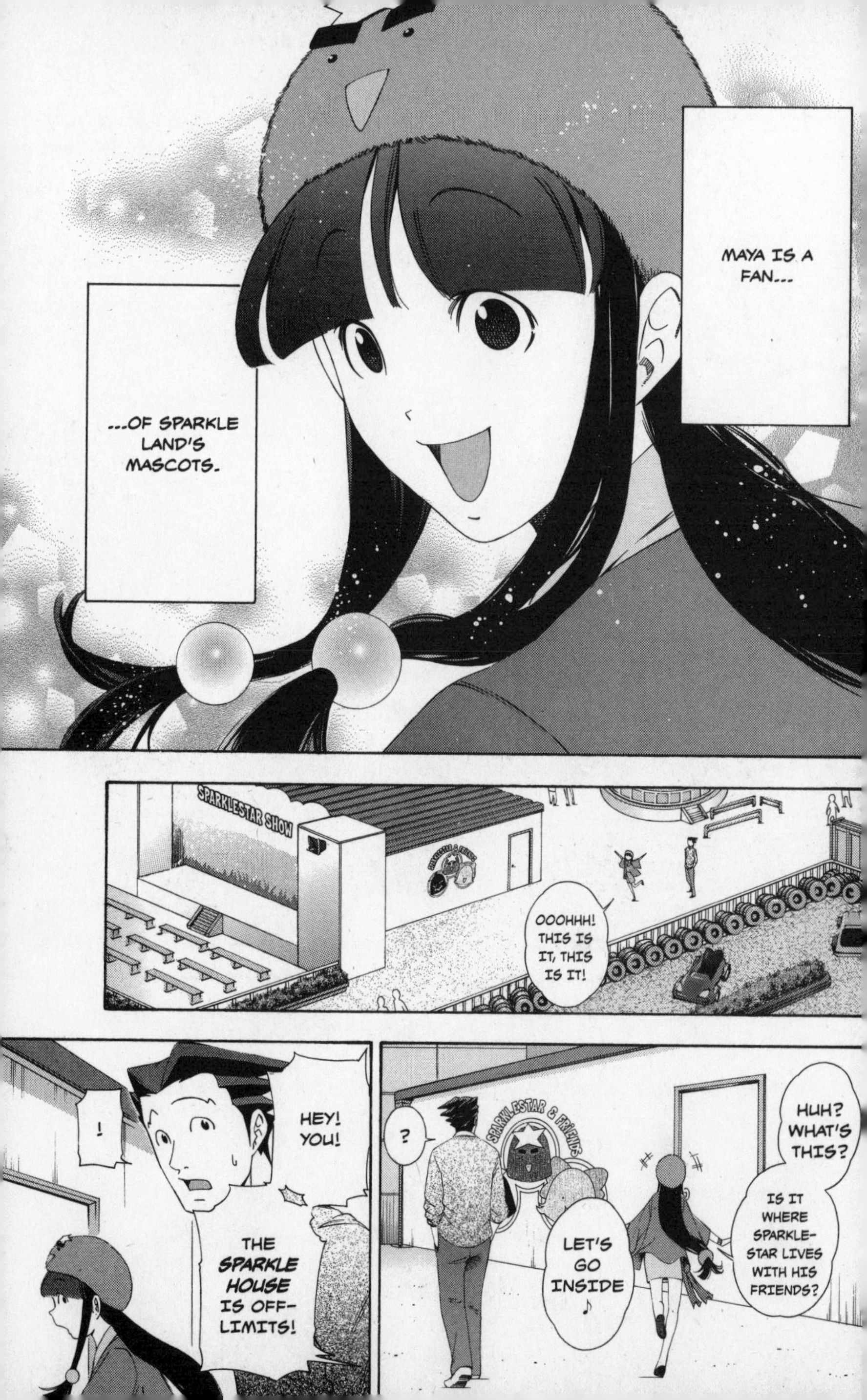
MAYA IS A FAN...
...OF SPARKLE LAND'S MASCOTS.
SPARKLESTAR SHOW
OOOHHH! THIS IS IT, THIS IS IT!
HUH? WHAT'S THIS?
IS IT WHERE SPARKLE-STAR LIVES WITH HIS FRIENDS?
SPARKLESTAR & FRIENDS
?
LET'S GO INSIDE ♪
HEY! YOU!
!
THE *SPARKLE HOUSE* IS OFF-LIMITS!

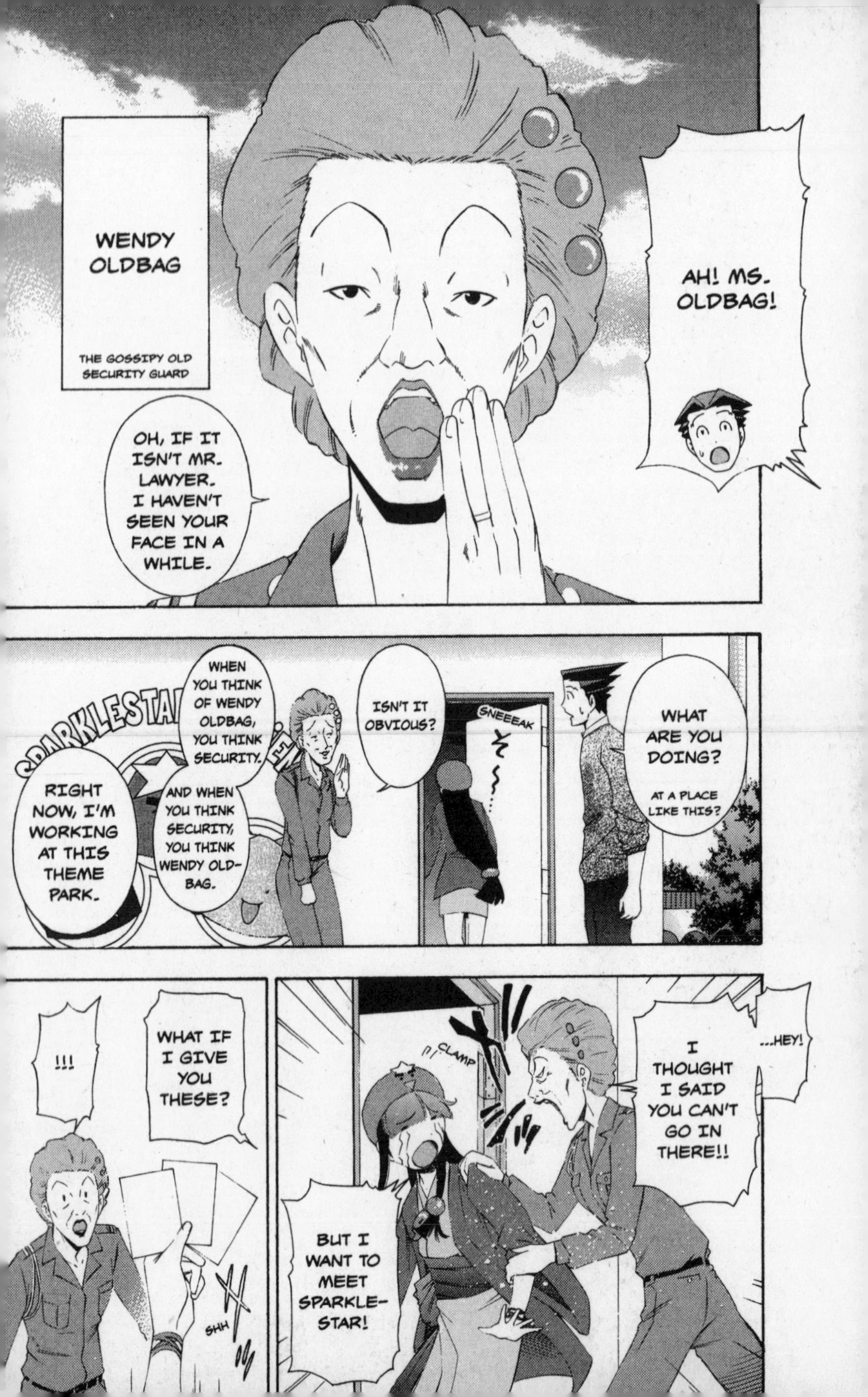
AH! MS. OLDBAG!
WENDY OLDBAG
THE GOSSIPY OLD SECURITY GUARD
OH, IF IT ISN'T MR. LAWYER. I HAVEN'T SEEN YOUR FACE IN A WHILE.
WHAT ARE YOU DOING?
AT A PLACE LIKE THIS?
SNEEEAK
ISN'T IT OBVIOUS?
WHEN YOU THINK OF WENDY OLDBAG, YOU THINK SECURITY.
AND WHEN YOU THINK SECURITY, YOU THINK WENDY OLD-BAG.
RIGHT NOW, I'M WORKING AT THIS THEME PARK.
...HEY!
I THOUGHT I SAID YOU CAN'T GO IN THERE!!
CLAMP
BUT I WANT TO MEET SPARKLE-STAR!
WHAT IF I GIVE YOU THESE?
!!!
SHH

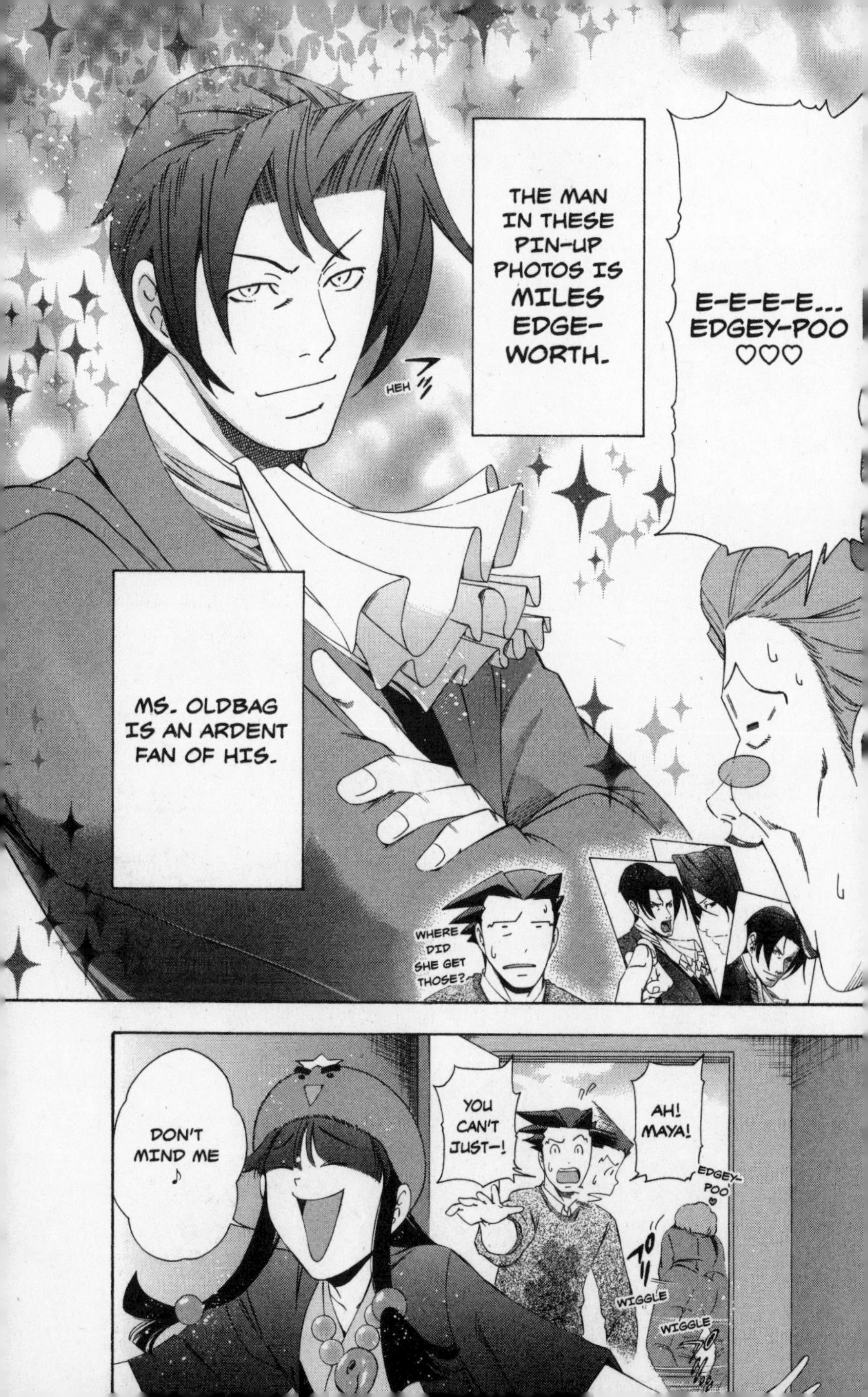
E-E-E-E... EDGEY-POO ♡♡♡
THE MAN IN THESE PIN-UP PHOTOS IS MILES EDGE-WORTH.
HEH
MS. OLDBAG IS AN ARDENT FAN OF HIS.
WHERE DID SHE GET THOSE?
AH! MAYA!
YOU CAN'T JUST—!
EDGEY-POO ♡
WIGGLE
WIGGLE
DON'T MIND ME ♪

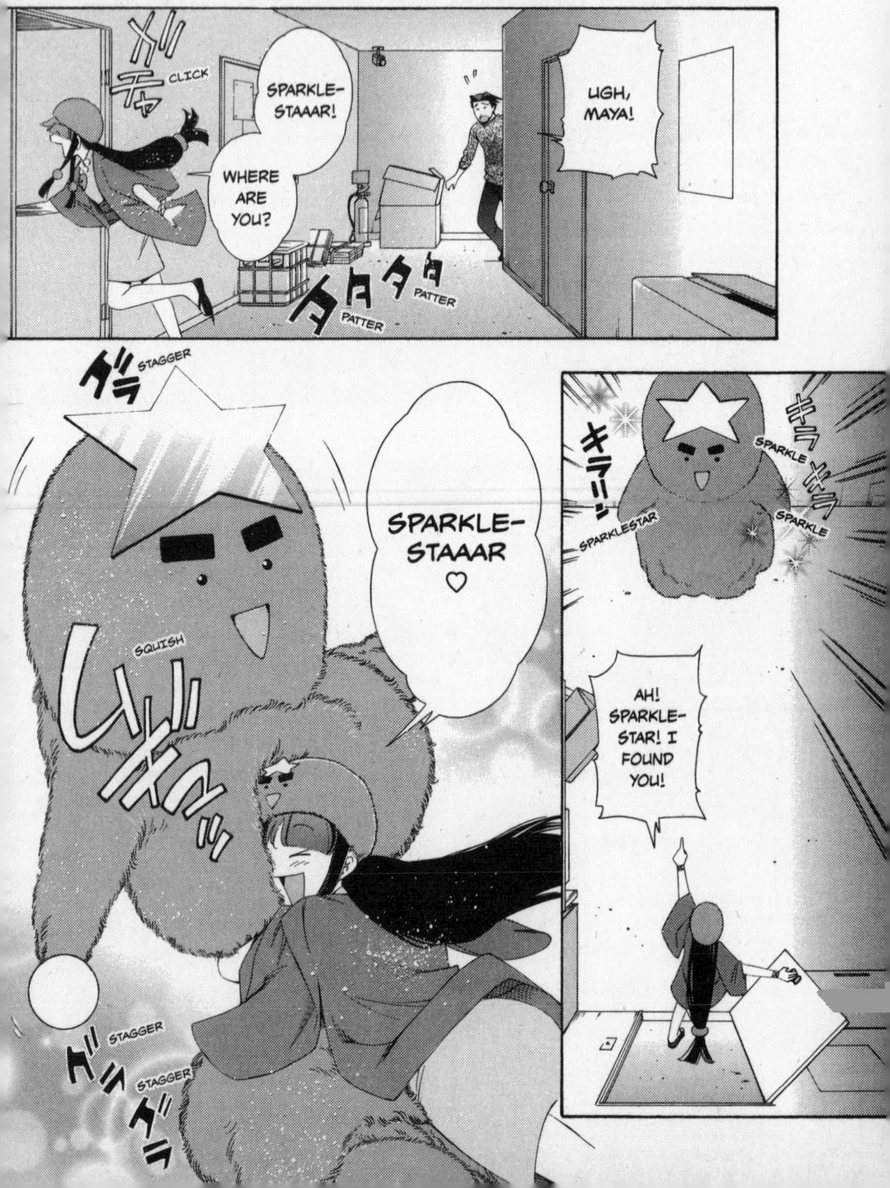
UGH, MAYA!
SPARKLE-STAAAR!
CLICK
WHERE ARE YOU?
PATTER
PATTER
SPARKLE
SPARKLE
SPARKLESTAR
AH! SPARKLE-STAR! I FOUND YOU!
STAGGER
SPARKLE-STAAAR ♡
SQUISH
STAGGER
STAGGER

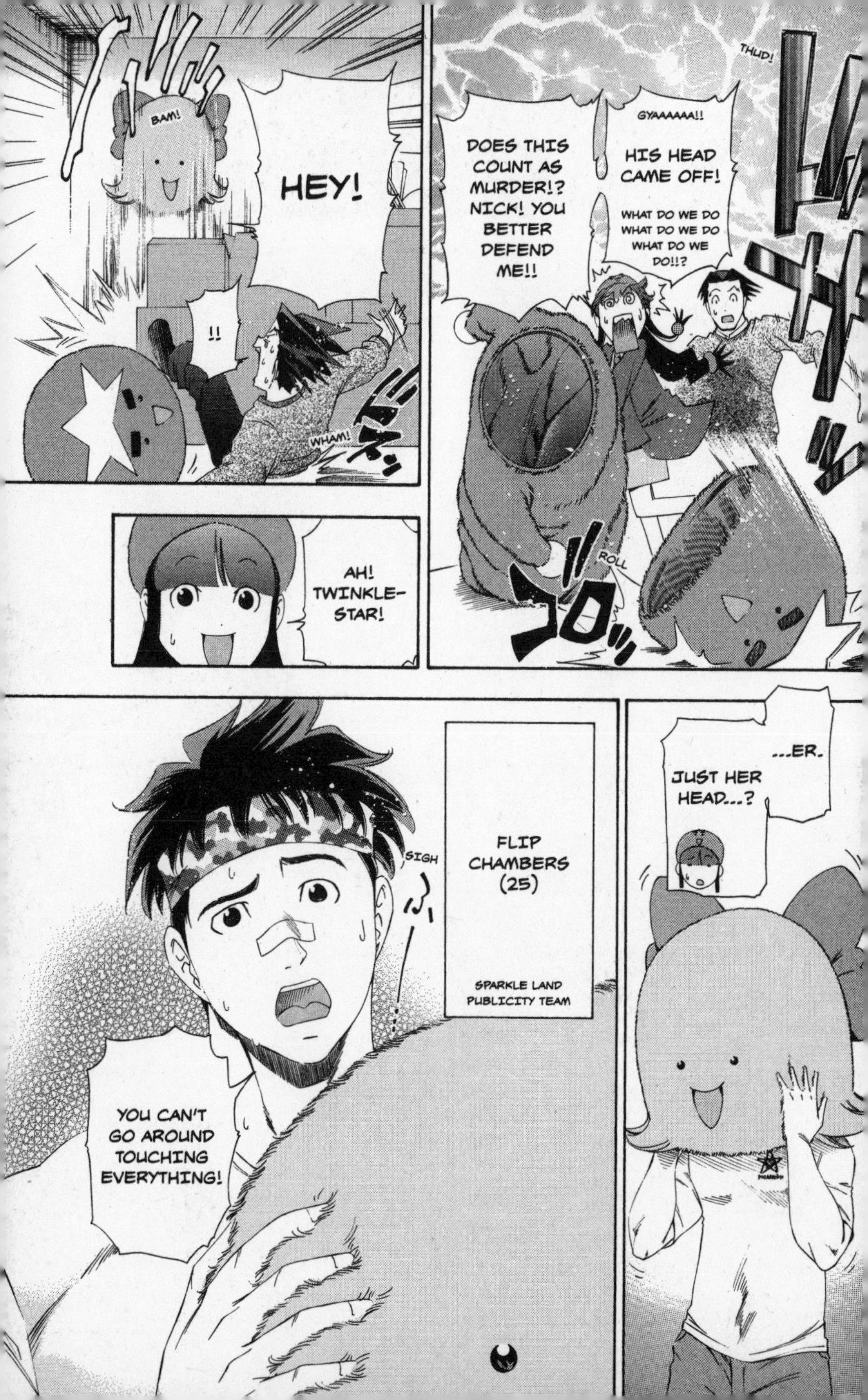
THUD!
GYAAAAAA!!
HIS HEAD CAME OFF!
WHAT DO WE DO WHAT DO WE DO WHAT DO WE DO!!?
DOES THIS COUNT AS MURDER!? NICK! YOU BETTER DEFEND ME!!
ROLL
BAM!
HEY!
!!
WHAM!
AH! TWINKLE-STAR!
...ER.
JUST HER HEAD...?
FLIP CHAMBERS (25)
SPARKLE LAND PUBLICITY TEAM
SIGH
YOU CAN'T GO AROUND TOUCHING EVERYTHING!

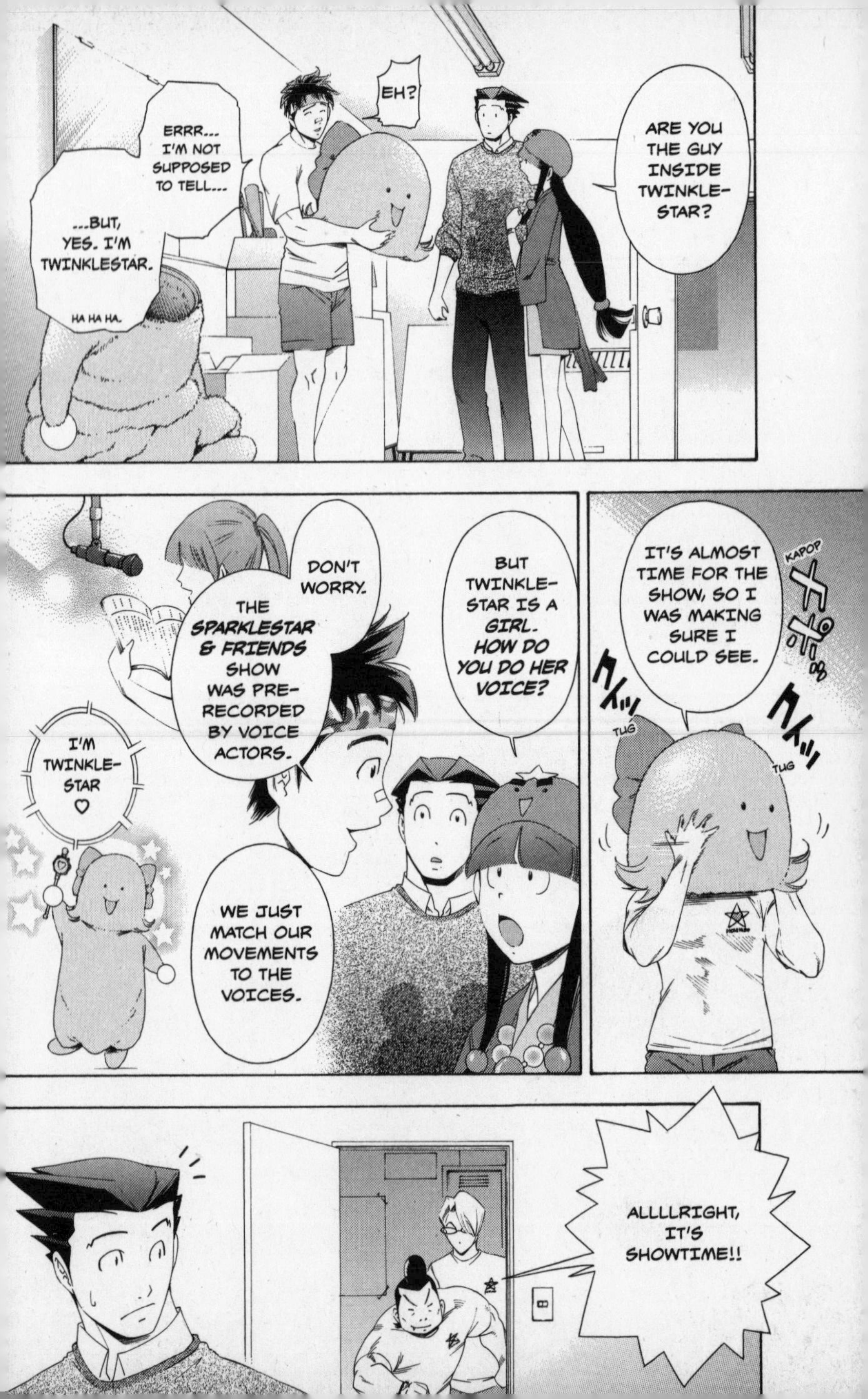
ARE YOU THE GUY INSIDE TWINKLE-STAR?
EH?
ERRR... I'M NOT SUPPOSED TO TELL...
...BUT, YES. I'M TWINKLESTAR.
HA HA HA.
KAPOP
IT'S ALMOST TIME FOR THE SHOW, SO I WAS MAKING SURE I COULD SEE.
TUG
TUG
BUT TWINKLE-STAR IS A GIRL. HOW DO YOU DO HER VOICE?
DON'T WORRY.
THE SPARKLESTAR & FRIENDS SHOW WAS PRE-RECORDED BY VOICE ACTORS.
I'M TWINKLE-STAR ♡
WE JUST MATCH OUR MOVEMENTS TO THE VOICES.
ALLLLRIGHT, IT'S SHOWTIME!!

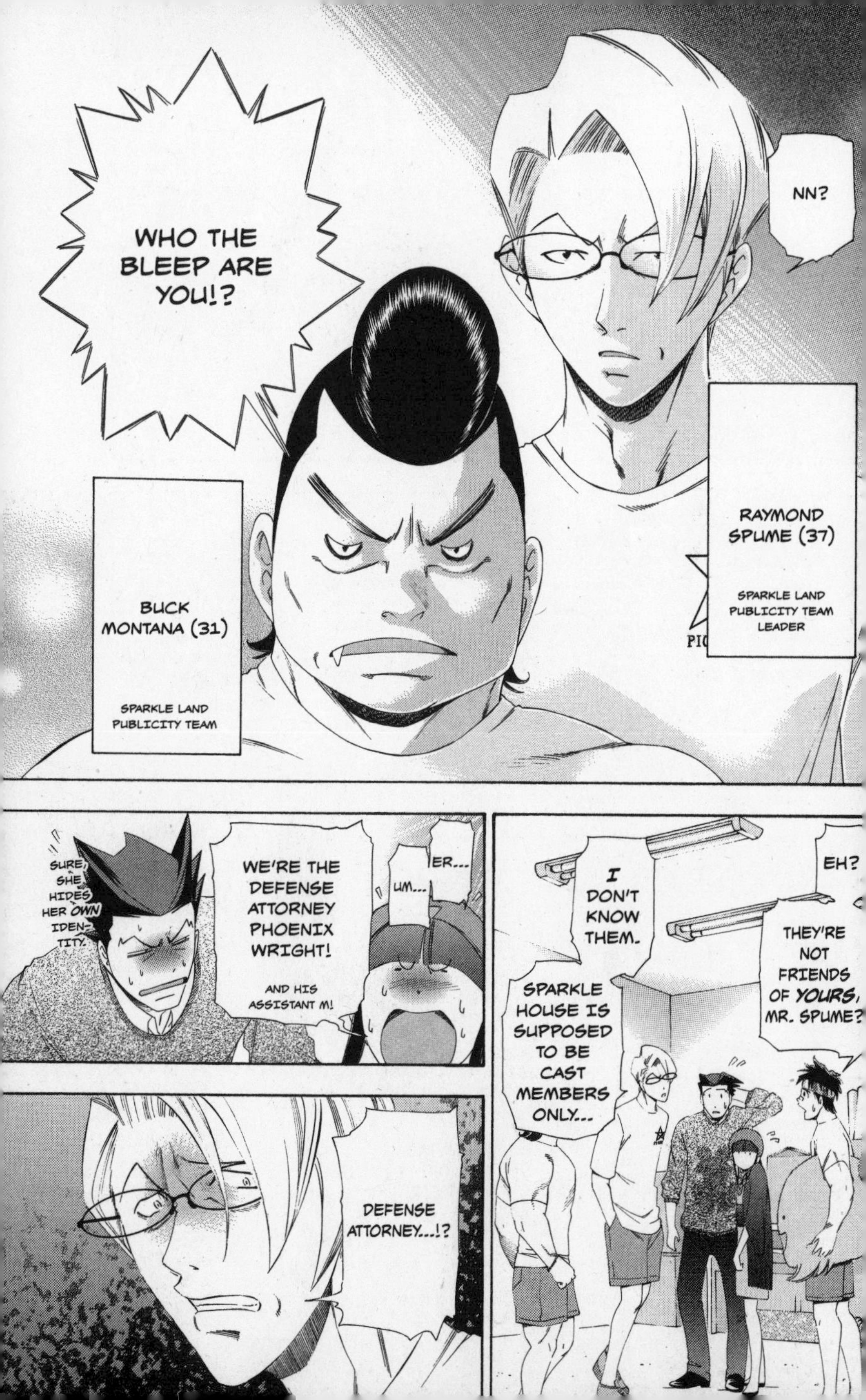

NN?
RAYMOND SPUME (37)
SPARKLE LAND PUBLICITY TEAM LEADER
WHO THE BLEEP ARE YOU!?
BUCK MONTANA (31)
SPARKLE LAND PUBLICITY TEAM
EH?
THEY'RE NOT FRIENDS OF *YOURS*, MR. SPUME?
I DON'T KNOW THEM.
SPARKLE HOUSE IS SUPPOSED TO BE CAST MEMBERS ONLY...
ER...
UM...
WE'RE THE DEFENSE ATTORNEY PHOENIX WRIGHT!
AND HIS ASSISTANT M!
SURE, SHE HIDES HER *OWN* IDENTITY.
DEFENSE ATTORNEY...!?

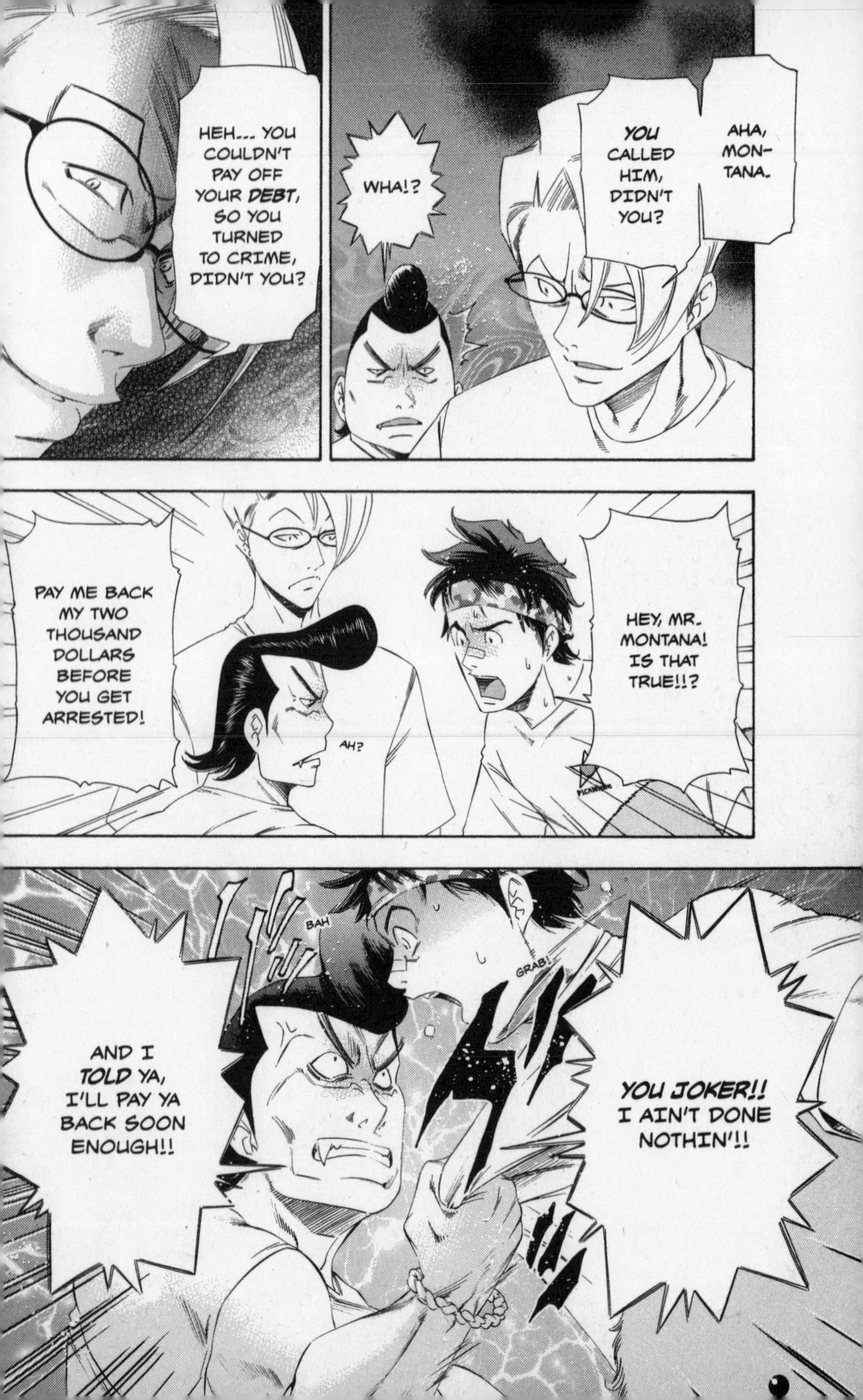

AHA, MON-TANA.
YOU CALLED HIM, DIDN'T YOU?
WHA!?
HEH... YOU COULDN'T PAY OFF YOUR DEBT, SO YOU TURNED TO CRIME, DIDN'T YOU?
HEY, MR. MONTANA! IS THAT TRUE!!?
AH?
PAY ME BACK MY TWO THOUSAND DOLLARS BEFORE YOU GET ARRESTED!
YOU JOKER!! I AIN'T DONE NOTHIN'!!
GRAB!
BAH
AND I TOLD YA, I'LL PAY YA BACK SOON ENOUGH!!

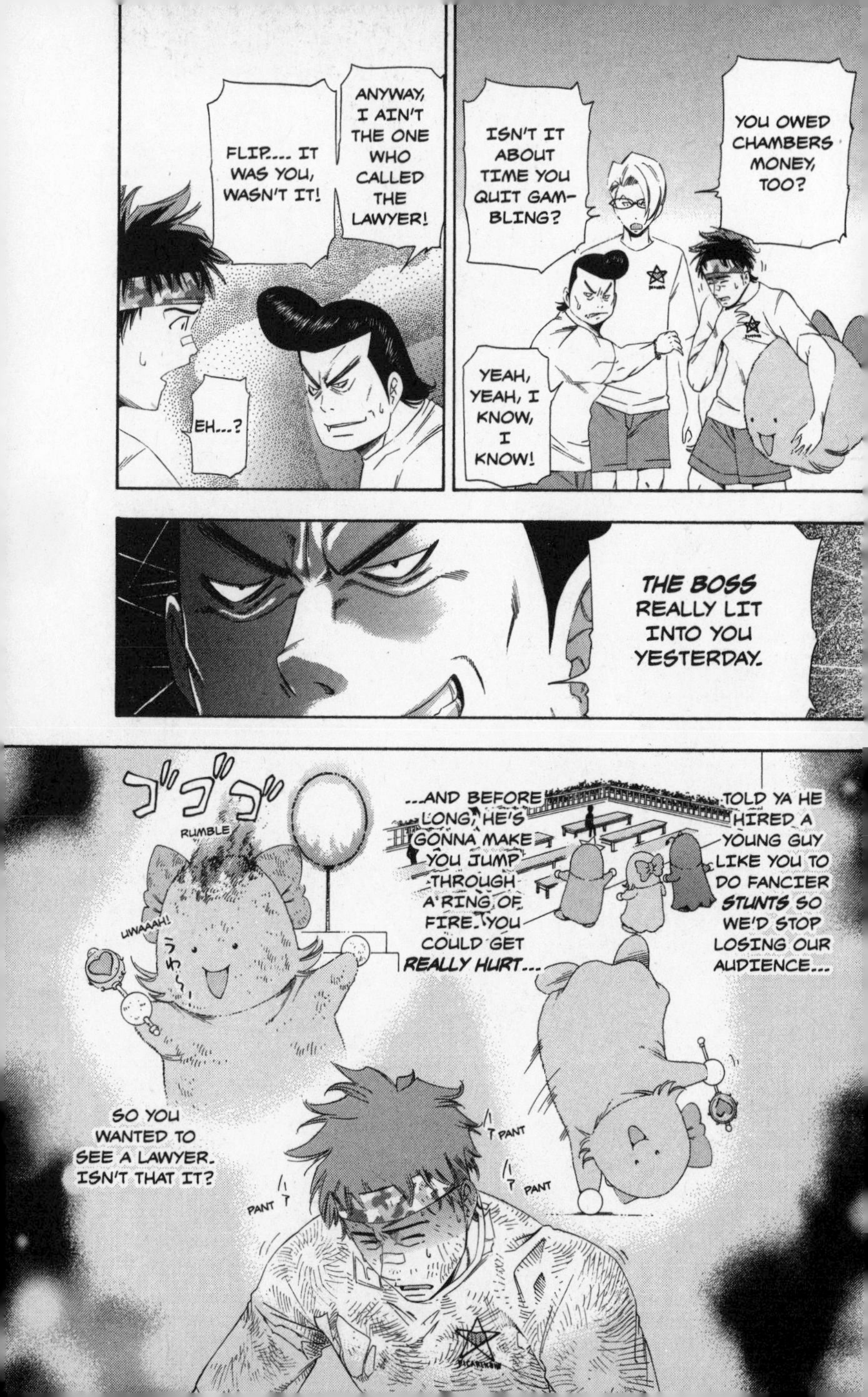
YOU OWED CHAMBERS MONEY, TOO?
ISN'T IT ABOUT TIME YOU QUIT GAM-BLING?
YEAH, YEAH, I KNOW, I KNOW!
ANYWAY, I AIN'T THE ONE WHO CALLED THE LAWYER!
FLIP.... IT WAS YOU, WASN'T IT!
EH...?
THE BOSS REALLY LIT INTO YOU YESTERDAY.
TOLD YA HE HIRED A YOUNG GUY LIKE YOU TO DO FANCIER STUNTS SO WE'D STOP LOSING OUR AUDIENCE...
...AND BEFORE LONG, HE'S GONNA MAKE YOU JUMP THROUGH A RING OF FIRE. YOU COULD GET REALLY HURT...
ゴゴゴ
RUMBLE
UWAAAH!
SO YOU WANTED TO SEE A LAWYER. ISN'T THAT IT?
PANT
PANT
PANT

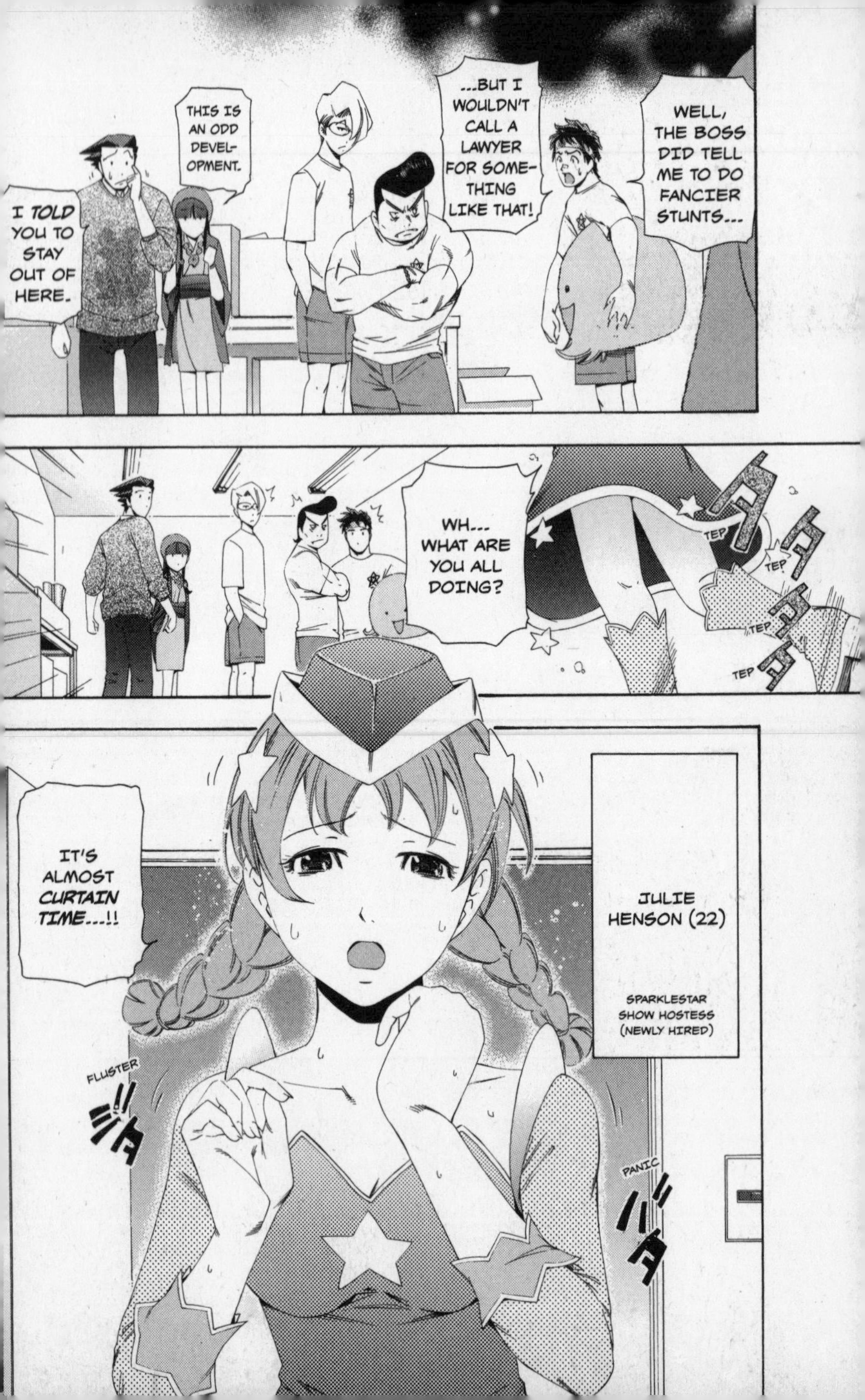
WELL, THE BOSS DID TELL ME TO DO FANCIER STUNTS...
...BUT I WOULDN'T CALL A LAWYER FOR SOMETHING LIKE THAT!
THIS IS AN ODD DEVELOPMENT.
I TOLD YOU TO STAY OUT OF HERE.
TEP
TEP
TEP
TEP
WH... WHAT ARE YOU ALL DOING?
JULIE HENSON (22)
SPARKLESTAR SHOW HOSTESS (NEWLY HIRED)
IT'S ALMOST CURTAIN TIME...!!
PANIC
FLUSTER

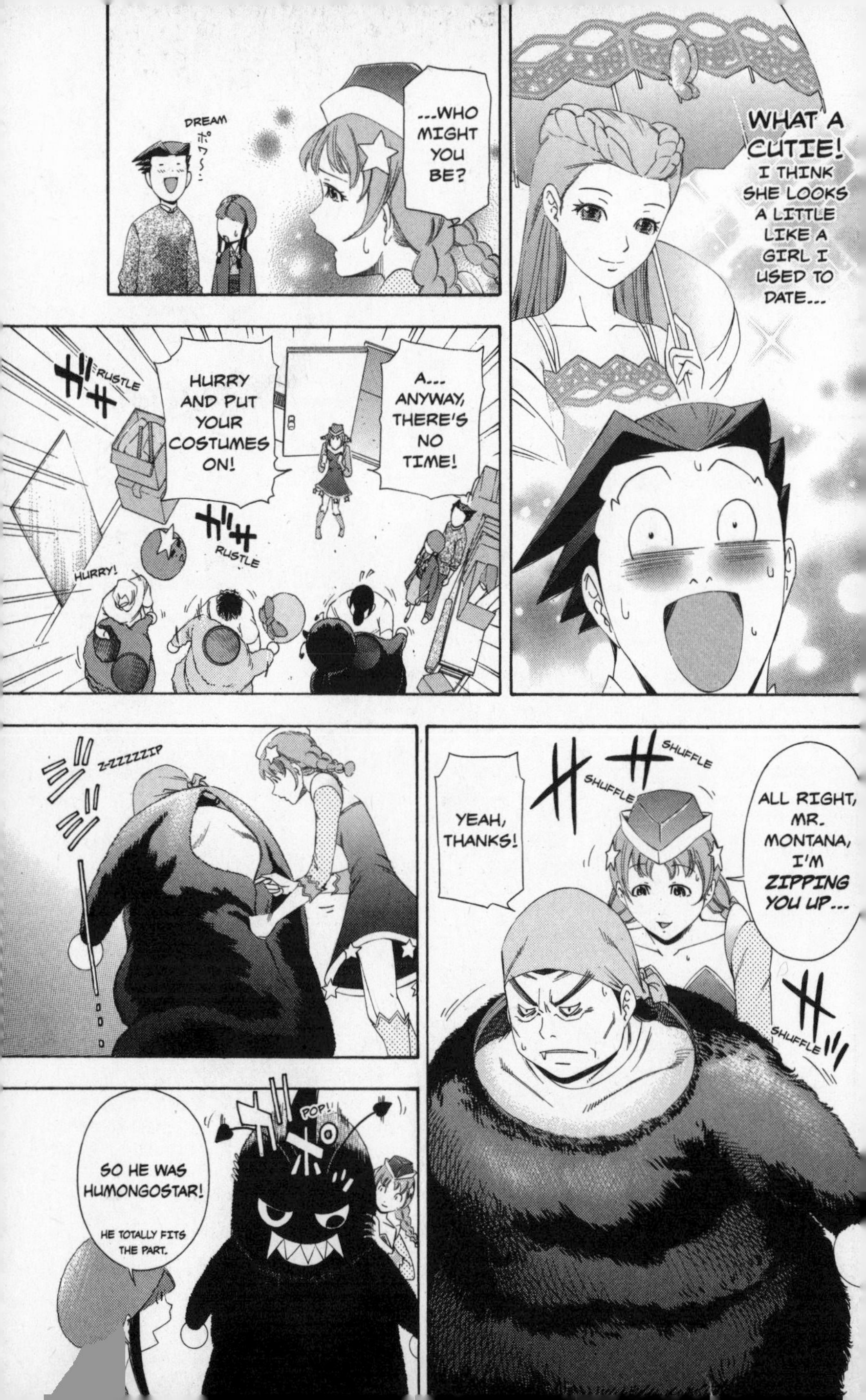
WHAT A CUTIE! I THINK SHE LOOKS A LITTLE LIKE A GIRL I USED TO DATE...
...WHO MIGHT YOU BE?
DREAM
A... ANYWAY, THERE'S NO TIME!
HURRY AND PUT YOUR COSTUMES ON!
RUSTLE
RUSTLE
HURRY!
SHUFFLE
ALL RIGHT, MR. MONTANA, I'M ZIPPING YOU UP...
SHUFFLE
YEAH, THANKS!
SHUFFLE
Z-ZZZZZIP
POP!
SO HE WAS HUMONGOSTAR!
HE TOTALLY FITS THE PART.

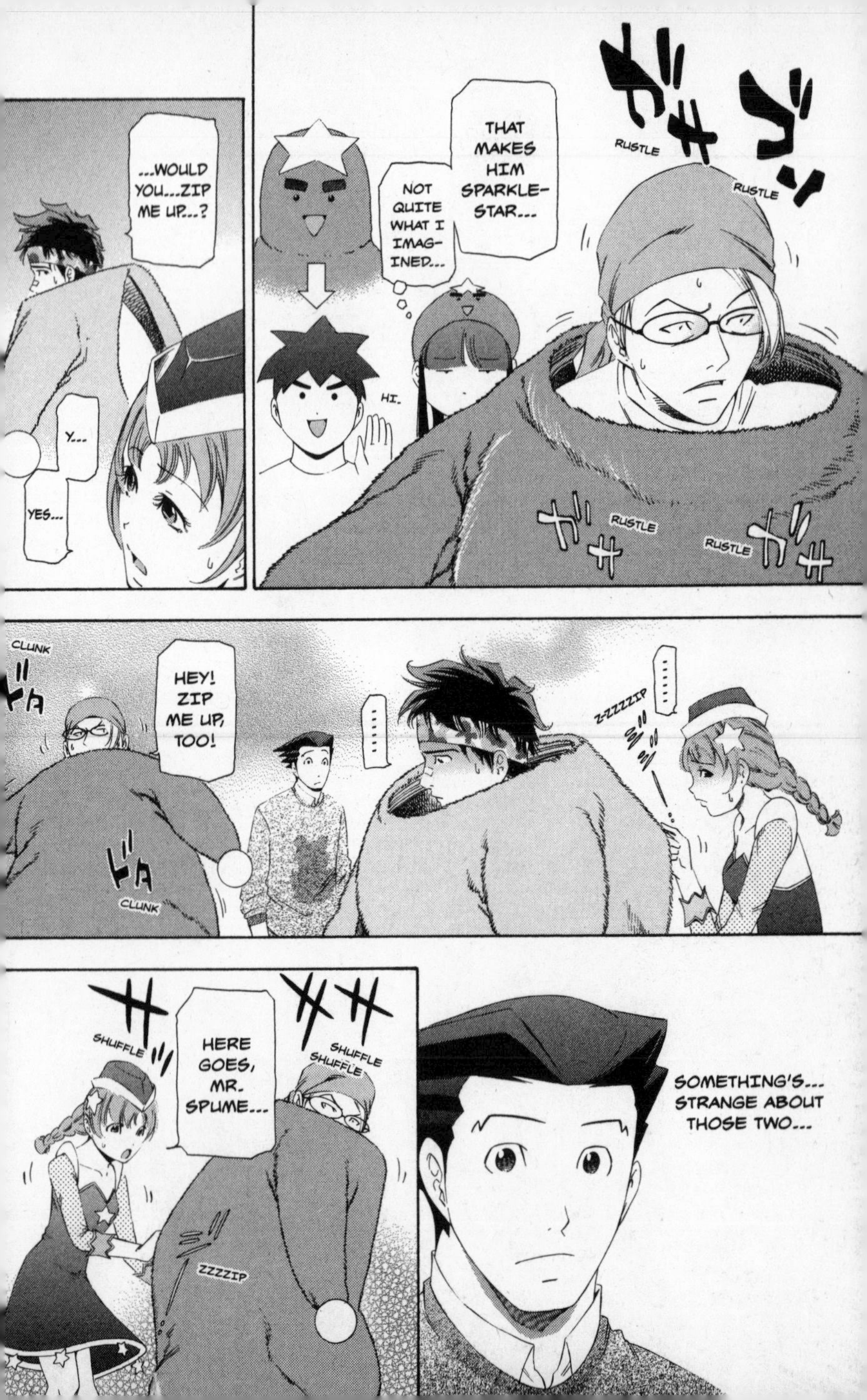
RUSTLE
RUSTLE
THAT MAKES HIM SPARKLE-STAR...
NOT QUITE WHAT I IMAG-INED...
HI.
RUSTLE
RUSTLE
...WOULD YOU...ZIP ME UP...?
Y...
YES...
......
Z-ZZZZIP
......
HEY! ZIP ME UP, TOO!
CLUNK
CLUNK
SOMETHING'S... STRANGE ABOUT THOSE TWO...
SHUFFLE
SHUFFLE
HERE GOES, MR. SPUME...
SHUFFLE
ZZZZIP

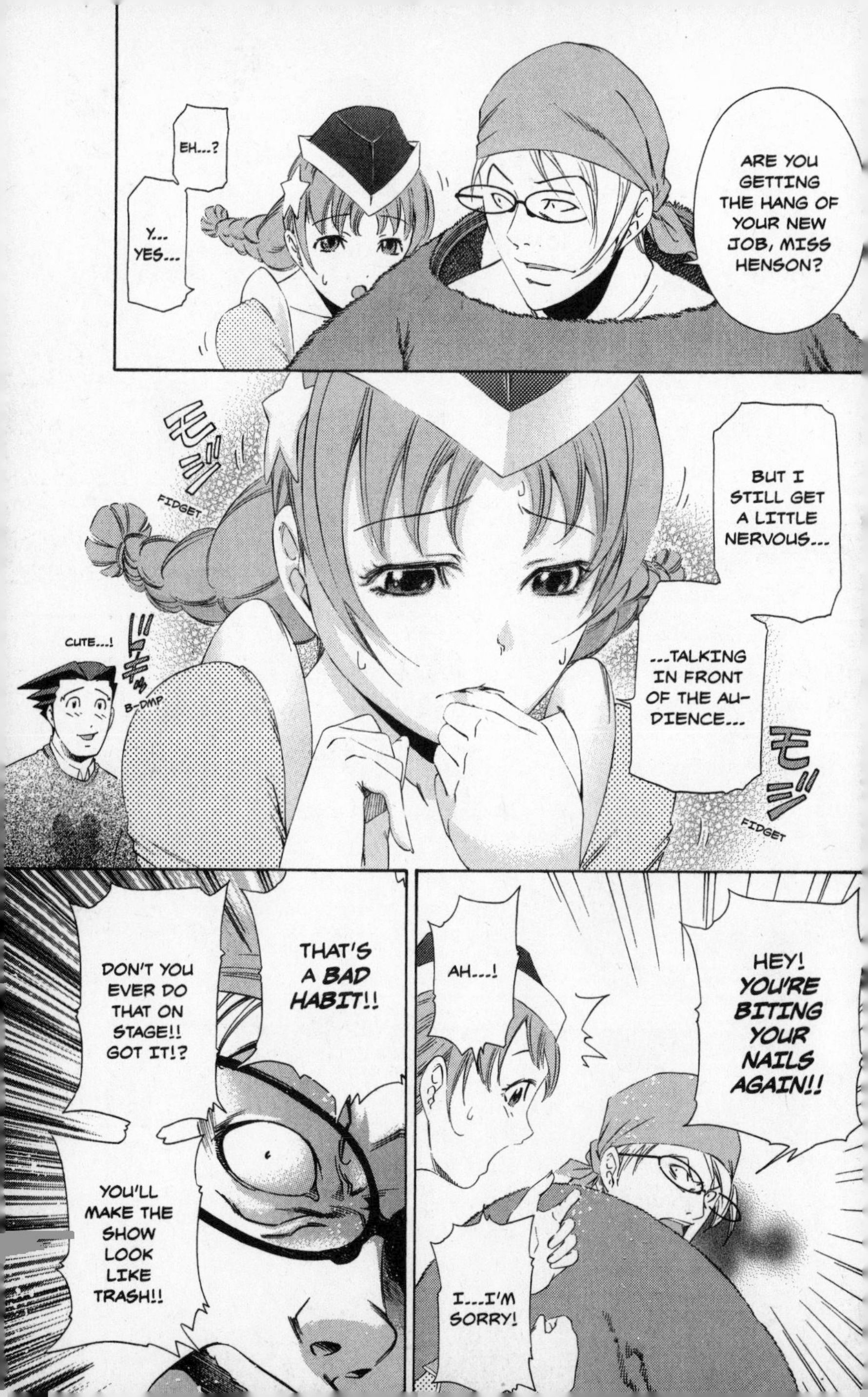
ARE YOU GETTING THE HANG OF YOUR NEW JOB, MISS HENSON?
EH...?
Y... YES...
BUT I STILL GET A LITTLE NERVOUS...
...TALKING IN FRONT OF THE AU- DIENCE...
FIDGET
FIDGET
B-DMP
CUTE...!
HEY! *YOU'RE BITING YOUR NAILS AGAIN!!*
AH...!
I...I'M SORRY!
THAT'S A *BAD HABIT*!!
DON'T YOU EVER DO THAT ON STAGE!! GOT IT!?
YOU'LL MAKE THE SHOW LOOK LIKE TRASH!!

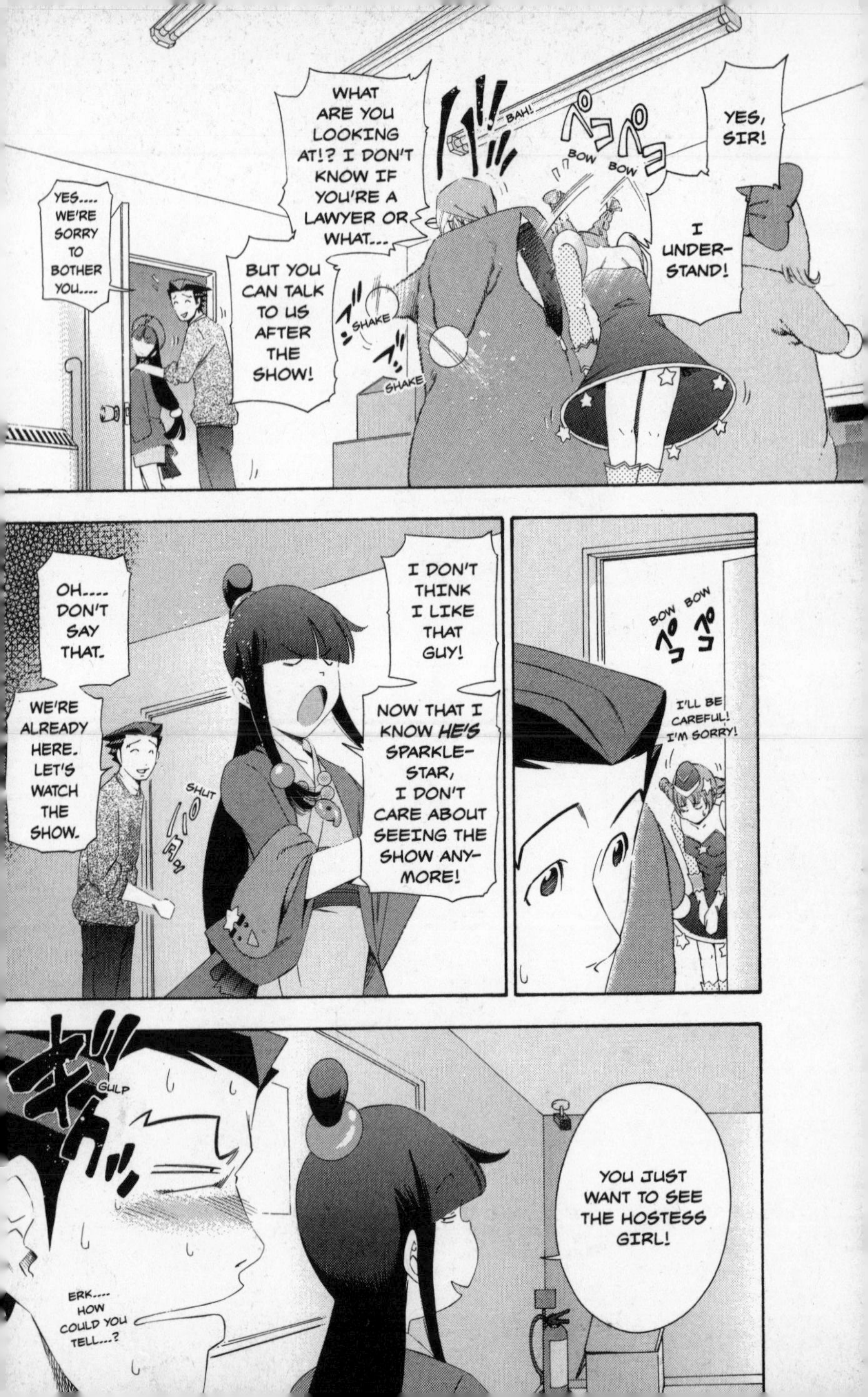
YES, SIR!
I UNDERSTAND!
BOW BOW
BAH!
WHAT ARE YOU LOOKING AT!? I DON'T KNOW IF YOU'RE A LAWYER OR WHAT...
BUT YOU CAN TALK TO US AFTER THE SHOW!
SHAKE
SHAKE
YES.... WE'RE SORRY TO BOTHER YOU....
BOW BOW
I'LL BE CAREFUL! I'M SORRY!
I DON'T THINK I LIKE THAT GUY!
NOW THAT I KNOW *HE'S* SPARKLE-STAR, I DON'T CARE ABOUT SEEING THE SHOW ANYMORE!
OH.... DON'T SAY THAT.
WE'RE ALREADY HERE. LET'S WATCH THE SHOW.
SHUT
YOU JUST WANT TO SEE THE HOSTESS GIRL!
GULP
ERK.... HOW COULD YOU TELL...?

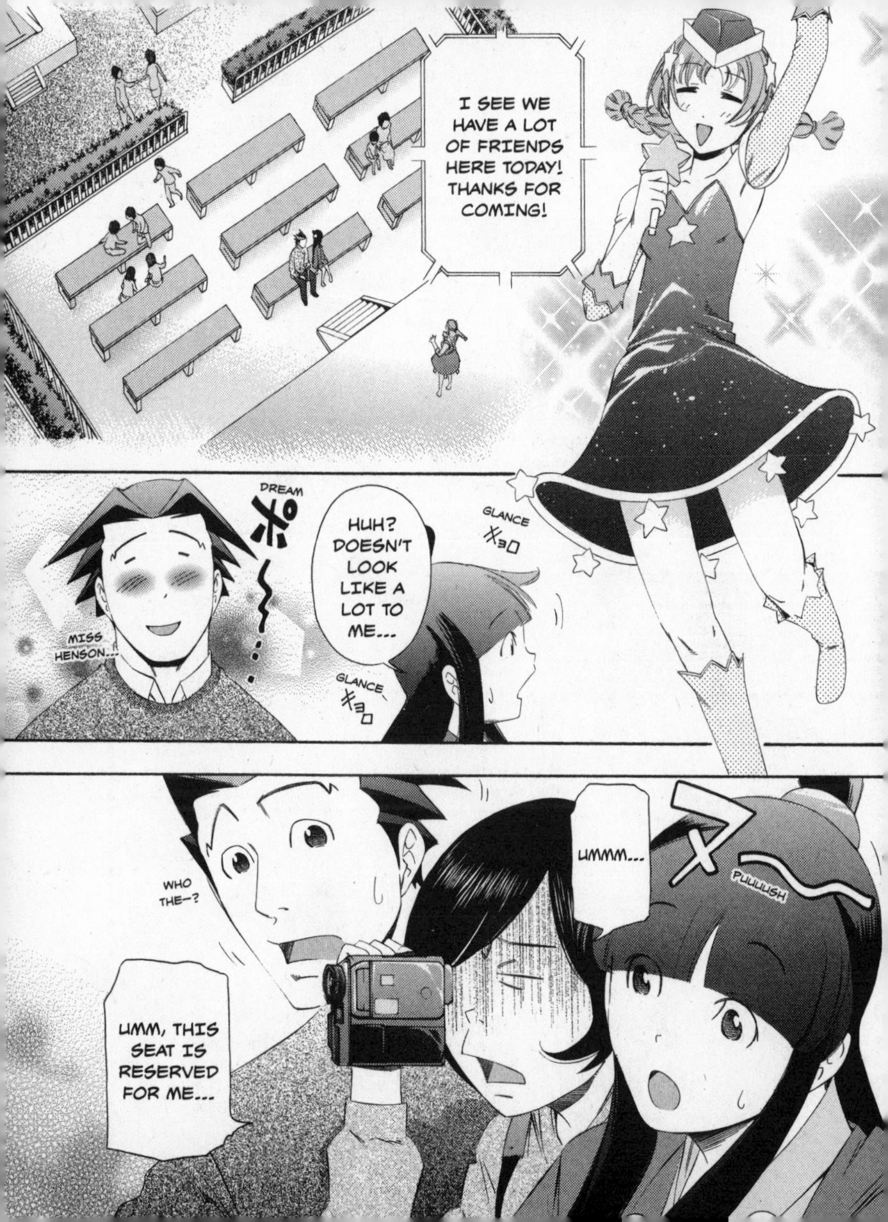
I SEE WE HAVE A LOT OF FRIENDS HERE TODAY! THANKS FOR COMING!
GLANCE
キョロ
HUH? DOESN'T LOOK LIKE A LOT TO ME...
GLANCE
キョロ
DREAM
ポ
MISS HENSON...
PUUUUSH
UMMM...
WHO THE–?
UMM, THIS SEAT IS RESERVED FOR ME...

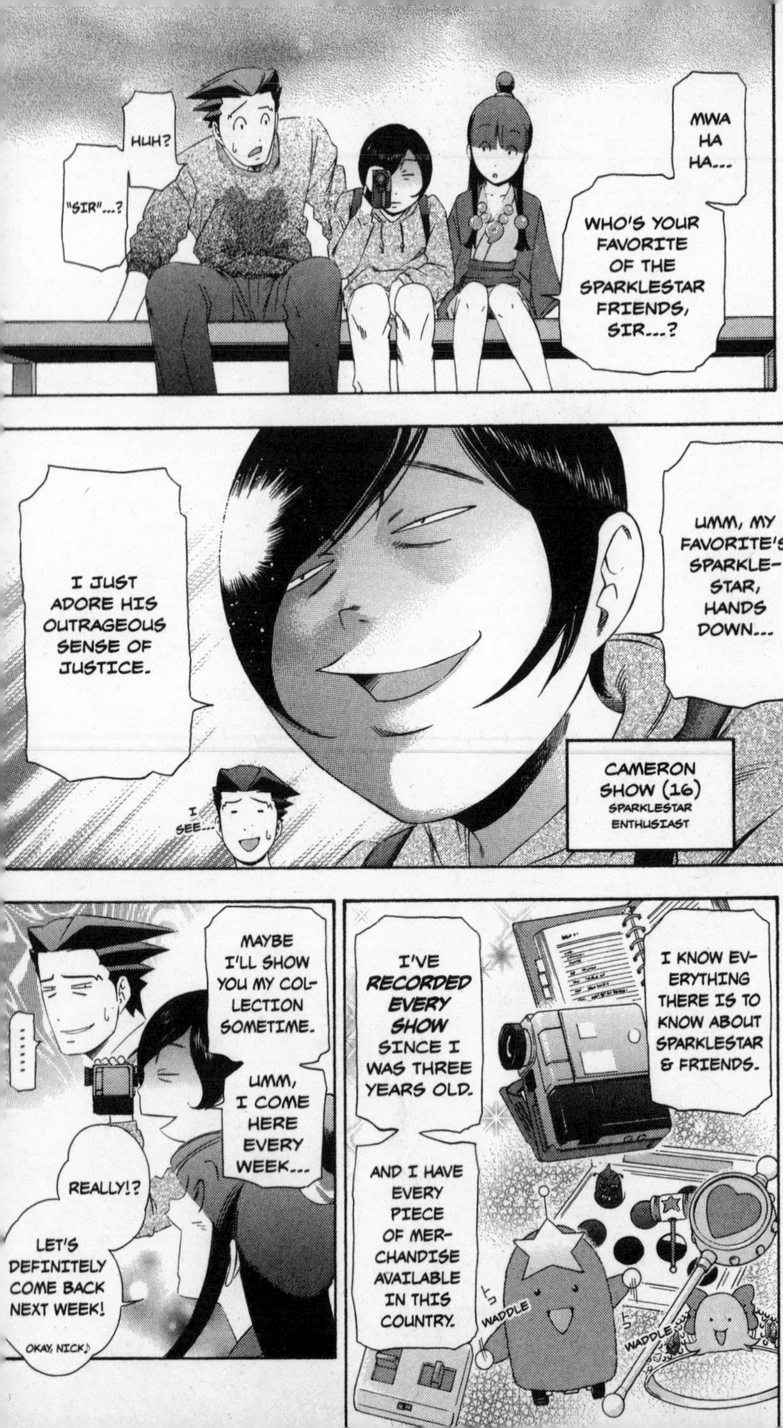
MWA HA HA...
WHO'S YOUR FAVORITE OF THE SPARKLESTAR FRIENDS, SIR...?
HUH?
"SIR"...?
UMM, MY FAVORITE'S SPARKLE-STAR, HANDS DOWN...
I JUST ADORE HIS OUTRAGEOUS SENSE OF JUSTICE.
CAMERON SHOW (16) SPARKLESTAR ENTHUSIAST
I SEE...
I KNOW EVERYTHING THERE IS TO KNOW ABOUT SPARKLESTAR & FRIENDS.
I'VE *RECORDED EVERY SHOW* SINCE I WAS THREE YEARS OLD.
AND I HAVE EVERY PIECE OF MERCHANDISE AVAILABLE IN THIS COUNTRY.
WADDLE
WADDLE
MAYBE I'LL SHOW YOU MY COLLECTION SOMETIME.
UMM, I COME HERE EVERY WEEK...
......
REALLY!?
LET'S DEFINITELY COME BACK NEXT WEEK!
OKAY, NICK♪

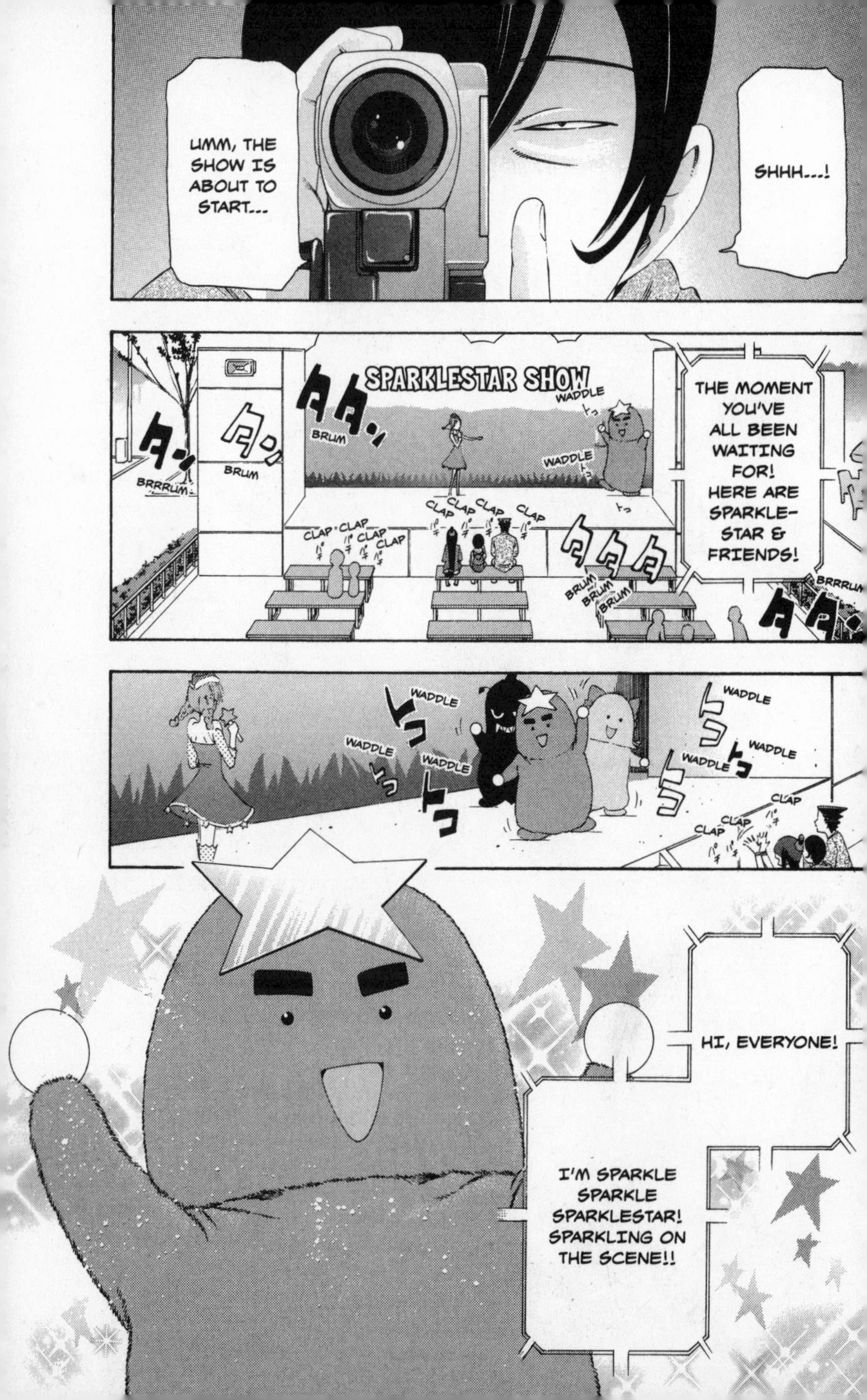
SHHH...!
UMM, THE SHOW IS ABOUT TO START...
THE MOMENT YOU'VE ALL BEEN WAITING FOR! HERE ARE SPARKLE-STAR & FRIENDS!
BRRRUM
WADDLE
WADDLE
SPARKLESTAR SHOW
BRUM BRUM BRUM
CLAP CLAP CLAP CLAP
BRUM
BRUM
BRRRUM
CLAP CLAP CLAP CLAP
WADDLE
WADDLE
WADDLE
CLAP
CLAP
CLAP
WADDLE
WADDLE
WADDLE
HI, EVERYONE!
I'M SPARKLE SPARKLE SPARKLESTAR! SPARKLING ON THE SCENE!!

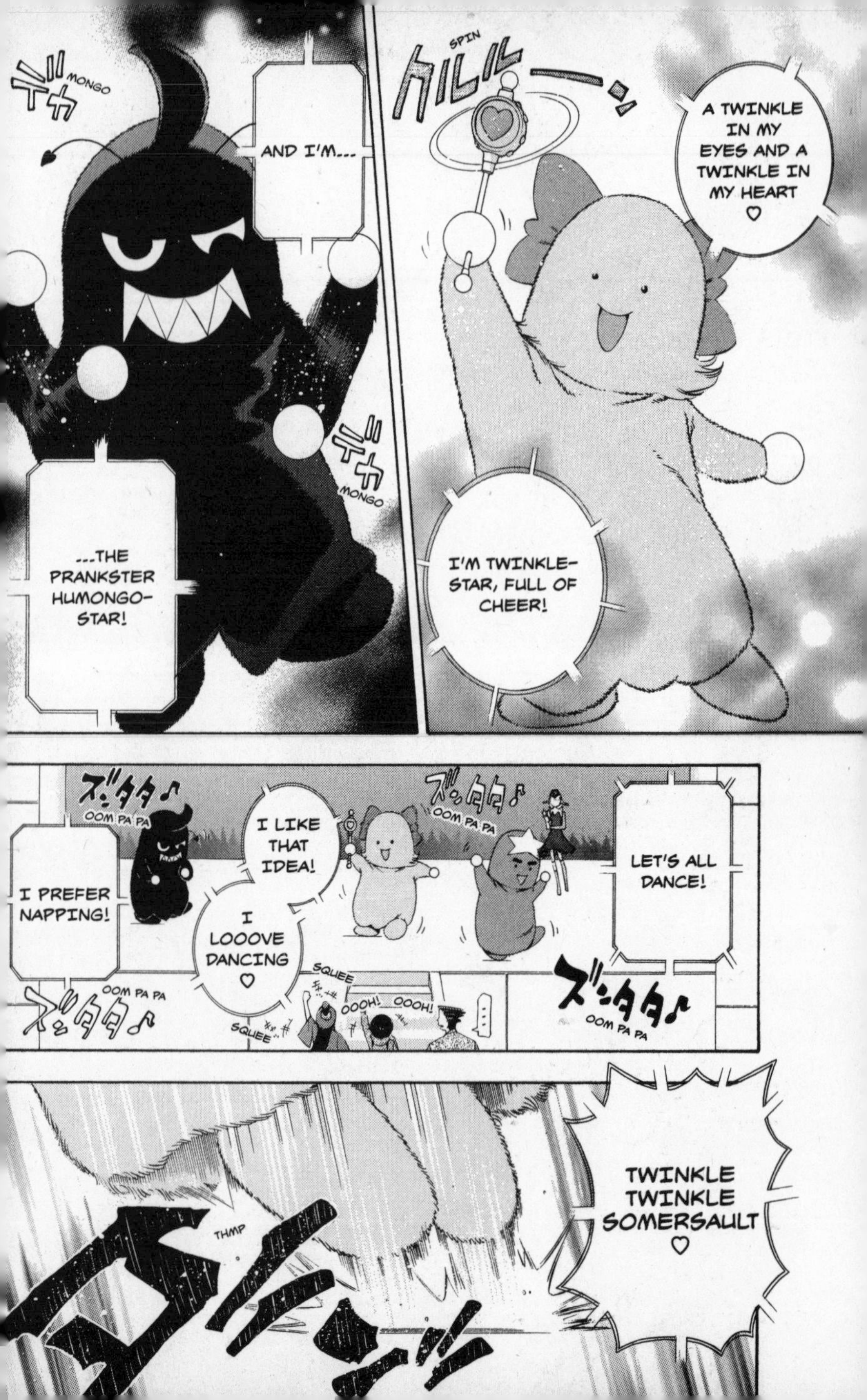
SPIN
A TWINKLE IN MY EYES AND A TWINKLE IN MY HEART ♡
I'M TWINKLE-STAR, FULL OF CHEER!
MONGO
AND I'M...
MONGO
...THE PRANKSTER HUMONGO-STAR!
LET'S ALL DANCE!
OOM PA PA
OOM PA PA
I LIKE THAT IDEA!
I LOOOVE DANCING ♡
SQUEE
OOOH! OOOH!
OOM PA PA
I PREFER NAPPING!
OOM PA PA
SQUEE
TWINKLE TWINKLE SOMERSAULT ♡
THMP

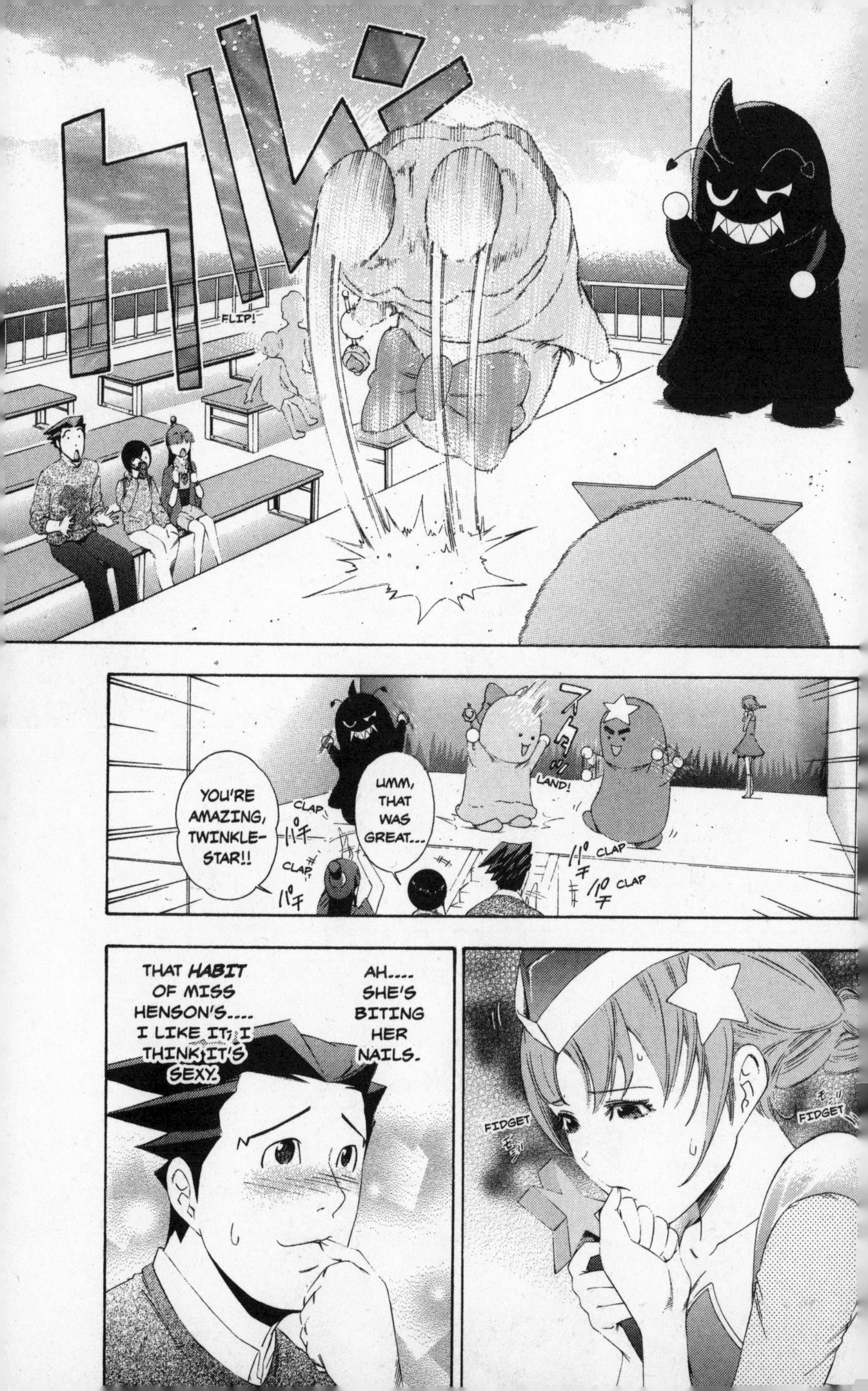
FLIP!
LAND!
UMM, THAT WAS GREAT...
YOU'RE AMAZING, TWINKLE-STAR!!
CLAP
CLAP
CLAP
CLAP
FIDGET
FIDGET
AH.... SHE'S BITING HER NAILS.
THAT *HABIT* OF MISS HENSON'S.... I LIKE IT; I THINK IT'S SEXY.

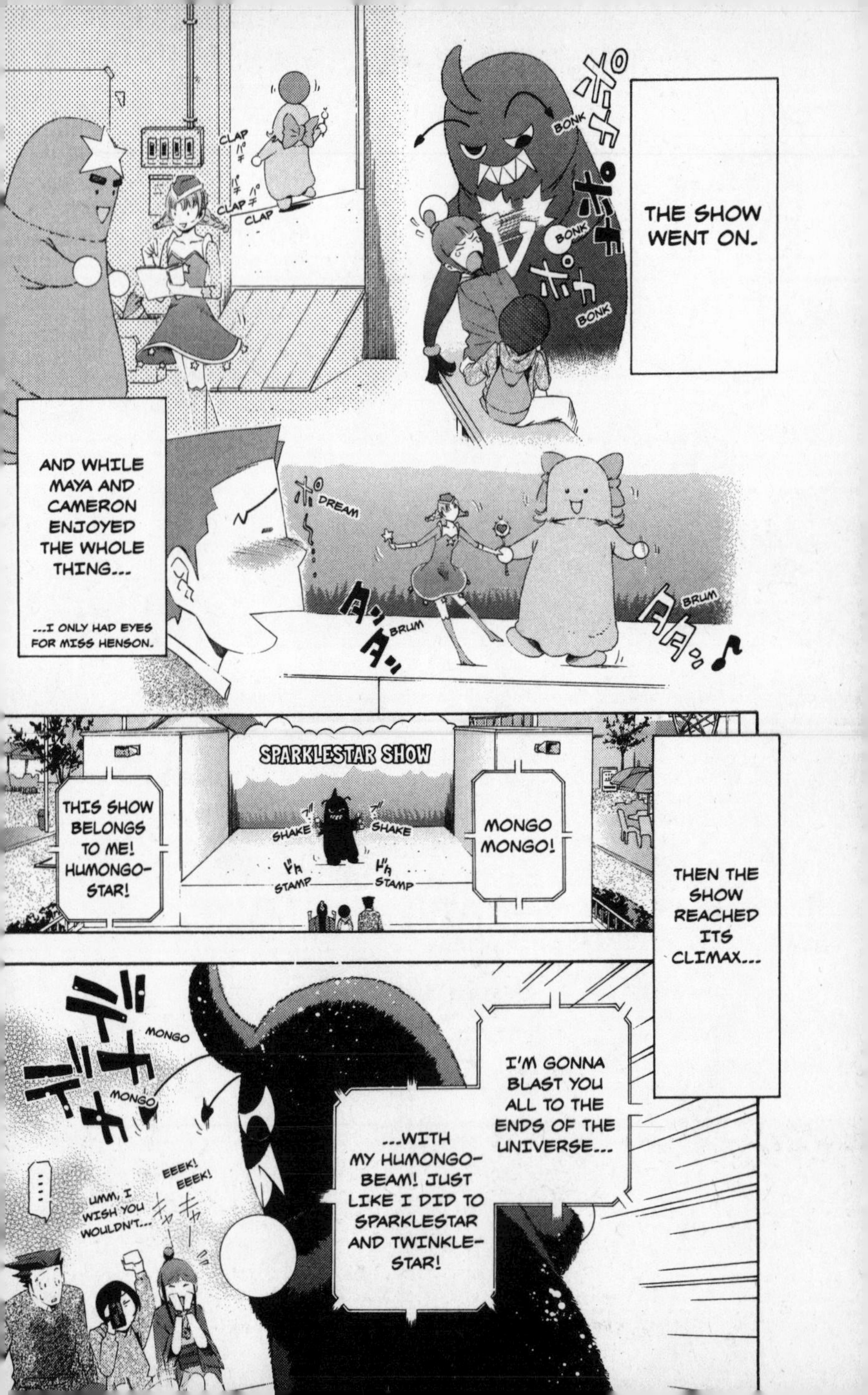
THE SHOW WENT ON.
BONK
BONK
BONK
CLAP
CLAP
CLAP
AND WHILE MAYA AND CAMERON ENJOYED THE WHOLE THING...
...I ONLY HAD EYES FOR MISS HENSON.
BRUM
DREAM
BRUM
THEN THE SHOW REACHED ITS CLIMAX...
SPARKLESTAR SHOW
MONGO MONGO!
SHAKE
SHAKE
THIS SHOW BELONGS TO ME! HUMONGO-STAR!
STAMP
STAMP
I'M GONNA BLAST YOU ALL TO THE ENDS OF THE UNIVERSE...
...WITH MY HUMONGO-BEAM! JUST LIKE I DID TO SPARKLESTAR AND TWINKLE-STAR!
MONGO
MONGO
EEEK! EEEK!
UMM, I WISH YOU WOULDN'T...
.....

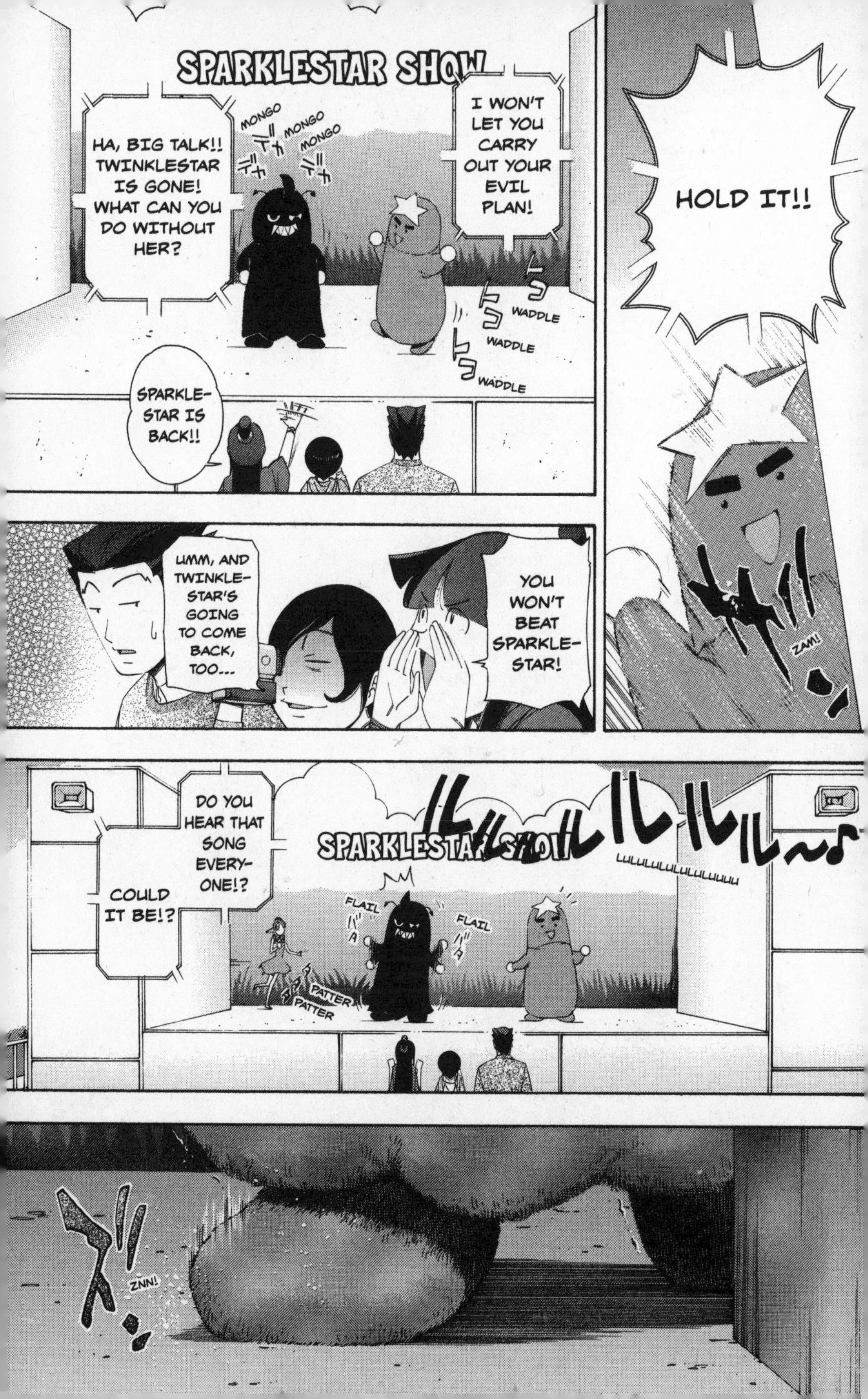
HOLD IT!!
ZAM!
SPARKLESTAR SHOW
I WON'T LET YOU CARRY OUT YOUR EVIL PLAN!
MONGO
MONGO
MONGO
HA, BIG TALK!! TWINKLESTAR IS GONE! WHAT CAN YOU DO WITHOUT HER?
WADDLE
WADDLE
WADDLE
SPARKLE-STAR IS BACK!!
YOU WON'T BEAT SPARKLE-STAR!
UMM, AND TWINKLE-STAR'S GOING TO COME BACK, TOO...
LULULULULULULULUUUU
SPARKLESTAR SHOW
DO YOU HEAR THAT SONG EVERY-ONE!?
COULD IT BE!?
FLAIL
FLAIL
PATTER
PATTER
ZNN!

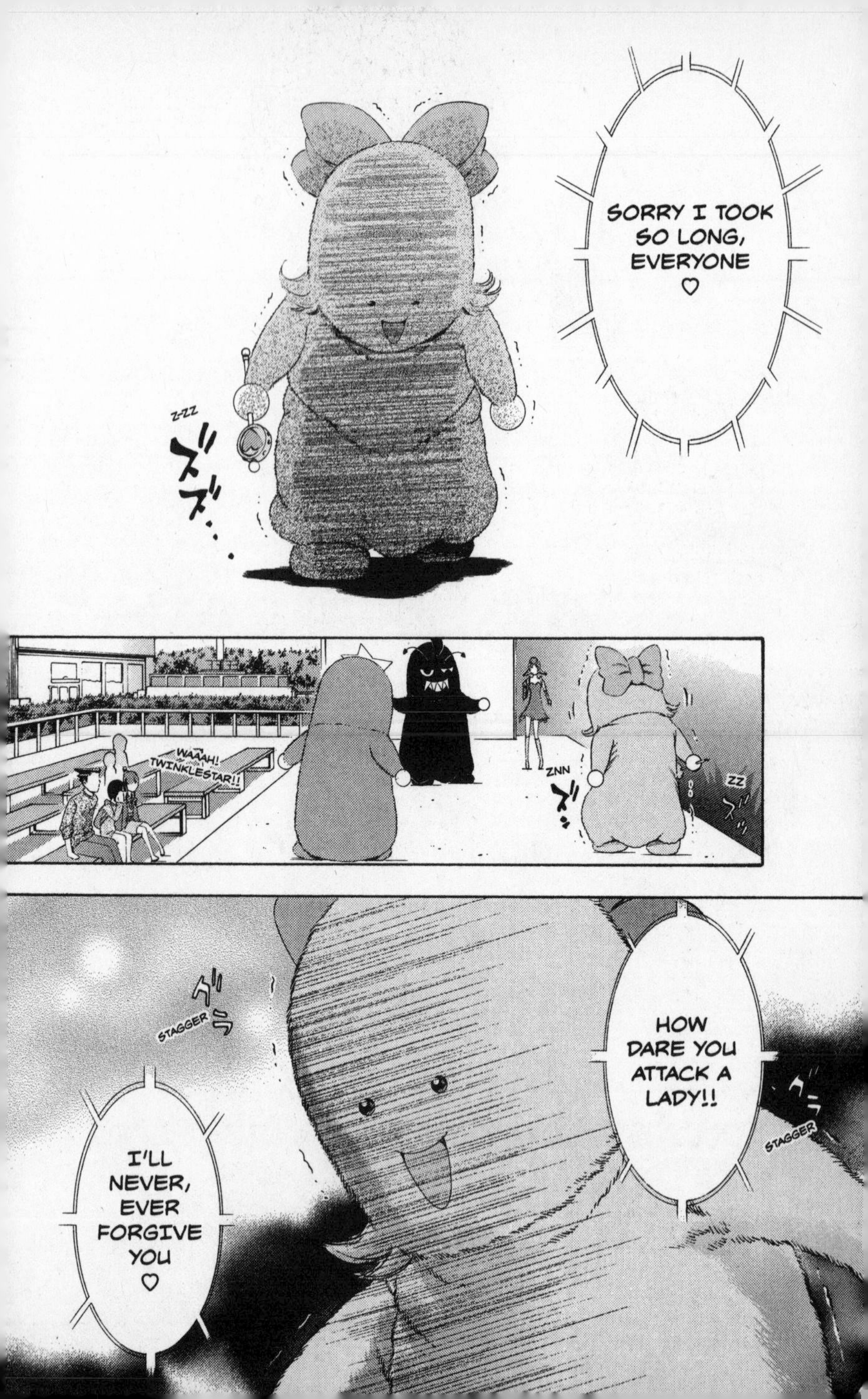
SORRY I TOOK SO LONG, EVERYONE ♡
Z-ZZ
ZZ
ZNN
WAAAH! TWINKLESTAR!!
HOW DARE YOU ATTACK A LADY!!
STAGGER
STAGGER
I'LL NEVER, EVER FORGIVE YOU ♡

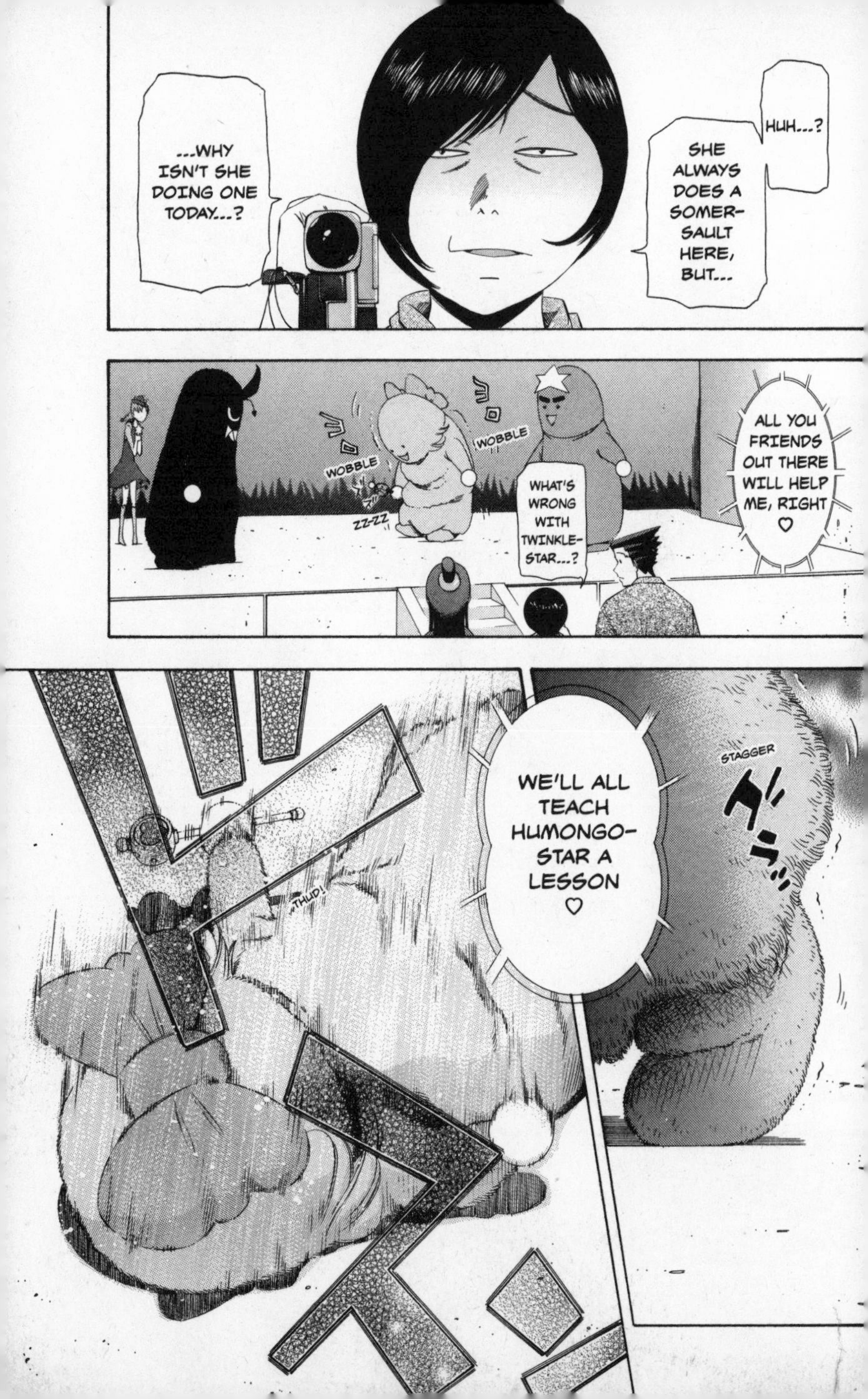
HUH...?
SHE ALWAYS DOES A SOMER-SAULT HERE, BUT...
...WHY ISN'T SHE DOING ONE TODAY...?
ALL YOU FRIENDS OUT THERE WILL HELP ME, RIGHT ♡
WHAT'S WRONG WITH TWINKLE-STAR...?
WOBBLE
WOBBLE
ZZ-ZZ
WE'LL ALL TEACH HUMONGO-STAR A LESSON ♡
STAGGER
THUD!

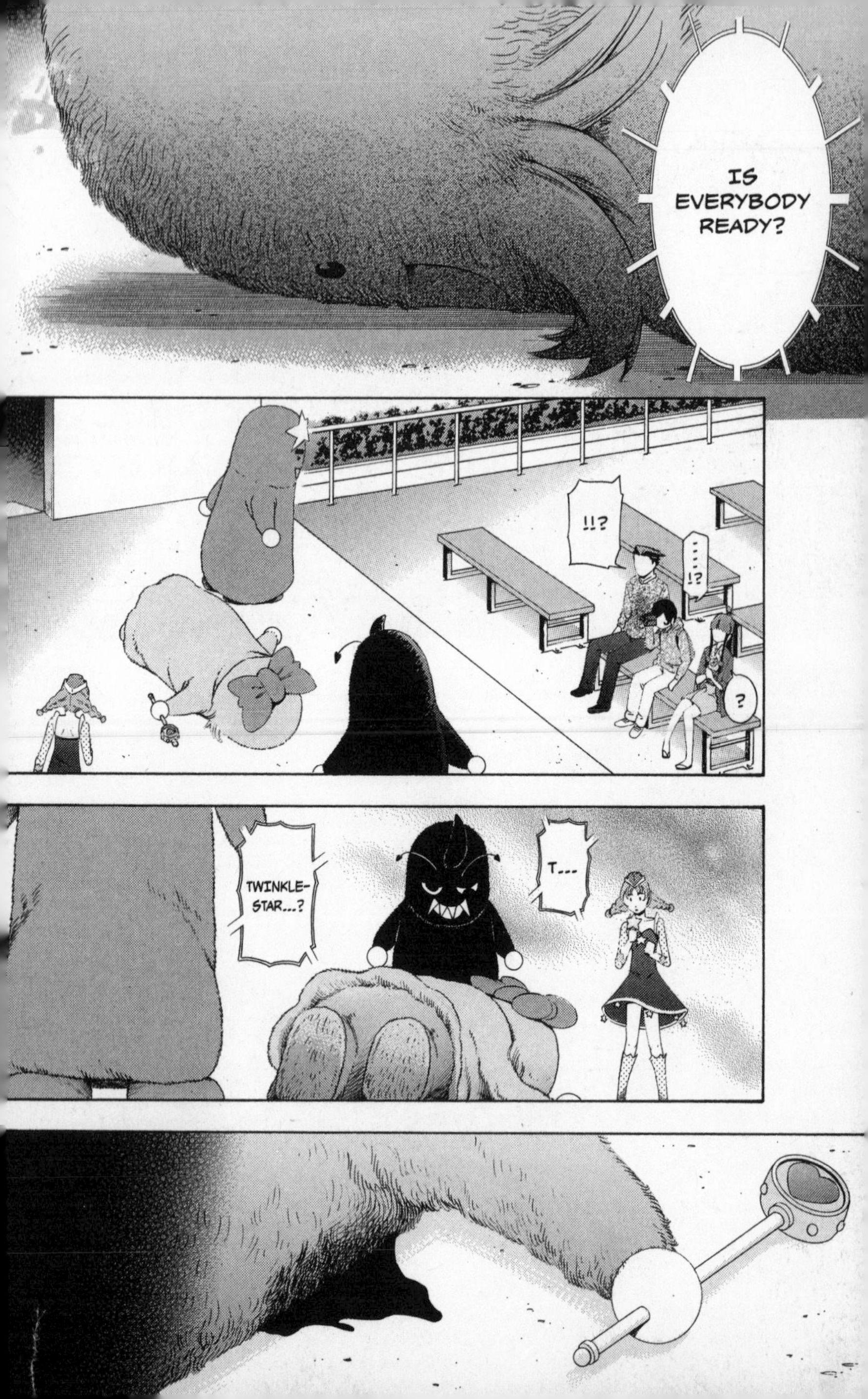
IS EVERYBODY READY?
!?
!!?
?
T...
TWINKLE-STAR...?

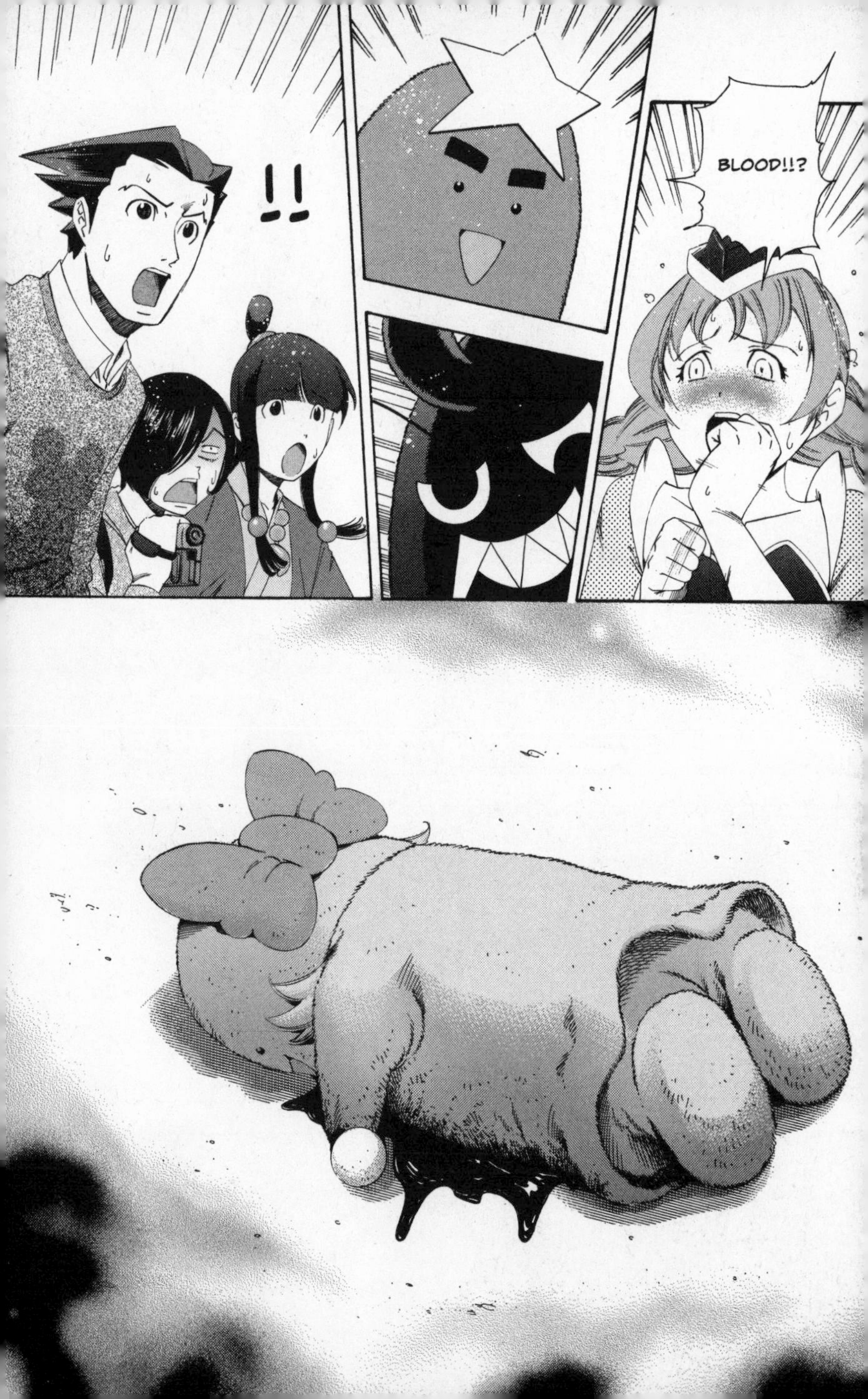
BLOOD!!?
!!

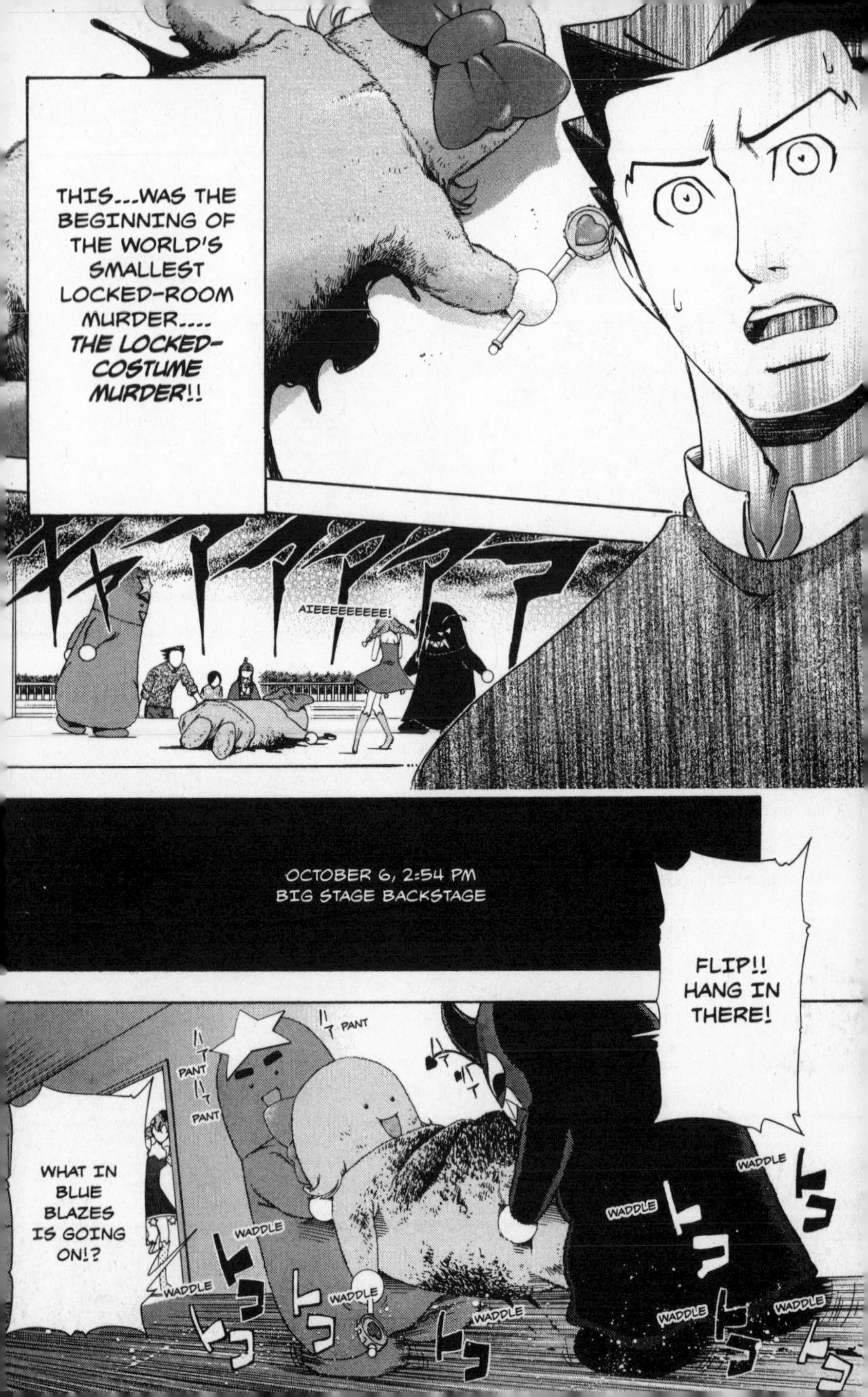
THIS...WAS THE BEGINNING OF THE WORLD'S SMALLEST LOCKED-ROOM MURDER.... *THE LOCKED-COSTUME MURDER*!!
AIEEEEEEEEEE!
OCTOBER 6, 2:54 PM
BIG STAGE BACKSTAGE
FLIP!! HANG IN THERE!
PANT
PANT
PANT
WADDLE
WADDLE
WADDLE
WADDLE
WHAT IN BLUE BLAZES IS GOING ON!?
WADDLE
WADDLE
WADDLE
WADDLE

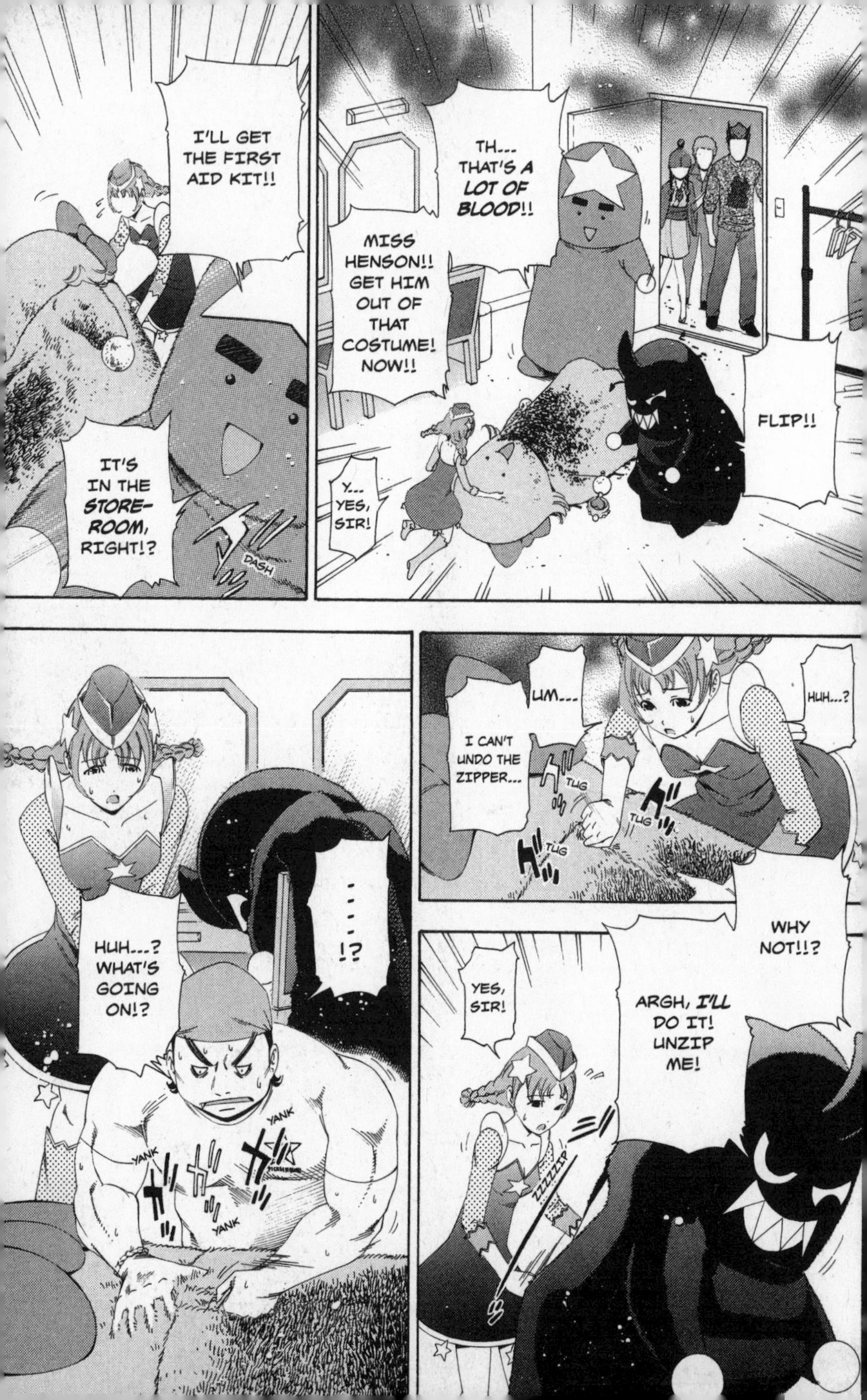
TH... THAT'S A *LOT OF BLOOD*!!
MISS HENSON!! GET HIM OUT OF THAT COSTUME! NOW!!
FLIP!!
Y... YES, SIR!
I'LL GET THE FIRST AID KIT!!
IT'S IN THE *STORE-ROOM*, RIGHT!?
DASH
HUH...?
UM...
I CAN'T UNDO THE ZIPPER...
TUG
TUG
TUG
WHY NOT!!?
ARGH, *I'LL* DO IT! UNZIP ME!
YES, SIR!
ZZZZZIP
......!?
HUH...? WHAT'S GOING ON!?
YANK
YANK
YANK

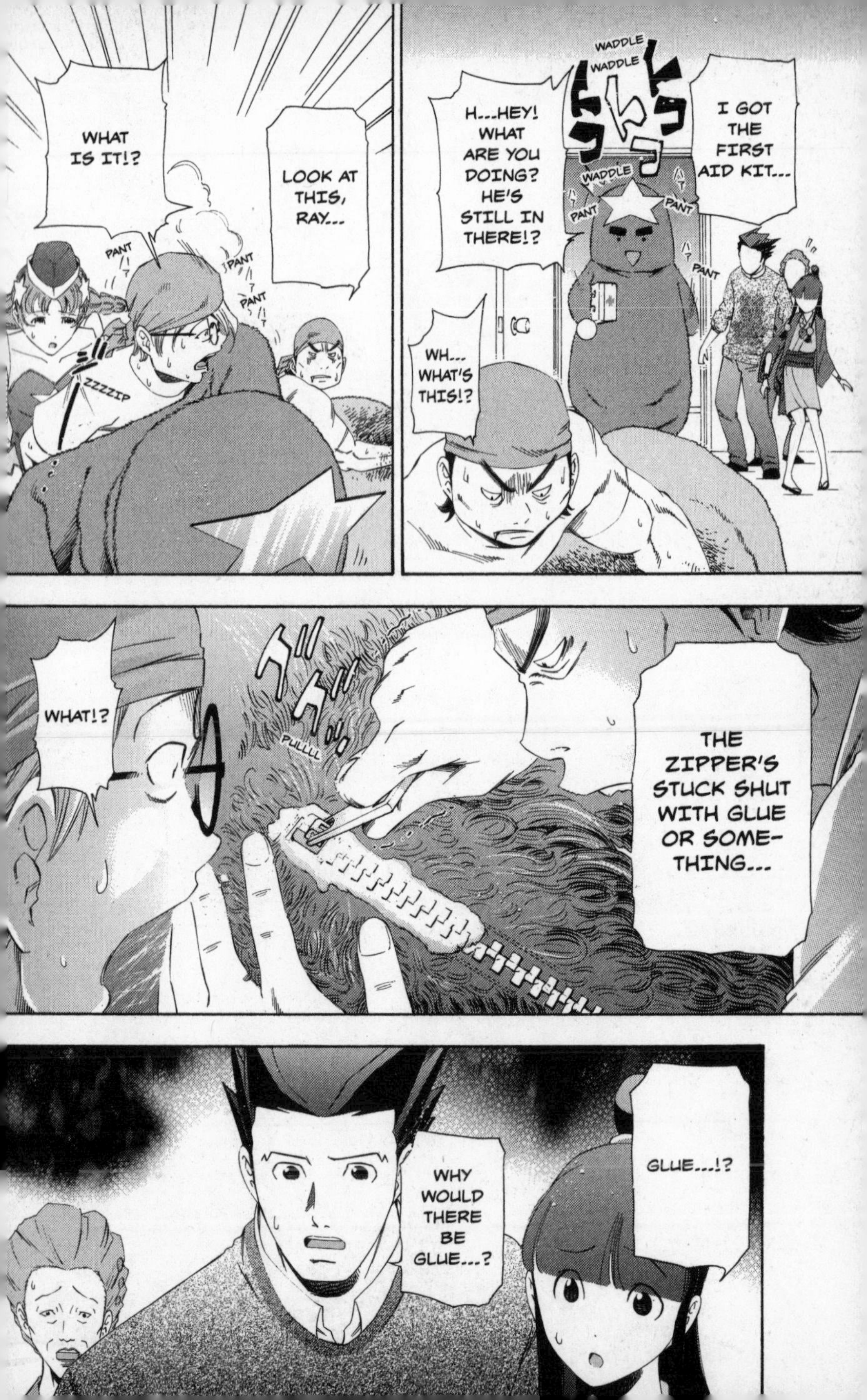
I GOT THE FIRST AID KIT...
WADDLE
WADDLE
H...HEY! WHAT ARE YOU DOING? HE'S STILL IN THERE!?
WADDLE
PANT
PANT
PANT
WH... WHAT'S THIS!?
LOOK AT THIS, RAY...
WHAT IS IT!?
PANT
PANT
PANT
ZZZZIP
THE ZIPPER'S STUCK SHUT WITH GLUE OR SOME-THING...
PULLLL
WHAT!?
GLUE...!?
WHY WOULD THERE BE GLUE...?

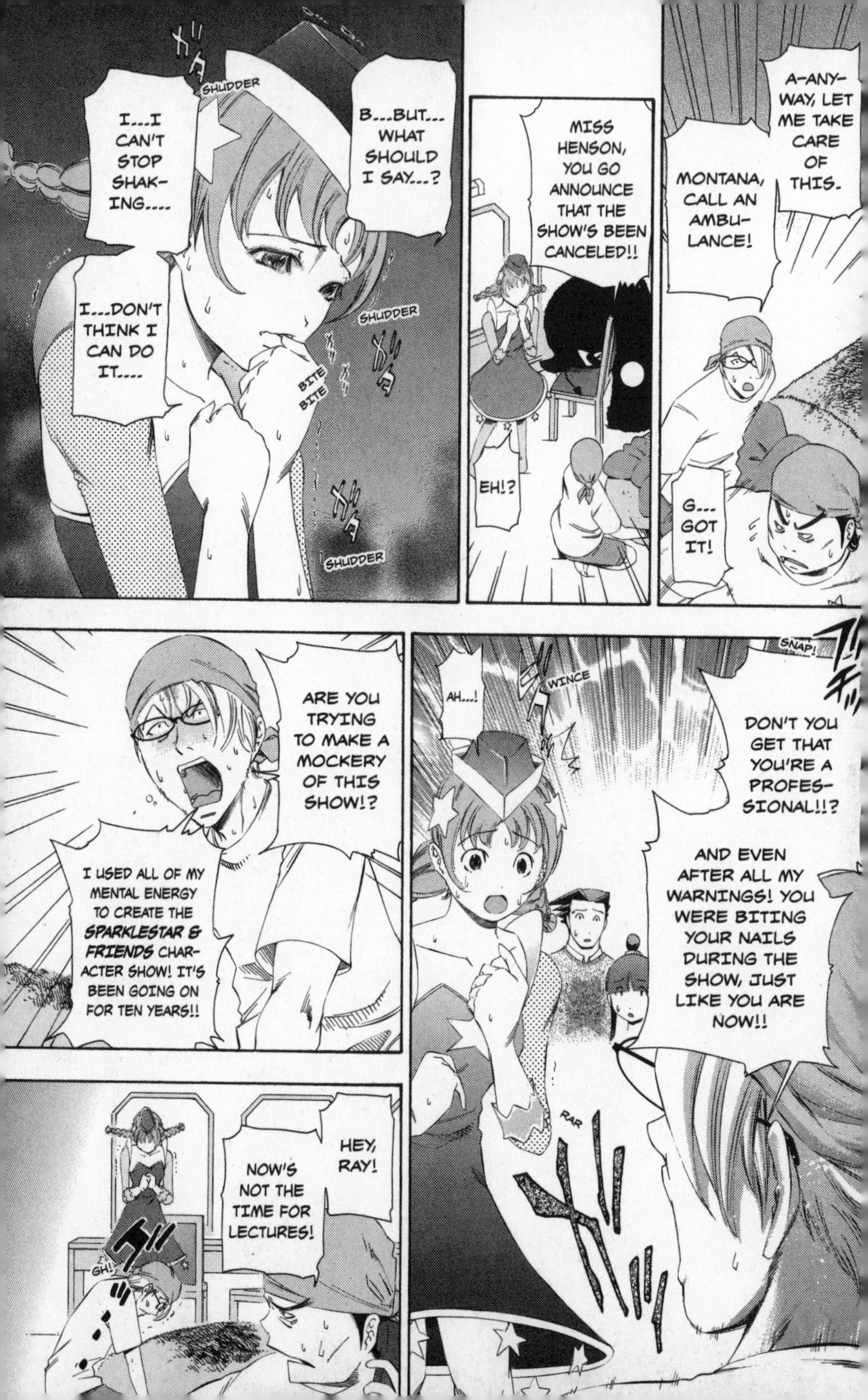
A-ANYWAY, LET ME TAKE CARE OF THIS.
MONTANA, CALL AN AMBULANCE!
G... GOT IT!
MISS HENSON, YOU GO ANNOUNCE THAT THE SHOW'S BEEN CANCELED!!
EH!?
B...BUT... WHAT SHOULD I SAY...?
SHUDDER
I...I CAN'T STOP SHAKING....
SHUDDER
BITE BITE
I...DON'T THINK I CAN DO IT....
SHUDDER
SNAP!
WINCE
AH...!
DON'T YOU GET THAT YOU'RE A PROFESSIONAL!!?
AND EVEN AFTER ALL MY WARNINGS! YOU WERE BITING YOUR NAILS DURING THE SHOW, JUST LIKE YOU ARE NOW!!
RAR
ARE YOU TRYING TO MAKE A MOCKERY OF THIS SHOW!?
I USED ALL OF MY MENTAL ENERGY TO CREATE THE SPARKLESTAR & FRIENDS CHARACTER SHOW! IT'S BEEN GOING ON FOR TEN YEARS!!
HEY, RAY!
NOW'S NOT THE TIME FOR LECTURES!
GH!

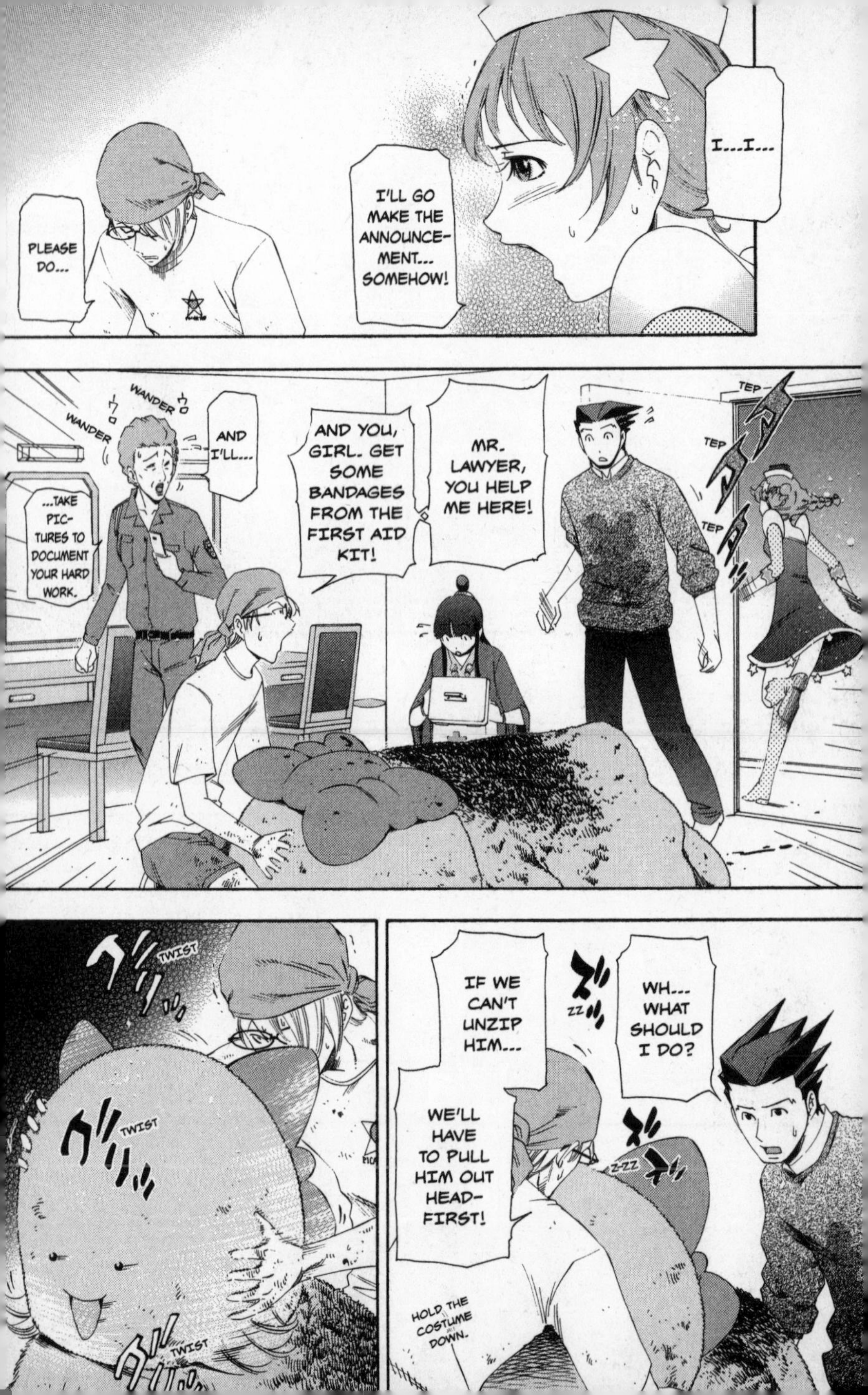

I...I...
I'LL GO MAKE THE ANNOUNCEMENT... SOMEHOW!
PLEASE DO...
TEP
TEP
TEP
MR. LAWYER, YOU HELP ME HERE!
AND YOU, GIRL. GET SOME BANDAGES FROM THE FIRST AID KIT!
AND I'LL...
WANDER
WANDER
...TAKE PICTURES TO DOCUMENT YOUR HARD WORK.
WH... WHAT SHOULD I DO?
ZZ
IF WE CAN'T UNZIP HIM...
WE'LL HAVE TO PULL HIM OUT HEAD-FIRST!
Z-ZZ
HOLD THE COSTUME DOWN.
TWIST
TWIST
TWIST

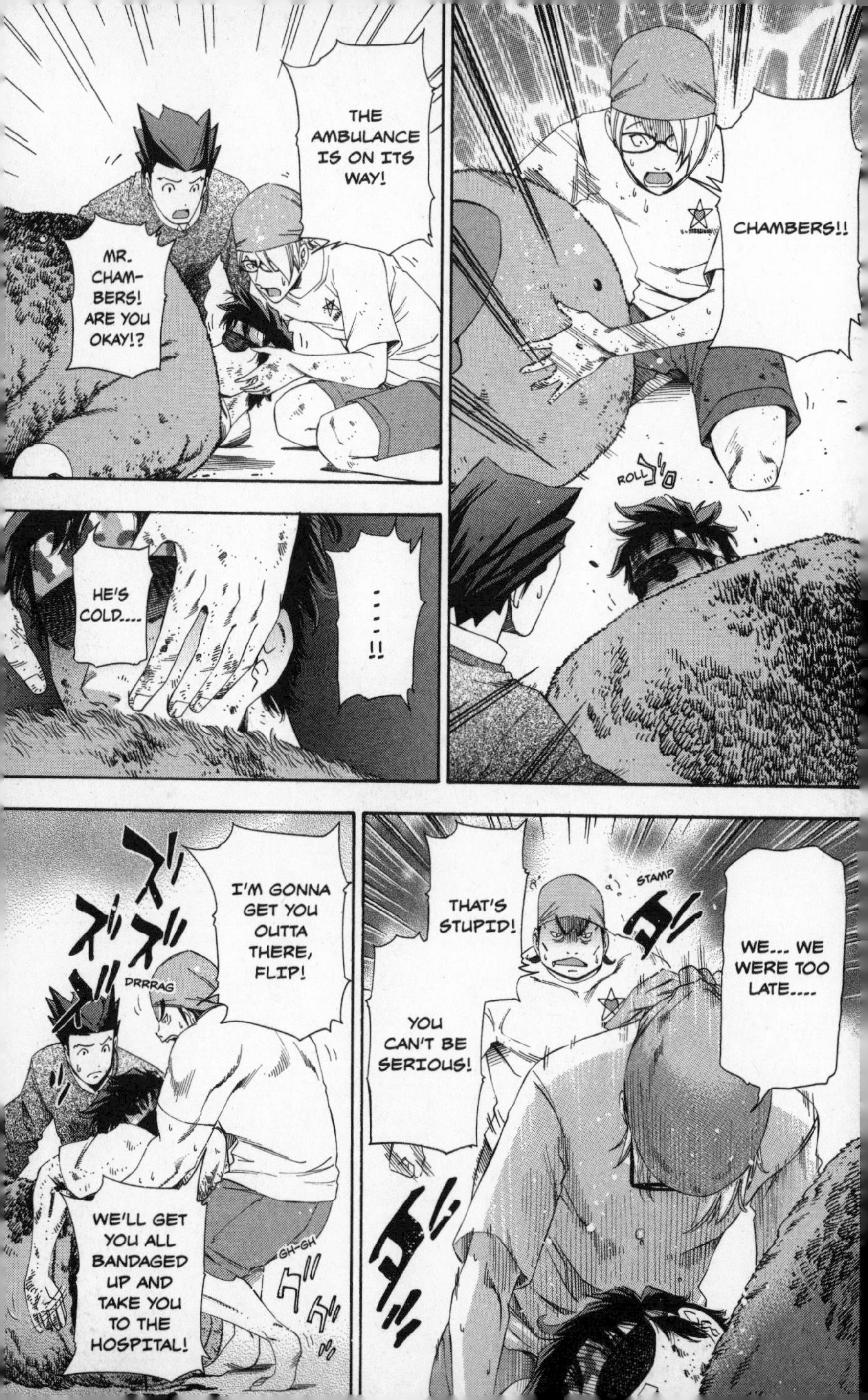
CHAMBERS!!
ROLL
THE AMBULANCE IS ON ITS WAY!
MR. CHAM-BERS! ARE YOU OKAY!?
HE'S COLD....
....!!
WE... WE WERE TOO LATE....
STAMP
THAT'S STUPID!
YOU CAN'T BE SERIOUS!
I'M GONNA GET YOU OUTTA THERE, FLIP!
DRRRAG
WE'LL GET YOU ALL BANDAGED UP AND TAKE YOU TO THE HOSPITAL!
GH-GH

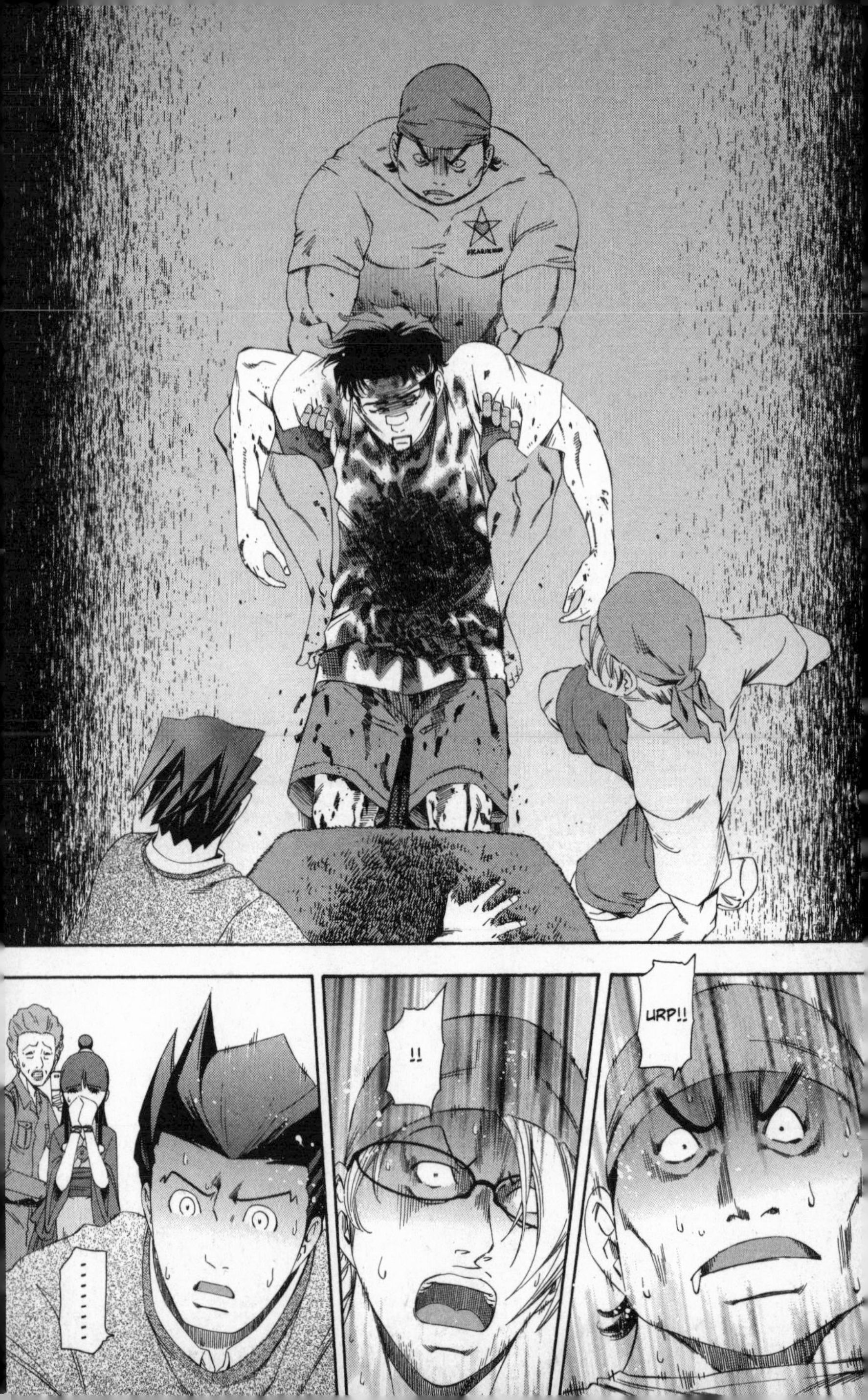
URP!!
!!
......!

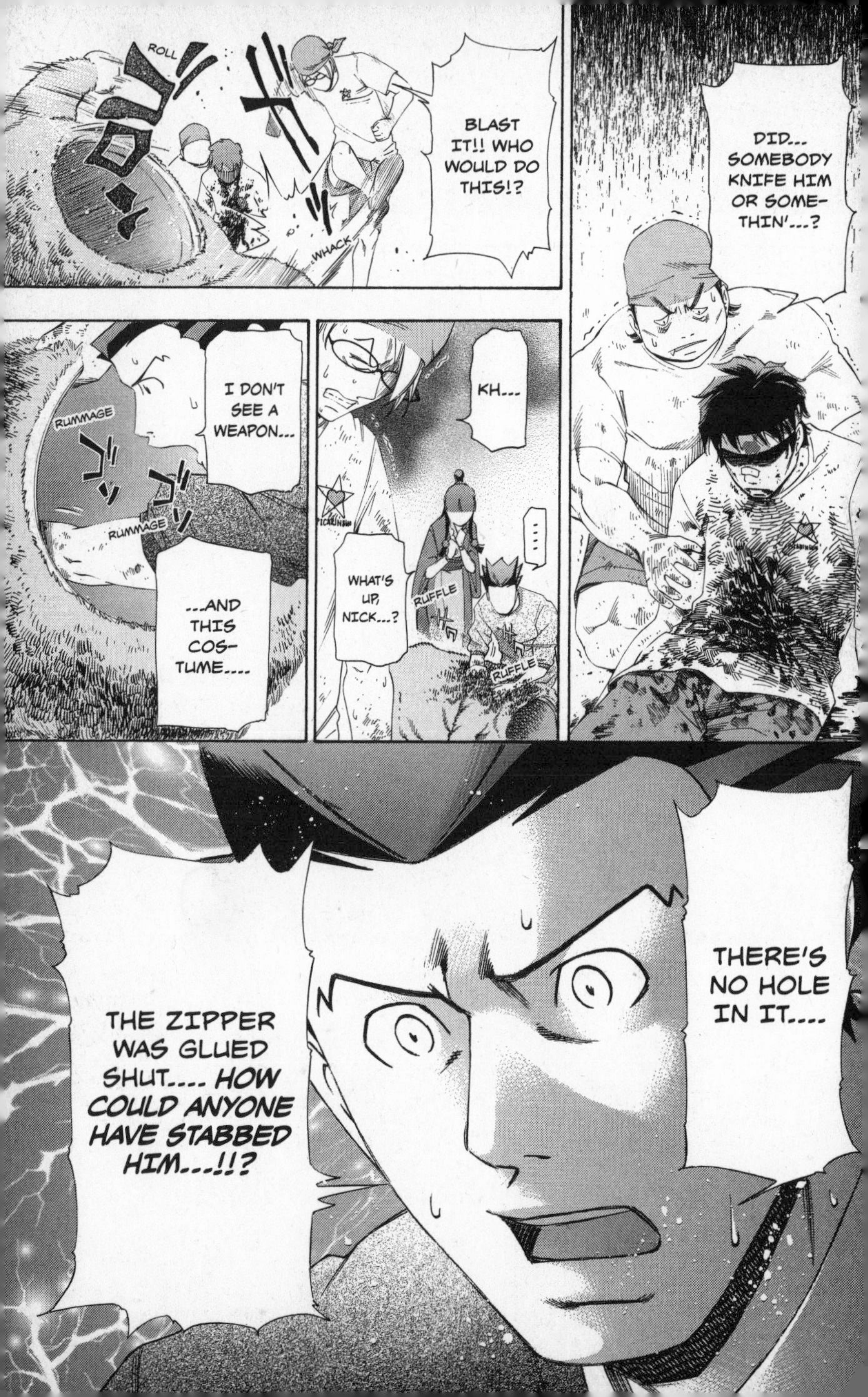
DID... SOMEBODY KNIFE HIM OR SOME- THIN'...?
BLAST IT!! WHO WOULD DO THIS!?
ROLL
WHACK
KH...
...
WHAT'S UP, NICK...?
RUFFLE
RUFFLE
I DON'T SEE A WEAPON...
RUMMAGE
RUMMAGE
...AND THIS COS- TUME....
THERE'S NO HOLE IN IT....
THE ZIPPER WAS GLUED SHUT.... *HOW COULD ANYONE HAVE STABBED HIM...!!?*

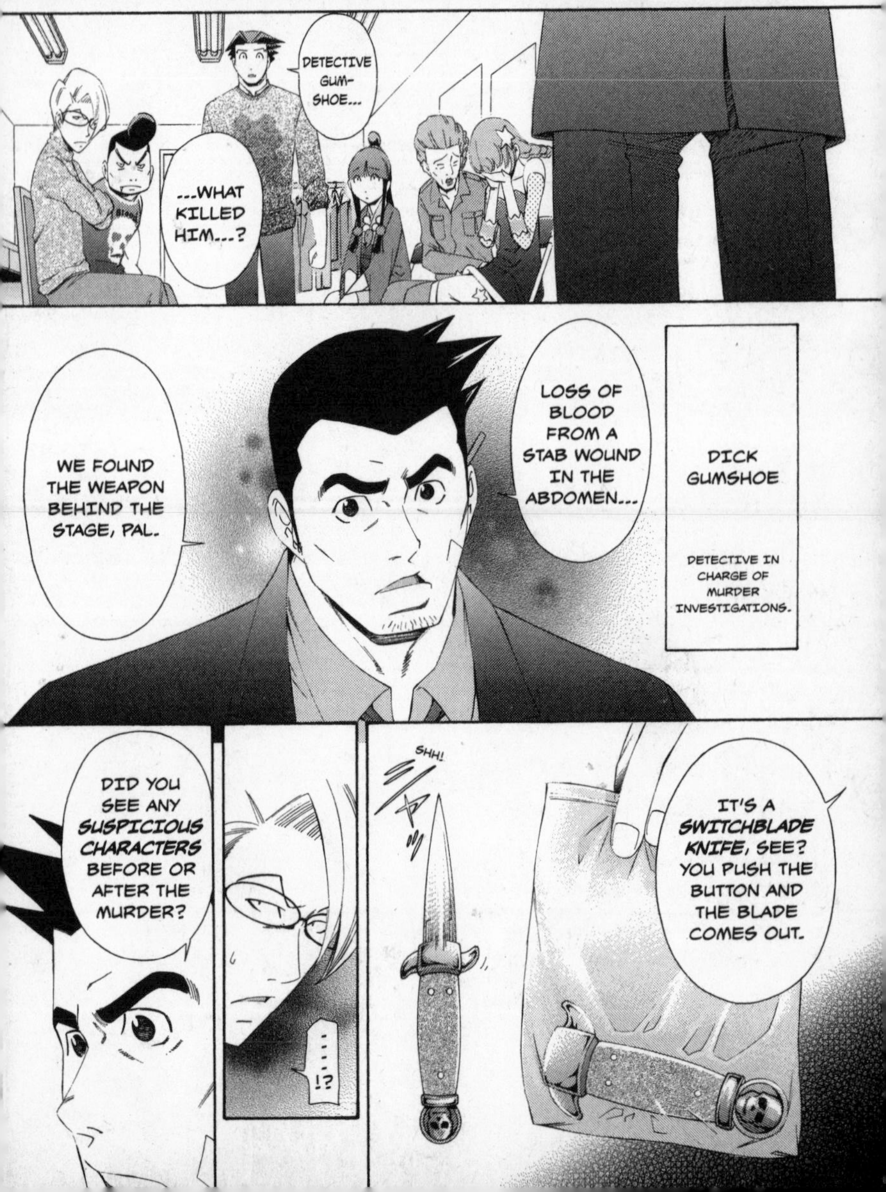
DETECTIVE GUM-SHOE...
...WHAT KILLED HIM...?
DICK GUMSHOE
DETECTIVE IN CHARGE OF MURDER INVESTIGATIONS.
LOSS OF BLOOD FROM A STAB WOUND IN THE ABDOMEN...
WE FOUND THE WEAPON BEHIND THE STAGE, PAL.
IT'S A *SWITCHBLADE KNIFE*, SEE? YOU PUSH THE BUTTON AND THE BLADE COMES OUT.
SHH!
......
!?
DID YOU SEE ANY *SUSPICIOUS CHARACTERS* BEFORE OR AFTER THE MURDER?

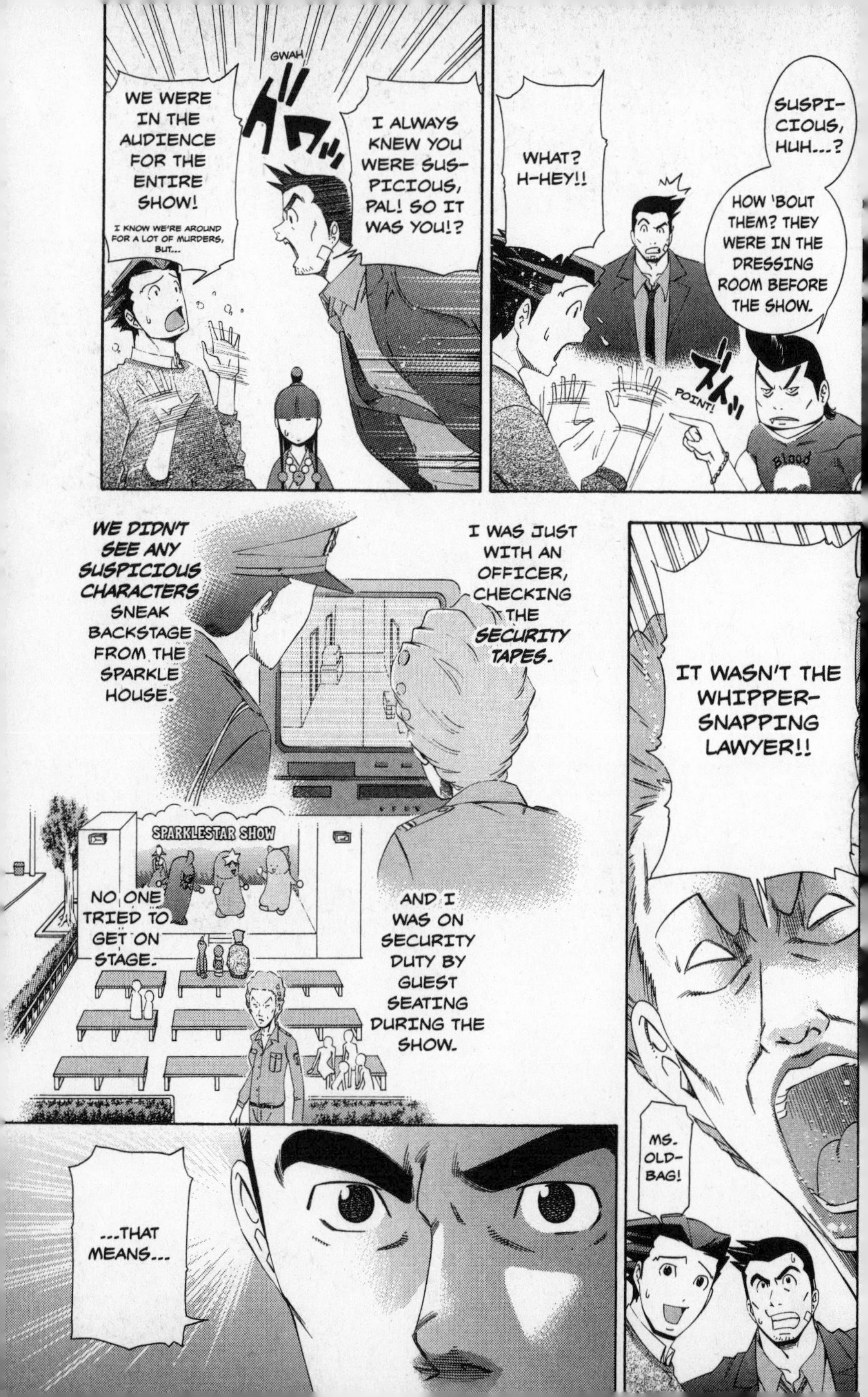
SUSPI-CIOUS, HUH...?
HOW 'BOUT THEM? THEY WERE IN THE DRESSING ROOM BEFORE THE SHOW.
WHAT? H-HEY!!
POINT!
GWAH
I ALWAYS KNEW YOU WERE SUS-PICIOUS, PAL! SO IT WAS YOU!?
WE WERE IN THE AUDIENCE FOR THE ENTIRE SHOW!
I KNOW WE'RE AROUND FOR A LOT OF MURDERS, BUT...
IT WASN'T THE WHIPPER-SNAPPING LAWYER!!
MS. OLD-BAG!
I WAS JUST WITH AN OFFICER, CHECKING THE SECURITY TAPES.
WE DIDN'T SEE ANY SUSPICIOUS CHARACTERS SNEAK BACKSTAGE FROM THE SPARKLE HOUSE.
AND I WAS ON SECURITY DUTY BY GUEST SEATING DURING THE SHOW.
SPARKLESTAR SHOW
NO ONE TRIED TO GET ON STAGE.
...THAT MEANS...

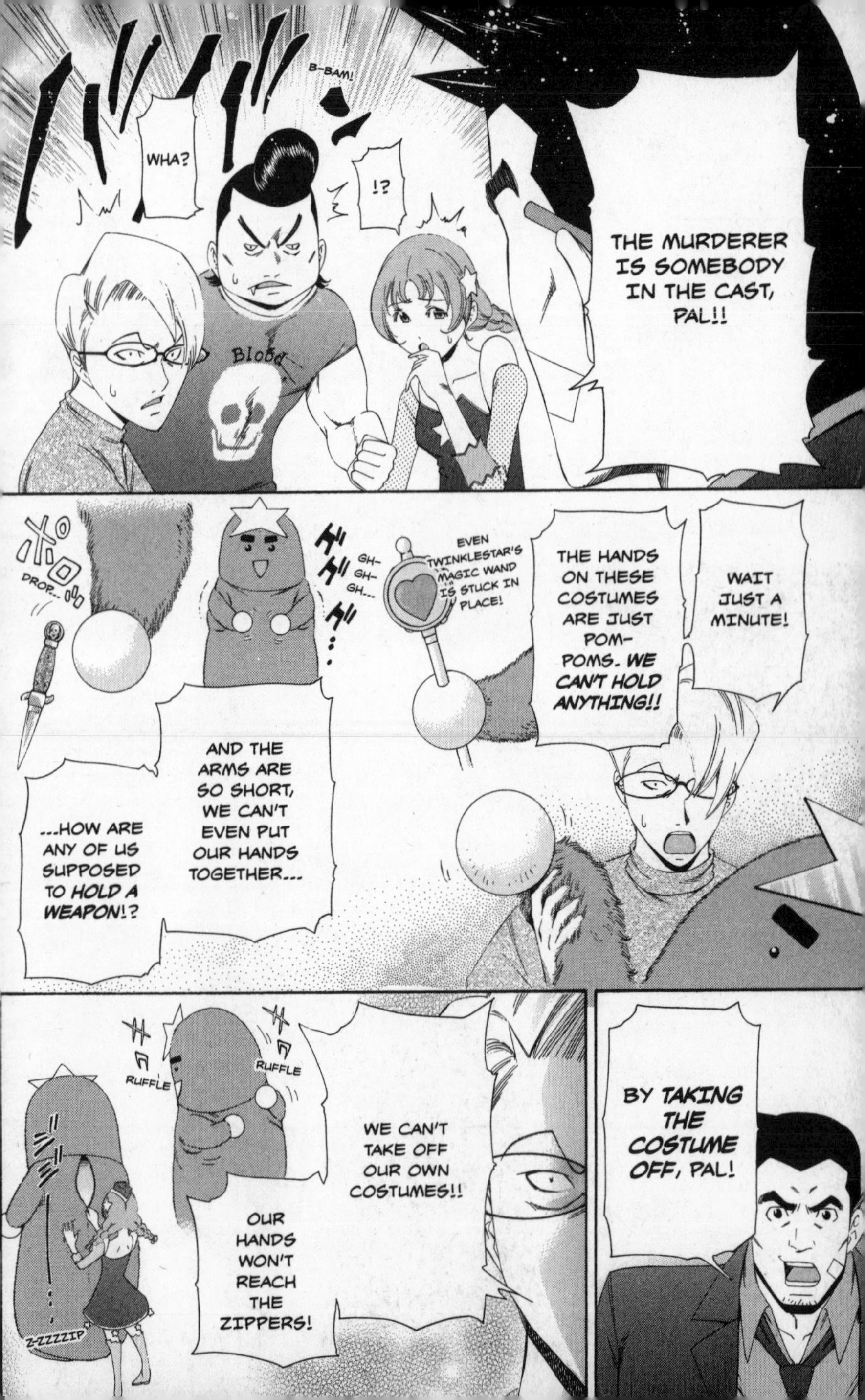
B-BAM!
THE MURDERER IS SOMEBODY IN THE CAST, PAL!!
!?
WHA?
WAIT JUST A MINUTE!
THE HANDS ON THESE COSTUMES ARE JUST POM-POMS. WE CAN'T HOLD ANYTHING!!
EVEN TWINKLESTAR'S MAGIC WAND IS STUCK IN PLACE!
GH-GH-GH...
DROP...
AND THE ARMS ARE SO SHORT, WE CAN'T EVEN PUT OUR HANDS TOGETHER...
...HOW ARE ANY OF US SUPPOSED TO HOLD A WEAPON!?
BY TAKING THE COSTUME OFF, PAL!
WE CAN'T TAKE OFF OUR OWN COSTUMES!!
RUFFLE
RUFFLE
OUR HANDS WON'T REACH THE ZIPPERS!
Z-ZZZZIP

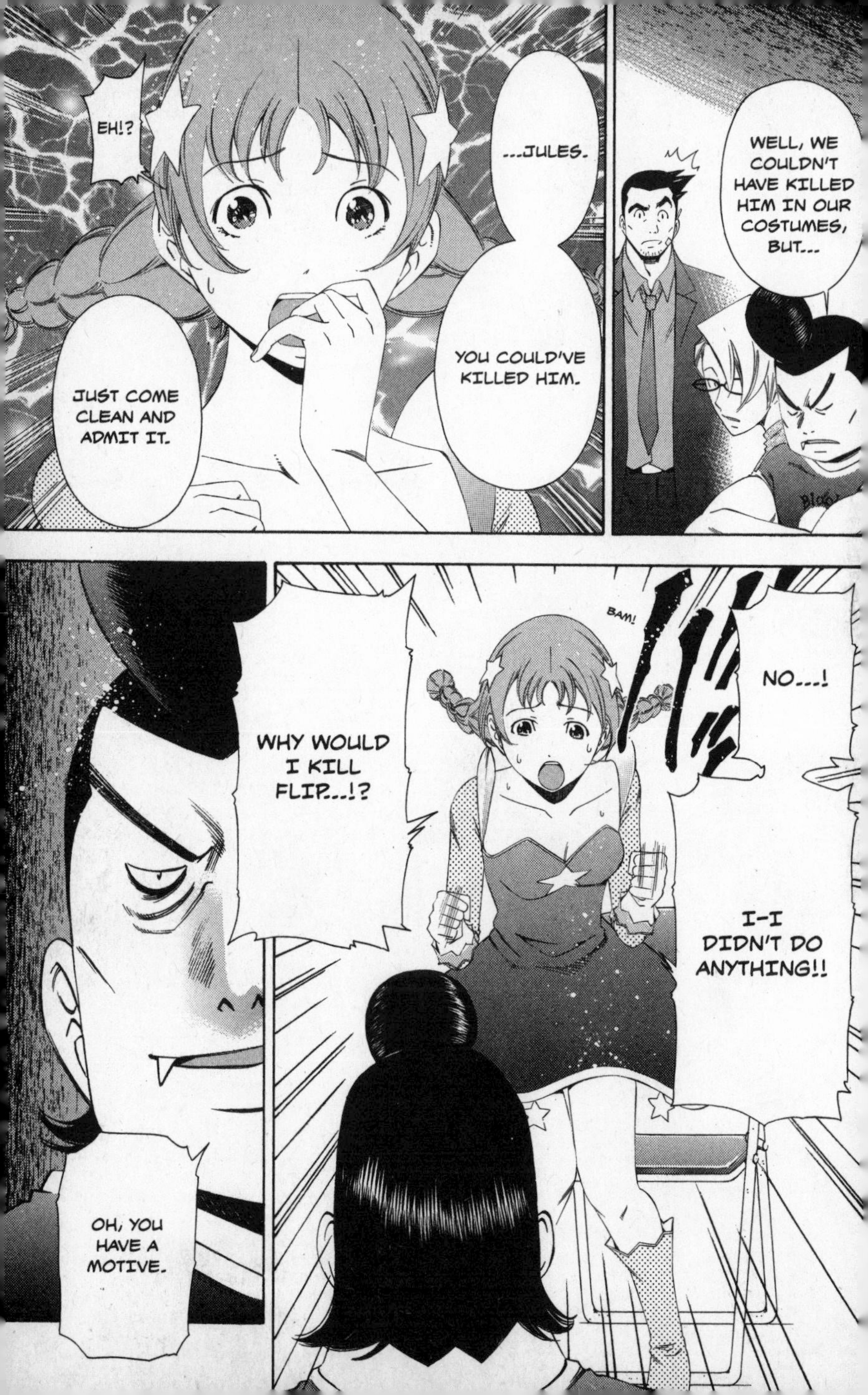
WELL, WE COULDN'T HAVE KILLED HIM IN OUR COSTUMES, BUT...
...JULES.
YOU COULD'VE KILLED HIM.
EH!?
JUST COME CLEAN AND ADMIT IT.
BAM!
NO...!
I-I DIDN'T DO ANYTHING!!
WHY WOULD I KILL FLIP...!?
OH, YOU HAVE A MOTIVE.

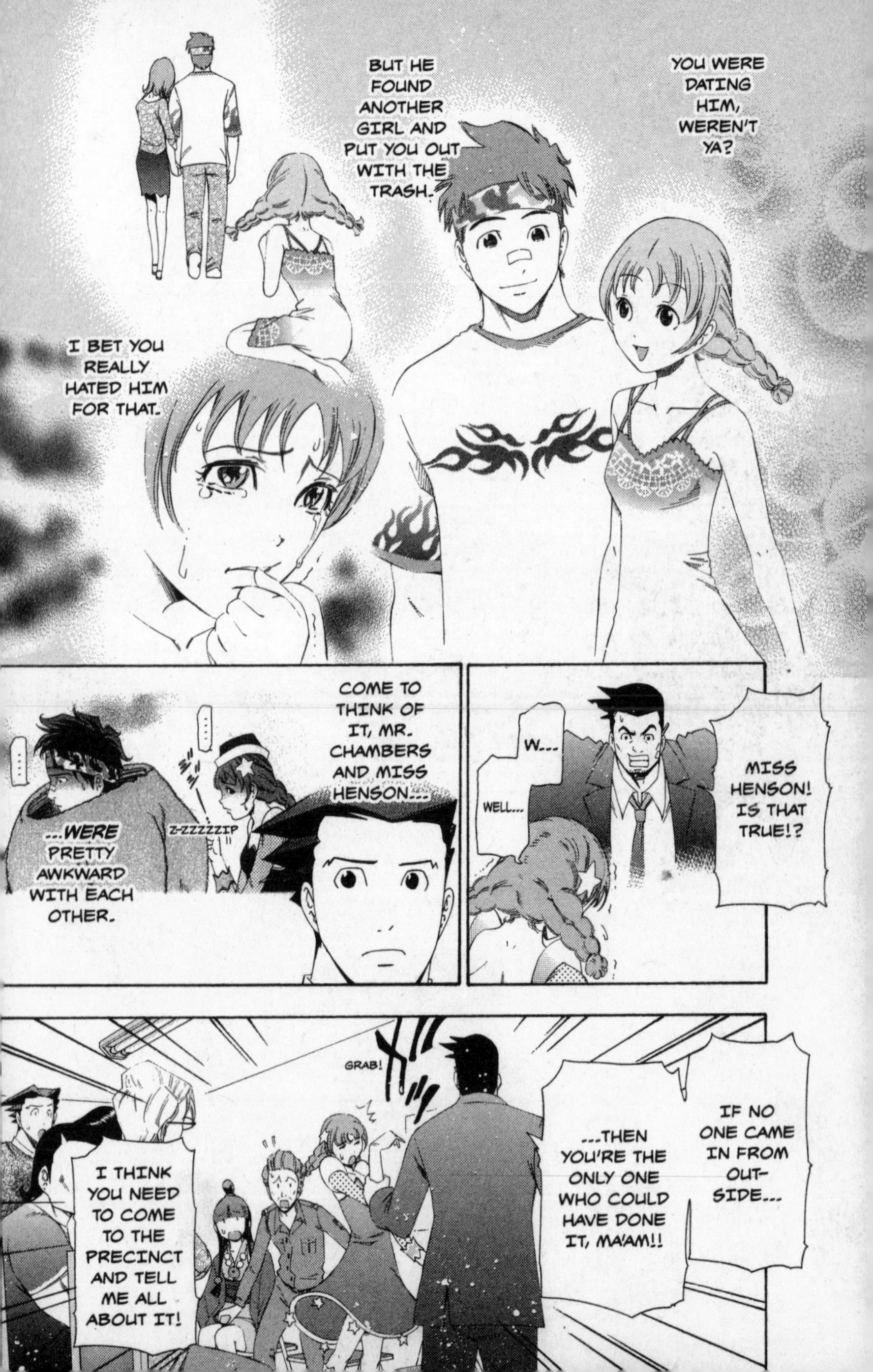
YOU WERE DATING HIM, WEREN'T YA?
BUT HE FOUND ANOTHER GIRL AND PUT YOU OUT WITH THE TRASH.
I BET YOU REALLY HATED HIM FOR THAT.
MISS HENSON! IS THAT TRUE!?
W...
WELL...
COME TO THINK OF IT, MR. CHAMBERS AND MISS HENSON...
...
...
Z-ZZZZZIP
...WERE PRETTY AWKWARD WITH EACH OTHER.
IF NO ONE CAME IN FROM OUT-SIDE...
...THEN YOU'RE THE ONLY ONE WHO COULD HAVE DONE IT, MA'AM!!
GRAB!
I THINK YOU NEED TO COME TO THE PRECINCT AND TELL ME ALL ABOUT IT!

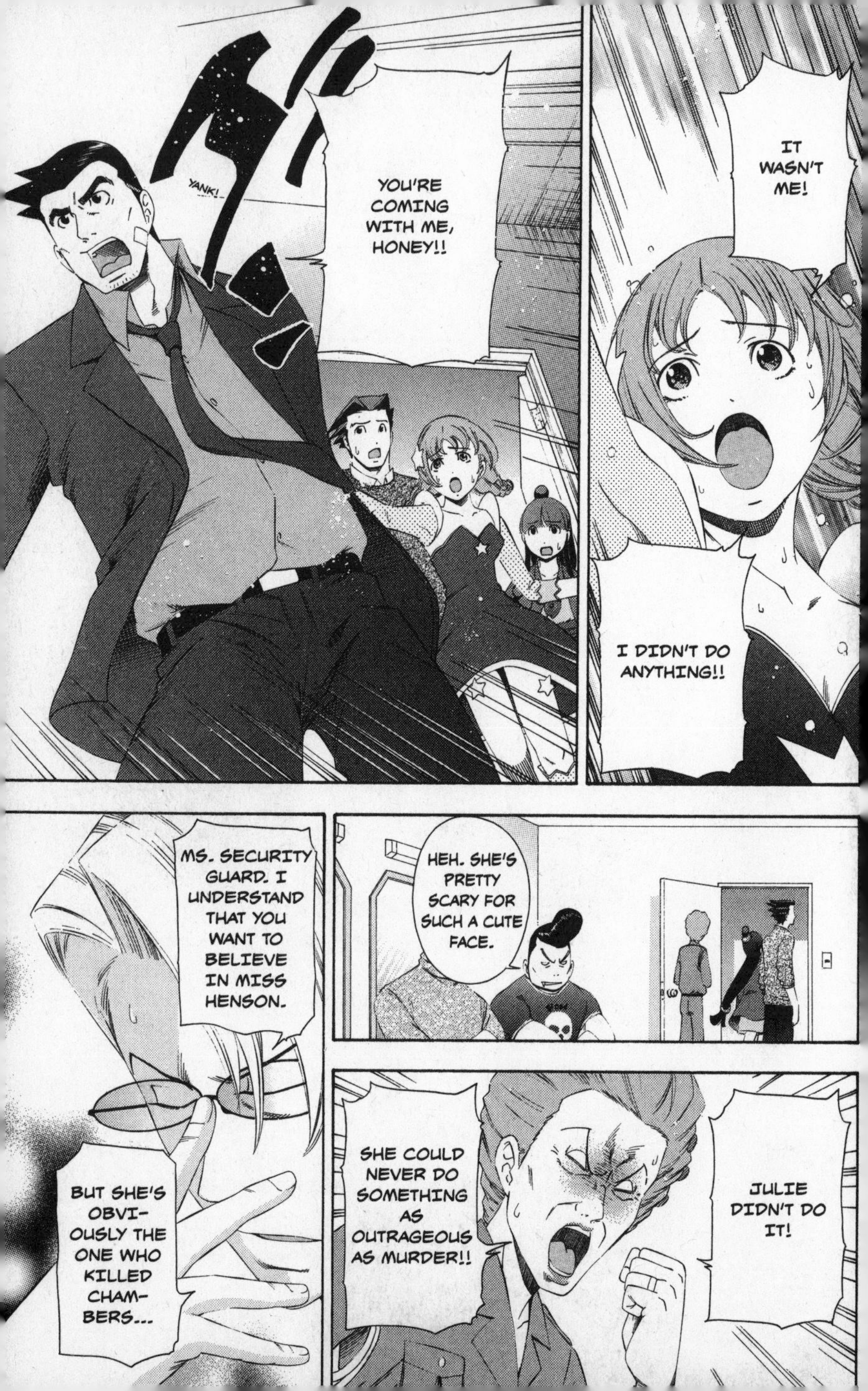
IT WASN'T ME!
I DIDN'T DO ANYTHING!!
YOU'RE COMING WITH ME, HONEY!!
YANK!
HEH. SHE'S PRETTY SCARY FOR SUCH A CUTE FACE.
JULIE DIDN'T DO IT!
SHE COULD NEVER DO SOMETHING AS OUTRAGEOUS AS MURDER!!
MS. SECURITY GUARD. I UNDERSTAND THAT YOU WANT TO BELIEVE IN MISS HENSON.
BUT SHE'S OBVI-OUSLY THE ONE WHO KILLED CHAM-BERS...

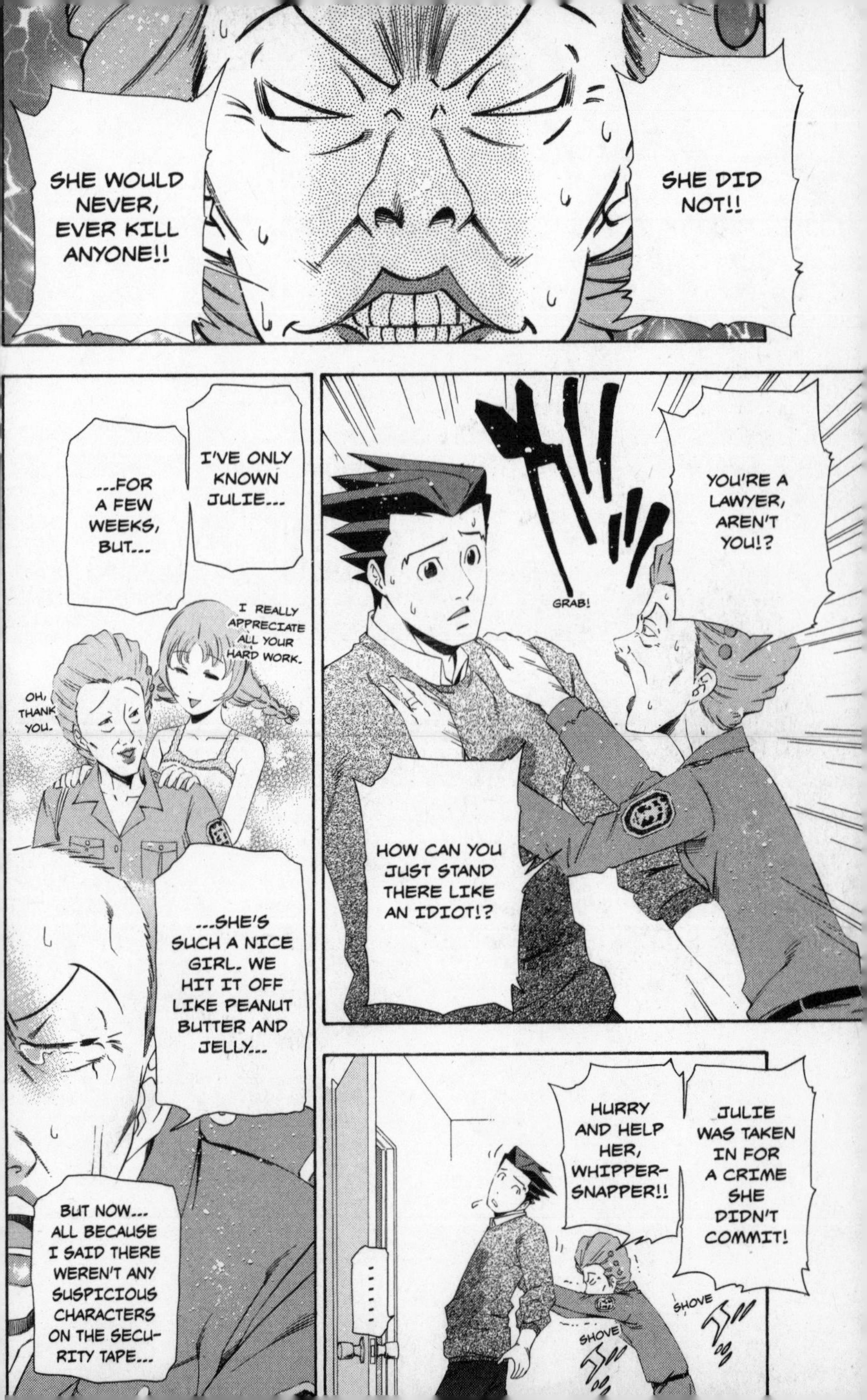

SHE DID NOT!!
SHE WOULD NEVER, EVER KILL ANYONE!!
YOU'RE A LAWYER, AREN'T YOU!?
GRAB!
HOW CAN YOU JUST STAND THERE LIKE AN IDIOT!?
JULIE WAS TAKEN IN FOR A CRIME SHE DIDN'T COMMIT!
HURRY AND HELP HER, WHIPPER-SNAPPER!!
SHOVE
SHOVE
I'VE ONLY KNOWN JULIE...
...FOR A FEW WEEKS, BUT...
I REALLY APPRECIATE ALL YOUR HARD WORK.
OH, THANK YOU.
...SHE'S SUCH A NICE GIRL. WE HIT IT OFF LIKE PEANUT BUTTER AND JELLY...
BUT NOW... ALL BECAUSE I SAID THERE WEREN'T ANY SUSPICIOUS CHARACTERS ON THE SECU-RITY TAPE...

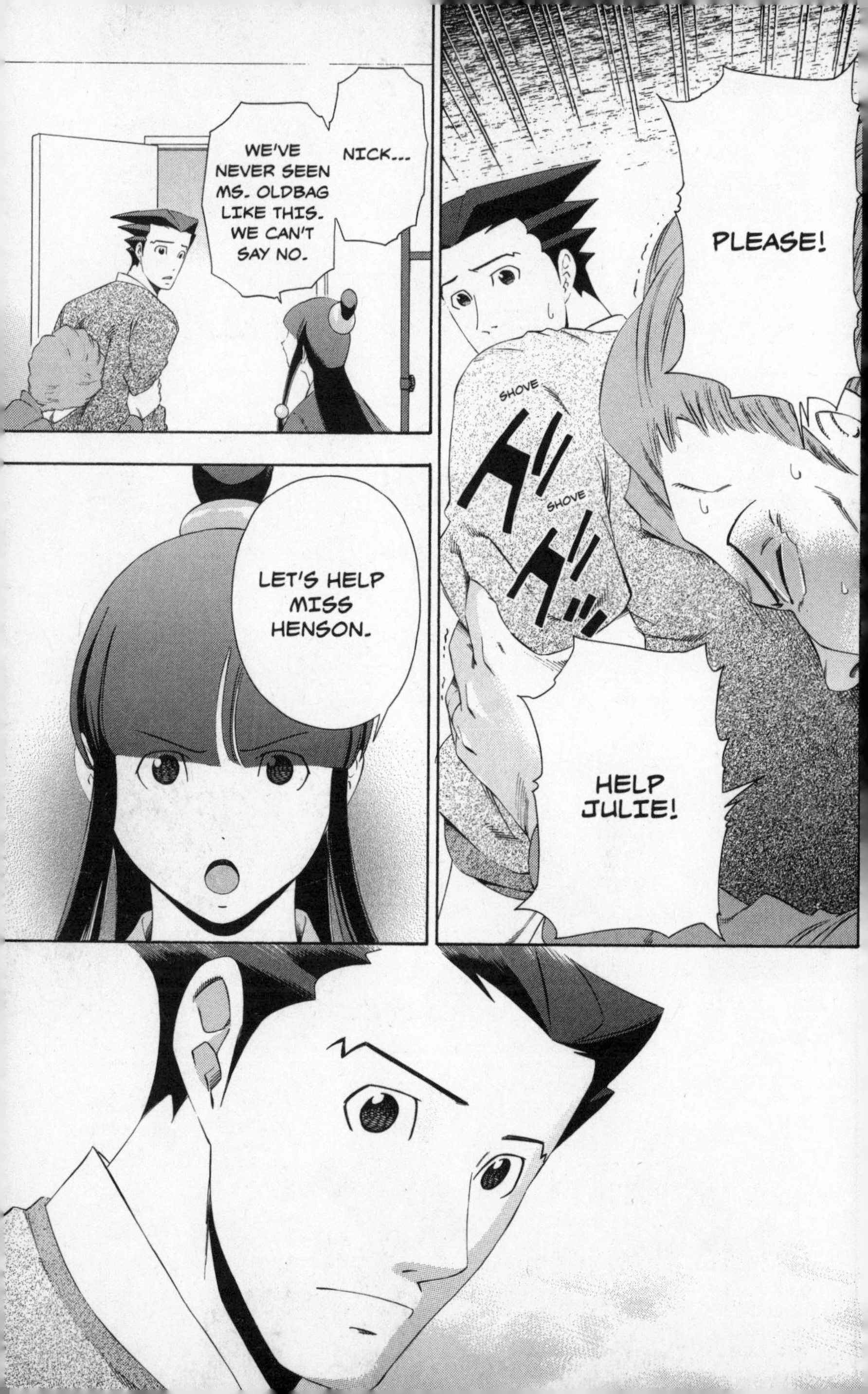
PLEASE!
SHOVE
SHOVE
HELP JULIE!
NICK...
WE'VE NEVER SEEN MS. OLDBAG LIKE THIS. WE CAN'T SAY NO.
LET'S HELP MISS HENSON.

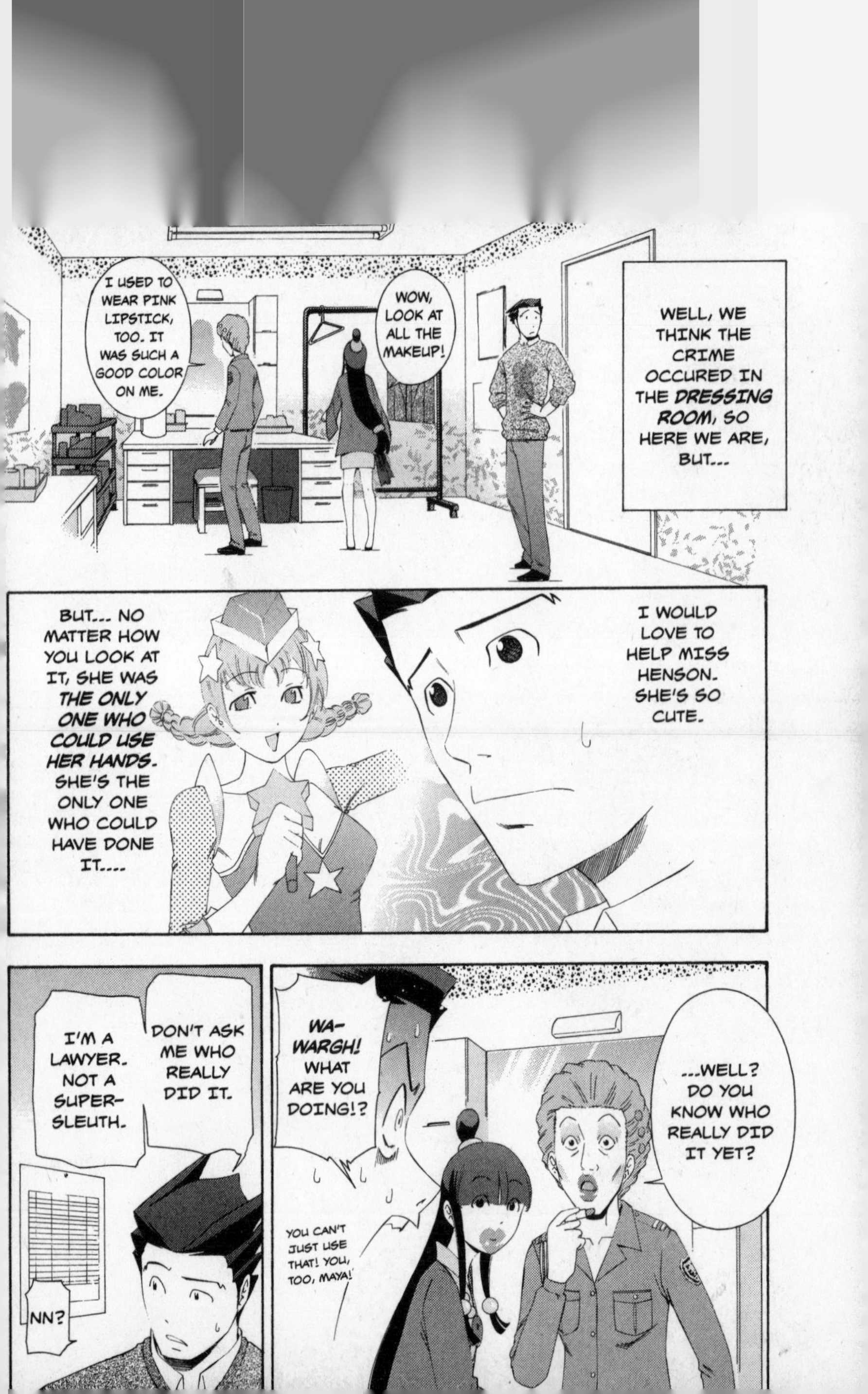
WELL, WE THINK THE CRIME OCCURED IN THE *DRESSING ROOM*, SO HERE WE ARE, BUT...
WOW, LOOK AT ALL THE MAKEUP!
I USED TO WEAR PINK LIPSTICK, TOO. IT WAS SUCH A GOOD COLOR ON ME.
I WOULD LOVE TO HELP MISS HENSON. SHE'S SO CUTE.
BUT... NO MATTER HOW YOU LOOK AT IT, SHE WAS *THE ONLY ONE WHO COULD USE HER HANDS*. SHE'S THE ONLY ONE WHO COULD HAVE DONE IT....
...WELL? DO YOU KNOW WHO REALLY DID IT YET?
WA-WARGH! WHAT ARE YOU DOING!?
YOU CAN'T JUST USE THAT! YOU, TOO, MAYA!
DON'T ASK ME WHO REALLY DID IT.
I'M A LAWYER. NOT A SUPER-SLEUTH.
NN?

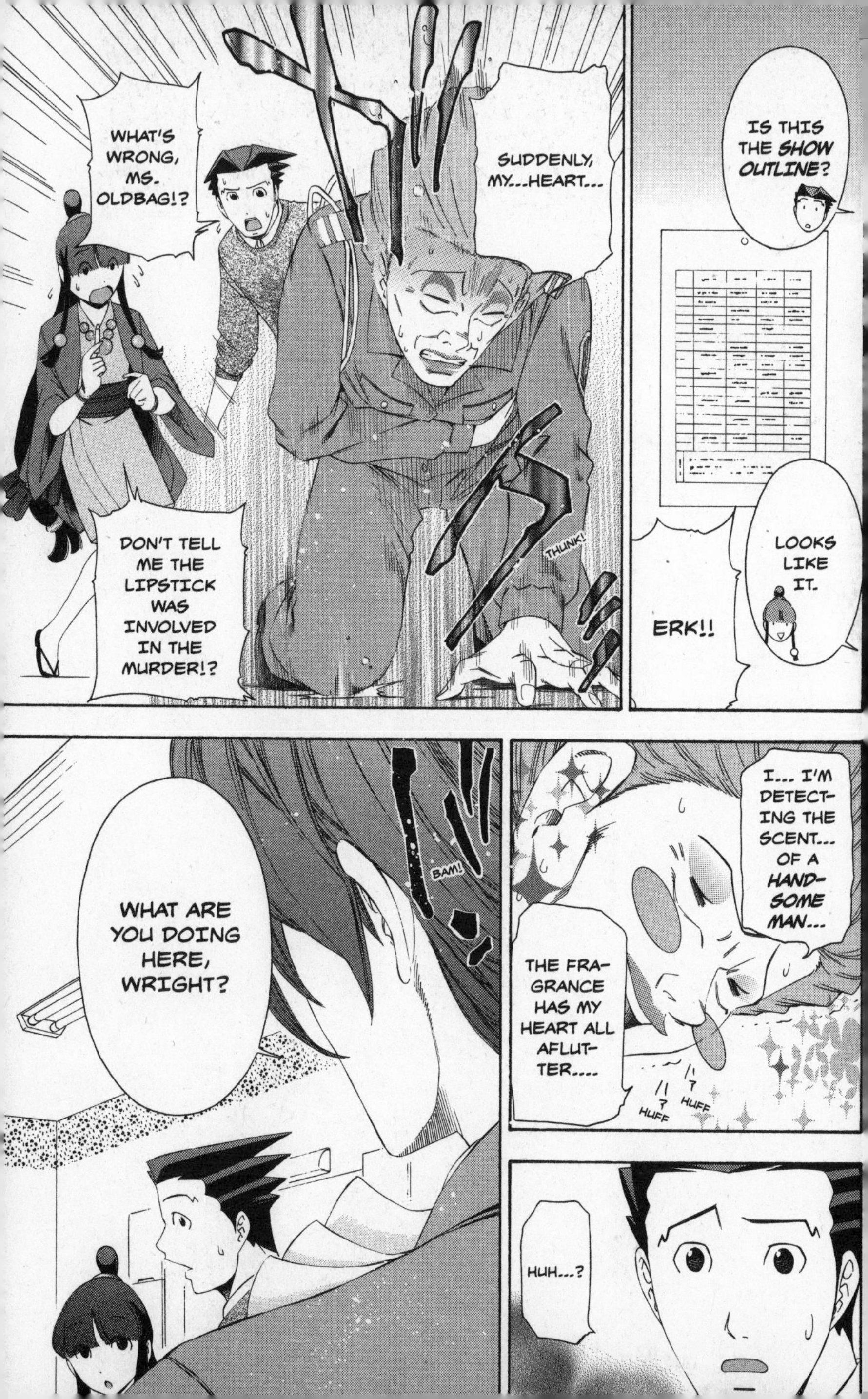
IS THIS THE SHOW OUTLINE?
LOOKS LIKE IT.
ERK!!
SUDDENLY, MY...HEART...
THUNK!
WHAT'S WRONG, MS. OLDBAG!?
DON'T TELL ME THE LIPSTICK WAS INVOLVED IN THE MURDER!?
I... I'M DETECTING THE SCENT... OF A HANDSOME MAN...
THE FRAGRANCE HAS MY HEART ALL AFLUTTER....
HUFF
HUFF
HUH...?
BAM!
WHAT ARE YOU DOING HERE, WRIGHT?

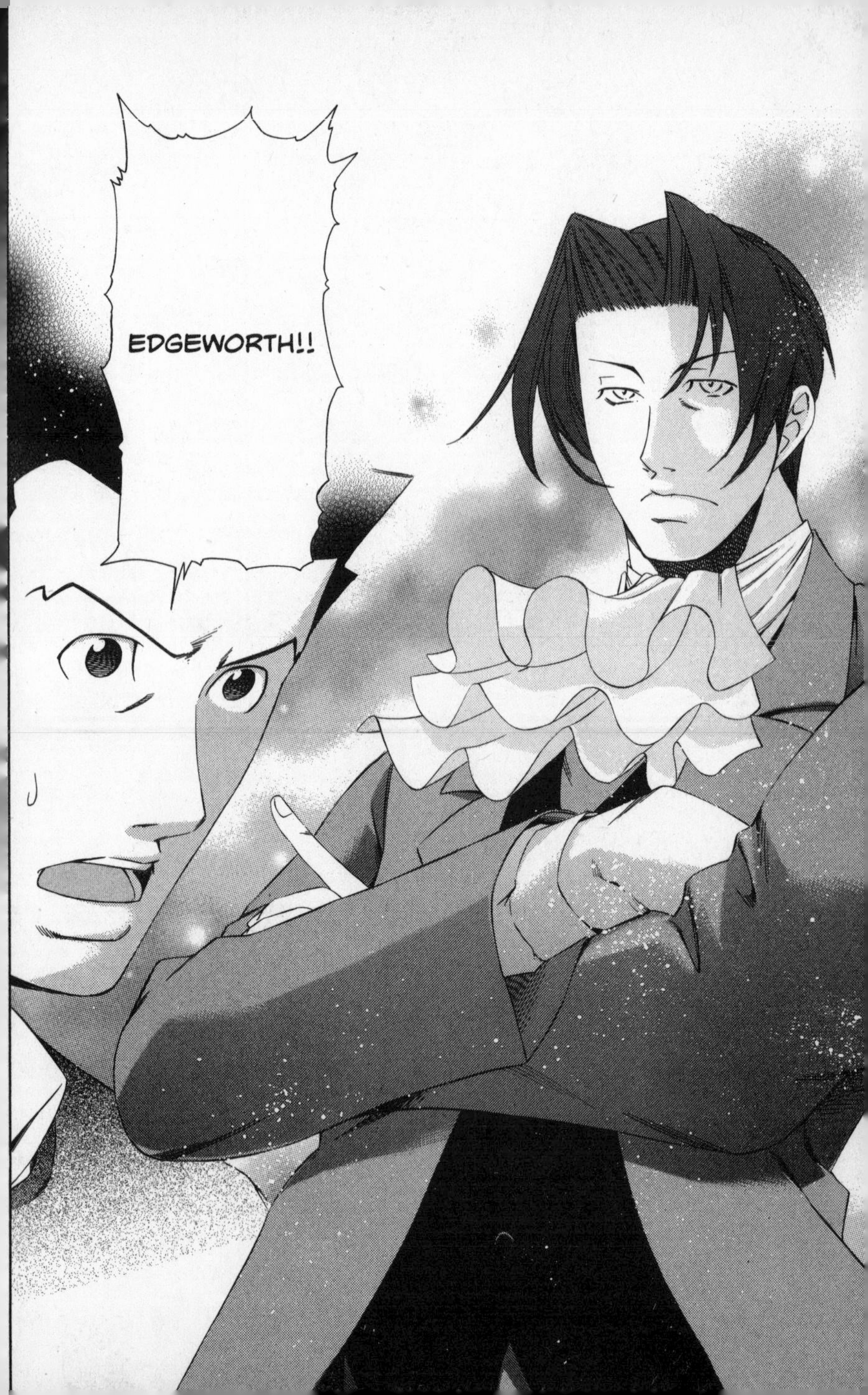
EDGEWORTH!!

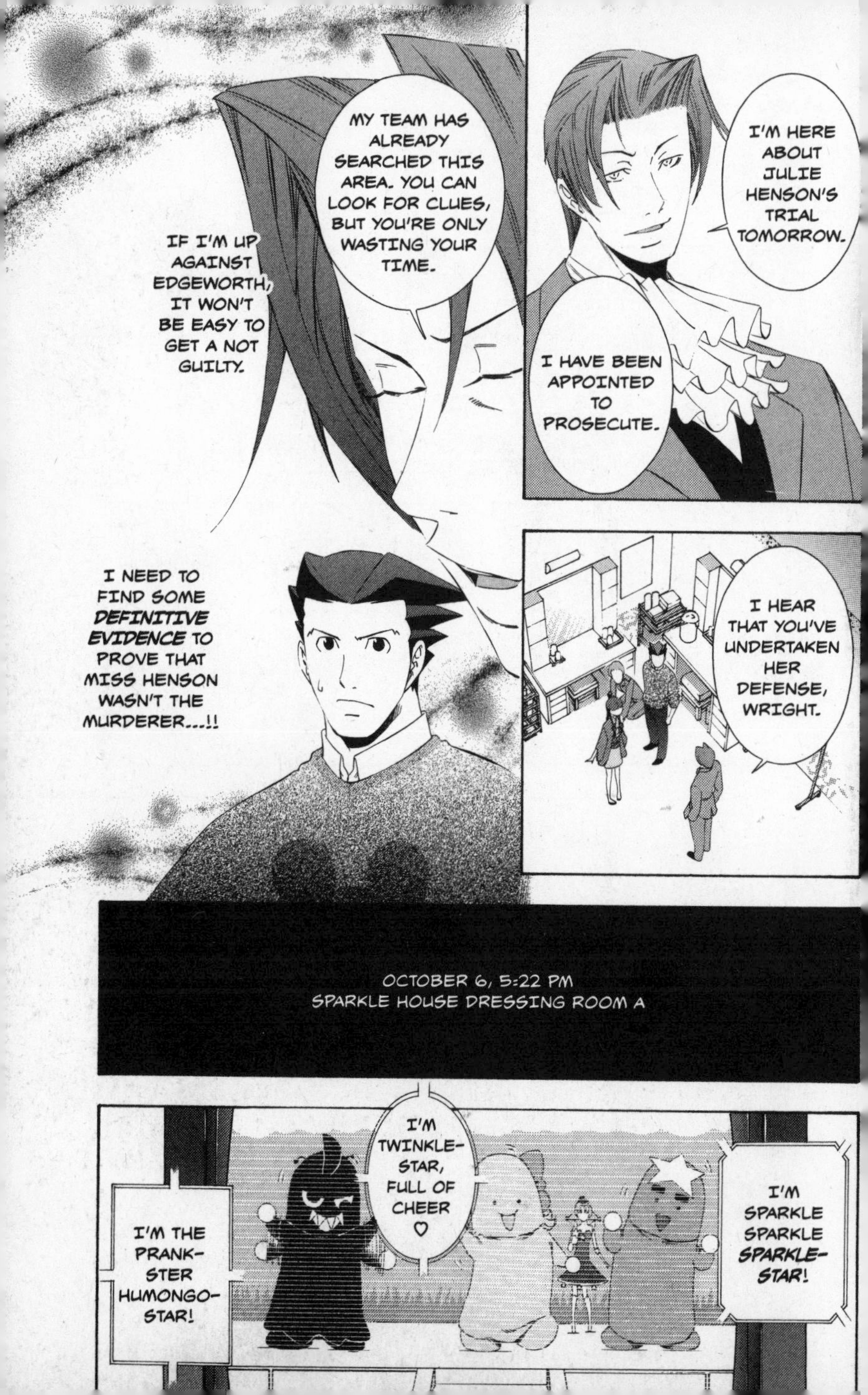
I'M HERE ABOUT JULIE HENSON'S TRIAL TOMORROW.
I HAVE BEEN APPOINTED TO PROSECUTE.
I HEAR THAT YOU'VE UNDERTAKEN HER DEFENSE, WRIGHT.
MY TEAM HAS ALREADY SEARCHED THIS AREA. YOU CAN LOOK FOR CLUES, BUT YOU'RE ONLY WASTING YOUR TIME.
IF I'M UP AGAINST EDGEWORTH, IT WON'T BE EASY TO GET A NOT GUILTY.
I NEED TO FIND SOME DEFINITIVE EVIDENCE TO PROVE THAT MISS HENSON WASN'T THE MURDERER...!!
OCTOBER 6, 5:22 PM
SPARKLE HOUSE DRESSING ROOM A
I'M SPARKLE SPARKLE SPARKLE-STAR!
I'M TWINKLE-STAR, FULL OF CHEER ♡
I'M THE PRANK-STER HUMONGO-STAR!

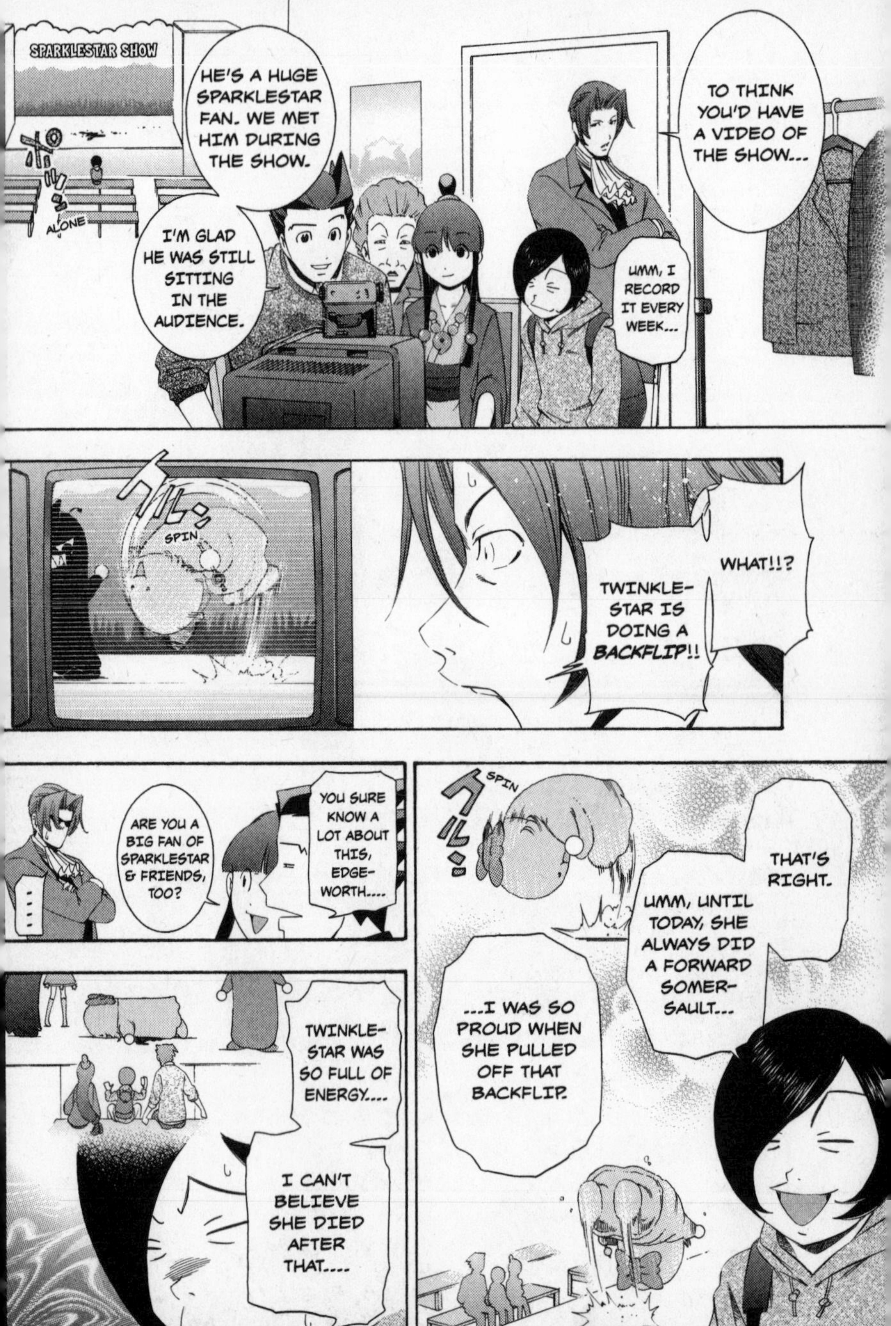
TO THINK YOU'D HAVE A VIDEO OF THE SHOW...
UMM, I RECORD IT EVERY WEEK...
HE'S A HUGE SPARKLESTAR FAN. WE MET HIM DURING THE SHOW.
I'M GLAD HE WAS STILL SITTING IN THE AUDIENCE.
SPARKLESTAR SHOW
ALONE
WHAT!!?
TWINKLE-STAR IS DOING A BACKFLIP!!
SPIN
SPIN
THAT'S RIGHT.
UMM, UNTIL TODAY, SHE ALWAYS DID A FORWARD SOMER-SAULT...
...I WAS SO PROUD WHEN SHE PULLED OFF THAT BACKFLIP.
YOU SURE KNOW A LOT ABOUT THIS, EDGE-WORTH....
ARE YOU A BIG FAN OF SPARKLESTAR & FRIENDS, TOO?
....
TWINKLE-STAR WAS SO FULL OF ENERGY....
I CAN'T BELIEVE SHE DIED AFTER THAT....

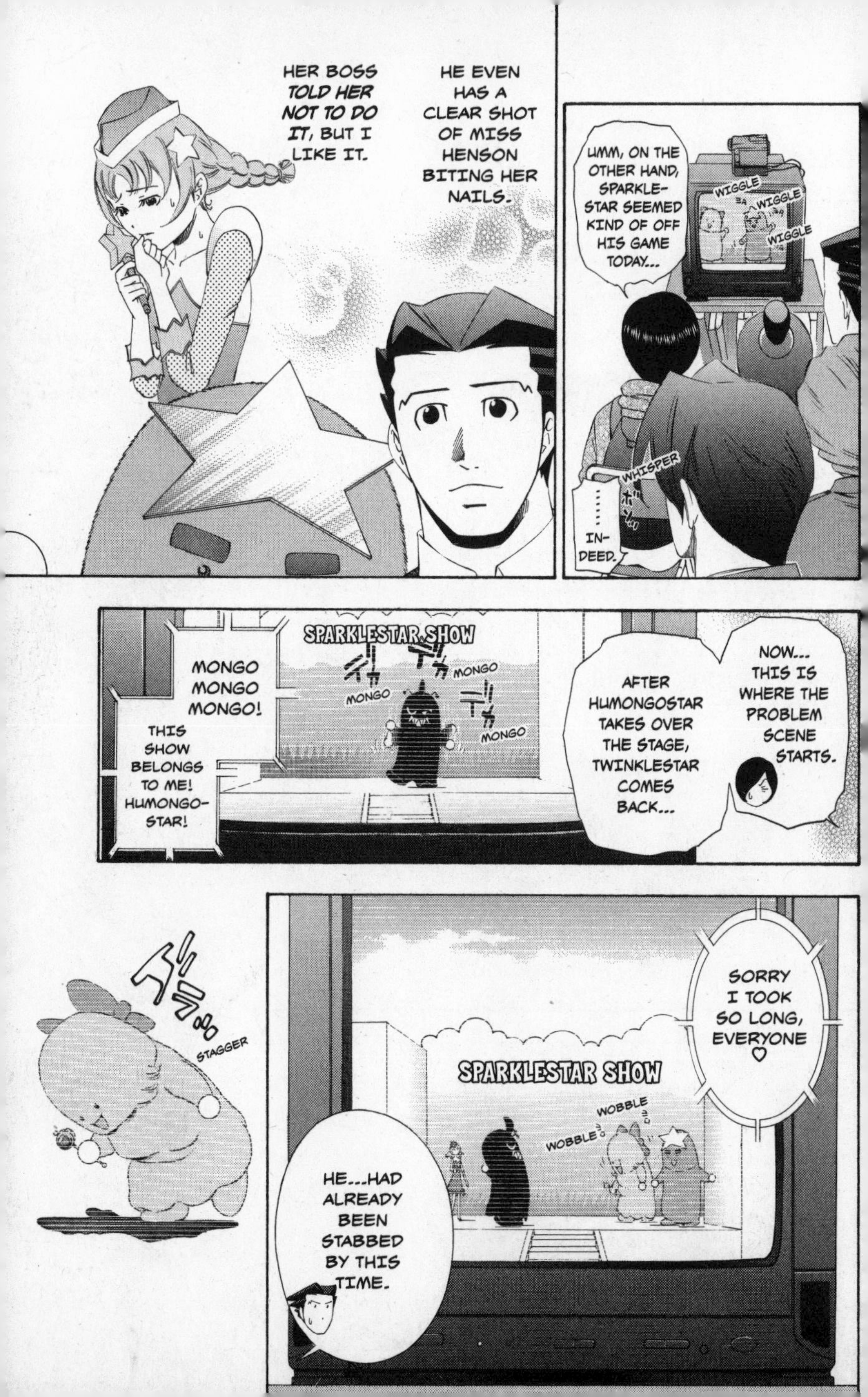
UMM, ON THE OTHER HAND, SPARKLE-STAR SEEMED KIND OF OFF HIS GAME TODAY...
WIGGLE
WIGGLE
WIGGLE
WHISPER
......
IN-DEED.
HE EVEN HAS A CLEAR SHOT OF MISS HENSON BITING HER NAILS.
HER BOSS *TOLD HER NOT TO DO IT*, BUT I LIKE IT.
NOW... THIS IS WHERE THE PROBLEM SCENE STARTS.
AFTER HUMONGOSTAR TAKES OVER THE STAGE, TWINKLESTAR COMES BACK...
SPARKLESTAR SHOW
MONGO
MONGO
MONGO
MONGO MONGO MONGO!
THIS SHOW BELONGS TO ME! HUMONGO-STAR!
SORRY I TOOK SO LONG, EVERYONE ♡
SPARKLESTAR SHOW
WOBBLE
WOBBLE
STAGGER
HE...HAD ALREADY BEEN STABBED BY THIS TIME.

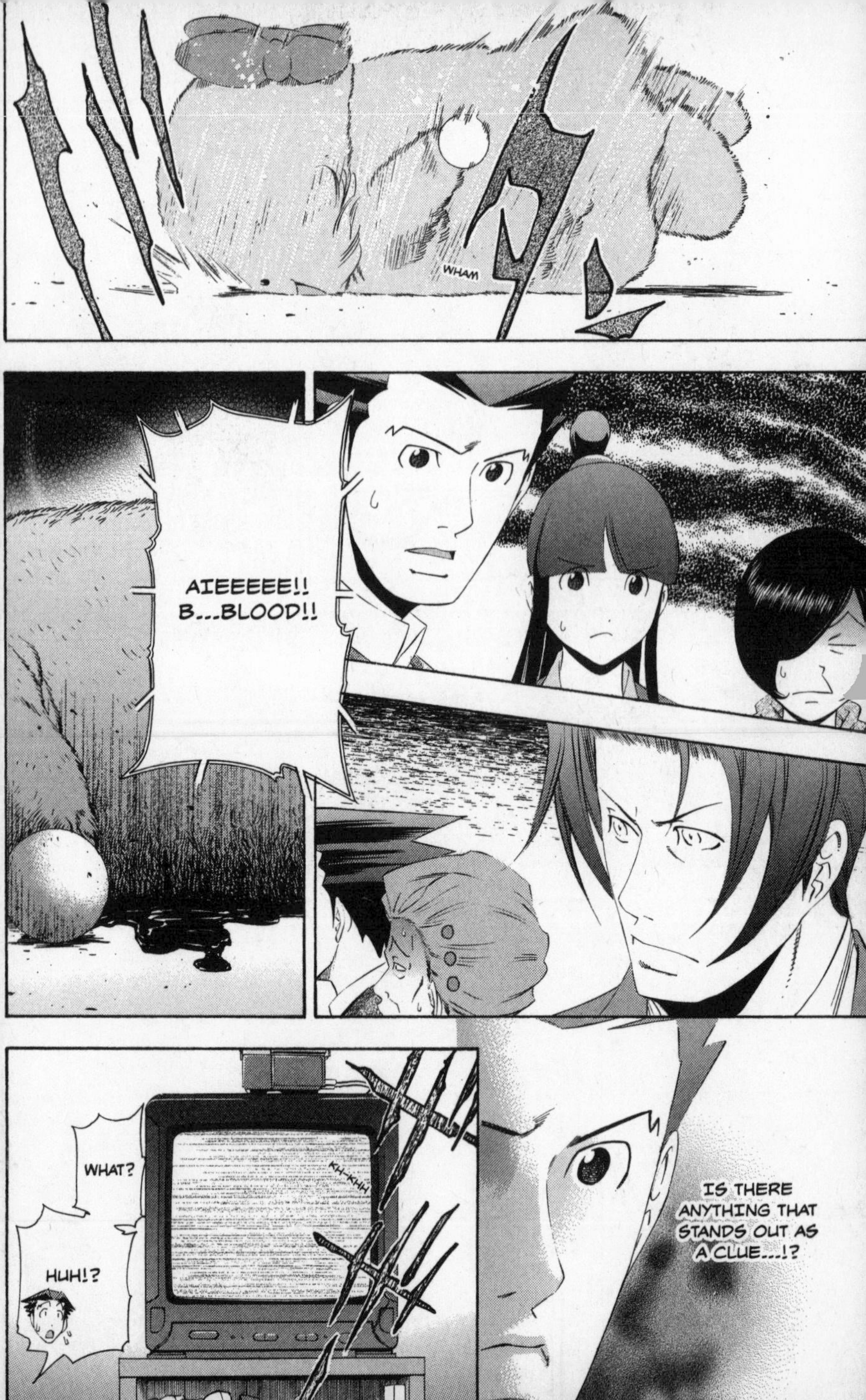
WHAM
AIEEEEE!! B...BLOOD!!
IS THERE ANYTHING THAT STANDS OUT AS A CLUE...!?
KH-KHH
WHAT?
HUH!?

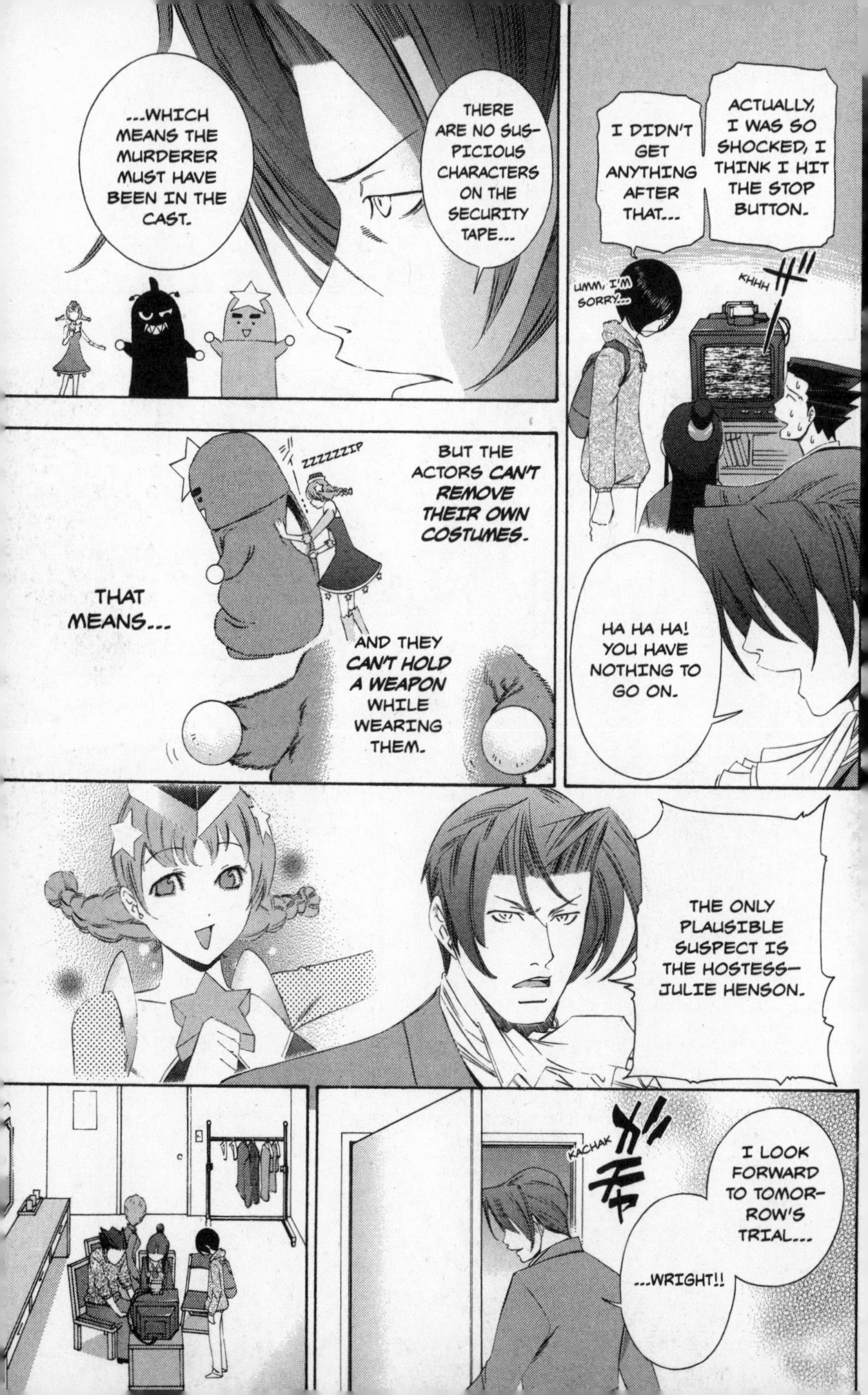
ACTUALLY, I WAS SO SHOCKED, I THINK I HIT THE STOP BUTTON.
I DIDN'T GET ANYTHING AFTER THAT...
KHHH
UMM, I'M SORRY...
HA HA HA! YOU HAVE NOTHING TO GO ON.
THERE ARE NO SUS-PICIOUS CHARACTERS ON THE SECURITY TAPE...
...WHICH MEANS THE MURDERER MUST HAVE BEEN IN THE CAST.
ZZZZZZIP
BUT THE ACTORS CAN'T REMOVE THEIR OWN COSTUMES.
AND THEY CAN'T HOLD A WEAPON WHILE WEARING THEM.
THAT MEANS...
THE ONLY PLAUSIBLE SUSPECT IS THE HOSTESS—JULIE HENSON.
KACHAK
I LOOK FORWARD TO TOMOR-ROW'S TRIAL...
...WRIGHT!!

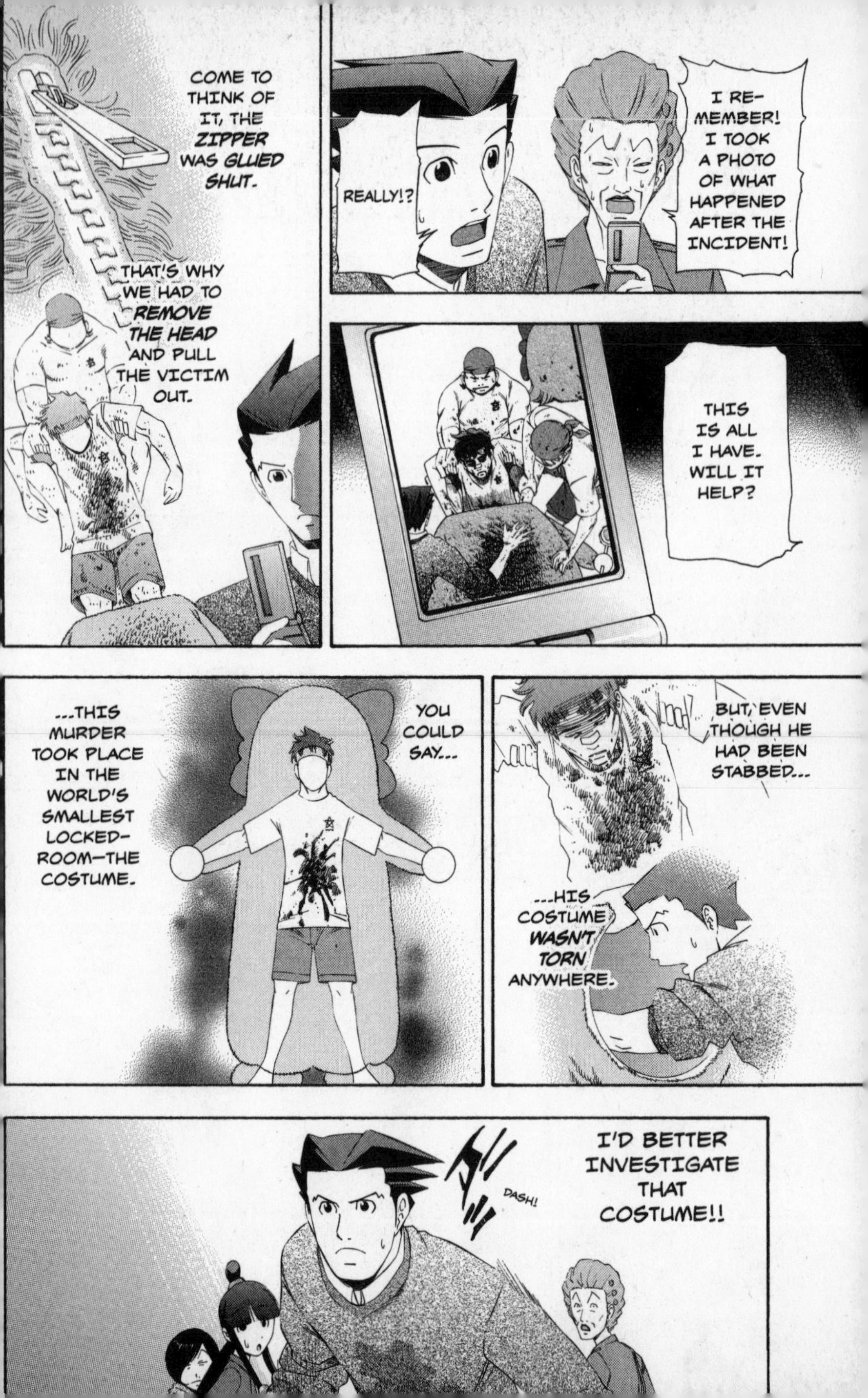

I REMEMBER! I TOOK A PHOTO OF WHAT HAPPENED AFTER THE INCIDENT!
REALLY!?
THIS IS ALL I HAVE. WILL IT HELP?
COME TO THINK OF IT, THE ZIPPER WAS GLUED SHUT.
THAT'S WHY WE HAD TO REMOVE THE HEAD AND PULL THE VICTIM OUT.
BUT, EVEN THOUGH HE HAD BEEN STABBED...
...HIS COSTUME WASN'T TORN ANYWHERE.
YOU COULD SAY...
...THIS MURDER TOOK PLACE IN THE WORLD'S SMALLEST LOCKED-ROOM—THE COSTUME.
I'D BETTER INVESTIGATE THAT COSTUME!!
DASH!

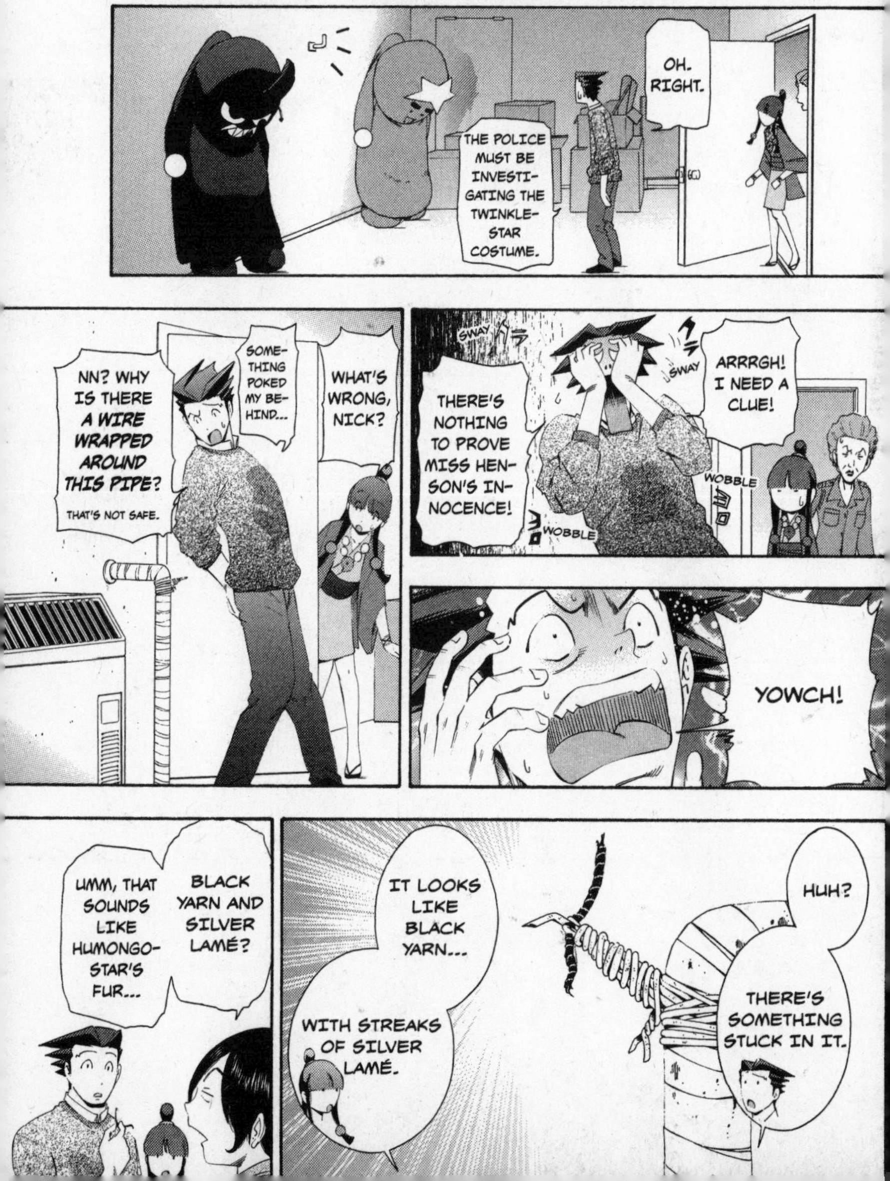
OH. RIGHT.
THE POLICE MUST BE INVESTIGATING THE TWINKLE-STAR COSTUME.
ARRRGH! I NEED A CLUE!
SWAY
SWAY
THERE'S NOTHING TO PROVE MISS HENSON'S INNOCENCE!
WOBBLE
WOBBLE
YOWCH!
WHAT'S WRONG, NICK?
SOMETHING POKED MY BEHIND...
NN? WHY IS THERE A WIRE WRAPPED AROUND THIS PIPE?
THAT'S NOT SAFE.
HUH?
THERE'S SOMETHING STUCK IN IT.
IT LOOKS LIKE BLACK YARN...
WITH STREAKS OF SILVER LAMÉ.
BLACK YARN AND SILVER LAMÉ?
UMM, THAT SOUNDS LIKE HUMONGO-STAR'S FUR...

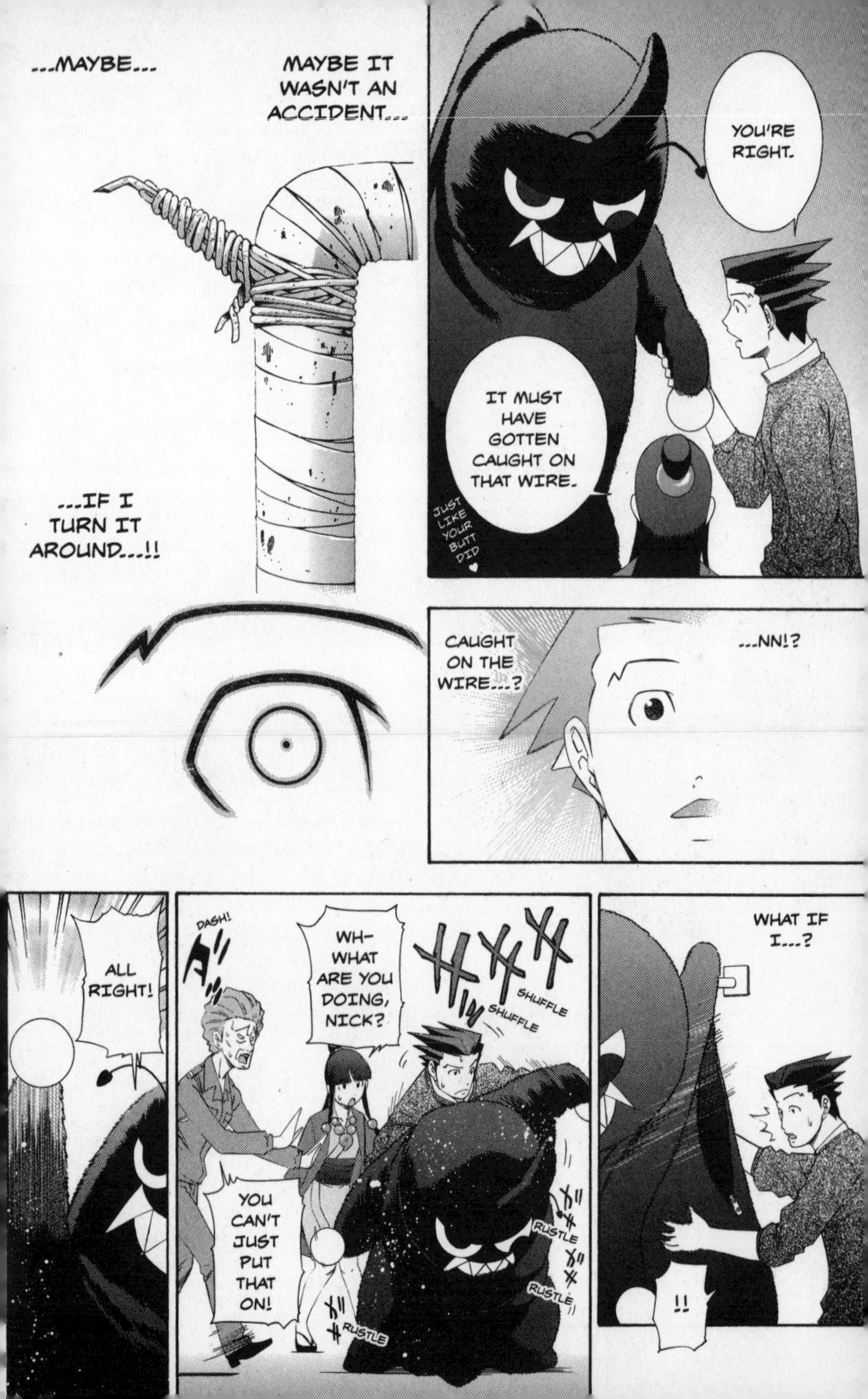
YOU'RE RIGHT.
IT MUST HAVE GOTTEN CAUGHT ON THAT WIRE.
JUST LIKE YOUR BUTT DID ♥
MAYBE IT WASN'T AN ACCIDENT...
...MAYBE...
...IF I TURN IT AROUND...!!
...NN!?
CAUGHT ON THE WIRE...?
WHAT IF I...?
!!
SHUFFLE
SHUFFLE
WH-WHAT ARE YOU DOING, NICK?
DASH!
RUSTLE
RUSTLE
YOU CAN'T JUST PUT THAT ON!
RUSTLE
ALL RIGHT!

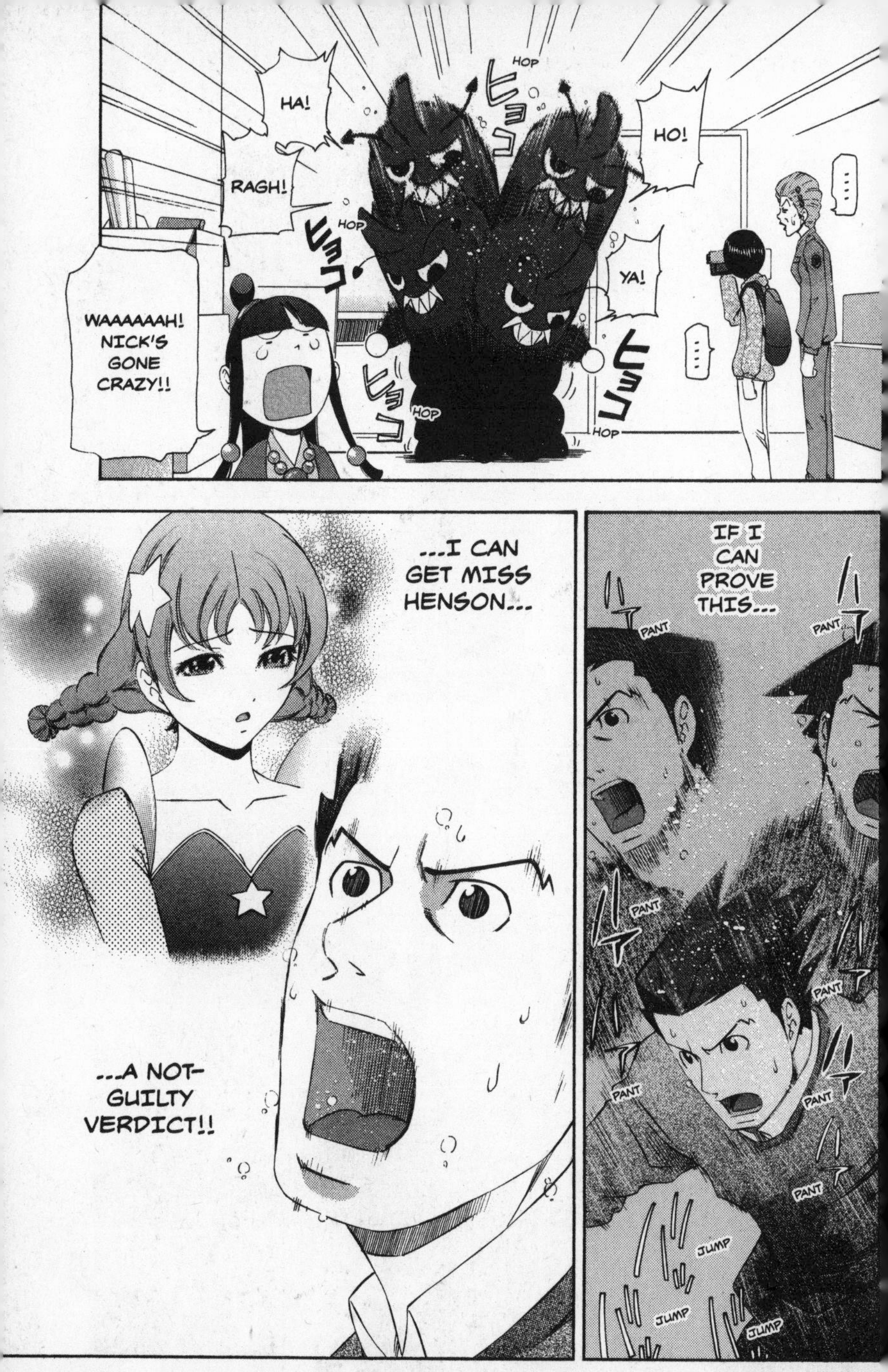

HOP
ヒョコ
HO!
....
YA!
....
HA!
RAGH!
HOP
ヒョコ
ヒョコ
HOP
WAAAAAAH! NICK'S GONE CRAZY!!
ヒョコ
HOP
IF I CAN PROVE THIS...
PANT
PANT
PANT
PANT
PANT
PANT
PANT
JUMP
JUMP
JUMP
...I CAN GET MISS HENSON...
...A NOT-GUILTY VERDICT!!

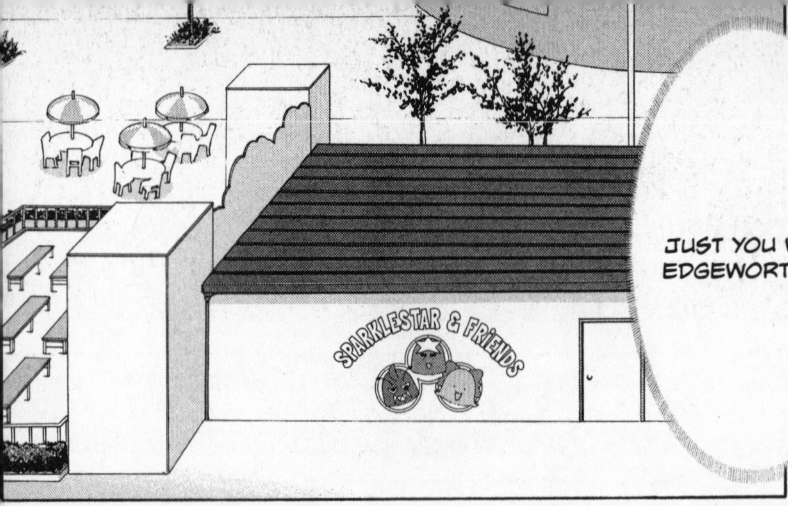
JUST YOU WAIT, EDGEWORTH...!!
SPARKLESTAR & FRIENDS
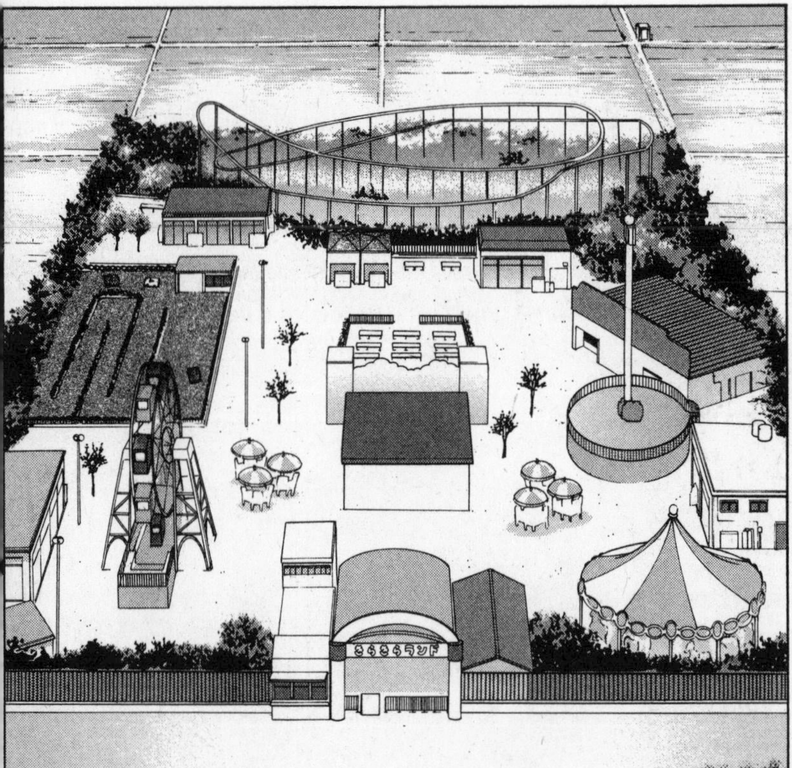
きらきらランド

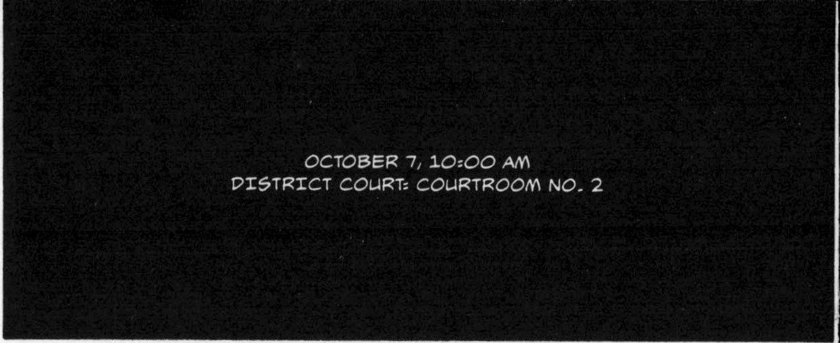
OCTOBER 7, 10:00 AM
DISTRICT COURT: COURTROOM NO. 2
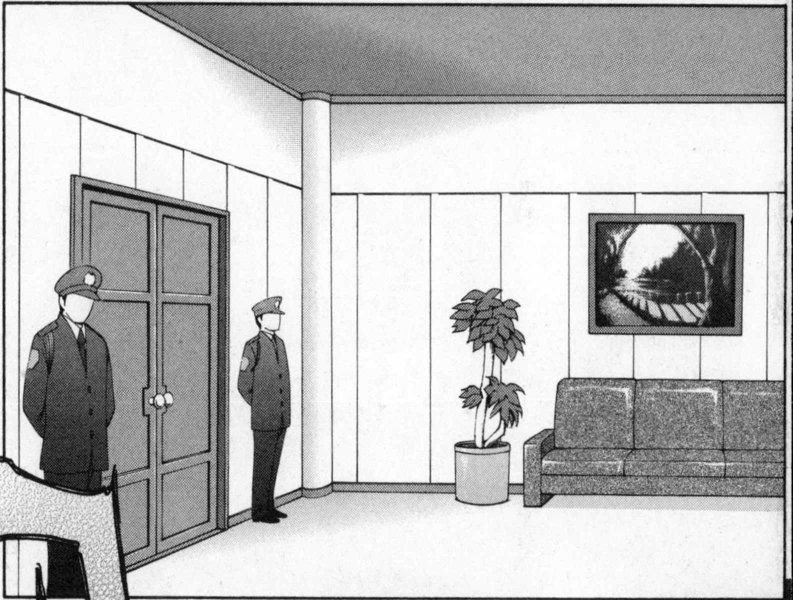
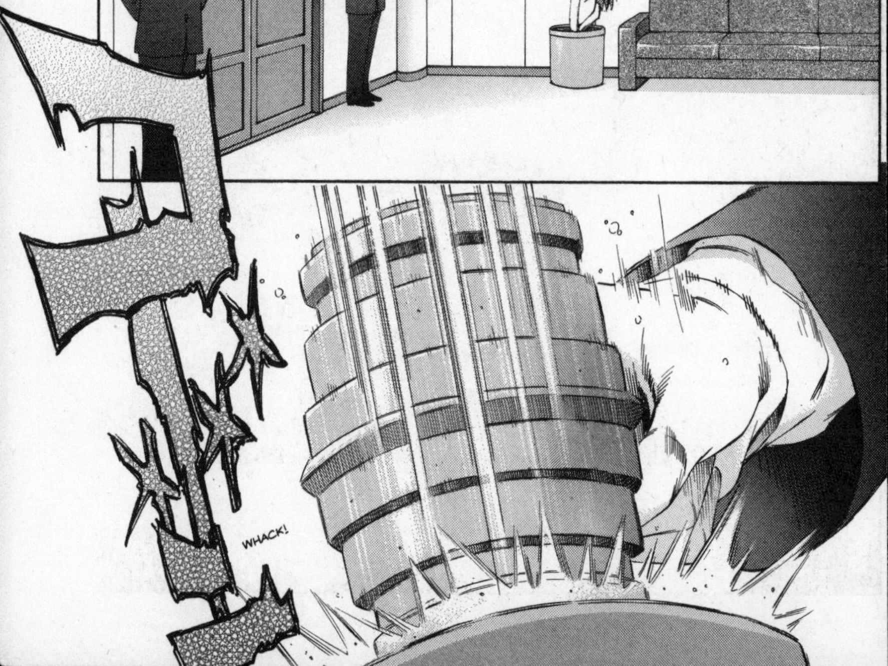
WHACK!

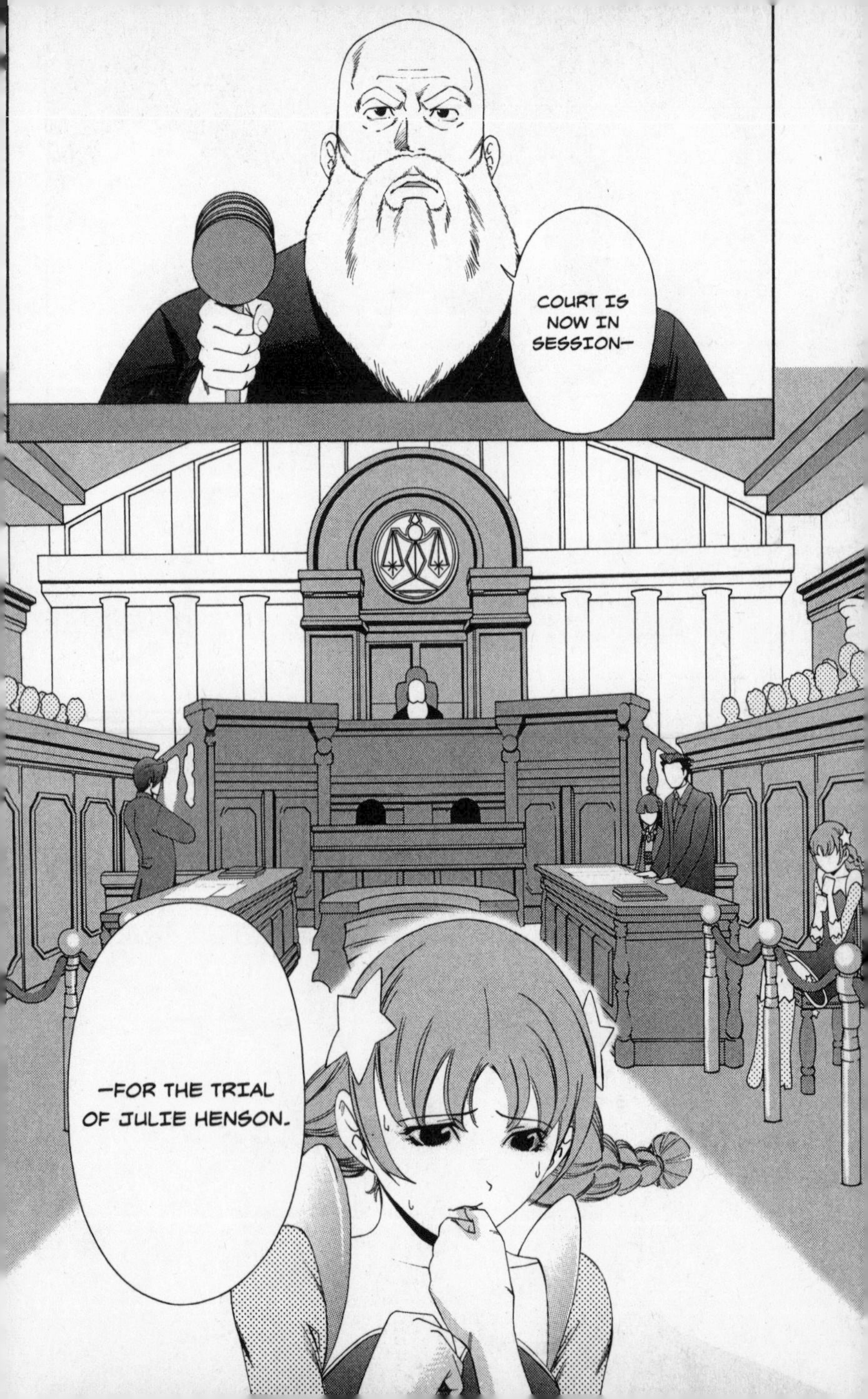
COURT IS NOW IN SESSION—
—FOR THE TRIAL OF JULIE HENSON.

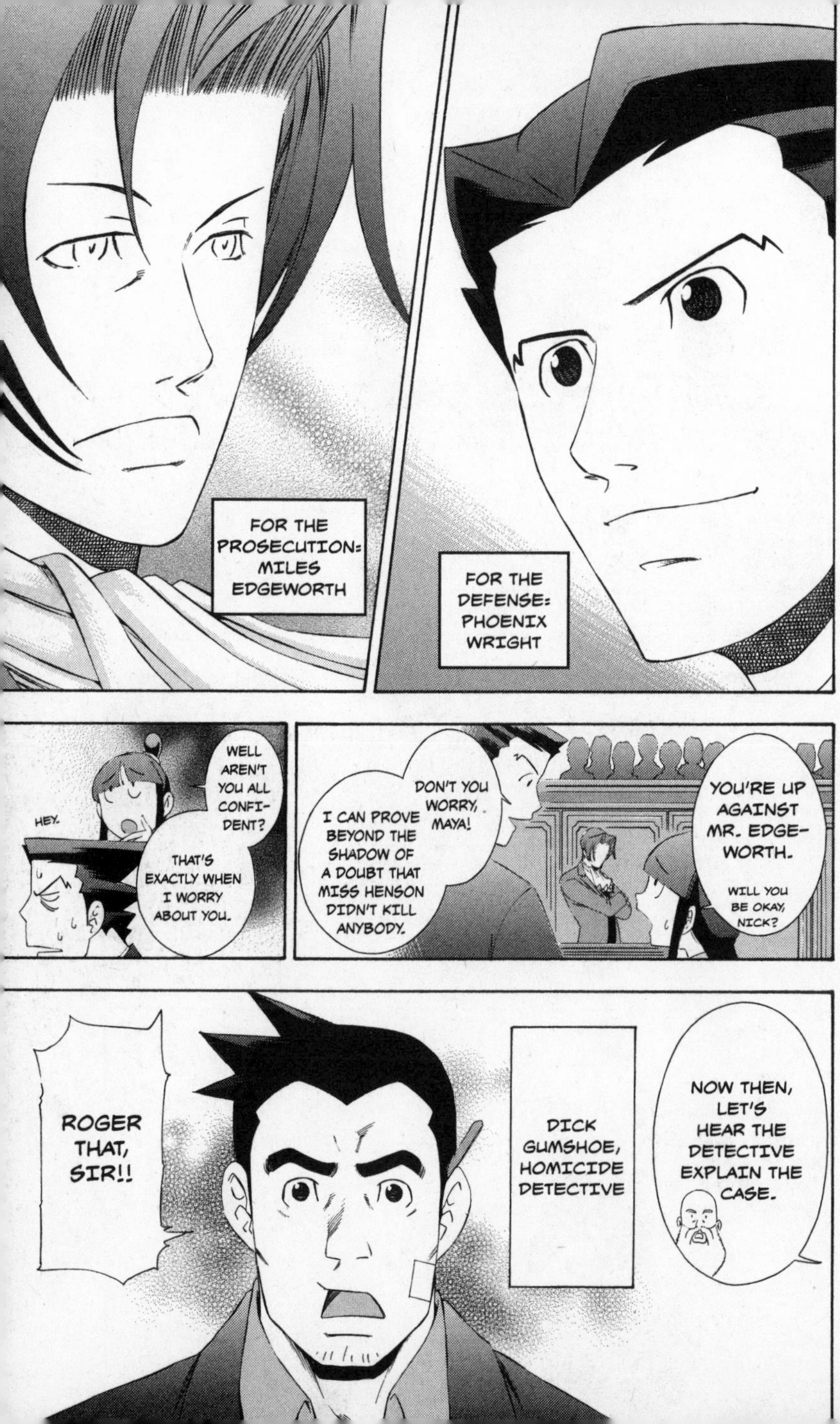
FOR THE DEFENSE: PHOENIX WRIGHT
FOR THE PROSECUTION: MILES EDGEWORTH
YOU'RE UP AGAINST MR. EDGEWORTH.
WILL YOU BE OKAY, NICK?
DON'T YOU WORRY, MAYA!
I CAN PROVE BEYOND THE SHADOW OF A DOUBT THAT MISS HENSON DIDN'T KILL ANYBODY.
WELL AREN'T YOU ALL CONFIDENT?
HEY.
THAT'S EXACTLY WHEN I WORRY ABOUT YOU.
NOW THEN, LET'S HEAR THE DETECTIVE EXPLAIN THE CASE.
DICK GUMSHOE, HOMICIDE DETECTIVE
ROGER THAT, SIR!!

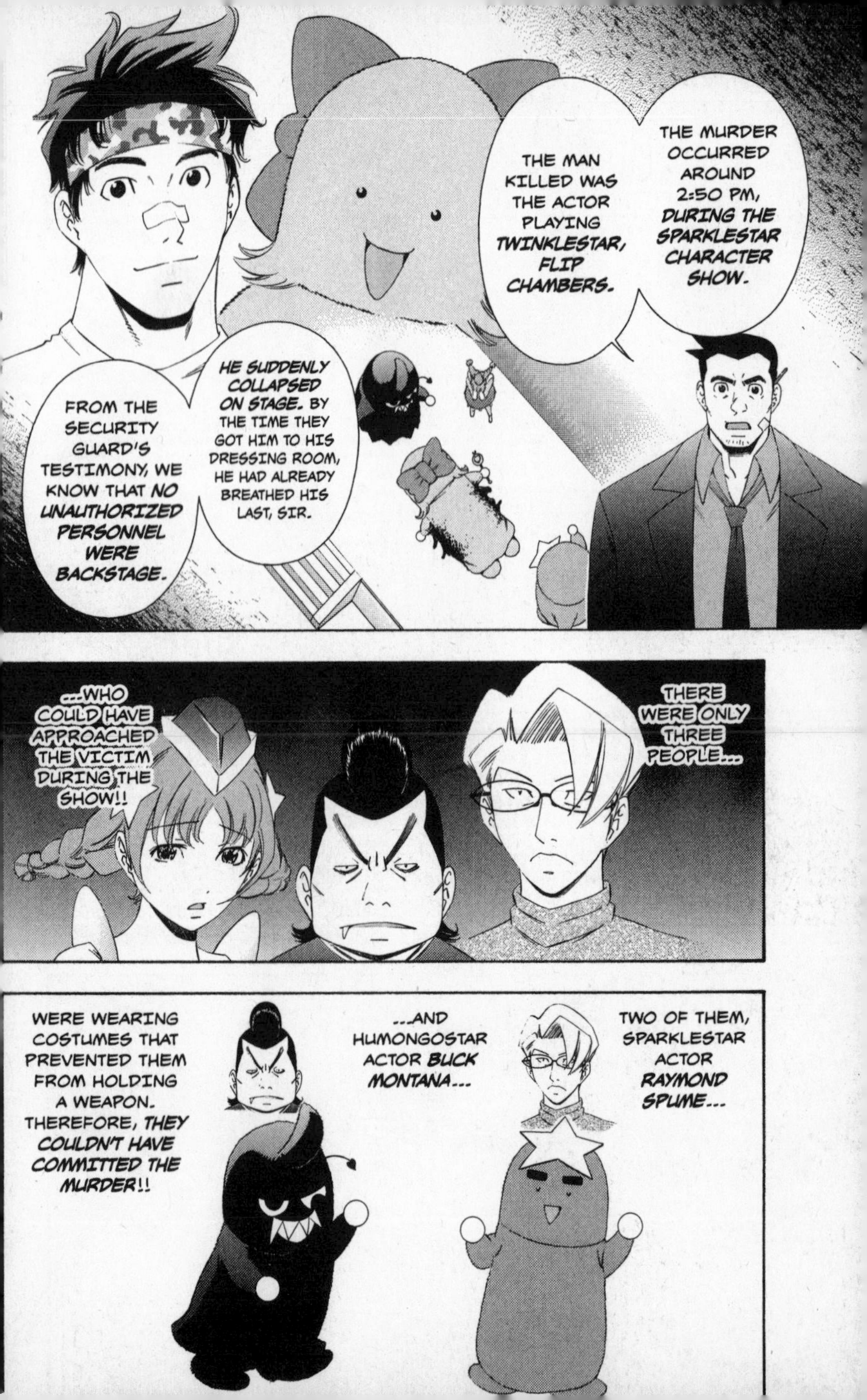
THE MURDER OCCURRED AROUND 2:50 PM, DURING THE SPARKLESTAR CHARACTER SHOW.
THE MAN KILLED WAS THE ACTOR PLAYING TWINKLESTAR, FLIP CHAMBERS.
HE SUDDENLY COLLAPSED ON STAGE. BY THE TIME THEY GOT HIM TO HIS DRESSING ROOM, HE HAD ALREADY BREATHED HIS LAST, SIR.
FROM THE SECURITY GUARD'S TESTIMONY, WE KNOW THAT NO UNAUTHORIZED PERSONNEL WERE BACKSTAGE.
THERE WERE ONLY THREE PEOPLE...
...WHO COULD HAVE APPROACHED THE VICTIM DURING THE SHOW!!
TWO OF THEM, SPARKLESTAR ACTOR RAYMOND SPUME...
...AND HUMONGOSTAR ACTOR BUCK MONTANA...
WERE WEARING COSTUMES THAT PREVENTED THEM FROM HOLDING A WEAPON. THEREFORE, THEY COULDN'T HAVE COMMITTED THE MURDER!!

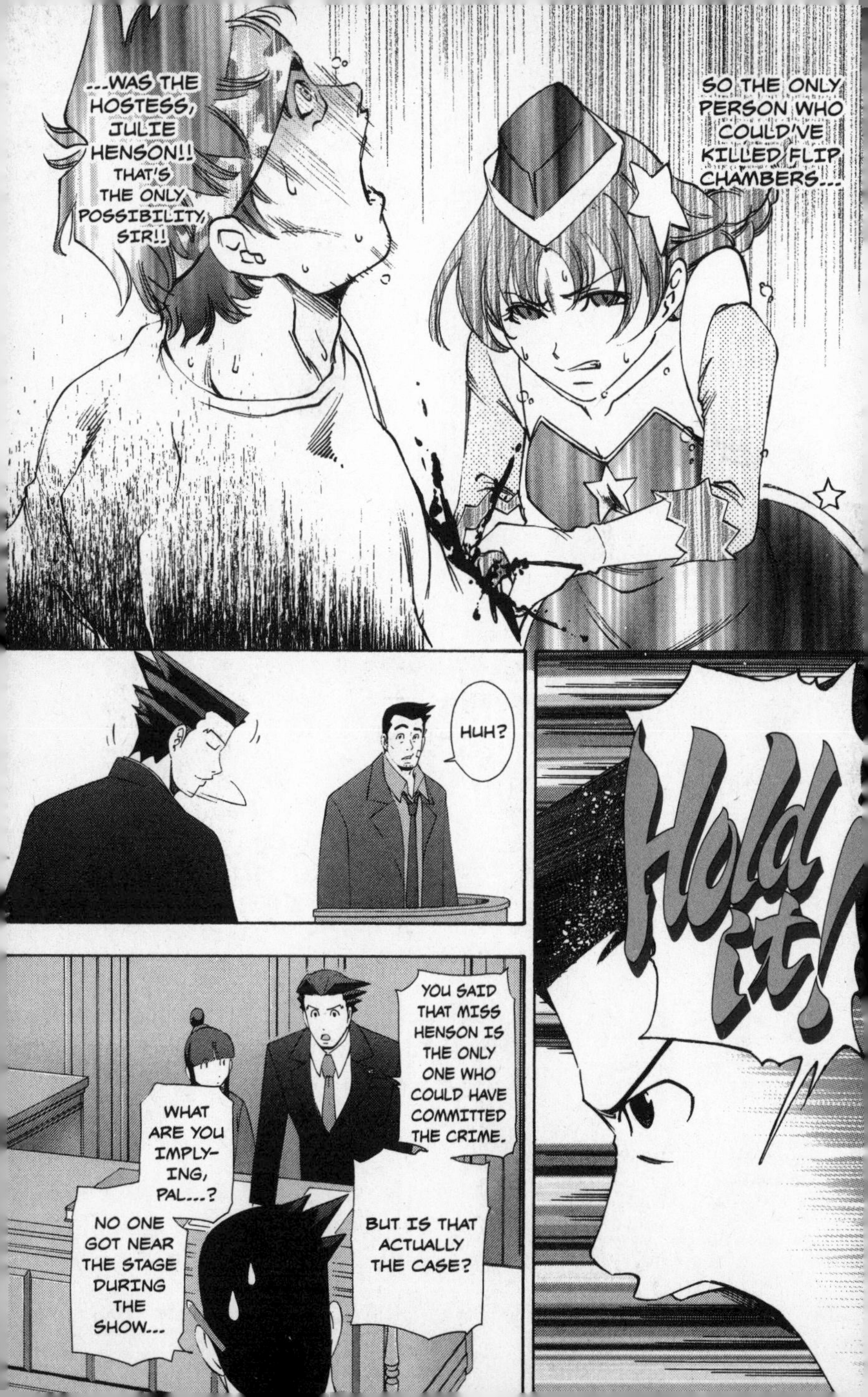
SO THE ONLY PERSON WHO COULD'VE KILLED FLIP CHAMBERS...
...WAS THE HOSTESS, JULIE HENSON!! THAT'S THE ONLY POSSIBILITY, SIR!!
Hold it!
HUH?
YOU SAID THAT MISS HENSON IS THE ONLY ONE WHO COULD HAVE COMMITTED THE CRIME.
WHAT ARE YOU IMPLYING, PAL...?
BUT IS THAT ACTUALLY THE CASE?
NO ONE GOT NEAR THE STAGE DURING THE SHOW...

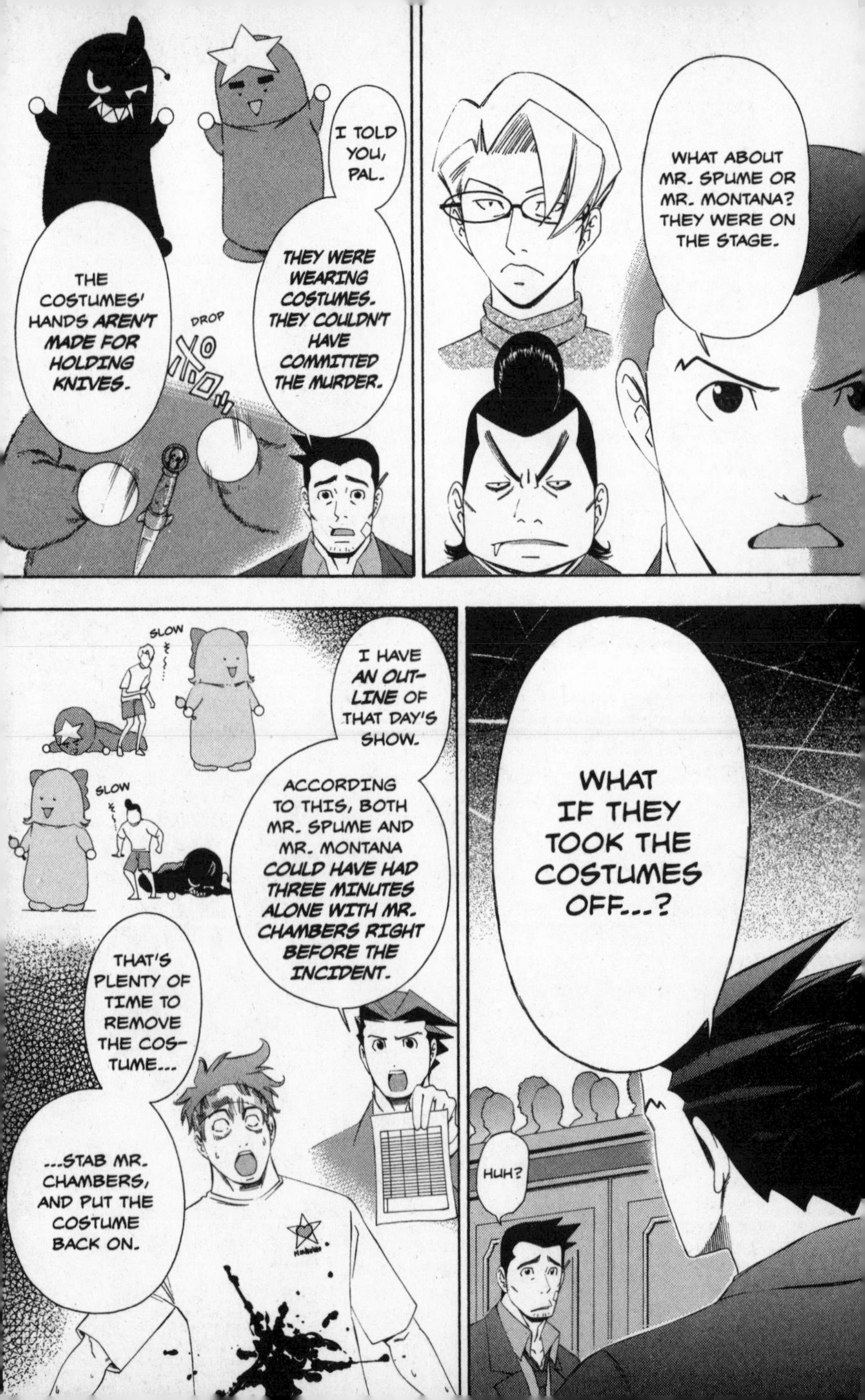
WHAT ABOUT MR. SPUME OR MR. MONTANA? THEY WERE ON THE STAGE.
I TOLD YOU, PAL.
THEY WERE WEARING COSTUMES. THEY COULDN'T HAVE COMMITTED THE MURDER.
THE COSTUMES' HANDS AREN'T MADE FOR HOLDING KNIVES.
DROP
WHAT IF THEY TOOK THE COSTUMES OFF...?
HUH?
I HAVE AN OUTLINE OF THAT DAY'S SHOW.
SLOW
SLOW
ACCORDING TO THIS, BOTH MR. SPUME AND MR. MONTANA COULD HAVE HAD THREE MINUTES ALONE WITH MR. CHAMBERS RIGHT BEFORE THE INCIDENT.
THAT'S PLENTY OF TIME TO REMOVE THE COSTUME...
...STAB MR. CHAMBERS, AND PUT THE COSTUME BACK ON.

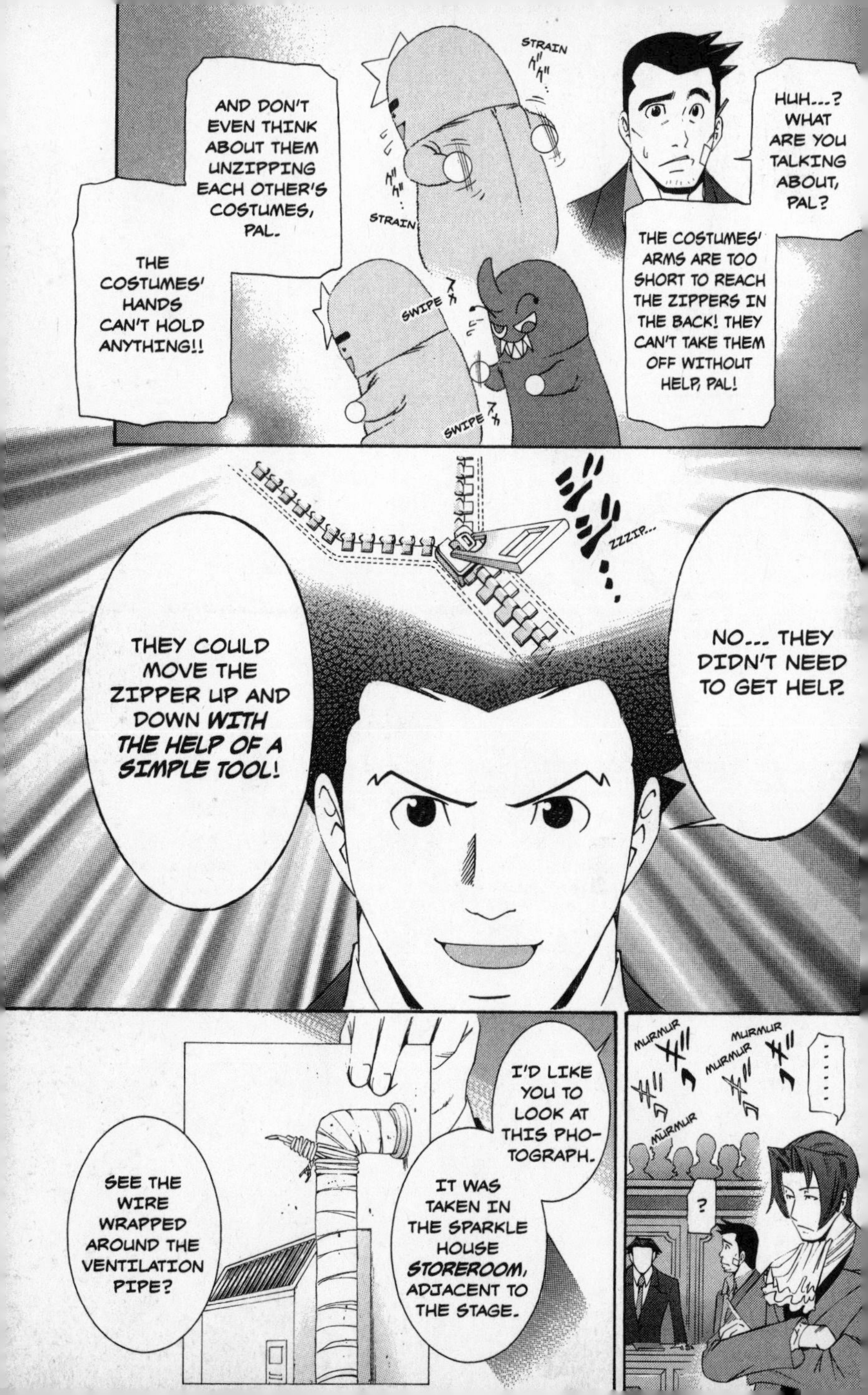
HUH...? WHAT ARE YOU TALKING ABOUT, PAL?
THE COSTUMES' ARMS ARE TOO SHORT TO REACH THE ZIPPERS IN THE BACK! THEY CAN'T TAKE THEM OFF WITHOUT HELP, PAL!
STRAIN
AND DON'T EVEN THINK ABOUT THEM UNZIPPING EACH OTHER'S COSTUMES, PAL.
STRAIN
THE COSTUMES' HANDS CAN'T HOLD ANYTHING!!
SWIPE
SWIPE
ZZZIP...
NO... THEY DIDN'T NEED TO GET HELP.
THEY COULD MOVE THE ZIPPER UP AND DOWN *WITH THE HELP OF A SIMPLE TOOL!*
......
MURMUR
MURMUR
MURMUR
MURMUR
?
I'D LIKE YOU TO LOOK AT THIS PHOTOGRAPH.
IT WAS TAKEN IN THE SPARKLE HOUSE *STOREROOM,* ADJACENT TO THE STAGE.
SEE THE WIRE WRAPPED AROUND THE VENTILATION PIPE?

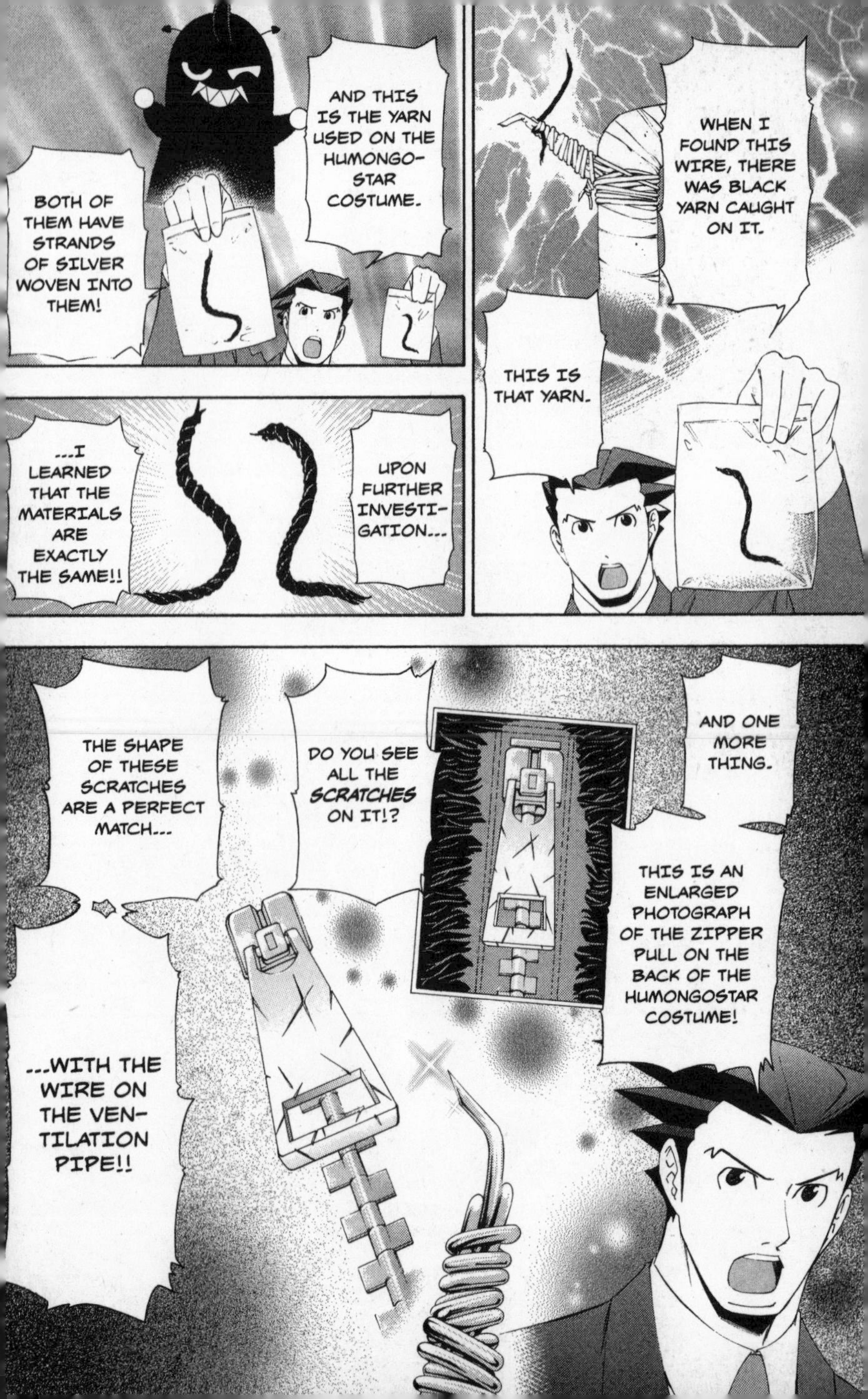
WHEN I FOUND THIS WIRE, THERE WAS BLACK YARN CAUGHT ON IT.
THIS IS THAT YARN.
AND THIS IS THE YARN USED ON THE HUMONGO-STAR COSTUME.
BOTH OF THEM HAVE STRANDS OF SILVER WOVEN INTO THEM!
UPON FURTHER INVESTIGATION...
...I LEARNED THAT THE MATERIALS ARE EXACTLY THE SAME!!
AND ONE MORE THING.
THIS IS AN ENLARGED PHOTOGRAPH OF THE ZIPPER PULL ON THE BACK OF THE HUMONGOSTAR COSTUME!
DO YOU SEE ALL THE *SCRATCHES* ON IT!?
THE SHAPE OF THESE SCRATCHES ARE A PERFECT MATCH...
...WITH THE WIRE ON THE VENTILATION PIPE!!

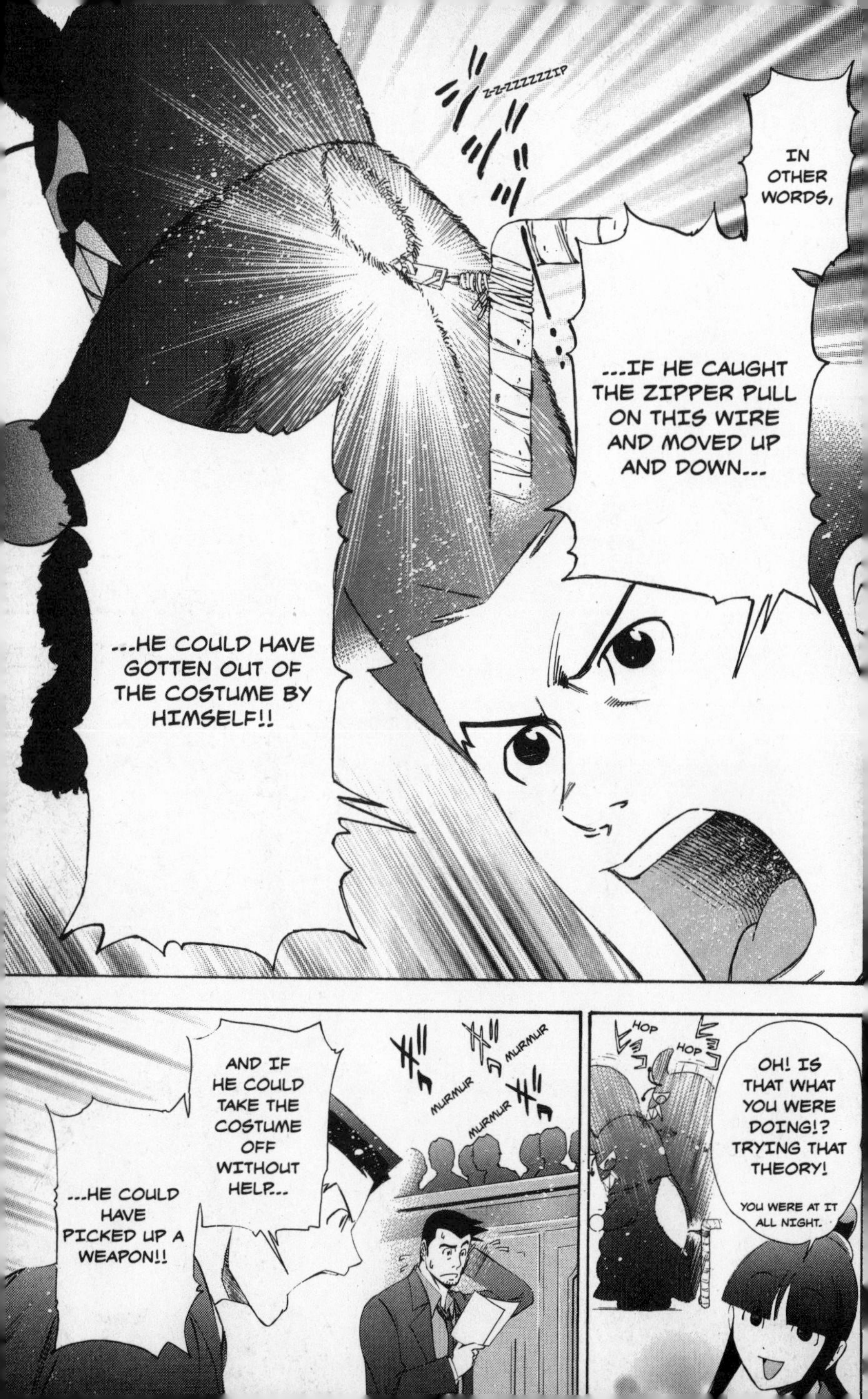
IN OTHER WORDS,
Z-Z-ZZZZZZIP
...IF HE CAUGHT THE ZIPPER PULL ON THIS WIRE AND MOVED UP AND DOWN...
...HE COULD HAVE GOTTEN OUT OF THE COSTUME BY HIMSELF!!
HOP
HOP
OH! IS THAT WHAT YOU WERE DOING!? TRYING THAT THEORY!
YOU WERE AT IT ALL NIGHT.
MURMUR
MURMUR
MURMUR
AND IF HE COULD TAKE THE COSTUME OFF WITHOUT HELP...
...HE COULD HAVE PICKED UP A WEAPON!!

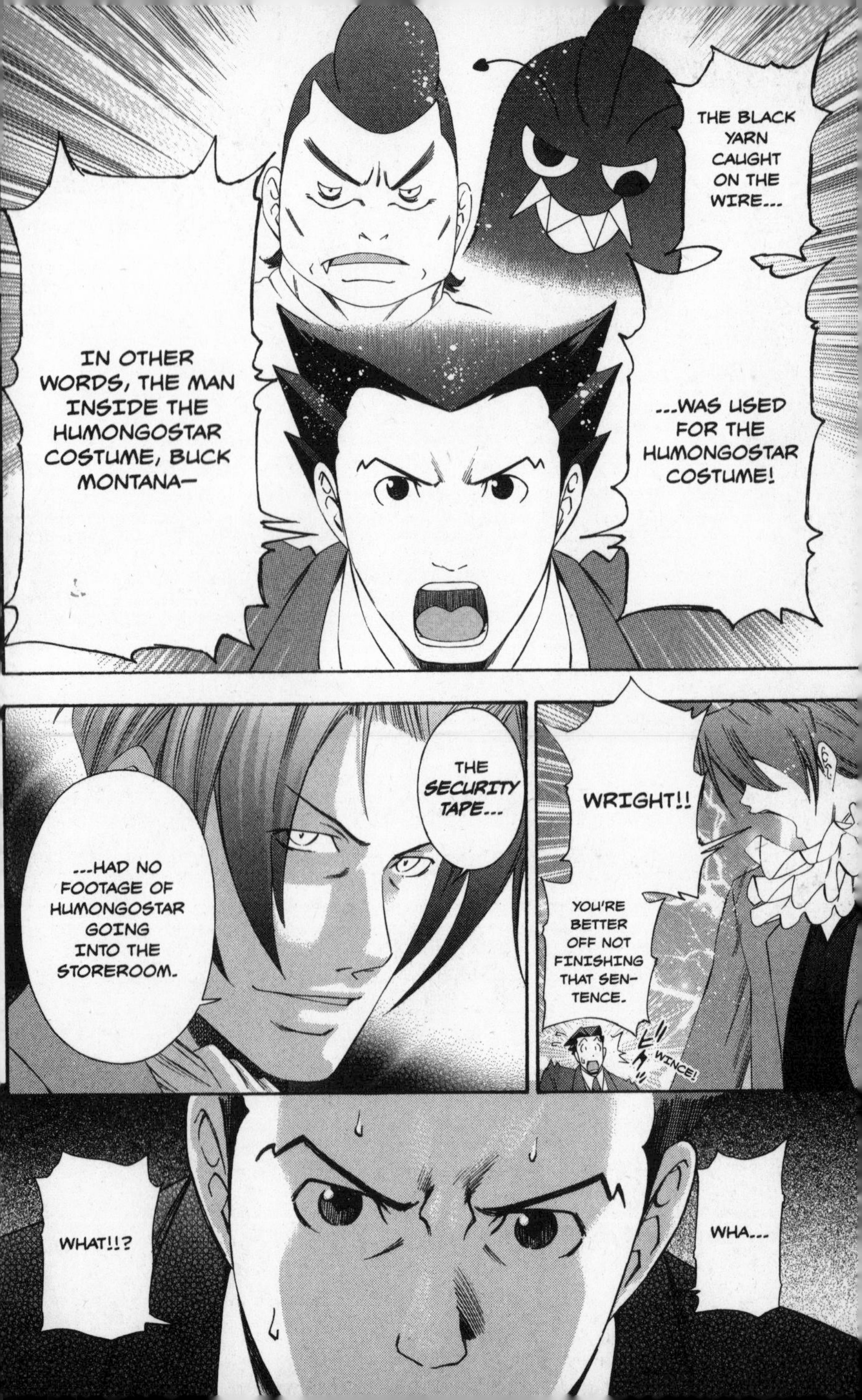
THE BLACK YARN CAUGHT ON THE WIRE...
...WAS USED FOR THE HUMONGOSTAR COSTUME!
IN OTHER WORDS, THE MAN INSIDE THE HUMONGOSTAR COSTUME, BUCK MONTANA—
WRIGHT!!
YOU'RE BETTER OFF NOT FINISHING THAT SEN-TENCE.
WINCE!
THE *SECURITY TAPE*...
...HAD NO FOOTAGE OF HUMONGOSTAR GOING INTO THE STOREROOM.
WHA...
WHAT!!?

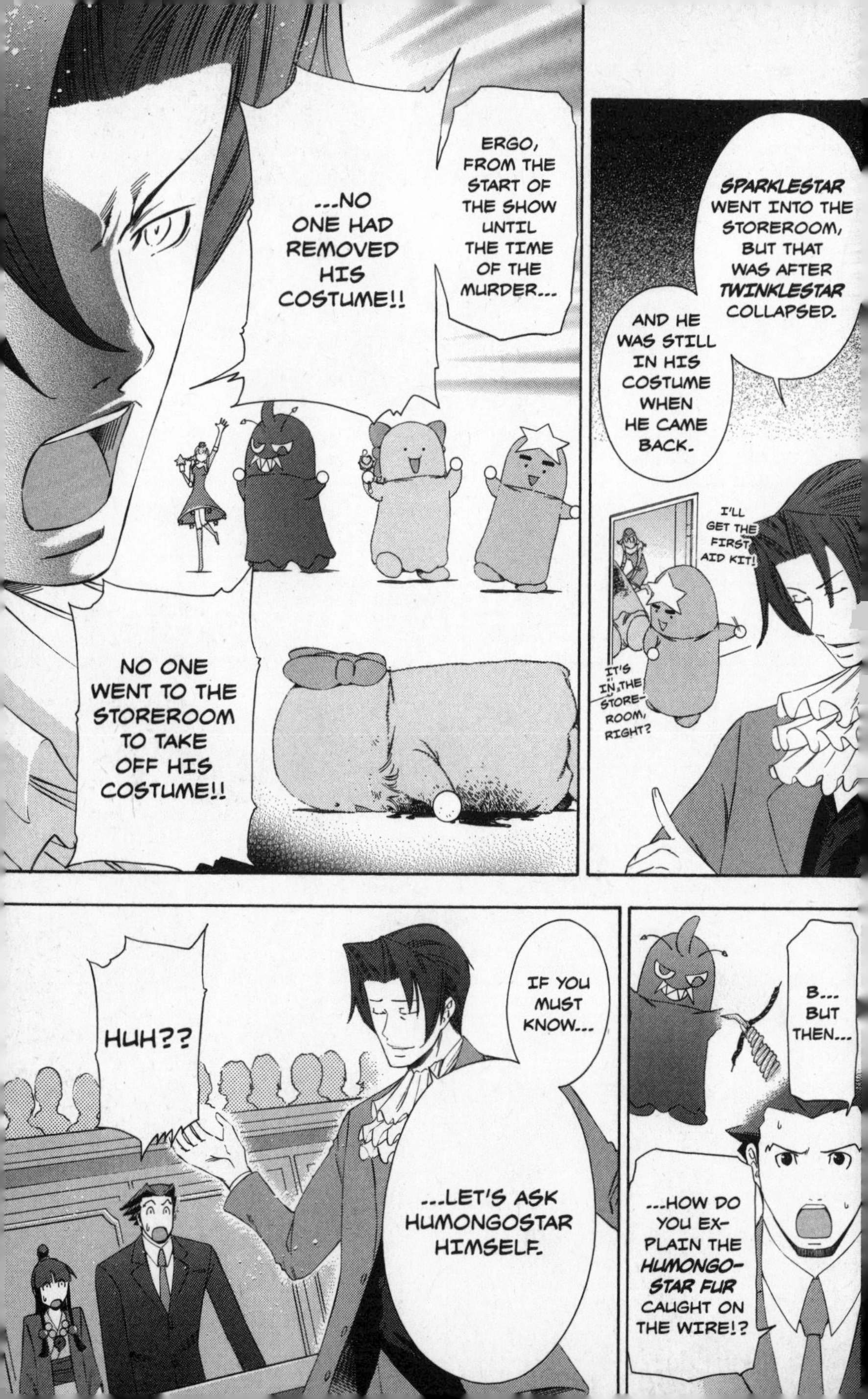
SPARKLESTAR WENT INTO THE STOREROOM, BUT THAT WAS AFTER TWINKLESTAR COLLAPSED.
AND HE WAS STILL IN HIS COSTUME WHEN HE CAME BACK.
I'LL GET THE FIRST AID KIT!
IT'S IN THE STOREROOM, RIGHT?
ERGO, FROM THE START OF THE SHOW UNTIL THE TIME OF THE MURDER...
...NO ONE HAD REMOVED HIS COSTUME!!
NO ONE WENT TO THE STOREROOM TO TAKE OFF HIS COSTUME!!
B... BUT THEN...
...HOW DO YOU EXPLAIN THE HUMONGOSTAR FUR CAUGHT ON THE WIRE!?
IF YOU MUST KNOW...
HUH??
...LET'S ASK HUMONGOSTAR HIMSELF.

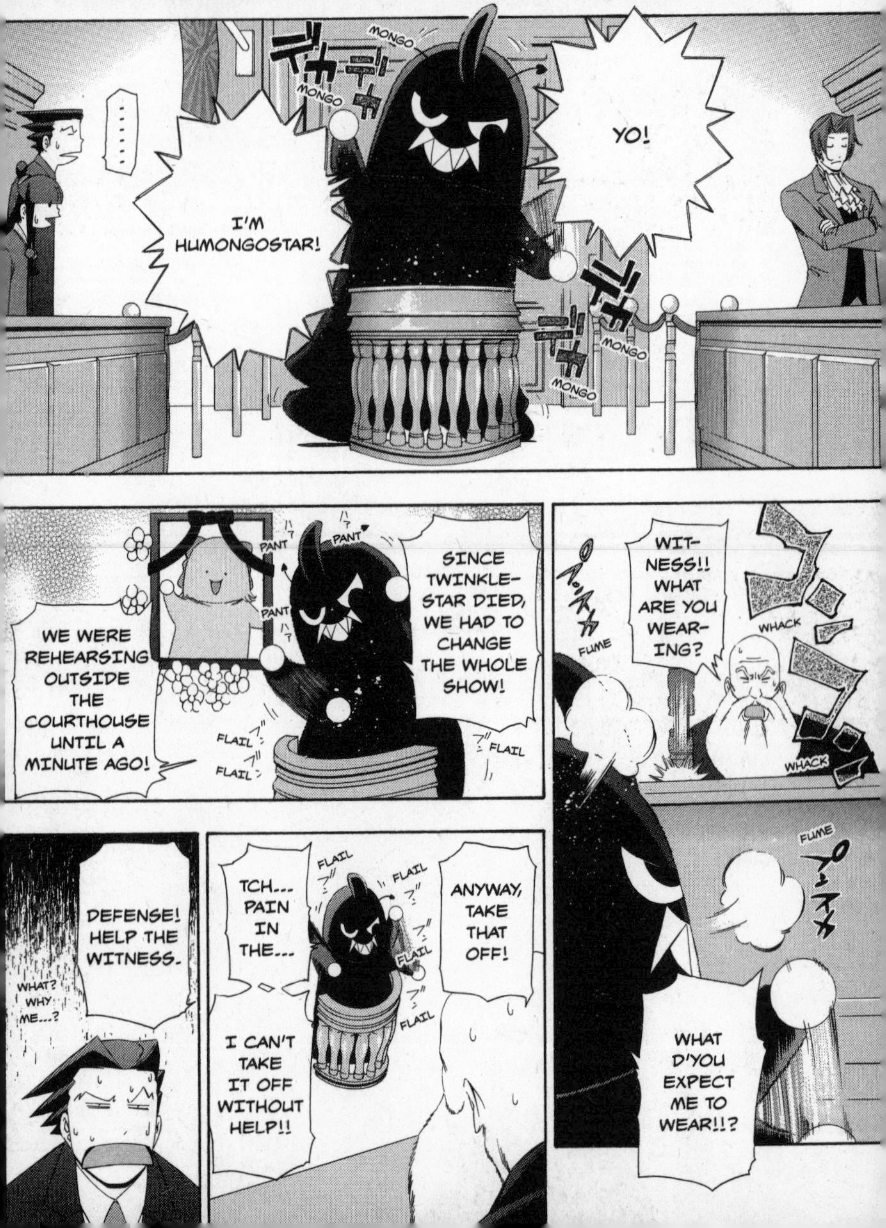
MONGO
YO!
MONGO MONGO
MONGO
MONGO
I'M HUMONGOSTAR!
......
FUME
WIT-NESS!! WHAT ARE YOU WEAR-ING?
WHACK
WHACK
PANT
SINCE TWINKLE-STAR DIED, WE HAD TO CHANGE THE WHOLE SHOW!
PANT
FLAIL
WE WERE REHEARSING OUTSIDE THE COURTHOUSE UNTIL A MINUTE AGO!
FLAIL
FLAIL
FUME
WHAT D'YOU EXPECT ME TO WEAR!!?
ANYWAY, TAKE THAT OFF!
FLAIL
FLAIL
TCH... PAIN IN THE...
FLAIL
FLAIL
I CAN'T TAKE IT OFF WITHOUT HELP!!
DEFENSE! HELP THE WITNESS.
WHAT? WHY ME...?

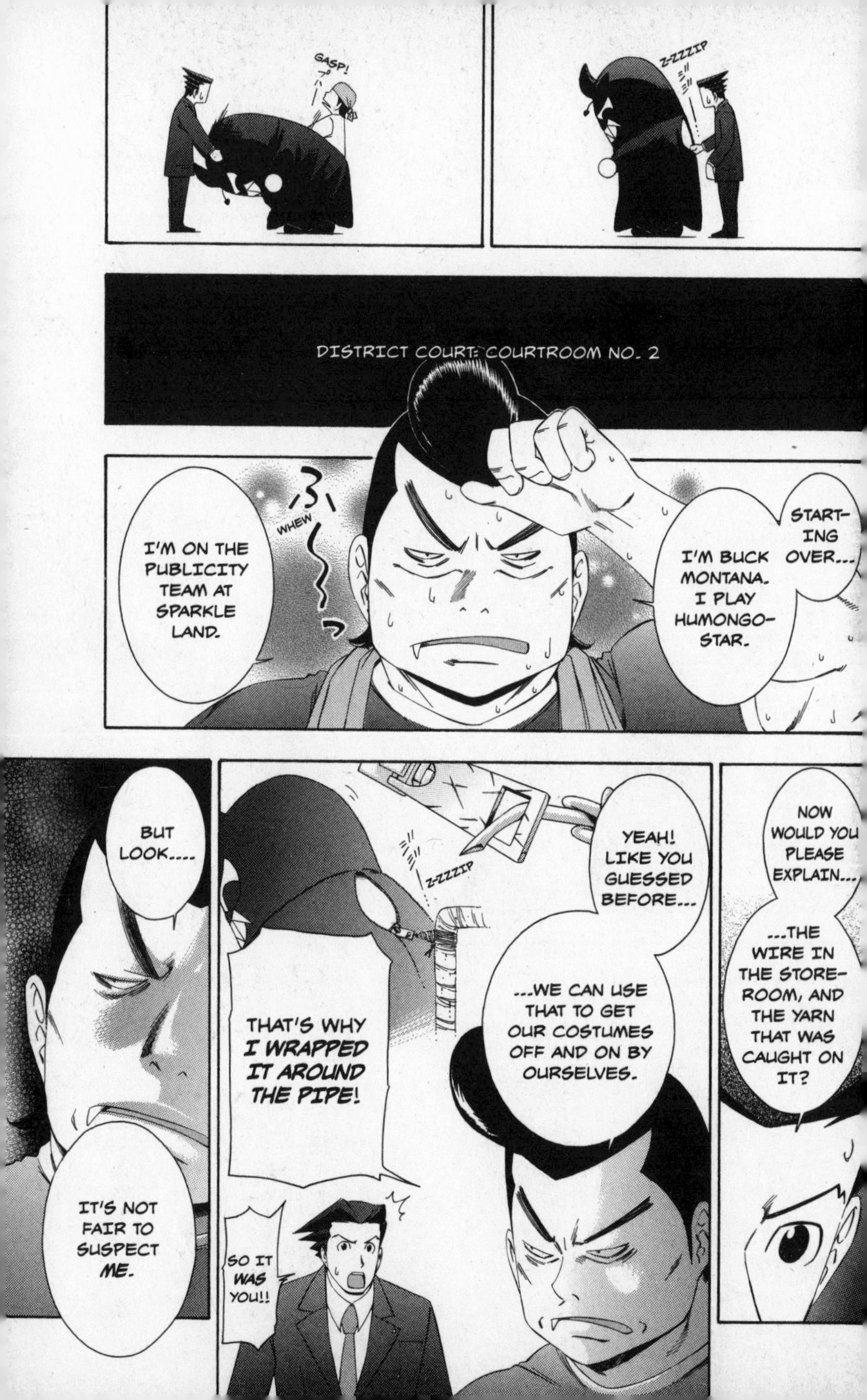
Z-ZZZIP
GASP!
DISTRICT COURT: COURTROOM NO. 2
STARTING OVER...
I'M BUCK MONTANA. I PLAY HUMONGO-STAR.
WHEW
I'M ON THE PUBLICITY TEAM AT SPARKLE LAND.
NOW WOULD YOU PLEASE EXPLAIN...
...THE WIRE IN THE STOREROOM, AND THE YARN THAT WAS CAUGHT ON IT?
YEAH! LIKE YOU GUESSED BEFORE...
...WE CAN USE THAT TO GET OUR COSTUMES OFF AND ON BY OURSELVES.
Z-ZZZIP
THAT'S WHY *I WRAPPED IT AROUND THE PIPE*!
SO IT WAS YOU!!
BUT LOOK....
IT'S NOT FAIR TO SUSPECT *ME*.

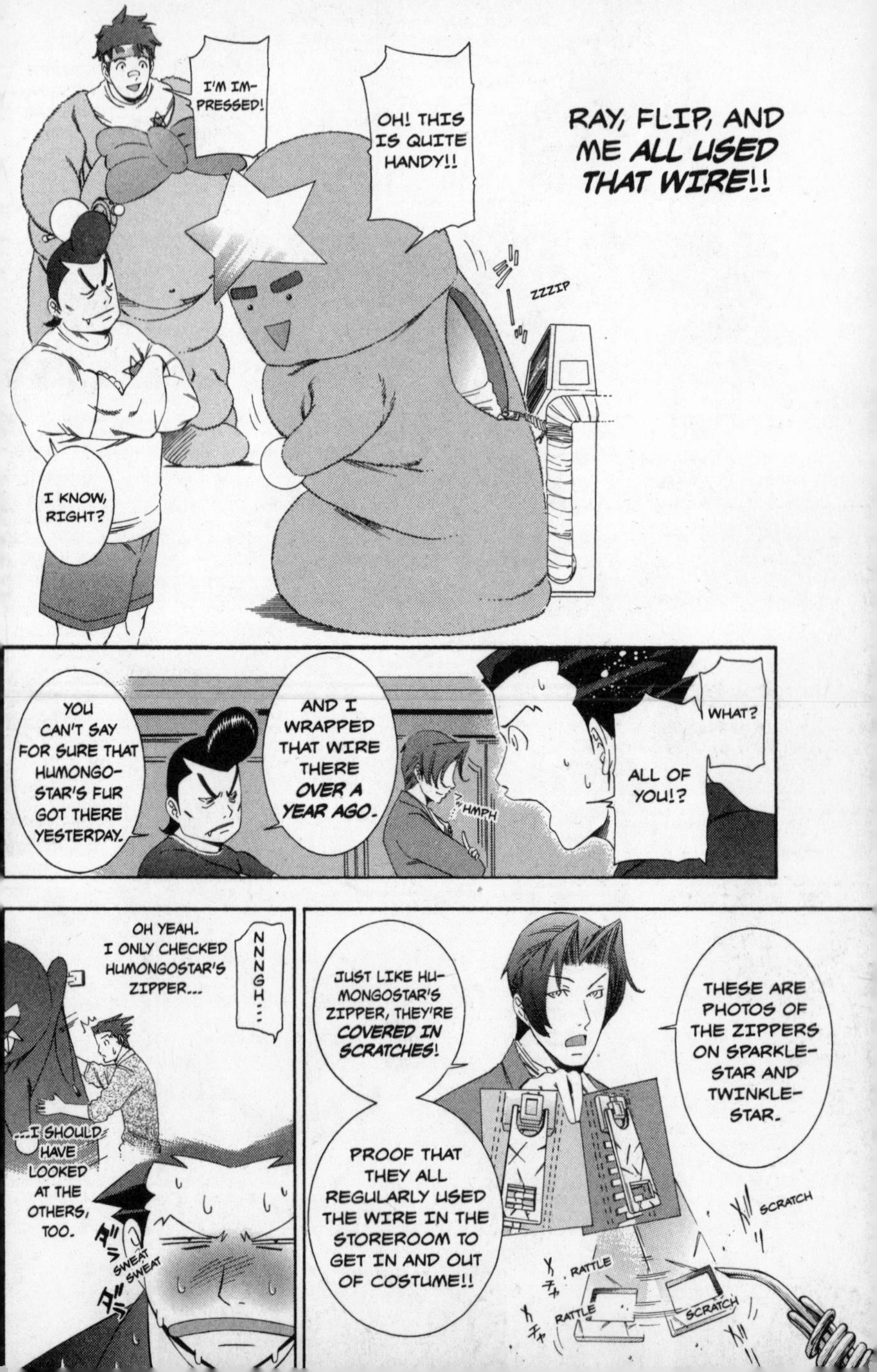
RAY, FLIP, AND ME *ALL USED THAT WIRE*!!
OH! THIS IS QUITE HANDY!!
I'M IM-PRESSED!
ZZZIP
I KNOW, RIGHT?
WHAT?
ALL OF YOU!?
AND I WRAPPED THAT WIRE THERE *OVER A YEAR AGO*.
HMPH
YOU CAN'T SAY FOR SURE THAT HUMONGO-STAR'S FUR GOT THERE YESTERDAY.
THESE ARE PHOTOS OF THE ZIPPERS ON SPARKLE-STAR AND TWINKLE-STAR.
JUST LIKE HU-MONGOSTAR'S ZIPPER, THEY'RE *COVERED IN SCRATCHES*!
PROOF THAT THEY ALL REGULARLY USED THE WIRE IN THE STOREROOM TO GET IN AND OUT OF COSTUME!!
SCRATCH
RATTLE
RATTLE
SCRATCH
NNNGH...
OH YEAH. I ONLY CHECKED HUMONGOSTAR'S ZIPPER...
...I SHOULD HAVE LOOKED AT THE OTHERS, TOO.
SWEAT SWEAT

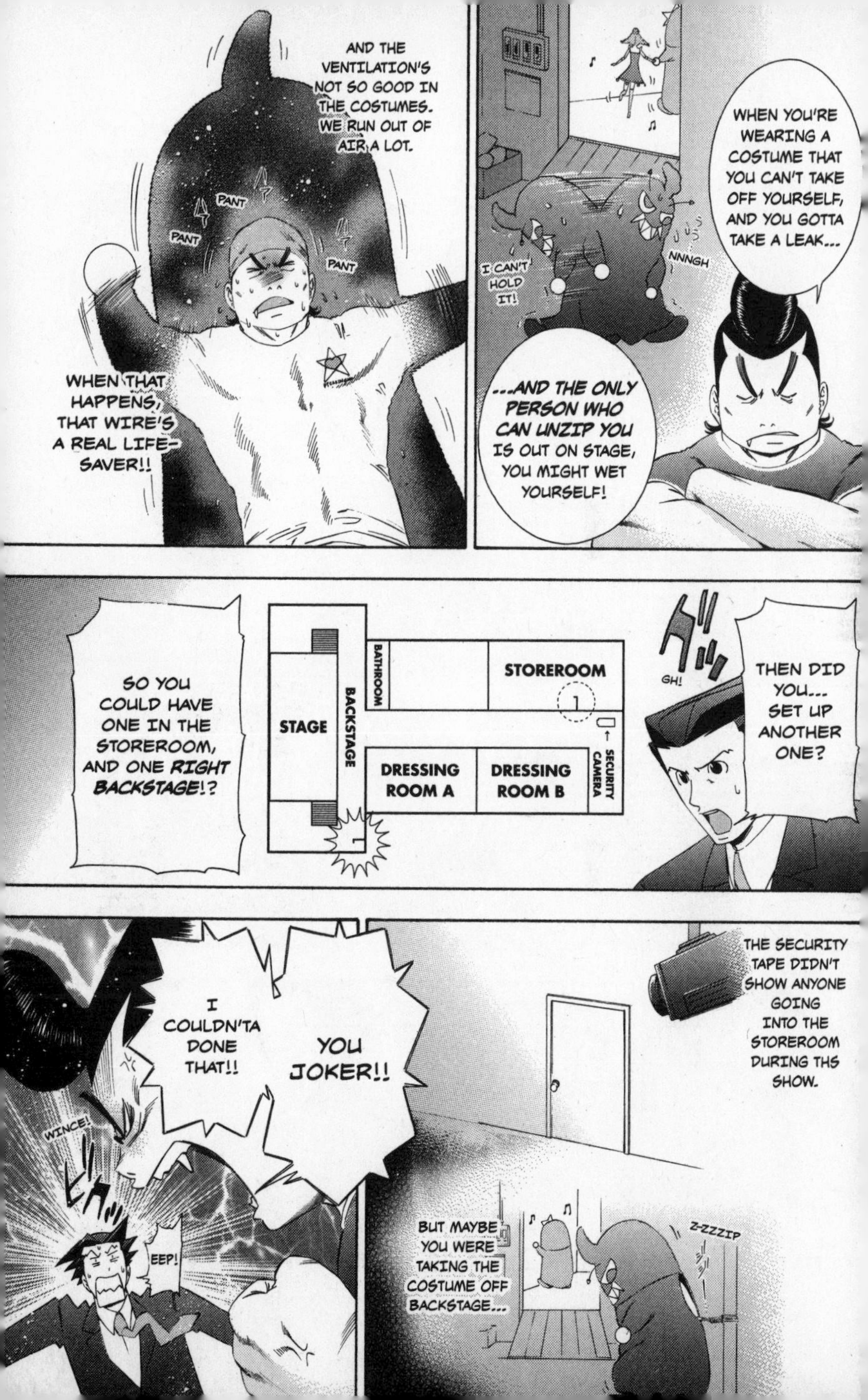

WHEN YOU'RE WEARING A COSTUME THAT YOU CAN'T TAKE OFF YOURSELF, AND YOU GOTTA TAKE A LEAK...
NNNGH
I CAN'T HOLD IT!
...AND THE ONLY PERSON WHO CAN UNZIP YOU IS OUT ON STAGE, YOU MIGHT WET YOURSELF!
AND THE VENTILATION'S NOT SO GOOD IN THE COSTUMES. WE RUN OUT OF AIR A LOT.
PANT
PANT
PANT
WHEN THAT HAPPENS, THAT WIRE'S A REAL LIFE-SAVER!!
GH!
THEN DID YOU... SET UP ANOTHER ONE?
STOREROOM
BATHROOM
STAGE
BACKSTAGE
DRESSING ROOM A
DRESSING ROOM B
SECURITY CAMERA
SO YOU COULD HAVE ONE IN THE STOREROOM, AND ONE RIGHT BACKSTAGE!?
THE SECURITY TAPE DIDN'T SHOW ANYONE GOING INTO THE STOREROOM DURING THS SHOW.
Z-ZZZIP
BUT MAYBE YOU WERE TAKING THE COSTUME OFF BACKSTAGE...
YOU JOKER!!
I COULDN'TA DONE THAT!!
WINCE!
EEP!

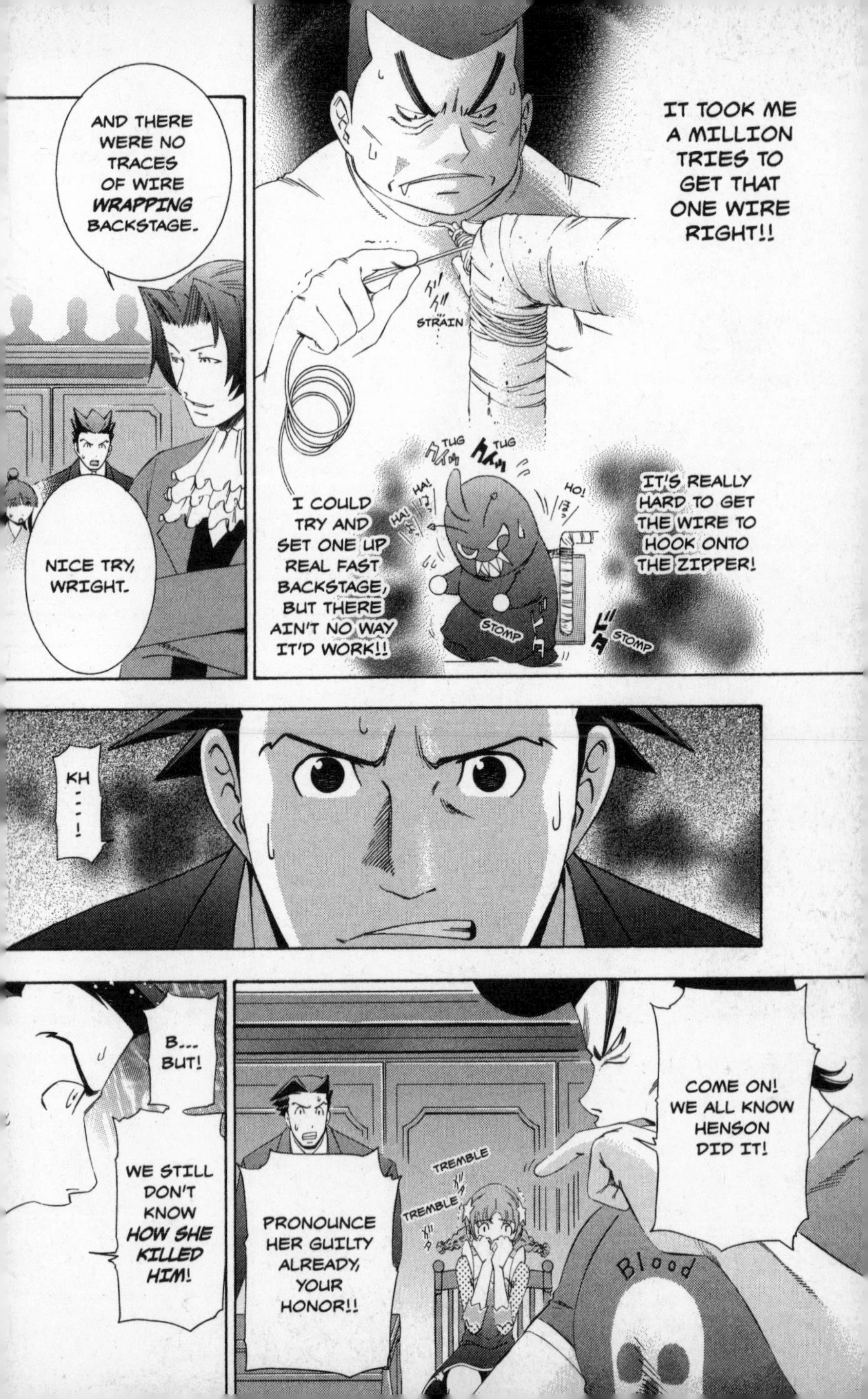
IT TOOK ME A MILLION TRIES TO GET THAT ONE WIRE RIGHT!!
STRAIN
IT'S REALLY HARD TO GET THE WIRE TO HOOK ONTO THE ZIPPER!
TUG
TUG
HO!
HA!
HA!
I COULD TRY AND SET ONE UP REAL FAST BACKSTAGE, BUT THERE AIN'T NO WAY IT'D WORK!!
STOMP
STOMP
AND THERE WERE NO TRACES OF WIRE *WRAPPING* BACKSTAGE.
NICE TRY, WRIGHT.
KH...!
COME ON! WE ALL KNOW HENSON DID IT!
TREMBLE
TREMBLE
PRONOUNCE HER GUILTY ALREADY, YOUR HONOR!!
Blood
B... BUT!
WE STILL DON'T KNOW *HOW SHE KILLED HIM*!

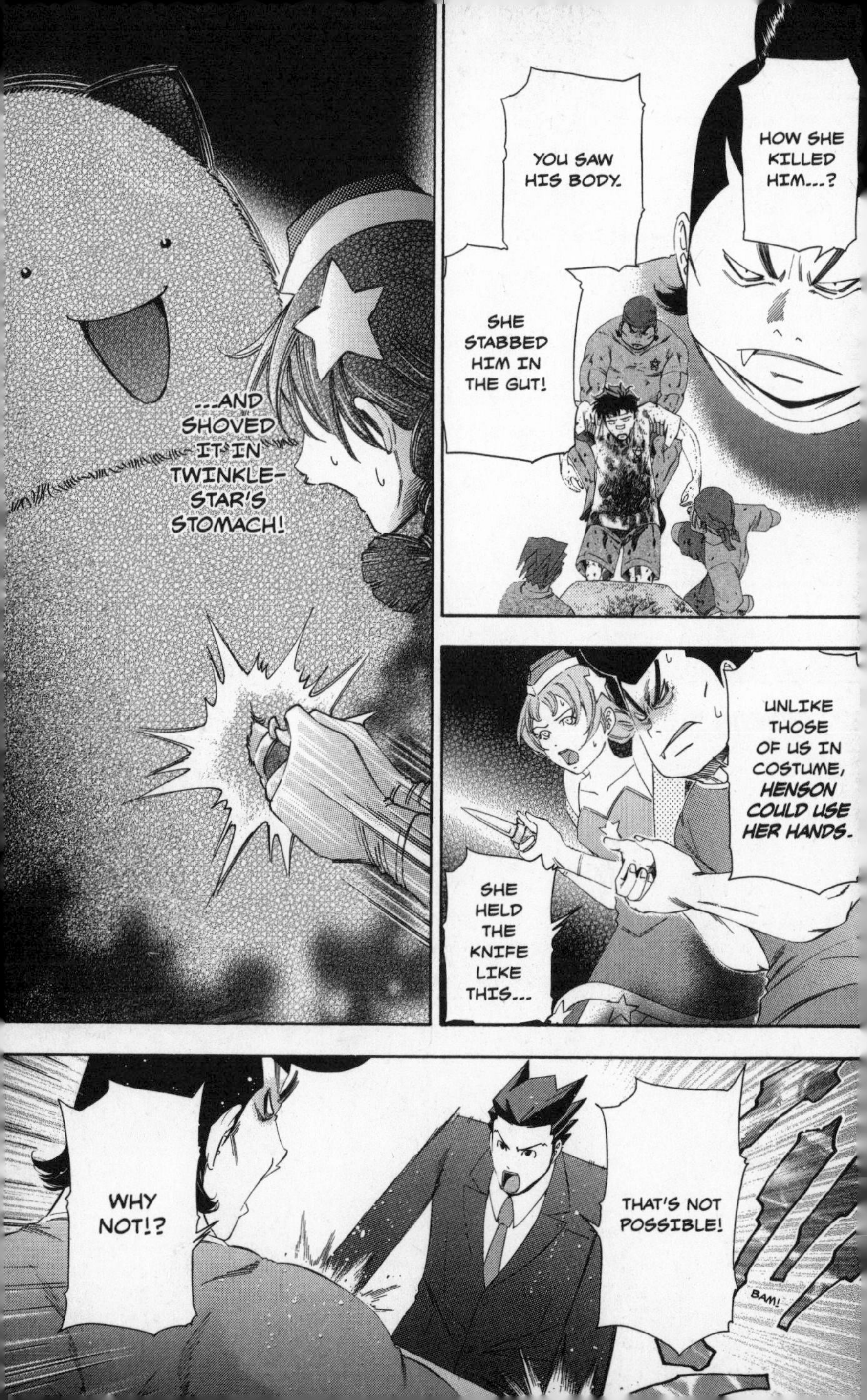
HOW SHE KILLED HIM...?
YOU SAW HIS BODY.
SHE STABBED HIM IN THE GUT!
UNLIKE THOSE OF US IN COSTUME, **HENSON COULD USE HER HANDS.**
SHE HELD THE KNIFE LIKE THIS...
...AND SHOVED IT IN TWINKLE-STAR'S STOMACH!
BAM!
THAT'S NOT POSSIBLE!
WHY NOT!?

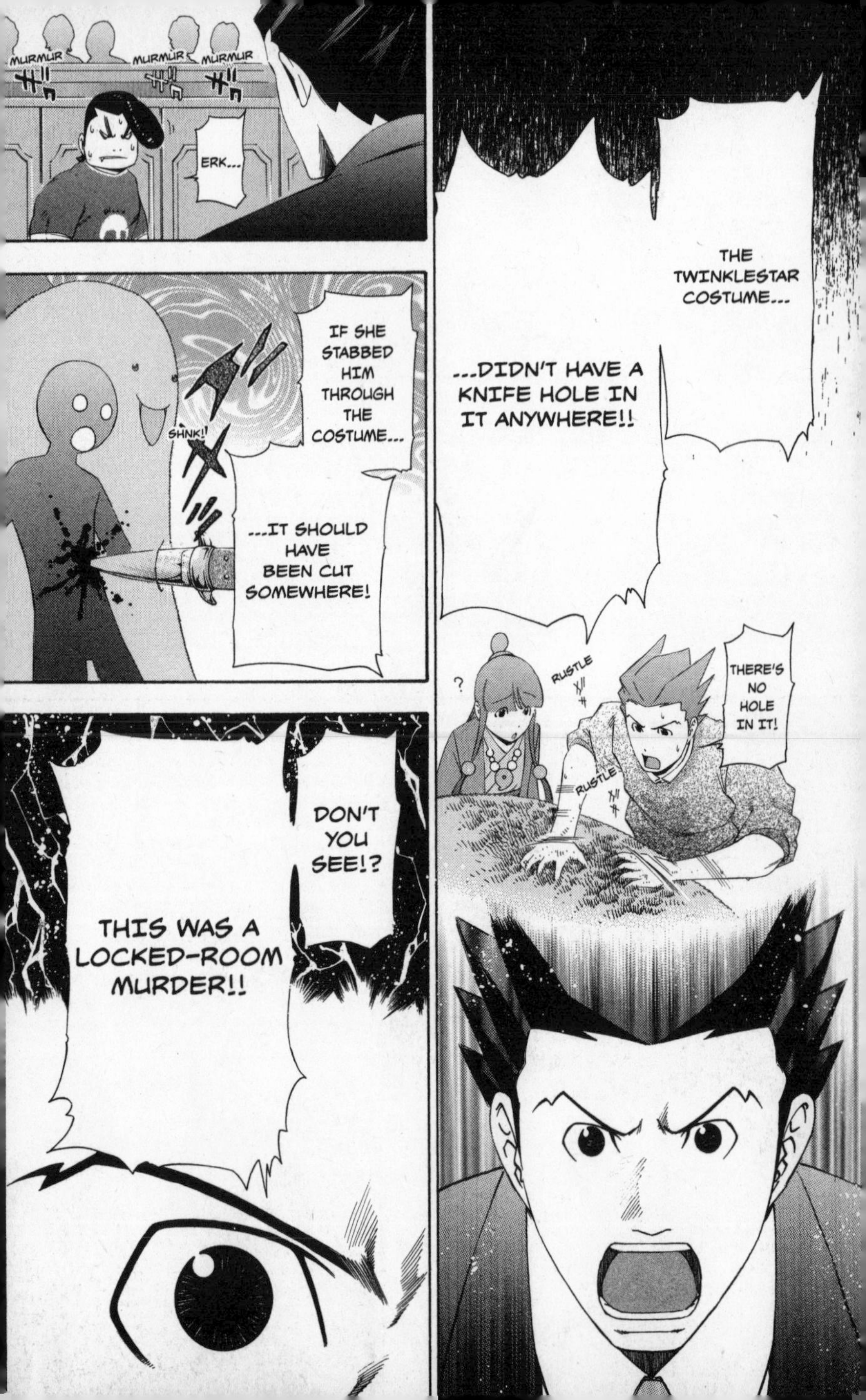
THE TWINKLESTAR COSTUME...
...DIDN'T HAVE A KNIFE HOLE IN IT ANYWHERE!!
RUSTLE
RUSTLE
THERE'S NO HOLE IN IT!
MURMUR
MURMUR
MURMUR
ERK...
IF SHE STABBED HIM THROUGH THE COSTUME...
SHNK!!
...IT SHOULD HAVE BEEN CUT SOMEWHERE!
DON'T YOU SEE!?
THIS WAS A LOCKED-ROOM MURDER!!

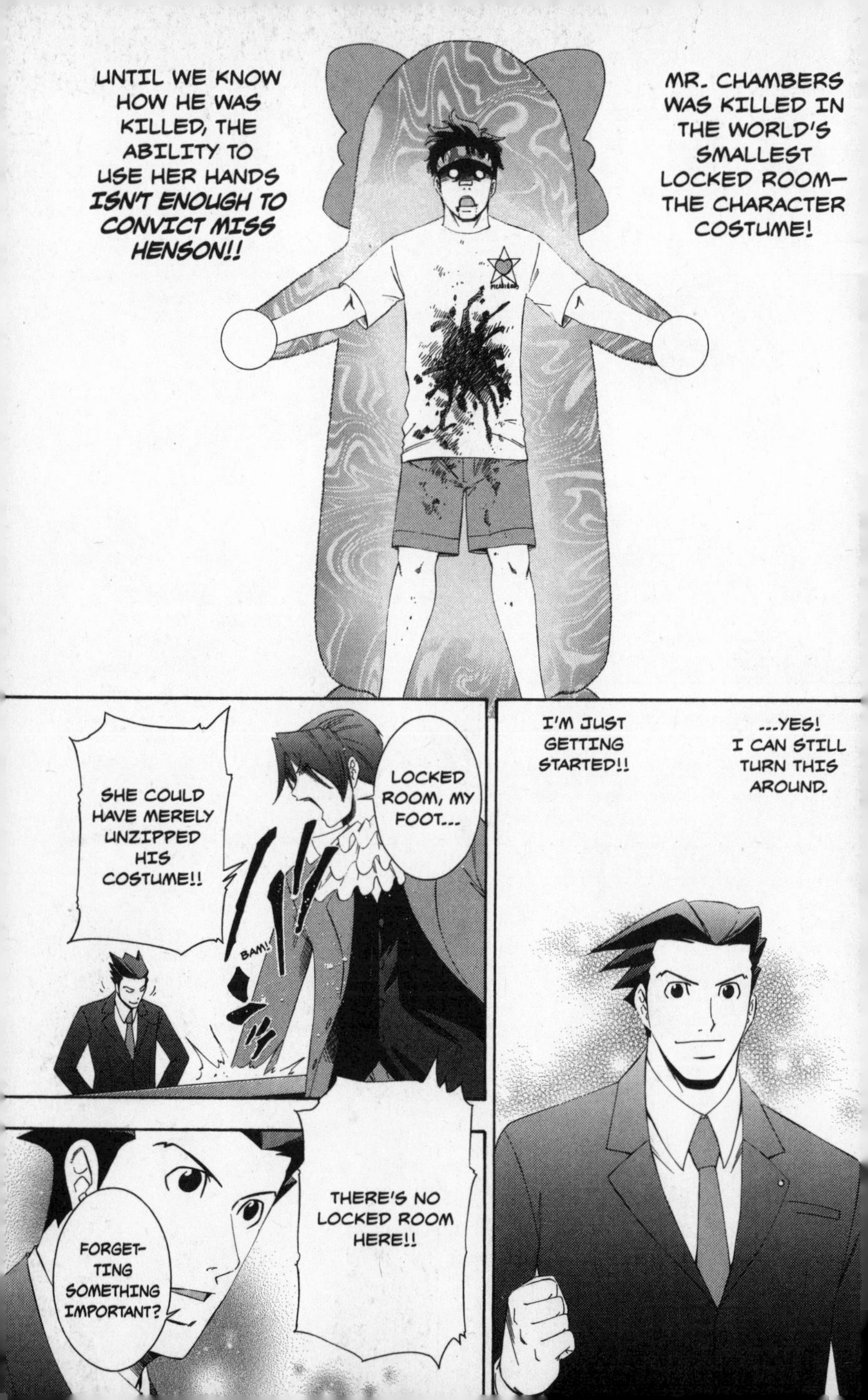
MR. CHAMBERS WAS KILLED IN THE WORLD'S SMALLEST LOCKED ROOM—THE CHARACTER COSTUME!
UNTIL WE KNOW HOW HE WAS KILLED, THE ABILITY TO USE HER HANDS ISN'T ENOUGH TO CONVICT MISS HENSON!!
...YES! I CAN STILL TURN THIS AROUND.
I'M JUST GETTING STARTED!!
LOCKED ROOM, MY FOOT...
SHE COULD HAVE MERELY UNZIPPED HIS COSTUME!!
BAM!
THERE'S NO LOCKED ROOM HERE!!
FORGET-TING SOMETHING IMPORTANT?

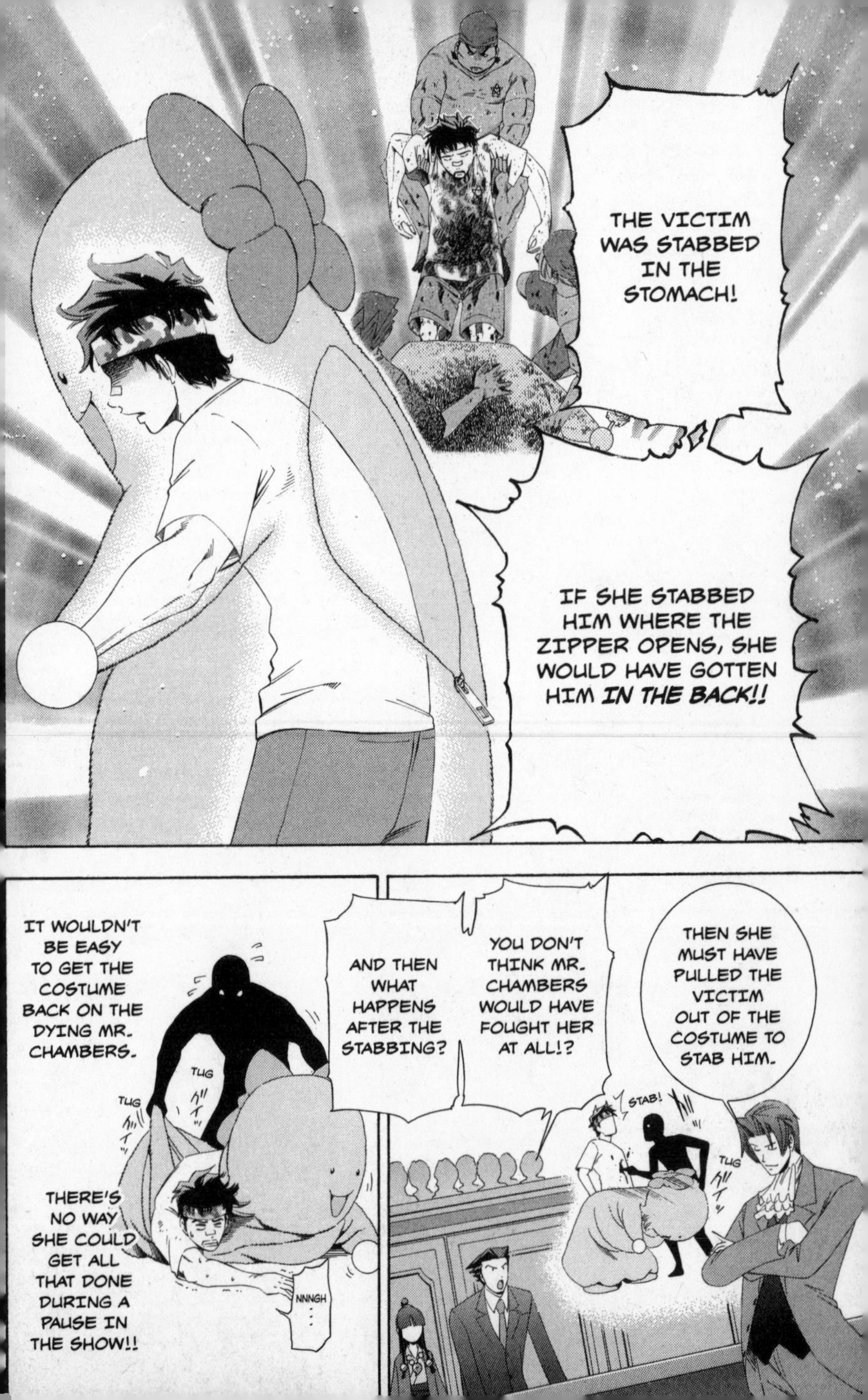
THE VICTIM WAS STABBED IN THE STOMACH!
IF SHE STABBED HIM WHERE THE ZIPPER OPENS, SHE WOULD HAVE GOTTEN HIM *IN THE BACK!!*
THEN SHE MUST HAVE PULLED THE VICTIM OUT OF THE COSTUME TO STAB HIM.
STAB!
TUG
YOU DON'T THINK MR. CHAMBERS WOULD HAVE FOUGHT HER AT ALL!?
AND THEN WHAT HAPPENS AFTER THE STABBING?
IT WOULDN'T BE EASY TO GET THE COSTUME BACK ON THE DYING MR. CHAMBERS.
TUG
TUG
THERE'S NO WAY SHE COULD GET ALL THAT DONE DURING A PAUSE IN THE SHOW!!
NNNGH...

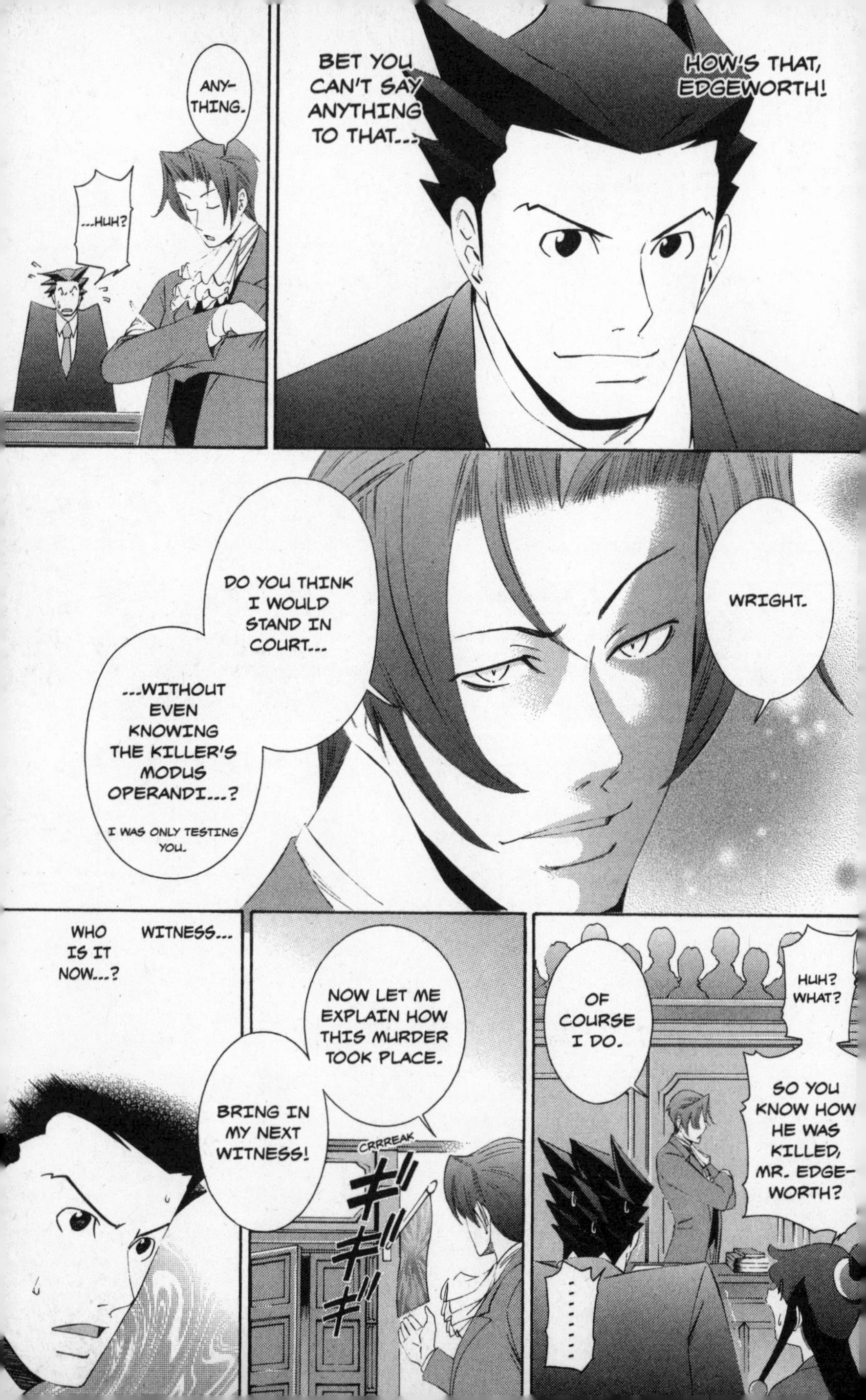
HOW'S THAT, EDGEWORTH!
BET YOU CAN'T SAY ANYTHING TO THAT...!
ANY-THING.
...HUH?
WRIGHT.
DO YOU THINK I WOULD STAND IN COURT...
...WITHOUT EVEN KNOWING THE KILLER'S MODUS OPERANDI...?
I WAS ONLY TESTING YOU.
HUH? WHAT?
SO YOU KNOW HOW HE WAS KILLED, MR. EDGEWORTH?
OF COURSE I DO.
......
NOW LET ME EXPLAIN HOW THIS MURDER TOOK PLACE.
BRING IN MY NEXT WITNESS!
CRRREAK
WITNESS...
WHO IS IT NOW...?

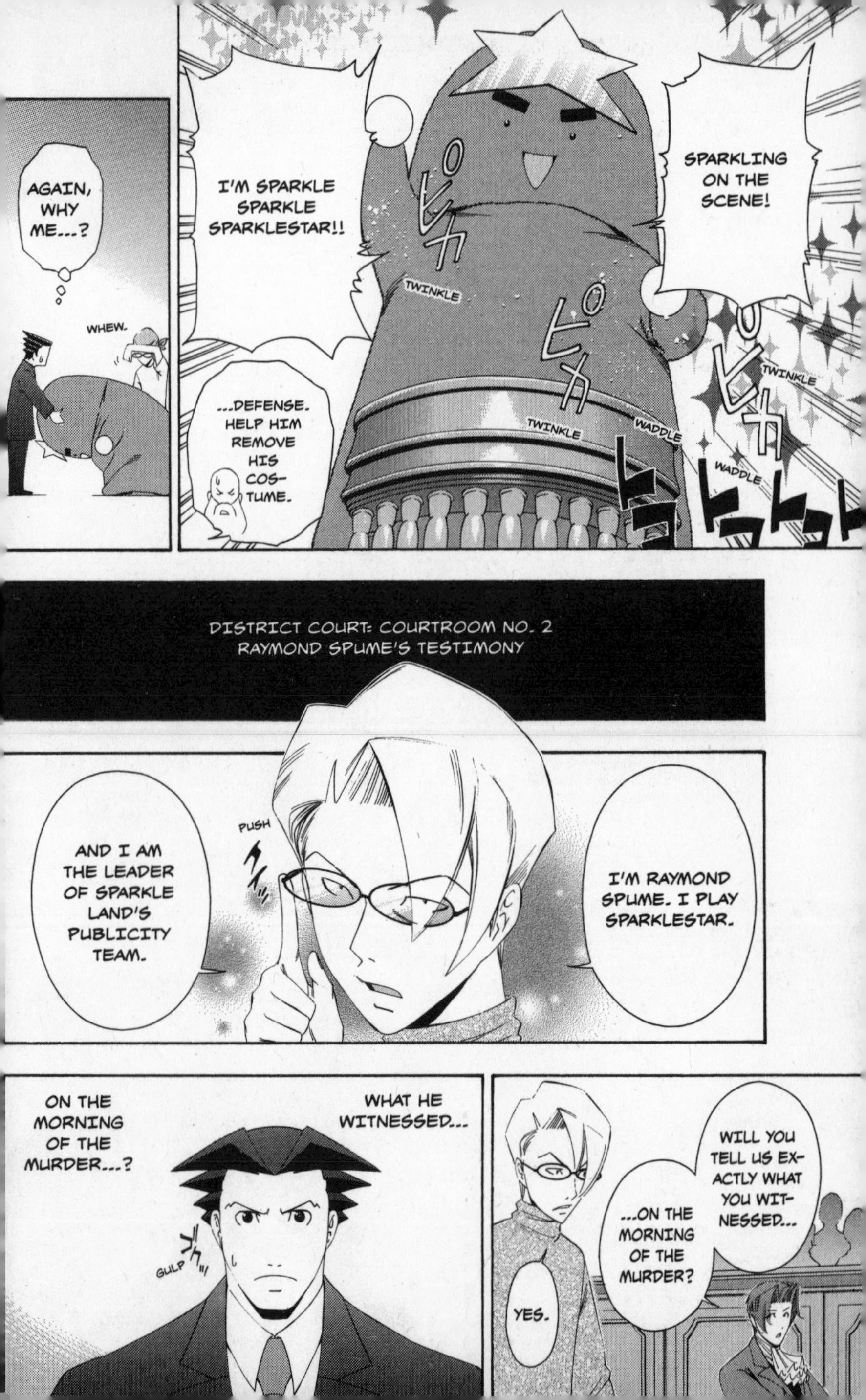
SPARKLING ON THE SCENE!
I'M SPARKLE SPARKLE SPARKLESTAR!!
TWINKLE
TWINKLE
TWINKLE
WADDLE
WADDLE
...DEFENSE. HELP HIM REMOVE HIS COS-TUME.
AGAIN, WHY ME...?
WHEW.
DISTRICT COURT: COURTROOM NO. 2
RAYMOND SPUME'S TESTIMONY
I'M RAYMOND SPUME. I PLAY SPARKLESTAR.
PUSH
AND I AM THE LEADER OF SPARKLE LAND'S PUBLICITY TEAM.
WILL YOU TELL US EX-ACTLY WHAT YOU WIT-NESSED...
...ON THE MORNING OF THE MURDER?
YES.
WHAT HE WITNESSED...
ON THE MORNING OF THE MURDER...?
GULP

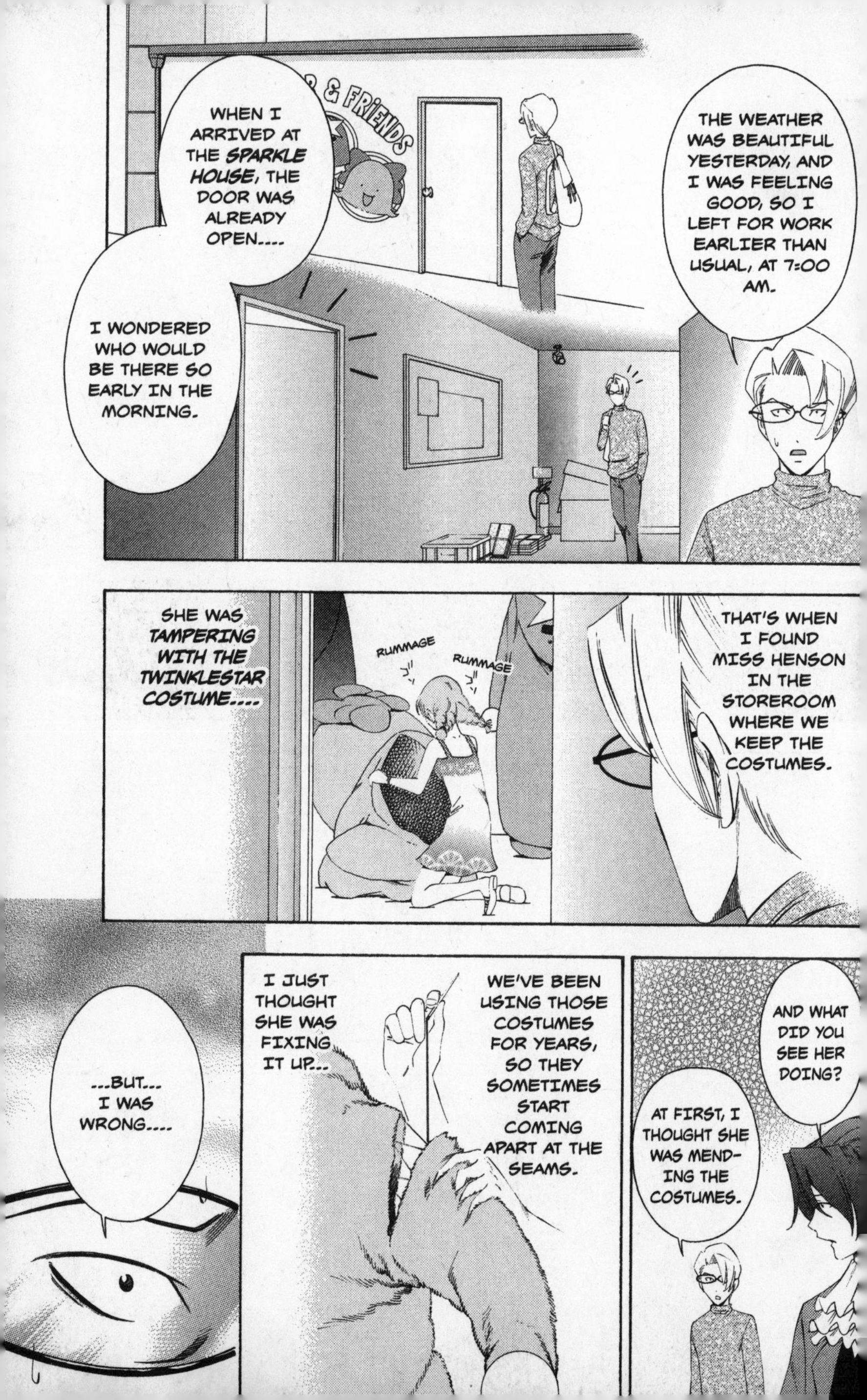
THE WEATHER WAS BEAUTIFUL YESTERDAY, AND I WAS FEELING GOOD, SO I LEFT FOR WORK EARLIER THAN USUAL, AT 7:00 AM.
& FRIENDS
WHEN I ARRIVED AT THE *SPARKLE HOUSE*, THE DOOR WAS ALREADY OPEN....
I WONDERED WHO WOULD BE THERE SO EARLY IN THE MORNING.
THAT'S WHEN I FOUND MISS HENSON IN THE STOREROOM WHERE WE KEEP THE COSTUMES.
RUMMAGE
RUMMAGE
SHE WAS *TAMPERING WITH THE TWINKLESTAR COSTUME....*
AND WHAT DID YOU SEE HER DOING?
AT FIRST, I THOUGHT SHE WAS MEND-ING THE COSTUMES.
WE'VE BEEN USING THOSE COSTUMES FOR YEARS, SO THEY SOMETIMES START COMING APART AT THE SEAMS.
I JUST THOUGHT SHE WAS FIXING IT UP...
...BUT... I WAS WRONG....

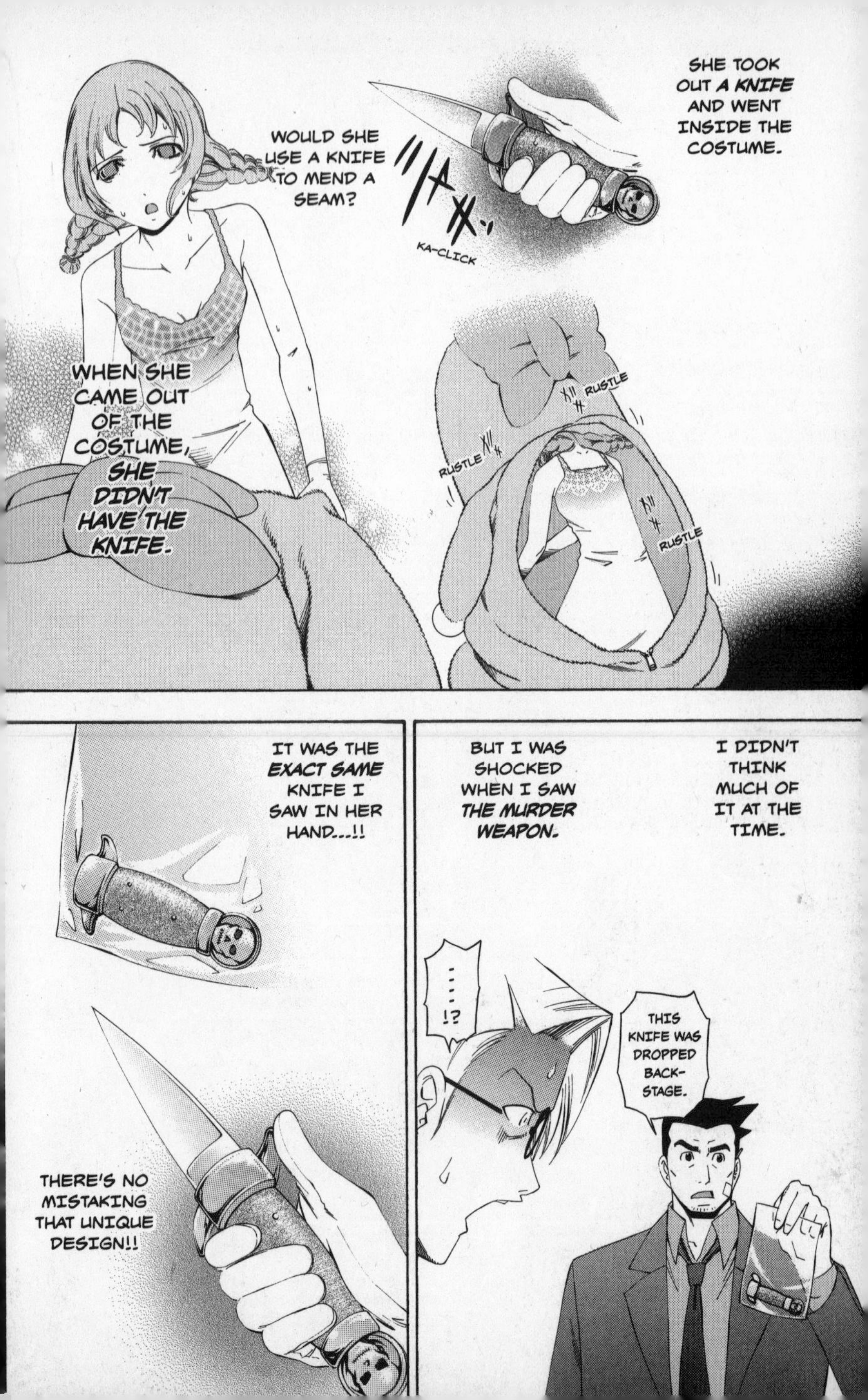
SHE TOOK OUT A KNIFE AND WENT INSIDE THE COSTUME.
KA-CLICK
WOULD SHE USE A KNIFE TO MEND A SEAM?
RUSTLE
RUSTLE
RUSTLE
WHEN SHE CAME OUT OF THE COSTUME, SHE DIDN'T HAVE THE KNIFE.
I DIDN'T THINK MUCH OF IT AT THE TIME.
BUT I WAS SHOCKED WHEN I SAW THE MURDER WEAPON.
THIS KNIFE WAS DROPPED BACK-STAGE.
......!?
IT WAS THE EXACT SAME KNIFE I SAW IN HER HAND...!!
THERE'S NO MISTAKING THAT UNIQUE DESIGN!!

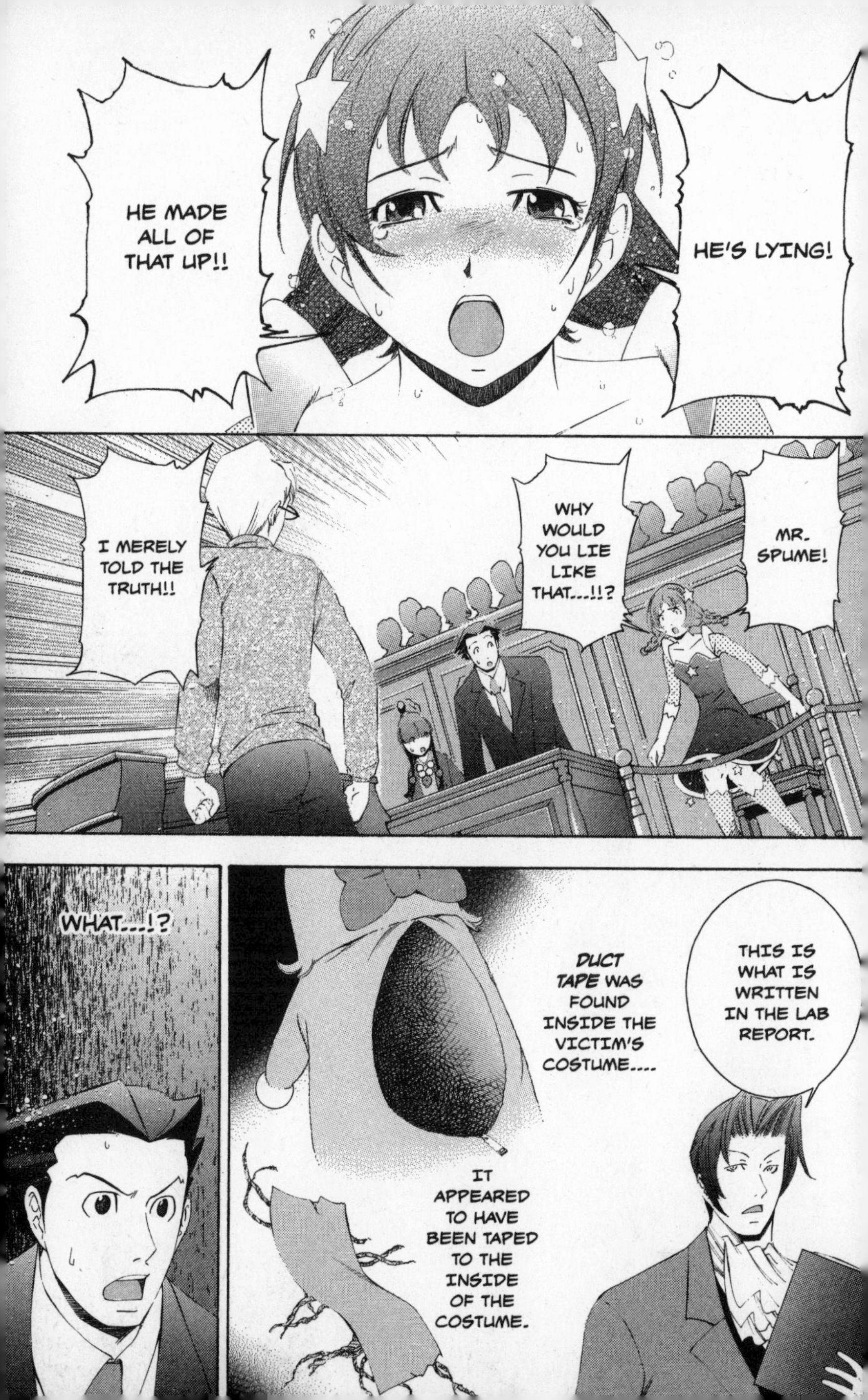
HE'S LYING!
HE MADE ALL OF THAT UP!!
MR. SPUME!
WHY WOULD YOU LIE LIKE THAT...!!?
I MERELY TOLD THE TRUTH!!
THIS IS WHAT IS WRITTEN IN THE LAB REPORT.
DUCT TAPE WAS FOUND INSIDE THE VICTIM'S COSTUME....
IT APPEARED TO HAVE BEEN TAPED TO THE INSIDE OF THE COSTUME.
WHAT...!?

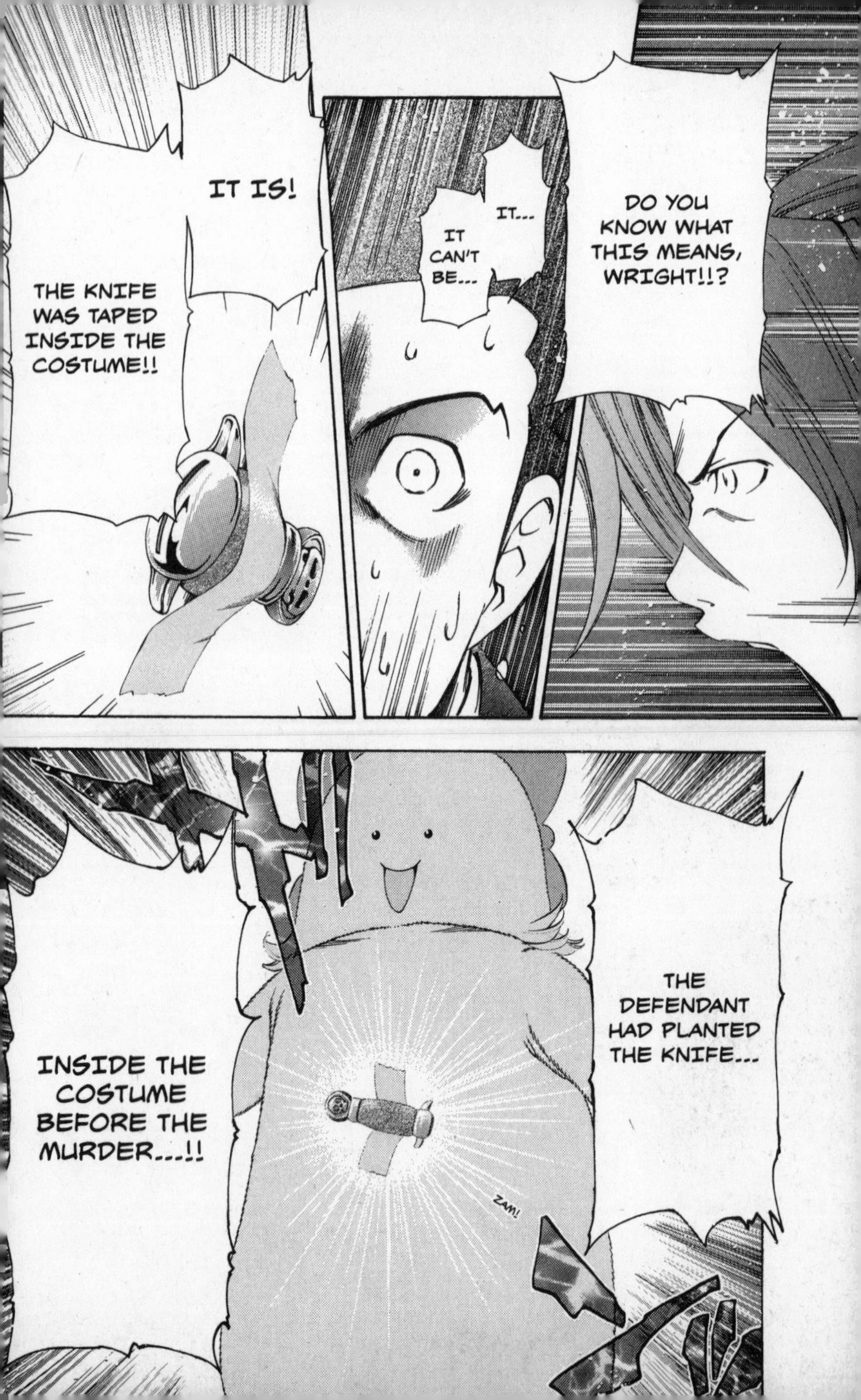
DO YOU KNOW WHAT THIS MEANS, WRIGHT!!?
IT...
IT CAN'T BE...
IT IS!
THE KNIFE WAS TAPED INSIDE THE COSTUME!!
THE DEFENDANT HAD PLANTED THE KNIFE...
INSIDE THE COSTUME BEFORE THE MURDER...!!
ZAM!

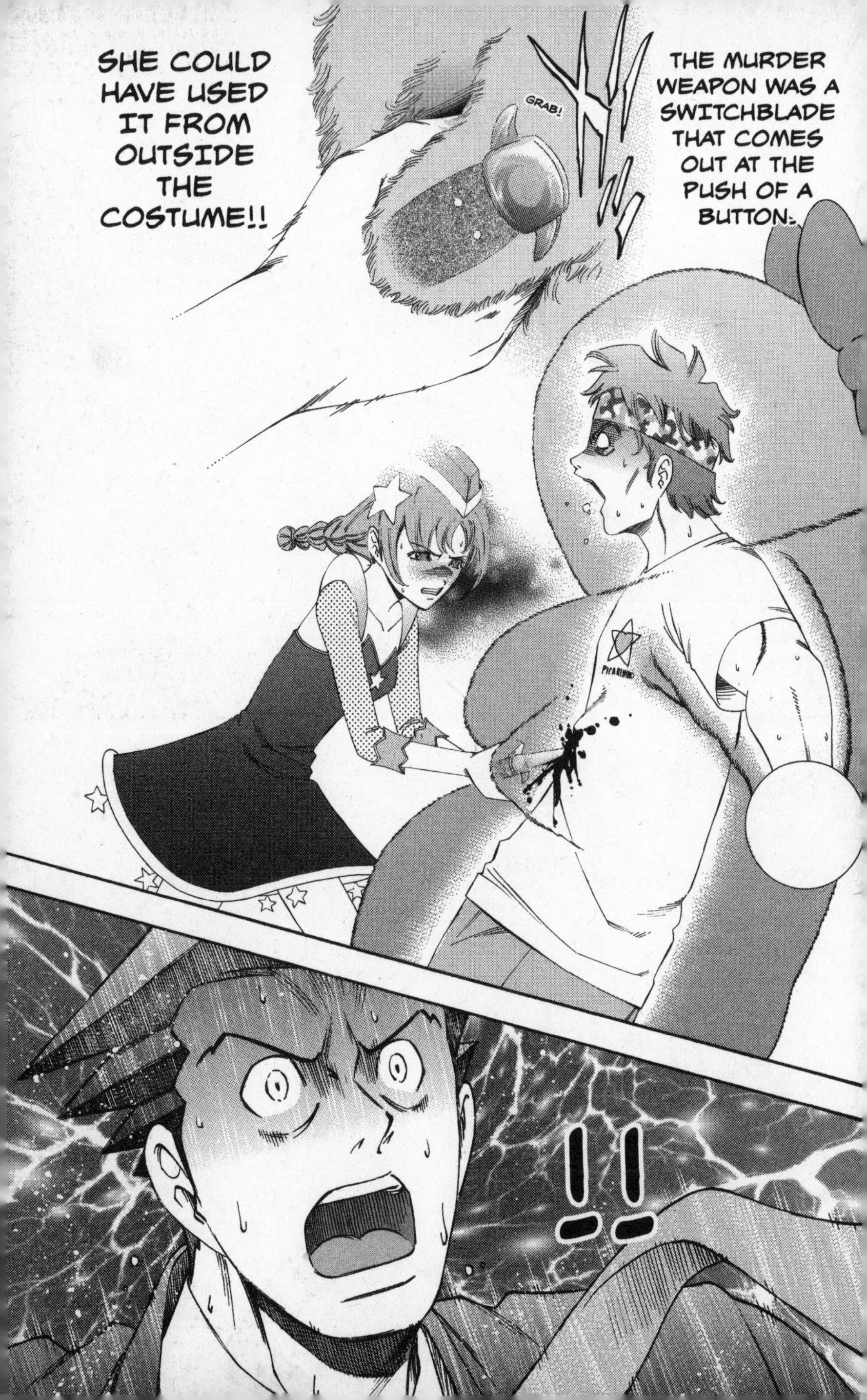
THE MURDER WEAPON WAS A SWITCHBLADE THAT COMES OUT AT THE PUSH OF A BUTTON.
GRAB!
SHE COULD HAVE USED IT FROM OUTSIDE THE COSTUME!!
!!

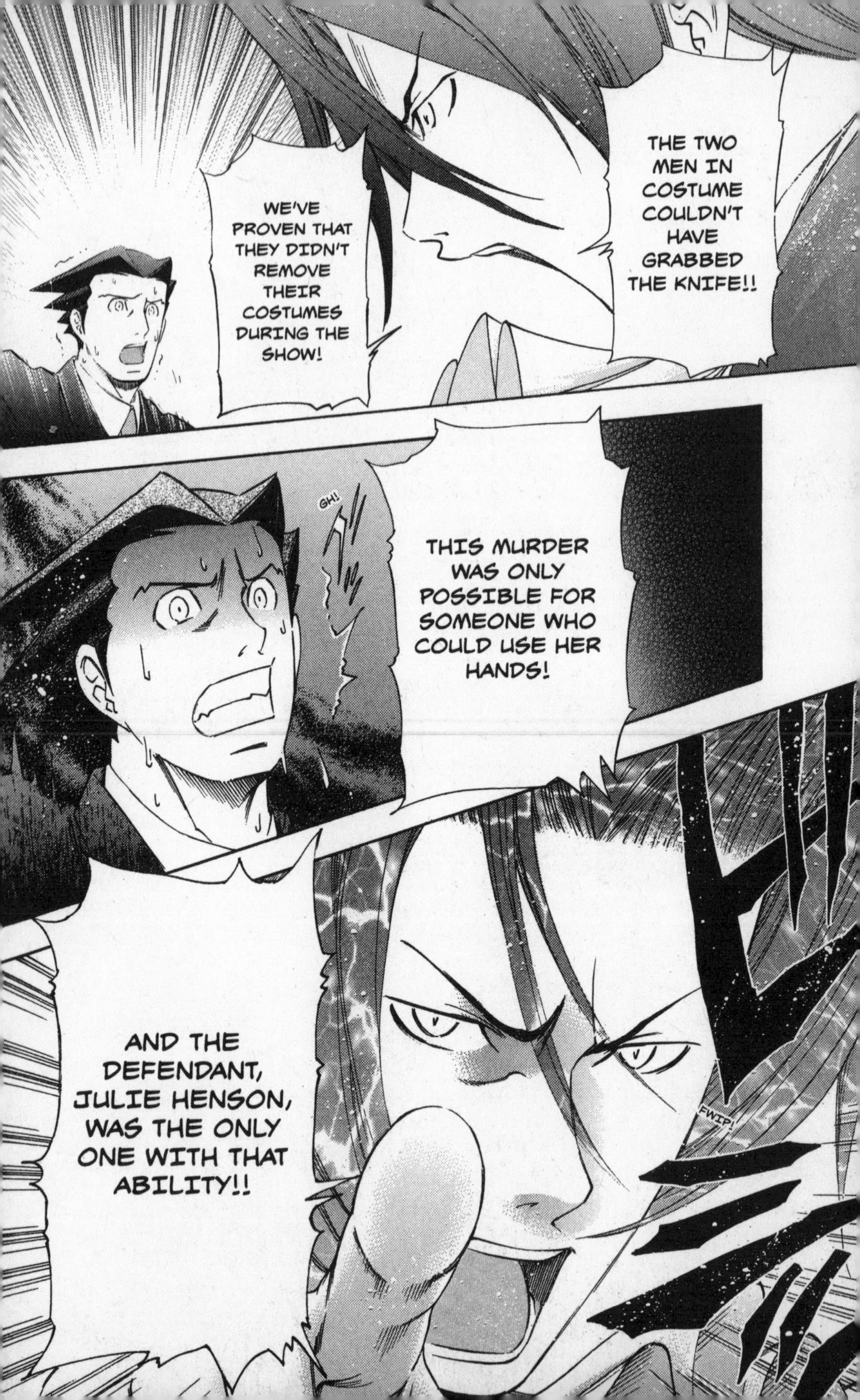
THE TWO MEN IN COSTUME COULDN'T HAVE GRABBED THE KNIFE!!
WE'VE PROVEN THAT THEY DIDN'T REMOVE THEIR COSTUMES DURING THE SHOW!
THIS MURDER WAS ONLY POSSIBLE FOR SOMEONE WHO COULD USE HER HANDS!
GH!
AND THE DEFENDANT, JULIE HENSON, WAS THE ONLY ONE WITH THAT ABILITY!!
FWIP!

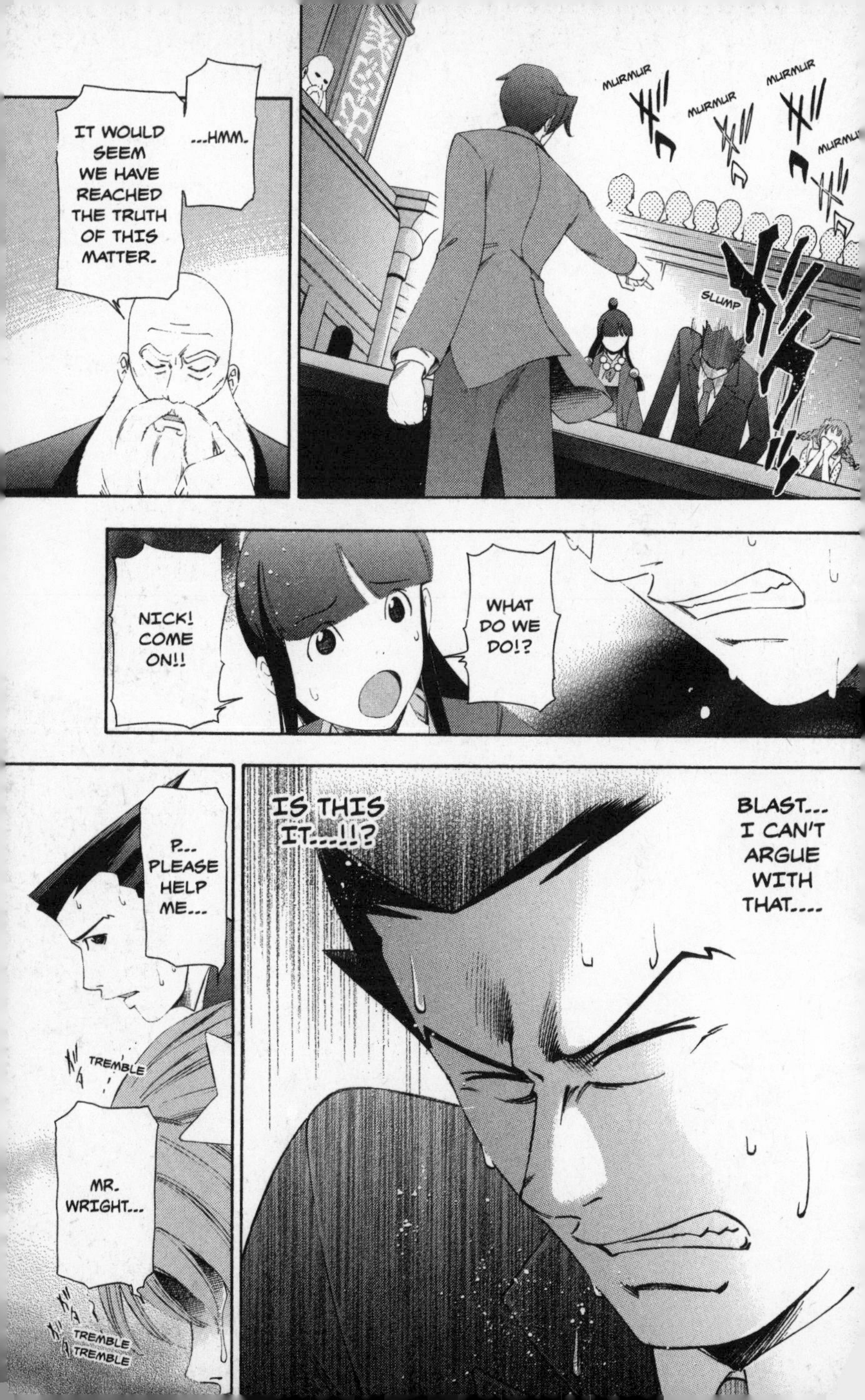
MURMUR
MURMUR
MURMUR
MURMUR
SLUMP
...HMM.
IT WOULD SEEM WE HAVE REACHED THE TRUTH OF THIS MATTER.
WHAT DO WE DO!?
NICK! COME ON!!
BLAST... I CAN'T ARGUE WITH THAT....
IS THIS IT...!!?
P... PLEASE HELP ME...
TREMBLE
MR. WRIGHT...
TREMBLE TREMBLE

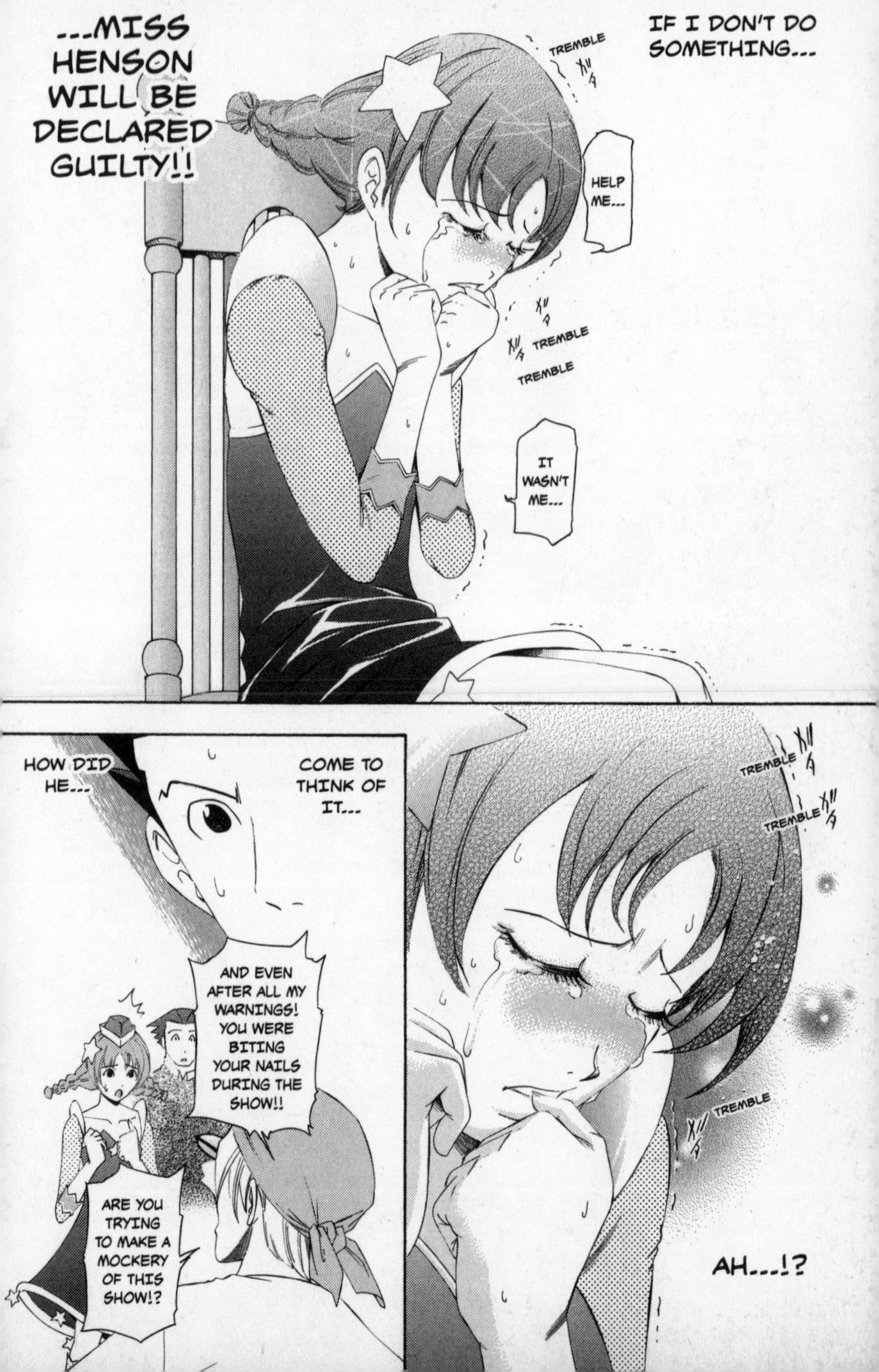
IF I DON'T DO SOMETHING...
...MISS HENSON WILL BE DECLARED GUILTY!!
TREMBLE
HELP ME...
TREMBLE
TREMBLE
IT WASN'T ME...
TREMBLE
TREMBLE
TREMBLE
AH...!?
COME TO THINK OF IT...
HOW DID HE...
AND EVEN AFTER ALL MY WARNINGS! YOU WERE BITING YOUR NAILS DURING THE SHOW!!
ARE YOU TRYING TO MAKE A MOCKERY OF THIS SHOW!?

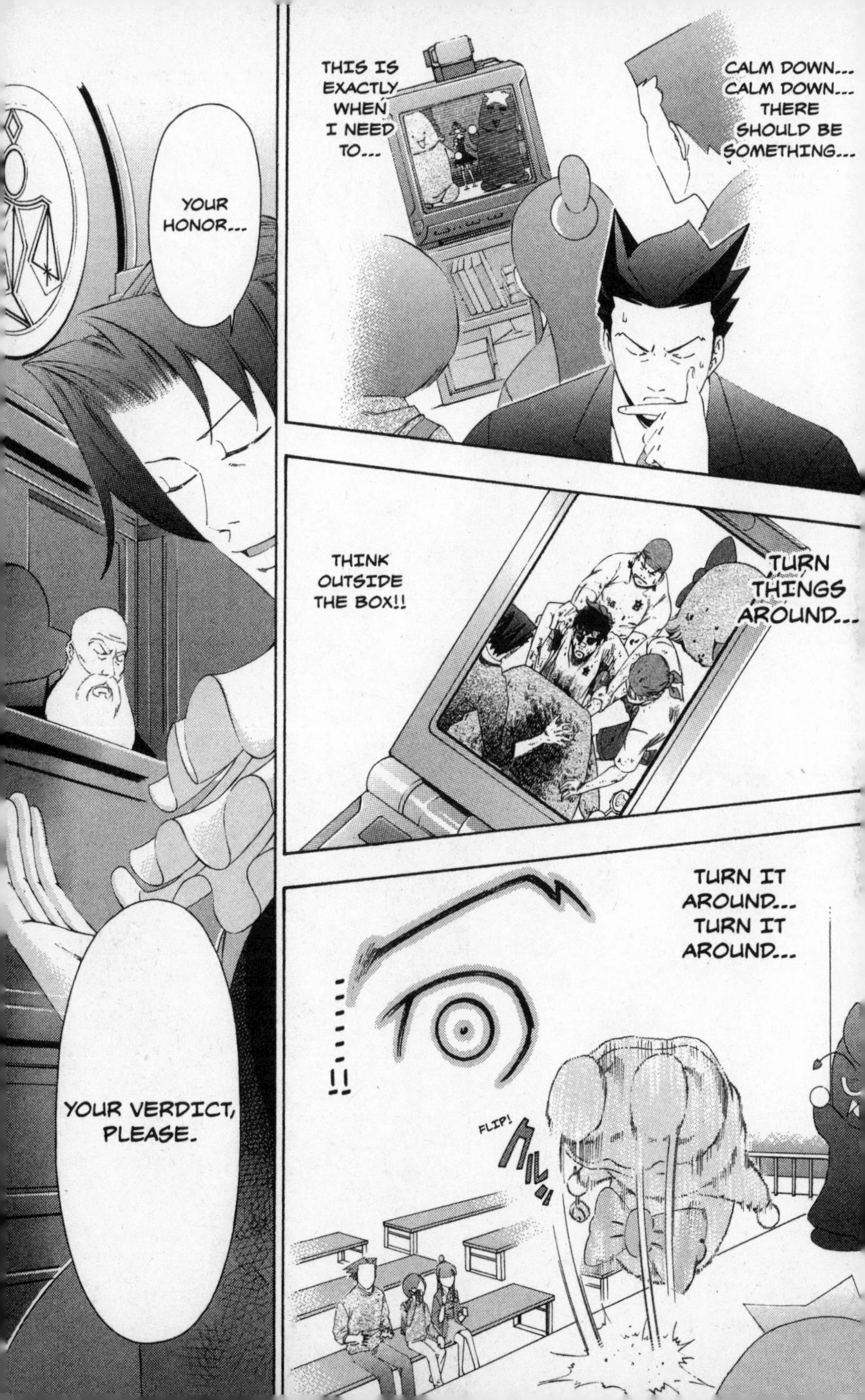

CALM DOWN... CALM DOWN... THERE SHOULD BE SOMETHING...
THIS IS EXACTLY WHEN I NEED TO...
TURN THINGS AROUND...
THINK OUTSIDE THE BOX!!
TURN IT AROUND... TURN IT AROUND...
......!!
FLIP!
YOUR HONOR...
YOUR VERDICT, PLEASE.

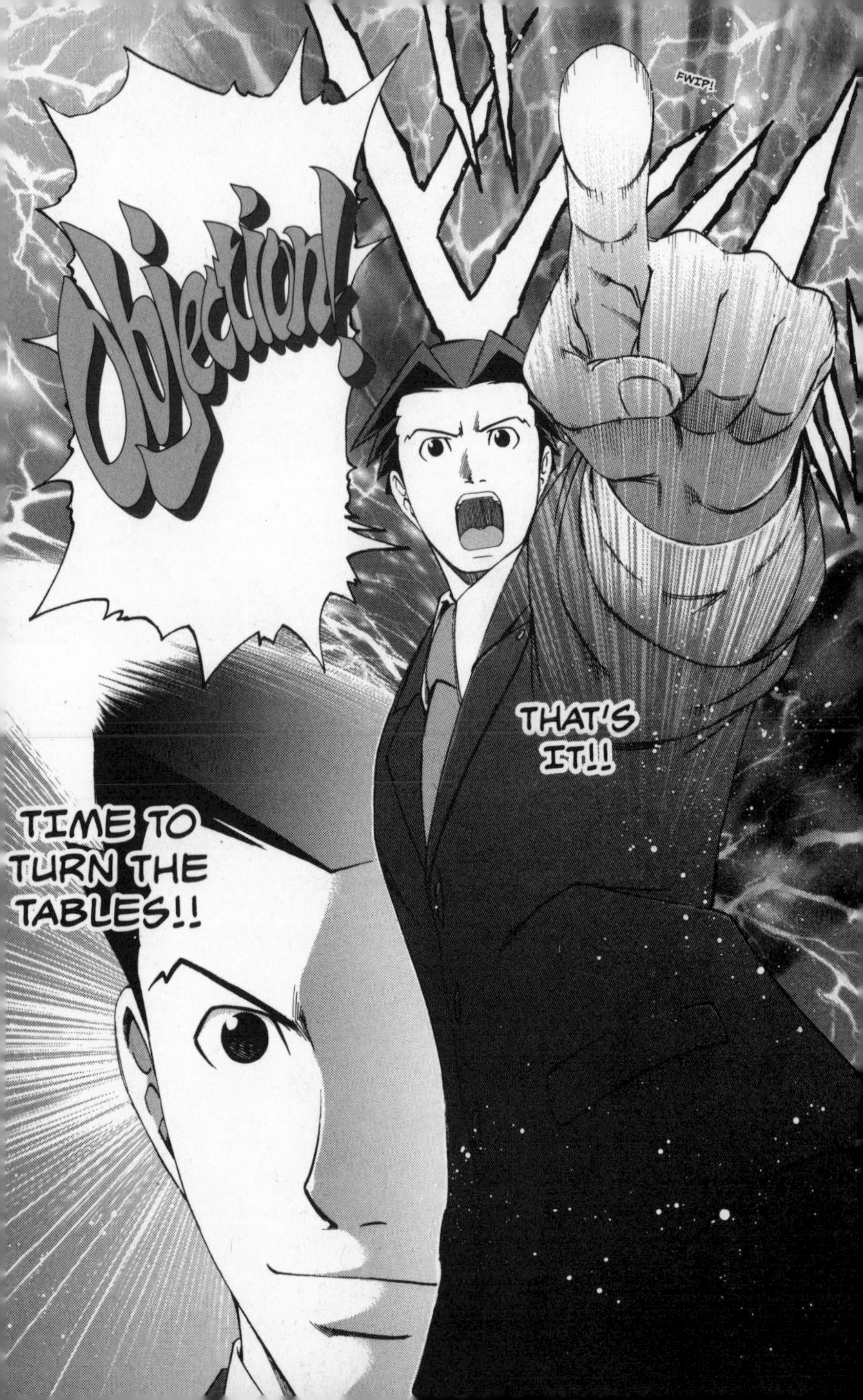
FWIP!
Objection!
THAT'S IT!!
TIME TO TURN THE TABLES!!

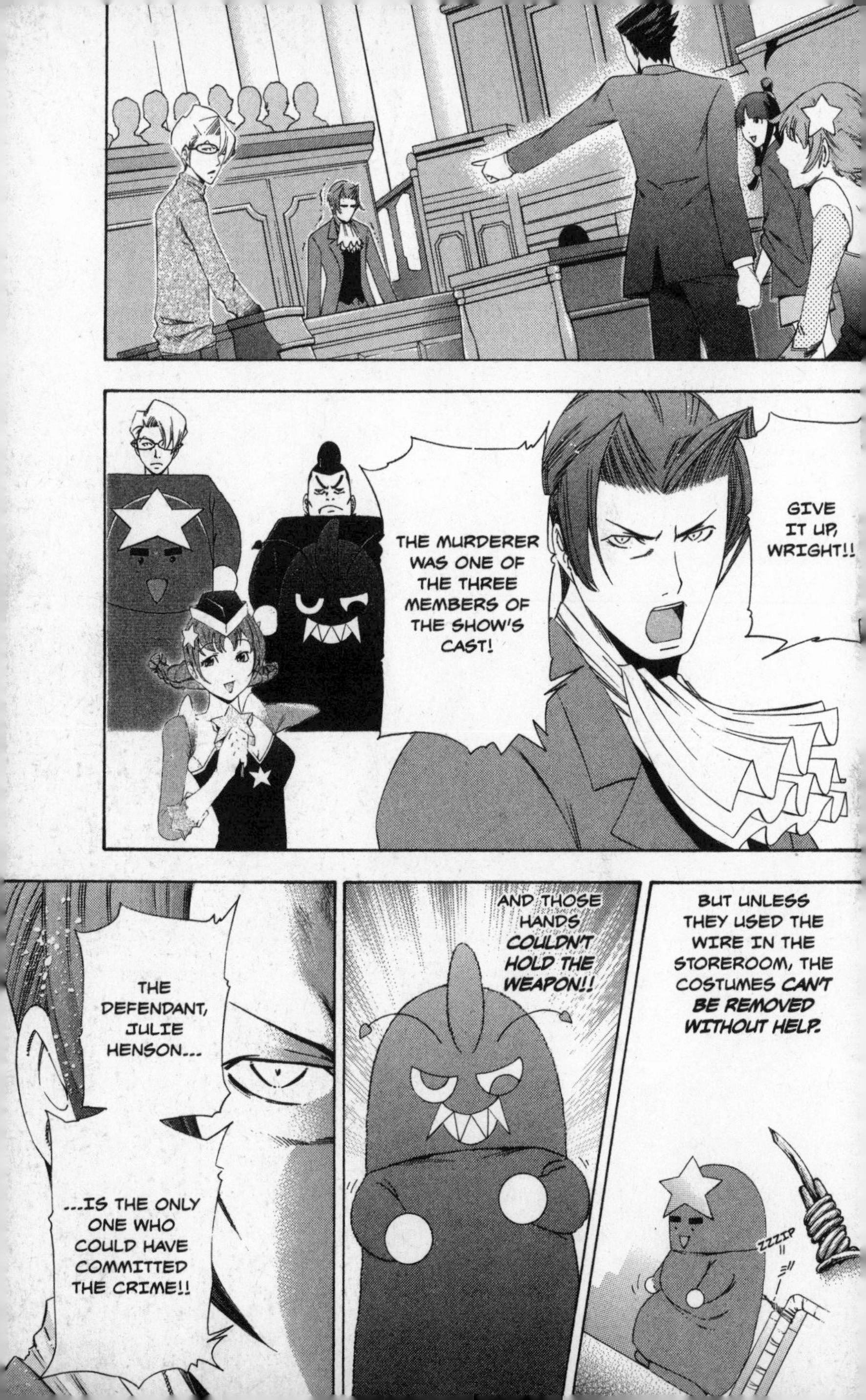

GIVE IT UP, WRIGHT!!
THE MURDERER WAS ONE OF THE THREE MEMBERS OF THE SHOW'S CAST!
BUT UNLESS THEY USED THE WIRE IN THE STOREROOM, THE COSTUMES *CAN'T BE REMOVED WITHOUT HELP.*
ZZZIP
AND THOSE HANDS *COULDN'T HOLD THE WEAPON!!*
THE DEFENDANT, JULIE HENSON...
...IS THE ONLY ONE WHO COULD HAVE COMMITTED THE CRIME!!

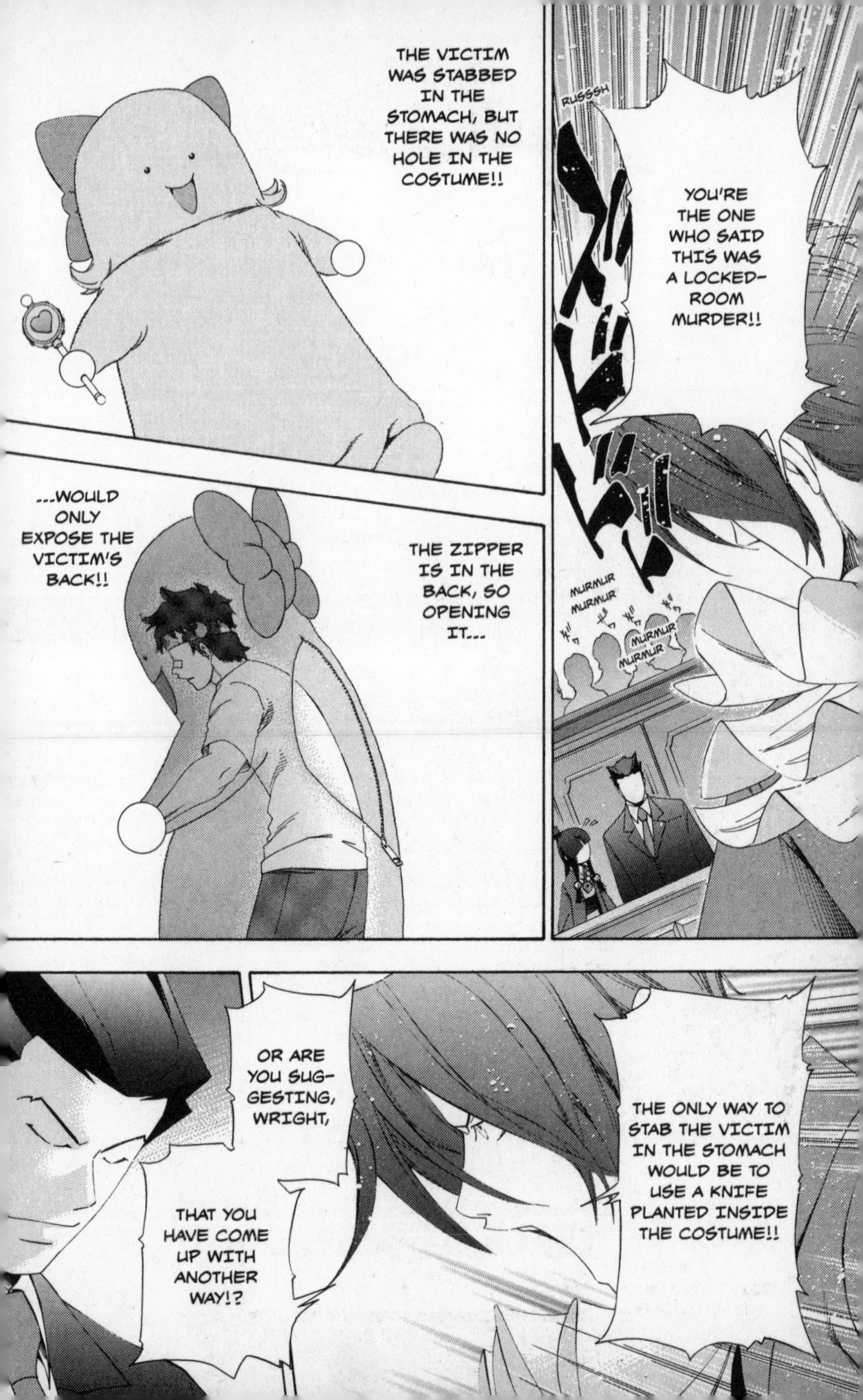
RUSSSH
YOU'RE THE ONE WHO SAID THIS WAS A LOCKED-ROOM MURDER!!
MURMUR MURMUR
MURMUR MURMUR
THE VICTIM WAS STABBED IN THE STOMACH, BUT THERE WAS NO HOLE IN THE COSTUME!!
THE ZIPPER IS IN THE BACK, SO OPENING IT...
...WOULD ONLY EXPOSE THE VICTIM'S BACK!!
THE ONLY WAY TO STAB THE VICTIM IN THE STOMACH WOULD BE TO USE A KNIFE PLANTED INSIDE THE COSTUME!!
OR ARE YOU SUG-GESTING, WRIGHT,
THAT YOU HAVE COME UP WITH ANOTHER WAY!?

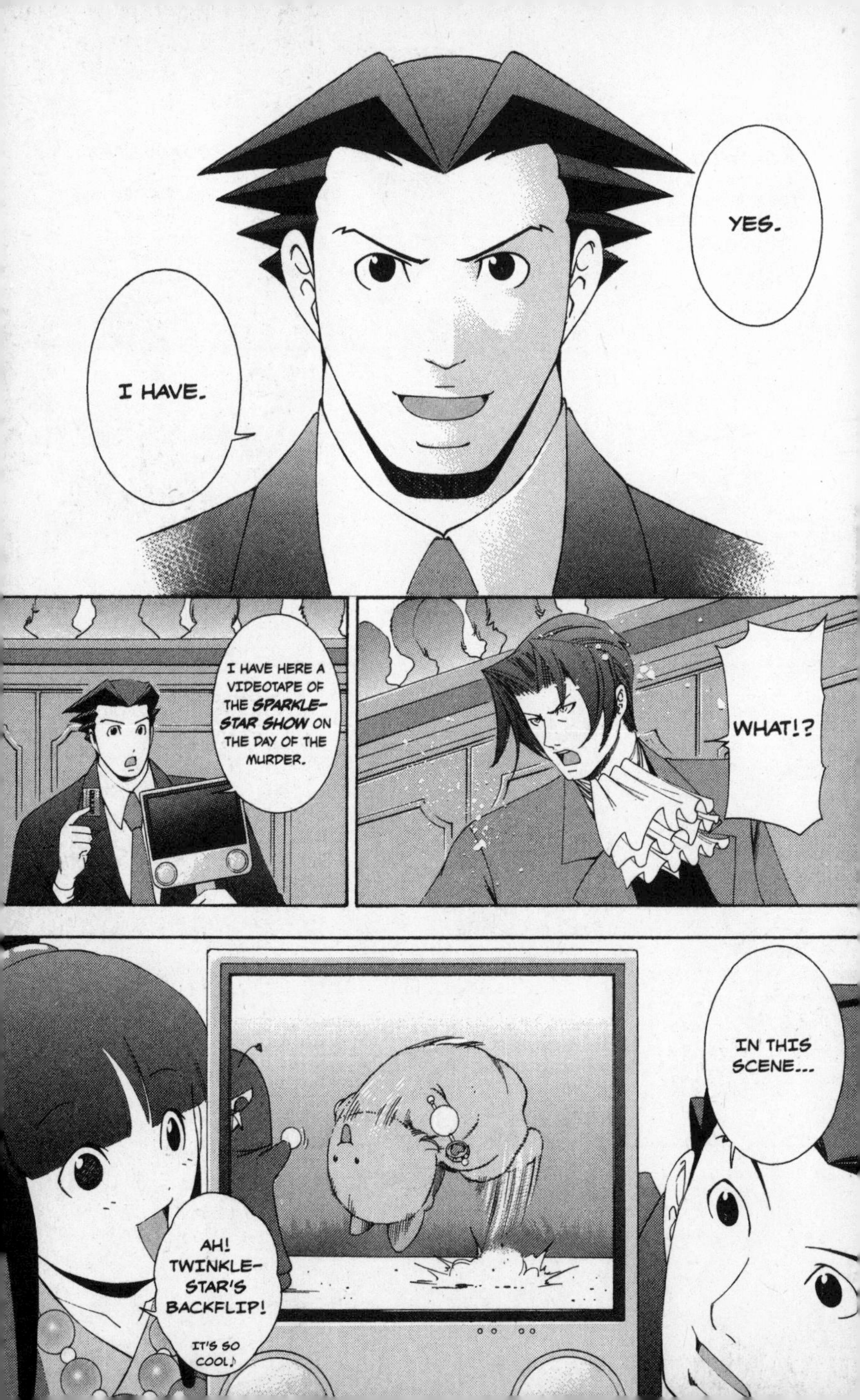
YES.
I HAVE.
WHAT!?
I HAVE HERE A VIDEOTAPE OF THE SPARKLE-STAR SHOW ON THE DAY OF THE MURDER.
IN THIS SCENE...
AH! TWINKLE-STAR'S BACKFLIP!
IT'S SO COOL♪

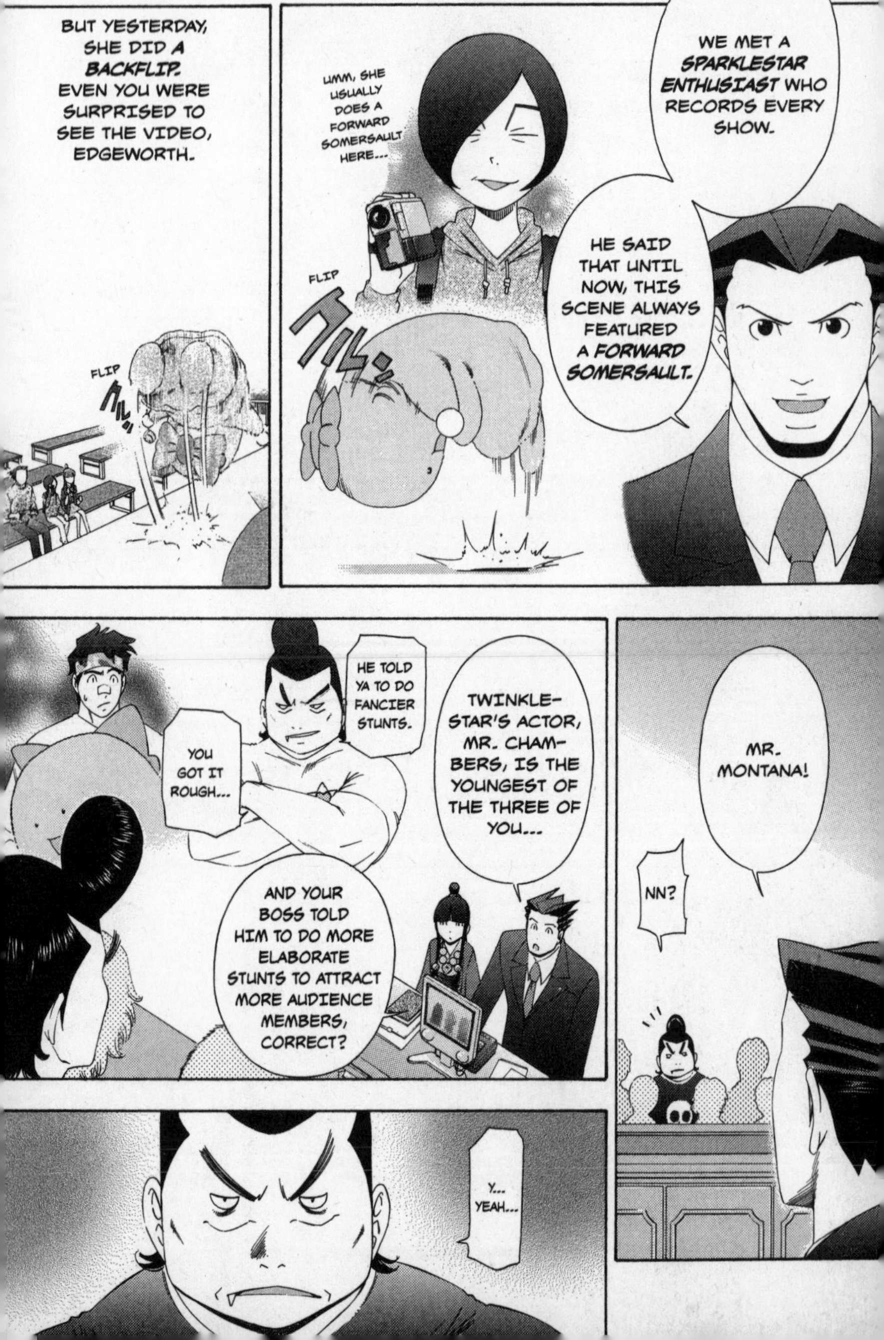
WE MET A SPARKLESTAR ENTHUSIAST WHO RECORDS EVERY SHOW.
HE SAID THAT UNTIL NOW, THIS SCENE ALWAYS FEATURED A FORWARD SOMERSAULT.
UMM, SHE USUALLY DOES A FORWARD SOMERSAULT HERE...
FLIP
BUT YESTERDAY, SHE DID A BACKFLIP. EVEN YOU WERE SURPRISED TO SEE THE VIDEO, EDGEWORTH.
FLIP
MR. MONTANA!
NN?
TWINKLE-STAR'S ACTOR, MR. CHAMBERS, IS THE YOUNGEST OF THE THREE OF YOU...
HE TOLD YA TO DO FANCIER STUNTS.
YOU GOT IT ROUGH...
AND YOUR BOSS TOLD HIM TO DO MORE ELABORATE STUNTS TO ATTRACT MORE AUDIENCE MEMBERS, CORRECT?
Y... YEAH...

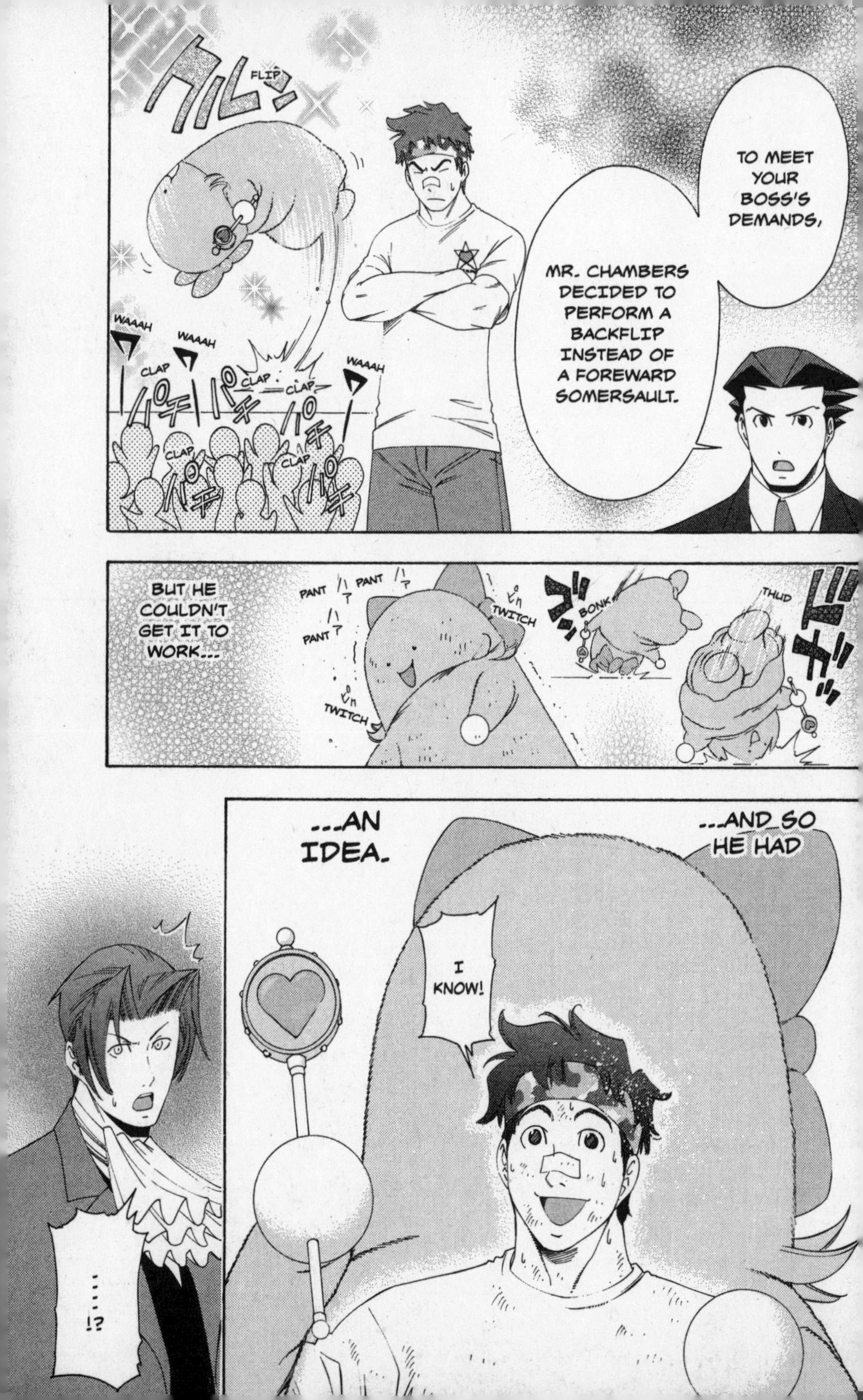
TO MEET YOUR BOSS'S DEMANDS,
MR. CHAMBERS DECIDED TO PERFORM A BACKFLIP INSTEAD OF A FOREWARD SOMERSAULT.
FLIP
WAAAH
WAAAH
WAAAH
CLAP
CLAP
CLAP
CLAP
CLAP
THUD
BONK
TWITCH
PANT
PANT
PANT
TWITCH
BUT HE COULDN'T GET IT TO WORK...
...AND SO HE HAD
...AN IDEA.
I KNOW!
......!?

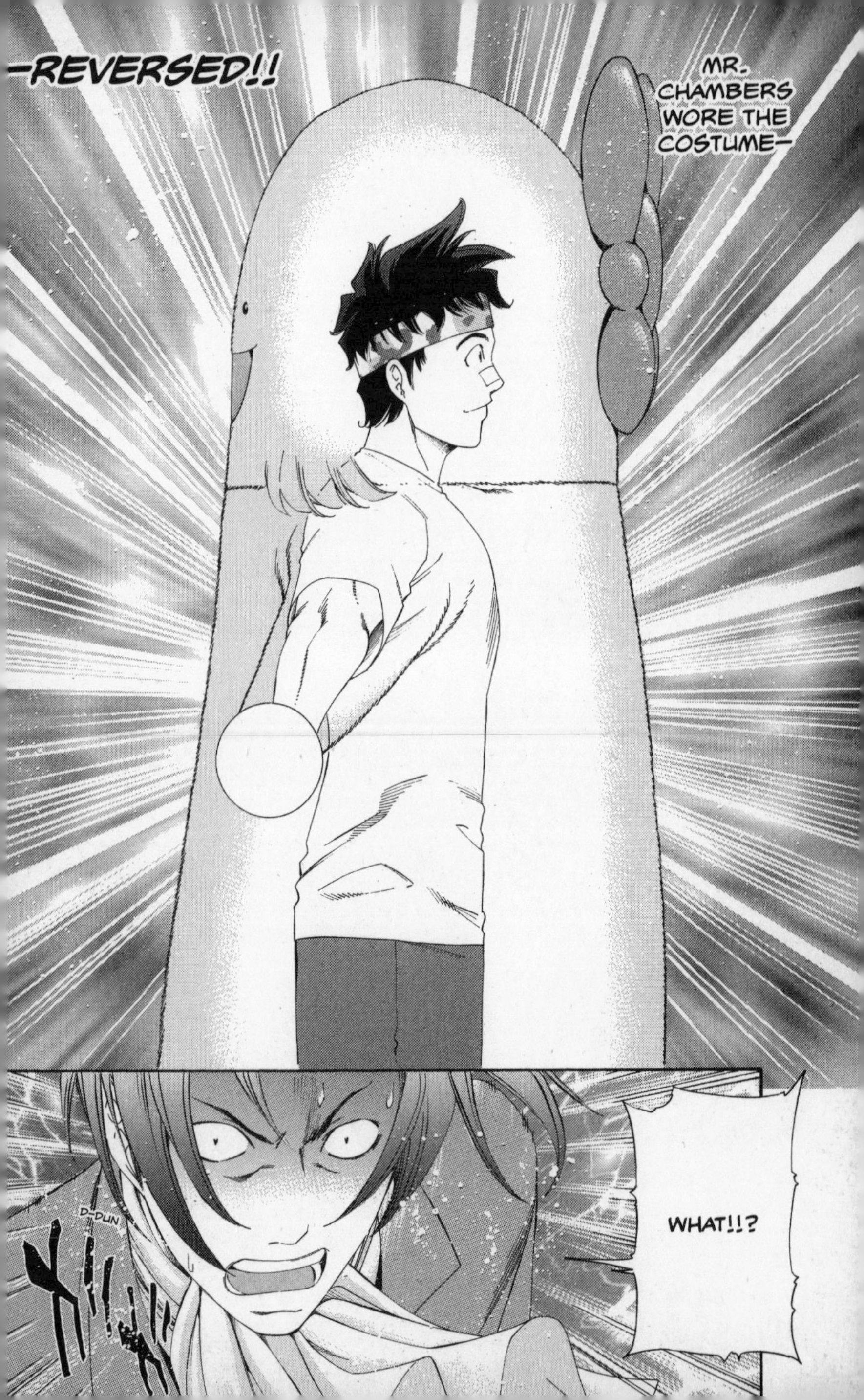
MR. CHAMBERS WORE THE COSTUME—
—REVERSED!!
WHAT!!?
D-DUN

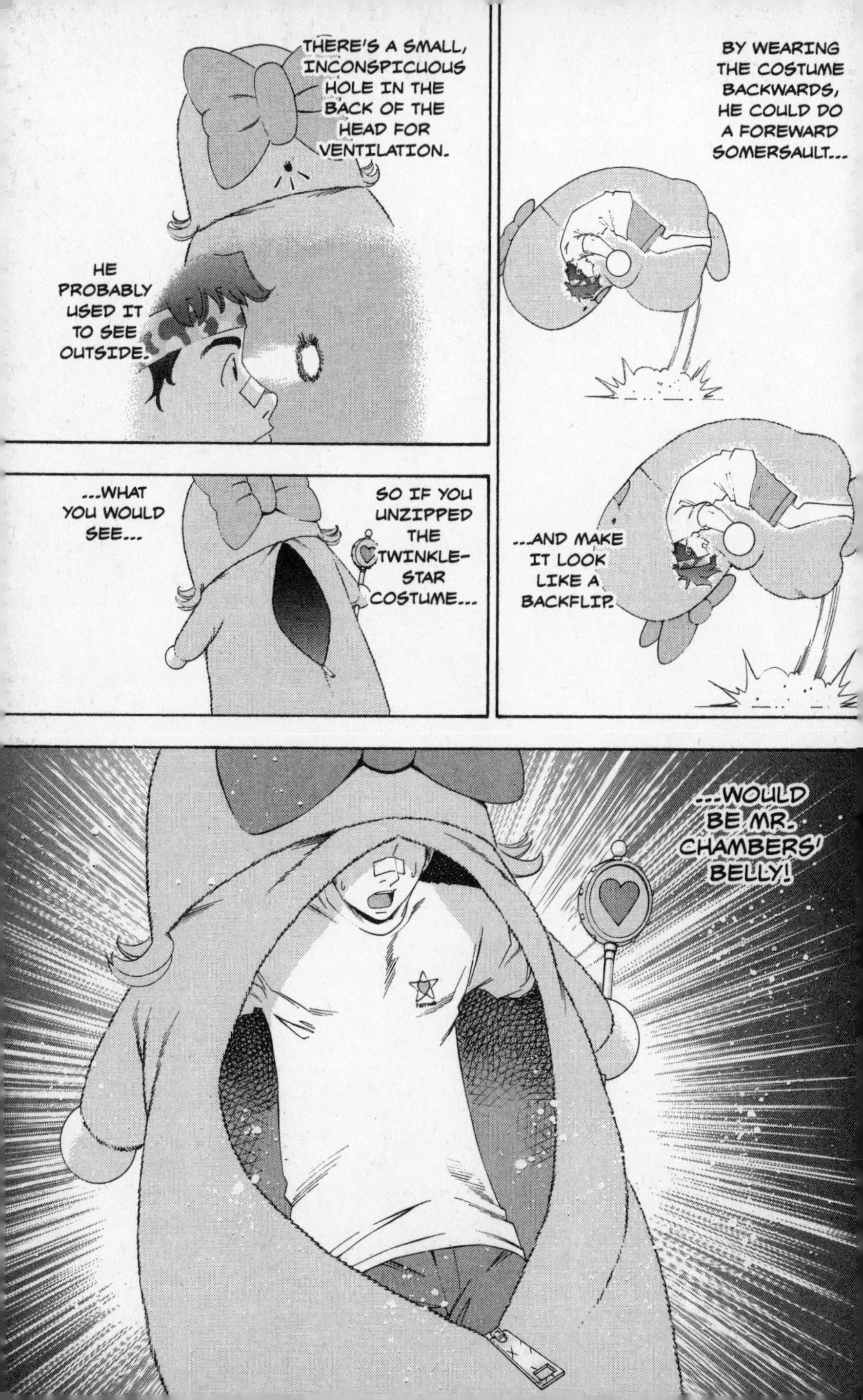
BY WEARING THE COSTUME BACKWARDS, HE COULD DO A FOREWARD SOMERSAULT...
...AND MAKE IT LOOK LIKE A BACKFLIP.
THERE'S A SMALL, INCONSPICUOUS HOLE IN THE BACK OF THE HEAD FOR VENTILATION.
HE PROBABLY USED IT TO SEE OUTSIDE.
SO IF YOU UNZIPPED THE TWINKLE-STAR COSTUME...
...WHAT YOU WOULD SEE...
...WOULD BE MR. CHAMBERS' BELLY!

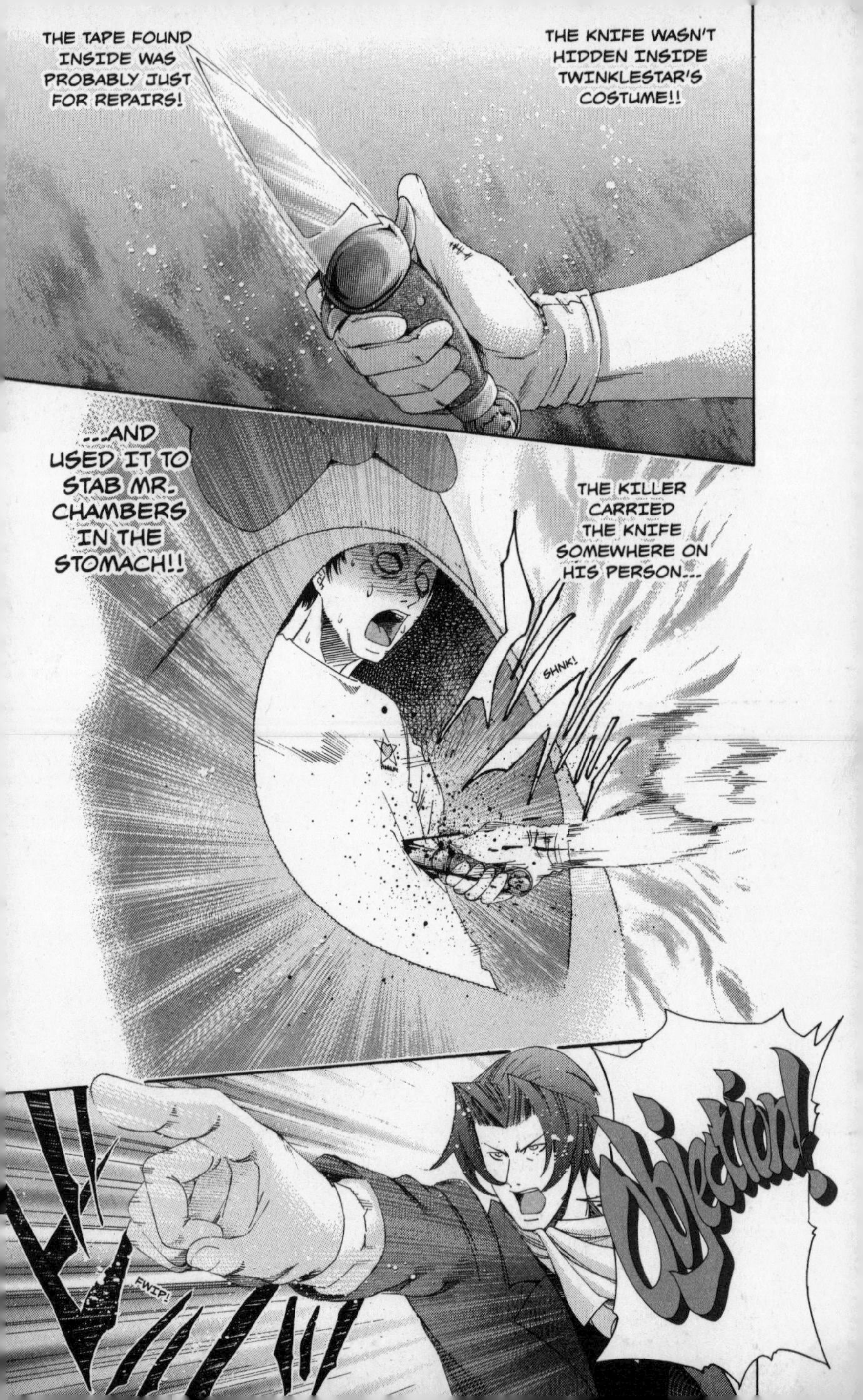
THE KNIFE WASN'T HIDDEN INSIDE TWINKLESTAR'S COSTUME!!
THE TAPE FOUND INSIDE WAS PROBABLY JUST FOR REPAIRS!
THE KILLER CARRIED THE KNIFE SOMEWHERE ON HIS PERSON...
SHNK!
...AND USED IT TO STAB MR. CHAMBERS IN THE STOMACH!!
Objection!
FWIP!

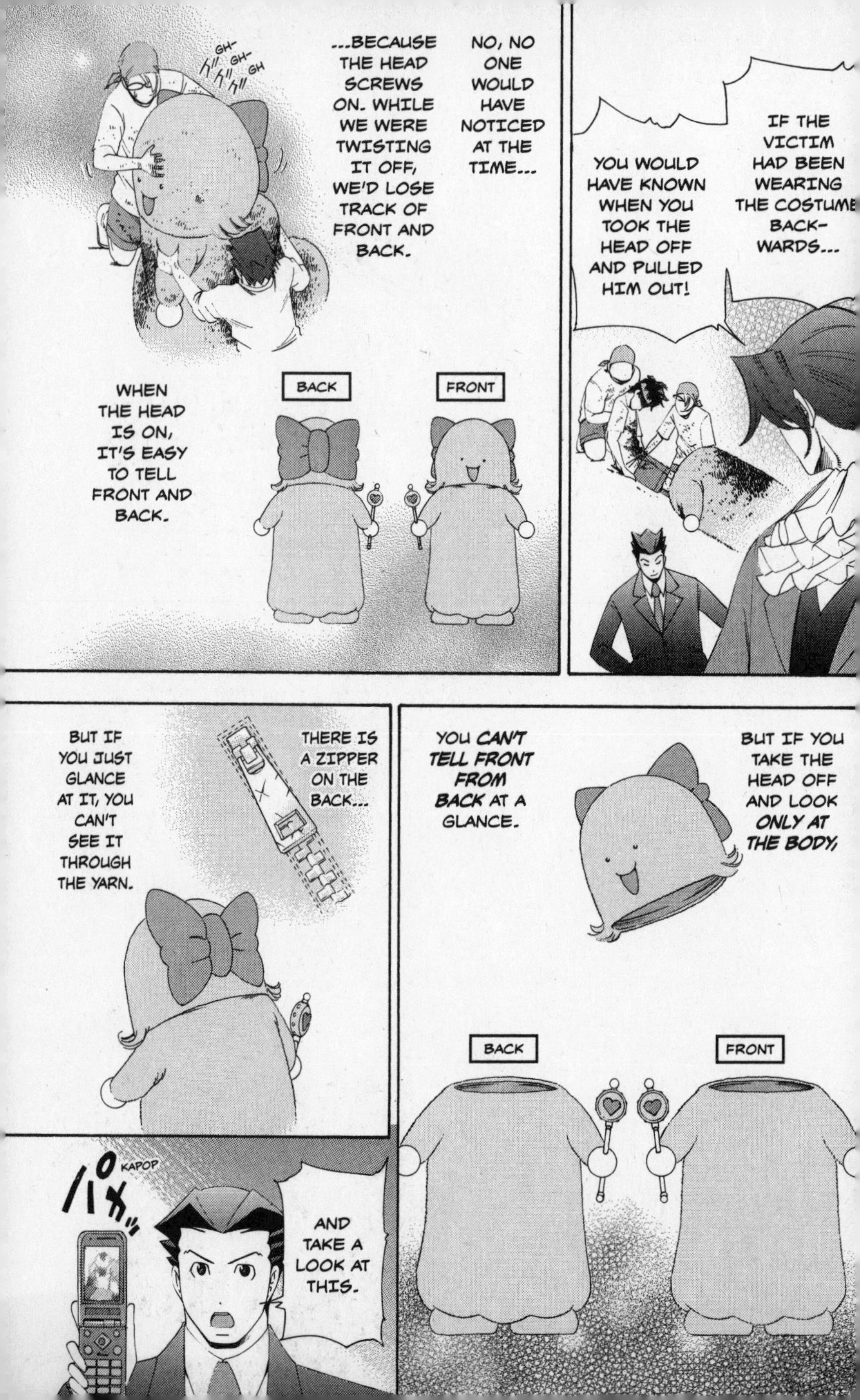
IF THE VICTIM HAD BEEN WEARING THE COSTUME BACKWARDS...
YOU WOULD HAVE KNOWN WHEN YOU TOOK THE HEAD OFF AND PULLED HIM OUT!
NO, NO ONE WOULD HAVE NOTICED AT THE TIME...
...BECAUSE THE HEAD SCREWS ON. WHILE WE WERE TWISTING IT OFF, WE'D LOSE TRACK OF FRONT AND BACK.
GH- GH- GH
FRONT
BACK
WHEN THE HEAD IS ON, IT'S EASY TO TELL FRONT AND BACK.
BUT IF YOU TAKE THE HEAD OFF AND LOOK *ONLY AT THE BODY,*
YOU *CAN'T TELL FRONT FROM BACK* AT A GLANCE.
FRONT
BACK
THERE IS A ZIPPER ON THE BACK...
BUT IF YOU JUST GLANCE AT IT, YOU CAN'T SEE IT THROUGH THE YARN.
AND TAKE A LOOK AT THIS.
KAPOP

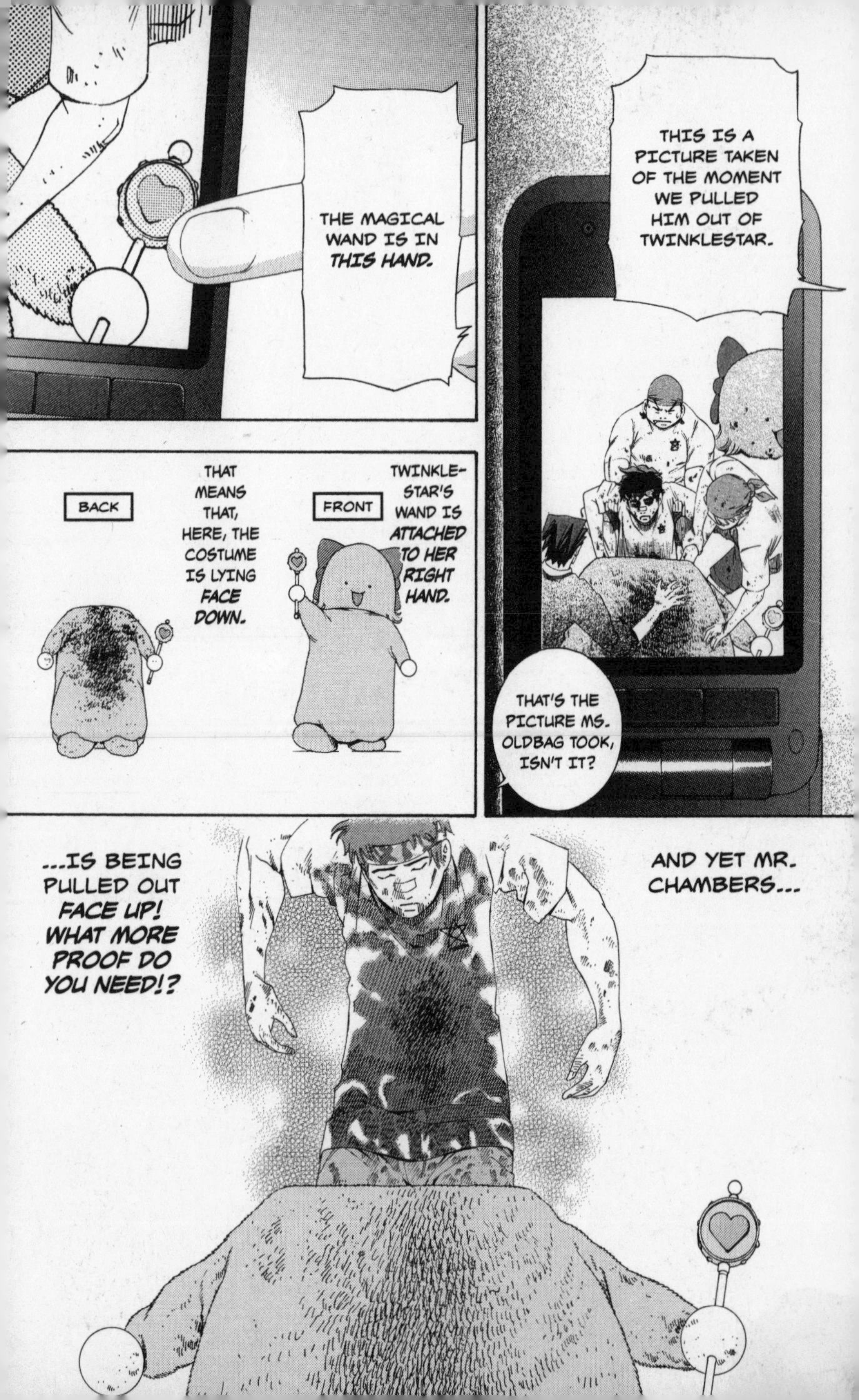
THIS IS A PICTURE TAKEN OF THE MOMENT WE PULLED HIM OUT OF TWINKLESTAR.
THAT'S THE PICTURE MS. OLDBAG TOOK, ISN'T IT?
THE MAGICAL WAND IS IN *THIS HAND.*
TWINKLE-STAR'S WAND IS *ATTACHED TO HER RIGHT HAND.*
FRONT
THAT MEANS THAT, HERE, THE COSTUME IS LYING *FACE DOWN.*
BACK
AND YET MR. CHAMBERS...
...IS BEING PULLED OUT *FACE UP! WHAT MORE PROOF DO YOU NEED!?*

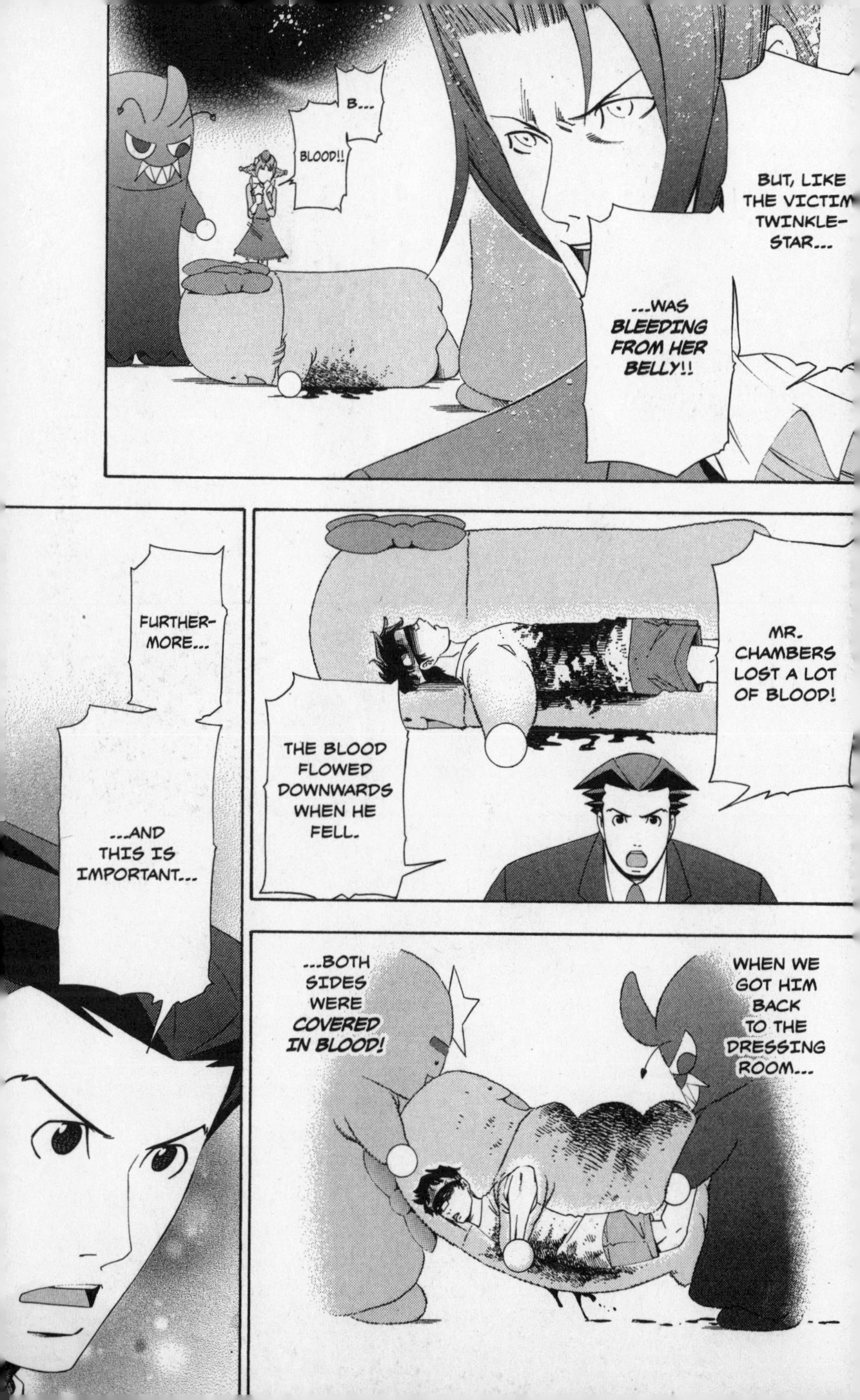
BUT, LIKE THE VICTIM TWINKLE-STAR...
...WAS *BLEEDING FROM HER BELLY!!*
B...
BLOOD!!
MR. CHAMBERS LOST A LOT OF BLOOD!
THE BLOOD FLOWED DOWNWARDS WHEN HE FELL.
WHEN WE GOT HIM BACK TO THE DRESSING ROOM...
...BOTH SIDES WERE *COVERED IN BLOOD!*
FURTHER-MORE...
...AND THIS IS IMPORTANT...

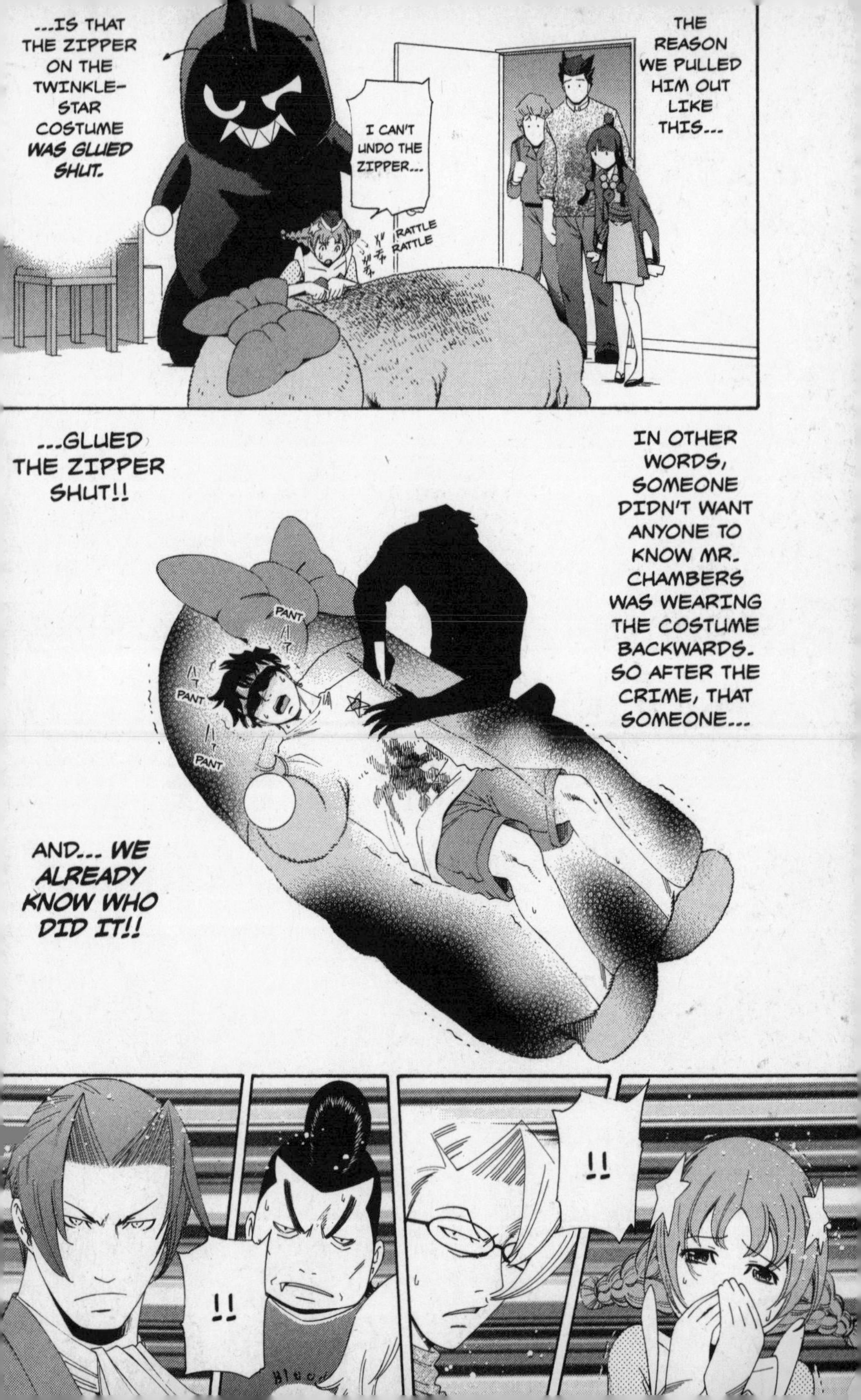
THE REASON WE PULLED HIM OUT LIKE THIS...
I CAN'T UNDO THE ZIPPER...
RATTLE RATTLE
...IS THAT THE ZIPPER ON THE TWINKLE-STAR COSTUME WAS GLUED SHUT.
IN OTHER WORDS, SOMEONE DIDN'T WANT ANYONE TO KNOW MR. CHAMBERS WAS WEARING THE COSTUME BACKWARDS. SO AFTER THE CRIME, THAT SOMEONE...
...GLUED THE ZIPPER SHUT!!
PANT
PANT
PANT
AND... WE ALREADY KNOW WHO DID IT!!
!!
!!

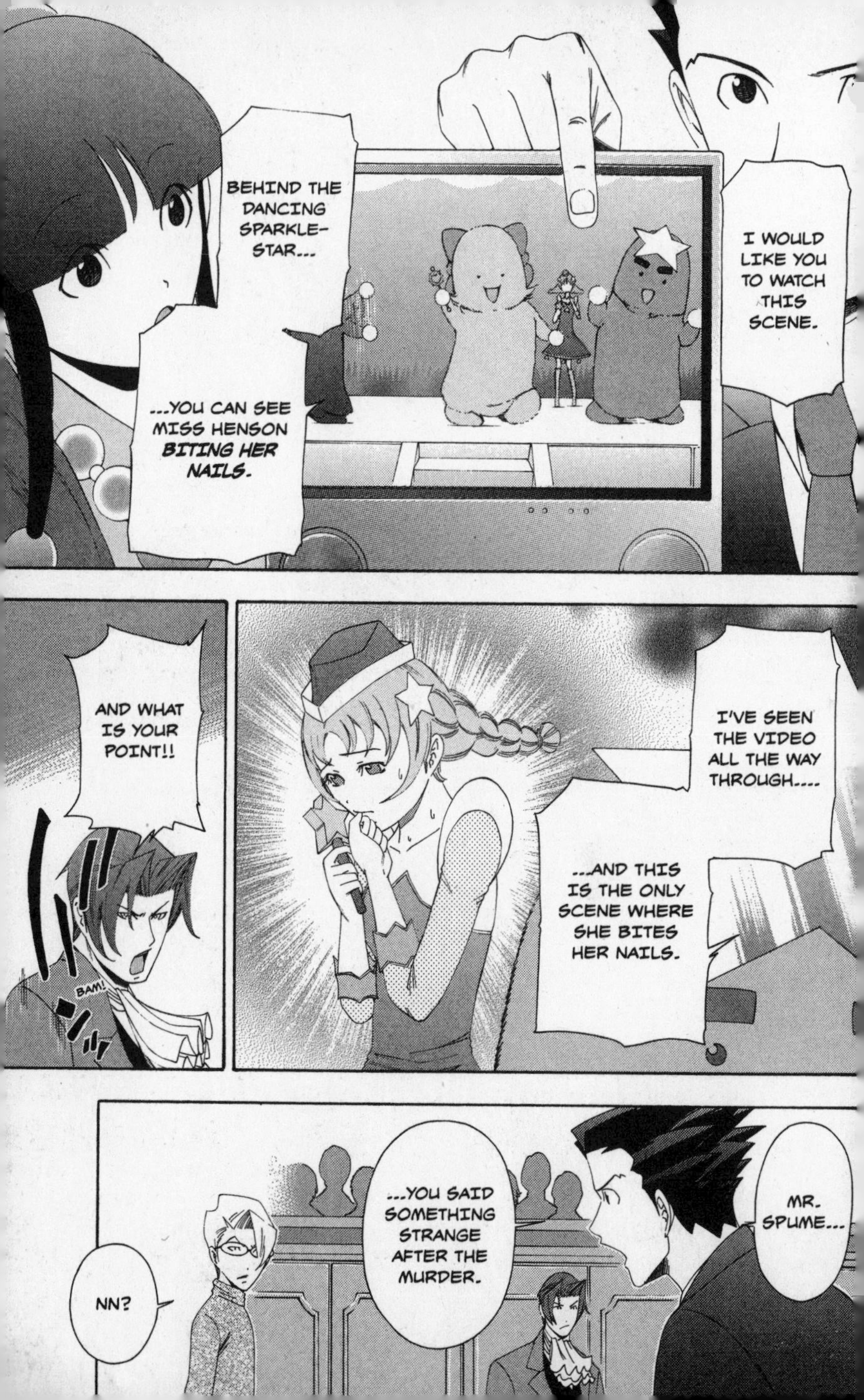
I WOULD LIKE YOU TO WATCH THIS SCENE.
BEHIND THE DANCING SPARKLE-STAR...
...YOU CAN SEE MISS HENSON BITING HER NAILS.
I'VE SEEN THE VIDEO ALL THE WAY THROUGH....
...AND THIS IS THE ONLY SCENE WHERE SHE BITES HER NAILS.
AND WHAT IS YOUR POINT!!
BAM!
MR. SPUME...
...YOU SAID SOMETHING STRANGE AFTER THE MURDER.
NN?

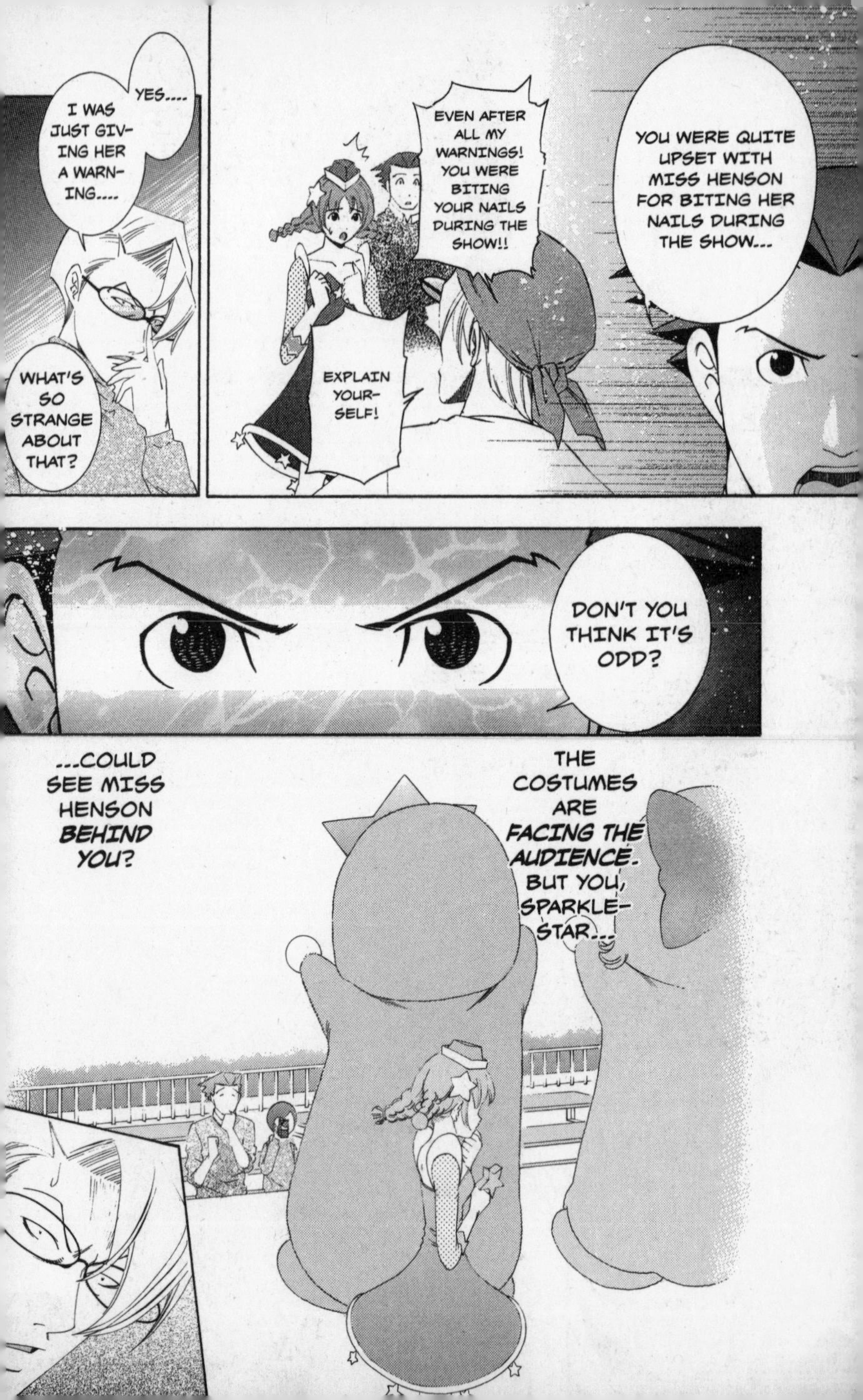
YOU WERE QUITE UPSET WITH MISS HENSON FOR BITING HER NAILS DURING THE SHOW...
EVEN AFTER ALL MY WARNINGS! YOU WERE BITING YOUR NAILS DURING THE SHOW!!
EXPLAIN YOURSELF!
YES.... I WAS JUST GIVING HER A WARNING....
WHAT'S SO STRANGE ABOUT THAT?
DON'T YOU THINK IT'S ODD?
THE COSTUMES ARE *FACING THE AUDIENCE.* BUT YOU, SPARKLESTAR...
...COULD SEE MISS HENSON *BEHIND YOU?*

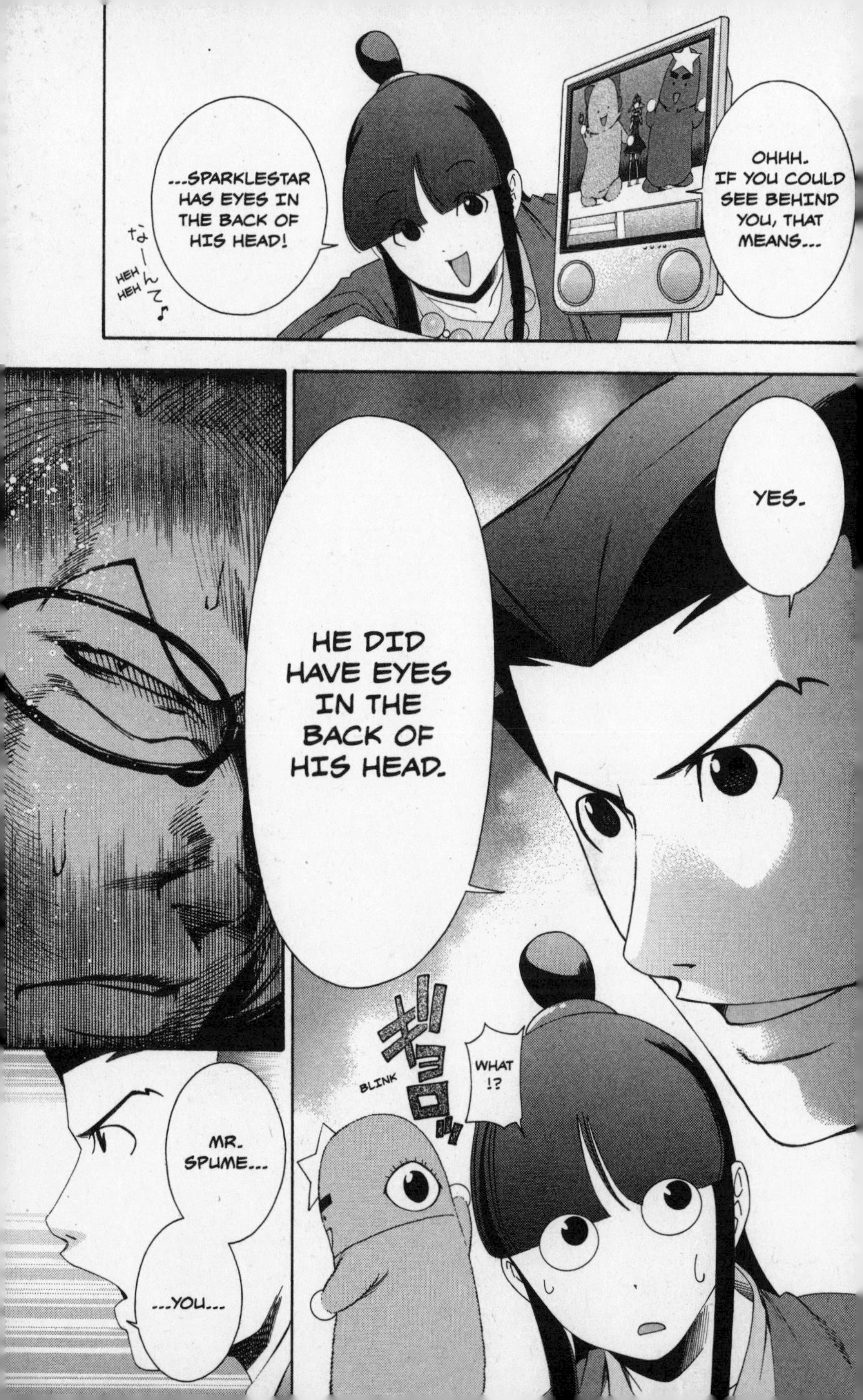
OHHH. IF YOU COULD SEE BEHIND YOU, THAT MEANS...
...SPARKLESTAR HAS EYES IN THE BACK OF HIS HEAD!
なーんて♪
HEH HEH
YES.
HE DID HAVE EYES IN THE BACK OF HIS HEAD.
WHAT !?
ギョロ
BLINK
MR. SPUME...
...YOU...

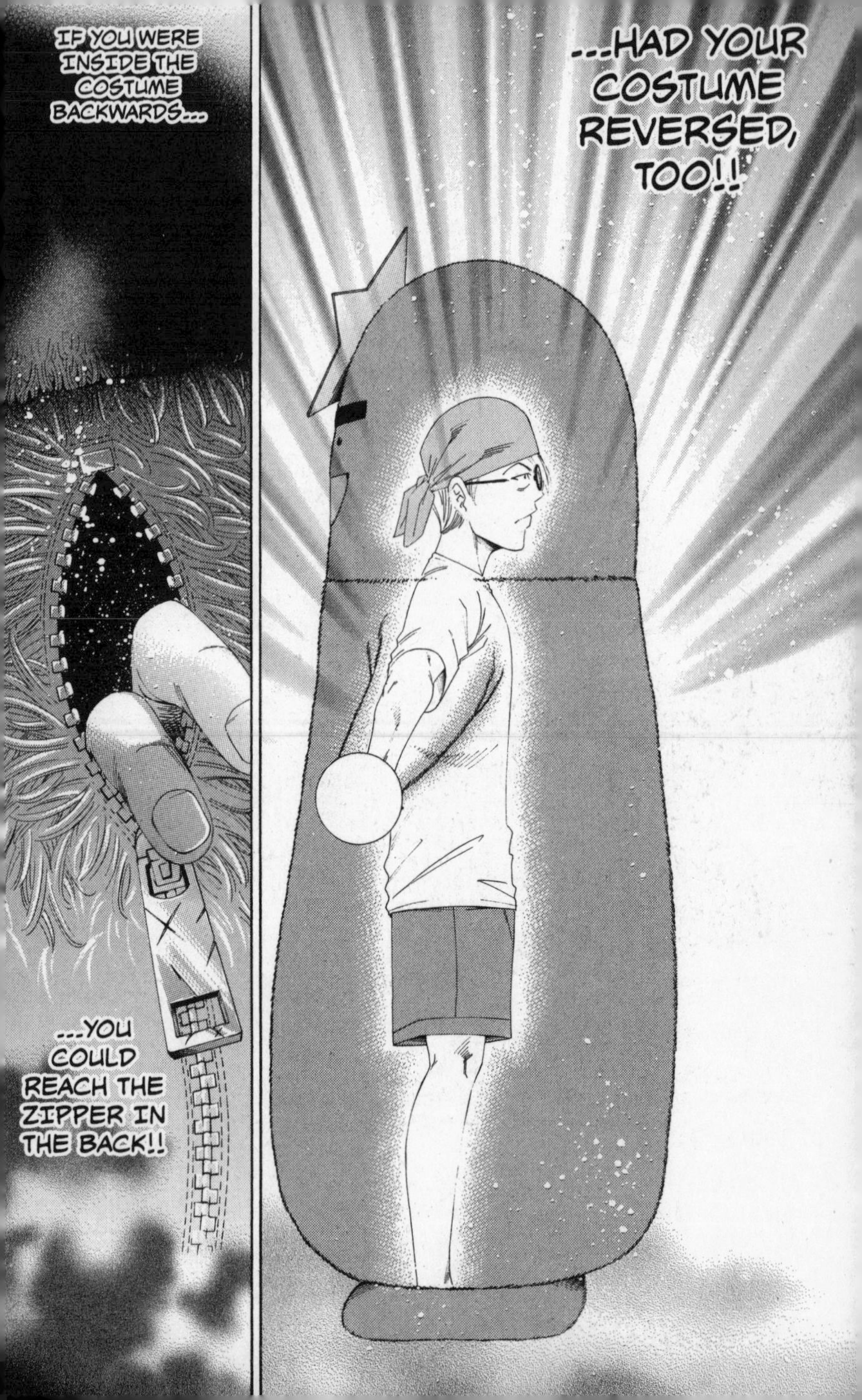
...HAD YOUR COSTUME REVERSED, TOO!!
IF YOU WERE INSIDE THE COSTUME BACKWARDS...
...YOU COULD REACH THE ZIPPER IN THE BACK!!

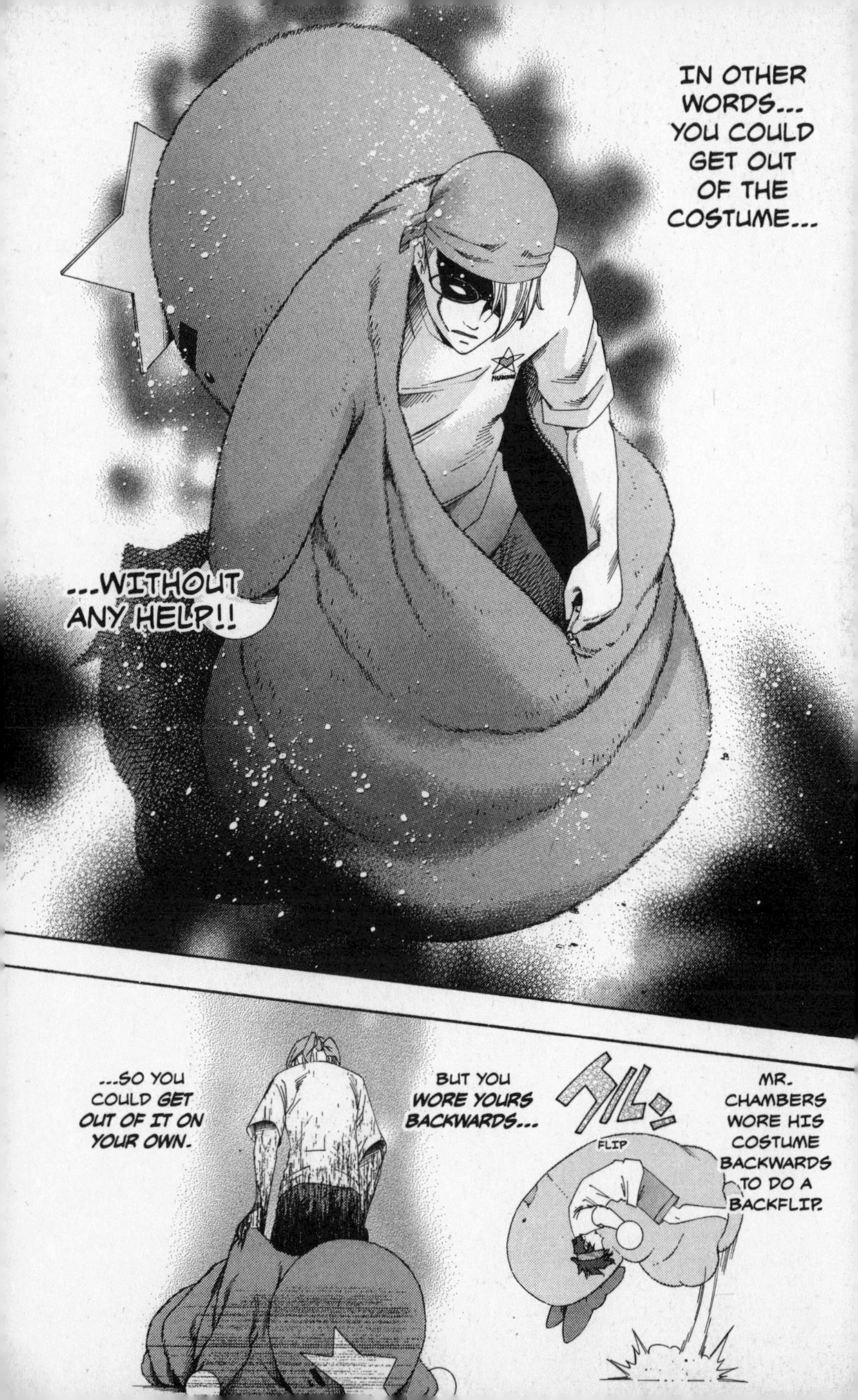
IN OTHER WORDS... YOU COULD GET OUT OF THE COSTUME...
...WITHOUT ANY HELP!!
MR. CHAMBERS WORE HIS COSTUME BACKWARDS TO DO A BACKFLIP.
FLIP
BUT YOU WORE YOURS BACKWARDS...
...SO YOU COULD GET OUT OF IT ON YOUR OWN.

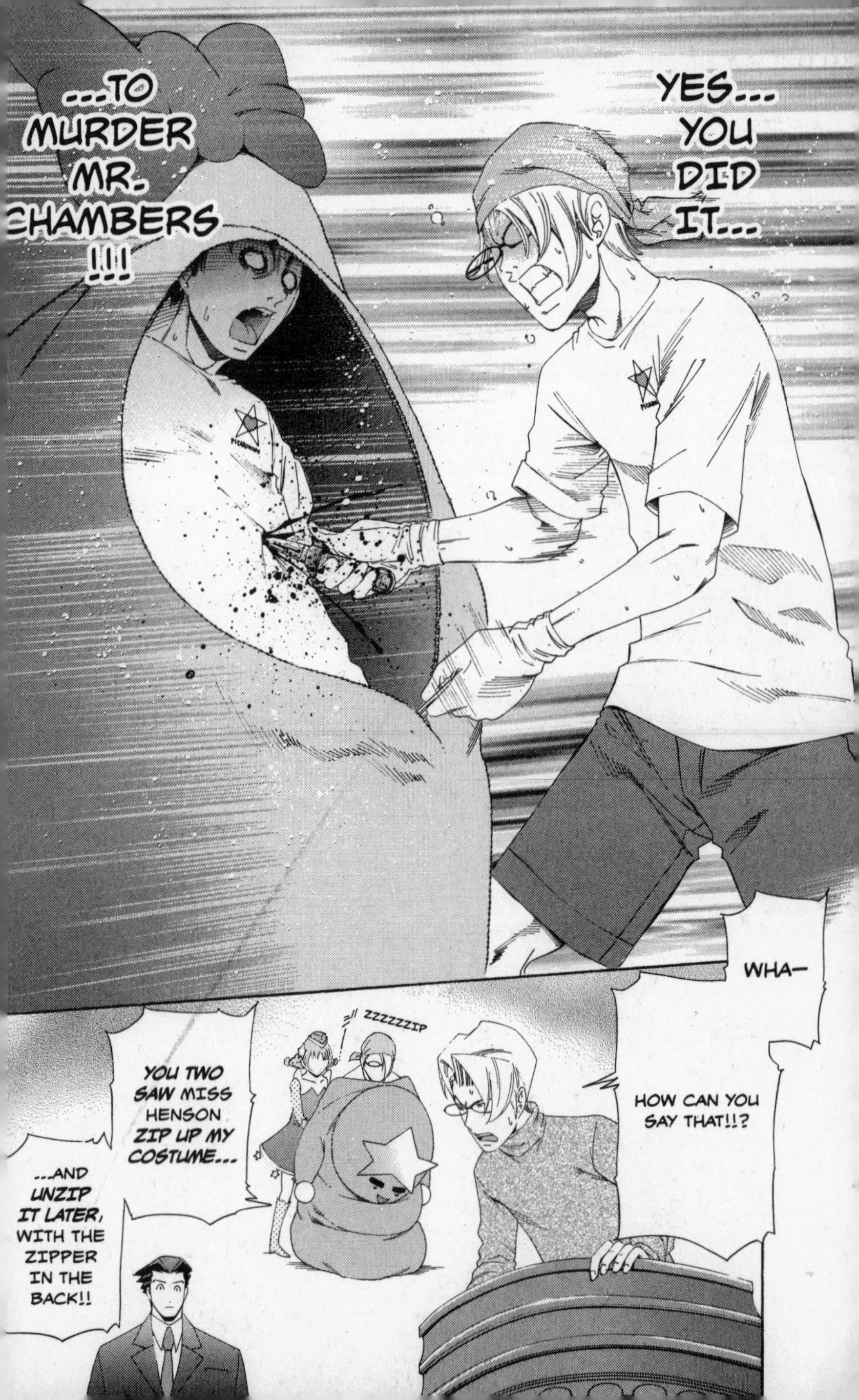
YES... YOU DID IT...
...TO MURDER MR. CHAMBERS!!!
WHA-
HOW CAN YOU SAY THAT!!?
ZZZZZZIP
YOU TWO SAW MISS HENSON ZIP UP MY COSTUME...
...AND UNZIP IT LATER, WITH THE ZIPPER IN THE BACK!!

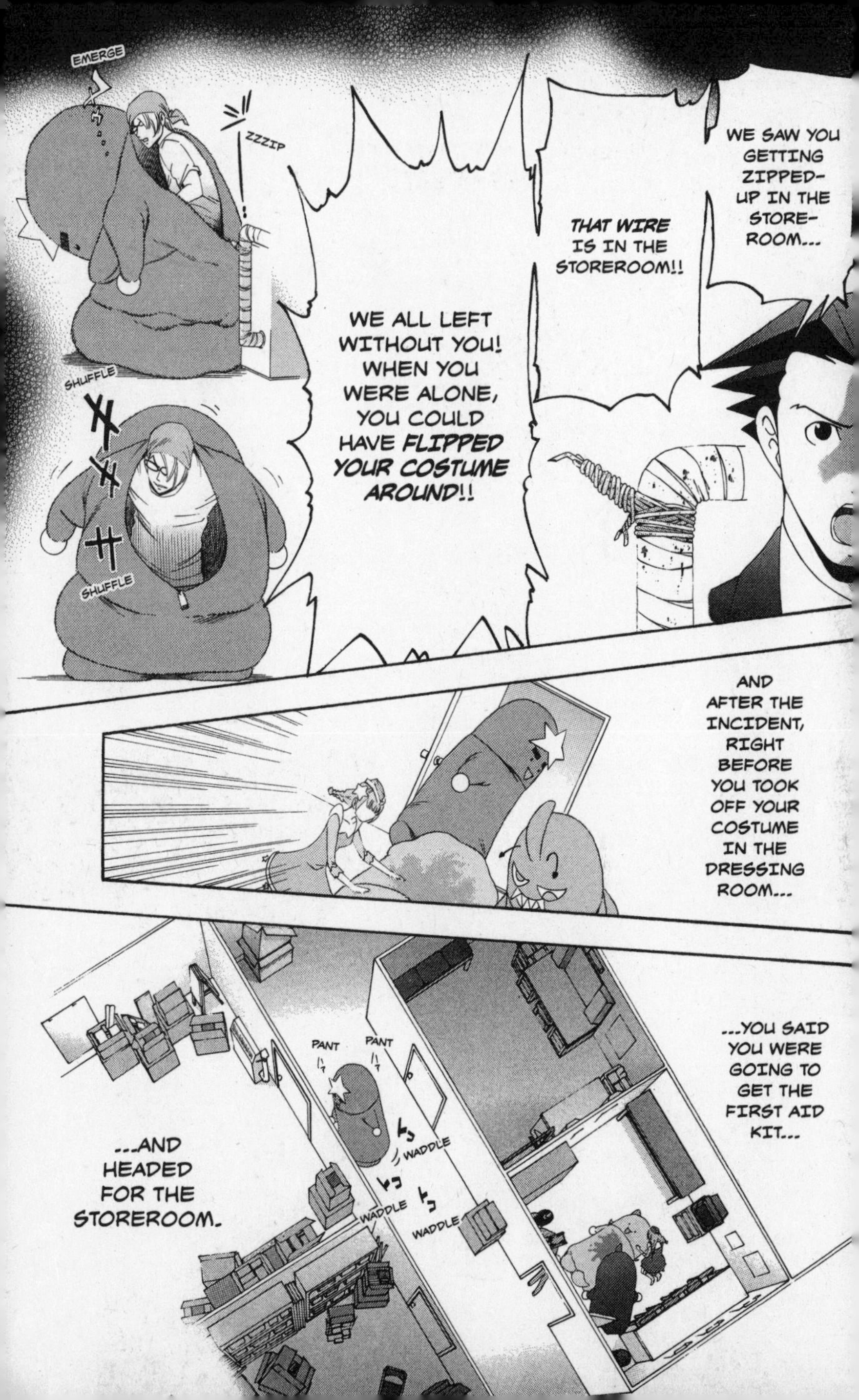
WE SAW YOU GETTING ZIPPED-UP IN THE STOREROOM...
THAT WIRE IS IN THE STOREROOM!!
WE ALL LEFT WITHOUT YOU! WHEN YOU WERE ALONE, YOU COULD HAVE FLIPPED YOUR COSTUME AROUND!!
EMERGE
ZZZIP
SHUFFLE
SHUFFLE
AND AFTER THE INCIDENT, RIGHT BEFORE YOU TOOK OFF YOUR COSTUME IN THE DRESSING ROOM...
...YOU SAID YOU WERE GOING TO GET THE FIRST AID KIT...
PANT
PANT
WADDLE
WADDLE
WADDLE
...AND HEADED FOR THE STOREROOM.

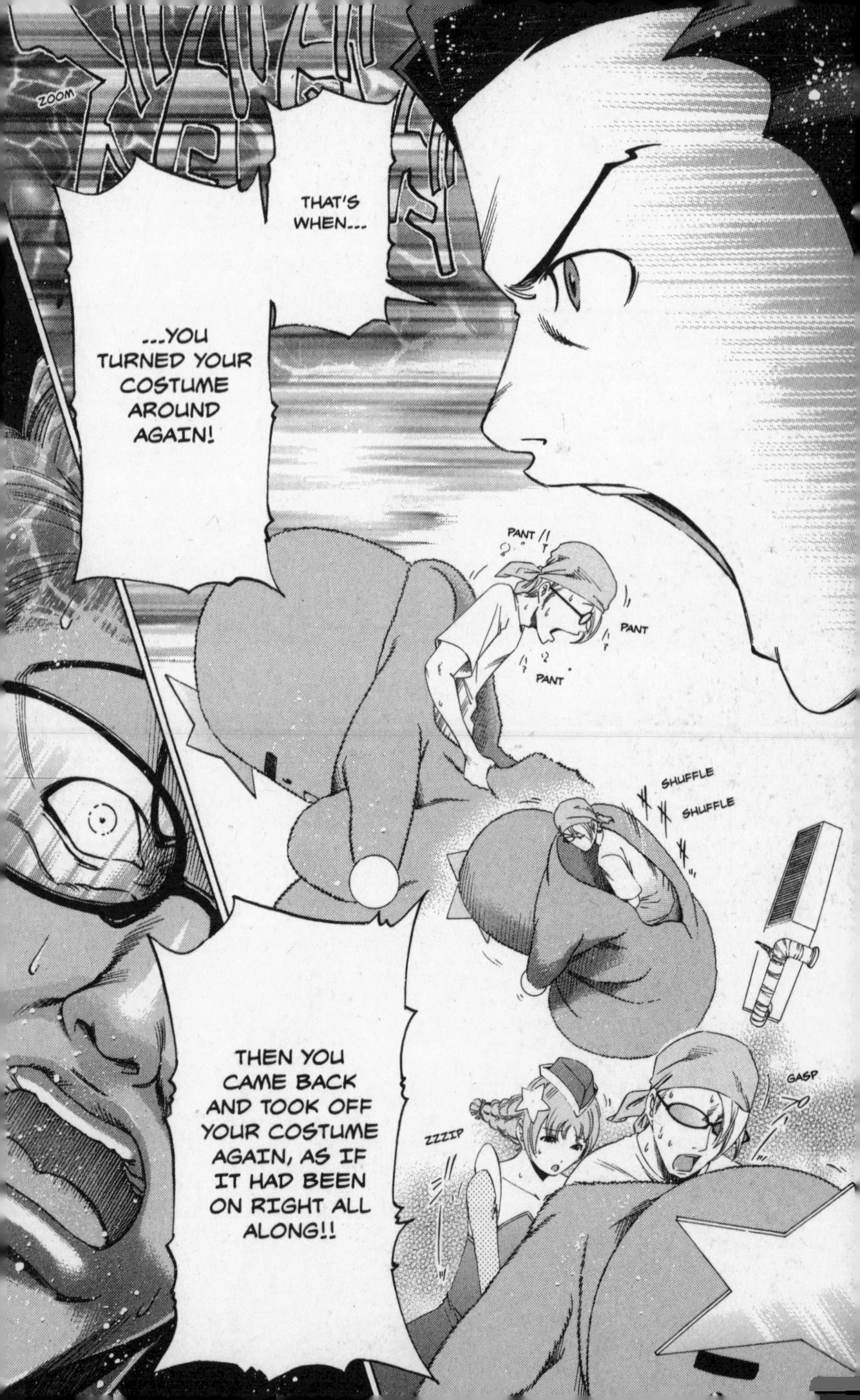
ZOOM
THAT'S WHEN...
...YOU TURNED YOUR COSTUME AROUND AGAIN!
PANT
PANT
PANT
SHUFFLE
SHUFFLE
GASP
ZZZIP
THEN YOU CAME BACK AND TOOK OFF YOUR COSTUME AGAIN, AS IF IT HAD BEEN ON RIGHT ALL ALONG!!

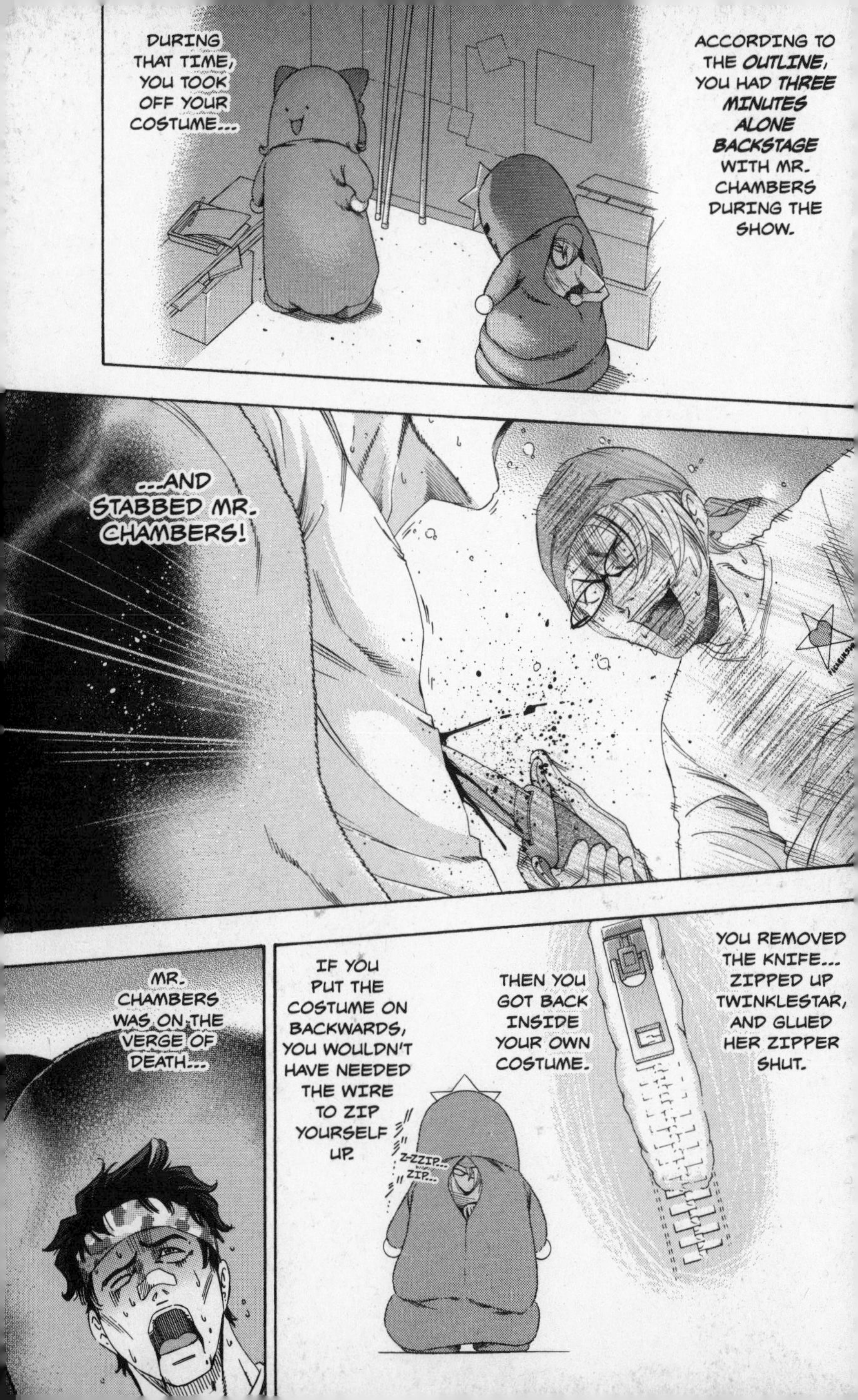
ACCORDING TO THE OUTLINE, YOU HAD THREE MINUTES ALONE BACKSTAGE WITH MR. CHAMBERS DURING THE SHOW.
DURING THAT TIME, YOU TOOK OFF YOUR COSTUME...
...AND STABBED MR. CHAMBERS!
YOU REMOVED THE KNIFE... ZIPPED UP TWINKLESTAR, AND GLUED HER ZIPPER SHUT.
THEN YOU GOT BACK INSIDE YOUR OWN COSTUME.
IF YOU PUT THE COSTUME ON BACKWARDS, YOU WOULDN'T HAVE NEEDED THE WIRE TO ZIP YOURSELF UP.
Z-ZZIP... ZIP...
MR. CHAMBERS WAS ON THE VERGE OF DEATH...

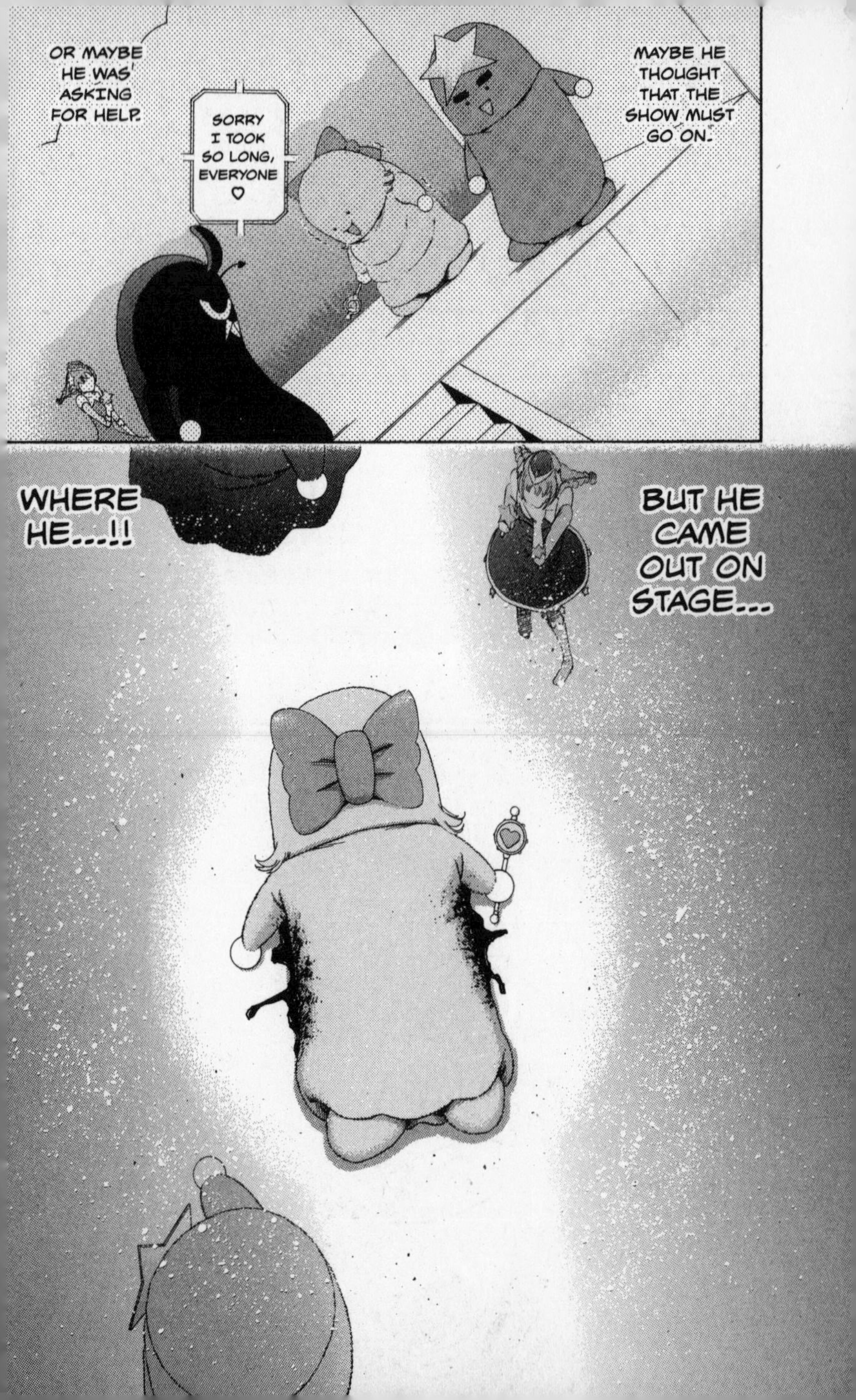
MAYBE HE THOUGHT THAT THE SHOW MUST GO ON.
SORRY I TOOK SO LONG, EVERYONE ♡
OR MAYBE HE WAS ASKING FOR HELP.
BUT HE CAME OUT ON STAGE...
WHERE HE...!!

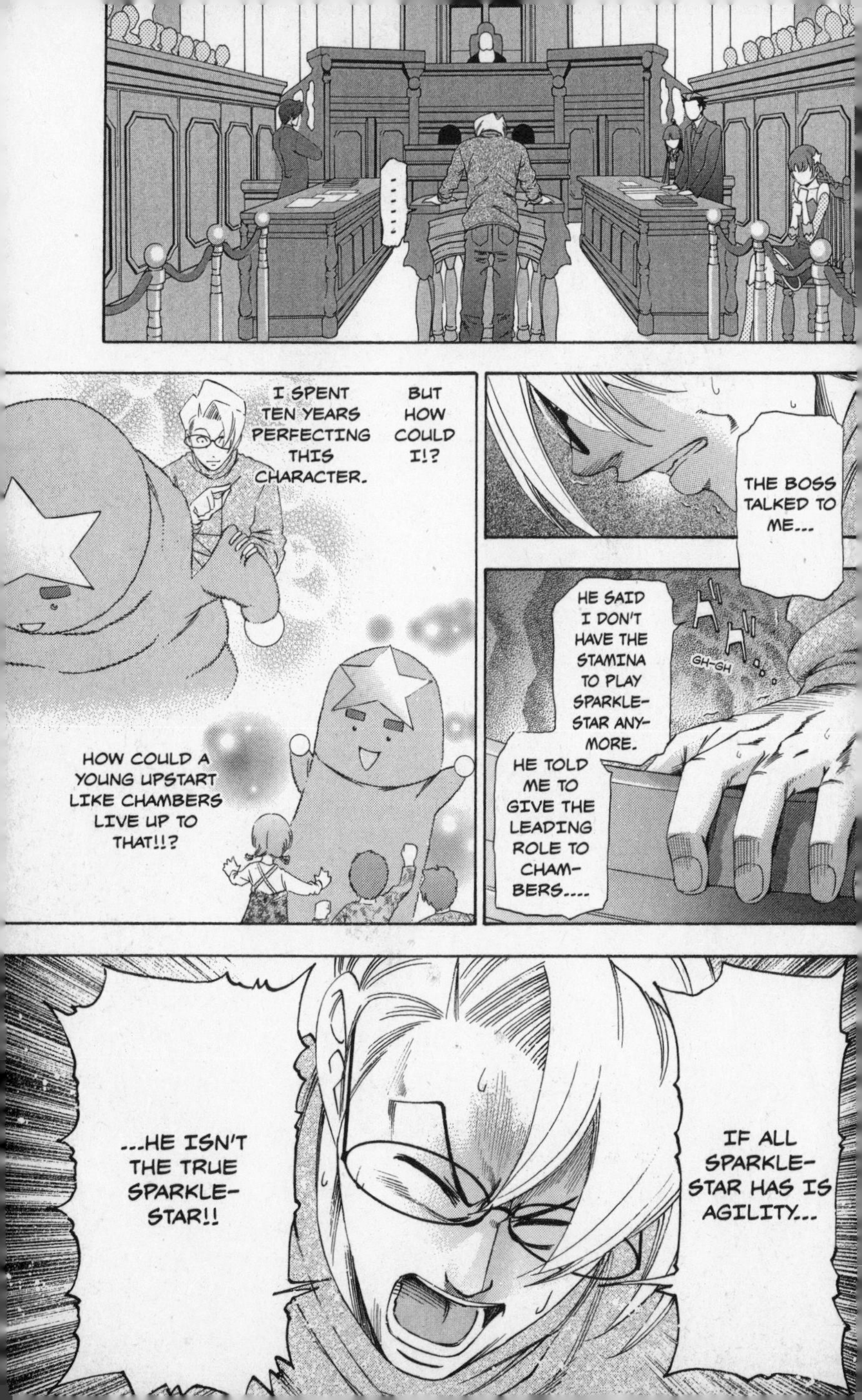
THE BOSS TALKED TO ME...
HE SAID I DON'T HAVE THE STAMINA TO PLAY SPARKLE-STAR ANYMORE.
GH-GH
HE TOLD ME TO GIVE THE LEADING ROLE TO CHAMBERS....
BUT HOW COULD I!?
I SPENT TEN YEARS PERFECTING THIS CHARACTER.
HOW COULD A YOUNG UPSTART LIKE CHAMBERS LIVE UP TO THAT!!?
IF ALL SPARKLE-STAR HAS IS AGILITY...
...HE ISN'T THE TRUE SPARKLE-STAR!!

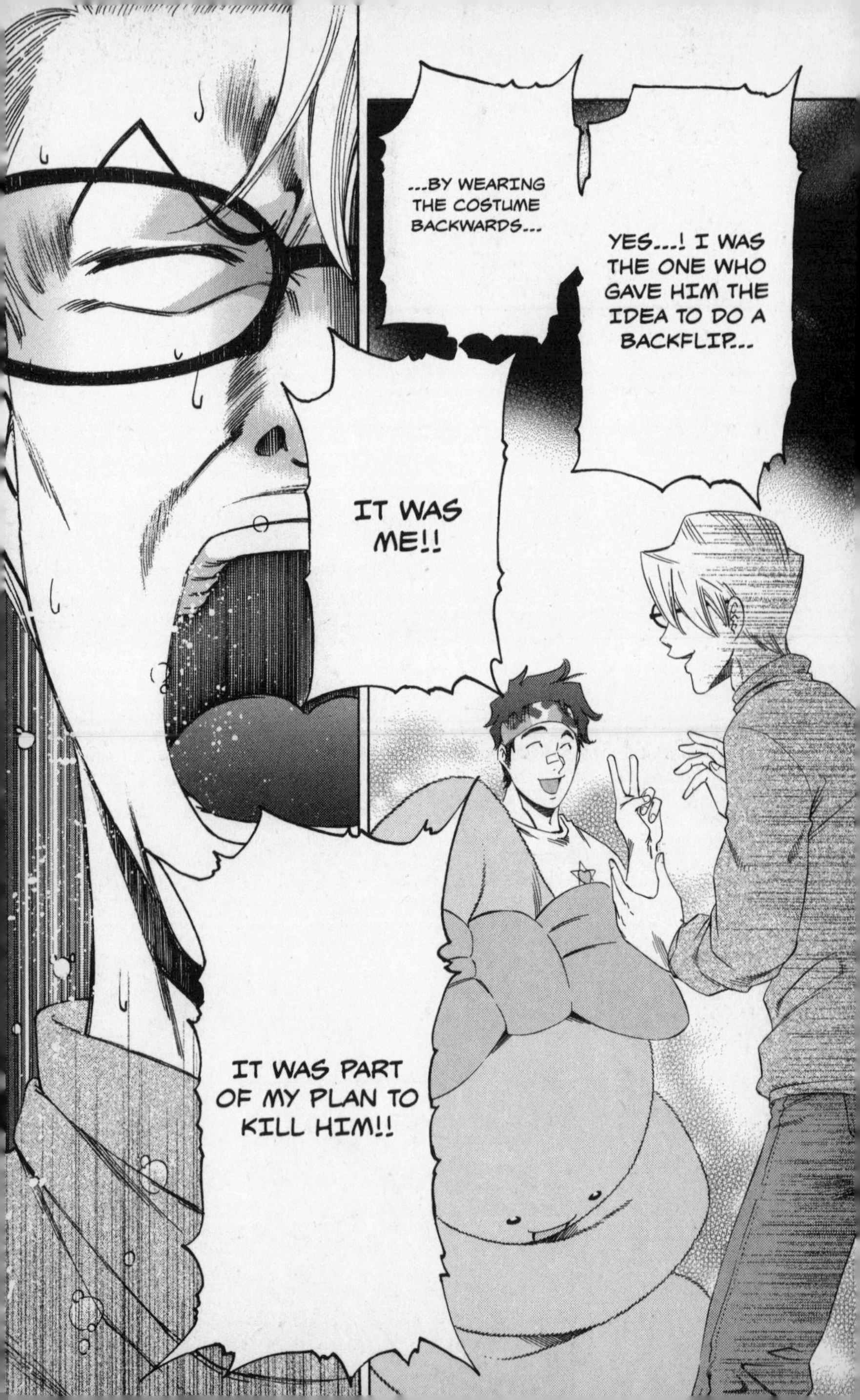
...BY WEARING THE COSTUME BACKWARDS...
YES...! I WAS THE ONE WHO GAVE HIM THE IDEA TO DO A BACKFLIP...
IT WAS ME!!
IT WAS PART OF MY PLAN TO KILL HIM!!

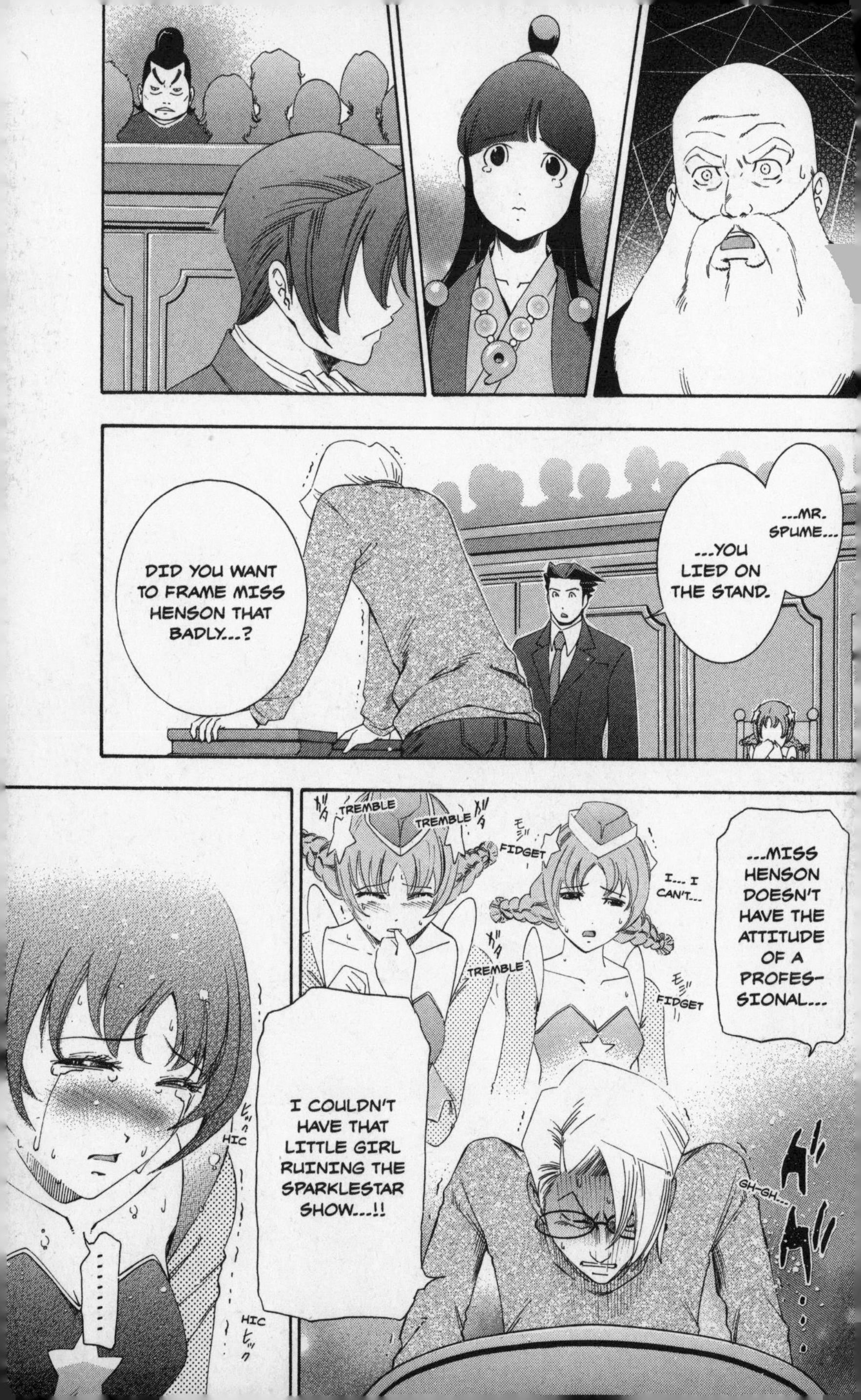
...MR. SPUME...
...YOU LIED ON THE STAND.
DID YOU WANT TO FRAME MISS HENSON THAT BADLY...?
...MISS HENSON DOESN'T HAVE THE ATTITUDE OF A PROFES-SIONAL...
TREMBLE
TREMBLE
FIDGET
I... I CAN'T...
TREMBLE
FIDGET
I COULDN'T HAVE THAT LITTLE GIRL RUINING THE SPARKLESTAR SHOW...!!
GH-GH...
HIC
HIC

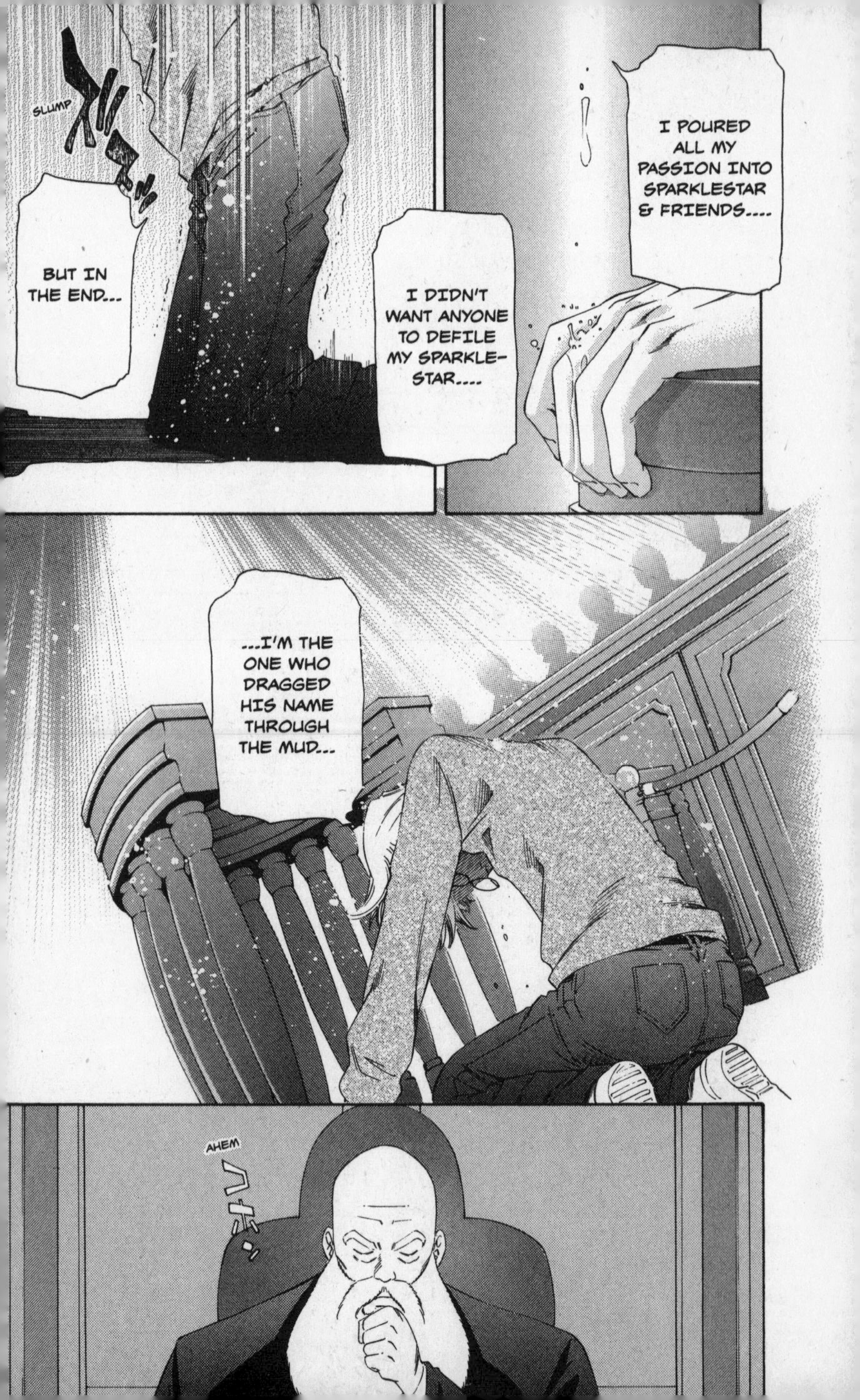
I POURED ALL MY PASSION INTO SPARKLESTAR & FRIENDS....
I DIDN'T WANT ANYONE TO DEFILE MY SPARKLE-STAR....
SLUMP
BUT IN THE END...
...I'M THE ONE WHO DRAGGED HIS NAME THROUGH THE MUD...
AHEM

I HEREBY

PRONOUNCE THE DEFENDANT, JULIE HENSON...

NOT GUILTY

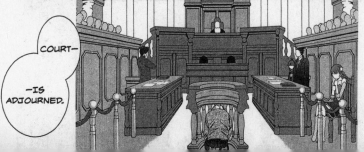

COURT—

—IS ADJOURNED.

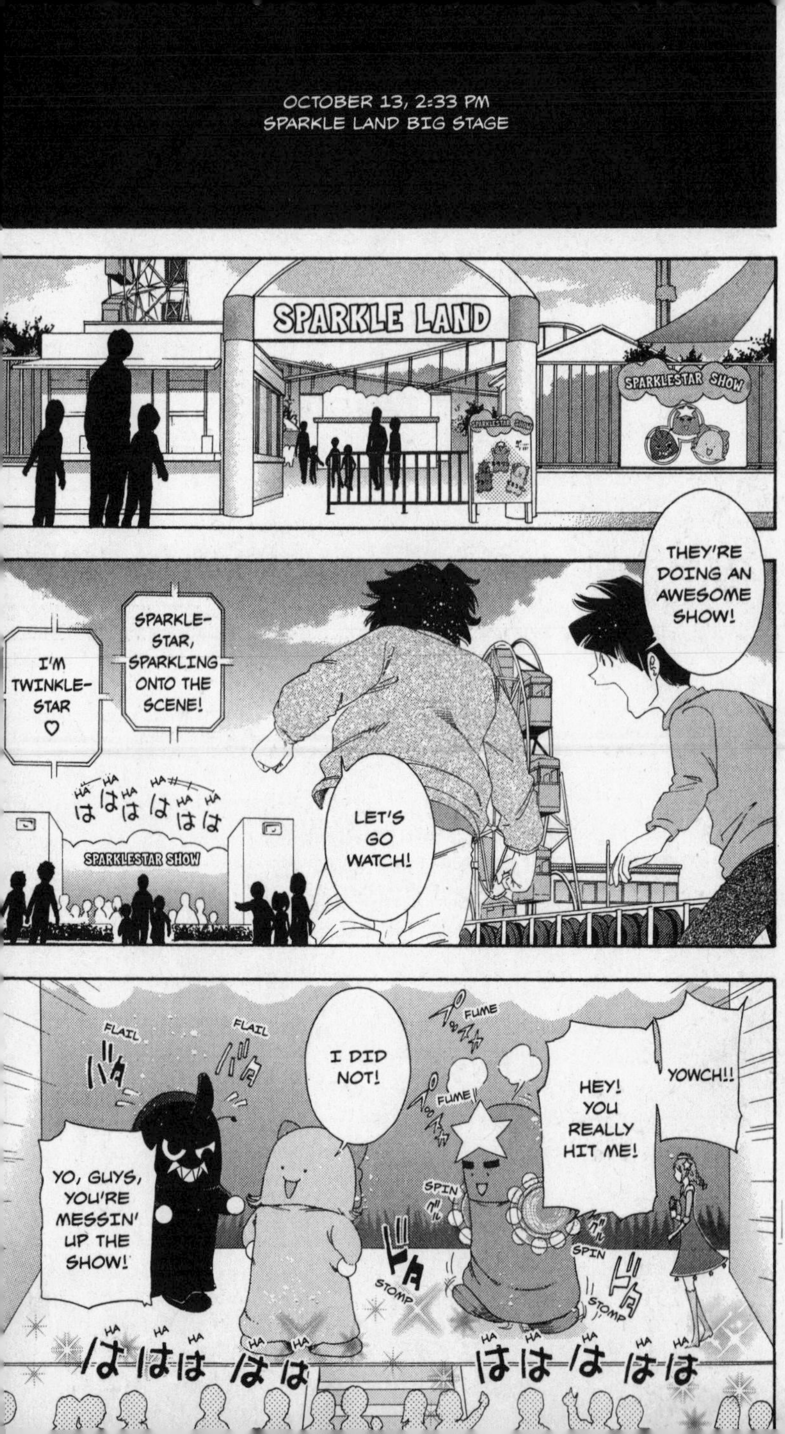

OCTOBER 13, 2:33 PM
SPARKLE LAND BIG STAGE
SPARKLE LAND
SPARKLESTAR SHOW
THEY'RE DOING AN AWESOME SHOW!
LET'S GO WATCH!
SPARKLE-STAR, SPARKLING ONTO THE SCENE!
I'M TWINKLE-STAR ♡
HA HA HA HA HA HA HA
SPARKLESTAR SHOW
YOWCH!!
HEY! YOU REALLY HIT ME!
FUME
FUME
I DID NOT!
FLAIL
FLAIL
YO, GUYS, YOU'RE MESSIN' UP THE SHOW!
SPIN
SPIN
STOMP
STOMP
HA HA HA HA HA
HA HA HA HA HA

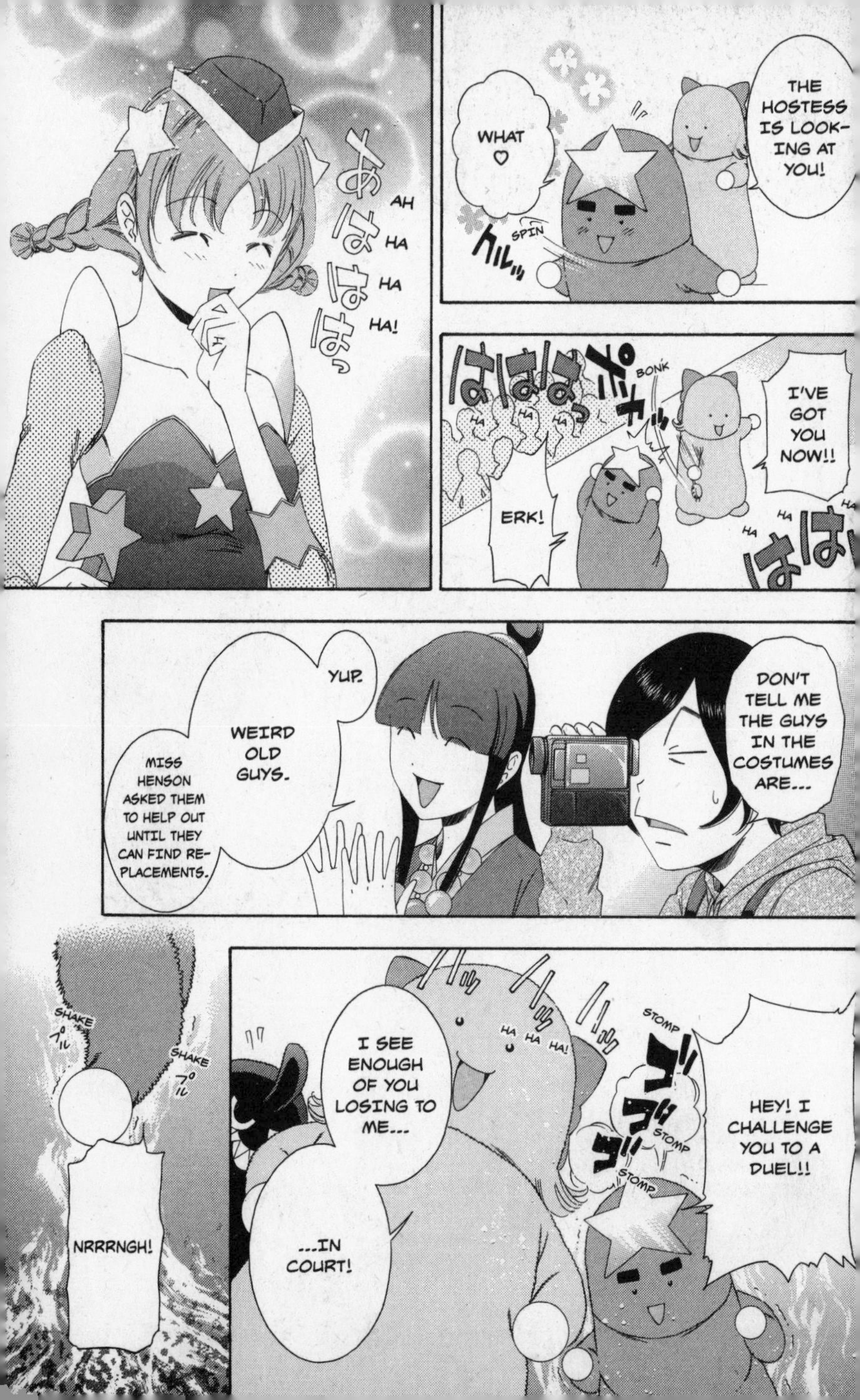
THE HOSTESS IS LOOKING AT YOU!
WHAT ♡
SPIN
I'VE GOT YOU NOW!!
BONK
HA HA HA
ERK!
HA HA
AH HA HA HA!
DON'T TELL ME THE GUYS IN THE COSTUMES ARE...
YUP.
WEIRD OLD GUYS.
MISS HENSON ASKED THEM TO HELP OUT UNTIL THEY CAN FIND REPLACEMENTS.
HEY! I CHALLENGE YOU TO A DUEL!!
STOMP
STOMP
STOMP
HA HA HA!
I SEE ENOUGH OF YOU LOSING TO ME...
...IN COURT!
SHAKE
SHAKE
NRRRNGH!

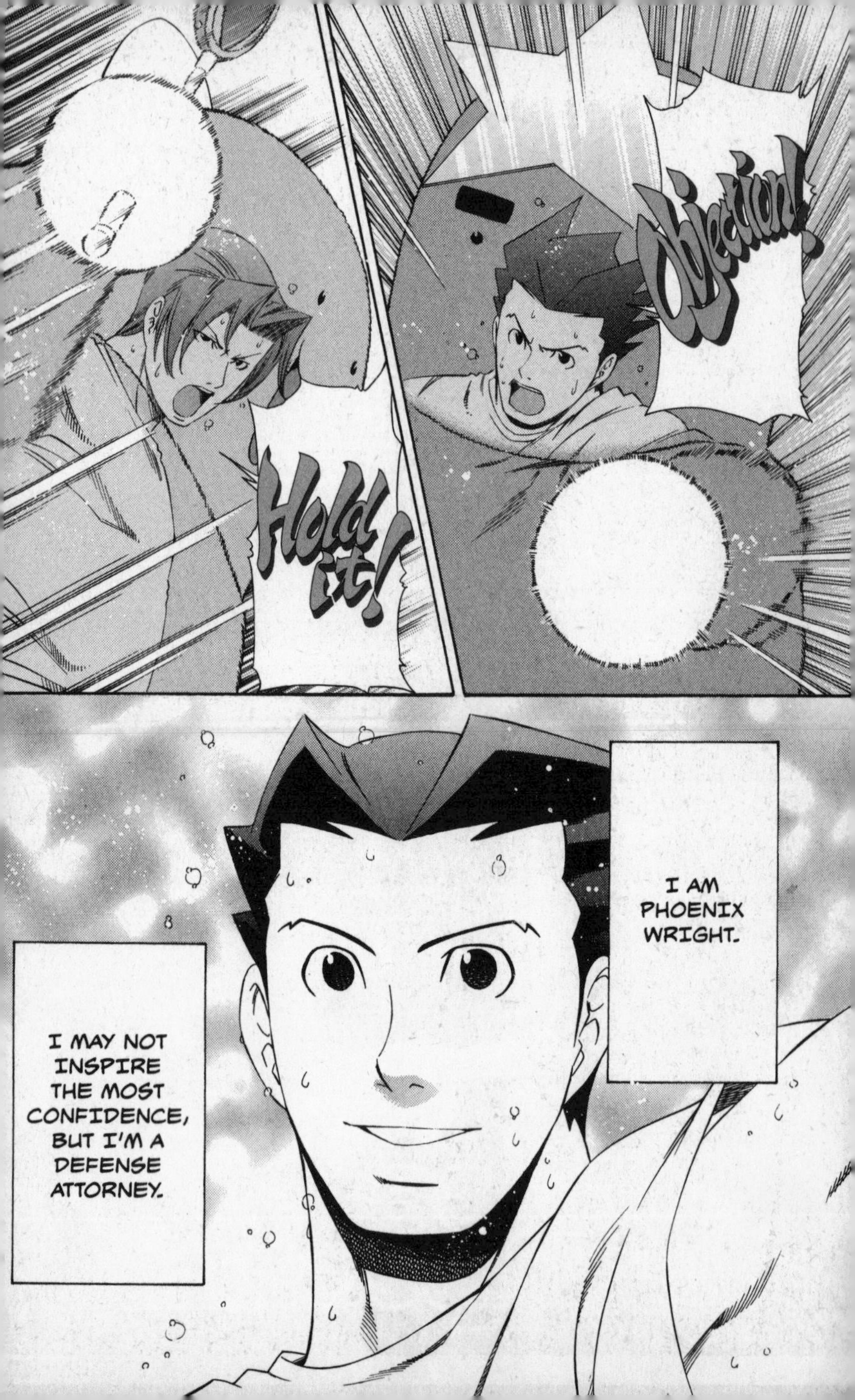
Objection!
Hold it!
I AM PHOENIX WRIGHT.
I MAY NOT INSPIRE THE MOST CONFIDENCE, BUT I'M A DEFENSE ATTORNEY.

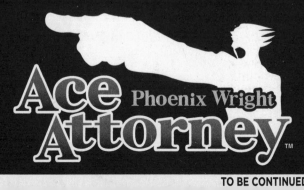

Ace Phoenix Wright Attorney™

TO BE CONTINUED.

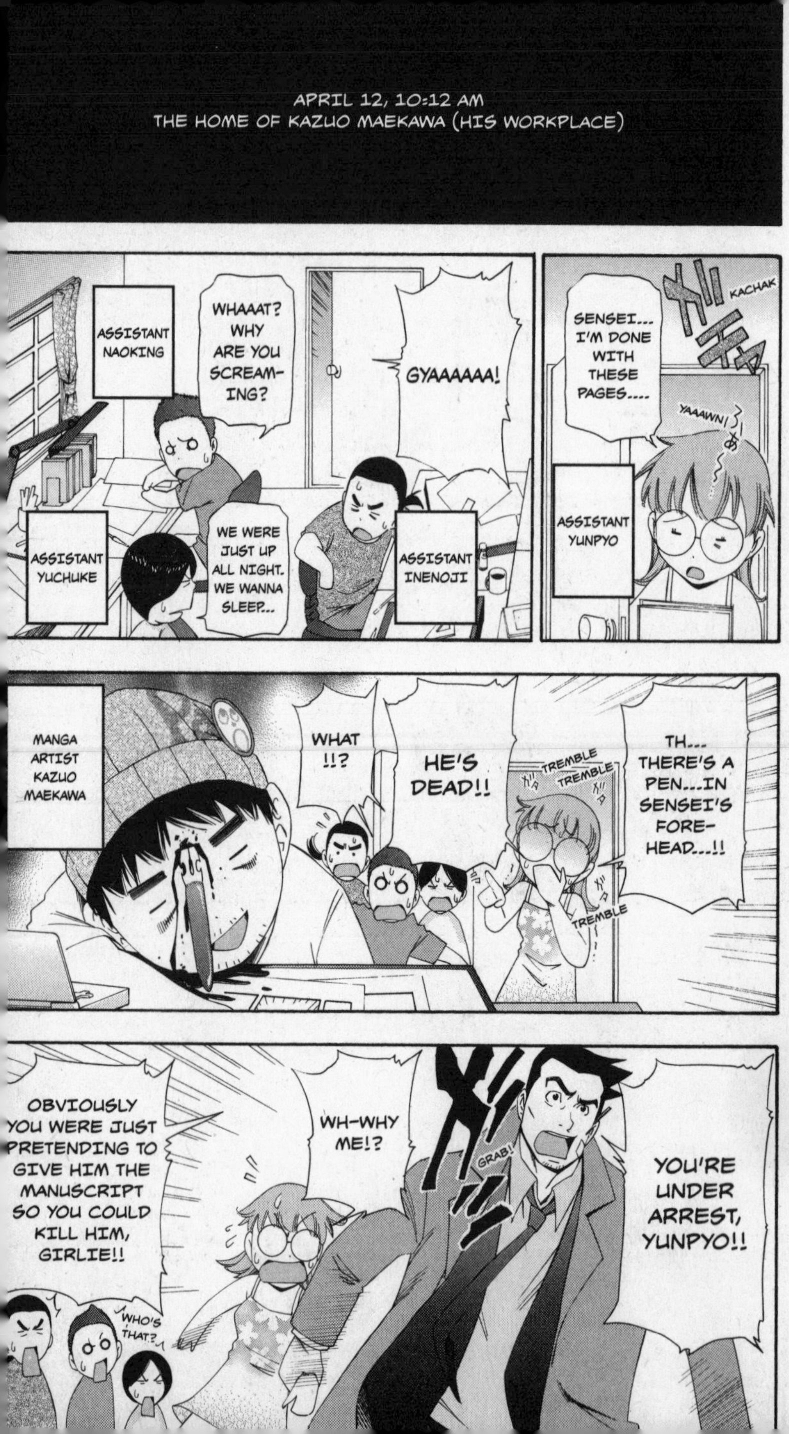
APRIL 12, 10:12 AM
THE HOME OF KAZUO MAEKAWA (HIS WORKPLACE)
KACHAK
SENSEI... I'M DONE WITH THESE PAGES....
YAAAWN!
ASSISTANT YUNPYO
GYAAAAAA!
WHAAAT? WHY ARE YOU SCREAM-ING?
ASSISTANT NAOKING
ASSISTANT INENOJI
WE WERE JUST UP ALL NIGHT. WE WANNA SLEEP...
ASSISTANT YUCHUKE
TH... THERE'S A PEN...IN SENSEI'S FORE-HEAD...!!
TREMBLE TREMBLE
HE'S DEAD!!
WHAT !!?
MANGA ARTIST KAZUO MAEKAWA
TREMBLE
YOU'RE UNDER ARREST, YUNPYO!!
GRAB!
WH-WHY ME!?
OBVIOUSLY YOU WERE JUST PRETENDING TO GIVE HIM THE MANUSCRIPT SO YOU COULD KILL HIM, GIRLIE!!
WHO'S THAT?

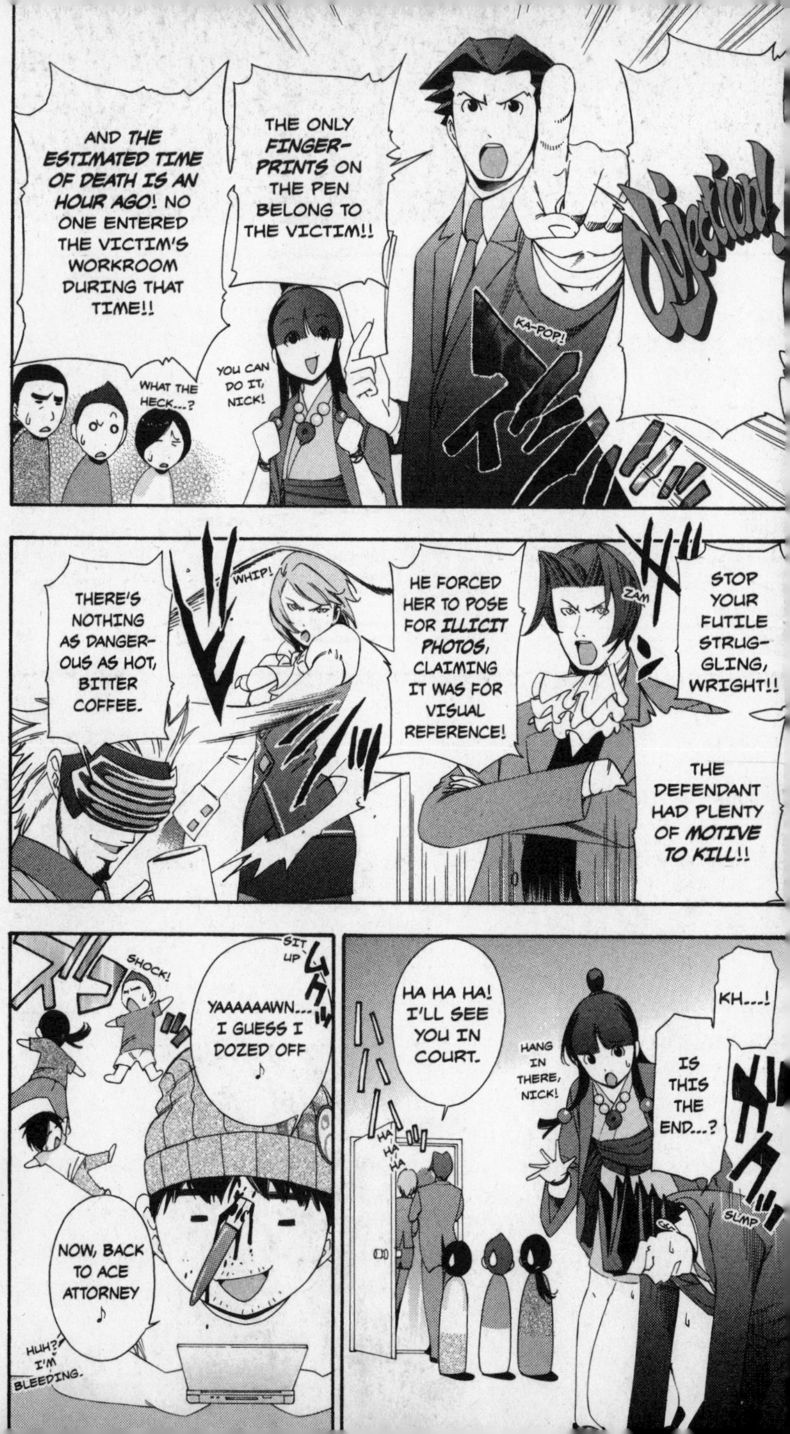
Objection!
KA-POP!
THE ONLY FINGER-PRINTS ON THE PEN BELONG TO THE VICTIM!!
AND THE ESTIMATED TIME OF DEATH IS AN HOUR AGO! NO ONE ENTERED THE VICTIM'S WORKROOM DURING THAT TIME!!
YOU CAN DO IT, NICK!
WHAT THE HECK...?
STOP YOUR FUTILE STRUG-GLING, WRIGHT!!
ZAM
THE DEFENDANT HAD PLENTY OF MOTIVE TO KILL!!
HE FORCED HER TO POSE FOR ILLICIT PHOTOS, CLAIMING IT WAS FOR VISUAL REFERENCE!
WHIP!
THERE'S NOTHING AS DANGER-OUS AS HOT, BITTER COFFEE.
KH...!
IS THIS THE END...?
SLMP
HANG IN THERE, NICK!
HA HA HA! I'LL SEE YOU IN COURT.
HA HA HA
SIT UP
YAAAAAAWN... I GUESS I DOZED OFF ♪
SHOCK!
NOW, BACK TO ACE ATTORNEY ♪
HUH?? I'M BLEEDING.

TRANSLATION NOTES

Japanese is a tricky language for most Westerners, and translation is often more art than science. For your edification and reading pleasure, here are notes on some of the places where we could have gone in a different direction with our translation of the work, or where a Japanese cultural reference is used.

Samurai manjû, page 62
Steamed yeast buns with filling, such as red bean paste.

Gyakuten Saiban name notes

Flip Chambers (Ichinomiya Junpei): Ichinomiya means "one palace," and we think it refers to the "locked-room" murder. Hence, Chambers. Junpei can also be spelled Jumpei, so we think this is a reference to his acrobatics. Hence Flip (nickname for Philip).

Buck Montana (Futagoyama Hôsaku): Both names probably refer to his size. Hôsaku also refers to an abundant crop, and is often paired with "binbô" as "hôsaku binbô (plentiful poverty)," a crop that is so abundant it becomes worthless. This may be a reference to his debt, so we went with Buck to refer to money. Futagoyama literally means "twin mountains," so we named him Montana, which means "mountain."

Raymond Spume (Kasugai Kôsuke): We were a little stumped for his name, but Kasugai can sound like "kasu (scum) guy," so we found a synonym for scum that sounded kind of like a name. We named him Raymond as in "ray of light" to indicate his role as SparkleStar.

Julie Henson (Okazaki Juri): Julie comes from Juri, because they sound alike. Henson comes from Jim Henson, as she is a human among monsters--the kind of scenario you'd find in Sesame Street or the Muppet Show.

Cameron Show (Sakae Shôtarô): Shôtarô probably comes from the word "show," so we left that as his last name. We named him Cameron because he's the guy with the camera.

BY KEN AKAMATSU

Negi Springfield is a ten-year-old wizard teaching English at an all-girls Japanese school. He dreams of becoming a master wizard like his legendary father, the Thousand Master. At first his biggest concern was concealing his magic powers, because if he's ever caught using them publicly, he thinks he'll be turned into an ermine! But in a world that gets stranger every day, it turns out that the strangest people of all are Negi's students! From a librarian with a magic book to a centuries-old vampire, from a robot to a ninja, Negi will risk his own life to protect the girls in his care!

Ages: 16+

Special extras in each volume! Read them all!

VISIT WWW.KODANSHACOMICS.COM TO:

- View release date calendars for upcoming volumes
- Find out the latest about new Kodansha Comics series

You are going the wrong way!

Manga is a completely different type of reading experience.

To start at the *beginning,* go to the *end!*

That's right! Authentic manga is read the traditional Japanese way—from right to left, exactly the *opposite* of how American books are read. It's easy to follow: Just go to the other end of the book, and read each page—and each panel—from right side to left side, starting at the top right. Now you're experiencing manga as it was meant to be.